SUCCESS IN
POLITICS

A COMPARATIVE STUDY FOR AS AND A2
SECOND EDITION

NEIL MCNAUGHTON

JOHN MURRAY

Success Studybooks

... and Promotion   Law

Book-keeping and Accounts   ...

Business Calculations   Marketing

Chemistry   Politics

Commerce   Principles of Accounting

Commerce: West African Edition   Principles of Accounting: Answer Book

Communication   Psychology

Economics   Sociology

Electronics   Statistics

European History 1815–1941   Twentieth Century World Affairs

Information Processing   World History since 1945

Insurance

First published 1996
by John Murray (Publishers) Ltd
50 Albemarle Street
London W1S 4BD

Second edition 2001 Reprinted 2002 (twice)

Typeset in 10.5/12pt Sabon by Wearset Ltd, Boldon, Tyne and Wear
Printed and bound in Great Britain by Alden Press, Oxford

A CIP catalogue record for this book is available from the British Library

ISBN 0 7195 7210 X

Contents

Foreword

The publication of the second edition of this book coincides with some of the biggest changes that have happened to the post-16 curriculum for half a century. All sixth form students are now being tested at the end of both their first and second years. Neil McNaughton has been heavily involved in changes to the specifications for Government and Politics and this book proves to be a comprehensive companion to those studying the subject at both AS and A2 levels. This new edition also provides valuable updated information on the progress of the first Blair administration as well as the important political landmark of Labour's second landslide election victory in June 2001.

Neil McNaughton has made major revisions to the first edition of *Success in Politics*, so that both the subject matter and the style are more focused to the needs of those sitting the new examinations. The structure of the book is helpful and the style throughout is clear and precise. AS students will find the early chapters of the book lively, accessible and a very useful introduction to what will be, to many, a new subject. Those following the A2 routes will find the later sections detailed, informative and geared to the increased demands of the second year of their studies.

Teachers and examiners are always encouraging students of politics to read newspapers and keep in touch with current events. This book will also stimulate its readers into looking at other sources in order to gain a wider insight into the issues that are discussed. However, the topics covered here are substantial and of direct relevance to AS/A2 studies and *Success in Politics* provides the knowledge, explanation, concepts and evaluation which is at the heart of the subject. The guide to examination questions will provide an indication as to how the contents of this book and the wider references may be brought together for best results in the unit tests.

Students usually do well if they know and enjoy their subject. I think *Success in Politics* will enable its readers to do both these things and ultimately the book will provide AS, A level and other students with the opportunity to achieve good grades in their examinations. General readers will also find much in this book that will aid in their understanding of the importance of politics, which at a time of low election turnouts, can be nothing other than worthwhile.

Chris Robinson
Principal Examiner for AS level Government and Politics
Chairman of The Politics Association

Acknowledgements

reproduce material and photographs.

Cover: *left* Ray Tang/Rex Features, *centre* John Townson/Creation, *right* Patsy Lynch/Rex Features; **pp.5,7,8** Economic Trends, National Statistics © Crown copyright 2000; **p.93** A. Giddens, *The Third Way*, Blackwell Publishers/Polity Press, 1998; **p.102** R. Rose, *Do Parties Make a Difference?*, with permission of Macmillan Ltd, 1984; **p.109** A. Adonis, *Parliament Today*, Manchester University Press, 1990; **p.117** Chris Ison/PA Photos; **p.124** Stefan Rousseau/PA Photos; **p.128** The Independent/Syndication; **p.132** R. Baggott, *Pressure Groups: A Question of Interest*, PAVIC Publications (Now Sheffield Hallam University Press), 1994; **p.138** Popperfoto/Reuters; **p.150** D. Butler and J. Butler, *British Political Facts 1900–94*, with permission of Macmillan Ltd, 1995; **p.151** Ben Curtis/PA Photos; **p.152** The Independent/Syndication; **p.153** PA Photos; **p.154** © *The Observer*, 4 May 1997; **p.156** D. Butler and J. Butler, *British Political Facts 1900–94*, with permission of Macmillan Ltd, 1995; **p.161** C. Rallings and M. Thrasher, *New Britain: New Elections*, Vacher Dod, 1999; **p.176** William Conran/PA Photos; **p.181** D. Butler and D. Kavanagh, *The British General Election of 1997*, with permission of Macmillan Ltd, 1997; **p.182** D. Butler and J. Butler, *British Political Facts 1900–94*, with permission of Macmillan Ltd, 1995; **p.191** PA Photos; **p.194** PA Photos; **p.195** Crown copyright is reproduced with the permission of the Controller of Her Majesty's Stationery Office; **p.207** Royal Commission on the reform of the House of Lords, Cm 4534, 1999, National Statistics © Crown copyright 2000; **p.208** Martin Beddall/Rex Features; **p.210** Sean Dempsey/PA Photos; **p.213** Womans Weekly/Rex Features; **p.214** Popperfoto/Reuters; **p.222** Associated Press; **p.223** J. P. Mackintosh, *The British Cabinet*, Routledge, 1962; **p.227** Popperfoto; **p.229** Popperfoto; **p.234** Popperfoto; **p.239** EPA/PA Photos; **p.242** Stefan Rousseau/Topham Picturepoint; **p.247** H. Young, *One of Us*, with permission of Macmillan Ltd, 1989; **p.251** Camera Press/Roger Taylor; **p.259** Crown copyright is reproduced with the permission of the Controller of Her Majesty's Stationery Office; **p.280** Ray Tang/Rex Features; **p.277** Wandsworth Council; **p.327** Associated Press/Topham Picturepoint; **p.329** With permission of Infoelect; **p.330** With permission of the European Communities; **p.331** Popperfoto/Reuters; **p.422** Brown Brothers, Sterling, PA; **p.426** © Ezio Petersen/UPI/Gamma/Frank Spooner Pictures; **p.450** Popperfoto/Reuters; **p.452** Popperfoto/Reuters; **p.455** Ron Edmonds/Associated Press; **p.462** Popperfoto; **p.482** Popperfoto/AFP; **p.484** Popperfoto; **p.485** Popperfoto; **p.487** Popperfoto; **p.492** Popperfoto/J. David Ake/AFP; **p.494** Popperfoto; **p.496** Popperfoto/AFP; **p.501** Topham Picturepoint; **p.486** Topham/ImageWorks; **p.515** © Mingasson Gilles/Gamma/Frank Spooner Pictures; **p.519** Erik Pendzich/Rex Features; **p.529** Popperfoto; **p.543** Kermani/Frank Spooner Pictures; **p.561** D. Kavanagh, *Thatcherism and British Politics*, by permission of Oxford University Press, 1990; Bill Jones, *Political Issues in Britain Today*, Manchester University Press, 1999; **p.562** Crown copyright is reproduced with the permission of the Controller of Her Majesty's Stationery Office.

While every effort has been made to trace copyright holders the publishers apologise for any inadvertent omissions.

Introduction

Success in politics

This book has been extensively revised and expanded in order to meet the requirements of the new specifications in government and politics that were introduced in September 2000. It fulfils four functions.

The first is to provide students with a thorough grounding in the study of government and politics. In this respect it follows the philosophy of political study that was established by Bernard Crick in the 1970s. It also reflects the contemporary interest in the concept of 'citizenship'. Thus it is designed to promote political literacy – a common language of politics – and to equip its readers with a knowledge of institutions, concepts and ideas that will enable them to become effective citizens of the modern state.

Second, it provides material that is required for all the new AS specifications approved by the Qualifications and Curriculum Authority (QCA) at the beginning of the year 2000. All the topics in the specifications of the major examination boards are included.

Third, *Success in Politics* includes units that are comprehensive enough to cover virtually all the optional specifications for the new A2 qualifications offered by the major boards. In this regard, it contains all the necessary content for the study of US government, issues concerning the European Union and its impact on the UK, aspects of political behaviour, political ideologies in the UK and the rest of the world and those major issues that have featured in the modern British political scene.

Finally, the book can be used as an introduction to the subject for all those who come to it new, for whatever reason. Thus it can be used by those who are beginning a degree course in politics or who have simply developed in interest in politics and wish to learn more.

The style of the book is designed to make it accessible. Thus it is carefully divided up into sections that enable the reader to follow arguments or narratives in a logical manner. This approach is also intended to reflect the style of questioning that typically occurs in AS- and A2-level examinations. In this way, a student who has followed the text carefully will be well prepared to tackle most of the tasks set by modern examiners.

How to use this book

The student who is new to politics faces two particular difficulties. One is that few political issues are clear cut. There are usually two or more sides to take on any idea or question. Used to being presented with relatively certain information at more elementary levels of education, the advanced student is confronted with a whole series of doubts about where truth and accuracy lie. The second problem involves understanding how to use examples and illustrations to underpin arguments. Examiners are all anxious that the better candidates in their examinations are able to demonstrate a good knowledge of relevant, contemporary political events and developments. The question is, what examples should be used? Which authorities should be quoted? In both cases this book attempts to provide help.

At the end of each section a summary is provided, usually in a convenient tabular form. As well as providing an aid to detailed revision of the material, the summaries also indicate the important elements of disagreement that can be identified among different political parties and philosophies. Students are encouraged to learn and understand all these key points. They are vital to good examination organisation and technique.

From time to time, brief narratives or quotations are included. These are designed both to help with an understanding of the text, and to provide suggestions for the illustrations and evidence that is needed to bring relevance and authority to any answer in politics examinations. Of course, the good student will add his or her own examples, but the illustrations shown can act as a guide to how such material can be effectively used.

Key terms and concepts

The nature of politics

One useful definition of politics is to describe it, as Professor Bernard Crick has done, as the peaceful resolution of conflict. This implies that the alternative is some form of violent means of settling differences, such as revolution, civil war or simply armed struggle, while in politics the clash of ideas and interests is resolved through legal, organised methods that have been agreed by consenting citizens. Under this definition, autocratic and totalitarian rule must also be ruled out as forms of politics. Instead they are merely means by which a state is governed.

Crick's definition of politics can be applied on any scale. Disputes within a family, for example, where there is a struggle for supremacy and possibly heated discussion about holidays, home alterations, education or pet keeping, could be described as the peaceful resolution of conflict. So, too, could manoeuvring for advantageous positions and promotion in a work situation. Above all, it can refer, of course, to the way in which whole states are run.

A more conservative and limited view has been described by the modern philosopher, Michael Oakeshott. He was attracted by the original Greek roots of the word *politiki*, meaning the affairs of the state. For him politics is, and should be, merely the organisation of the running of the state. This implies doing whatever may be necessary to preserve the security and promote the well-being of the people. This shares common ground with Crick's definition, but also allows for other forms of rule.

So, politics can relate to the power struggles on the high peaks of government, to the internal disputations of parties, the campaigns of local groups of activists, elections to a school sixth-form committee or even contests for influence among groups of friends. All these circumstances may conform to one or the other of our two alternative descriptions.

To sum up a definition of politics, three ideas can be identified:

- Politics concerns the resolution of conflicts by non-violent means.
- It necessarily involves a struggle for power and influence.
- In its fullest sense, it refers to the manner in which a state is organised and run.

Here we will confine ourselves to treating politics as the manner in which the affairs of government are handled and the conflicts that are involved in the running of those affairs. For our 'scale' we will be dealing with government at local, regional, national and supra-national level. The 'micro-politics' of the home, the classroom and the workplace need not concern us here.

A glossary of common political terms is to be found on pages 564–71.

nature of state and government

These two terms cause considerable confusion to new students of politics. This is with good cause. They can, indeed, be difficult to define and distinguish from each other. As with the term 'politics', a number of different descriptions could be adopted without harm to our general understanding. In this book the ~~terms are generally~~ applied.

The state

The term 'state' refers to the permanent institutions that exercise sovereign power within a defined territory. 'Sovereign power' may be defined as the monopoly of the right to enforce laws. These institutions are permanent in the sense that they do not change when a new government is elected or when new political leaders replace existing ones. State institutions in the UK include the following:

- Those bodies that administer laws – the courts, police and other enforcement agencies, the tax and welfare authorities.
- Those public bodies, often known as 'quangos' (quasi-autonomous national government organisations), which carry out many of the functions of government, such as the allocation of public funds, the regulation of large private organisations and the development of policies.
- Local and regional levels of government that either make decisions themselves or administer services whose nature has been determined by central government institutions.
- Parliament itself, which may be considered to be part of the state. Although its personnel may change after each general election, it is permanent as an institution.
- The civil service, including the executive agencies that have now replaced parts of the old bureaucracy, is very much at the heart of the state, establishing a stability that does not exist in ever-changing government structures.
- The armed forces, including the security or intelligence services, which play a vital role in the protection of the state.

The Head of State is the monarch (a term referring to the individual who holds the position) or Crown (referring to the office itself). This implies that there is one personality who has the authority to speak on behalf of, and represent, the whole nation. Though this may theoretically be the case, a problem arises in that the monarch is not elected and cannot be held accountable to the people for what she does. In those systems – the majority in the world of politics – where the Head of State is elected and is normally known as 'President', this difficulty does not arise. Thus, although the Queen may have the technical authority to speak for all her subjects, it is not expected in a modern democracy that she should attempt to do so without guidance.

The British non-political monarch, therefore, cannot represent the state. In her place the Head of Government must do so. This is the Prime Minister. The confusion between the role of Head of State and Head of Government presents problems, as we shall see below.

The government　Although the word 'government' can refer to the 'act of governing' and often does so, 'the Government' itself is a more specific term. It applies to those elected ministers who claim the authority to run the state that is described above.

We have seen that the institutions of the state are permanent; the Government, on the other hand, is transient. It represents a temporary majority thrown up in Parliament by the results of the previous general election. By their votes the people give it a temporary mandate (authority) to control the institutions of the state, pass laws and administer services in accordance with the manifesto that it put before them at the election.

The idea that the Government controls and runs the institutions of the state is not quite sufficient for the fullest understanding of the relationship between the two. We must also take into account certain other realities:

- For its period of office the British government effectively *is* the state. It is almost impossible to distinguish between the two. All key national decisions – when to hold elections, whom to appoint as ministers, what foreign treaties to sign, what military actions to take – are taken by the Government.
- The Head of State (the monarch) does have reserve powers that may be used in exceptional circumstances. Thus, the Queen could theoretically dismiss a minister or the whole Government, could refuse to give Royal Assent to legislation and could command her troops not to take action ordered by the Government. Whether this would be tolerated by those troops or by the people remains an open question.
- Parliament also enjoys the power to veto Government legislation. Though rarely used, this is a real power. When it is used we can say that Parliament is working on behalf of the state, in the sense that it is acting in the national, long-term interest against a temporary, partisan Government.
- The situation is now further complicated by the European Union. In some areas of jurisdiction, such as trade and environmental protection, the Council of European Ministers is the government of the UK. Short of leaving the Union, there is nothing the British Government or Parliament can do about the Council's decisions where there is no national veto available. Similarly, the permanent institutions of the Union – the Commission, the European Parliament and the Court of Justice – are now part of the state. Unlike specifically British state institutions, however, the Government cannot speak on their behalf.
- The new devolved administrations in Scotland, Wales and Northern Ireland may also be described as 'government', but it should not be forgotten that the power of such regional governments can be withdrawn by Parliament in London. This is what occurred in February 2000, when the Northern Ireland Executive was suspended. They are, in effect, 'delegated governments'.

The social and economic structure of the UK*

Although a detailed factual knowledge of the social and economic structure of the UK is not required in AS- and A2-level studies, it is nevertheless important and students should familiarise themselves with such information. Some of the principal changes occurring in the modern era are described below.

The population

The total size of the population of the UK has become remarkably stable. However, the raw figures disguise three developments that are having marked effects on the making of policy.

The first trend is for the population to become older. This means that an increasingly large proportion of the population is over 60. Conversely, of course, this means that there is a lower proportion of younger people and this fact, in itself, is likely to reduce birth rates in the future. The data shown below do not indicate dramatic change, but there is no doubt that the ageing of the population is accelerating.

Second, the UK is increasingly becoming a **multicultural** society. Indeed, much of the population rise has been caused by net immigration, rather than high birth rates or falling death rates.

These first two developments have policy implications:

- The ageing population places greater burdens on that proportion of the population which is still working. That is to say, the **dependency ratio** – the relationship between those who are producing and those who are not – is growing. It also means that there are growing demands on the pension system and the health service as older people tend to require more medical treatment. Policies concerning care of the elderly will play a greater part in British politics in the future than in the past.
- The growing proportion of the population who come from ethnic minorities has increased the need for measures to prevent racism and discrimination or to promote integration and racial harmony. Much of the responsibility for these policies falls upon the law enforcement system and upon education.

Thirdly, there has been a long-term drift of population away from the regions towards the more prosperous south-east corner of the country. This is largely the result of a restructuring of the UK's economy. Traditional manufacturing industries in Wales, Scotland and the north are in long-term decline. Similarly, the contraction of employment in agriculture has tended to depopulate large parts of west and north Wales, northern Scotland and the south-west of England. Conversely, the service and financial industries, which are concentrated in the south, have been expanding. Transport and housing policies must absorb the main impact of these movements.

* All statistics from the Government Statistical Service.

Some key population statistics					
	1984	**1994**	**1995**	**1997**	**1998**
Population (millions)	56.5	58.4	58.6	59.0	59.2
Ethnic minorities (millions)	2.31	3.21	3.24	3.60	3.66
Proportion over 75 years old (%)	6.3	6.8	7.0	7.2	7.3

The economic structure

The most striking feature of the UK's economy, apart from the steady rise in prosperity that all developed countries have enjoyed in the modern age, has been the changing balance between manufacturing and service industries. There has also been a relative decline in agriculture. The table below shows the way in which the output of various industries has changed in recent years. It is expressed in index numbers, so that growth rates can be compared.

Index of output for various industries (1995 = 100)					
	1950	**1975**	**1995**	**1997**	**1998**
Agriculture	39.1	65.1	100	103.5	102.6
Construction	47.3	73.1	100	104.7	106.0
Textiles	100.9	129.9	100	96.4	88.9
Engineering	52.0	87.9	100	104.1	108.8
Services	34.4	61.9	100	107.8	111.8
Manufacturing	46.0	85.0	100	101.7	102.1

Although most sectors have been growing since 1950, it can be clearly seen that the **relative** importance of agriculture and manufacturing has declined compared to service industries.

These changes require policies to ease the problems associated with restructuring, including unemployment and shifts in population. Decisions have to made as to which industries are worthy of government support and which should be allowed to decline naturally. There are also education and training requirements as employment and skill needs change.

The impact of restructuring is also felt in Europe. As a member of the European Union, the UK is part of a European single economy and single market. To some extent this ties the hands of policy-makers, who are not always permitted to intervene in industrial policy by European regulations. It also means that there is now greater **interdependence** with the rest of Europe. What happens in the UK has an impact in Europe. More importantly, changes in the structure of the European economy **as a whole** affect the British economy.

Education Although the actual **structure** of educational provision in the UK changed little over the last two decades of the twentieth century, this should not disguise the fact that education became a key element in social policy during the period.

Most children are still educated in non-selective comprehensive primary and secondary schools – about 92 per cent in 1999 – with only a small minority in private schools or selective grammar schools. The higher education sector, post-18, has, however, expanded hugely. The proportion of the post-18 age group who are in full-time further and higher education rose from 14 per cent in 1982 to 34 per cent in 1999. At the same time, the number of pupils obtaining qualifications at GCSE, A-level and their equivalents has grown steadily.

In the primary and secondary sectors, there has been growing concern with raising standards. This has been pursued by the imposition of the National Curriculum, the regular testing of pupils at various stages of their education and efforts to improve the quality of the teaching profession. Despite these efforts, standards in education remain a major concern for all policy-makers.

It is now recognised that the UK's ability to adapt to the rapidly changing global economic environment, and to be flexible enough to develop new industries that require higher skill levels, depends on educational standards. Further growth in the higher education sector and increases in expenditure on schools are therefore likely.

Health and social security

As we have seen, the ageing population of the UK is placing a growing burden upon the National Health Service (NHS). As with education, the basic structure of health care in the UK has not changed significantly in recent years. The stresses in health care, however, certainly have changed.

New treatments, notably in transplant services, cancer treatment and control of heart disease, have meant that there are new and growing demands on the NHS. The result is that, although expenditure on health care has been rising continuously, the apparent shortfall in spending is also increasing. The gradual rise in the use of private health schemes has not been able to make up the difference. The medical professions remain under intense pressure and the demands for more spending on new medicines and treatments continues unabated. Governments have constantly to make critical decisions both about how much to spend on health care, and about how expenditure is to be distributed among competing needs.

The social security system, on the other hand, has been undergoing fundamental reforms since the mid-1990s. Four developments stand out:

- There has been a continuing attempt to eliminate from the system those who are not **entitled** to benefits. For example, the unemployed are required to attend regular job interviews if they are to claim their payments. Straightforward unemployment benefit has been largely replaced by the 'jobseeker's allowance', which places the onus on the recipient to be genuinely searching for work.
- The emphasis of the welfare system has shifted away from merely operating a kind of 'safety net' for those in need, towards a range of incentives designed to help people out of poverty and need. For example, single parents are now offered help with child care if they find employment.

- The welfare and tax systems have been adjusted so that there are incentives for those at the lower end of the income scale to improve their earning potential without being penalised by the tax system. This effectively means that every working family will have a minimum standard of living. Allied to the introduction of a national minimum wage, these developments are beginning to make inroads into poverty in the UK.
- While tax and welfare systems have been reformed to improve living standards, the state pension system has been steadily eroded. This is partly because private pension schemes have grown in importance, and partly because the state pensions burden has increased markedly. The elderly are increasingly expected to rely on their own resources; the state is beginning to withdraw from this aspect of social policy. The growing pensions bill is indicated by the table below, showing the marked rise in the numbers entitled to the state pension.

Year	State pensioners (millions)
1976	8.1
1986	9.2
1996	9.7
1998	9.9

The numbers claiming unemployment benefit or poverty relief may ebb and flow according to economic conditions, but the number of pensioners is set to rise continuously until well into the twenty-first century.

Crime

The apparently inexorable rise in crime levels that characterised most of the twentieth century seemed to level off in the 1990s. However, the total numbers remain extremely high. There is also a trend towards offenders becoming younger.

The main increases in crime have tended to be in offences against the person, especially street robbery (mugging) and housebreaking. Meanwhile, the prison population has risen considerably. This has been the result less of increases in crime levels than of changes in sentencing policy. More offenders now tend to be sent to prison, as opposed to receiving non-custodial sentences, and for longer periods.

The continued high crime levels have placed greater burdens on the police and courts system. Expenditure has had to rise on both, but this does not mean that the UK's police force has grown in size. In fact, it has remained relatively static in recent years. Policing has become more expensive and this has inhibited the ability of governments to recruit more officers of the law.

Crime and punishment have moved steadily up the political agenda over the past two decades. The implications for education, law making, policing and sentencing have become important themes in inter-party debates. In general, a more 'hard-line' stance has been adopted by all the parties in response to public opinion.

Some key crime and punishment statistics (England and Wales)							
	1900	1925	1950	1975	1981	1991	1998
Total recorded crimes (thousands)	77.9	114.0	479.4	2,105.6	2,794.2	5,073.5	5,109.1
Prison population (average)	17,435	10,509	20,474	39,820	43,311	45,897	65,298
Proportion of crimes solved (%)	N/A	N/A	45	44	38	29	29
Number guilty of motoring offences (thousands)	1	137	358	1,181	1,211	713	665
Number guilty of violent crime (thousands)	1	1	4	40	56	67	61
Number of police officers (thousands)	N/A	56.5	63.1	107.1	119.6	127.5	126.5

Political concepts

Introduction

Politics has its own vocabulary, much of which is familiar to us in everyday speech. However, if we are to be serious students of the science of politics, it is essential that we understand that common terms may have different meanings and usages. The expression 'usage' refers to the fact that many political concepts are treated in a particular way by people who hold differing philosophical outlooks. In other words, the 'use' of political terms may vary greatly. For example, the word 'freedom' may mean one thing to a liberal, but another to a traditional Conservative. In the former case, it may suggest the idea of an absence of restrictions, as in 'free speech' or 'free movement'. To a Conservative, freedom may express the idea of maximum opportunity. Thus the concept 'freedom' must be used carefully and explained fully according to its context.

Similarly, a number of political terms are used in one way in everyday language, but can mean something different or more precise to the student of politics. For example, the word 'responsible' can imply behaviour that is sensible, perhaps caring for the feelings of others. This is too vague for the political scientist. Responsible **political** action specifically means action for which an individual may be held to account, just as ministers must be **responsible** to Parliament. We also tend to treat the words 'power' and 'authority' as meaning roughly the same thing. In politics, however, the distinction is crucial, as we shall see below.

Professor Bernard Crick's work on political literacy in the 1970s suggested that concepts fall into three broad categories, which provide us with a useful scheme. These were:

- concepts concerning the process and status of government
- concepts concerning the status and interests of individuals in society
- concepts concerning relationships between government and the people.

We will consider below the following concepts within these three categories.

Government	Individuals	Relationships
• Order	• Freedom	• Representation
• Power	• Individualism	• Responsibility
• Authority	• Rights	• Law and legal justice
• Legitimacy	• Welfare	• Social justice
• Consent	• Equality	
• Sovereignty		

Concepts concerned with government

Order At first sight, the concept of social order may appear to be simple and ~~however, a number of different political perspectives~~ can be applied to the subject. Not least is the question of how fundamental order is to the human condition. For some, such as the seventeenth-century English philosopher **Thomas Hobbes** (1588–1679), or the early conservative commentator **Edmund Burke** (1729–97), the need and desire for order is man's most basic instinct once he has provided for himself in a material sense. Others, such as the nineteenth-century liberal **John Stuart Mill** (1806–73), have argued that individual freedom comes first.

> *'Good Order is the foundation of all Good things.'*
> Edmund Burke, 1790

To simplify the issues surrounding order, we can identify four political traditions that have their own view of what the term implies.

Authoritarian conservatism or totalitarian dictatorship Here order is considered to be so vital that the means by which it is achieved are less important than the result of those methods. All that matters is that sufficient **force** can be exerted upon society and in extreme cases even **terror**. Thus order is maintained by propaganda and fear of punishment and not just by law alone.

Mere conservatives would tend to stress the use of law more than the totalitarians, but both would agree that there may be times when pure force is justified in order to preserve the security of the state and the individuals who live in it. Typical of this view was the Italian Renaissance writer **Niccolo Machiavelli** (1469–1527). He argued that wise and successful rulers should use a shrewd combination of legal and military methods to maintain their own power, as well as the internal and external security of the state. But we should not think that this is a purely historical idea. Twentieth-century dictators such as Mussolini and Stalin adopted much the same view.

Traditional conservatism The maintenance of order and security is just as important to traditional conservatives as it is to those described above. However, they approach the problem from a very different perspective. For them there is a **'natural order'** in any society: that is, a social structure which has developed over a long period of time. It becomes part of the traditions of the people and they feel comfortable and secure within it.

Possibly the most striking example was the feudal system that flourished in Europe throughout the Middle Ages. There, every individual knew their position within the structure, understood their rights and duties and rarely questioned the system. The result was long periods of peace and order. There were, of course, periodic breakdowns in order, when thrones and territory were disputed, or when poor harvests or disease created unrest, but for the most part feudalism was a guarantee of good order. A more extreme form of this kind of stratified society is the Indian **caste** system. Each person is born into a caste or level of society, connected to specific occupations and roles in that society. It is forbidden, under strict Hindu religious teaching, to leave one's caste or marry out of it. The reward for caste loyalty is spiritual salvation and the result has been a remarkably well-ordered society.

It can be seen that, as long as such natural forms of order are maintained, society is likely to enjoy peace and security. Conservatives have, therefore, observed that the best way for governments to maintain order is to respect traditions. The greater individual liberty or social equality that liberals and socialists have sought has, they believe, caused upheaval and disorder.

> '*What is the fundamental principle of the feudal system, gentlemen? It is that the tenure of property shall be the performance of its duties. Why, when William the Conqueror carved out parts of the land, and introduced the feudal system, he said to the recipient, "You shall have the estate, but you shall do something for it; you shall feed the poor; you shall endow the Church; you shall defend the land in case of war; and shall execute justice and maintain truth to the poor for nothing."*'
>
> Benjamin Disraeli, 1882

Feudal order has all but disappeared in the modern world, but traditionalists still believe that an ordered society can be promoted if time-honoured institutions are preserved and respected. The conventional family, established religion, moral principles and traditional political bodies are examples of how security can be carried forward from one generation to the next.

Liberalism and democracy

Liberals and democrats attempt to reconcile the principles of freedom and self-determination of peoples with the need to maintain order. The conservative notion that it is sufficient for the people to respect traditional forces of order is rejected by liberals. There must, instead, be a specific and explicit agreement by the people as to how they are to be governed. The system of government and its laws must enjoy, broadly, the consent of the people. Thus, even if there are political disagreements and different parties may compete for power, order is maintained because people respect the **principle** of democratic government.

This is not to say that force is never required to maintain good order. It is understood that there will always be those of a criminal frame of mind, and others who disagree fervently with the actions of government and are therefore prepared to break the law in pursuit of their beliefs. Nevertheless, the principle holds good that order will be preserved only if there is popular consent to government.

> '*The basis of order in any society is agreement upon how we are governed.*'
>
> John Hume, Northern Ireland MP, 1994

The practical implications of this liberal–democratic view of what constitutes order can be identified as follows:

- The vast majority of the people support the system of government.
- The rule of law prevails – governments are subject to legal constraints.

- Only a small minority are prepared to break the law for political reasons.
- There is an organised and effective law enforcement system.
- Power is transferred ~~peacefully from one government to the next.~~

Anarchism and communism

All the views on order described above depend upon the existence of a political state that has powers to maintain security. Both anarchists and Marxist-inspired communists, however, oppose the existence of a state. While they accept that the state maintains some form of order, it is seen as an artificial creation that is an unwarranted interference in people's true freedom.

Anarchists, for example, believe that good order is possible without a state, provided conditions exist within which people can exercise their own judgements, free from the many corruptions of modern society such as private property, the use of force and the existence of class distinction. The communist view is remarkably similar. For communists it is a just **economic** order that must be imposed in order to remove the need for the powerful state. In the latter case, the equal distribution of income and wealth, together with the absence of private ownership, constitutes such an order.

> 'We know that, if our descendants are to reach their high destiny ... they will owe it to their coming together more and more intimately, to the incessant collaboration, to this mutual aid from which brotherhood grows little by little.'
>
> E. Reclus, nineteenth-century anarchist

Power

Power is the ability that an individual or a body has to make others do something. We may qualify this by adding that we assume that the subject of power is doing something **that they would otherwise not do**. We can also differentiate between different **degrees** of power.

Degrees of power

Power may be **absolute** in the sense that we can say the subject will obey **virtually without fail**. Of course, no power can be totally absolute in this sense as, if a person is willing to die, there can be no way of forcing him to act in a certain way. The political or religious martyr who will sacrifice himself for his belief cannot be controlled and power ceases to have any meaning. Power may also be relatively weak. Here we are suggesting that power merely means affecting people's behaviour without fully controlling it. In this sense, power is better described as **influence**. In between these two extremes is an infinite number of levels of power.

To illustrate, we can say that military leaders of totalitarian states have absolute power. They control all the forces of law and order and may put to death, or at least imprison, any opponent. There may be a few brave individuals willing to risk death to defy a dictator's power, but he has virtually absolute power. At the other end of the spectrum, we often speak of the 'power' of trade unions or of big business. Clearly, such bodies cannot physically force anybody to act in a certain way, but they do possess influence. By threatening sanctions, such as strikes or lack of co-operation, they may influence governments or other bodies and individuals to behave in a particular way that suits them. In

between the two, we can point to democratic governments that
power through legitimate institutions. Ultimately, they are in t
of the people who have elected them and who may, in th
remove them from office. Between elections, however, they are generally
able to get their way.

How power is exercised How and why is power exercised? To answer this question we must
examine the basis of power.

Coercion is perhaps the clearest source of power. It concerns the use
of **force** to secure compliance. Force implies threat of torture or execution in extreme circumstances, but more commonly uses the threat of
imprisonment if its subjects will not obey.

It should be emphasised at this point that **all** states reserve the use of
coercive power, no matter how peaceful or democratic the government
may be. This is because states are not voluntary organisations, so that it
is almost inevitable that there will be people who will not agree with
some of its laws and customs. Such people must, therefore, be forced
to conform in the interests of the security of others. If they will not
conform, they must be removed from society by imprisonment or even
execution.

By contrast, if we freely join a club, society, business/company or
college, for example, we have voluntarily joined and, by so volunteering,
have agreed to abide by its rules. Should we find the rules unacceptable,
we may leave or be expelled. By and large, states do not have these
options. Instead they must reserve the right to force people into compliance.

Of course, states do not need to exercise such coercive power most of
the time. Most people will conform either through natural consent or
through fear of punishment. Thus, coercive power is usually reserved or
latent: that is, it exists and people know it exists, even when it is not in
use. In peaceful ordered states, notably western democracies, coercive
power remains on the whole latent. On the other hand, in less stable
situations, such as Northern Ireland from the 1970s to the 1990s, when
sections of the population did not consent to the regime that governed
them, open force is needed. Thus, in Northern Ireland there were soldiers in the streets and many individual rights were suspended. The same
has been true in military dictatorships such as Chile or Cuba.

'Political power grows out of the barrel of a gun.'
Mao Tse-tung, 1938

Despite Mao's extreme view, political power is that which is exercised
without force, but which is nevertheless highly effective. Governments
and law-making bodies possess such power because they enjoy the force
of law behind them. They can use laws, but also persuasion, offers of
rewards and threats of sanctions to get their way. How, for example,
does the British Cabinet exert political power over Parliament? The
answer is that it can reward those MPs who are loyal to the Cabinet
(e.g. advancing their careers) and threaten sanctions against those who
defy them (e.g. reducing their career prospects or even expelling them
from the party in extreme circumstances). Of course, in this particular
example, Parliament as a whole can defy such **political** power by exert-

ing the **coercive** power that it possesses as the supreme law-making body. In other words, the forces of law and order – the police and courts – must enforce Parliament's wishes above those of the Cabinet if there is a conflict.

Finally, **influence** refers to the ability to affect decisions in the political arena, but it is not real power in the sense of being able to ensure that certain actions are undertaken. Thus, pressure groups often influence government, but none of them can actually make decisions and carry them through to implementation. We can now rank forms of power in descending order of effectiveness:

1. Coercion
2. Political power
3. Influence

So far we have not discussed the question of whether these types of power are being **rightfully** exercised. The sources and levels of power tell us nothing about this issue. In other words, power can be judged by its **results**, but this does not tell us anything about its justification. To examine this issue we must introduce the concept of **authority**.

Authority

As we have suggested above, the terms 'power' and 'authority' are often treated as interchangeable terms, but this would be inaccurate. While 'power' refers to the ability to achieve certain ends, 'authority' refers to the right to exercise that power.

Hereditary authority

Until the sixteenth century, questions about authority were largely redundant in Europe. A combination of the doctrine of the 'Divine Right of Kings' and the strength of the tradition of the hereditary principle prevented any questioning of the sources of royal power. Divine Right referred to the widely held belief that monarchs owed their right to govern to the sanction of God. They were, in other words, God's servant on earth, doing his will. The hereditary principle was a matter of both tradition and expediency. It was the accepted way of determining who should govern, but also provided a peaceful means of transferring power on the death of a ruler. (Of course, it did not always work perfectly and disputes over succession to the throne were not uncommon.)

Hobbes's interpretation of authority

Thomas Hobbes (1588–1679), writing at the time of the English Civil War and the execution of King Charles I, asked who was the real 'author' of the King's power. His answer was that 'authority' can only be granted by the people. The notion that God or tradition could sanction the use of power must, he argued, be rejected just as Parliament had abolished (though only temporarily) the monarchy. But Hobbes was not a democrat. He asserted that popular authority could not be granted to each individual ruler, and could not be removed by the people. Rather, authority was given to an absolute, all-powerful ruler on the grounds that this was necessary to ensure peace and security. Thus, Hobbes's kind of ruler was little different from any existing seventeenth-century monarch. However, he had found a basis for his authority, a better justification for the use of power. In short, he had developed the concept of political authority.

Weber's alternative sources of authority

With the growth of democratic ideals in the nineteer
Hobbes's limited notion of authority became increasingly u
The German sociologist **Max Weber** (1864–1920) understc
cal authority could have more than one single source, any
could be considered as legitimate. Three such sources were identified.

<u>Traditional</u>   This is the idea that if the exercise of power by an institu-
tion has been accepted by the people over a long period of time, certainly several generations, it has gained real authority. In other words, it
has stood the test of time. Hereditary monarchy is an obvious example,
but the British House of Lords could also be included. The ruling families in a variety of Arab states in the Middle East certainly base their
authority on tradition and there is relatively little challenge to the principle.

<u>Charismatic</u>   The term 'charisma' refers to the ability to inspire others
and to attract a following. Originally applied to actors or religious
leaders, it has come to have political significance. Here authority is
granted purely on the basis that leaders are so persuasive and respected
that they are allowed to exercise power over their followers. Such
examples as Mahatma Gandhi and Benito Mussolini may be said to
have been granted such authority by large numbers of people.

<u>Legal–rational</u>   This refers to any organised system for establishing
proper authority. In the modern world this is likely to consist of free
elections. It may, therefore, be described today as 'elective' authority. In
democracies it has become the only fully acceptable basis for authority,
though it is often combined with traditional or charismatic forms. Thus,
a Prime Minister such as Margaret Thatcher could claim special authority on the grounds of charismatic appeal in addition to her elected position. Similarly, some democracies such as the UK's still accept the
authority of traditional institutions alongside elected bodies.

Before leaving the subject of authority it is worth noting how different political movements tend to deal with it.

Conservatives have been much more willing to accept traditional
forms of authority, especially in the nineteenth century. Of course,
during the twentieth century elective authority became increasingly
important, but there remains an acceptance of some traditional sources
of authority relating to the House of Lords, the Church and the monarchy. In addition, conservatives have placed great store by leadership,
so that charismatic authority is accepted more readily by them as a
legitimate basis for power than it is, for example, by liberals. Individuals
such as Churchill and Thatcher illustrate such beliefs.

Liberals are very much more concerned with popular authority and so
accept only fair and free elections as a basis for authority. Furthermore,
they believe that government must be fully responsible to the people in
order to retain that authority.

Socialists too insist on elective authority and completely reject the
claims of traditional regimes. Nevertheless, there are occasions when the
implementation of socialist objectives may clash with the will of the
people, precipitating a crisis of authority. This is particularly the case
when socialist governments are especially dogmatic in their ideological
outlook.

Power and authority

We can see from the above that power and authority are closely related concepts, but do not mean the same thing. It should also be noted that there can be circumstances where power is being exercised without recognised authority, as in unpopular military dictatorships. It may also be that an individual or body is exceeding the authority which it has been granted. Thus, a hereditary monarch might have some traditional authority, but nevertheless be acting in a dictatorial manner by not consulting others in the exercise of power.

In some unusual cases it could also occur that authority has been granted to an individual, but they are unable to exercise power because they do not have control of sufficient force. For example, the Pope is unable fully to enforce his rulings on the personal conduct of Catholics today, even though they may pay lip service to his authority.

Ultimately, it is likely that, where an institution or an individual enjoys the broad **consent** of those who are being governed, and if sufficient **coercive power** is also available to deal with those who do not consent, then power and authority may coincide in the most effective way. Stable liberal democracies, on the whole, conform to this pattern.

Legitimacy

The concepts explored above – of order, power and authority – are all descriptions of circumstances we may observe in the real world. They are theoretically measurable and there are few disputes as to their meaning or significance. The term 'legitimacy', however, presents us with considerable problems.

When we ask the question, 'Is power being rightfully exercised?' there is no indisputable reply. It depends very much on what we consider to be legitimate authority, what we believe is the justified use of power. Democrats, for example, only accept elections as a means of bestowing authority, while many conservatives argue that tradition is an acceptable basis for the exercise of power. Who is right? The answer is that there is no single answer. Legitimacy is a matter of opinion. It depends entirely upon the individual's political outlook. There is a considerable selection of versions of what constitutes legitimate rule. The principal examples are as follows.

Tradition

As we have already seen, a regime that has held power without serious popular challenge for a long period of time could claim legitimacy.

Control

Some would say that any ruler who can control the state, provide internal security and protect it from external attack has a right to govern. This theory, sometimes called 'might is right', is often accepted as the basis for the international recognition of a regime. It can be argued that, once a government has proved that it controls a territory, it deserves to be recognised by other states, even if they disapprove of the way it has achieved power.

Religion

Some Islamic regimes today, such as Iran or Libya, argue that the basis of their authority is religious belief. As long as the rulers are following the teachings of Mohammed the Prophet, this is sufficient reason for the people to obey them. Such **theocracies** have flourished from time to time in the name of other religions too.

Legality It could be suggested that, if there is a recognisable system of laws in a state, and if the government operates within those laws, it is a legitimate regime. There is, of course, a major problem with this proposition, since we must also ask how the laws came about, but it can also be said that such a regime does at least accept limitations on its own actions.

Morality Here judgements about the conduct of a regime must be made in order to assess a claim to legitimacy. Questions such as 'Are human rights respected?', 'Does the government respect large minorities?' and 'Is true democracy allowed to flourish?' may be asked. Naturally such criteria must be subjective, so legitimacy based on moral grounds may be hotly disputed.

Consent Possibly the most widely accepted basis for legitimacy is that a regime enjoys the consent of its people to govern them. This is examined in more detail below.

Consent

It is a fundamental principle of modern democratic societies that they should feature government by consent. Without this the whole basis of government can be called into question.

Nevertheless, the concept of political consent causes great difficulty among scholars. Superficially, it may often seem clear when a regime enjoys the consent of its people to govern; yet it is often a problem to determine whether people are so much in fear of their government that there appears to be no significant opposition. It was not clear, for example, whether the rulers of the former Soviet Union did, as they claimed, enjoy the support of their subjects or whether the sanctions against opposition were so great that little of it was seen. Only when Mikhail Gorbachev opened the country to free expression and Boris Yeltsin inspired the people to embrace political reforms was it apparent that real consent had been absent.

Though faced with such problems, some attempt has to be made to identify positive signs of consent in order to make a valid judgement as to whether regimes are legitimate. The following may be used as criteria:

- There is a widespread participation in free elections. Where turnouts at the polls are very low, it can be deduced that there is little confidence in the regime. In countries such as the UK or France, where 60–80 per cent of the electorate vote without the need to make voting compulsory, as is the case in Australia, it is clear that broad consent does exist. It should be stressed here that there may be periods when the government in power is unpopular, but this does not mean that the system itself is opposed.
- In the absence of truly free elections, it might be tempting to say that there can be no proof of popular consent. This would not be valid, however. There may, for example, be clear and regular demonstrations of support for a regime in ways other than voting. Distasteful though we may find it, there is little doubt that Hitler's Third Reich enjoyed a long period of strong support even when democracy had been suspended. Less controversially, the Sheikhdoms of the Middle East certainly appear to be well loved even though they are far from free societies in western terms.

- While open manifestations of support give us strong clues as to a regime's popularity, it is less clear when we observe a state in which the people are enthusiastic in neither support nor opposition. ~~governme~~ ~~The~~ populations of east European socialist regimes up to the 1990s, the largely silent masses of China and the apparently peaceful societies of south-east Asia could be the result of either of two phenomena. As we have said above, it may be that the people simply live in abject fear of their rulers. On the other hand, the silence of the people could signify unenthusiastic yet genuine consent. However, it can certainly be argued that lack of any significant opposition over a long period of time suggests that a people are content to be governed as they are.
- Finally, there are political systems that have survived for such a long period of time and are so absorbed in the traditions of a society that consent can be assumed. Few questioned the right of hereditary monarchies to rule for many centuries largely on the grounds that many generations before had accepted them as a reality. Today some traditional regimes of the Middle East fall into this category.

Sovereignty

In general terms, the expression 'sovereignty' simply means 'supreme power', but an investigation into most political systems reveals that a more sophisticated approach is needed. It is useful to divide sovereignty into two main types: that is, legal and political sovereignty.

Legal sovereignty

This describes the point where the ultimate ability to make laws, which will be enforced, resides. Thus, in the UK this point is indisputably Parliament. The police, the courts and other law enforcement agencies will only administer laws that have been properly passed in Parliament and given the Royal Assent by the Queen. It may sometimes appear that other bodies are making law, such as ministers or local authorities, but in reality they are acting only on the authority of Parliament. They may be overruled or have their powers cancelled by Parliament at any time. The legislative powers granted to the Scottish Parliament and Northern Ireland Assembly in 1999 did not confer sovereignty. The power to make laws could always be taken back by London. In some other 'democracies', legal sovereignty may be divided, often between a legislative assembly and an elected presidency.

Regimes that are not democratic in nature usually grant legal sovereignty to a ruler or ruling body which governs 'by decree', but the principle holds good that, if such decrees are enforced, the ruler is indeed sovereign. This illustrates that the concept of sovereignty has nothing to do with questions of legitimacy or genuine authority.

Political sovereignty

Here we are concerned with effective, rather than merely legal power. The difficulty arises when we ask the question, 'Where does ultimate political power reside?' Most states have written constitutions that describe who is legally sovereign and, even where there is no such constitution, as in the UK, it is usually clear who has such sovereignty. Power, on the other hand, is a more elusive idea.

The UK provides us with an ideal example of the problem. As we have said, Parliament alone is legally sovereign, a reality that is explored further in Unit 7. But real power seems to lie elsewhere. The Cabinet, in particular, is considered the centre of power. Yet it must not be forgotten that Parliament can, and sometimes does, overrule the Government. Then there are the people. At the polls it is they who decide who shall form the government. Thus, the people could be considered to be 'politically sovereign', at least at election time.

Sovereignty and the European Union

Membership of the EU means that each member state agrees to accept and enforce decisions made by the Council of Ministers rather than by their own government or Parliament. Although such jurisdiction lies over a limited range of functions such as trade, agriculture and consumer protection, it is often said to mean a **transfer of legal sovereignty** from member states to the EU. Is this so? The answer lies with voting arrangements in the Council of Ministers. On some key issues a unanimous vote is required. In other words, each member has a **veto**. In these cases sovereignty is **not** lost. However, where only a **majority** vote is needed, there is a loss of sovereignty since each member state can be outvoted.

We should not forget, however, that any member may withdraw from the Union, so the loss of sovereignty is not irrevocable. It should also be stressed that any loss of legal sovereignty is accompanied by a gain in the influence that each member has over the affairs of all the others. In other words, there is a trade-off between national sovereignty and international influence. In other words, there can be a 'pooling' of sovereignty.

In other political systems, the political sovereignty of a President may be considerably more important than the legal sovereignty of a legislative body. In present-day Russia, for example, the power of Parliament is relatively weak in comparison to the power of the Head of State.

The two types of sovereignty described above refer to the internal workings of a political system. However, the term does have a further connotation. This concerns the status of political rulers in relation to other states.

Northern Ireland sovereignty

Since the partition of Ireland between North and South in 1921, the sovereignty of Northern Ireland has been hotly contested. The dispute also concerns an issue of consent. The claim of the Republic of Ireland and of the Republicans in the North is that the people of the **whole** of Ireland did not consent to partition. Furthermore, they argue, since Ireland is traditionally a single community it should not be split. Thus, sovereignty is claimed rightfully to lie in Dublin. The British claim to sovereignty, supported by the Loyalist community in Ulster, is that the majority of the people of Northern Ireland **alone** wish to remain part of the United Kingdom. Thus, both communities argue that their claim is the more legitimate. The Good Friday Agreement of 1998 attempted to settle the issue of Northern Ireland sovereignty through a compromise. However, despite the agreement's widespread support in the province, sovereignty remains a disputed issue.

International or external sovereignty

This refers to the criteria by which we judge who is actually in control of a certain territory. In practice, this opens the question of which government should be officially recognised by other governments. There are two principal ways of viewing this problem.

First, we can ask who is effectively in control of a territory: that is, which institution or institutions possess coercive power. This says nothing about the morality, legitimacy or desirability of the regime in power. It is simply a pragmatic question. If we accept the reality of the situation and we wish to have dealings with a regime – economic or diplomatic – we might put aside our opinions and simply recognise the rulers in power. Second, we might care more about the legitimacy of the regime. If it does not come up to certain standards of behaviour, we might choose not to grant recognition of its sovereignty. Its record on human rights or the effectiveness of its democratic institutions might be the criteria we use.

China and the USA

The strange case of American reluctance to recognise the People's Republic of China illustrates the problem of external sovereignty. In 1949, led by Mao Tse-tung, the communists took control of China following a civil war. The deposed rulers, under Chiang Kai-shek, fled to the offshore island of Taiwan and set up a rival government, still claiming to be the rightful government of all China. The USA continued to recognise the government-in-exile until 1977, arguing that they had been wrongfully deposed and were the only elected government of China. Most of the world, however, took a more realistic view and accepted the regime in Peking on the grounds that they controlled the country and there was no real prospect of a return to the former government.

Concepts concerned with the individual

Freedom At first sight, the concept 'freedom' or, as it is often termed, 'liberty' might seem reasonably straightforward. On the whole, we think of it as meaning an 'absence of restraint'. Prisoners, for example, are said to be given their freedom at the end of their sentence; the bars that imprisoned them have been removed. When whole peoples – colonies, conquered territories and the like – are released from subjugation by a foreign power, we say they are now 'free'. But this is a limited interpretation of freedom. Political thinkers and politicians alike have used freedom to describe a number of different phenomena. In some cases, as we shall see below, complete political doctrines are based on a specific usage of the concept. It is, therefore, crucial that its various meanings are understood.

Licence If there were to be absolutely no restraints upon man's actions, a state of complete 'licence' would exist. Some philosophers, notably **Thomas Hobbes,** the seventeenth-century English writer, imagined mankind in a total 'state of nature'. This refers to pre-history when there was no state, no laws and no form of social organisation. This would indeed have been a state of complete licence. However, Hobbes pointed out that this would certainly not constitute true freedom simply because there were no artificial controls. Rather, mankind would be enslaved by a constant state of fear. The individual's property and even his life would be threatened by all the other free individuals in the world. Thus, licence leads to the utter loss of real liberty.

Hobbes's close contemporary, **John Locke,** developed a similar analysis of pre-society, but suggested that man is subject to natural laws that are rules of conduct instinctively understood. These include social feelings and an understanding that each individual should respect the lives and property of others. At first sight this may appear to suggest that no artificial restraints are needed, that there is no such condition as complete licence, since we will control our own behaviour. However, Locke realised that not all people would follow these laws of nature so that there would indeed be a need for man-made laws.

Freedom as 'private judgement' The philosophy of anarchism, which developed during the nineteenth century, suggested an optimistic view of mankind living in such a state of nature. In the view of most anarchists, mankind is naturally sociable, uncompetitive and co-operative. People do not need to be guided towards 'good actions' and do not naturally wish to harm their fellow human beings. It follows from this belief that it is possible to achieve real freedom without recourse to artificial laws. In short, the state becomes unnecessary (the term 'anarchism' literally means 'absence of government', not chaos as many believe).

The early English anarchist **William Godwin** (1756–1836) referred to man's potential to use complete freedom positively and for good ends as the exercise of private judgement. This is not the same as 'licence' because people actually **restrain themselves.** They are certainly not free to do absolutely anything. Indeed, the Russian anarchist **Mikhail Bakunin** (1814–76) insisted that people were actually subject to social necessities so that, even in the total absence of laws and government, there can be no such thing as complete freedom.

> *'It is earnestly to be desired that each man should be wise enough to govern himself, without the intervention of any compulsory restraint.'*
>
> William Godwin

Negative liberty

The terms 'negative' and 'positive' liberty were coined by a modern English philosopher, **Isaiah Berlin**, in 1958. However, the meanings of these two concepts were of particular relevance to the development of liberal principles in the seventeenth, eighteenth and nineteenth centuries. It is therefore convenient to employ the two expressions in this context, even though they had not been developed at the time.

John Locke (1632–1704) and **Jean-Jacques Rousseau** (1712–78) both understood that people can only be truly free when they place the protective cloak of laws around themselves and others. Locke referred to this as 'freedom within the laws', while Rousseau suggested an even more striking 'paradox'. He suggested that people are naturally reluctant to be bound by laws but find themselves in a dilemma. People not being perfect, as anarchists were later to accept could be the case, realise that the absence of laws creates more limitations than the laws themselves. As Hobbes had said, a state of licence leads men to fear each other. Therefore, argues Rousseau, man must be 'forced to be free'. In other words, he must be compelled, however reluctantly, to accept laws which he dislikes, in order to be truly free.

The idea of the freedom of action we possess within laws can be described as **negative liberty**. It was **John Stuart Mill** – England's most celebrated nineteenth-century liberal – who developed the idea of negative liberty to its fullest extent. In his view, we have a right to be free to undertake any action that does no harm to others. He called these **self-regarding actions**. In practice, this referred to most personal conduct and it certainly implied thoughts and beliefs. These areas constituted the realm of negative liberty. **Other-regarding actions**, on the other hand, do affect others and must be subject to legal controls. Here negative liberty exists only within the laws, as Locke had insisted.

The importance of safeguarding the maximum amount of such negative liberty became the central value of nineteenth-century Classical Liberalism. Its most important arena was the economic sphere, where it was felt that capitalism could achieve its full potential only if the maximum degree of economic freedom could be guaranteed. This theme was later to be resurrected by the 'New Right' which was successfully led by Margaret Thatcher in the 1980s. In practice, the maximisation of negative liberty requires that the power of the state be reduced as far as possible, while laws or regulations are kept to a minimum.

> *'The only purpose for which power can be rightfully exercised over any member of a civilised community, against his own will, is to prevent harm to others.'*
>
> John Stuart Mill, *On Liberty*, 1859

Positive liberty

For liberals, as their name suggests, liberty is a fundamental value. It therefore became a major problem for them when the accepted notion of negative liberty was seriously called into question later in the nineteenth century. At that time, excessive liberty was creating a society in which large sections of the population were experiencing extremes of social and economic deprivation. The freedom of the more able and fortunate to benefit from capitalism was balanced by the freedom of others to fail to do so, often through no fault of their own.

But if the state or any other organisation were to step in to alleviate such suffering, there would be a loss of negative liberty for all. Taxation to fund such social welfare, for example, would seriously curtail individuals' freedom to spend their income as they wished. It therefore became necessary for liberals to attempt to redefine freedom.

Without abandoning negative liberty as a desirable end, liberals began to see that, by maximising the opportunities open to people to realise their full potential and to lead the kind of life they prefer, a new form of freedom could be created. This was a 'positive' kind of freedom resulting from better social conditions and welfare, such as education, training, health care, good housing, employment opportunities and pension provision. 'Positive liberty', as Berlin was later to describe such an idea, became the new central belief of the liberal movement as well as that of modern socialism and social democracy. Indeed, by the 1940s it was a concept around which moderate politicians from all political traditions could rally.

Collective freedom   A considerably more difficult conception of freedom has been offered by such philosophers as **Friedrich Hegel** (1770–1831) and **T.H. Green** (1836–82). For them, personal freedom, meaning the pursuit of our own self-interest, does in fact enslave us. We are not really free under such circumstances because we are forced to battle against a world that we see as separate from us. We are, in other words, alienated by the rest of the world and society. Even if that society places few restrictions upon our actions, it still confronts us threateningly. In practical terms, for example, we may be forced to compete against our fellow human beings in our economic lives, to struggle against economic forces that seem to be beyond our control. Yet it is the very freedom in modern liberal societies that has unleashed those forces against us.

In a contemporary setting we may consider that those consumers who have adequate means are free to purchase whatever goods they wish. In reality, however, the producers of those goods have already decided what is available and so the apparently free choice of the consumer is actually in the hands of those producers.

True freedom, Hegel and Green suggest, can flourish only if each individual is totally at one with the rest of society. This implies that each individual should lose their own personal identity into that of society as a whole. In this way there is no contradiction between the goals of society and the goals of any individual within it. Everyone is now 'free' because there is no contradiction between the actions of individuals and the actions of all.

This need not be such a dangerous concept if we consider such a state as one of perfect harmony between the actions of the individual and the needs of society as a whole. For Green, a liberal, it suggested nothing more radical than a welfare state in which all freely contribute to the protection of others. However, it is also an idea that has been taken up by **fascists** to justify the totalitarian state, and by some **Marxists** to justify the imposition of communist ideology at the expense of individual liberty. In other words, this difficult conception of freedom is extremely flexible in its implications.

Forms of freedom	
1. Licence	The complete absence of artificial restrictions.
~~2. Private judgement~~	...wherein each individual is guided by their own conscience.
3. Negative liberty	The freedom that exists within the laws. For early liberals this was the only practical form of freedom.
4. Positive liberty	Associated with modern liberals and socialists, this refers to circumstances where opportunities for people are maximised.
5. Collective freedom	The belief that we are only truly free if there is no distinction between the goals of individuals and those of society as a whole.

Individualism

Closely allied to ideas of freedom is individualism, a concept that has been adopted by conservatives, liberals and socialists alike.

It encompasses a number of goals that individuals may wish to attain, including maximising personal opportunities, realising one's potential, the fulfilment of aspirations, and the enjoyment of wealth, property and privacy as well as the security that results from a well-ordered and peaceful society. These are all qualities that may allow us to enjoy and express our own individuality.

The idea has coincided with freedom as a desirable end for the simple reason that, for many, it is personal liberty which is the best guarantee of one's ability to express such individuality. For example, only if we are free to enjoy our own private property without threats from others or interference by the state can we pursue a truly individual lifestyle. However, various political philosophies have stressed different aspects of individualism and have proposed radically different ways of achieving it.

Conservatism

For conservatives, the key lies in the creation of a well-ordered and secure society. Individualism certainly cannot flourish, they argue, if we are constantly in fear of encroachments on our property or attacks on our person. Similarly, there must be a regulated economic, social and political environment in which individuals feel secure enough to be able to engage in freely chosen activities in the knowledge that the future will be much like the past, that there will be no violent social upheavals which may create uncertainty.

The liberal–conservative economist **John Maynard Keynes** (1883–1946) used such an argument to promote his proposals for extensive state intervention in the national economy. The free working of the capitalist system was all very well, he observed, but it resulted in too many uncertainties for individual economic enterprise to flourish. The Great Depression of the 1930s, for example, created a climate in which there was insufficient optimism for individuals to undertake new economic enterprises. Intervention by the state could have prevented the slump and protected individuals, both workers and entrepreneurs, from its worst effects.

Conservatives have always insisted that there should be a strict dividing line between matters which should be in the public domain and thus be the concern of the state – such as maintenance of law and order, or measures to alleviate the conditions of the poor – and those which should remain in an individual's control: that is, in the private sphere – such as the enjoyment of property and the nature of family life. It is this observance of a protecting barrier around private concerns that distinguishes conservatism from forms of totalitarianism. The latter recognises no such divisions; everything becomes the legitimate business of the state. The scope for individualism is, thus, eliminated.

Liberalism

For the original eighteenth- and nineteenth-century liberals, the so-called classical liberals, individualism was best served by reducing external interference with individual action to a minimum. Freedom of thought, belief, expression and action were manifestations of individualism and should therefore be jealously guarded.

More modern liberals, however, have modified this view, arguing that such freedom is not the only guarantee of individualism. There must also be equality of opportunity through such devices as accessible education, career chances and the elimination of artificial privilege. Also they have accepted that social evils such as poverty, unemployment and poor housing reduce the scope for individualism. Thus, the state can be justified in stepping in to reduce such disadvantages.

Socialism

It is often argued that socialism is the enemy of individualism. Its emphasis on **collective** solutions to economic and social problems appears, at first sight, to preclude any scope for significant individual action. However, this would be a false assumption. Socialists have suggested that the creation of greater equality in the economic world, together with greater control by workers over their own labour activities, does increase the scope for individuals. While they have accepted that education, welfare, housing and industrial relations may be better managed by collective action (through the state or trade unions), freedom from the uncontrolled forces of capitalism does release the individual from economic struggle.

The moderate social democratic element of the socialist movement, often referred to in the modern Labour Party as the 'Third Way', shares the liberal view, however, by stressing equality of opportunity and welfare capitalism as the main guarantees of individualism.

Rights

Feudal rights

Until the seventeenth century, the notion of 'rights' was a relatively limited one. They were only considered to exist in relation to the strict hierarchy that existed in society. Thus, slaves or medieval serfs had very few rights, being limited in their movements, work and personal lives. The nobles, on the other hand, possessed extensive rights, including entitlement to own and manage property and to exercise control over large expanses of land.

Not only were rights limited, but also they were sometimes only granted in return for performing specific duties. The more rights one possessed, the more duties one was expected to perform. The role of maintaining the peace was, for example, carried out by those who were also entitled to ownership of great estates. In practice, therefore, rights were both traditional and an integral part of the social hierarchy. The Magna Carta of 1215 was an expression of this hierarchy of rights and an attempt to remind the King of their existence.

Natural rights In the seventeenth century came the first conceptions of natural rights, opening the door to a whole new world of political ideas. Two English philosophers of the period, Hobbes and Locke, both asserted that men are actually born with rights. These rights come into existence as soon as an individual enters the world. For Hobbes they consisted of the right to life, to liberty and to the pursuit of happiness. Locke added the enjoyment of property to Hobbes's list.

It followed from this new belief that any attempt to curtail these rights was against nature. Man alone could give up his rights; they could not be limited by others unless it were with his consent. This firmly put paid to the controlled forms of feudal rights described above and set strict limits on the ability of rulers to exercise their powers.

Ironically, though the concept of natural rights was developed largely in England, their practical application was at first confined to France and America. The American Declaration of Independence, part of which is shown below, was written by **Thomas Jefferson** in 1776 as a direct challenge to the absolute colonial monarchy of George III.

> 'We hold these truths to be self-evident, that all men are created equal, that they are endowed by their Creator with certain inalienable rights, that among these are Life, Liberty and the Pursuit of Happiness. That to secure these Rights, Governments are instituted among men, deriving their just powers from the consent of the governed. That whenever any form of Government becomes destructive of these ends, it is the right of the people to alter or abolish it.'
>
> American Declaration of Independence, 1776

Similar declarations were made by the French revolutionaries, inspired by another Englishman, Tom Paine, in 1789. We can see from the Declaration that the notion of natural rights opened the door to a number of political principles including:

- limited government
- government by consent
- responsible government
- individual liberty
- equal rights.

The absolute belief in natural rights went into something of a decline during the nineteenth century, replaced largely by concerns with the idea of freedom, but it returned to favour in the second half of the twentieth century as will be indicated below.

Equal rights As we have seen above, a natural result of the idea that everyone is born with equal rights is the belief that we must all enjoy equal rights. After all, why should nature (or indeed God) endow us with unequal rights? So it was that the early revolutionary liberal movements were based on equality of rights. They sought to sweep away the hierarchical system of rights that remained from the feudal age.

It has since become a basic principle of all societies which profess to be just and democratic that every citizen shall enjoy equal rights under the law and in their dealings with government. During the twentieth century, equal rights were steadily extended to women, who had been left behind by all but the most radical of liberal thinkers.

Citizenship

Before the development of ideas about natural and equal rights, all people, other than monarchs, were known as subjects. This meant that all were 'subject' to the power of the Crown and to the strict legal structure at whose head the monarch stood. Citizens did not exist and had not done so since the classical civilisations of Greece and Rome.

The term 'citizen' implied the holding of certain rights that could not be removed or curtailed except by proper process of law. Thus, the prominent members of ancient Greek and Roman society were given privileges under the law: for example, to travel or to take part in political decision making – rights that others did not possess. In the Middle Ages no such concept existed, since all were subject to the absolute authority of the monarch.

When the notion of equal rights became established, the concept of citizenship returned. This time, however, citizenship was not limited to a privileged few, but applied to everybody by virtue of their equal entitlement to rights. Indeed, in the days following the French Revolution it was customary for people to address each other as 'Citizen' in celebration and recognition of their new-found equal status.

Thus, in modern democracies we are all both citizens and subjects. We are subject to the laws, but we also have rights with regard to those laws and the governments that enforce them. In order to qualify as citizens, however, we must also accept our **obligations** under the law. It is expected that we obey the law, that we pay our taxes and that we respect properly constituted authority. In some states, though not the UK, there is even a legal obligation to vote in elections. Sometimes, too, in the interests of defence, citizens may be obliged to serve in the armed forces. This was the case in the UK during both World Wars and into the 1950s. Thus, citizenship implies a balance between our civil rights and obligations.

Human rights

After the Second World War and the defeat of a number of totalitarian dictatorships, academics and world statesmen began to search for a new universal conception of rights. These were rights that all people in all parts of the world could hope to enjoy. In 1948 the United Nations (UN) Declaration of Human Rights was formulated and signed by all members of the UN. This represented a new and fuller description of basic rights and was the modern version of the original concept of natural rights.

It contains a vast array of rights, both traditional and modern. As well as legal and political rights, such as free speech, movement and association, there are also economic and social rights. All people are considered entitled to education, health care, employment opportunities and welfare.

Of course, it would be intensely optimistic to expect all such rights to be respected everywhere and there is certainly no way of enforcing them. It is also true that some of the poorest countries simply cannot afford to guarantee many of them. Nevertheless, such conceptions of human rights do provide a standard by which political systems can be tested.

Apart from the UN Declaration, many states have their own Bill of Rights within which governments and law-makers are forced to operate. The European Convention of Human Rights, administered by its own court in Strasbourg, ~~is~~ ~~~~ ~~many European~~ states are now subject. Even the UK has now accepted the terms of the Convention by adding it to domestic law under the Human Rights Act. It is still not binding on Parliament, which remains sovereign, but all other public bodies must respect its limitations.

Legal or civil rights

Since many modern states have codified constitutions, setting out the rights that citizens enjoy both collectively and individually, it is often the case that rights are legally **guaranteed**. These can be described as **civil rights**. This term has almost become synonymous with the struggle waged by black Americans for full legal and political rights in the 1950s and 1960s. Up to that time they did not enjoy the same legally guaranteed, or 'civil', rights as whites, so the movement came to be known as the 'Civil Rights Movement'.

Rights and ideologies

Although a number of institutions now lay down basic human rights, attitudes towards rights still differ among various political philosophies. British **conservatives**, for example, have traditionally been suspicious of most abstract concepts. The idea of natural or universal human rights, has, therefore, never been fully embraced by them. They prefer instead to think of rights as **traditional**. That is, rights have a valid existence only within the context of a particular society. This implies that rights evolve and develop with society. They are not an unchanging concept and so will vary at different times and between different communities. Thus, for example, rights that may suit Americans do not necessarily belong in the UK or other societies. For instance, it is a closely guarded principle of American life that there is a right to carry weapons for self-defence. The British are, on the whole, fearful of such a practice; even the police are not normally armed.

For **liberals** rights remain paramount. There is very little justification for individual rights to be limited. Wars and other emergencies may be an acceptable reason for their suspension, and there must be some balance between the needs of the whole community and the rights of individuals. Nevertheless, liberals have always been antagonistic towards threats to basic rights that they perceive as highly valued and in need of clear protection. Unlike conservatives, liberals do see some rights – such as freedom of thought and of expression – as universally applicable.

Socialists are often accused of being careless of individual rights. Their beliefs in collectivism and the power of the state are seen as threats to the individual. Certainly the track record of many socialist states in eastern Europe was very poor in terms of respect for human rights. However, modern democratic socialists and social democrats have accepted the value of rights and now insist they must be safeguarded. Indeed, it has normally been socialists who have most effectively championed the cause of equal rights for such groups as women and ethnic minorities. In addition, certain economic and social rights have entered the socialist creed. Ideas such as the **right to work**, to a decent **education**, to a decent wage and to **welfare** provision have largely been the result of socialist thought. Many consider such rights to be a basic necessity to ensure a minimum standard of life.

Welfare Welfare can be defined as the achievement of goals and the satisfaction of demands of individuals through the **collective** provision of goods and services. It follows from the idea of collective provision that there must be **general** agreement as to what shall be provided.

The philosophical ideas behind welfare provision are explored in some detail in Unit 3, notably in the sections on democratic socialism and liberalism. However, a number of more practical considerations have resulted in the state provision of welfare in the UK. Essentially, there are two non-ideological reasons for providing welfare services:

- Some aspects of the quality of life may be considered vital in a civilised society. Personal medical care, relief from the effects of involuntary unemployment, low-cost housing and education are among these. It follows that some provision must be made by the state for those who are unable to provide them for themselves.
- Most members of a community would agree that there are some minimum obligations of care which everybody has for those who are less fortunate than themselves. State welfare thus becomes the vehicle for the performance of these obligations.

Clearly socialists and many liberals would add that welfare should be used to create greater social equality between the classes, and it can ensure that some services are paid for by those who can best afford it. Thus, welfare provision can be seen by those on the centre-left of British politics as an essential aspect of social justice.

A more extreme view is associated with a broad conception of rights. It can be argued that a decent standard of living, education, good housing, etc. are actually **human rights**, so that all societies should provide them, in the form of welfare, to all their people.

It was the link between the concept of rights and that of welfare which inspired liberal social reformers such as **William Beveridge** and **John Maynard Keynes** in the 1930s and 1940s. They viewed a good standard of living, regular and secure employment, and decent housing as basic human rights even more important than the civil rights upon which liberals had traditionally concentrated. Indeed, they represent the central theme in the transformation of liberalism from a purely political movement to one that embraced **social reformism** – a key element in mid-twentieth-century British politics.

Equality The breakdown of the rigid types of social hierarchy in the eighteenth and nineteenth centuries cleared the way for various new liberal- and socialist-inspired concepts of social equality. The notion of natural rights, which had been developed in the seventeenth century, provided the foundation for ideas of equal rights, but this could not take hold until the traditional social order had declined. Once established, however, the concept of equality quickly grew and expanded into a number of different applications.

Equal rights   The development of ideas about equal rights has been described in the section 'Rights', on page 25 above. It is notable for its influence upon the revolutionary movements in Europe and America which flourished in the late eighteenth and early ~~~~~~~~~~~~ ~~~~~~ ~~~~~, the principle of equal rights under the law has become established as an essential feature of any political system that claims to be democratic.

While most political philosophies accept that humans possess unequal powers and abilities, there is almost universal acceptance today that all are born with **equal worth**. It is equality of worth upon which the idea of equal rights is based.

Women's equality   Apart from a brief period in the 1640s when the English 'New Levellers' suggested that women should have equal political and property rights alongside men, the issue of women's equality has been relatively late in appearing within political thought as a viable proposition.

One of the earliest English campaigners for women's equality was **Mary Wollstonecraft** (1759–97), wife of the most celebrated English anarchist, William Godwin. Wollstonecraft firmly believed that women have the same potential abilities as men and are therefore entitled to equal treatment. It was not just equal political and legal rights that she wanted to see for women, but also equality of opportunity. Education and career possibilities must be equally open to women, she argued.

Despite much interest in women's equality after the French Revolution, little progress was made for women until the second half of the nineteenth century. John Stuart Mill and his wife, Harriet (née Taylor) Mill, led the way in Britain. John Stuart Mill's principal target was the notorious Married Women's Property Act, which denied married women the right to own property and so condemned them to arranged marriages and no opportunity to divorce. Meanwhile, Harriet was more concerned with voting rights. Many other social reformers were also campaigning for equal pay and employment rights for women, including the Chartist movement of the 1840s.

Nevertheless, lack of success in the economic and social fields achieved by the early campaigners for women's equality led to a belief that true progress would be made only if women were granted equal voting rights with men. Thus, movements for women's suffrage grew up all over America and Europe in the late nineteenth century. During the first quarter of the twentieth century, most western democracies granted votes to women.

Even then, equality for women was far from assured. Only when the feminist movement gathered strength in the 1960s were the final steps towards full equality made. Such objectives as equal pay, employment rights, and equal opportunities in education and careers have largely been achieved. In the USA the battle to enshrine women's equality through the **Equal Rights Amendment** has not yet been won, but most legal statements of rights now include some guarantees of women's equality.

There are still a number of important exceptions to this steady movement towards women's equality in the world community. One is Muslim countries, where there is most resistance to change. This has a religious basis since the Koran appears to grant women a different, perhaps inferior, status to that of men. The religious–cultural barrier to women's equality in such countries seems unlikely to change in the foreseeable future. For similar cultural reasons, many poor countries, especially in Africa, also deny equal rights to women.

Equality of opportunity

It is now widely accepted that considerable natural inequalities exist among people. Only a few extreme thinkers of the anarchist or communist varieties base their political ideas on the belief that we can be equal in our powers and abilities. However, this is not to say that all people should not be given equal chances in life, since we have equal rights and are of equal worth as human beings.

So it is that societies which claim to be both democratic and just have sought to create greater equality of opportunity. The key element in this regard is the provision of good quality education that is accessible to all. In addition, supporters of such equality have advocated the opening up of careers to all with the relevant skills and an end to artificial privileges being granted to a fortunate few.

After the Second World War, many of these objectives were achieved, but sociologists continued to point out that those who had been brought up in relatively 'deprived' backgrounds continued to 'fail' in both education and employment. Even with free education and improved opportunities in many of the professions, equality of opportunity did not seem to be working. Why was this so? The answer, the same sociologists (led in the UK by **Peter Townsend**) suggested, was that inequality results from causes more complex than simple lack of educational and employment opportunities. The effects of poverty, poor housing, unsettled family background and racial prejudice were also key factors. In other words, whatever the state did to try to promote equality of opportunity, social background would continue to inhibit real equality.

This problem gave rise to suggestions for the introduction of **positive discrimination** (known in the USA as **affirmative action**). This device not only attempts to eliminate disadvantages, but also substitutes deprivation with positive advantages. Thus, inner city schools were to be granted extra resources. Measures were to be taken to promote employment opportunities for members of ethnic minorities and the disabled. Better housing and support for deprived families were seen as vital ingredients in promoting opportunities for children. More recently, attempts have also been made, notably within the Labour Party organisation, to discriminate positively in favour of both women and black or Asian members. Thus, equality of **political** opportunity can also be a goal of egalitarians.

So we see that equality of opportunity is a social issue as well as a legal one. It can never realistically be fully achieved, perhaps, but liberals and socialists especially continue to struggle to reduce the unnatural inequalities that still abound.

Racial equality

Aspirations for racial equality have only become an issue in modern times with the advent of multiracial societies. Throughout history it has been acknowledged that there are important differences between races and national conflicts have often been exacerbated by racial rivalry. However, modern theories of racial superiority and inferiority have given rise to considerable controversy over the significance of racial differences.

J.A. Gobineau (1816–92), the French social theorist, and **Houston Chamberlain** (1855–1929), an Englishman who was an early adviser of Adolf Hitler, popularised theories of racial inequality. Such theories had considerable influence on right-wing ~~~~~~~~~~~~~~~~~~~ fascism.

Similarly, the post-war white regime in South Africa adopted a policy of **apartheid**, which systematically discriminated against non-whites, based on a fundamental belief in the racial superiority of the white races.

But it has not only been pseudo-scientific theories that have created the problem of racial inequality. Racism and racial prejudice, often fuelled by economic deprivation, have taken hold in many societies, not in terms of theory but simply in people's minds and emotions. This has led to considerable discrimination against racial minorities, resulting in a loss of equality in education, employment and other legal and social rights.

As a result, the search for racial equality has become a key issue at the beginning of the twenty-first century. To some extent, solutions have been legal and constitutional in nature. Thus, race relations laws in the UK, civil rights legislation in the USA and a variety of international declarations of human rights have sought to establish racial equality. However, it is also widely recognised that prejudice is one of the main causes of unequal treatment for racial minorities. Solutions to this aspect of the problem are more difficult to find. They centre on education and public campaigning and, as such, remain long-term goals.

Equality of outcome   Also referred to as **economic equality**, this concept is usually associated with socialism and communism. It is an idea based on ethics or morality, arguing that all are of equal worth, even though they may make a different contribution to society. What is considered important is that all who make the best contribution they can, should be entitled to equal rewards.

In its most extreme form, this suggests that all who work will receive exactly the same income. Certainly after the Russian Revolution in 1917, Lenin intended this to be the case. Very soon, however, he learned that this took away the incentives which could persuade individuals either to work diligently or to undertake long periods of education and training in order to carry out more socially valuable jobs. Thus, he introduced limited inequality in wages. Nevertheless, it was still claimed to be a 'just' system, since each was paid on a rational basis, according to the social value of their contribution. Capitalism, communists claim, grants rewards according to market forces, which results in random and unjustifiable inequalities that have nothing to do with the true value of one's contribution.

> '[Society can inscribe on its banners] "From each according to his ability, to each according to his needs".'
> Karl Marx, *Critique of the Gotha Programme*, 1875

Milder forms of socialism do not go as far. Rather, the idea of equality of outcome implies that gross inequalities should be reduced and that rewards should be more fairly distributed than the free market capitalist system usually achieves. It remains a moral question for socialists. Equality is seen as the natural state of mankind, rather than inequality as liberals and conservatives believe.

Concepts concerned with relationships between citizens and the state

Representation   When ideas concerning popular government emerged in the seventeenth and eighteenth centuries, when the notion arose that the authority to govern must be granted by the people and that mere tradition or divine right was no longer acceptable, immediate problems presented themselves. Three principal difficulties can be identified:

- Most people at that time were either illiterate or only semi-educated. They would have had difficulty reading about, let alone understanding, political issues. Even the most tolerant, liberal of thinkers such as **John Stuart Mill** recognised this difficulty.
- The demands and beliefs of the mass of the people would most likely be incoherent, driven by emotion rather than reason, and subject to undue influence by dictatorial leaders. The American democrat **James Madison** understood this when contributing to the shape of the United States Constitution in 1787.
- Such ideas of pure democracy would result in the people making decisions derived from pure self-interest. The good of the community as a whole could be overlooked. Even the eighteenth-century French philosopher of the Enlightenment, **Jean-Jacques Rousseau**, rejected popular democracy altogether on these grounds.

Thus, representative systems were developed to deal with such problems. Although there are a number of forms, which are described below, in all cases the same principle applies – that the people do not govern themselves, but have representatives who govern on their behalf.

Burke's model   The eighteenth-century English politician **Edmund Burke** became concerned that new ideas emerging from Europe and the USA would lead to Parliament becoming merely a forum for the promotion of sectional interests and demands. For him the role of a representative should be to promote the **national** interest, not the interests of a minority or even the majority. True, MPs might hold particular views and be influenced by their own philosophy, but in the end they should seek to further their own view of the interests of the whole community.

So, Burke's model of the ideal representative suggests an independent individual who takes into account the mood and sentiments of his constituents, but then uses his own judgement in making decisions. Ultimately, if his judgement is flawed or becomes unacceptable to the voters, he can be removed at the next election.

The balance between political philosophy and national interest is nicely expressed in Burke's definition of a political party:

> *A body of men united for promoting by their joint endeavours the national interest upon some particular principle in which they are all agreed.'*
> Edmund Burke, *Reflections on the Revolution in France,*
> 1790

Social representation   A related idea to that of Burke is the creation of a body which is a **microcosm** or miniature version of the community that it is representing. For example, such a group would be likely to be half women, half men, would reflect the social class structure and would include a representation of ethnic minorities as well as a good age range. In this way, it might be expected to make the same kind of collective decisions that the whole community would make if it were to meet together. Here again, representatives would be using their own judgement as well as taking account of the way other like-minded people might act.

The jury system operates on this principle in the legal rather than the political field, but illustrates its value in ensuring just decision making. In addition, to some extent, any elected body may be considered to be more democratic if it can be socially representative. Thus, there are calls to increase female membership of the British House of Commons and for more members of ethnic minorities to be represented. Even by 1997 there were still only just over 100 women out of 659 in the House of Commons (though there was a woman speaker, Betty Boothroyd, and a recent woman Prime Minister for eleven years), and only a handful of Afro-Caribbean origin. A similar principle can be applied to the civil service, in view of its influence over policy making. The higher levels of the civil service have been notorious for their bias towards Oxford and Cambridge graduates, who have invariably come from middle-class backgrounds (a tendency that is, more recently, less marked). There are also very few women in the higher echelons of Whitehall.

However, the representatives of the people, it can be argued, ought to be superior to the majority of the community. We should, perhaps, expect representatives to be better educated and more experienced than most of us. It therefore becomes inevitable that there will be a majority of the better-educated, older and more successful individuals in our governmental institutions.

It is sometimes suggested that, in order to encourage the election of more women and members of ethnic minorities, positive discrimination should be applied whereby a quota, or minimum number, drawn from such groups, are guaranteed places. The Labour Party operates such a system on behalf of women within certain sections of its internal organisation. There is, indeed, a feminist pressure group, known as the Three Hundred Group, which aims to increase the number of women MPs to the number suggested in its title. Opponents of positive discrimination, however, point out that such quotas may result in some inferior individuals gaining seats simply to fulfil the requirements of the system.

Delegation   This is the clearest form of representation. A delegate is one who is elected or appointed to mirror accurately the views of those whom they represent. In the most extreme of circumstances, a delegate may have no flexibility whatsoever, having instead to follow a specific mandate or strict instructions. Parties in the USA, for example, hold **Primary Elections** to choose delegates who will support a particular candidate for office. These delegates **must** follow the instructions of their party voters, at least until their chosen candidate is knocked out of the race.

The example described above is the strictest form of delegation. In practice, delegates are expected almost invariably to follow the wishes of their electorate, but may stray from these in certain circumstances. Again, the USA provides a useful example here. Members of the House of Representatives must seek re-election every two years. They must, therefore, pay special heed to the wishes of their constituencies. Too much independent action, as Burke recommended, is likely to result in loss of their seat.

Totalitarian representation

As we have seen above, Rousseau suggested in the eighteenth century that representative democracy was likely to be flawed by the dominance of sectional interests. He was concerned that the collective good of the whole community, what he called the **general will**, should be served. Since the people or their representatives could not be trusted to establish the general will, it must be left to a single superior individual to establish that will. This person – called the 'legislator' – would govern as a **representative** of the community **as a whole**, as a single **collective** body. This highly controversial position has often been used to justify totalitarian government, and certainly the dominant Jacobin Party, led by the notorious **Robespierre** during the French Revolution, claimed to represent the mass of the people in such a way.

Summary of representative forms	
1. Burke's view	Representatives should use their judgement and not slavishly follow the beliefs of their constituents.
2. Social representation	A representative body should be a microcosm of the community that it represents.
3. Delegation	A representative who follows closely or exactly the instructions of those who appointed or elected him.
4. Totalitarianism	The idea that an individual or small elite party can represent the collective interests of a society.

More recently, such communist leaders as Lenin and Mao Tse-tung have adopted a similar position. They both led elite parties that claimed to represent the best interests of the masses. Since communist ideology was, in their view, clearly in the best interests of the people, its ruthless imposition could be justified in terms of representative government.

The case of British MPs

In some ways, the position of British MPs summarises the variety of representative forms that can flourish. We should bear in mind that they are members of a highly disciplined party, largely united in purpose and with a clear election manifesto expressing its policy intentions. They are also elected to represent a constituency, are expected to consider the national interest and may be sponsored by an interest or pressure group to provide publicity and influence for their cause. Yet voters rarely elect MPs for their personal qualities and beliefs. Instead, they generally elect them because they are members of the party that they wish to support. Thus, MPs may experience a number of conflicting influences in their representative role. We can summarise these as follows:

- The party whips expect them to 'toe the party line'. Their constituents may do the same.
- Sometimes the interests of their constituency may conflict with government policy.
- They may support a particular cause that leads them into conflict with party policy.
- If they believe their party's policy is not in the national interest, they face a dilemma.
- Their own personal principles may cut across some considerations shown above.

In the face of these potentially difficult conflicts, consider how an MP should react in the following circumstances:

- He is anti-European when his party policy is for closer European integration.
- His own party proposes an unpopular new motorway in his constituency.
- He is sponsored by the National Union of Students and his party proposes cuts in student grants.
- His party supports the return of the death penalty, to which he is morally opposed.
- His constituency party wants him to vote one way on a key issue against party policy. His party whip insists he takes the opposite, official party line. His constituency threatens to 'de-select' him so that he will not be their official candidate at the next general election. This will guarantee defeat for him at that election.

Responsibility

It is a general principle of any representative system that government should be responsible to those who have elected it. This can imply two principles.

Responsible government

First, electors have opportunities to find out what government is doing, can subject its actions to scrutiny and, in extreme circumstances, can remove it if it is proving unsatisfactory. The performance of our representatives must be judged before we can know whether to renew their mandate. This idea is often known as **accountability**.

Second, it can mean that government acts in a way which is in the genuine national interest and is not merely concerned with satisfying the demands of a section of the population, or is not only concerned to ensure its own re-election in the future. Such governments need to be relatively free from constant control by the electorate. They need the opportunity to ignore short-term popularity concerns in order to benefit the long-term interests of the community.

In either case, responsibility is a vital partner to representation. It is also crucial to the effective operation of democracy. Power without responsibility is indeed a recipe for absolute, autocratic government. All rulers need the discipline of responsibility if they are to keep in touch with the people.

Responsibility in practice

There are a number of ways in which government can be made responsible in practice. The British system of parliamentary accountability is perhaps the most ancient. Just as absolute monarchs were required to report their actions to Parliament on a regular basis, modern ministers are also called to account regularly.

Such responsibility applies both individually and collectively, as follows.

<u>Individual ministerial responsibility</u> The doctrine of individual ministerial responsibility insists that every government minister must attend Parliament regularly to answer questions, to justify decisions, to explain the thinking behind policy and to be subject to cross-examination by MPs. In effect, the minister is being held accountable to the people, but MPs are performing the function on behalf of the community.

It is also argued that a minister whose department makes a serious error should actually resign. In recent years, this principle has fallen into disrepute, so reluctant are ministers to relinquish their posts despite strong parliamentary pressure to do so.

The question may be asked, 'Why must ministers answer for their department when most of the work and most of the decisions are taken by civil servants?'. The answer lies in the principle that all civil servants must remain politically anonymous in order to protect their neutrality. Thus, their political boss, the minister, must be prepared to answer for them.

The minister who resigned and the minister who didn't . . .

In 1982, when the UK was caught unprepared for the Argentine invasion of the Falkland Islands, it was clear that someone in government was to blame and would have to accept responsibility. In the event, it was Lord Carrington, the Foreign Secretary, who 'did the honourable thing' and resigned.

In February 1996 the report of Sir Richard Scott into the Government's handling of the sale of arms and arms-related equipment to Iraq in the lead-up to the Gulf War of 1990 strongly criticised the conduct of William Waldegrave, who had misled Parliament over changes in official policy on such arms sales. Despite much condemnation from Parliament and the media, Waldegrave refused to resign and survived in the Cabinet.

<u>Collective responsibility</u> This refers to the fact that the Government is collectively responsible for its actions and the quality of its performance. Of course, it is at general elections that a government is principally called to account, but continuous scrutiny is exercised by Parliament. The ultimate sanction is the passage of a 'vote of no confidence' in the House of Commons, which must result in the removal of the Government, but this is rare as the Government usually commands a loyal majority. The Labour Government of 1979 is the only modern example of such an occurrence. In practice, it is merely in the course of debates that government accountability is exercised.

The doctrine is so important in British politics that individual ministers are required to defend the Government's position even if they disagree privately. By insisting on such loyalty, the Government stands or falls together. A minister who is not willing to accept responsibility for a government decision must resign his post. Michael Heseltine's resignation after the Westland affair in 1986 was the most significant example in recent times.

Law   Here we can define law as a body of rules that is binding within the whole of a community. Many other types of rules may exist, of course, such as military law, church law, and regulations within clubs, societies, schools and ~~~~~~~~ ~~~~ ~~ ~~~~~ ~~~~~ ~~~~~ in particular circumstances and among certain sections of the community. Law itself is binding on all and, as such, must effectively be enforced by the state. Three main reasons exist for the creation and enforcement of laws:

- State laws are not the only rules by which people abide. Many are guided in their conduct by their own sense of morality or by religious principles. Indeed, in an ideal world, the laws would conform to a common sense of moral behaviour. However, views on morality vary from individual to individual, so the state must set standards for all to follow.
- In addition to such rules of conduct, laws are needed to ensure that government policy is properly implemented. Thus, for example, business must abide by laws that govern the employment of their staff and the quality of the goods they sell, individuals must pay various taxes and schools must implement educational objectives.
- The modern world can prove extremely competitive and circumstances frequently arise where individuals may come into conflict with one another. To avoid the disordered and sometimes violent settlement of such conflicts, laws act as a guide for the resolution of disputes.

Purposes of law

1. Setting common standards of behaviour.
2. Ensuring that government policy will be implemented.
3. Dealing with disputes which may arise between citizens.

Types of law   <u>Statute law</u>   This refers to those laws that have been passed by Parliament. These are known as statutes or Acts. If there is any conflict between a statute and any other kind of law, the statute is considered superior.

<u>Secondary legislation</u>   This is produced by bodies that are sanctioned to do so by Parliament. In the main these are government ministers, local authorities and public corporations. Such secondary authorities act within powers granted to them by primary or **enabling legislation** and the orders and by-laws that they make are as binding as any other laws. Thus, the Secretary of State for Trade and Industry may be granted powers to establish a wide range of industrial or commercial regulations. Similarly, local authorities have statutory powers to regulate vehicular traffic and to set building regulations.

<u>Common law</u>   This is uncodified (that is, not written in an organised form). It is a body of rules that has evolved over a long period of time. Although such law has not been passed by Parliament, it is considered binding by the courts. Much common law has now been replaced by statutes that are more precise. It is still often applicable in commerce and family law, but it is in the process of being phased out.

Lawyers are charged with the task of studying past legal judgments in order to discover what the common law says about a particular case with which they are involved. In practice, it is judges who declare how common law applies and these judgments must be followed in any similar case.

<u>Case law</u> This is developed where judges must decide how a law, whether common or statute, should apply in a particular case. Such principles having been established, any future similar case must be treated in the same way. For example, the equal opportunities laws seek to establish equal rights for women. However, there may be many instances where it is not clear whether these rights are being abused. So a body of case law builds up over the years until a new statute can be passed that tidies up such practical applications. This kind of law is often referred to as **judge-made law** because the interpretation is made by the judge in each case and becomes binding on all other courts.

<u>Constitutional law</u> Such law is normally superior to other kinds of law. That is, all actions by government or laws passed by a legislature must conform to constitutional principles. In the UK this is not the case, however, since constitutional statutes are no different from ordinary laws. The doctrine of the sovereignty of Parliament means that the legislature cannot be limited by any superior law. This is not to say that there are no constitutional statutes in the UK – the laws governing local government, ministerial powers and citizens' rights fall into this category. What it does mean is that they are not binding on Parliament.

In either the British case or that of other liberal democracies, the functions of constitutional law are the same:

Functions of constitutional laws

1. Determining the distribution of power between the various institutions of government.
2. Setting the limits to those powers.
3. Establishing the rights of citizens, in relation both to each other and to the state.
4. Defining the territory controlled by the state and the nature of citizenship.
5. Setting out procedures for amending the Constitution itself.

Further details and issues concerning the British Constitution are included in Unit 12.

The rule of law It is clear that all organised societies need laws which can be enforced by the state. It is only liberal democracies, however, which lay claim to the principle of the 'rule of law'. In a very general sense, this principle simply refers to systems where government always operates within the laws rather than in an arbitrary fashion, which was the custom of medieval absolute monarchs. In 1885 Professor A. V. Dicey set out a full and precise definition by which all democracies can be judged. His definition has four parts:

- All are equal before the law. No one, including government, is above the law and no one should be at a special disadvantage when being dealt with in law.

- Citizens may be punished only through the proper application of law. In other words, the law enforcement agencies must abide by legal procedures.
- ~~Only laws passed by~~ Parliament or under authority granted by Parliament (in other states this would be applied to whatever constituted the sovereign body) can be enforced.
- Laws should be just and respect the rights of citizens.

Few would argue that the first three principles hold largely true in the UK and in most democratic countries, but the fourth, concerning rights and justice, is open to considerable question. In states with a codified constitution and/or a guaranteed Bill of Rights, rights may well be protected, but the UK's lack of such features creates a major problem. Rights are at the mercy of the sovereign Parliament. The rule of law is, therefore, always vulnerable.

Law and justice   There is often confusion between these two terms. If we define justice in a general way, as 'fairness', it may certainly conflict with law. We all have our own conception of what is 'fair' in any particular circumstance. The laws cannot hope to reflect all these different views of justice. If each judge were to attempt to take into account various ideas, the outcome of the law would be too uncertain. Those who come to be involved in legal cases can only hope to be treated according to the law as it stands, whether it is 'fair' in our eyes or not. As Dicey argued, as long as we are all treated equally under laws that are consistently enforced, we can at least be sure that we have been treated with 'justice'. If we do not like the laws as they are applied, the best we can do is to seek to influence the political system so as to have those laws changed.

The consistent and equal application of the law, including fair trials and impartial judges or juries, can be described as **legal justice**. This should not be confused with **social justice**, which is the final concept to be described here.

Social justice   Social justice can be defined as different conceptions and beliefs about how goods should be distributed within a community. Here the term 'goods' refers not only to material goods and services or money income, but also to desirable conditions such as rights, power, status, freedom or welfare. In other words, everything that most would describe as desirable.

The use of the word 'beliefs' above gives a clue to the nature of social justice. It is an evaluative term: that is, its meaning depends upon the ideological or philosophical standpoint of the person using it. For example, socialists do not mean the same as conservatives or liberals when describing social justice because their beliefs and values are different. By contrast, 'legal justice', as described by Dicey, is a positive or universal term that can be generally applied.

The table below indicates a number of commonly held principles that can be described as conceptions of social justice. In each case the particular philosophies that incorporate the beliefs are identified.

The beliefs shown above can be studied in more detail in Units 3 and 14.

There are a few extreme thinkers who deny the validity of social justice at all. Such **libertarians**, as they are known, envisage a society where no such principles exist. Each becomes responsible totally for their own welfare and no one has any obligation to ensure justice for others. However, as a concept, social justice is the most important characteristic of all political beliefs.

Principles of social justice	Philosophies supporting the principle
• Equality of outcome where all are given approximately equal economic rewards	• Communism • Anarchism • Extreme socialism
• Equality of opportunity where inequalities are accepted but artificial advantages and disadvantages are reduced	• Socialism • Modern liberalism • Social democracy
• Equal legal and political rights	• Socialism • Social democracy • Modern and classical liberalism
• Economic rewards awarded strictly according to merit	• Classical liberalism • Conservatism • New Right neo-liberalism
• The use of taxation and welfare to reduce income inequalities	• Socialism • Social democracy
• The provision of welfare only to ensure all have a minimum standard of living	• Conservatism • New Right neo-liberalism
• Economic rewards determined only by markets	• Classical liberalism • New Right neo-liberalism

Democracy

There are two commonly held beliefs about the term 'democracy', both of which are misleading. These are:

- that democracy is one specific form of government and society which can be readily identified
- that democracy has been, and still is, considered a universally 'good thing', to be supported by all right-thinking people and pursued by all good governments.

We can illustrate the first fallacy by considering two political systems, both of which have described themselves as 'democracies'. First, the former East Germany, acknowledged widely as one of the most autocratic and intolerant regimes of the twentieth century, nevertheless described itself as the 'German Democratic Republic'. Second, the USA has extensive guarantees of rights and liberties, and in the West we would probably hold it up as an ideal model of democracy. How can two such contrasting systems both claim the title 'democracy'? The answer is that the term can be used to mean whatever we want it to mean. Above all, its meaning is determined by one's own general political philosophy, be it conservative, liberal, communist or fascist.

As to the second common error – that democracy has been a universally popular system – we shall see below how, during much of the history of human society, democracy has either not existed in any form, or been viewed with deep suspicion. It is only since the First World War that democracy has become the accepted form of government for most advanced societies.

Professor Bernard Crick's colourful comment on the concept of demo-cracy may serve to illustrate these problems. 'Democracy', he argues, 'is perhaps the most promiscuous word in the world of public affairs. She is everybody's mistress and yet somehow retains her magic even when a lover sees that her favours are being, in his light, shared by many another.'

First we will explore the origins of the idea of democracy, taking us to around 1800, by which time France, the USA and Britain had estab-lished the basis of modern western political systems. Following from these early developments, we will see how differing interpretations and forms of the idea arose, just as traditional kinds of regime were declin-ing. Finally, we look at the continuing problems that exist in a modern democratic society.

In an investigation into the theory and practice of democracy, the best place to begin is at the beginning, with its origins in Greece.

The origins of democracy   Classical Greece was not one single state, but a series of city states, each of which developed its own political system, ranging from despotic monarchy to extremely open forms of direct popular rule. Thus there was more than one form of 'democracy' flourishing in this region. Undoubtedly the best known, however, was the system operating in Athens in the sixth and fifth centuries BC.

The basis of Athenian democracy was that all citizens were granted the right to attend a regular assembly where laws were enacted, executive decisions made and general policy formulated. There was also the opportunity to scrutinise and criticise those city officials who had also been elected by the popular assembly. In order for this to take place, the citizens had to be granted political equality, which included the rich and the relatively poor together. In many ways, this political equality was the most radical feature of the system. The participation of sections of the wider population was not unusual at that time in Greece, but the concept of granting nearly universally equal status was certainly controversial. Women and slaves were still excluded from such equality, but it was really the equal treatment of different classes that conservatives could not accept.

As Athens, like its Greek neighbours, was a relatively small state, it was quite feasible for the citizenry to gather in one single location for their deliberations, so that the process is often described as 'market place democracy'. Great orators and ambitious politicians addressed the assembly, but any member of the crowd had the right to take part in debates if he could gain a hearing. Thus we can see that Athenian demo-cracy contained several elements to which we can still relate today:

- popular participation in politics
- political equality (at least for free male adults)
- the notion that government should be responsible to the people.

Plato and Aristotle   These three principles are all ones that we in so-called liberal democracies find both familiar and desirable, but at the time not all Athens' citizens were seduced by the apparent attractions of the system, among them its greatest philosopher, **Plato**.

In fact Plato was democracy's most scathing critic at the time of its heyday. He began his criticism by making clear that he did not believe that the mass of the people were wise or knowledgeable enough to make important decisions. On a more fundamental level, he objected to the fact that, as a system, it gave everybody an equal voice even though they were not equal in other ways, especially in education and judgement; he feared that it could lead to dictatorship. To him the common people were too ready to follow great orators with a broad emotional appeal. Such leaders, able to exert charismatic control over the people, would become too powerful. Thus he tells us, 'So, from an extreme form of liberty one is likely to get, in the individual and in society, a reaction to an extreme form of subjection, and if that is so, we should expect tyranny to result from democracy, the most savage subjection from an excess of liberty.'

On balance, therefore, he preferred rule by a small group or **oligarchy** of wise, responsible (by implication also wealthy) rulers.

His pupil, **Aristotle**, took a similar view, but he was more particularly concerned that the people might not respect the laws which they, themselves, had made. The fear was that, feeling free and self-responsible, the people could make and unmake laws to suit themselves. Why obey a law that no longer conforms to one's wishes if one can simply set the law aside?

We can now summarise the criticisms that Plato and Aristotle laid on democracy:

- The mass of the people are not fit to make laws for themselves.
- An open system gives the opportunity for dictators to arise, raised up by the masses, who have been too easily swayed by emotional rhetoric.
- Democracy imposes an unnatural equality upon people. In fact, some are more fit to govern than others.
- People will not respect laws they have made for themselves.

In modern terms, these would be seen as conservative views on democracy, but much time was to pass before the serious political battles over democracy were to be waged.

Locke and Rousseau Following the decline of Greek classical civilisation, democracy, in a limited form, made a brief reappearance in Ancient Rome, but then largely disappeared, to be replaced in most parts of the civilised world by absolute monarchies, until the seventeenth century. The English Civil War in the 1640s raised questions about what form of political authority could replace the traditional or divine rule of the Stuart monarchy. In Cromwell's army and among the Levellers, an embryonic socialist organisation, there was much talk of popular forms of government.

The Levellers produced a document in 1647 entitled the 'Agreement of the People', which contained a radical programme for a representative democracy with most, though not all, adults having voting rights. At the great debate in Putney, which took place in Cromwell's army as a result of its publication, General Ireton, a close colleague of Cromwell, argued that if the propertyless were to be granted the vote they would surely vote for the abolition of property itself. In other words, he saw democracy as a precursor of communism. The Levellers were quickly defeated, in the event. The propertied middle classes were the true driving force of the Parliamentary rebellion and, since they had much to lose from Levellers' ... that the more radical elements were excluded from power. England, though perhaps the most politically advanced nation of the day, was not ready for modern democracy.

Following the Glorious Revolution of 1688 and the advent of truly parliamentary government in England, the ground was more fertile for the seeds of democracy to be sown again. The Whig philosopher **John Locke** expounded his theories of representative rule in his *Two Treatises on Government* in 1689. The first principle for Locke was that government must be based on the consent of the people. Nobody is entitled to judge on our behalf, as individuals, what is best for us. We are the best judges of what is in our interests. Therefore, government must be set up by the people, by a free agreement among them. (This is his so-called 'Social Contract', which gives rise to the term 'Contract Theory' for much of Locke's work). Second, Locke insisted that, once set up, government should be continuously responsible to the people. Indeed, he gave the people the right to remove a government, by force if necessary, if it broke the trust placed in it by the people. Third, Locke envisaged a representative assembly whose role would be to maintain control, on behalf of the people, over government.

Here we can see a much more recognisable conception of a democratic form of government, closer to contemporary forms. However, there needs to be a word of caution here. Locke was very much a representative of the property-owning middle classes, so his representatives would be safeguarding and advancing the interests of property. He did not believe that the uneducated, unpropertied mass of the people should be included in such government. (In this respect, he was still close to the outlook of Plato and Aristotle.) This is not to say they were to be ignored. Rather, their interests could best be understood by the more responsible middle classes. The ownership of property was seen as crucial by Whigs such as Locke, for it gave the individual a greater stake in the maintenance of good order. Thus property owners could be trusted to behave and think in a responsible manner.

Nearly a century later, the French philosopher **Jean-Jacques Rousseau** was to introduce serious reservations over the growing enthusiasm for Locke's style of democracy, much as Plato had done in Greece. Rousseau's reflections, however, were considerably more sophisticated than those of Plato. He wrote against a background of French political philosophy that much admired the English system of parliamentary government. For him, though, the English were only free at election time. Between elections there was no guarantee that government would act in the interests of the people.

Rousseau's starting point is that man has a right to freedom, but as soon as government is set up over him he loses his freedom, hence his famous maxim, 'Man is born free but is everywhere in chains.' To solve the problem, government must be set up by the people and come broadly under their control. However, for the first time in the history of democratic thought, Rousseau recognised the dangers of majority rule if decisions were to be based on a popular vote. He asked, 'On what basis will people make their decisions?', giving the answer that we are driven largely by self-interest, what is best for ourselves. It follows that the will of the majority is bound to conflict with the interests of the minority. Thus simple, popular democracy, based on majority rule, is unjust and dangerous. Of course, he pointed out, if all men were truly enlightened and understood the interests of the whole community as well as their own, the problem would not exist. Thus he tells us, 'Were there a people of gods, their government would be democratic. So perfect a government is not for men.'

Instead, Rousseau discusses the concept of a 'general will', a difficult idea over which scholars have argued ever since. Broadly, it seems to refer to the interests of the people collectively, rather than simply the will of the majority based on a collection of self-interests. So, for example, the majority might vote against a general rise in taxation to improve the public finances, or for relief of the poor, but the true interests of the whole community might lie with such a rise. How then can the 'general will' be arrived at? Rousseau's solution – that only a single, enlightened, perfectly moral individual could perform such a task – has been seen by many commentators as a recipe for a kind of totalitarian rule. Thus, paradoxically, Rousseau has been seen as both a democrat and a supporter of so-called benevolent despotism (sometimes referred to as enlightened dictatorship).

We can sum up the contributions of Locke and Rousseau in the following principles:

- Government must rest on the consent of the people.
- There must be safeguards to ensure that government acts in the interests of the people.
- Government must represent the interests of the people. In Locke's case, this means the interests of the majority of voters; in Rousseau's case, it refers to the collective will of the people.

Paine and Madison   If Rousseau proved to be the guiding light of the French Revolution, it was **Thomas Paine** and **James Madison** who inspired the American rebels on the other side of the Atlantic. Their conceptions of democratic principles were to be discovered in the American Declaration of Independence of 1776 and the Constitution that was written in 1787. The American Constitution still forms the basis of American government and remains, for many, the clearest example of democracy ever codified.

Tom Paine, celebrated for his authorship of *The Rights of Man*, held almost socialist views, similar to those of the English Levellers. For him, democratic equality meant more than political and legal justice; it also included a fairer distribution of property. Yet it was not his socialist leanings that endeared him to the American revolutionaries. Rather, it was his insistence that any government must be based on the principle that all men are free and have rights which are inalienable: that is, incapable of being removed by government, however fairly elected it might be. Such ideas were added to the American Constitution almost immediately after it was first drafted, and form the first ten amendments known as the Bill of Rights.

Madison, a contemporary of Paine, was less radical but made an equally important contribution to the development of ~~~~~~~~ theory. His best-known ~~~~~~ ~~~~~~~~~~~~~ in the Federalist Papers', a ~~~~~ ~~ ~~~~~~ written at the time of the American Revolution to air the various issues that the newly independent country would have to face. Madison's concerns centred on two main problems. First, he was concerned with how to stop an elected government becoming too dictatorial. He recognised that, enjoying the increased authority of having been elected by a popular majority, a government might feel it has a mandate to take too much power. Second, like Plato, he did not trust the judgement of the mass of the people. They might elect leaders for the wrong reasons and, having elected them, might support them in oppressing minority interests. His greatest fear was the establishment of a political party that would represent a permanent majority and dominate the system indefinitely.

In answer to these problems, Madison proposed that government should contain, within itself, checks and balances or internal limitations to its own powers. In other words, for every branch of government there should be another branch able to control it. This would reduce the likelihood of an over-powerful government arising. The problem of the excessive power of the majority was a more difficult one. He hoped to see a democracy work without political parties at all, but this very soon proved to be impractical. More realistically, Madison introduced the notion of indirect democracy. Having rejected outright the idea of a direct democracy of the Athenian kind, he developed a system where the people would elect intermediate bodies between themselves and government. These bodies would serve the purpose of filtering public opinion and reducing the effects of more extreme proposals. Thus, for example, the President would be elected not directly, but by an electoral college of representatives of the people. The college would be guided by the people but would not be its slaves.

Although Madison's ideas were eventually overtaken by the rapid development of democracy during the nineteenth century, his principles still have influence, particularly the notion of self-limiting government. So, from the American experience, we can see further progress towards modern democracy, notably:

• Individual rights could not be sacrificed to the power of government.
• Government should be limited.
• The influence of popular opinion should be moderated by representative institutions.

As the nineteenth century dawned, the idea of democracy was established as a serious threat to more traditional forms of government. Yet it still had more enemies than friends. The experiences of the French Revolution, the infamous 'Reign of Terror' in particular, and the radical ideas of the USA's Founding Fathers sent shock waves through Europe. But rapid industrialisation, and the large capitalist middle class who came with it, ensured that popular forms of government would inevitably emerge. It was only a question of how long traditional forms could endure and, when they were replaced, what would be the precise form of democracy to replace them.

Although the democratic spirit began to spread through Europe in the nineteenth century, its implementation had, at first, to be tempered with a need for order and stability. In particular, the role of monarchy and the institutions connected with monarchy, such as the British House of Lords, became a matter of controversy. Could non-elected institutions have any place in a modern democracy? In France the answer was a resounding 'no' and by 1871 it had gone the way of the USA and established a pure republic following several past flirtations with the idea.

The forms of democracy Unfortunately for students of the concept of democracy, no sooner had it begun to gain popularity than its theory and practice split into a variety of forms. We can now see how, over the ensuing two centuries, it gained a number of contrasting types.

The first modern democracies were essentially mixed systems. Popularly elected parliaments (invariably elected only by a limited proportion of the population through various limiting voting qualifications) found their authority set against the power of hereditary monarchy. England had set out on the road as long ago as 1688 when the principle was established that, while the King may rule, the elected Parliament should enact laws. Variations on this theme flourished in Europe through the nineteenth century. In Britain, indeed, the concept of combining elected with traditional institutions was turned into a philosophy and became one of the founding principles of the Conservative Party. This was known as 'Tory democracy'.

<u>Tory democracy</u> This philosophy, largely associated with **Benjamin Disraeli** and **Randolph Churchill**, was principally concerned with balancing the interests of the different social classes who had grown up as a result of the Industrial Revolution. Full-scale popular democracy, while desirable in principle, would lead to social conflict, argued the Tories. One fear was that the working class, now the huge majority, would be able to command large numbers of votes and parliamentary seats. The danger here was that such a huge numerical superiority would sweep away the traditional ruling classes. A second concern for Tories was that the newly wealthy capitalist middle classes, who now held economic power, might convert their wealth into political power. There was a danger that such power in the hands of capitalists could be used to damage working-class interests and provoke revolution, as was common on the continent of Europe. The traditional rulers, drawn from the numerically weak landed gentry and aristocracy, would be powerless to mediate in the great clash of interests that would result. Since the maintenance of order and security was the dominant goal of conservatism, a solution was imperative.

The answer was to balance the power of elected institutions, notably the House of Commons and its representatives in government, with that of traditional institutions such as the monarchy, the aristocracy (represented in the House of Lords) and the Church of England. Furthermore, if the working class could be persuaded to vote Conservative in large enough numbers, the possibility of a 'tyranny' of a working-class majority could be avoided. In this way, the clear need to accept the democratic spirit of the age could be reconciled with the desire for stability.

In the event, this model of limited democracy was short-lived. As the nineteenth gave way to the twentieth century, it was the elected institutions, and the parties that dominated them, which came to be seen as the true bearers of democracy. When the principle of adult suffrage had been established, and when the experiences of the First World War made the satisfaction of working-class demands essential, only elected institutions could claim real authority to govern.

Democratic elitism   After the First World War, the idea of popular democracy ceased to instil fear into those who had a vested interest in maintaining the status quo. At worst it was accepted as an inevitable development; at best it was welcomed as the final maturity of liberal political thought. Few now feared that the capitalist West would be swamped by working-class parties, elected on the back of universal suffrage and dedicated to the introduction of Marxist-inspired socialism. President Woodrow Wilson's so-called Fourteen Points, introduced as part of the post-war settlement that set out the future of international relations, finally gave official approval to popular sovereignty and self-determination constituting the only acceptable basis for a modern state.

Yet democracy was still in its infancy as a political system. The modern notion of a society where the citizenry are intensively and constantly active in politics, where information is widespread and sophisticated, and where active participation is common, had not arrived. The political system, and the number of people actively involved in it, remained limited in scope. In effect it was, during the first part of the twentieth century, operated by a small political leadership. The clearest description of such a narrow form of democracy is provided by the economist **J. A. Schumpeter** (1883–1950). Schumpeter understood that the role of the people in political decision making was inevitably limited. It was simply not realistic for people with relatively little knowledge or understanding to become continuously involved in complex political argument. Rather, he observed, their role is reduced to being able to choose freely between different groups of politicians, each presenting competing sets of policies. These groups, or political 'elites', would submit themselves regularly to free and fair elections and would usually be open to entry by anyone with sufficient ability and ambition. Between elections, however, the role of the people was only slight. They could not expect to exercise continuous influence or to be regularly involved. He characterised such a democracy as 'public competition between open elites'. As a further illustration it can be compared to the economic process. The people are the 'consumers' of politics while the elites are the 'producers'. The consumers may choose between competing products in the store, but they have little influence over their design and production.

Several other theorists since Schumpeter, largely from American schools of political science, have followed this elitist analysis of democracy. **C. Wright Mills** referred to a 'power elite' in political society incorporating leaders of business and commerce, the military and politics itself, who continuously hold real power. The democratic competition between parties is, therefore, a mere façade behind which the true decisions are made.

By the 1950s and 1960s such elitist theories had been superseded b
new theories, but there are still many who see democracy in terms o₁
such a model. Its main conclusions can be identified as follows:

- Political issues are, on the whole, too complex for most people to be
  intimately involved in policy making.
- For most, political participation must be confined to choosing
  between competing elites at free elections.
- The system can still be described as democratic if these elites are open
  for most members of the public to join if they have the necessary
  political skills and will.
- It can further be described as democratic if the competition between
  these elites is based on a desire to act in the public good.

Pluralist democracy   The term 'pluralism' is one that can be applied to
political processes in general. It refers to any scenario where a variety of
beliefs, demands and interests are permitted to flourish together. Thus,
for example, the former Soviet Union could not have been described as
pluralist since competing political ideologies and religious creeds were
forbidden. On the other hand, the USA is often held up as the perfect
model of pluralism since many political, religious and moral beliefs are
tolerated. In the context of democratic politics, we may also look to the
USA to provide us with an example of how these two concepts – pluralism and democracy – can be synthesised.

As long ago as 1835, the French democratic theorist **Alexis de Tocqueville** commented on American society that its potential for true
democracy lay in its tolerance of many interest groups standing between
the mass of the people and their government. At the same time, he noted
the tendency of the American people to involve themselves enthusiasti-
cally in the activities of such groups. The danger of democracy lay predominantly in the fact that majority government might feel itself
unfettered by public opinion and so at liberty to adopt dictatorial
methods. The best protection against such a danger, observed Tocqueville, was this continuous participation of the people in intermediate
political groups.

Over a century later, in the 1960s, Tocqueville's ideas on democracy
were echoed in the sociological studies of American political scientists
such as **Robert Dahl** and **David Trueman**. They rejected the elitist
theories of Schumpeter and Mills, replacing them with observations
that much of American society was pluralist in nature and that the
true character of the political system was extremely complex. It was
simplistic, they claimed, to see power as lying exclusively in the hands
of a few political elites. Whatever the outcome of elections and the
size of the voting turnout, in reality the political process consisted of
the interplay of many pressure and interest groups. The role of government was to mediate between the demands of such groups in such a way
as to discover a consensus. There were, thus, no majority groups in
control, but rather a large number of minorities competing for the attention and favours of the elected government. This process took place
from Washington in the centre, to city and country government at
the periphery. Such an analysis seems particularly compelling when we
consider that in the UK of the early twenty-first century considerably

more people are members of environmental pressure groups such as Friends of the Earth and the Woodland Trust than of the major political parties.

Indeed, the pluralist analysis of modern democracies ~~see representation~~ as acting through specialised pressure groups that have direct links with government, rather than through the traditional media of parties and legislatures. In the USA, where parties are diffuse, relatively loose-structured organisations, much political influence now centres around various kinds of interest groups or policy communities, notably 'political action committees' that seek to build temporary coalitions for the purpose of securing the passage of legislation. Thus, the pluralist model suggests that there exists an active, politically aware public who see democracy in terms of a series of issues rather than the broader clash of competing parties and philosophies.

Liberal democracy   All contemporary political systems that can be described as 'popular government' are, to a greater or lesser extent, pluralist or elitist as described above. Yet these definitions are not precise enough for the purpose of categorising regimes into more specific types. Perhaps a better description is 'liberal democracy', the common title given to those states which broadly follow a liberal tradition that can be traced back to the eighteenth century. Before establishing detailed criteria, there are two essential prerequisites for maintaining that a system is liberal in nature. These are:

• government is based on the free consent of the people
• government is responsible to the people.

Such requirements correspond essentially to Abraham Lincoln's renowned description of democracy as 'government of the people, by the people, for the people'. But the details are more instructive:

• Government is chosen as a result of regular, free and fair elections in which the whole adult population (with a few justified exceptions) is entitled to take part. It is implied by this description that ballots are secret and that there are adequate safeguards to ensure results are accurate. The question of what kinds of electoral system are compatible with the description 'fair' can be left open in this context and is discussed later.
• Such elections should be freely competitive. Within reason any political party should be entitled to field candidates (exceptions are likely to be those parties that have illegal aims).
• Government must be continuously responsible to the people, either directly or through representative institutions such as parliaments. It is not sufficient for government only to make itself responsible at elections.
• The rights and liberties of individuals must be protected, preferably in a constitution. These rights should be enjoyed equally by all citizens.
• A wide variety of beliefs should be tolerated, provided they do not threaten the peace of the community and the existence of the state.
• There should be peaceful transition of power from one government to the next. It is a vital principle of democracy that, should a government be removed from power by a popular vote, it should accept the

popular decision, step down peacefully from power and agree to obey those laws which may be established by the victors; so too should the supporters of the defeated government.

- The rule of law should prevail. In essence, this implies that government must be subject to its own laws, i.e. should not attempt to place itself above the law and should not act in an arbitrary fashion. In addition, all citizens should be equal under the law and entitled to a fair trial by a judiciary that is independent of government.
- Government must be limited: that is, its powers should be exercised within parameters laid down in a constitution.

Of course, no single political regime could hope to meet such stringent conditions in all respects and without some failings. Nevertheless, they do serve as a useful yardstick against which we can assess the democratic credentials of any state.

Representative and direct democracy   Before moving away from what may be termed 'orthodox' conceptions of democracy, it will be useful to cast a glance back to ancient Athens and to compare the merits of direct democracy and the representative forms that now flourish in most economically developed countries. The case against direct democracy has not been proved, nor has representative democracy established itself without serious criticism.

For the past two centuries, the practice of expressing the demands and interests of the people through chosen representatives, normally elected, has been known as 'representative democracy'. Virtually all the celebrated democratic theorists, including Locke, Rousseau, Madison and J. S. Mill, have insisted that such a device is vital to the just and effective operation of a state for the following three principal reasons:

- For many, the activity of government is seen as one which can only be undertaken by those who are considered to possess superior knowledge and personal qualities. In short, they would prefer to be governed by their betters. This may seem unconvincing in an age when politicians are frequently brought into disrepute, yet it is still true that most of the electorate do seek to support individuals whom they can respect.
- The electorate may well demonstrate an emotional response to issues which, in reality, demand a more measured, rational consideration. Representatives, removed from the ebb and flow of public debate, may be in a position to judge matters dispassionately. The classic example is the debate over capital punishment. Elected representatives, through the medium of rational and calm discussion, are likely to consider all the practical and moral issues, while the voters are more inclined to display a narrower and more emotional reaction. Such a conclusion is not watertight, of course, since in this particular case there are strong moral considerations. Certainly elected representatives cannot be said to enjoy a monopoly of the proverbial 'moral high ground', even if they can claim to carry out their deliberations in the peaceful environment of Washington or Westminster. The matter of taxation is a clearer example of how rational thinking may be more desirable than the emotional response. Most of us will feel we would like to pay less tax, but politicians have to weigh up our demands against the broader needs of the country.

- On the assumption (possibly not as over-optimistic as one might believe) that representatives embody a well-developed degree of integrity, there is a good possibility that those whom we elect can reach decisions which are genuinely in the national i̶n̶t̶e̶r̶e̶s̶t̶ ̶T̶h̶e̶ ̶a̶l̶t̶e̶r̶native is the politics of self-interest, where decisions are made to the benefit of narrow sections of the community. Understandably, individuals may wish to support measures that will be to their advantage. The representative may be in a better position to balance the interests of one section of the population against another. The wealthy, for example, may not wish to pay more tax than those of more modest means, but it may be in the interests of the whole community for them to do so. Such a solution is a modern example of what Rousseau meant by his term, the 'general will'. More will be said on this issue when we consider the relative merits and demerits of direct democracy below.

> The theory of parliamentary sovereignty might suggest that if Parliament enacts legislation all must obey, but the reality is that people are far more likely to conform if a strong case has been made to them and if they themselves have approved the measure.

Anthony Batchelor, 'Referendums and Initiatives',
Politics Review, Vol. 1, No. 3 (February 1992)

A sceptic might view the arguments presented above as hopelessly utopian. Are our representatives really wiser than the collective judgement of the people? Do they pursue the national interest or merely that of the section of the community from which they themselves have emerged? Perhaps they pander to the irrational excesses of public opinion in the hope of ensuring their future re-election. Perhaps by considering the main alternative to representative government – direct democracy – it might be possible to assess the relative virtues of the two forms.

Direct democracy   In today's large-scale societies, the 'market place' democracy of Greek antiquity is clearly not appropriate. However, modern versions of it are emerging. The marketing techniques now used by political parties to gauge public opinion are a good example. Instead of mass turnout voting, smaller 'focus groups' can be used to measure opinion. The Labour Party after 1997 assembled a panel of 5000 people – a typical cross-section of society – in order to test reactions to different policy options. TV and radio surveys are now common and Internet opinion polls are increasingly used as opinion guides. In all these cases, people are making their views known directly rather than having them filtered by elected representatives.

However, it is the referendum, whether national or local, that is the main modern equivalent of direct democracy. Politicians, ever afraid of alienating public opinion, are resorting more and more to these kinds of poll. Local councils now frequently hold opinion surveys about their services and central governments have realised that a referendum is a useful way of avoiding controversial decision making.

Two criticisms often levied against the use of referenda initiatives and other forms of direct democracy can be dispensed with at the outset of this discussion. The first is purely logistical. It is often argued that it would simply be impractical and too slow a process to decide issues by direct popular vote. But technology has now overtaken such an objection. Many hundreds of thousands of viewers now vote in TV talent shows or take part in multiple-choice quizzes through telephone lines or even with the use of interactive TV sets. It seems highly likely, then, that it will soon be reasonable to connect all members of the public to a system capable of recording votes instantaneously.

Second, there exists a common argument that referenda undermine the authority of elected institutions by removing their decision-making discretion. However, this argument is not particularly clear. The referendum, by its nature, has invariably been used to fill gaps in decision-making processes left by representative institutions. In other words, if referenda are needed, our representatives have accepted their own inability to come to a decision. The Labour Government's recourse to a referendum over the UK's membership of the European Community (now Union) in 1975 was such a case. The party, and indeed the Cabinet itself, was hopelessly split on the issue. Asking the people to decide removed the problem as supporters of both sides of the argument were forced to accept the decision of the people. The campaign conducted by Sir James Goldsmith's Referendum Party in 1997 again centred on the issue of the UK's relationship with the EU in the context of a split within the Conservatives between 'pro-Europeans' and 'Eurosceptics'. Goldsmith argued that in a case affecting British sovereignty, the people should be allowed to decide. There are problems, however, with such an argument:

- Many issues are extremely complex and might be beyond the understanding of a high proportion of the electorate. It is certainly doubtful whether the voters of France, the Irish Republic and Denmark understood all the implications of the Maastricht Treaty when asked to approve it in 1992 and 1993.
- There is a danger that voters, much as they do in British local elections, will use the referendum as a vote of confidence, or disapproval in the government of the day. The true judgement of the people is thus lost.
- Just as Plato and Madison feared, the electorate might be easily swayed by emotional arguments when issues require a more rational response. One only has to consider the excesses of the tabloid press in the UK over recent years to appreciate such a danger.
- Voters might behave in an illogical and contradictory manner. In the USA, for example, where state-level referenda or initiatives are used, the people of California voted for reductions in taxation in 1978 – the notorious Proposition 13. What the voters had failed to appreciate was that such a measure would lead to drastic reductions in the provision of public services, notably the police and emergency services. Shortly afterwards the reduction had to be reversed. The danger that Rousseau identified – that people will vote out of self-interest unless properly informed – is fully illustrated by California's experience.
- Although we now have the technology to hold frequent referenda, there is a strong possibility that 'voter fatigue' will set in. Apathy could become so serious that results, based on very low turnouts, will become meaningless and lack sufficient authority to be implemented.

- Where questions excite the interest of powerful pressure groups, there is a danger that the huge financial resources which such groups may possess will distort the referendum campaign. It is, for example, suspected that in the UK's 1975 referendum on European Community membership, the fact that business interests were broadly in favour of a 'Yes' vote gave rise to a more effective public campaign in favour than against.

Despite these objections many states do use the referendum as a means of confirming key constitutional changes where a consensus of support is required. The French voters in 1969 were thus instrumental in the removal of President de Gaulle, while in 1993 the Italians voted to ditch proportional representation just when New Zealanders opted to introduce it. The 1997 election manifestos of all three main parties in the UK promised a referendum on whether the country should join a European monetary union, while Labour was offering additional votes on Scottish and Welsh devolution as well as a proposed change in the electoral system. The referendum principle seemed to have been firmly established by the mother of parliamentary government.

There are, in addition, a number of strong reasons why referenda could be acceptable as a **complement** to existing decision-making institutions, rather than as an **alternative**. On some occasions, party politicians might recognise the need for decisions, but be unable to agree on action. In such cases the clear verdict of the people might help to overcome the log-jam. This has been perfectly illustrated by the UK's inability to reach consensus over its involvement in the European Union. Certainly, if a democracy needs to ensure that key decisions enjoy popular consent, the device of the referendum might prove to be an ideal way of preserving such democratic principles. Direct democracy may be 2500 years old, but there is still no conclusion as to its desirability.

A common objection to the use of referenda is that they are merely tools employed by politicians to deal with their own insoluble problems. Where the **initiative** system is used, decision making is placed more firmly in the hands of the people. Used in parts of the USA and Switzerland, for example, the initiative is a referendum demanded by the people rather than the Government. Where it operates, a minimum number of petition signatures is required in order to trigger a referendum.

Use of referenda in the UK		
Year	Subject	Result
1975	Whether UK should remain in the European Community	Decisive 'yes' vote
1979	Devolution to Wales	Rejected
1979	Devolution to Scotland	'Yes' vote but insufficient majority to go ahead
1997	Devolution to Wales	Very narrow 'yes' vote on a low turnout
1997	Devolution to Scotland	Decisive 'yes' vote
1998	Northern Ireland Good Friday Agreement	Decisive endorsement of the agreement
1999	Whether to introduce an elected mayor in London	Decisive 'yes' vote

The **Political Parties, Elections and Referendums Act, 2000** regulate: use of referenda. An Electoral Commission will ensure that they carried out fairly, will attempt to ensure that the wording of the questions is clear, and will control the funding of campaigns to ensure that both sides have equal expenditure levels. It is also an acknowledgement that the use of referenda is here to stay and is now a part of the UK's constitutional arrangements.

The main arguments for and against the use of referenda

Arguments against	Arguments in favour
1. Issues might be too complex for the general public to understand (e.g. the single European currency).	1. Referenda are the most direct form of democracy.
2. The response of the public might be over-emotional and irrational (e.g. the death penalty).	2. The people might respect decisions if they have made them themselves (e.g. devolution of power to Scotland, Wales and Northern Ireland).
3. Referenda might become mere public opinion polls on the popularity of the government and ignore the issues.	3. When government itself is divided, referenda might help to avoid damaging splits and instability (e.g. the single European currency).
4. The media might have undue influence (e.g. membership of the European Union).	4. The electoral mandate is not precise enough because it does not distinguish between individual issues, whereas referenda do.
5. Referenda might undermine the authority of elected institutions such as Parliament.	5. Referenda are an opportunity for a full debate on key issues.
6. Wealthy pressure groups might have undue influence (e.g. licensing laws).	
7. If the turnout is low, the decision will lack authority and might not be accepted.	
8. If there is a very close result, it will split the nation on a vital issue.	

<u>Other forms</u>   What we have been dealing with so far is a conventional western-liberal type of democracy. But there are democratic theories that stray a good deal from these typical ideals. It may seem paradoxical to western ears, for example, when the term 'totalitarian democracy' is used, yet it can have some meaning if one is viewing the concept from a particular perspective. It was Rousseau in the eighteenth century who suggested that a single enlightened ruler, the 'legislator', could express the 'general will' on behalf of the people. The nature of such rule could be considered democratic in a broad sense, since the interests of the people were being served. It must also be considered totalitarian, however, since the regime would need wide powers in order to prevent minority interests operating against the collective good. The operation of such powers would thus entail the loss of many other liberties. Indeed, history is scattered with dictators who laid claim to such democratic authority even though the conventional institutions of democracy were absent. Napoleon was perhaps the first who drew inspiration from Rousseau's analysis, while others such as Bismarck and Stalin have made similar claims.

The communist argument, that social equality and democracy are synonymous, was not as modern as it might have appeared. As long ago as the 1830s, the French democratic theorist, Tocqueville, had expressed the belief that the true ~~~~ ~~~~ ~~~~ and American revolutions had been to create more equality between the classes. This, he argued, was part of a long historical process during which democracy would ultimately prevail over aristocracy and the system of class privilege. Almost prophetically, however, Tocqueville warned that such democracy could result in the kind of tyranny experienced under Stalin. The class system had created stability at least. Social equality introduced the danger of a disordered society and so opened the door for totalitarianism. As we saw earlier when we looked at pluralist democracy, only an active, enlightened, participatory society could prevent this development.

Equally, as C.B. MacPherson has pointed out in his influential work *The Real World of Democracy*, we should not be mesmerised by the existence of so-called democratic institutions such as parliaments and elections. Rather, the true test of a democracy is whether it serves the broad interests of its people. In this regard, MacPherson suggests we should not reject out of hand the claims of many one-party states to be democratic. They are one-party states often because they have a necessity for singleness of purpose. They may require rapid economic development, as is often the case in Asia, or may be searching for a national identity, frequently the problem for former African colonies. Whichever, the existence of a plurality of parties and ideologies would endanger such processes. As long as these regimes do not abuse civil liberties on a wide scale, and as long as the single legal party displays a reasonable degree of internal democracy, they are indeed democratic themselves. MacPherson does not extend his blessing of such 'one-party democracies' to the communist type, however, since their widespread abuse of human rights disqualifies them.

The democratic case for communist regimes is made most persuasively by V.I. Lenin, who developed a theory known as **democratic centralism**. As the name suggests, this contains two elements. The term 'democratic' refers to the ultimate goals of the system – equality and justice – which are clearly in the interests of the people according to classical Marxist theory. It also paid at least lip-service to the idea that all were entitled to participate in the process (though they must accept the parameters of socialist doctrine) and to the acceptance of a certain amount of free dialogue within the ruling party. The 'centralist' element was that, once firm decisions had been reached, discussion and opposition would end. The higher echelons of the system would impose the decisions upon those below them. In other words, influence was to spread down through the system from the centre, rather than up as is the case in the liberal form of democracy. Ultimately, Lenin's successor, Stalin, was to bring the principles of democratic centralism into disrepute by establishing autocratic government that engaged in the systematic abuse of human rights. Nevertheless, Lenin's argument that equality itself could constitute democracy, and that so-called liberal democracy was merely a charade to disguise the institutionalisation of class rule, has enjoyed widespread popularity, at least until recent years.

We may perhaps end this section on democracy where we began, with Professor Bernard Crick. He suggests that we should not seek to classify regimes as either democratic or undemocratic. Democracy, he suggests, is more a 'spirit' than a set of institutions. We should judge political systems according to the extent to which they embody such spirit and contain democratic elements. He sums this idea up thus: 'Democracy, then, if we give the word the fairest meaning we may want to give it – if we value liberty, free choice, discussion, opposition, popular government, all of these things together – is still but one form of politics, not something to be hoped for at every stage of a country's development or in every circumstance.'

A summary of democracy

1. Historically there have been a number of usages of the term 'democracy', in particular:

   - Plato's description of a direct, popular decision-making process with equal political rights
   - The idea of a representative system of government, favoured by English liberals such as John Locke and John Stuart Mill and the American, James Madison. Decisions should be made on behalf of the people by elected representatives
   - Rousseau's difficult concept of a powerful leader able to discern and carry out the 'general will' of the people
   - The meaning used by Tocqueville of a society where there is social equality and an absence of class hierarchy and privilege
   - Lenin's communist doctrine of democracy as economic equality with the interests of the people (essentially the working classes) served by a single party
   - Modern 'liberal' ideas of a highly tolerant, pluralistic society with widespread popular participation and influence over government. This is normally characterised by the presence of free elections, competing parties, representative and responsible government and a free media.

2. The type of democracy described immediately above, variously described as 'liberal democracy', 'pluralist democracy' or 'democratic elitism' and often containing features of all three, has steadily gained ascendancy during the past two centuries. Of all the political systems that exist today, it appears to be the most popular and the most sought after. This development became even more marked during the 1980s and 1990s

3. Despite their apparent success, there remain problems with such democratic systems. They may lack the ability to take decisive action when it is clearly necessary. There are dangers that minorities may be ignored or persecuted in the face of majority rule. Furthermore, if the modern form of direct democracy is used – the referendum – there is a fear that irrational, over-emotional decisions will be taken.

4. A number of solutions have been adopted to reduce the problems described above. Both consensus and pluralist politics go some way to providing safeguards. Individual and minority rights may be protected in various ways, while a well-informed and sophisticated people could prove capable of handling the responsibility placed upon them in a democracy.

For exam questions relevant to this unit, see page 555.

Introduction

Outside Northern Ireland, Britain has an essentially two-party system, with some challenge from third parties – Liberal Democrats in various regions and nationalists in Scotland and Wales – yet its ideological background is considerably more complex and fragmented. It is therefore inevitable that these ideological traditions do not coincide precisely with the party structure.

We can divide political traditions into as many as seven main philosophical movements, all of which are still flourishing at the beginning of the twenty-first century. These may be described as:

- traditional conservatism
- authoritarian–nationalistic conservatism
- 'New Right' conservatism
- liberalism
- democratic socialism
- social democracy
- 'Third Way'
- liberal nationalism.

At first sight this list may appear confusing when set against the simpler party system. The reason is that each party is really a coalition of groups who belong to these ideological movements to a greater or lesser extent. If we place each movement into the party structure, we obtain the following scheme.

Ideological movements and the party structure			
Conservative Party	**Labour Party**	**Liberal Democrat Party**	**Scottish and Welsh Nationalists**
• Traditional conservatism	• Democratic socialism	• Liberalism	• Liberal nationalism
• Authoritarian nationalists	• Social democracy	• Social democracy	• Liberalism
• 'New Right' neo-liberals	• Liberalism	• Liberal nationalism	• Social democracy
	• 'Third Way'		

We can now see that three identifiable forms of conservatism flourish within the same Conservative Party and that liberalism and social democracy can be discovered in four different parties. It is even the case that some members of the Conservative Party on its moderate wing hold views in common with pure liberals or even social democrats.

So we must be careful to distinguish between the political parties (with their various internal factions) and their ideological traditions, which we will now examine.

Traditional conservatism

The most effective and convenient way to trace the development of traditional conservatism is by reference to a number of individuals who have either proposed or practised political principles that can be grouped into this category of belief. Having reviewed the ideas of these conservatives, we can summarise the position as it stands today.

Foundations of traditional conservatism

Opinions vary considerably as to when British conservatism came into existence. Some go back as far as the English Civil War in the 1640s, citing the supporters of the Stuart monarchy as the original conservatives, reacting against the new ideas of the parliamentary faction. Others suggest it began with the opponents of the Whig Party who established parliamentary sovereignty and a limited, constitutional monarchy following the 'Glorious Revolution' of 1688. Indeed, it was at this time that the term 'Tory' was first introduced to describe such a conservative faction. For convenience, the actual formation of a 'Conservative Party' by **Sir Robert Peel** in the 1840s could be used as a starting point. However, the period which can, perhaps, best be selected as seeing the birth of the tradition is the years immediately following the French Revolution: that is, the 1790s. The key figure was, ironically, a Whig MP rather than a Tory, but his philosophy was unmistakably conservative. He was **Edmund Burke**.

Edmund Burke (1729–97)

After the French Revolution in 1789, and more particularly the 'reign of terror' of 1792–3 when many aristocrats and opponents of the ruling party lost their lives or their liberty, fear gripped much of the British political establishment that the radical ideas of the revolutionaries would be exported across the Channel, sweeping away the authority of traditional institutions such as the monarchy, the landed aristocracy and the Church of England. These ideas included such principles as equal political rights, democratically elected institutions and religious freedom. Burke was among the reactionaries or 'conservatives' who opposed the radical new ideas. His major work, entitled *Reflections on the Revolution in France*, expressed these fears, but went further still, developing into a full account of early conservative principles.

His ideas follow a logical series of steps:

- Man is not a rational creature, but is driven by basic instincts and emotions. The new ideas of the eighteenth century, often referred to as the 'Age of Reason' or the 'Enlightenment', assumed that people were capable of rational thought and action, so that society and politics could be moulded in such rational ways. Burke would have none of this. Not only did mankind follow emotions rather than reason, but man responded to such base instincts as selfishness and greed. It would therefore be futile to conduct politics in a rational manner. The imperfections of man had to be recognised.
- Since man is imperfect and, furthermore, is not capable of being made perfect through education or moral example, he must have disciplines imposed on him, just as children must be disciplined. Such control can only be imposed from above, by some form of superior force.

Democracy and equality, he argued, involved man being able to control his own actions rationally. He was not capable of this, Burke insisted.

- The most basic ~~~~~~~~~~~~~~~~~~ order and security. Such qualities in a society are far more desirable than characteristics such as individual freedom and tolerance. Thus, the purpose of political power is to create and to maintain good order.
- Order and security are best achieved through continuity and respect for traditional institutions. By preserving strong links between the past, present and future, security is maintained. The preservation of traditional institutions such as landed interests, the family and the Church could provide such continuity.
- Violent and rapid change is, thus, to be avoided. There might be times when gentle reforms are required, but these should be undertaken only when absolutely necessary and with regard to traditional practices.
- Property ownership brings with it a sense of responsibility. Not all are capable of this, so property ownership cannot be shared by all. However, those who are privileged enough to own property have a duty to protect the security of the whole of society, including the propertyless.

Sir Robert Peel (Prime Minister 1834–5, 1841–6)

After Burke the conservative movement fell into danger of becoming a purely reactionary movement, opposed to any form of social reform or progress. Thus, conservatives were opposed to reform of the political system (which was a key issue in the early 1830s), to the introduction of free trade rather than protectionism during the same period and to equal political rights for Catholics. Peel recognised that such a reactionary movement would be politically doomed.

In his 'Tamworth Manifesto' issued in 1834, he urged conservatives to accept reforms if they were clearly desirable and inevitable. Thus, he linked the movement to progress and reform. His maxim was that it was sometimes necessary to 'reform in order to preserve'. However, he insisted that such change should be moderated and, to achieve this, traditional forms of authority would need to be combined with the new democratic institutions that were promoting reform. Thus, the conservative movement added the principle of a 'mixed' political system to Burke's earlier ideas. More popular democracy could be accepted provided some power was retained by traditional institutions.

Peel's support for an ordered society was demonstrated by perhaps his best-known achievement, the creation of an organised police force when he was Home Secretary in 1822.

Benjamin Disraeli (Earl of Beaconsfield, Prime Minister 1868, 1874–80)

Disraeli had formed his political beliefs under Peel, and the two men had a great deal in common. Disraeli took the idea of the mixed political system and developed it further into the concept of 'Tory democracy'. He urged conservatives to accept the right of all people to a share in democracy. In effect, they should be granted voting rights. Recognising the dangers of democracy, however, he proposed a political system designed to reduce the threat to society. For him, the dangers were as follows:

- The huge voting power of the working classes might create revolutionary change, sweeping away order and authority, and replacing it with anarchy or even socialism.
- Alternatively, the wealth of the newly enriched capitalist middle classes could be converted into political power. If they were to exercise power in their own interests – and he believed they would – the working class would be disadvantaged, creating the seedbed for discontent and revolution (1848 had seen a series of revolutionary upheavals in various parts of Europe). Capitalist power, he predicted, was creating 'two nations', one of the rich and powerful, the other of the poor and powerless.
- The traditional power of the aristocracy, monarchy, landed gentry and Church had always been a moderating and unifying influence. If their power were to be undermined by democracy, moderation would disappear. The landed classes were the natural ruling class, since they alone could govern in the interests of the whole nation rather than purely in their own interests.

Thus Disraeli warned against a divided nation, torn by class conflict and destroyed by the uncontrolled pursuit of self-interest by the two great social classes. The answer was to ensure that Britain remained 'one nation', living with order and security, so as to preserve the power of traditional institutions and to combine it with new democratic institutions. This was Disraeli's vision of Tory democracy. He also believed that a strong sense of nationalism and pride in the Empire (which was at its height then) could unite the nation.

On a more philosophical level, Disraeli believed that society was a single organism, one great united whole that could exist in a state of harmony if the 'natural order' were preserved. He firmly believed that people are not equal, but that some are naturally superior to others. Any social and political system, therefore, had to reflect that social order and not destroy it, as nineteenth-century liberals and socialists were proposing. Each level in society had its part to play in preserving order and creating prosperity, so the levels depended on each other. But this did not mean that rank and privilege should be abolished. On the contrary, they should be maintained. At the top there should be a permanent ruling class made up of the traditionally superior class – the aristocracy and landed gentry.

In summary, Disraeli's contributions to the conservative tradition can be described as follows:

- Popular democracy is necessary, but carries such dangers of disorder that democratic institutions must share power with traditional centres of power which have proved themselves to be superior and more responsible in the past.
- It is vital for peace and prosperity to unite the nation (his views are often described as 'one nation Toryism'). Unity can only be preserved if no section of society is able to profit unduly at the expense of others.
- Nationalism is to be encouraged as a further means of unifying society.
- There is a natural order in society which should be preserved. This order serves to unify and not divide the nation. At the top is a natural ruling class who should govern fairly and responsibly. Ideas of social equality are, therefore, artificial and false.

**Michael Oakeshott
(1901–90)**

For nearly a century after Disraeli the conservative movement, and much of the Conservative Party itself, adopted his principles. As with Peel, they learned to accept reforms where they were necessary and to argue that Conservati~~...~~ ~~...~~ ~~...~~ ~~...~~ suited to manage such changes for the good of the whole nation and not just sections of it. However, by the mid-twentieth century this was not enough. The steady march of liberal and socialist ideas represented a threat to traditional conservative beliefs. A restatement of philosophy was needed, and it was provided by the modern conservative philosopher Michael Oakeshott.

Faced with increasingly high levels of involvement by the state in society, Oakeshott questioned the basis upon which any political action should be undertaken. His answer was to oppose all forms of action that were based on abstract principles or artificial ideologies. Thus, for example, 'equality' was an abstract principle, not natural to mankind. If political measures were simply designed to promote greater equality **for its own sake** – a socialist objective – it would be seen as unnatural and would lead to disruption in society. Ideologies too are to be treated with great suspicion, he suggested.

Like all conservatives, Oakeshott opposed the imposition of rigid ideologies on the grounds that this could easily lead to tyranny – political leaders who were driven by the desire to impose the ideology would tend to accept no opposition, often ruthlessly putting down any resistance to it. This had clearly occurred after the French Revolution of 1789 when the Jacobins hunted down all opponents, whether real or imagined. Similarly, in the twentieth century, communism adopted tyrannical methods in order to impose itself upon society. Oakeshott, however, added a further objection: ideology and abstract principles do not take account of the traditions and sentiments of the people. **All** political action, Oakeshott said, must take account of such natural features of a society. If not, the people will not readily accept it and disorder is likely to result. He suggested that politics should be 'a conversation, not an argument'.

The implication of Oakeshott's beliefs is that there should be no sense of **progress** in politics. Politicians should not see their task as moving society in a particular direction, towards a goal or a series of goals. Rather, they should allow the people to set their own direction naturally and should simply ensure that the state is maintained in a safe and secure condition. For Oakeshott, the art of politics was something similar to steering a ship. The course is set by the passengers and the politician should merely ensure it keeps safely to that course. It is this particular aspect of Oakeshott's philosophy that perhaps defines the term 'conservatism' most aptly today. It includes the idea of conserving what is good and what is in accordance with the wishes of the people. The alternative is to lead the people towards goals that they may not desire, with unpredictable consequences that may threaten the preservation of the better features of society.

'If the main strength of Conservatism is adaptability, its main enemy is ideology.'
Francis Pym (Conservative Cabinet minister 1979–83),
The Politics of Consent, 1984

Harold Macmillan (Prime Minister 1957–63)

From the First World War onwards, there was a steady expansion in the activities and scope of the state. For conservatives, traditionally suspicious of state power, this represented a major challenge. Macmillan adopted the approach of Peel and Disraeli to such developments, while updating their beliefs to suit the second half of the twentieth century. Thus he 'modernised' the conservative tradition without distorting it.

He recognised that the new powerful state should play a similar role to that of the ruling class in the nineteenth century. It should prevent class conflict and act as a neutral arbiter between the competing claims of different sections of society. By creating a stable society, the state would maximise the opportunities for individualism to flourish. Thus the powerful state would not threaten individual action, but would enhance it. In practice, this implied such policies as firm economic management, control and support for industrial development, protection of the rights of both employers and trade unions, and maintenance of an effective welfare state for the benefit of all. Since the Labour Party could support such objectives, the period surrounding Macmillan's premiership is often referred to as a time of 'consensus politics'.

Macmillan also understood that, if the state were to remain benevolent and popular, it was necessary to involve the representatives of important sections of society in the governing process. Thus trade union leaders, employers, financiers, agricultural and military interests were incorporated into the state. So far did the process go, in fact, that Macmillan's vision was often described as the 'corporate state'.

His objectives were still those of Disraeli. He believed that those of a conservative disposition should govern. He saw social unity and harmony as vital. He understood that all should feel they have a stake in the activities of the state and that no single class should be allowed to dominate.

Traditional conservatism today

Margaret Thatcher transformed the nature of the Conservative Party during the 1980s. Many of the traditional values described above were abandoned. Those members of the party who adhered to them were steadily removed from power and declined in numbers. They referred to themselves as 'one-nation' Tories, as 'Disraelian Conservatives' or sometimes merely as 'traditional' Tories. Thatcher's supporters disparagingly dubbed them 'wets' on the basis that they had insufficient nerve to support the radical reforms that were being proposed. Such proponents of the tradition as **Francis Pym**, **John Biffen** and **Ian Gilmour** were driven from office and fought a losing rearguard action against radical Thatcherism.

> 'The aim [of Conservatism] has always been to conserve what is good and to improve what is bad.'
> Francis Pym (Conservative Cabinet minister 1979–83),
> *The Politics of Consent*, 1984

During the 1990s, traditional conservatism was forced into progressively deeper retreat. Senior figures who were seen as the heirs to Peel and Disraeli, such as **Kenneth Clarke** and **Michael Heseltine**, have become increasingly marginalised. To add to their growing isolation, they are in favour of closer integration with the European Union at a time when the conservative movement as a whole has become exceptionally 'Eurosceptic'.

Under William Hague, the Conservative Party also moved towards a more authoritarian, nationalistic position, which might have increased its appeal in the country, but lost many of its long-standing supporters from the traditional wing. Ironically, the 'New' Labour Party under Tony Blair seemed the natural home for the traditionalists. Its moderate policies became more attractive to traditional conservatives than the more extreme views of such leading party figures as Michael Portillo and John Redwood.

Summary of traditional conservative beliefs

1. People are imperfect, irrational and imperfectible, so no political action should be based on rational ideas or be designed to grant excessive amounts of personal freedom.

2. The desire for order is the most important instinct of mankind, so any political system should be aimed at preserving order.

3. Rapid and radical social change should be avoided. Reform if necessary should be gradual and carried out in accordance with traditions. Whatever changes are allowed, what is good in society should be conserved.

4. Traditional institutions and an established ruling class are crucial in maintaining continuity between the past and the present.

5. There is a natural order in society that should be preserved.

6. Society should be a unified, harmonious whole and political action should be designed to preserve such a situation.

7. Abstract political principles and ideologies are to be treated with great suspicion and generally opposed.

8. The state should take into account the interests of all sections of society in creating order and general prosperity. In so doing, it should promote individualism and maximum opportunities for the people.

9. Ownership of property is a privilege and brings with it the responsibility to preserve and maintain an ordered society.

Authoritarian–nationalist conservatism

This flourished on the margins of the movement for most of the twentieth century, but from time to time it moved to the forefront of conservative politics, notably in the 1930s and the 1960s. In the latter period it was led by **Enoch Powell**. Powell opposed immigration into the UK and championed the idea of repatriating existing ethnic minorities to the country from which they had come. He combined this with a fierce determination to prevent the break-up of the UK into separate, devolved administrations in Wales, Scotland and Northern Ireland. He did not live to see the realisation of devolution.

This 'right wing' of the Conservative Party survived under Margaret Thatcher, even achieving some representation in her Cabinets. **John Redwood** and **Michael Portillo** (who has modified his views since then) became leading protagonists. The movement grew under John Major and William Hague in the 1990s. The huge Conservative Party defeat at the 1997 general election provided a boost for the right-wingers, who believed that John Major had moved the party too far towards the moderate centre. In addition, the party began to believe that the only way it could challenge the position of the popular Blair Government would be to take up a strong anti-European position. This gave a further boost to the nationalists. Steadily they moved to the leadership of the Conservative Party as William Hague's position weakened. This split the party fundamentally, but nationalism continued to grow in influence.

Principal beliefs of authoritarian–nationalist conservatism

Authoritarian ideas

1. A very strong position on law and order. They favour the death penalty, longer prison sentences, increased police powers and a hard line against young offenders.
2. Opposition to liberal and progressive theories concerning education, the family, homosexuality and other moral issues.
3. A strong defence of the rights of property owners.
4. Support for traditional institutions such as the monarchy, the Church of England and the House of Lords.
5. Support for private provision of health and education.
6. A belief in the centralised state and therefore opposition to the power of regional and local government.

Nationalist ideas

1. Preservation of the 'Union' of the United Kingdom. This implies opposition to the devolution of power to national regions. Once devolution had taken place in 1999, they opposed any further loss of power to these regions.
2. Opposition to greater integration with the European Union. Most oppose the UK **ever** joining a single European currency. They oppose any further losses of sovereignty and the more extreme members of the movement favour the UK's complete withdrawal from the EU.
3. Opposition to substantial immigration into the UK and suspicion of refugees who come to the UK seeking political asylum.
4. Support for an influential British position in world affairs. In order to achieve this, defence expenditure should be maintained at a high level and the nuclear deterrent retained. They strongly support the maintenance of NATO as the means by which collective security in Europe can be maintained. Related to this is a belief that the USA should remain the UK's principal ally.

'New Right' conservatism

Although various elements of New Right conservatism have flourished separately over the centuries, it was only in the 1980s that they were brought together into a single ideology. It came to dominate the political agenda in western Europe and the USA and was led by its best-known proponent **Margaret Thatcher** (Prime Minister 1979–90). She and her close political allies, such as **Sir Keith Joseph**, fused a number of political traditions into a single philosophy.

In broad terms, the New Right is a synthesis of what have been called 'neo-liberalism' and 'neo-conservatism' – in other words, modern versions of two traditional nineteenth-century movements. However, we can divide it further into as many as four historical tendencies.

Classical liberalism With the growth of the Industrial Revolution in Britain and the capitalist system that was a natural companion to it, there developed the study of economics as a science. The early economists, such as **Adam Smith** and **David Ricardo** in the late seventeenth and early eighteenth centuries, believed that the reason for the extraordinary growth in production and wealth resulting from capitalism was the degree of individual freedom that the system allowed in the economic sphere. This freedom released the forces of enterprise and innovation that facilitated such progress. At the same time, the preservation of such freedom required that governments should resist the temptation to interfere in economic affairs. Any such interference would inevitably reduce the wealth-creating capacity of capitalism. These economists further believed that all would benefit from the free operation of capitalism – workers, consumers and employers alike – as it guaranteed that production could be carried out at the most efficient level possible.

As the eighteenth century progressed and the political movement known as liberalism advanced, these **economic** theories came to be linked with the new **political** interest in personal liberty. Thus, the original – now known as 'classical' – liberals, such as **John Stuart Mill**, **Richard Cobden** and **Herbert Spencer**, advocated free trade and competition, the absence of state interference in the operation of product and labour markets, and control of monopoly power resulting from large companies squeezing out smaller firms. (More detail on classical liberalism can be found in the section on liberalism page 69.)

Classical liberal ideas were falling out of favour by the end of the nineteenth century, to be replaced by political doctrines that involved more state interference in social and economic affairs. However, in the 1970s economic progress in the developed world seemed to be faltering. Interest was revived in the classical liberal ideas of a hundred years before. The Swiss philosopher **Friedrich Hayek** and American economist **Milton Friedman** suggested that excessive interference by the state in economic affairs, together with a growth in the influence of trade unions, were robbing capitalism of its ability to promote real growth in prosperity. Not only that, but unduly high taxes, over-regulation of industry and high levels of public expenditure were reducing economic and political liberty unjustifiably.

Margaret Thatcher and her close adviser Sir Keith Joseph were heavily influenced by these neo-classical liberals and set about converting fellow conservatives to their beliefs. Their goal was to 'roll back the frontiers of the state', as they put it. This involved reducing public expenditure and taxation, removing state control over industry and restoring the operation of free markets wherever possible. At the same time, what was seen as the undesirable influence of trade unions was to be destroyed. It is these beliefs that are now referred to as 'neo-liberalism'.

American populism

The term 'populism' refers to any political movement that appeals to the mass of the people. The American populist party that flourished in the 1890s, however, was considerably more. It championed opposition to any form of vested interest that threatened the independence of the individual. The targets were big business, big government and especially excessive taxation. In a modern context, a number of institutions have come under attack, such as the civil service (including the bureaucracy involved in the European Union), over-powerful local government, trade unions, monopolies, the established Church and the welfare state.

Populism also appeals to the feelings of extreme individualism, self-responsibility and independence that are so widespread in the USA. Welfare, for example, is believed to rob people of the necessity to provide for themselves. If there is over-reliance on the state, families will lose the will to fend for themselves. Big business and over-regulation reduce the effectiveness of small business. Thus, populism appeals to the 'small man', the rugged individualist. It follows that those who are unwilling to support themselves should not be rescued by the state.

Whiggism

In the nineteenth century, the Whigs were essentially liberals who adapted their belief in individual liberty to defend the interests of the capitalist and property-owning classes. The New Right is also a neo-liberal movement and, in common with the Whigs, wishes to defend the importance of property ownership. Thatcher added a modern aspect to the movement by encouraging widespread ownership of shares in private industry. The opportunity to accumulate wealth and property is seen as fundamental and the role of the state should be to sponsor and defend such rights.

Conservative authoritarianism

Although the New Right opposes the over-powerful state and defends the rights of individuals against it, there remains an acceptance that individuals need to be protected in their lives and property against attacks from others. Small though the state may be, therefore, it should be a powerful, centralised institution. In common with traditional conservatives, the New Right takes a strong position on law and order issues. Its attitude to crime is to concentrate on punishment rather than social cures, while on social issues generally, a conservative line is taken.

Although there was an element of moralism in the British New Right, greater stress was placed on it in the USA. It was certainly recognised that the increases in personal freedom that were resulting from New Right policies created the danger that society would disintegrate, with individuals in permanent conflict with each other and lacking any sense of moral responsibility. The answer lay in a stress on traditional values of family and religious morality. Such apparent immoralities as crime, homosexuality, single parenthood, pornography and sexual permissiveness were opposed. They threatened the integrity and security of society in a way that was unacceptable to any brand of conservatism. Patriotism has been promoted as an additional unifying force in a potentially fragmented society, forming a bond with the nationalist form of conservatism described above. It is this modern application of traditional conservative values that is often described as 'neo-conservatism'.

New Right and neo-liberalism

1. Great stress on economic freedom.

2. Disengagement of the state from economic control.

3. Restoration of free markets wherever possible.

4. Dependence on the welfare state discouraged, self-responsibility in its place.

5. Opposition to vested interests such as trade unions, big business, bureaucracy.

6. Support for small independent businesses.

7. Encouragement for widespread property and share ownership.

8. Stress on morality and traditional values.

9. Maintenance of a limited but disciplinarian state.

Conservatism and the Conservative Party

At the start of the twenty-first century, the Conservative Party has not found itself in such a state of turmoil since the 1920s. Derived, as the party is, from the three movements described above, the shock of a disastrous defeat at the polls in 1997 and continued unpopularity had the effect of fragmenting the party. Two trends can be discerned. The first is the synthesis of 'New Right' conservatism with the authoritarian–nationalist tradition. This appears to be crystallising into the central position of the new party. The second is that the traditional one-nation Toryism that began to decline in the 1980s has become only a distant influence on modern conservatism.

Nevertheless one conservative tradition remains intact. The movement has always adapted itself in opposing new political doctrines that threaten the status quo. New Labour's success in the 1990s has provided such a threat. As it has done throughout its history, therefore, conservatism has taken on a new form to combat its opponents.

Liberalism

Origins

During the eighteenth century, two major developments were occurring in Europe. First, the traditional forms of authority and the existing social order – both political and religious – were coming under challenge. Second, the Enlightenment ushered in new forms of rational, scientific thought.

The challenge to traditional authority and order

The religious Reformation that had earlier gripped much of northern Europe was not only of spiritual significance. The traditional authority of the Papacy and the religious intolerance that had characterised Roman Catholicism were also called into question. The rigid doctrines of Rome, including its insistence on the authority of the Church, had been defeated by free-thinking, radical members of the Protestant movement. At the same time as papal authority was being weakened, the institution of hereditary, absolute monarchy was also coming under attack. The execution of Charles I in England represented a warning shot. It was soon followed by the 'Glorious Revolution' of 1688, which ushered in a limited, constitutional form of monarchy. A century later both the French and the Americans rid themselves of hereditary monarchy (the French temporarily) and replaced it with more rational forms of government, based on a limited degree of democracy.

Along with these challenges to traditional authority there arrived a new outlook on human society. The notion of a 'natural order' in society was soundly rejected in favour of the view that each person is an individual with unlimited potential. The traditional order stratified humanity into social layers. This order was rigid and denied people their individuality. As the nineteenth century dawned, bringing with it the onset of capitalism and industrialisation, this insistence on individuality became an essential ingredient in economic development.

The Enlightenment

The Enlightenment, which underpinned the historical developments described above, challenged existing religious and irrational modes of thinking. The movement encompassed the worlds of science, politics, religion, the arts and literature. Enlightenment philosophers were offering rational explanations of the world and suggested new ways of ordering society along such rational lines. They stressed the ability to apply reason to problems instead of merely responding in an emotional, instinctive manner.

Rational thinking gave rise to such possibilities as equal rights, individual liberty, government by popular consent and even full-scale democracy. The old order had denied the possibility of any of these new ideas.

The original ideas of liberalism

1. Tolerance of new beliefs and ideas.
2. Rejection of traditional forms of religious and political authority.
3. Replacement of the philosophy of a 'natural order' by a stress on individuality.
4. Rational analyses of society and proposed social reforms.
5. Belief in the importance of 'government by popular consent'.
6. The possibility that equal rights could be introduced.

Classical liberalism

The term 'classical' refers to the early form of liberalism that flourished for much of the nineteenth century. However, before it came to maturity, liberalism was preceded by two parallel movements, **natural rights and utilitarianism.**

Natural rights

The doctrine of 'natural rights' had been developed in seventeenth-century England by **Thomas Hobbes** and **John Locke**. They argued that each man is born with certain rights which are natural and cannot, therefore, be denied to him by other men. These suggested rights included the right to life and liberty, to pursue happiness, avoid pain and enjoy one's own property. It followed that these rights could only be limited if man himself consented to accept controls. Thus, government had to be founded on consent and, at least in Locke's case, was subject to some degree of popular control.

This philosophy viewed man very much as an individual, entitled to be free yet understanding that, in order to enjoy his freedom successfully, he would have to set up government over himself.

By the end of the eighteenth century, natural right philosophy had been taken further by the French romantic thinker **Jean-Jacques Rousseau** and the British revolutionary **Tom Paine**. They suggested that all men have not only **natural** rights but also **equal** rights and **equal** potential. By contrast, the inequality of rights that had existed within traditional society was artificial and could not be justified.

Utilitarianism

Like Locke and Paine, **Jeremy Bentham** (1748–1832), the founder of the **Utilitarian** movement, saw men essentially as individuals. However, he rejected the notion of natural rights, calling it 'nonsense on stilts'. In its place he developed the principle of utility. This was based on the belief that man is motivated by the desire to achieve happiness and to avoid pain. Happiness, for utilitarians, meant the consumption and enjoyment of goods and property. The provision of such happiness was described as **utility**. Pain meant the deprivation of such pleasures and was referred to as **disutility**.

The kind of society that was envisaged was one of free individuals, pursuing their own interests as workers, producers and consumers. The role of government was to ensure that these individuals enjoyed a society where their utility was maximised. This would imply little action by government, save to ensure the free operation of the economy. However, where state action could be seen to increase the **total sum of utility** in a society, it could be justified. Thus, the goal of any political system was to achieve the 'greatest good for the greatest number'. All government action could be judged on rational grounds. To ensure that the state pursued such goals, the utilitarians insisted on a large degree of democracy and that government be answerable to the people. Indeed, popular control of government was essential, since each individual knows what is best for himself. It is not for governments to decide what is best for their people. These beliefs suggested a number of principles:

- Each individual should be free to pursue his own goals.
- No person has a right to determine what is best for another individual.
- Each has an equal right to opportunities to achieve his own happiness.
- The role of government should be limited to maximising utility.

The most important disciple of Bentham was the son of James Mill, one of Bentham's close associates. This was **John Stuart Mill** (1806–73). J.S. Mill (to distinguish him from his less liberal father) synthesised many of the earlier principles of liberalism with utilitarianism and became the founder of classical liberalism in the nineteenth century. His views have since been at the centre of British political philosophy.

John Stuart Mill Though he rejected the concept of natural rights, J.S. Mill was close to Locke in his view that each individual has a basic right to be free. He also accepted Bentham's belief that social utility should be maximised if possible. But he differed from the Utilitarians on two important points:

- He believed that people could have higher personal goals than merely the consumption of goods and the accumulation of property. Governments that acted on this limited view were arrogant and mistaken. Human individuality in thought, belief and action should be recognised. He argued that 'it is better to be a human being dissatisfied than a pig satisfied; better to be Socrates dissatisfied than a fool satisfied'.
- If governments concentrate only on achieving maximum social utility, there is a danger that this will interfere with the basic freedom of action and thought of the individual. In order to determine how much freedom individuals should be allowed, he suggests a basic rule – if an action does no harm to others, it should suffer no outside interference.

> *'The only purpose for which power can be rightfully exercised over any member of a civilised community, against his own will, is to prevent harm to others. His own good, either physical or moral, is not a sufficient warrant.'*
> John Stuart Mill, *Utilitarianism*, 1841

Other classical liberals The so-called **Manchester School** of liberalism, led by **Richard Cobden** and **John Bright**, concentrated on freedom in the economic life of the country. They advocated free trade and the retention of 'market forces'. Following the theories of the economist **David Ricardo**, they argued that only free trade and free markets could ensure maximum wealth creation. J.S. Mill himself had agreed that freedom in economic life would release the innovative and enterprising spirit in the individual.

On the extreme wing of the classical movement lay **Herbert Spencer** (1820–1903). Spencer was a follower of the evolutionary theories of Charles Darwin. He applied them to human society by arguing that individuals who adapt best to their environment – principally the economic environment – will progress. Those who fail to do so will fall behind. Similarly, he believed that people are naturally unequal, just as animals are, so that some will inevitably do better than others. Governments were beginning, in the second half of the nineteenth century, to interfere with the natural state of society by providing education, welfare and a variety of local services. Spencer believed this was tampering with the processes of nature and so was to be opposed.

Samuel Smiles, a contemporary of Spencer, campaigned against welfare provision on the grounds that it is up to individuals to make the best of their own lives according to their abilities, without relying upon others. Thus, Smiles and Spencer were both fervent opponents of state interference in society.

Summary of classical liberal ideas

1. The most basic value that must be preserved in society is individual liberty.
2. The free working of the economic system is vital in maximising prosperity.
3. The state should play a minimal role in society.
4. Inequality is natural. Creating greater equality is an interference with nature.
5. On the whole, individuals are responsible for themselves and their own welfare.

New liberalism

The problems of classical liberalism

As the nineteenth century progressed, the apparent divide between rich and poor widened, and concern grew that the exceptional spread of industrialisation and capitalism was resulting in excessive levels of deprivation. It was becoming clear that, while there were many beneficiaries of the new prosperity, there were even more losers. Two main concerns taxed liberal minds in the second half of the century:

- How to deal with the clear evidence that free market capitalism combined with an inactive state was actually **causing** poverty and social ills among the masses.
- The realisation that, while individual freedom might be desirable, and while it might seem just that people should be responsible for their own successes or failures, there was also fundamental **injustice** in the system. This was that individuals may be disadvantaged simply by circumstances of birth and social environment. In other words, not everyone begins life from the same starting point.

Thus, solutions were required to these two problems: first, how to alleviate the condition of the poor without interfering too much in society and so reducing individual freedom; second, how to provide **equality of opportunity**, again without jeopardising freedom.

Three liberal philosophers and three politicians were the principal architects of a new form of liberalism aimed at providing such answers.

T.H. Green (1836–82)

Green was a moral philosopher who re-examined the nature of freedom. The earlier liberals saw freedom only in terms of freedom from the restrictions of laws and over-powerful governments. Green argued that we are not **truly** free if we do not have a sense of caring, or obligation, towards our fellow human being. As Rousseau had argued a century before, we may be **enslaved** by the pursuit of our own self-interest. Such a pursuit was very much what liberals had been advocating. According to Green, we must balance our own personal liberty with our obligations to others. In so doing we achieve harmony with the society in which we live. With this harmony comes a higher form of freedom.

William Ewart Gladstone (Prime Minister 1868–74, 1880–5, 1886, 1892–4)

Gladstone, who effectively founded the modern Liberal Party, shared Green's sense of social morality as well as recognising the growing injustices in late Victorian society. He was mostly concerned to increase opportunities by providing some degree of education for all and to encourage local government to be more active in the care of the poor. At the same time, he attempted to open up access to British institutions to a broader section of the population, in particular the civil service, higher education and the military. For Gladstone injustice was itself a barrier to freedom, so that stronger government measures to restore justice could not be considered illiberal.

Leonard Hobhouse (1864–1929)

At the 'socialist' end of the new liberal movement, Hobhouse argued that the poor and the low-paid workers had no control over the operation of capitalism. They were, therefore, not free, but subject to economic forces beyond their control. It was up to the state to free them from such forces by ensuring a decent standard of living and the right to work. His contribution to the debate was essentially to justify considerable extensions in the activities of the state.

Joseph Chamberlain (1836–1914, Mayor of Birmingham and Cabinet minister)

In common with Hobhouse, Chamberlain argued that the state should step in to improve the conditions of the poor and underprivileged. He believed that it was local government which should achieve this and so he urged municipal provision of hospitals, housing, schools, parks and libraries. Like Hobhouse, he was very much a socialist-style liberal. Indeed, his brand of politics was known as 'municipal socialism'. Although Chamberlain left the Liberal Party at the end of his career, he did not join the new Labour Party, which appeared to be his natural political home. Nevertheless, he represents the beginning of a style of liberalism that was closer to socialism than classical liberalism.

J.A. Hobson (1858–1940)

Unlike Chamberlain, Hobson did transfer to the Labour Party later in life. As a liberal he had developed a test against which to judge any extension of the activities of the state. For him, if an action extends the social freedom and opportunities for individuals, if it maximises the possibility for each to reach their desired potential, it can be justified. Thus, for example, compulsory education might seem a threat to liberty, but its effects – to enhance opportunities for all – justify its provision.

David Lloyd George (Prime Minister 1916–22)

The culmination of the transition from classical to new liberalism was largely realised in the achievements of Lloyd George, both as his predecessor Asquith's Chancellor of the Exchequer and later as Prime Minister himself. It was he who extended the provision of education and public housing, and introduced pensions and a system of state-organised welfare to cushion individuals against poverty and unemployment. Fear of state intervention as a threat to individual liberty was finally placed in the background of liberal thinking. Since then the Liberal Party has championed the cause of the poor and underprivileged and has accepted that the state must play a vital role in creating greater social justice.

Ironically, Lloyd George was perhaps the most effective, but also the last, Liberal Prime Minister of the twentieth century. The rise of the Labour Party squeezed the Liberal Party out, especially as many of its ideas were adopted by Labour. There was simply too little difference between the two parties for voters to differentiate between them. Nevertheless, prominent Liberal politicians have continued to be influential in British politics.

Summary of new liberal ideas

1. Liberty does not only consist of freedom from restriction. There is a higher form of freedom that results from a collective sense of harmony and co-operation.
2. The state is justified in intervening to reduce clear social injustices.
3. Equality of opportunity is essential to maximise each individual's potential.
4. The state has an obligation to care for those who are unable to support themselves.

Modern liberalism

Just as the Liberal Party was entering a catastrophic decline in its electoral fortunes, a report published in 1942 by a committee led by a leading civil servant and liberal, William Beveridge, set out a blueprint for post-war British society. It was based on the idea that liberty was less threatened by laws and governments than by social evils such as poverty, unemployment, ill health and generally poor living conditions. It followed from this that state action to reduce such evils would provide greater freedom. For liberals this was the end of Samuel Smiles' old idea, that individuals must fend for themselves. Beveridge now proposed that the state has a responsibility to care for all, 'from the cradle to the grave'.

William Beveridge (1879–1963)

The practical results of Beveridge's thoughts were the introduction of a compulsory welfare state, free provision of secondary and higher education, the National Health Service and large increases in the social activities of local government. Once again, however, it was for others, not the Liberal Party, to implement such plans.

> To my mind there are three things above all that every citizen of this country needs as a condition of a happy and useful life after the war. He needs freedom from Want and fear of Want; freedom from Idleness and fear of Idleness enforced by unemployment; freedom from War and fear of War.
> Sir William Beveridge, Why I am a Liberal, 1945

State economic management – John Maynard Keynes (1883–1946)

Keynes was the leading economist of his day. Like Beveridge he found further cause for the state to intervene in order to enhance personal liberty. For him, a stable economy was vital to provide the environment in which every individual – worker, consumer or employer – could fulfil their potential. Free market capitalism was characterised by periods of boom and slump, the worst example of the latter having occurred in the Great Depression of the 1930s. If governments could reduce these natural economic cycles, replacing them with steady growth and stability, all individuals would be freer to pursue their own goals.

Constitutional reform

The Liberal Party enjoyed a political revival in the 1970s, but it was still searching for a distinctive identity. The only area where it has been decisively successful concerns proposals for constitutional reform. Three successive party leaders, **David Steel**, **Paddy Ashdown** and **Charles Kennedy** have been instrumental in supporting these reform proposals.

Their view is that British parliamentary democracy is flawed, largely as a result of the two-party system, which has resulted in government that is too powerful, too centralised, too uncontrolled and too secretive. As a result, individuals have become politically powerless, lacking influence and sufficient opportunities to participate.

Their solutions to these problems lie in proposals for extensive reform of the political system. The introduction of proportional representation in voting is a central feature, reducing the stranglehold of the two main parties. Of almost equal importance is their support for a 'Bill of Rights' to guarantee the rights of individuals and important minority groups. Other measures include reform of the House of Lords, introducing fixed-term parliaments, forcing government to be more open and restoring powers to local and regional government.

Just as Liberal Party fortunes were reviving in the 1970s, Scottish and Welsh nationalism experienced growth in popular support. Such nationalist sentiments were seen as manifestations of people's desire to take control of their own lives and to have greater influence over the activities of government. It was not, therefore, surprising that Liberals took up the nationalist cause.

Environmentalism

As interest in environmental issues grew during the 1970s and 1980s, liberals came to be aware that individuals were feeling that the quality of their lives was under threat from excessive industrialisation, intensive agriculture and urbanisation. It was seen as an appropriate concern for them on the grounds that freedom was threatened by reductions in the quality of life.

Equality

Although liberals have always believed that inequalities among people are natural, they have also insisted that all individuals, no matter what their qualities and abilities, should have equal rights. The battles for equal legal and political rights have largely been won. However, equal rights for women, for various groups of the underprivileged and for ethnic minorities have not yet been fully secured. This objective remains, therefore, a central element in modern liberalism.

A summary of modern liberalism

1. Individual freedom is still its main goal.
2. Equality of opportunity should be promoted.
3. Social justice should be created, if necessary by the state.
4. The political system should promote opportunities for individuals to influence and participate in government.
5. Government should be as locally based as possible.
6. Equal rights should be protected.
7. State action is justified if it enhances individual opportunity and freedom.
8. It is the role of the state to protect the physical environment in order to enhance the quality of life.

Where is liberalism today?

The ideas of both 'classical' and 'new' liberalism have largely been incorporated into other political movements. As we have seen above, much of the liberalism of Lloyd George and Joseph Chamberlain, Green and Hobhouse, Beveridge and Keynes, was soon absorbed by the new successful Labour Party. Indeed, once 'consensus' politics had set in after the Second World War, much of the Conservative Party was happy to accept the same principles. At the same time, there has been a resurrection of neo-classical liberal ideas by such thinkers as Friedman and Hayek and their implementation by 'New Right' conservatives, led by Margaret Thatcher.

In both cases the Liberal Party itself (now the Liberal Democrats) has found itself without its own distinctive policies. It must be stressed, however, that liberalism itself has been a highly successful movement, challenging both conservatism and socialism with great effect. It is only the Liberal Party that has declined. In short, most of the liberal clothes have been stolen by others and are still being worn by them.

Democratic socialism

Like conservatism and liberalism, the term 'socialism' does not have a

~~single meaning. But unlike the UK the European traditions which have existed~~

~~Britain~~ ditions, British democratic socialism has taken on a quality that is noticeably distinct from its counterparts in Europe. How could there be, for example, any relationship between the kind of philosophy adopted by the Labour Party and the ideology of the former socialist republics of eastern Europe? Even the socialist parties of France and Spain have emerged from a very different tradition.

We should be alerted to the distinctive nature of British 'socialism' by the very fact that the party which was its home for the whole of the twentieth century did not choose to title itself a 'Socialist' party at all, preferring the somewhat ambiguous name 'Labour' to inscribe on its banners. Indeed, those socialists who expressed admiration for such regimes as the Soviet Union or the People's Republic of China have always been marginalised in the Labour Party, and often expelled, on the grounds that their views are revolutionary and anti-democratic.

Some terms defined

The term 'socialism' in the context of western democracy is, therefore, an imprecise one, so much so that it is more helpful to consider it as essentially three separate movements.

Social democracy

In its most moderate form it has come to be known as 'social democracy', which should not be confused with an earlier revolutionary movement flourishing particularly in Germany, Russia and much of central Europe in the late nineteenth and early twentieth centuries. Modern social democracy, by contrast, is neither revolutionary nor truly socialist in nature. It is described in some detail later in this unit.

State socialism

More extreme forms of the movement have been described as 'state' or 'revolutionary' socialism. Its followers reject the notion of parliamentary and pluralist democracy in which parties with differing philosophies may compete freely for power. Rather, the state is to be taken over as the main instrument for the transition to a socialist society. In such circumstances, only limited opposition is envisaged. Democratic institutions would also be severely restricted in their role. This extreme form of socialism is described in Unit 14.

Democratic socialism

The form of socialism that represents the central origin of the British Labour Party and many other left-wing parties in Europe has come to be known as 'democratic socialism'. As its name suggests, it proposes to retain a democratic system of government, but is, at the same time, more committed to a radical socialist programme than are social democrats. It is this branch of the movement that we are considering here.

In the context of the British Labour Party we can certainly assert that the radical, revolutionary form of state socialism now has relatively little influence in the party. The efforts of **Neil Kinnock** in the mid-1980s to rid Labour of its extreme left wing proved largely successful. The schism between the moderate centre of the party – the 'democratic socialists' – and the moderate 'social democrats' (who have always refused to accept such a description of their beliefs) has continued since the 1950s when leader **Hugh Gaitskell** attempted to shift the party to the centre ground, with a certain amount of success. By the 1990s, under the reforming leaderships of **John Smith** and **Tony Blair**, the term 'social democrat' became both widespread and acceptable within the party. Indeed, so extensive were the Blair reforms that his party came to be known as 'New Labour'. However, it is democratic socialism, which has been the principal philosophy of Labour for much of its life, that is considered in this section.

The perhaps unique form of socialism that has flourished in the UK has been the result of a wide variety of influences. It is that variety which has given it its unusual character. We shall examine these origins first.

Origins

Trade unionism

The British trade union movement grew steadily through the nineteenth century. Unlike its contemporary counterparts in Europe, however, it rarely assumed a radical political character and kept some distance between itself and the main political arena until the turn of the century.

Instead the trade unions tended to concentrate upon economic, social and industrial issues, such as decent wages, improved factory conditions, safety and bargaining rights. There were few attacks on the capitalist system in general, and more on those individual businesses and entrepreneurs who were guilty of using their economic power against the interests of workers. Of course, the trade union movement has had its fair share of revolutionary socialists and Marxists in its ranks, including in recent times the miners' leader **Arthur Scargill**, but these have been exceptions and not the norm.

As far back as 1848, when much of Europe erupted in a series of revolutionary upheavals and continental European workers and trade unionists played a leading part in attempts to bring down the established order, Britain remained largely calm. The **Chartist** movement of the 1830s had made some radical demands – for example, for trade union recognition, votes for the working classes and negotiating rights with employers – but it did not threaten the existing political and economic order. Since then the picture has remained much the same. Despite widespread union membership and periodic outbreaks of militant action, such as the general strike of 1926 and the campaign against extensive reform of industrial relations in 1971, British trade unionism has remained moderate and limited in its aims.

This form of non-radical trade unionism is sometimes described as 'labourism', a working-class struggle that does not assume the full characteristics of class warfare. The movement accepts capitalism as a necessary vehicle for wealth creation, but wishes to mitigate its worst effects through state-led controls and an extensive and powerful trade union movement.

Despite the relatively limited horizons of the trade union movement, it has been a major influence upon the nature of British socialism. The central position that unions have enjoyed within the Labour Party itself is testimony to its importance.

Christianity Many British socialists derived their belief in social justice and equality from firmly held Christian faith. For them there was no essential difference between the basic teachings of Christ and the socialist creed. The virtues of shared wealth, caring for the poor, equal rights and pacifism were, for them, the essence of basic Christian values.

The historian **R.H. Tawney** (1880–1962), for example, rejected scientific analyses of capitalism, such as Marx's, to justify its overthrow. Instead he concentrated on the idea that the 'injustices' of capitalism, such as wide disparities in wealth and opportunities, were matters of conscience and morality rather than class conflict. Indeed, such figures as Tawney and the contemporary socialist **Tony Benn** are notable for their rejection of class warfare as the basis for socialism. For them the clear **justice** that they feel is inherent in socialism should be enough to persuade people to vote for such a future.

Nonconformism In the traditional industrial regions of Britain, such as the north of England, South Wales and the Scottish Clyde Valley, a particular brand of Protestant Christianity took hold during the eighteenth and nineteenth centuries. Such varieties as Methodism, Presbyterianism and Congregationalism were all manifestations of the movement that was collectively known as Nonconformism. In such cases the motivation that lay behind their formation was a reaction to the conservatism and paternalism of the Church of England.

The established Church was seen as a representative of the landed gentry and the middle classes. The working classes could not identify with its traditionalism, its strict hierarchy and its association with the ruling class. The nonconformist churches, each with its own characteristics, had in common a sense of internal democracy, equality among their membership and a strong sense of brotherhood and social solidarity.

The specific influence that Nonconformism had upon British socialism is widely acknowledged, yet difficult to define. Certainly there was a strong sense of social equality present, derived from a certainty that all people were created equal by God. It could also be argued that a strong commitment to democracy arose out of these egalitarian churches, as well as a distrust of all powerful vested interests. Above all, however, a well-developed sense of local community was associated with Nonconformist churches and chapels, which helped to form close bonds between Church, trade union and local Labour Party branch. Certainly British socialism has been especially deeply rooted in such small communities.

Fabianism

In 1884, when a modest British interest in Marx's radical and revolutionary brand of socialism was first awakening, a group, composed mainly of middle-class intellectuals, formed the **Fabian Society**. Named after the Roman general Fabius, who fought wars by a process of long-term attrition rather than by attempting a decisive military blow, it was a movement committed to a gradual transition to a socialist society.

Its founders, who included the playwright **George Bernard Shaw** and the celebrated socialist couple **Sidney and Beatrice Webb** (the former of whom founded the London School of Economics), believed that capitalism was a doomed system. There was no need for revolution, since socialism would naturally evolve out of capitalism. Thus, what was required was for intellectuals and workers to prepare themselves for the inevitable onset of socialism. This was to be largely achieved through education and planning the form of the future socialist state. This movement, which was extremely influential around the turn of the nineteenth century, went some way to ensuring that British socialism remained evolutionary rather than revolutionary in nature.

Fabianism was unusual in another more important regard, however. Its leaders were committed to the idea of a form of socialism to be run by a centralised state. This state would take over the principal industries and commercial activities, running them in the interest of the whole community, with fair wages and guaranteed employment. However, this was not to be a workers' state. The Fabian leaders did not believe that the working class was able to govern itself. Instead they were elitist paternalists, believing that intellectuals would understand how best to realise a socialist future. These ideas contrasted sharply with many of those of the European socialist movement. There, especially in France, it was envisaged that workers themselves would take over the means of production, distribution and finance. The state was seen as the potential enemy of the working class. Thus it was expected to remain limited in size and weak in nature. The Fabians, on the other hand, were committed to a strong, wide-ranging state.

> 'Labour works by the inevitability of gradualness. Building democratic socialism is an existential process, done slowly by perseverance, patience and education.'
>
> Austin Mitchell, *The Case for Labour*, 1983

Liberalism and parliamentary democracy

As we have seen above, when the liberal movement of the nineteenth century was transformed from its 'classical' to its 'new' variety, it took on many characteristics now described as socialist. Such liberals as **Hobhouse** and **Hobson** preached the virtues of **equality of opportunity** and the notion of **state-sponsored welfare**. At the same time, liberals had always promoted equal rights and protection for the especially weak in society. All these ideas appealed greatly to the moderate form of socialism that the British seemed to prefer.

British socialism is also notable for its strong attachment to parliamentary democracy. In much of continental Europe, socialists have been traditionally less concerned with individual liberty and democratic institutions. On the whole they have been more interested in a powerful centralised state and other collective institutions which tend to operate in opposition to individualism. In Britain, however, there has always been a strong bond between liberal democracy and mainstream socialism.

In practice this has created a commitment to such principles as equal political rights, pluralist party politics and guarantees of individual liberty through democratic institutions. Apart from the Social Democratic Federation, led by the neo-Marxist **H.M. Hyndman** (1842–1921) who was suspicious of parliamentary politics, preferring instead a more direct transition to a socialist system, British socialists have mostly been committed to liberal democracy. Even the **Independent Labour Party** – the more radical of the two main working-class parties that emerged around the turn of the nineteenth century – chose the parliamentary route to power. It was finally squeezed out by its more moderate and powerful counterpart, the orthodox Labour Party, in the 1930s. As we have seen above, such liberal figures as Lloyd George, William Beveridge and J.M. Keynes have had more influence on the British socialist movement than the great European socialists such as Marx, Bernstein and Blanqui, all of whom favoured direct action to achieve working-class goals.

> *'Of political parties claiming socialism to be their aim, the Labour Party has always been one of the most dogmatic – not about socialism, but about the parliamentary system.'*
> Ralph Miliband, *Parliamentary Socialism*, 1972

Miscellaneous influences

There is a remarkable richness in British socialism, which is largely the result of the wide variety of influences that have moulded it. The principal examples are described below.

Robert Owen (1771–1858), a philanthropic industrialist, believed that capitalists themselves had a moral obligation to ensure the welfare of their workers. His experimental **New Lanark Mill** provided the employees with education, health care, housing and subsidised goods in the hope that it would provide a model for all employers to follow. In the event, the experiment failed, but his ideas were largely instrumental in moulding the character of British trade unions. Unions might have become politically radical and revolutionary in character, as they had done in parts of Europe. Instead they tended to concentrate on achieving the kind of benefits that Owen had provided for his own workers. Thus, ironically, Owen, one of the most radical socialists of his day, went some way to moving unions into a moderate position on workers' conditions.

The **co-operative movement**, which was founded in 1844, differed from its European counterparts in that its objectives were to protect the interests of **consumers** from capitalist 'profiteering'. By contrast, the producer co-ops, which particularly flourished in France and Spain, were designed to free **workers** and **small producers** from exploitation by big business. Ever since the development of the co-operative movement, British socialism has included a commitment to protect the interests of consumers from the monopoly power of capitalism.

William Morris (1834–96) is still celebrated today for his contribution to interior design, but it was his **romantic** and **anarchistic** brand of socialist principles that endeared him to many trade unionists during the twentieth century. Morris was suspicious of the centralised state and abhorred the effects of large-scale industrialisation on the lives of workers. He favoured the small-scale workers' co-operative as the ideal form of economic organisation. He practised his own beliefs in the company that he set up and ran in consultation with the workforce. As we have seen above, the workers' co-operative movement has had little success in Britain, despite many attempts to popularise it. Nevertheless, Morris remained a model for the many small craft unions that flourished through much of the twentieth century. Such unions have had some success in protecting the interests of their members and ensuring organised training facilities and expanded educational opportunities.

Guild socialism, the inspiration of the socialist historian **G.D.H. Cole** (1889–1959), was a similarly romantic ideal to that of Morris. Cole also advocated a system of small, powerful trade unions, akin to the ancient craft **guilds** that had protected free, skilled workers within the feudal order. These unions would be granted democratic rights within each business. They would not be producing organisations, however. Instead they would ensure a degree of worker influence over capitalist organisations, guaranteeing both the welfare of employees and some say for them in the running of enterprises. As with Morris, there was little practical application of these ideas, but they had considerable influence. Such measures as employment protection, minimum wages and better working conditions were achieved through a system of **trades councils** which became a model of small-scale, decentralised socialism at work. Their influence over industrial relations continued until the 1980s.

Summary of British democratic socialist origins

1. Trade unionism	A particularly moderate form with largely economic rather than political goals. The influence of a non-radical working class has resulted in a moderate form of socialism.
2. Nonconformism	This reinforced the social solidarity of socialism and rooted it firmly in local communities.
3. Fabianism	This imbued British socialism with a sense of gradualism and paternalism. Socialist goals were to be achieved by evolution not revolution.
4. Liberalism	Most modern liberal aims have been absorbed within the socialist movement, especially the pursuit of equal rights and a commitment to popular parliamentary democracy.
5. Christianity	A strong moral atmosphere was added, arising out of an interpretation of Christian teaching which proposed social justice and equality.
6. Other influences	These include consumerism, industrial democracy and a strong attachment to welfarism.

Characteristics of British democratic socialism

Collectivism

It is the basis of **all** socialist thought that there are a large number of human goals that are better achieved by **collective** than by **individual** action. This is based on assumptions that this is both the **most efficient** and the fairest way of providing a wide variety of services. Some examples will serve to illustrate this idea.

Health care could be arranged so that individuals pay for care as they receive it, perhaps through voluntary private health schemes. This is very much how health care is organised in the USA. Thus, it would be up to each individual how much care they receive, how often and of what type. The collective road to health care is likely to involve either a **national health care** system, where everybody who is able must contribute but everybody receives free health care on demand, or a state-run **health insurance** system, where all contribute to an insurance scheme and claim back any expenditure on health provision that may be needed. In either case, a collective health system requires compulsory contribution, while an individualistic solution does not.

The pay and conditions of workers of any kind could simply be left to free market forces and individuals negotiating the terms of their own employment. Socialists support strong **trade unions** that negotiate collectively on behalf of their members. However, for unionism to be effective it is almost essential that all or most workers are prepared to support the union and take industrial action where required. If not, employers will be able to divide their employees and weaken their collective bargaining power.

Finally, **welfare** is a typical example of collective action. Here it is expected that all should contribute through various forms of tax, so that all, however rich or poor, may be relieved from such problems as poverty, homelessness and unemployment.

Collectivism can also be applied to such provisions as education, housing, industrial training, child care and employment creation, all of which have, from time to time, been the responsibility of central or local government in Britain. The key philosophy behind collectivism is that contributions should be calculated according to **ability to pay**, but care, welfare and services should be given equally on the basis of **need**. Virtually the whole of the socialist movement has been based on this fundamental belief.

> 'Socialism is the creation of a society in which it is easier to secure self-fulfilment through serving society than through the exclusive pursuit of self alone.'
> Stuart Holland, *The Socialist Challenge*, 1975

Distributive justice

The effect of free market capitalism is to distribute rewards, in the form of incomes, corporate profits and wealth, unevenly. It is inevitable that some workers, investors and entrepreneurs will do better than others financially. For socialists this is both random and unjust. For them, rewards should be distributed according to merit. The capitalist system takes no account of this, operating merely on the basis of an individual's position in the market.

It would be an error to assume that socialists advocate that financial rewards should be distributed **equally**. Such a belief belongs in communist philosophy rather than among less radical socialists. Instead, socialists wish to see the distribution of rewards made on a rational basis, most commonly according to how much an individual's work is perceived to be worth to society. How is such 'distributive justice' to be achieved?

The simplest solution lies with the **tax system**. By implementing a progressive tax system – where those with higher incomes pay a larger proportion in taxation – the inequalities in income can be reduced. At the same time, accumulations of wealth in too few hands can be broken up by **taxes on inheritance** or even through **wealth taxes** based on the value of total assets owned rather than on income. Company profits can be redistributed more evenly through **corporate taxation**.

The **welfare system** can also be used in the redistributive process. Those on particularly low incomes can receive financial subsidies from the proceeds of taxation. This can be in the form of family benefits, housing subsidies, unemployment benefit and a host of other benefits.

The state can have a more direct effect on income distribution through its own **employment policies**. Government employees might be offered wages higher than those that would normally prevail in markets operated by private companies. There might also be a tendency to employ more workers than private companies would normally use. In this way some workers, who would otherwise be unemployed and on very low incomes, receive decent incomes and job security.

The most radical measure that can be adopted to achieve such economic 'justice', short of complete control of commerce and industry by the state, is to introduce strict controls over incomes, forbidding excessively high wages and adopting minimum wage legislation. In practice, the former is virtually impossible to implement, but a national minimum wage has long been a socialist dream and it was finally realised in the UK with the election of the Labour Government in 1997.

Welfarism

We have seen above that welfare can be used as a means of redistributing income to the less well off. However, it can also be seen as a desirable end in itself. Socialists accept that there are some who are unable to provide adequately for themselves, such as the old, the very poor, the disabled, the unemployed and the long-term sick. Society, therefore, has an obligation to contribute to their welfare so that all can enjoy at least an acceptable standard of living.

The principal means of achieving this is the **welfare state** itself, a system where all who are able make compulsory contributions to a state-run organisation which then distributes welfare benefits on the basis of need.

Social ownership of the means of production

Possibly the most controversial issue among British socialists surrounded the commitment that the Labour Party appeared to make in Clause IV of its constitution formulated in 1918. The wording of the main part of this clause is shown below:

> '[we aim] to secure for the workers ... the full fruits of their industry and the most equitable distribution thereof that may be possible upon the basis of the common ownership of the means of production.'
>
> Clause IV, The Labour Party Constitution, 1918

The questions that have been asked since are: 'How is this to be achieved?', 'Does it really imply the complete takeover of production and distribution?' and, in the 1990s, 'Is this an ~~outdated~~ ~~~~~ ~~~~~ ~~now~~ ing the ~~privati~~ ~~~~~ ~~~~~ ~~state-run~~ industries in the 1980s?'

The first issue was largely resolved in the UK when **Herbert Morrison**, a leading member of the post-war Labour Government, produced a blueprint for the creation of publicly owned and state-run industries. While 'syndicalists', mostly on the continent of Europe, were arguing for the takeover of major industries by trade unions, Morrison was convinced that ownership by the central state was the most effective form of social ownership. This would ensure that major industries were run for the benefit of the **whole community** and not just for the workers in them.

The extent of collective ownership was also hotly disputed. Candidates for **nationalisation** – the Morrisonian method for bringing economic enterprises under public control – were:

- **natural monopolies** such as railways and gas supply
- **public utilities** that the whole community consumes, such as electricity and telecommunications
- **infrastructure** industries upon which all other enterprises rely, such as iron, steel and coal
- **very large companies** on the grounds that their economic power might operate against the interests of workers and consumers.

In the event, nationalisation was confined to the first three categories, although more radical members of the movement advocate public ownership of all large enterprises.

The purposes of nationalisation were several. In general, any profits from a nationalised industry can be distributed throughout the community rather than to a small group of shareholders. More specifically, prices can be controlled, workers' pay and conditions protected, and output geared to the needs of the economy in general rather than purely to the making of profit. Finally, nationalised industries can protect the less fortunate in society by ensuring that they receive goods and services which might not be supplied to them by private enterprise. Thus, for example, transport and other utilities can be subsidised to serve isolated communities or special low prices might be charged to old-age pensioners.

The issue of Clause IV and its implications was transformed when **Tony Blair** became Labour leader in 1994. He was determined to modernise the party in general and Clause IV in particular. After a short struggle against radical elements in the party and some of the larger trade unions, he succeeded in changing the clause fundamentally. The commitment to public ownership was dropped and replaced by the goal of achieving full employment opportunities and the control of large-scale industry for the public good, rather than public ownership itself.

Equality of opportunity   In common with liberals, socialists argue that the state should create conditions that will give maximum opportunity to all sections of society. Education, from the nursery through to higher institutions of learning, should thus be open to all and should not discriminate on the grounds of wealth or privilege. A strong, comprehensive system of secondary schooling, colleges and universities that are accessible to everyone, and the provision of student grants have all been supported to enhance equality of educational opportunity.

Socialists oppose entrenched privilege. Measures to open up career opportunities are an essential feature of the socialist goal of creating a society based purely on merit. Discrimination against women, ethnic minorities, the disabled or any other minority group has been firmly opposed. More radical proposals for **positive discrimination** in favour of disadvantaged groups have been suggested, underpinned by specific legislation to outlaw discrimination.

Trade unionism

Although the main agent of socialist collective action has, in the UK, been the state, through both central and local government, unions are seen as playing a key role in protecting workers' rights. Without the **collective** power of unions, individual workers are powerless in the face of market forces and control exercised by large employers.

Socialists therefore insist on the preservation of union privileges, including the guaranteed right to undertake collective bargaining, to take industrial action without undue fear of legal restrictions and to be recognised by employers if sufficient workers wish to be represented.

In addition to their right to defend the interest of workers at the place of their employment, unions are expected to play a key role in the state planning of industrial development and economic management. It is not sufficient, argue socialists, for workers to be able to express their aspirations through the ballot box every few years. They must also have a continuous role in public policy making if their interests, are to be properly protected. Thus the state is expected to be a 'corporate state', where employees as well as employers are fully represented on official policy-making bodies.

The 'dirigiste' state

It can be seen from many of the features described above that British democratic socialism has been very much the friend of the powerful state. The collective goals that democratic socialists wish to pursue are seen as the business of the state rather than of voluntary secondary groups. In addition to welfare provision and the redistribution of income, socialists have supported a 'dirigiste' state, meaning one that seeks to direct and control key aspects of the economy.

Centralised planning has long been a socialist dream. Indeed, in 1964 a Labour Government was elected with a commitment to implementing a **National Plan** detailing future raw material, production and employment requirements. The state was to establish targets for all aspects of industrial and commercial activity. The achievement of these targets was to be facilitated by the state, both through the enterprises under its direct control and through private companies. The incentive for these companies was a guarantee of a healthy, growing economy.

In the event, the National Plan failed after less than two years of life simply because the state could not deliver its promises of economic growth and so failed to secure the co-operation of those who were to implement the plan. It was not only economic circumstances that destroyed this unique experiment with state planning in a liberal democracy. For many, both in and out of the Labour Party, it was simply too radical an idea, threatening as it did opportunities for individual initiative.

In addition to full-scale planning, socialists have also promoted ~~interference in industrial relations~~, the supply of finance and investment for industry, the provision of grants and incentives for businesses to set up in areas of high unemployment, and even nationalisation of land.

Municipalism

Somewhat ironically, it was a Liberal – **Joseph Chamberlain** – who inspired the Labour Party to adopt local government as a suitable vehicle for a number of socialist endeavours. It is at this level that such provisions as subsidised housing, public health protection, social services to protect families in need and support for the elderly were introduced by early Labour administrations. It is in this regard that the community-based, Nonconformist roots of socialism in Britain have been particularly influential. There is a residual fear among socialists that the centralised state could become excessively powerful. The best protection against this, many have argued, is a strong, independent system of local government. In the modern era, **Ken Livingstone**, London's first elected mayor, has remained a champion of this kind of municipal socialism.

The end of democratic socialism?

Between 1979 and 1992 the Labour Party suffered four successive election defeats. During this period the onslaught of Thatcherite, New Right policies shifted the centre of British political opinion markedly to the right. The 'frontiers' of the state had been rolled back, trade unions had been stripped of most of their influence, and individualism and private enterprise were widely preferred over the collectivist ideals of traditional socialism.

In eastern Europe all the 'socialist' regimes fell to democratic movements that adopted free market capitalism to replace state-run socialist economic systems.

Thus, democratic socialism had become discredited and unpopular. Many of its cherished monuments had been destroyed or were suffering threatening attacks. Privatisations removed huge sections of British industry from state control. Reforms demolished many of the trade unions' rights and privileges, the functions of local government were reduced and its independence severely curtailed. Direct taxes on incomes and profits were reduced dramatically, having the effect of increasing the gap between rich and poor. The National Health Service was reformed by introducing an internal market. Even the welfare state, possibly the greatest jewel in the socialist crown, was being threatened in the 1990s.

The reaction of socialists was not to fight back, but to respond by adopting a more moderate position. A few stalwarts of the movement continued to struggle against the tide as the twentieth century came to a close, but most socialists drifted towards social democracy.

British democratic socialist achievements

1. Nationalisation of natural monopolies including

   - water
   - electricity generation and supply
   - gas
   - telecommunications
   - railways
   - municipal public transport

2. Nationalisation of other key industries.

   - iron and steel
   - airports
   - national airline
   - seaports
   - oil exploration
   - British Leyland (Motors)
   - British Aerospace

3. Steeply progressive personal taxation with a top rate of 83 per cent rising by another 15 per cent for investment income.

4. Municipal socialism including

   - child and ante-natal care
   - subsidised council housing
   - grants to students in higher education
   - care of the elderly
   - subsidised public transport
   - colleges of higher education
   - adult education

5. Protection for private tenants against landlords

6. Equal pay for women

7. Employment protection and compulsory redundancy pay

8. Free state education for all from 5 to 18 years of age

9. The welfare state

10. The National Health Service

Social democracy

Philosophical Socialists are frequently accused of a slavish attachment
~~background~~ that have ~~...~~ meaningless or placed too little importance on
the individual. The role of trade unions is a prime example. It is a funda-
From institutions to mental aspect of the socialist creed that strong, active unions are essen-
values tial in the protection of workers' rights and conditions. This does not
present a problem until the suspicion takes hold that over-powerful
unions and their leaders might hold back the aspirations of some
workers while appearing to protect their interests. At the same time, the
'conservatism' of unions in terms of work practices and new technology
might hold back economic progress. Social democrats, therefore, recognise the need for worker protection, decent pay and fair conditions, but
also understand that each individual worker is entitled to choose
whether to participate in union activity, and should certainly have the
opportunity of influencing the way in which unions operate on their
behalf. Thus it becomes more important to create a better **climate** of
industrial relations, and to establish **agreed values** about how workers
should be treated, than merely to allow powerful unions to struggle
against stubborn employers.

The nationalised industries were a further example of how important
cherished institutions had become to the socialist movement. They were
designed to act in the interests of their workers and of the whole
community. Yet many of them, such as gas, electricity and the railways,
were simply state monopolies that had replaced private monopolies. Not
only did they not always operate efficiently or sensitively enough, but
also they stifled much economic initiative in the community, owing to
their enormous market power. Again, social democrats are concerned
more with how industry can best benefit the community than with the
form it takes. Large or small scale, state-run or private, protected or
subject to full competition, free or controlled, enterprises should be
judged by how well they serve consumers and employees, rather than by
whom they are run. **Prosperity with social justice** is what social democrats wish to see achieved by industry, rather than mere state control.

We can perhaps say, therefore, that social democracy represents original socialist values, such as equal rights, equality of opportunity and
social justice, but is not inevitably linked to any specific socialist institutions.

Pluralism Traditional socialism has always been associated with an analysis of
society which suggests that **class differences** are crucial, in particular
that the middle classes, composed of professionals, managers and business owners, have gained at the expense of the working classes under
capitalism. In short, the interests of the two great classes are seen to be
in conflict. Social democrats believe that society is more complex than
this simple class analysis would suggest. They see, instead, a community
of individuals and many different interest groups. Class interest thus
becomes outdated in such a **pluralist** society.

A further criticism of socialism has been that it is too rigid and intolerant in its outlook. We have seen above that it has been firmly attached to certain institutions and has been reluctant to accept that there might be a number of alternative ways of achieving the same goals. In addition, it has made assumptions that all people will ultimately benefit from such socialist objectives as social equality, public ownership of major industries and the imposition of comprehensive education. Social democrats are willing to accept that it is for individuals to **choose** what type of services they wish to consume and whether they wish to make their own arrangements for education, health care, pensions and the like.

It follows from this that a vital goal of social democracy is to enhance and facilitate choices for individuals and therefore to oppose socialist measures that might limit such choices. For example, a well-resourced and organised state education system might be vital for the creation of equality of opportunity, but this should not preclude the existence of private education alongside the state provision. Both should flourish together to provide maximum choice and opportunity. Similar arguments can be brought to bear in the field of a large number of welfare and social benefits that may be provided in a variety of different ways.

> 'Pluralism offers the prospect of a more interesting, relevant and stimulating democracy, where difficult problems will evoke different solutions and where decisions more fully reflect the wishes of particular communities.'
>
> David Owen, *Face the Future*, 1981

Individualism

While socialism has been an essentially collectivist doctrine, insisting that many goals are better achieved by collective action than by individual endeavour, social democracy places greater emphasis on the individual. Indeed, for the latter, the only acceptable purpose for collectivism is to improve opportunities and choices for those individuals. In other words, collectivism is a desirable **end in itself** for socialists, but it is only a **means to an end** for social democrats.

> 'The essential principle of the left of centre – whether democratic socialists or social democrats – is the belief that society must work together for the individual to succeed.'
>
> Tony Blair, 1994 speech

Freedom

The American philosopher **John Rawls** in his theory of **distributive justice**, has asserted that, while there should be a fair distribution of income in society, this should not be achieved at the expense of personal liberty. Social democrats, many of whom follow and admire Rawls' work, accept the importance of such freedom. Socialism has often been accused of curtailing freedoms through its insistence on compulsion in such areas as taxation, contributions to welfare and industrial regulation. Collective values, in other words, have often pushed individual liberty into the background.

Social democrats, by contrast, believe both that liberty should be better protected than it has been in the past by socialists, and also that the creation of wider opportunity and choice ~~is, in itself, an enhancement of freedom~~. The state should not, therefore, concentrate on prohibiting activities on the grounds that they may not promote greater equality, but should try to improve the range of opportunities open to citizens. Housing provision is a good example of the distinction. Socialists have tended, in the past, to argue that local council-owned housing is the fairest way of providing homes for the less well-off. The private rented sector and opportunities for home ownership have, meanwhile, been either opposed or discouraged. Social democrats accept the need for some public provision of low-cost housing, subsidised out of taxes, but also wish to encourage **all** types of housing provision to increase choice and to encourage a free housing market.

Equality of opportunity

Equality of outcome has been a central objective of traditional socialism. This ignores the possibility that individuals are unequal in their abilities and the contribution they make to society, replacing it with the idea that all are of equal worth. The implication is that all are deserving of equal rewards.

Social democrats prefer to accept **natural inequality**, which implies that individuals enjoy different levels of merit and potential. Artificial advantages or disadvantages, based on inherited privilege, gender, ethnic origin or a deprived childhood should be removed, but thereafter we are not of equal worth so that rewards must reflect this in a just society. Like liberals, therefore, it is equality of opportunity, not of outcome, that social democrats prefer.

Distributive justice

What degree of inequality should be allowed in a just society? This is a question that taxes social democrats. Democratic socialists have less problem with the same question. For them the answer is simply 'relatively little'. The former, however, have more difficulty, as inequality is both inevitable and necessary in any economic system that seeks to maintain incentives for enterprise and endeavour.

An answer has been supplied by Rawls again. He argues that inequalities can be justified if they do not interfere with the liberty of others, and if the least well-off in society are not made worse off as a result of those inequalities. For example, it can be justified for capitalist entrepreneurs to make very large profits, provided they are not benefiting directly from losses suffered by the lowest-income groups. Indeed, the incentive of high profits might result in more enterprise, leading to greater income and employment for others.

Key distinctions between social democracy and democratic socialism

1. Social democrats are more concerned with values, while democratic socialists wish to preserve socialist institutions.

2. Democratic socialists analyse society in simple class terms, while social democrats have a more pluralist approach to both social organisation and political ideas.

3. While socialism has always been a collectivist doctrine, social democrats lay greater stress on individualism.

4. Social democrats criticise traditional socialism's apparent disregard for individual freedom.

5. Social democrats stress the need for equality of opportunity, while democratic socialists are more concerned with equality of outcome.

6. Social democrats are prepared to accept greater economic inequalities than democratic socialists, provided this can be shown to benefit society.

Social democratic values

It will quickly become apparent here that the principal values of social democracy bear a resemblance to those of both democratic socialism and modern liberalism. It is certainly true that the movement is something of a synthesis of liberal and socialist ideals, though this is often denied by its supporters. It is for the uncommitted observer to decide from the following descriptions.

Equality of opportunity

The very same goal is pursued by liberals and socialists. However, like liberals, social democrats would not feel it necessary to destroy such 'artificial' advantages as inherited wealth and private education, as purer socialists might.

The mixed, pluralist economy

It was the leading moderate Labour Party ideologue of the 1950s and 1960s, **Tony Crosland**, who suggested that the idea of the state controlling the **commanding heights** of the economy – the great industries, financial institutions and communication facilities – was no longer desirable. He asserted instead that there should be a pluralist approach to ownership of the means of production, distribution and finance. Some enterprises were ideal for private ownership, some for local government control, some for producer co-operatives and only some for the central state to run. In other words, there should be a **mixed economy**, with the type of ownership depending on circumstances. His views are now fully accepted by social democrats.

The welfare state   The main development here is that the welfare system should not stifle individual enterprise, but rather enable people to widen their own opportunities. For example, single parents should not be subsidised to stay at home and merely receive benefit ~~......~~ the facilities to be able to return to work and support themselves, possibly through child care and retraining. The same applies to the unemployed and young school-leavers as well as to the homeless.

> 'With a few inevitable exceptions, welfare should be an investment in productive and capable people, not a last resort for the incompetent.'
>
> Ralph Miliband, *Reinventing the Left*, 1994

Pragmatic economic management   Both New Right conservatives and traditional socialists have tended to link themselves firmly to one particular style of economic management, the former to **monetarism** and **laissez-faire**, the latter to **Keynesian** policies. Social democrats reject such a dogmatic stance. They accept the need for a pragmatic and pluralistic approach to economic policy.

Constitutional reform   Social democrats believe that the centralised state is too powerful. They accuse both conservatives and democratic socialists of carrying the process of centralisation too far, to the detriment of popular democracy. Thus, like liberals, they propose decentralisation, open government, reform of the second chamber and enhanced powers for Parliament. Some, but not all, advocate reform of the electoral system.

Social justice   Although this principle is much vaunted among all members of what is called the 'centre left' of British politics, it is extremely difficult to define. Indeed, it can mean anything that its advocates want it to mean. It must, therefore, be left somewhat flexible as a concept. In practice, it concerns such policies as **fair taxes**, involving a certain amount of redistribution of income, the use of **welfare** to protect the vulnerable in society, the establishment of **equal rights** for all sections of the community and the use of **public expenditure** to aid parts of the country that suffer economic disadvantages.

Employment   Without being dogmatic about methods, social democrats would claim to place greater emphasis on the creation of employment than other political creeds. Whether it be through economic management, public expenditure or job creation schemes, social democrats place a high priority on keeping unemployment at low levels.

New Labour and the Third Way

During the 1980s and 1990s, three successive Labour leaders – Neil Kinnock, John Smith and Tony Blair – moved the party firmly towards a position of 'social democracy'. By the mid-1990s, however, a further adaptation of social democratic values was emerging. This came to be known as the **Third Way**, a term coined by Professor **Anthony Giddens** of the London School of Economics. As the Labour Party absorbed these ideas, it came to be known as **New Labour**. The purpose of the new title (still not the official name of the party) was to distinguish it from the 'old' movement that had been associated with the discredited policies of the early 1980s. Tony Blair hoped that it would represent a fresh start and would persuade sceptical voters to support the party at the 1997 election. It worked. Once in power, Blair was in no hurry to drop the term 'New' and it has remained.

The expression 'Third Way' implies that there must have been first and second 'ways'. The **first way**, argues Giddens, was traditional socialism. It proposed collectivist solutions to most social and economic problems – state ownership of major industries, an extensive welfare state, strong trade unions and high levels of personal taxation to finance the redistribution of wealth and income. The **second way** comprised the New Right policies of Margaret Thatcher and her followers. These championed free market capitalism, the pursuit of individual self-interest, a much reduced role for the state, free labour markets and low levels of personal taxation. To a great extent these two ways were seen as complete enemies, implacably opposed to each other.

The Third Way has been viewed as an attempt to get away from this futile struggle. Its critics have suggested that it is merely a compromise between the two other 'ways'. Its supporters, on the other hand (including most of the leadership of the Labour Party after 1997), see it as a completely new political doctrine that can inspire support from all sections of British society.

> 'Classical social democracy thought of wealth creation as almost incidental to its basic concerns with economic security and redistribution. The neo liberals placed competitiveness and the generating of wealth much more to the forefront ... Third Way politics, it could be suggested, advocates a new mixed economy ... The new mixed economy looks instead for a synergy between public and private sectors, utilizing the dynamism of the markets, but with the public interest in mind.'
>
> Anthony Giddens, *The Third Way*, 1998

The principles of the 'Third Way' are as follows:

- Free market capitalism is the most effective way of producing wealth. The state should step in only ~~~ economic enterprise when ~~~ is clearly failing or when it is operating against the public interest. Consumers and workers should be protected from excessive economic power through the regulation of high prices or low wages.
- Where the state is running social activity – health, education and transport, for example – it should co-operate fully with the private sector in order to raise finance and maintain efficiency. In other words, the state should operate in partnership with private enterprise, rather than in opposition to it.
- It is understood that free market capitalism creates sectors of society who are 'socially excluded'. These are people and families who, through no fault of their own, are not able to take a full part in the freely operating economy. The state should, therefore, actively address the problems of social exclusion. The groups concerned include lone parents, the long-term unemployed, children failing in school, the disabled, families in poverty who are suffering from general deprivation and disaffected youth, including drug users.
- The welfare system should attempt, wherever possible, to solve the problem of social exclusion described above. By preference it should help to remove the **causes** of exclusion. If this is not possible, it should ensure a minimum standard of living for all. The old welfare system, it is argued, had simply given financial and material support without attempting to solve the roots of the problem.
- As the New Right had advocated, the scope for the pursuit of economic self-interest should be widened as far as possible. Nevertheless, this should be combined with a new sense of what is called **active citizenship**. This suggests that all citizens should also adopt a responsible attitude to the rest of society. In practice, this means actively supporting the welfare of one's local community. It might involve voluntary action or merely political participation in local affairs. Citizens should also develop a sense of national and global responsibility, taking account of issues concerning the environment and the plight of the world's poor. In the past, socialists have left such duties to the state, but the Third Way suggests that all individuals should play their part.
- The main vehicle for the cultural changes that are needed to achieve these aims should be education. There is a belief that many social problems can be prevented through a strong, effective education system.
- Despite the faith in education, the Third Way stresses relatively authoritarian policies on law and order. There is a partial rejection of liberal policies towards dealing with continuing high levels of crime in society.
- Although the UK should continue to play a leading role in world affairs, as conservative nationalists advocate, it should adopt an 'ethical foreign policy'. In practice, this implies active opposition to regimes that deny human rights and democracy.

The table below summarises the policies of New Labour and the ideas of the Third Way in the light of past socialist and New Right doctrines.

Third Way policies			
Subject	New Right doctrines	Socialist doctrines	Third Way
• Capitalism and the free market	• Should operate freely.	• Should be very limited by the state.	• Should operate freely, but excessive economic power should be regulated.
• Role of the state	• Should be very limited.	• Should be active in redistributing wealth and income. • Should promote social change.	• Limited but should co-operate where possible with the private sector.
• Social exclusion	• Individuals are responsible for their own lives. The state is not responsible.	• The state should be highly active and support all those in need through welfare.	• The state and welfare system should concentrate on eliminating the causes of exclusion.
• Citizenship	• All are responsible for themselves and their own conduct.	• The state carries out social responsibilities on behalf of citizens.	• Citizens have a responsibility to take an active role in their communities.
• Education	• Should be subject to free choice.	• Should promote social equality through a uniform comprehensive system.	• A highly formalised system designed to promote national standards. Designed to reduce social problems.
• Foreign policy	• The UK should take a leading role on a purely pragmatic basis.	• Minimising the UK's world role. • Defence expenditure should be low to finance social policies.	• The UK to play a world role, but with ethical policies.
• Law and order	• An authoritarian position. • Stress on punishment rather than prevention.	• A liberal, tolerant view. • Stress on solving the social causes of crime rather than mere punishment.	• An authoritarian position, but combined with measures to deal with causes such as social exclusion.

Students of politics may decide for themselves whether the Third Way is indeed a new philosophy or merely a series of compromises. They might also wish to judge the extent to which New Labour is implementing its principles.

Liberal nationalism

The liberal form of nationalism that fl~~ouri~~ ~~Britain~~ should not be ~~con~~f~~used~~ ~~with the so-called~~ 'British nationalism'. The latter is an extreme right-wing movement, often described as 'neo-Nazi' or 'neo-fascist', which is concerned with maintaining British unity, discouraging immigration, laying stress on patriotism, isolationism and the restoration of the UK's pre-eminence in world affairs, and establishing a strong, authoritarian state.

By contrast, Scottish and Welsh nationalism are essentially liberal movements with completely different roots and aspirations. (Nationalism in the context of Northern Ireland is dealt with in Unit 15.)

Welsh nationalism

The principal vehicles for Welsh nationalism are **Plaid Cymru** (the Welsh National Party), the **Welsh Language Society** (a political and cultural campaign group) and **Sons of Glendower** (a militant separatist group).

The last named is committed to an independent Wales, with its own sovereignty and, therefore, political institutions. It operates outside democratic politics, preferring direct, sometimes violent, action to further its aims. It is a small, relatively insignificant movement.

The Welsh Language Society, despite its apparently innocuous title, has proved an effective force in Welsh politics. As its name suggests, it is concerned with the preservation and extension of the use of the Welsh language. However, it goes further than that. It is also committed to safeguarding and promoting Welsh culture in general, including literature and the arts. It has become political in the sense that English culture is seen as the main threat to its objectives. Thus, greater independence for Wales in the political and social spheres is also likely to preserve the culture. It is, naturally, closely allied to Plaid Cymru.

Few Welsh nationalists wish to see full political independence for Wales. However, they do campaign for a greater degree of self-determination for the Welsh people and for the preservation of a separate Welsh identity. Some of their principal objectives have been:

- an elected Welsh assembly to oversee government
- local control over education, social services, higher education, health and transport
- greater Welsh control over funds for local industry and commerce
- equal status with English for the Welsh language
- local control over funding for the arts and broadcasting.

The implementation of devolution of power has gone some way to meeting these demands. However, nationalists still wish to see greater independence and there remains a minority who wish to convert devolution into full independence.

Scottish nationalism

Unlike Wales, Scotland has long enjoyed a good deal of administrative independence from England. Since the nineteenth century there has been a Scottish Office, with its own funds for the administration of education, health, transport and a wide range of other services. In addition, Scotland has its own legal system, very different from that of England and Wales, and its own laws, although these have to be passed by Parliament in London. There is a separate education system, from primary through to universities, and the Church of Scotland has long been distinct from its Anglican counterpart.

Thus Scotland has been able to retain a good deal of its own political, social and cultural identity. Nevertheless, Scottish nationalism, represented by the Scottish National Party, has become more radical than its Welsh equivalent. Indeed, one wing of the party now supports full independence from the UK. Those nationalists who stop short of demanding full Scottish sovereignty have wished to see a large degree of 'devolution' of power. Among their demands have been:

- a Scottish legislative assembly that would make laws and oversee government
- a Scottish executive drawn from the assembly and responsible to it
- power to raise taxes in Scotland for the direct finance of public expenditure
- control over existing services maintained and some extension into other services
- more control over industrial and economic policy in relation to Scotland itself
- a large share in the revenues from North Sea Oil
- a more independent Scottish voice in the European Union.

As in Wales, Scottish nationalism realised many of its aspirations when power was devolved to a new parliament and executive in Edinburgh in 1999. Unlike their Welsh counterparts, however, Scottish nationalists are enthusiastic about full independence in the future. Indeed, should the nationalists win a majority in the Scottish Parliament in the future, they are committed to holding a referendum on the issue.

The growth of European integration has fuelled nationalist hopes still further. On its own, Scotland might well not be a viable state. The financial burden of defence, agricultural and industrial support and the need for regional development might not be sustainable by a small country. Within Europe, on the other hand, much of this responsibility would be shared. Thus the slogan 'An independent Scotland within Europe' has become the nationalist maxim.

A summary of nationalist aspirations other than full independence

1. A greater degree of self-government, with regional elected assemblies.
2. Protection for the national culture.
3. An extension in the number of services being locally controlled.
4. More influence within the European Union.
5. Greater control over the local economy.

For exam questions relevant to this unit, see page 555.

4 Political parties

In this chapter the functions of political parties **in general** will be described. Although political parties exist in a number of different types of regime, we will concentrate here on those that flourish within essentially democratic systems. British parties are very much like others in western Europe, but important differences will be identified.

It is usually suggested that the UK's is a 'two-party system' and that the whole of the political system can only be understood in terms of two-party dominance. Thus the meaning and significance of the phenomena of 'party government' and 'two-party government' must be explored. Despite the apparent control exercised by the Labour and Conservative Parties in modern times, however, there are contrasting analyses of the party system that deserve consideration. One is that the two-party system is likely to be an enduring phenomenon. The other suggests that the true position is that we are a multiparty system. This second idea is the result both of consideration of votes cast rather than seats won and of the election outcomes seen in local government and the devolved assemblies in Scotland, Wales and Northern Ireland.

Prior to 1997, it had been suggested that there was a **dominant party** system in the UK. The Conservative Party had been continuously in power for eighteen years and had dominated British politics for most of the second half of the twentieth century. Labour's striking victory in that year, however, together with its success in making fundamental changes in the political culture, has effectively destroyed the dominant party theory.

The basic philosophies that have inspired members of British parties have been described in Unit 3. However, those descriptions do not tell the full story of the actual **policies** that have been proposed and implemented during the modern era. Therefore, the **practical** aspects of party politics will be discussed, with special reference to the period since the Second World War.

The internal structures and procedures of the main parties must also be described. The workings of the party system cannot be understood without reference to the contrasting ways in which British parties go about the business of making policy, selecting candidates for election and raising finance. The various factions and internal groups that make up the parties will also be described.

The functions of political parties

The articulation of demands

Individuals and groups in a community place a wide variety of demands upon the political system. These demands might be the result of **values**, **beliefs** and **ideologies** that prevail in any society. They might also represent the **interests** of specific sections of the community. Examples of such demands are given in the following

Demands on the political system	
Values, beliefs, ideologies	**Interests**
• Greater freedom	• Demands by the poor for better welfare
• More social equality	• The well off demanding lower taxation
• A welfare state	• Women seeking equal rights
• Greater law and order	• Industry asking for more government aid
• Environmental protection	• Unions demanding employment protection
• Better health care	• Consumers requiring better protection
• Constitutional reform	• Isolated communities needing transport provision

The left-hand column refers to concerns that might benefit the whole community, while on the right are demands that would benefit only a particular section of the population. In both cases, there is only a prospect that the demands will be met by government if they are properly expressed or articulated, and if it can be demonstrated that there is reasonably widespread support for them.

Two principal methods of furthering one's demands are available. One is to form special pressure or interest groups that will campaign for a particular issue on behalf of a section of the community. The activities of such groups are described in Unit 5. The other is to persuade a political party to adopt one's demands as part of its own policy programme. Since parties form governments, control parliamentary voting and have constant channels of communication with both government and Parliament, they are often preferred to pressure groups.

The recruitment of political leaders

Parties perform a key role in training and identifying effective leaders. The skills of persuasion, organisation of support, public speaking, committee work and public campaigning are all required if ambitious individuals are to rise through party ranks and assume public office. Thus, parties are a training ground and also act as a filter, separating the able from the less competent.

Ultimately, it is the parties that select candidates for election to local government and to Parliament. In addition, the parties nominate individuals to important positions in the public service, such as school governing bodies, hospital trusts and a variety of committees charged with the task of protecting the public interest.

Sustaining the system

Any democratic political system requires widespread support among the people whom it governs. Without this continuous 'consent', major problems arise in the implementation and enforcement of laws. It is, therefore, a basic principle of democratic politics that the parties, which ~~ably flourish~~ in pluralist systems, should sustain broad public support for the system. Of course, ~~they will~~ concentrate on mobilising support for their own particular policies, but underlying this ~~political~~ activity there will normally be an understanding that the institutions and processes of politics must be defended. Some examples from the UK's political system will illustrate this principle:

- Following a general election, losing parties will confirm the **authority** of the winning party to exercise power. Though they may keep up implacable opposition to that party's policies, they will not normally deny its right to govern.
- As it is agreed that Parliament is at the centre of the system and that all politicians should be responsible to it, the parties respect its importance and are generally scrupulous in upholding its traditions and procedures, and in confirming its importance.
- Though the monarch has no political power, his or her status as Head of State is acknowledged and respected.
- In times of crisis, war or other threat to national security, competing parties often suspend political hostilities in the interests of national unity. This has occurred in the two world wars and in matters of policy on many lesser crises, including the disorders in Northern Ireland. There are, of course, some parties that are committed to radical changes in the political system, even to its total destruction. Far left 'communists' and the neo-Nazi right wing are examples. However, they are both small and insignificant, and largely exclude themselves from the mainstream of democratic politics through their beliefs and methods.

Operating the system

As part of their involvement in sustaining the system, parties play a key part in the 'mechanics' of organising political activities within the various institutions involved. In many cases, these institutions could not effectively operate in their existing form without the involvement of the parties and their leaders. Once again, examples will illustrate:

- Possibly the most vital role that parties play in a modern system is the formulation of coherent policy programmes. In this way, when a new government is formed, it will indeed be ready to govern. Its election manifesto will be broadly known not only to many electors, but also to the administrators who will have to implement policy. This gives direction and organisation to the decision-making process. That does not mean, of course, that such policies will prove effective or popular, but at least they are likely to be understood by those who need to understand them. Without the policy-making functions of parties, there is likely to be incoherence, delay and contradiction in the political process.

- As we have seen above, parties recruit candidates for election and then act as a filter to try to ensure that the more able become available for positions of power and influence.
- They also help to run the elections themselves. They 'get the vote out' by ensuring that as many people as possible turn up at the polls, both by giving information and often also by organising transport for the frail and the reluctant. A healthy democracy relies upon good voting turnouts to ensure continuous support among the people. On an administrative level, party representatives also play a vital role in ensuring that elections are conducted honestly and fairly.
- The timetable of Parliament is controlled by the party 'business managers'. Naturally, it is the governing party that dominates, but all play some part in organising the legislative and scrutinising functions of Parliament. Important parliamentary committees constantly need informed, able and committed members. It is the parties who provide the personnel for these committees.

Summary of how parties sustain and maintain the political system

1. Ensuring the peaceful transition of power from one government to the next.

2. Maintaining public support for the institutions of the system.

3. Ensuring national unity in times of danger and crisis.

4. Developing legislative programmes, so maintaining some coherence in policy making.

5. Recruiting candidates for election and identifying leaders.

6. Helping with the administration and controlling of elections.

7. Organising the business of Parliament.

Informing the public

Although we might perceive the parties to be interested only in promoting their own policies, they are also playing a wider role. Without the collective activities of the parties, the public would be deprived of a large amount of information concerning the great issues of the day. The state of the economy, the country's role in world affairs, the major social and legal problems within the community and the transport needs of the country are all examples of issues that have been the subjects of political controversy. As long as the parties seek to mobilise support for their own stance on these issues, they are, in so doing, also informing the public about the problems and the various options available for their solution.

The nature of party government

'The conventional view of Westminster democracy [...] for granted that party government was both necessary and desirable. Only by placing the powers of government in the hands of a single party could a country be effectively governed by politicians strong enough to take unpopular but necessary decisions. Only by offering the electorate a choice between the record of the party in office and the criticism of the opposition could the electorate effectively hold politicians accountable.'

Richard Rose, *Do Parties Make a Difference?*, 1984

Professor Rose's view of how party government is generally seen tells us much about its perceived nature in the context of British politics. However much Rose may find it an unfortunate and undesirable feature of the system, there can be no doubting that it dominated the political scene for much of the twentieth century. British government cannot be understood, nor could it have survived in its present form, without the existence of strong, effective political parties. In practice, what does the term 'party government' mean? The following features can be identified:

- It is normally the case that one **single party** is able to dominate Parliament and to take complete control of the government, including the whole machinery of administration. In only one election since the Second World War, that of February 1974, has no party succeeded in gaining an overall majority in the House of Commons, thus laying claim to undisputed entitlement to form the Government. Even on that occasion, when Labour was the largest party in the Commons, no coalition was formed and a single party formed a minority government. By 1976 Labour had lost its majority through by-election defeats, but it continued to try to govern alone, with a loose agreement with the Liberals for support in return for a few minor concessions. Thus we have come to expect a single party to take control, even in difficult circumstances.

- The doctrine of **mandate and manifesto** plays a key role in British politics. Each party enters an election campaign with a manifesto, a statement of its intended programme, should it gain office. If it should win the election, the manifesto is expected to form the basis of its actions. It has, we can say, a 'mandate' to carry out its policies, granted by the electorate at the polls. So we expect a single party's programme to be implemented following election success. In a broader sense too, the doctrine suggests that the winning party enjoys a 'doctor's mandate'. This refers to the idea that the Government must have the authority to act in whatever way it feels necessary to deal with a particular problem, even if this was not specifically mentioned in its manifesto. Normally it is unforeseen circumstances that lead to such a situation.

- Parliament is effectively controlled by the parties and dominated by the governing party. Its **legislative agenda** and general business are controlled by party managers; its committees are staffed by party appointees and their agendas are, in turn, arranged by party bosses. There is some room for independent activity by MPs, free of party control, in the departmental select committees that scrutinise the conduct of government. A few pieces of private members' legislation may find sufficient time and support within a crowded parliamentary agenda to come into effect. Yet on the whole the parliamentary scene is dominated by the parties.
- The appointment of all grades of ministers, as well as the senior staff of important committees and other public bodies, is in the hands of the party leaderships. This power of **patronage** ensures a great degree of loyalty to such leaders and again helps the parties to dominate the scene.
- Effective **opposition** is largely confined to the main parties in Parliament that have been unable to form a government. Though pressure groups and the public may demonstrate their disagreement with government action, it is still the other parties that are able to make their voices most clearly heard in the majority of cases.

So we can see that the whole of the British political scene is dominated by the parties and their leaders. There are, of course, many other actors on this stage, but they are rarely as effective as parties in influencing the decision-making process.

Summary of features of party government

1. It is almost always the case that one party wins a parliamentary majority and so forms a government alone.

2. Parties create policy programmes in the form of election manifestos and have a mandate to carry them out if they secure government office.

3. Parties control the parliamentary agenda.

4. All government posts and many other official positions are under party patronage.

5. The main opposition to government is in the hands of other parties.

Criticisms of party government

Regret is often expressed that the processes of legislation and government cannot be carried out without the influence of parties. As long ago as the 1780s, the American constitutionalist and later President, James Madison, was warning against the dangers of party power.

> *'Complaints are everywhere heard from our most considerate and virtuous citizens, equally the friends of public and private faith, and of public and personal liberty, that our governments are too unstable; that the public good is disregarded in the conflicts of rival parties; and that measures are too often decided, not according to the rules of justice, and the rights of the minor party, but by the superior force of an interested and overbearing majority.'*
>
> James Madison, Federalist Paper 10, 1787

Since then the criticisms have continued, both along the lines of Madison's concerns and including some new objections.

The doctrine of the mandate

Madison referred to the dangers of majority rule and many still argue today that the 'winner takes all' nature of party government is unhealthy. The doctrine of 'manifesto and mandate' dictates that a winning party has clear authority to carry out **all** its policies. The defeated opposition parties in the UK are given no part in the policy-making process.

Yet the concept of an electoral mandate is flawed. There is no guarantee that a particular policy in the manifesto does indeed enjoy the support of the electors. The party as a whole might enjoy greater support than any other, but this says little about **all** its policies. Despite this clear truth, the winning party claims the right to implement every policy, popular or not. It was clear to many, for example, that the introduction of a Poll Tax, which was in the 1987 Conservative manifesto, was highly unpopular, yet it was implemented after the Tory victory. Subsequent events, including violent riots, a campaign of non-payment of tax and the fall from power of Margaret Thatcher, proved the fallacy of claiming a mandate for such a policy.

What is a majority?

While majority rule might indeed be a dangerous phenomenon, the British electoral system virtually ensures that the winning party in a general election **does not** gain a majority of the popular vote. Since 1945 no party has gained such a majority. Thus there is no real majority rule, yet party government gives the impression that it does exist. The Conservative vote between 1983 and 1992 held steady at about 43 per cent of the popular vote, but it enjoyed 100 per cent of governmental power over that period. The Labour Government which took office in October 1974 was even less favoured, with only 39 per cent of the vote and a very narrow Commons majority. Madison would indeed have been dismayed!

Conflict and consensus

British politics are essentially **adversarial** in nature. It is expected that the governing party will defend all its policies while the other, opposition parties will oppose all that the Government proposes. At first sight this might appear inevitable and healthy. On the other hand, it can be seen as counter-productive. The alternative model is one of **consensus**, where policies are adopted only if there is widespread agreement as to their desirability. This might weaken the influence of individual parties, but does ensure more acceptance of policies than can be guaranteed if only those of the governing party are implemented.

Do parties make a difference?

The view of Professor Richard Rose is that party government is merely an illusion. In practice, the government of the UK is largely out of the hands of the party in power. Instead, government is a process of acting in response to events whose course is determined elsewhere. International organisations including the European Union and NATO, together with such international economic phenomena as currency speculation and fluctuating world trade, do more to influence the economy than do party politicians. Even domestically, economic and social problems might not be capable of radical solution by the Government. Small, incremental changes can be made, but certainly not the dramatic solutions that party leaders often claim to be able to offer.

Since Rose wrote his analysis of party government, the process of **globalisation** has become an increasingly important factor in domestic politics. As the governments of the world – especially the economically developed world – become more interdependent, the scope for national action is further limited. This applies principally to economic policy, but is increasingly making an impact on policies on the media, including the Internet, international crime, drug enforcement and issues concerning human rights. When we add foreign and defence policy to this analysis, we can see that British governments are remarkably constrained by global considerations. Political parties that seek to fly in the face of the reality of globalisation are thus likely to be thwarted.

Rose's **ungovernability thesis** is not merely a description of the political system. It is also a criticism, since it suggests that the public are being effectively duped by the parties into believing that they are responsible for successful policies while their opponents are responsible for failures.

The benefits of party government

It would be wrong to suggest that party government is universally criticised. It does have a number of discernible advantages:

- The fact that a single party invariably wins the general election outright and is able to form a government alone gives considerable direction and stability to British government. Major splits in the
  Government are rare, since party solidarity is usually maintained,
  both within the Cabinet and in Parliament.
- The doctrine of manifesto and mandate, which has been examined
  above, means that the electorate can be reasonably certain of what
  policies they are voting for at a general election. They may indeed not
  support all of their favoured party's policies, but they do at least
  know what to expect.
- Adversarial politics provide the public with a clear examination of the
  Government's policies and of the alternatives presented by the opposition parties. Parliamentary business might appear at times to be
  excessively hostile in nature, but democracy is being served by the certainty that the Government will be forced to justify itself and its policies.

Summary of advantages and disadvantages of party government	
Disadvantages	**Advantages**
1. Winning parties are granted too much power to implement policies without effective opposition.	1. It creates clear, united decisive government.
2. The British electoral system means a party can win power without a majority of popular support.	2. The policies of the Government can be readily understood as they are based on a party manifesto.
3. Adversarial politics leads to unpopular policies succeeding at the expense of consensus policies that can produce more widely supported programmes.	3. The adversarial model makes government accountable and presents clear choices to the electorate.
4. The claim that parties control policy may be a dangerous illusion, since external factors outside of government control are more powerful.	

The two-party system

The conventional view of British politics suggests that it is dominated by a two-party system. In many ways this is undeniably true and this system will be described below. Nevertheless, there are competing theories of British party politics. The first, and most prominent, is that we now experience single-party dominance and will do so for the foreseeable future. The other is that the UK is a multiparty state in reality, but that various aspects of the political system disguise and inhibit this reality. To begin, we will examine the main aspects of the two-party state.

Voting support

The table below shows how voting support for the two main parties has developed since 1945.

Election year	% votes won by Labour and Conservative Parties together
1945	87.6
1950	89.6
1951	96.8
1955	96.1
1959	93.2
1964	87.5
1966	89.8
1970	89.4
1974 (Feb.)	75.0*
1974 (Oct.)	75.0*
1979	80.8*
1983	70.0*
1987	73.2*
1992	76.3*
1997	75.5*
2001	72.6

* From 1974 Ulster Unionist votes were counted as separate from the Conservatives. This accounts for a small drop in voting for the main parties (about 2%).

There are two main conclusions to be drawn from this table. The first is that two parties do indeed dominate voting in British general elections. They have always succeeded in gaining over 70 per cent of the total vote and, if we ignore the special circumstances of 1983 and 1987 when a strong alliance between the Liberals and the short-lived Social Democrat Party achieved unusual popularity, the figure has never been below 75 per cent.

Second, it is possible to suggest that there is a long-term decline in support for the main parties. There might have been 'blips' along the way, but there is a clear trend d~~own~~, generalisations about ~~the two-party~~ system must be treated with great suspicion.

Seats in the House of Commons

If we examine the same general elections in terms of the **seats** won by the two main parties, rather than the percentage of votes cast, the picture is considerably clearer.

Election year	% of seats won by Labour and Conservative Parties together
1945	94.6
1950	98.1
1951	98.6
1955	98.6
1959	98.9
1964	98.6
1966	97.6
1970	98.0
1974 (Feb.)	94.2*
1974 (Oct.)	93.9*
1979	95.7*
1983	93.2*
1987	93.1*
1992	93.2*
1997	88.5*
2001	85.3

* From 1974 the Ulster Unionists were counted as separate from the Conservatives. This accounts for some decline in the percentage of seats won by the main parties.

The dominance of the two parties is now very evident. The discrepancy between the percentage of votes cast and seats won, which becomes marked after 1970, is due to the unusual electoral system that the UK operates. Whatever the causes, there is no doubt that seats in the House of Commons are almost totally monopolised by the Conservative and Labour Parties.

Agenda and procedures of Parliament

Approximately 67 per cent of the time of the House of Commons is directly in the control of the Government or the main opposition party. This is made up as follows:

Debates on Government Bills	34%
Government Motions	6%
Opposition Motions	6%
Money Resolutions and Estimates	9%
Addresses and Queen's Speech	2%
Others	10%

Source: Andrew Adonis, *Parliament Today* (Manchester University Press, 1990), relating to 1987–88.

If we were to include Question Times, which are also dominated by the leaderships of the two big parties, the true figure approaches 80 per cent. The minor parties are limited to a few days a year for discussion of their interests in addition to the very limited opportunities their back-benchers might have to raise particular issues.

The same is true of committee work and personnel. The Liberal Democrats, Nationalists and Northern Ireland MPs are awarded individual places here and there on select and standing committees. Otherwise their influence is minimal. The agendas of committees are totally determined by the big party business managers.

The only important exceptions concern the select committees on Wales, Scotland and Northern Ireland, whose work may be influenced to some small degree by these smaller parties. Similarly with the 'Scottish Grand Committee', which is made up of MPs representing Scottish seats and discusses less controversial pieces of legislation relating only to Scotland. Here again, there is slightly enhanced minor party participation.

The story is similar in the House of Lords, even though the two main parties do not enjoy the same dominance in the holding of seats. Indeed, the control is perhaps even more marked with 61 per cent of its business accounted for by Government-sponsored Bills compared to only 34 per cent in the Commons (figures from Adonis, see above table).

Party finance

Winning elections in the UK today is an expensive business. Expenditure on broadcasting, poster campaigns and administration must run into many millions if an election is to be fought successfully. To illustrate the problem, it is estimated that James Goldsmith, who formed the Referendum Party from scratch in 1997, had to spend £20 million to make any impact. Even then he failed to win a single seat!

It is the Liberal Democrats who suffer most from the problem of finance. The Labour and Conservative Parties have ~~vast~~ ~~amounts~~ of potential funding. They can ~~call~~ ~~on the~~ ~~generosity~~ of a large member-~~ship~~ ~~and attract large~~ single donations from wealthy individuals or companies, while the Labour Party has access to finance from the trade union movement. The Liberal Democrats (and indeed the nationalist parties) have small memberships and find it difficult to attract rich sponsors.

The spending on the 1997 general election by the three main parties has been calculated as follows:

Conservatives	£28.3 million
Labour	£25.7 million
Liberal Democrats	£2.3 million

This indicates quite starkly how far ahead the two main parties are. The Neill Commission, which produced these figures in 1999, has recommended that a ceiling of £20 million be placed on general election spending, that curbs be placed on individual donations and that parties should receive some state funding. However, until these or similar measures are introduced, the reality of finance is likely to underpin the two-party system into the future.

The political agenda

Much of the conduct of British political processes concerns the presentation to the electorate of a clear choice between just two competing sets of policies. Manifestations of this limited choice are to be seen in a number of circumstances.

- Elections are fought largely on the basis that there are two manifestos, presented by the only two parties that have a realistic chance of being elected. Once a party is elected, it is expected that it will seek to implement most of its programme. The Opposition, by contrast, will have no access to the decision-making process and must therefore wait its turn.
- In parliamentary debates a clear struggle is waged between the proposals of the Government and the criticisms of the Opposition, together with their alternative policies. There is rarely any question of more subtle negotiations with a larger number of options being considered. The choice between just two alternatives is maintained by the two dominant parties.

Is the UK a multiparty state?

The argument that points to the UK being a two-party state is very compelling. Yet there are four senses in which a case could be made for it being a multiparty system.

Voting in general elections

Since the mid-1970s, smaller parties have enjoyed considerable success in winning votes. Although support is variable, depending on region, the overall results are striking as the following table illustrates.

Small parties' performance in general elections (%) (Scottish and Welsh results in those countries only)			
	Liberals*	Scottish Nationalists	Plaid Cymru**
1974 (Feb.)	19.3	21.9	10.7
1974 (Oct.)	18.3	30.4	11.1
1979	13.8	17.3	8.1
1983	25.4	11.8	7.8
1987	22.6	14.0	7.3
1992	17.8	21.5	8.8
1997	17.1	22.5	10.0
2001	18.3	20.1	14.3

*Fought as Liberal/Social Democrat Alliance in 1983 and 1987, and as Liberal Democrats since 1992.
**The name of the Welsh Nationalists.

The electoral system has meant that these votes have not been converted proportionately into seats, so the three parties shown gained only a small foothold in Parliament. Nevertheless there is clearly considerable support for these parties in the regions.

Elections to devolved assemblies and the European Parliament

Three forms of proportional representation were used in the elections to the Welsh and Northern Ireland assemblies, to the Scottish Parliament and to the European Parliament in 1999. It is not surprising, therefore, that the smaller parties did relatively well, as the table below shows.

Seats won by parties in 1999 elections					
	Labour	Conservative	Liberal Democrat	Nationalists	Others
Welsh Parliament	28	9	6	17	0
Scottish Parliament	56	18	17	35	3
European Parliament	30	36	10	3	8

It is clear from this table that, were Britain to adopt a proportional system, the multiparty nature of voting would indeed break the dominance of the two parties. In Northern Ireland the situation is yet more complex. In the devolved elections there in the same year, a large number of political groups won representation, together with some independents. However, it should be noted that Northern Ireland is an atypical political system and that generalisations should not be made from it.

Local elections

Local authorities have experienced multiparty politics for many years. The 1999 and 2001 elections confirmed this. The table below indicates how evenly spread representation is, certainly among the three main parties.

Total seats won in 1999 local elections (all Britain)				
Labour	Conservative	Liberal Democrat	Nationalists	Others
9,140	6,144	4,493	447	2,030
Total seats won in 2001 county council elections (England)				
Labour	Conservative	Liberal Democrat	Independent	Others
843	1,093	449	67	28

This leads to a situation in many councils where two or more parties share control and where politics is complicated by the fact that the two-party system is the exception rather than the rule.

So we must be careful before we assert that the two-party system dominates the UK. It can be argued that it is only the electoral system that maintains the dominance of the Labour and Conservative Parties. If we look beyond the raw results, the party system does appear more pluralist in nature.

Membership

Traditionally, it was the Labour and Conservative Parties alone that enjoyed large, mass memberships. This gave them both funds and support at election times. In recent years, however, there has been a dramatic fall in membership of both parties. Figures are difficult to collect and hotly disputed, but it seems likely that membership of both parties has fallen to about 350,000 from high points close to one million. The leakage has been partly to pressure groups, and partly to smaller parties, often interested in single issues. Thus nationalists, the UK Independence Party and the Greens have experienced some gains.

The loss of funds has not been serious, as large sponsors have arrived to fill the gap. More seriously, the big parties have lost many of the activists who were so important in gathering electoral support. This might have been an important factor in the inroads that smaller parties have made into Labour and Conservative support.

Summary of arguments concerning the party system		
Dominant party	Two party	Multiparty
• Theory ended in 1997.	• The two main parties dominate seats in the London Parliament. • They have also dominated voting, though less so in recent years. • They dominate the business of parliament. • They dominate the policy agenda. • They have vastly more financial backing than other parties.	• Small parties have won significant numbers of votes in general elections since 1970, but few seats. • Small parties have significant regional support. • The devolved assemblies are multiparty. • Many local authorities are multiparty. • The two main parties have lost their mass memberships.

The Labour Party

Origins and brief history

Early days

In 1900 the **Labour Representation Committee (LRC)** was formed in order to campaign for the election of Members of Parliament who could represent the interests of the trade unions in particular and the working classes in general. It was not, strictly speaking, a political party, but rather an action committee. It was the result of a major initiative by a number of different sections of the working-class political movement. The unions were the major element, but other groups were also involved. Radical socialists from the **Independent Labour Party (ILP)**, which had already been in existence for several years, and the **Social Democratic Federation** had come to the conclusion that parliamentary representation was necessary to further working-class aims. The more moderate **Fabian Society** and the **Co-operative movement** lent weight to the Committee, which was led by the legendary socialist figure, **Keir Hardie**.

By 1906 it had become clear that, in order to achieve long-term success, the Committee should transform itself into a full-blown political party with a mass membership to add to its union representatives. Thus the **Labour Party** was founded in that year.

Three aspects of these early years are instructive and relevant. First, it was clear from the outset that the party was a federation of groupings from a variety of socialist traditions, and that it encompassed a wide range of philosophies from both radical and moderate wings of the whole movement. Second, it was formed **outside** Parliament. Thus its most important institutions are not parliamentary, but external party organs. This has created constant tension between those parts of the party that are inside and those that are outside Westminster. Third, the influence of trade unions existed from the very beginning, when they were the dominant force. Their central position remained crucial throughout the twentieth century.

Growth and consolidation

Support for Labour grew slowly and steadily, with 40 candidates elected in 1910. The Constitution of the party was drawn up in 1918. This asserted its aims and objectives, including the notorious Clause IV which committed the party to common ownership of industry and commerce. It also set up the organisation and procedures of the party, a system which endured largely unaltered until 1981.

Some Labour members chose to join the Lloyd George coalition in 1918–22, and until 1945 the party spent most of its time in coalition with other parties, apart from the period 1922–31. In 1929 the party achieved a landmark when, in the election of that year, it won more seats than any other party (288 out of 615). However, Labour could still not form a majority government on its own.

Compromise and controversy

In the 1930s, during the dual crises of the Great Depression and the rise of fascism, the party became severely split. Broadly, the controversies included: whether to co-operate with the National Coalition Governments of 1931–45, which were Conservative-dominated (ultimately ~~Labour~~ ~~lost their first~~ Prime Minister, **Ramsay MacDonald**, as their leader over this issue); whether to accept a policy ~~of appeasement~~ with Hitler (**George Lansbury**, leader from 1932 to 1935, was an avowed pacifist); and what was to be the future form of common ownership of industry if and when a future Labour Government was elected. The onset of the Second World War brought these issues to an end and real planning for the future could begin.

The socialist reforms, 1940–51

Senior members of the party played a leading role on the domestic front during the war years. Party leader **Clement Attlee** (effectively Deputy Prime Minister), **Herbert Morrison** (Home Secretary) and, above all, **Ernest Bevin** (Labour and National Supply) largely governed the country while Churchill and the leading Conservatives ran the war. At the same time as these Labour members were acting as key ministers, they were also planning for the future. Thus the **Beveridge Report**, setting out the nature of the future welfare state, was produced in 1942 with much input from the Labour Party. A system of free secondary education for all was introduced through the **1944 Education Act** (introduced by R. A. Butler, a leading Conservative, but inspired by Labour). Above all, the success of national control and planning of production and distribution, which had to be introduced for war purposes, convinced the party and much of the electorate that a limited form of socialist planning was desirable after the war.

The landslide Labour election victory of 1945 led to six years of dramatic socialist reforms. A number of large industries were nationalised and local government social and personal services, including housing, were extended. The welfare state and the National Health Service were introduced among a host of lesser measures.

Consensus politics

After the rush of reforms of 1945–51, Labour spent most of the years from 1951 until 1974 in opposition. Apart from the Wilson Governments of 1964–70 – when technological advances, improvements in the legal and economic status of women and racial minorities, employment protection for workers and the growth of higher education were Labour's main achievements – Labour could only watch while Conservative governments avoided major political controversies by governing the UK on the basis of consensus. Consensus politics ensured the adoption of broadly agreed and moderate policies that consolidated and built on the reforms of the 1940s. Radical changes were avoided while sound management of the mixed economy and the welfare state were claimed, with invariable electoral success for the Conservatives.

Lurch to the left   Successive election defeats in 1979 and 1983, together with the clear shift to the 'New Right' neo-liberal policies by the Thatcher-led Conservatives, led to a distinct movement to the left within the Labour Party. A radical leader, **Michael Foot**, was elected in 1980, an internal reorganisation of the party took place in 1981 giving more influence to the traditionally left-wing grass roots membership, and a number of 'extremist' policies were adopted. These were dark days for Labour. Its proportion of the popular vote fell to 27.6 per cent in 1983 and was still at only 30.9 per cent in 1987. A splinter group broke from the party in 1981, naming itself the **Social Democrat Party** and claiming to espouse the true, traditional philosophies of the modern Labour movement. For a few years it threatened, in combination with the Liberal Party, to replace Labour as the main opposition party.

The election of **Neil Kinnock** to replace Foot in 1984 was the beginning of the party's long climb back to moderation and electoral success.

New Labour under Blair   Three successive leaders of the party – Kinnock, **John Smith** (1992–4) and **Tony Blair** (1994–) brought Labour back to a less radical position and made it electable again. In particular, the **Policy Review** of 1989–9, which Kinnock ordered, set the agenda for Labour's new philosophy. Then Blair's successful battle to revise Clause IV of the party Constitution ultimately symbolised Labour's transformation. Formerly, Clause IV committed the party to state ownership and control of industry, distribution and finance. By replacing it in 1995 with a more general commitment to equality of opportunity, social justice and the search for maximum employment opportunities, Blair brought to a climax the changes proposed by his two predecessors. Indeed, so great were the changes made by Blair, that the party campaigned in the 1997 election as 'New Labour.' Following its second successive election victory in 2001, Labour remained committed to extend further the policies it had introduced in the previous few years.

Labour policies   The beliefs and philosophies behind the current Labour Party's policies should be viewed in terms of the sections on social democracy and democratic socialism, described in Unit 3. It should also be noted that true policy, whichever the party in question, can only be fully established when election manifestos have been produced and when programmes have been unfurled before Parliament. Nevertheless, general intentions can be established. The schedule shown on page 116 is not exhaustive and must, by the very nature of political change, be subject to constant alteration. Yet it does indicate the main thrusts of Labour policy at the time of the 2001 election.

Labour Party policy in 2001

...a	Policy
...rol	• keeping inflation under control. • Prudent approach to public spending – 'golden rule' forbids government borrowing except for long-term investment.
• **Employment**	• Stress on training and retraining. • More tax and welfare incentives to encourage people to seek work. • Stress on education to create a more flexible workforce.
• **Welfare**	• A tax and welfare system that encourages all to find work and support themselves. • Tighter controls to prevent benefit fraud. • Principle of a minimum level of income for all working families. • Help available for child care for single parents who wish to work. • Support for the child benefit system. • The state pension to become less important, largely to be replaced by private pension schemes.
• **Taxation**	• General level of personal taxation to be reduced except at the top levels. • Extensions of a 10 per cent tax band at low income levels. • Vague commitment to reducing the total burden of taxation. • More stress on taxes on expenditure. • Reductions in tax on business, especially small companies.
• **Education**	• Continued stress on education. • Increased expenditure and a long-term goal to reduce class sizes and to drive up standards. • Increased number of teachers, but pay increases linked to performance. • Further expansion of higher education, partly funded by a fee system for students. • Stress on Information and Communication Technology at all levels. • Citizenship education also encouraged.
• **Health**	• Increased real expenditure on the NHS, above inflation levels. • Commitment to retain the basic system. Stress on primary health care.
• **Industry**	• Reluctance to intervene directly in maintaining industries. • Restructuring of the British economy away from manufacturing towards service industries allowed to occur. • Strong support for small businesses, especially those involved in technology. • Strengthened controls over competition and consumer protection. • Large Competition Commission formed to implement this.
• **Law and order**	• Generally tough approach. • Attempts to speed up the judicial process including reduction in use of trial by jury. • Continued opposition to legalisation of drugs. • Increases in size of police forces.
• **Europe**	• Support for closer integration with the European Union. • Leading the movement towards a common European defence and foreign policy. • A referendum on joining the Euro system as soon as economic conditions are favourable.
• **The Constitution**	• Most proposed reforms had been achieved by 2000. • Some support for strengthening local government, including more elected city mayors. • Completion of reform of the House of Lords.

| • Foreign/
defence
policy | • The UK to maintain a leading role in world affairs.
• Strong support for both NATO and a European Union common policy on defence and foreign affairs.
• Willingness to intervene in international conflicts. |
| • Transport | • Increased expenditure on public transport.
• Partial privatisation of London Transport. |

Labour Party organisation

Annual Conference

The main structure of the party is described below.

The Annual Conference is made up of delegates from trade unions and constituency parties, MPs, Members of the European Parliament (MEPs) and representatives from co-operative societies and other socialist societies. Voting is dominated by trade union delegates, who account for 70 per cent of total representation (reduced from 90 per cent in 1995).

It is the 'sovereign body' of the party which has ultimate power over decisions. However, its resolutions, while being party policy, do not bind the leadership either to placing those policies in the election manifesto or adopting them as government policy if the party should win power.

The Conference elects the National Executive Committee of the party.

2000 Labour Party Conference

National Executive Committee

The National Executive Committee (NEC), elected annually at Conference, contains twelve members elected by unions, five by constituency parties and one by socialist associations. In addition, the NEC must include at least five women. Four officers are automatically members – the party Treasurer, Chair of the Young Socialists, party leader and deputy leader. It therefore represents the broad range of the party membership.

Its role is to determine party policy on the advice of the Conference and under the strong influence of the party leader. Before elections it writes the party manifesto, although it is accepted that the leader has a veto over individual items.

The NEC also handles party discipline and approves candidates to be chosen by constituency parties.

Constituency Labour Parties	The Constituency Labour Parties (CLPs) contain the grass roots members of the party. The CLPs discuss their attitude to policy and may propose resolutions at the Conference. They also send delegates to that Conference and often instruct those delegates on how to vote on each issue. In each constituency the General ~~~~~~~~ Committee chooses candidates for election to Parliament. Smaller committees in each ward (sub-division of the constituency) choose candidates for local government office.
Leader and deputy leader	Both are elected by a ballot of union members, constituency members and MPs. The weighting given to each of these groups is one-third. The roles of the leader and deputy leader are ill-defined but in practice they are the leading figures in policy making, with special control over the election manifesto. Clearly, too, if the party wins power they become the two leading members of the Government itself and so gain considerable authority. In particular, a Labour Prime Minister chooses his Cabinet and other ministers, whereas as mere Leader of the Opposition he does not choose the Shadow Cabinet (see below).
Parliamentary Labour Party	Made up of all Labour MPs, the Parliamentary Labour Party (PLP) attempts to exert influence over policy, especially when Labour is in power. It is divided into a number of policy committees and meets regularly to make its general views known to the leadership.
Shadow Cabinet	Of course, this only exists when Labour is in opposition. Its membership of twelve (plus the leader and deputy) is elected by the MPs annually, but the leader may add members and decides for which policy area each shall be spokesperson. It is a guide as to who is likely to be in a future Labour Government, but no guarantee since, once in office, the leader alone appoints the Cabinet. The Shadow Cabinet meets regularly to discuss and arrange parliamentary business for the Opposition, determining tactics, main speakers in debates and general policy lines. However, its role in long-term policy making is less significant.

Power in the Labour Party

As we have seen, Labour has a wide and complex structure. Traditionally, power and influence have been dispersed throughout the party, avoiding the possibility of too much concentration of power in one place. The different sections of the party balance each other in terms of influence, with particular emphasis on serving the interests of union and constituency members. Since 1981, however, distinct changes in the distribution of power have taken place. These, together with other key features, are described below:

- It must be stressed that, when Labour gains government office, its leader becomes Prime Minister, so there is a marked shift in power. The leader then has enormous powers of patronage, carries the fate of the Government very much in his or her own hands, and becomes chief policy-maker (see Unit 8).
- Before 1981 the leader was elected by MPs alone. At that time, however, a new procedure was introduced. Election was to be by the whole party, with 40 per cent of the votes being carried by trade union leaders. It was assumed and feared in some quarters that this would lead to the election of more radical leaders, but this has not occurred as union leaders have proved to be increasingly moderate.

- In 1994 the party adopted further reforms proposed by John Smith, who died before they could be implemented. In particular, the trade union 'block vote' was abolished. The block vote meant that union leaders could vote, at Conference and in leadership elections, on behalf of **all** their members. Under a system of 'One Member One Vote' (OMOV) each member of the party votes separately both for the leader and for parliamentary candidates. At Conference, meanwhile, union delegates are free to vote as they wish. Block delegate voting is now outlawed. This has been seen as a major step forward in internal democratisation of the party. The following year, the 'weighting' of union votes at Conference was also reduced from 90 per cent to 70 per cent.
- It used to be the case that the Annual Conference could force policies on to the parliamentary leadership. In the 1980s, for example, the party had to accept nuclear disarmament as a policy when it was clear that this would be unpopular in electoral terms. By the 1990s, however, it had become accepted that, while Conference may embarrass the leadership, it cannot really force it to accept policies that it cannot present to Parliament or the electorate. This was demonstrated in 1994 when a resolution to retain Clause IV was passed after leader Tony Blair had made it clear he wished to reform it. What would, in the past, have been a major internal crisis for the party proved to be a minor difficulty soon to be resolved. In 1995 Blair was able to force the revision of Clause IV through a special conference.
- It is certainly true that Labour remains slightly more internally democratic than the Conservative Party. The Labour leader is not as powerful as the Conservative Leader and is constrained by a number of other influential bodies in the party. Yet there has been a shift in the distribution of power towards the leader and his or her parliamentary colleagues. The desperate need to 'stop the rot' and win a general election went a considerable way to force such changes upon the party's membership. Following the Clause IV revision in the spring of 1995, more internal reforms were promised by Tony Blair to modernise and democratise the party further. The party's draft manifesto for the 1997 election was submitted to a vote of approval of all members as an indication of his determination to involve the grass roots.

Summary of Labour Party internal reforms in the 1990s

1. The union block vote was abolished inside constituency parties when selecting candidates for parliamentary and council elections, and also at Annual Conference, special conferences and in NEC and leadership elections. Each individual union member's vote is counted separately, instead of being cast on the member's behalf by a union delegate.
2. All constituency party members now have a say in the selection of parliamentary and council election candidates.
3. The proportion of weighting given to union votes in leadership elections was reduced from 40 per cent to one-third.
4. The weighting of union voting at Annual Conference was reduced from 90 per cent to 70 per cent.
5. Clause IV was revised from a commitment to public ownership of industry to a broader statement of aims concerning social justice, equality of opportunity and reduced unemployment.

The Conservative Party

Origins and brief history

Unlike Labour there is no specific starting point for the Conservative Party. Its appearance as a coherent group in Parliament was possibly first evident in the 1830s when ... Peel gathered around him a group of MPs and peers who had opposed the economic, social and political reforms of the time, but who were prepared to accept them in the interests of the stability and unity of the nation.

However, it was Disraeli in the 1870s and 1880s who actually created a political party in the modern sense of the word. Although it was still a party rooted in the House of Commons, there now began the development of Conservative Associations up and down the country, comprising leading local citizens who wished to ensure the election of Conservative MPs and to sustain them in Parliament. The philosophies of this group were to unite the nation by accepting social and political reforms, to support the Empire and the nation, to oppose Irish independence and to uphold traditions.

Wilderness years

After Disraeli the reformers among the Conservatives largely deserted the party in favour of Gladstone's new Liberal Party. The rest of the party soon lapsed into a reactionary stance, opposing the rush of reforms that were led by Gladstone. As a consequence, the Conservatives enjoyed only brief periods of government office. Between 1902 and 1922 there was no Conservative Government, with only a progressive section of the party joining Liberal coalitions. Conservatives could only attract about one-third of the working-class vote and a minority of middle-class support, so electoral success was difficult to achieve.

Recovery and protectionism

After the period of extensive reform and progress over which the Liberal Party had presided in the first twenty years of the twentieth century, the Conservatives were able to present themselves as the party of consolidation and stability. With the decline of the Liberal Party and before Labour was able to mobilise enough support to form its own government, the party dominated the political scene through to the 1940s.

The Conservatives governed on the basis of sound public finance, protectionist economics and reliance upon the Empire for economic prosperity. Led by the non-interventionist **Stanley Baldwin** (Prime Minister 1923–4, 1924–9, 1935–7), the party commanded widespread support even during the dark days of the Great Depression. Above all, conservatism was seen as representing stability while the other parties suggested upheaval and uncertainty. Baldwin himself represented this sense of security under the Tories.

Consensus and corporatism

After the shock of election defeat in 1945, the Conservatives had to take stock of the socialist reforms which were then in full swing. It was the moderates and reformers, led by **Anthony Eden** (Prime Minister 1955–7), **R.A. Butler** and **Harold Macmillan** (Prime Minister 1957–63), who brought the party into the consensus era of politics.

They accepted the new reforms and campaigned on the grounds that the Conservatives were the best party to build on and to manage the new age of the mixed economy and the welfare state. Macmillan in particular recognised that there was general agreement about the nature of the reforms, so there was no future for the Conservatives if they were to oppose them.

In addition, Butler and Macmillan recognised that the country should be governed in consultation with the representatives of both employers and trade unions. Thus, steady growth and progress, sound economic management and constant consultation with the major interests in society – a form of politics known as 'corporatism' – were adopted with great success.

Selsdon Man and Thatcherism

In the late 1960s a group of prominent Conservatives met at Selsdon Park in Surrey to map out a new form of conservatism. This group, known as 'Selsdon Man', was concerned that the enormous power of the state, excessively high taxation and the destructive power of trade unions were hindering the UK's economic progress. The first signs of economic stagnation were becoming apparent. They recommended a great reduction of state interference in industry and the economy, large-scale tax reductions, restoration of free markets and curbs on union power.

They persuaded party leader **Edward Heath** (Prime Minister 1970–4) to adopt their position and reforms were commenced in 1970. A succession of economic crises brought these changes to a sudden halt, but this new kind of neo-liberalism had taken hold in the party. When **Margaret Thatcher** was elected in 1979, she revealed herself as a convert to this 'New Right' form of conservatism, as it was becoming known. The next decade saw a transformation in British economic and social life as dramatic as that of 1945–51. It was a decade of privatisation, reductions in personal and corporate taxes, union reform, deregulation of industry and reductions in local government functions. At the same time, opposition to European integration became an important feature of the party. By the 1990s, after Thatcher, the question for the party was whether to continue with the process begun by the New Right, or to institute a period of consolidation.

Conservative policies

The divisions within the Conservative Party that re-emerged in the 1990s make it difficult to establish the future direction of policy. The schedule below describes the 'central' and most generally accepted aspects of party policy. However, there are important variations of many of these policies that attract significant support within the party. As with the Labour Party, the following descriptions of Conservative policy should be read in conjunction with the analyses of the three types of conservatism in Unit 3.

Defeat in the 2001 general election led the party to reconsider its policies over the course of the next parliament. Inevitably most of its efforts, however, were focused on opposition to early entry into the European Monetary Union.

Conservative Party policy in 2001	
Policy area	**Policy**
• **Economic control**	• Very similar to Labour. • A commitment to keep down public expenditure and inflation. • Largely pragmatic.
• **Employment**	• Similar to Labour. • The principal attack on unemployment should be through a tighter benefits system.
• **Welfare**	• A harder line is taken on benefits fraud. • Regulations on benefits to be further tightened. • Welfare to be used purely as a safety net for those who have no alternative.
• **Taxation**	• A strong commitment to reducing levels of personal and business taxation. • Basic rate of taxation to be reduced to at least 20 per cent. • The total burden of taxation in relation to national income to be reduced.
• **Education**	• Firm commitment to performance targets in the National Curriculum. • Teachers to be paid according to results. • Commitment to further reductions in class sizes. • Expansion of the higher education system. • Generally similar to Labour.
• **Health**	• A commitment to further increases in health expenditure. • Where necessary the private sector may be used by the NHS.
• **Industry/agriculture**	• Similar to Labour, with great stress on position of small businesses. • Where possible, industries should be protected from falling employment. • Strong support for the agricultural sector.
• **Law and order**	• A slightly harder line than Labour. • Special measures to reduce youth crime. • Longer sentences and more custodial punishments. • A tougher stance on the admittance of asylum seekers to the UK.
• **Europe**	• Opposition to the introduction of a single European currency for the foreseeable future. • Opposition to further European integration. • No support for a common European defence and foreign policy system. • No further political integration in Europe. • There is a stress on the UK's defending its national interests in European decision making. • However, there is no policy to leave the Union.
• **The Constitution**	• General opposition to any further reforms. • However, there is no policy to reverse the reforms made by the Labour Government after 1997.
• **Foreign/defence policy**	• Similar to Labour. • However, there is no support for the common European defence and foreign policy system. • Support for NATO is strong. • More emphasis than Labour on defence spending.

Important variations

Unlike the Labour Party in 2000, which is remarkably united at its upper levels, the Conservative Party contains leading members who have fundamental disagreements with some of the policies listed above.

A major division in the party concerns the UK's place in Europe. There are still some members – mostly older, well-established ones – who are supportive of the idea of a single European currency and would like the UK to join it when conditions are favourable. A former Chancellor of the Exchequer, **Kenneth Clarke**, is one of these, as is a former Prime Minister, **Edward Heath**. They represent a minority in the party and there are signs that their numbers are waning.

On the other hand, there is a strong, possibly growing, **Euro-sceptic** wing, led by such figures as **John Redwood, Bill Cash** and **Lord Tebbitt**. They would like to see the party make a firm commitment **never** to enter a single currency system. Indeed, there is a growing faction that now wishes to see the UK leave the European Union altogether. As this is against official party policy, the view has been largely suppressed. Privately, however, there is little doubt that it is a growing emotion within the Conservative Party.

There remains in the party a 'liberal' wing, sometimes described as the **one nation** Conservatives, who draw their inspiration from the older traditions of the Conservative Party, before it was transformed by Margaret Thatcher in the 1980s. They include the former ministers **Lord Hurd, Lord Howe** and **Michael Heseltine**. They are uneasy about the hard line the party has taken on such issues as welfare, law and order, and immigration. They have also been content to support some of the constitutional reforms made by the Labour Party. In essence, their ideas do not vary greatly from those of the Labour and Liberal Democrat parties. They can, therefore, be seen as 'consensus' politicians who prefer to see general national agreement on policies, rather than constant adversarial conflict. This wing of the Conservative Party is, however, in steep decline.

Conservative Party organisation

Leader

As recently as 1963, the Conservative Party did not elect its leader at all. Before then the position was largely in the gift of the outgoing leader and/or the leading members of the parliamentary party. Since then the party has steadily democratised itself to the point where, in 1998, it was decided that the party leader should be elected by all members of the party. In this way the Conservatives have actually overtaken the Labour Party in democratising the process of leadership selection. To date no leader has been elected by this system, so it remains to be seen how much influence the new system actually has.

Once elected, the party leader enjoys a dominant position in the party. While it is certainly true that the Conservative Party is considerably less united than it used to be before 1990 and it is also likely that a popularly elected individual will have to take more account of grassroots opinion, the leader's power should not be underestimated. He or she has responsibility for writing the party election manifesto and sets the policy agenda. There are no institutional constraints on the leader's power. The annual conference does not set policy and the party headquarters is under the leader's control. The Conservatives therefore remain a 'leadership-orientated' party.

1922 Committee   The 1922 Committee is the collective title of all Conservative back-bench MPs. This semi-formal organisation has an influential chairperson and meets on a regular basis, often questioning Conservative prime min-isters or lesser ministers over policy and tactics. Heath, in particular, learned that it pays a leader to inform and consult with the 1922 Committee as they have the power to remove him or her. Thatcher (1990), Heath (1975) and Home (1965) were all ousted by discontented MPs. MPs are also divided into a number of policy committees that seek to influence the leadership, though ultimately it is only influence that they possess and not power itself.

Party Headquarters   Party Headquarters comprises both the administrative organisation of the party, or **Central Office**, and its **Research Department**. It is headed by the influential **Party Chairman**. The role of the Chairman and the Headquarters staff is to organise the selection of a short list of possible parliamentary candidates, to maintain discipline and to handle party publicity and image. As the Conservative Party relies heavily upon its public face, the activities of Central Office are especially important. The Research Department used to have a good deal of influence over the leadership, but Margaret Thatcher's preference for external advice moved it into the background. Since 1999 there has been a **Policy Forum**, which is designed to maintain contact with ordinary members. How much influence it will have remains to be seen, but it is potentially an important development.

Michael Portillo, Ann Widdecombe and David Heathcoat-Amory at the Conservative Party Conference 2000

Conservative Associations

Conservative Associations comprise the grass-roots members of the party. There is an Association in each parliamentary constituency. Strictly speaking, they are not part of the main organisation of the party itself, but are local organisations that exist to support the real party in Parliament. Although they send delegates to the annual conference, they do not expect to influence policy a great deal. In the main their role is to raise finance, select candidates for office from a list presented by Headquarters and organise electoral support. In 1997 some associations added deselection of candidates to their role with two members – Sir Nicholas Scott and Sir George Gardiner – losing their seats in the face of local opposition.

Annual Conference

Annual Conference is really the regular meeting of the **Union of Conservative Associations**. Ministers (mere front-bench MPs if the party is in opposition), including the party leader, are invited to speak but do not have an automatic right to do so. Since this is not really a gathering of the party itself, but only its local support groups, Conference has no decision-making power. Instead it has a number of lesser functions. It is a public relations exercise to demonstrate unity and purpose, designed to transmit the general 'mood' of supporters to the leadership, and it is a rally of the faithful, an exercise in morale boosting and a time to inspire. There have been occasions when it has sought to shift party policy in a particular direction. In the 1990s, for example, strong anti-European and pro-authoritarian sentiments were expressed at Conference.

> 'It is a Conservative article of faith that splits spell electoral suicide, which is why the party traditionally conducts its quarrels in private or in code. Voters expect Labour, not the Conservatives, to brawl in public.'
>
> Ivor Crewe, in *The Major Effect*, 1995

Power in the Conservative Party

The Conservative Party is very much a 'top-down' party, with power concentrated in its central leadership. It is also predominantly a parliamentary party – a reflection of its origins as well as its belief that its natural position is in government. The ordinary grass-roots members have relatively little influence, while the Members of Parliament do not expect to exert very much control unless a particularly controversial issue arises. While in the Labour Party the financial backing of trade unions is matched by their important status in the party organisation, the Conservatives' corporate backers – a number of large private companies – do not enjoy such a privileged position. Having said this, the influence of these companies on the party is difficult to assess.

As we have seen, the position of the leader can be somewhat ambiguous. On the one hand, a leader has great powers of patronage and of policy formulation. On the other, MPs have shown themselves not averse to removing a leader whom they feel is damaging the fortunes of the party. The halcyon days of Margaret Thatcher's leadership, from 1982 to 1989, indicate the enormous potential power of the leader. By contrast, the less secure leadership of John Major demonstrated the potential power of the parliamentary party and determined groups within it.

The Liberal Democrat Party

Origins and brief The modern Liberal Party formed itself into a formal organisation under
William Gladstone in the 1870~~s~~.

reformist Tories, Radicals and even some quasi-socialists. Under Gladstone's dynamic leadership they soon came to dominate the political scene. Backed by a network of local party organisations and effective discipline in Parliament, they held power for most of the years between 1880 and 1922, either alone or in coalition with others.

These 40 or so years saw the liberals lead the way in reforming the machinery of government, including the civil service, extending the franchise to women, granting freedom to Ireland, establishing education for all, pensions, municipal housing and a wide variety of other local authority services. Both they and the Conservatives were pledged to improving the condition of the people, but it was the Liberals who held most of the power to achieve these goals.

This success came to a rather abrupt end in the early 1920s. The growing Labour movement and a revived Conservative Party began to squeeze the Liberal vote. The reforming stance of the party was taken over by Labour, while the Conservatives stood for stability at a time of great economic uncertainty. There now began a steady decline in support for the Liberals.

The darkest days for the party occurred after the Second World War. In 1951 they won only 2.5 per cent of the popular vote and six seats in the House of Commons. It was even feared that the party might go out of existence.

In the 1970s, however, support for the major parties began to wane. General dissatisfaction with the performance of both major parties set in. The Liberals, together with Scottish and Welsh Nationalists, began to win votes and seats slowly but surely.

When the Social Democrat Party (SDP) broke from Labour in 1981, advocating moderate, centrist policies, it was clear that the new party bore a considerable resemblance to the Liberals. The two leaders, **David Steel** for the Liberals and **Roy Jenkins** for the SDP, reached an agreement known as the **Alliance**, which was to fight the forthcoming election along a broadly common front. In 1983 the Alliance won 25 per cent of the votes and 23 seats in the Commons. Despite a number of crises in the relationship, the Alliance staggered on to the 1987 election, where it did almost as well as it had four years earlier. However, the hoped-for breakthrough to challenge the hegemony of the two main parties had not occurred. Faced with internal dissension, the two parties merged to form the Social and Liberal Democratic Party. The smaller Liberal and Social Democrat Parties retained separate identities, supported by a small number of enthusiasts, but these 'rumps' soon passed into political oblivion.

The SLD Party soon dropped its 'Social' tag in order to distance itself from any links with former socialists. It became the Liberal Democrat Party, which it still is today. Despite the name change, it can be said that the Liberal Democrats are the genuine heirs to the former Liberal Party. In the 1990s support appeared to have stabilised at between 15 and 20 per cent of the electorate, with occasional dramatic victories at by-elections, where sometimes huge Conservative majorities were overturned.

Liberal Democrat policies

It should be stressed at the outset that **Paddy Ashdown,** the party leader between 1988 and 1999, and his successor, **Charles Kennedy,** both accepted that the Liberal Democrats should not be driven solely by rigid ideology, but should be willing to be pragmatic in their approach. Nevertheless, there are some firm policies to which the party is committed.

Liberal Democrat Party policy in 2001

Policy area	Policy
• **The economy**	• Very much a pragmatic approach that mirrors Labour policy.
• **Taxation**	• There is a difference here. • The Liberal Democrats oppose tax cuts if this reduces expenditure on vital public services such as health and education. • Indeed, the party would support higher taxes if these were necessary to maintain such services.
• **The Constitution**	• The party supports all the reforms made by the Labour Party. However, it wishes to go further. • An elected second chamber. • A stronger Freedom of Information Act. • Greater independence for local government. • A stronger Human Rights Act. • Devolution of power to the English regions.
• **Law and order**	• Generally the party opposes the very hard line taken by the two large parties. • It stresses policies to tackle the causes of crime rather than mere punishment.
• **Welfare**	• Liberal Democrats would support maintenance of the value of old age pensions. • Further steps to be taken to take people out of the poverty trap. • Greater support for minority groups as such as the disabled and single parents.
• **Moral issues**	• While the party does not have very specific proposals on a variety of moral issues, it does wish to see a more open debate on drugs, sex education, the age of consent, etc.
• **Europe**	• The Liberal Democrats are the most enthusiastic supporters of European integration and the single currency. • They believe that there will be more local and regional autonomy within an integrated Europe.
• **The environment**	• The party is more 'green' than its main rivals. • It supports radical transport measures to reduce pollution and to improve public transport. • Greater controls on emissions. • GM foods and energy production to be instituted.
• **Health**	• Similar policies to Labour, but the party lays more stress on the need for higher levels of spending.
• **Education**	• Again similar to Labour, but the Liberal Democrats support higher spending. • They oppose the imposition of fees on higher education students.
• **Defence/ foreign policy**	• Similar to Labour. However, the party wishes to see a more 'ethical' foreign policy than has been adopted by either of the two main parties. • It would take a hard line against regimes that are not democratic and abuse human rights.

Liberal Democrat Party organisation

It has to be borne in mind when considering the distribution of power and influence in the Liberal Democrat Party that it operates without a realistic prospect of achieving governmental power on its own. The best it can hope for in the foreseeable future is to share power with a bigger party. It can, therefore, afford the luxury of indulging in extremes of internal democracy, controversy and radicalism without being too concerned with the reaction of the electorate. Its two most recent leaders, **Paddy Ashdown** and **Charles Kennedy**, have attempted to curb the independence of local and regional bodies in the party in the interests of unity and clarity of purpose. They have had some success, but the party remains more decentralised and internally democratic than its larger rivals.

Liberal Democratic Party Conference 1994 – Charles Kennedy (left) became leader five years later

Leader

The leader of the party is elected by the most 'democratic' process of the three principal parties: that is, by all the members of the party, by postal ballot. The small size of the Liberal Democrat Party inevitably means that the leader appears to dominate. Certainly in parliamentary affairs the leader is pre-eminent and is very much the spokesperson of the party as a whole. The only two other significant figures in a national context are the **Party President** and the **deputy leader**. In practical terms, this triumvirate has a dominant role to play in policy making.

Party Headquarters

Party Headquarters has some input on policy, but is mainly concerned with the business of raising money and of drumming up sufficient publicity to challenge the attention paid to the two bigger parties.

Federal Policy Committee The Federal Policy Committee rivals the leader, the President and the deputy leader in deciding on Liberal Democrat policy. As its name suggests, it comprises representatives from different parts of Britain: that is, England, Scotland and Wales. In addition, it is staffed by four MPs, representatives from Liberal local councils and from the House of Lords. Thus, it reflects all aspects of party activity.

Federal Conference The Federal Conference meets annually. It is served by regional conferences that take place earlier in the year. These conferences feed in policy proposals to the main conference. At the latter, representatives from all constituencies act as delegates and pass resolutions that are strongly advisory, but not binding on the leadership. As a body it is known for its independence and often for its radicalism. In the 1990s, for example, there were calls for the abolition of the monarchy, the legalisation of cannabis and for an electoral pact with the Labour Party from significant sections of the party, but against the wishes of the leadership.

Constituency parties Constituency parties are, in keeping with the democratic and individualistic philosophy of the party, extremely autonomous. As we have said above, they may take an extreme line on policy, are relatively free in the choice of parliamentary and local government candidates, and tend to adopt their own independent procedures.

Small parties

Before reviewing the nature and role of Britain's very small parties, we must consider the reasons why political support is so concentrated on just three parties, at least in England: in other words, why smaller 'fringe' parties are so unsuccessful. The following reasons may be considered:

- Britain is an unusually homogeneous culture. There are few major conflicts of interests within the country. Compared to many other, less prosperous states, there are relatively small differentials in wealth and income among the majority of the population. There is an uncomplicated class structure, with no significant peasant class and a largely unified working class that does not include a significant radical element, as do several of its European counterparts. There is also only a weak tradition of extreme right-wing nationalism. Most members of the population are moderate in their political outlook, so their views and interests can be articulated by a small number of parties.
- The electoral system discriminates against small parties. Only those parties with concentrated support – the two main parties and the nationalists in restricted parts of Scotland and Wales – can hope to win significant numbers of parliamentary seats. The electorate, perceiving that a vote for a very small party is likely to be a wasted one, are therefore reluctant to support such a party even if they feel politically inclined to do so.

- Finance has become increasingly important in the process of winning votes and parliamentary seats. Without a significant financial base, small parties are at a serious disadvantage.
- Possibly as a result of the factors described above, Britain's large parties are broad coalitions of belief and interest. Internal discipline enables them to remain relatively unified while, at the same time, being able to attract a wide range of support. This takes the ground away from minority parties.
- An active and influential system of pressure groups flourishes in the British political system. It is therefore unnecessary for parties that represent minority interests and philosophies to exist, as many such demands may be successfully articulated in other ways.

Despite the features of the British political culture described above, some small parties do still function. Among them are the following.

The Green Party   A former environmental pressure group, it turned itself into a quasi-political party known as the **Ecology Party**, fought a few election campaigns but was not seriously pursuing significant representation. Following the success of its counterparts in Germany, its name was changed to the **Green Party** in 1985 to signal its serious intention to win seats in Parliament.

Its high point came in 1989 when the party won 15 per cent of a low turnout in the elections to the European Parliament. No seats were won, but the other parties were severely shaken. They reacted by taking the environmental lobby more seriously. Green policies appeared higher on their political agenda. The Liberal Democrats in particular adopted many of the party's policies.

Partly as a result of its political 'clothes' being stolen by the main parties, and partly as a result of a destructive internal schism over tactics and organisation, the tide of Green Party fortunes soon ebbed away. In the 1992 general election its vote fell below 1 per cent. Other than winning a few rural local government seats, the Greens have ceased to be a significant electoral force.

Nationalists   The aspirations of the nationalist parties in Wales and Scotland – Plaid Cymru and the Scottish National Party (SNP) respectively – were hugely boosted when devolution was granted to their countries in 1999. Yet this also presented them with a problem. Having achieved most of their objectives, what was to be their new identity?

One aspect of this was relatively predictable. Happy though they are with devolved power, they would like to see yet more independence from government in London. The SNP tentatively supports full independence for Scotland, but promises that this would occur only following a positive referendum result. Plaid Cymru is less interested in full independence, but is campaigning for greater powers to be exercised by the Welsh Assembly.

Both the nationalist parties also support policies that allow their countries to be more **distinct** from England. In practice, this means greater support for regional industries, a fair allocation of resources to health and education and a more autonomous local government system.

Others Many small political groupings flourish in Northern Ireland. The political system there, of course, is very different from the rest of the UK, so it is impossible to generalise from the Ulster experience. It should be noted, however, that the electoral system there – the Single Transferable Vote (STV) – is one of the most proportional, so small groups can gain electoral success.

In the rest of the UK it is the emergence of **single-issue parties** that has been most striking. The **Referendum Party**, backed by one wealthy businessman, James Goldsmith, fought the 1997 election purely on the issue of Europe. Similarly, the more permanent **UK Independence Party (UKIP)** is concerned only with Europe. The **Pro-Life Alliance** (anti-abortion) put up candidates in 1997, though it remains to be seen whether it continues to fight elections in the future. It is generally expected that, in the future, there will be a proliferation of single-issue parties. They have more chance of winning seats in the devolved assemblies and parliament, but will also fight for seats at Westminster. They depend on finance, of course, as they need maximum publicity. But there do seem to be sufficient wealthy individuals and pressure groups willing to seek influence in this way to provide the money.

A few tiny ideological parties put up candidates for election. On the left, the **Socialist Workers Party** (SWP) and on the right the **British National Party** (BNP) are examples. They show no signs of growing in the modern age and attract only a tiny handful of votes in elections, although the BNP did win substantial votes in Oldham at the 2001 election, largely as a result of racial tensions which had broken out in the town that summer. The **Natural Law Party** has been branded variously as eccentric, ideological and spiritual, but it does attract enough funds to put up large numbers of candidates. Its policies – a mixture of holism, mysticism, liberalism and environmentalism – are little understood and it remains an interesting footnote to most elections.

Minor parties are likely to remain minor while general and local elections remain based on the first-past-the-post system of voting. They may make some inroads where proportional representation operates in Wales, Scotland and Northern Ireland, but in England they have little chance to grow significantly.

For exam questions relevant to this unit, see page 555.

Introduction

Perhaps the two leading authorities on British pressure groups are Robert Baggott and Wyn Grant. They have offered the following definitions of a pressure group:

> 'an organisation which seeks to influence the details of a comparatively small range of public policies and which is not a faction of a recognised political party'
>
> Robert Baggott

> 'an organisation which seeks as one of its functions to influence the formulation and implementation of public policy, public policy representing a set of authoritative decisions taken by the executive, the legislature and the judiciary, and by local government and the European Community [now Union]'
>
> Wyn Grant

> Both quoted in R. Baggott, *Pressure Groups: A Question of Interest*, 1994

From this pair of definitions we can extract a number of key facts about pressure groups:

- They are **organisations**, which suggests that they have a formal structure of some kind.
- They seek to **influence**, indicating that they have fairly precise goals.
- Their goals are relatively **narrow**, which means that they do not concern themselves with the full range of public policy.
- They are **not political parties** or parts of parties.
- They operate on **any public decision-making body**, whichever is appropriate.

The nature of pressure

In politics, pressure is the means by which **influence** is exercised. As is the case with influence, there is no certainty that pressure will actually achieve its ends. Only pure **coercive power** can guarantee success in virtually all circumstances.

While power operates through the ultimate use of **force**, pressure does not enjoy such luxuries. Those who wish to exercise it must, therefore, use more subtle means. Among these are the following.

Reasoned argument

In an ideal world we might expect that political decisions are all based upon rationality, but it is only on rare occasions that reason alone prevails. Groups that have campaigned for constitutional reforms, such as **Charter 88**, or those that are concerned with rights – of both humans and animals – such as **Liberty** and the **League Against Cruel Sports**, hope that politicians will be persuaded by the force of their argument. However, sterner measures are normally required.

Threats of sanctions

Since reason often does not prevail, decision-makers usually need clearer messages in order to stir them into action. Thus, negative pressure may be used. Here the threat of action that will damage, embarrass or hinder the purposes of the Government can be effective. In extreme circumstances, law breaking may be involved, such as the 'tax strike' organised by the anti-Poll Tax movement in the 1980s. The withholding of local taxes created havoc for local authorities, expense for the Treasury and chaos in the courts, which were attempting to prosecute the non-payers. Trade unions might organise strikes or lesser industrial action and producer groups might threaten to thwart government economic policies, should they not receive favourable treatment.

Rewards

Few politicians can resist the lure of the promise of large numbers of voters granting their support at the next election. The achievement and retention of governmental power are meat and drink to these politicians. Pressure that promises to satisfy these appetites is, therefore, likely to be the most successful. It is the large interest groups such as trade unions, home owners and taxpayers which offer these rewards in the greatest numbers. **Finance** is another powerful carrot to attract the attention of the political parties. Groups from both sides of industry – unions and employers – have supported parties in the expectation that they will have some influence over policy. The threat that financial support might be removed can exert as much pressure as voting strength.

There have also been occasions when co-operation, and the promise of it in the future, has been used as a means of persuasion. In the latter half of the 1970s, for example, trade unions were able to stave off the threat of significant reductions in their power by agreeing to co-operate in the Government's battle against high inflation. The agreement, known as the 'Social Contract', was a clear case of political rewards being used as a successful bargaining counter.

Pressure group classification

We can divide pressure groups into two broad types: interest or sectional groups on the one hand, and ~~promotional~~ ~~groups~~ ~~on~~ ~~the~~ ~~other.~~

Interest or sectional groups

Here a specific part of the population is being represented by a group. Hence we may call it a **sectional group**. It is also known as an **interest group**, in that its role is to further the interests of that section of the population. 'Interests' may involve economic well-being, quality of life, rights, or any other desirable goals.

In some cases, membership of these groups may be restricted only to those whose interests are being pursued, as is the case with trade unions or the motoring organisations. These may be described as **restricted membership groups**. In others, membership may be open to all who are concerned, whether or not they stand to benefit. These have been called **cause groups**, as members often feel they have a duty to campaign for those less fortunate than themselves. **Child Poverty Action Group** and **Age Concern** fall into this sub-category.

A slight complication may occur when groups are concerned with foreign countries, as is the case with **Amnesty International**, which campaigns for political prisoners around the world. However, this should not interfere with the basic distinction.

Some of the UK's principal interest or sectional groups are shown below, together with their main goals.

Principal interest groups in the UK	
Interest group	**Goals**
• Trade unions	• Furthering the interests of specific groups of workers, including better pay, working conditions, pensions, health and safety, employment prospects, job-security and training opportunities.
• Confederation of British industry (CBI)	• Securing economic, industrial and financial policies favourable to British industry. Supporting the interests of British industry in European and world trade bodies.
• Automobile Association (AA)	• Pursuing policies favourable to the private motorist, including road building, road safety measures and lower fuel prices.
• Child Poverty Action Group (CPAG)	• Securing policies favourable to poor families, especially welfare benefits, lower taxation and better housing.
• MIND	• Pursuing the interests of the mentally ill, mainly the provision of research and care facilities.
• National Farmers' Union (NFU)	• Securing treatment beneficial to British farmers, including provision of subsidies, favourable trade agreements and environmental policies. Largely now concerned with the European Union's agricultural policies.
• Countryside Alliance	• Preserving traditional life in rural areas. This includes the defence of fox hunting and seeking financial aid to agriculture.

Promotional or issue groups

These organisations may appeal to all sections of the community, but are concerned with a particular issue or group of related issues. We can further divide them into those groups that are likely to remain **permanent,** since the issue is likely to persist, and those that might be **temporary** because they will disappear when their goals have been achieved. Of course, some organisations might **hope** to be temporary, but lack of success might turn them into permanent campaigns.

Some prominent examples are shown below.

Principal issue groups in the UK	
Permanent issue groups	**Goal(s)**
• Friends of the Earth	• Achievement of policies to improve and protect the natural environment including the protection of endangered animal and plant species and opposition to genetically modified (GM) crops.
• Transport 2000	• Promoting the cause of public transport, securing more public funds and support for such transport.
• Viewers' and Listeners' Association	• Preventing the presentation of explicit sex and violence in public performances, mainly the broadcasting media.
Temporary issue groups	**Goal(s)**
• Campaign for Nuclear Disarmament (CND)	• Securing the worldwide abolition of all nuclear weapons.
• Campaign for Lead-Free Air (CLEAR)	• Achieving the abolition of lead-additives in motor fuel.
• Electoral Reform Society	• Securing a change in the British electoral system to some form of proportional representation.
• Snowdrop Campaign	• The banning of private ownership of handguns, following the Dunblane primary school massacre.
• Animal Liberation front (ALF) • Anti-Vivisection League	• The banning of experimentation on animals.

Pressure groups and parties

What distinguishes a pressure group from a party? The similarities are overwhelming. Both are formal organisations with specific goals, engaged in campaigns to achieve them, often using similar methods and seeking to influence the political system. Yet there are crucial differences.

Attitude to governmental office

Political parties seek governmental office, either alone or in partnership with others. Pressure groups do not. Any pressure group that adopts the aim of achieving government office automatically turns itself into a political party and must change its approach. There may be some confusion where pressure groups put up candidates at elections. Anti-European groups adopted such tactics in the 1990s and local campaign groups have often put up candidates for councils, sometimes successfully. However, this is not the same as running for office. The purpose of such an action is to seek greater publicity, but little more.

Some confusion has been caused by electoral tactics. The **Ecology Party**, which has since become the **Green Party**, has itself been split on the very issue of whether it is a pressure group or a political party. **Sinn Fein**, too, can scarcely hope to gain office with its very restricted aim of the reunification of Ireland, but it fights elections and has regularly won seats in both Dublin and London. The Sinn Fein President, Gerry Adams, refused to take up the seat he had won at Westminster in 1987. Adams lost his seat in the 1992 general election, but after the IRA cease-fire that began in the autumn of 1994, he began negotiations with the Government on behalf of both Sinn Fein and the IRA. Thus he resumed full-scale political activity. He and fellow Sinn Fein candidate Martin McGuinness both won their seats in the 1997 election.

Breadth of aims

Parties must be willing to accept the responsibilities of government, should they be successful at elections. Thus, they must adopt policies across the **whole range** of national concerns. Pressure groups do not have such a problem. They will never seek office and so their aims can be narrower. More importantly still, they do not have to concern themselves with the full potential consequences of their proposals.

In this respect, problems arise in distinguishing between pressure groups and factions **within** parties. Such factions also have relatively narrow aims and may neglect the wider implications of their goals. For example, the Conservative **Bruges Group** campaigns against the UK's closer integration in Europe. Similarly, **trade unions** have institutional links with the Labour Party and so form an internal interest group. However, since these groupings exist within the parties, their members are ultimately hoping to enter government in some respect.

Legal status

Finally, political parties are subject to legal constraints that do not apply to pressure groups. Parties must account for the sources of their funds to reduce the likelihood of undue influence. The way in which they choose their leaders, select candidates and operate within political institutions are all carefully scrutinised and controlled by Parliament and its committees. Pressure groups must, of course, abide by the laws, but they are much more free in the way in which they conduct their internal affairs.

Methods

As we have seen above, pressure groups are more flexible than parties in the methods they can adopt. This means that there is a wide variety of devices used to influence the governing process. These are described below.

Mobilising public support

If a group is to 'catch the eye' of the Government or of Parliament, its most effective method is to demonstrate that there is widespread popular support for its aims. High-profile campaigning, the organisation of public demonstrations and the dissemination of information are all means by which such support may be attracted and then demonstrated to those in power.

The late 1980s anti-Poll Tax movement was a typical example, as was organised opposition to the imposition of VAT on domestic fuel in 1994. A few years before, a huge campaign to stop the closure of coal pits was almost enough to create a reversal of government policy and certainly wrung a number of important concessions from the Department of Trade and Industry. The widespread protests against high petrol duties and the Countryside Alliance's mass campaigns in support of fox-hunting and agricultural support in 2000–1 are more recent examples.

Incorporation or 'insider status'

In the long term, any pressure group is almost guaranteed greater success if it can achieve **incorporation**, or what Professor Wyn Grant has called 'insider status'.

Much government work is carried out through a variety of official committees, staffed by ministers, officials and other invited members. These committees and quangos make key decisions concerning the allocation of expenditure, licensing of various activities and proposed future legislation. If representatives of pressure groups can be incorporated into these bodies, or be regularly consulted by them, they have penetrated the heart of the decision-making process. They have become **insiders**.

Of course, such a status carries responsibilities, but in return pressure groups can expect to be able to exert considerable influence. This applies not only to central government in Whitehall, but also to local government and the European Commission in Brussels.

Examples of groups that have achieved such a status are:

- National Farmers' Union
- Friends of the Earth
- National Trust
- Confederation of British Industry
- Institute of Directors
- Royal Society for the Protection of Birds
- Royal National Institute for the Blind.

Yet more crucially, some groups have achieved the ultimate level of incorporation by becoming government-sponsored bodies themselves. Here, certain interest groups are considered so important that their cause must be represented directly. Such quangos undertake research, propose legislation, organise campaigns and may even enforce laws on behalf of key sections of the community or popular interests. Examples include:

- Equal Opportunities Commission (women)
- Commission for Racial Equality (ethnic minorities)
- Office of Fair Trading (consumers)
- National Heritage (traditional architecture)
- Countryside Commission (environment).

Grant's analysis also identifies groups that are 'outsiders'. These do not have the formal links with political institutions that insiders enjoy. They may be outsiders through choice, as was the case with the Campaign for Nuclear Disarmament (CND), or simply because they have been unable to find acceptance in the political establishment. Greenpeace falls into this latter category.

WPC and animal rights protester outside London's High Court, 12 April 1995

Outsiders tend to concentrate on mobilising public support in order to put pressure on politicians by the sheer force of numbers and opinion. They often take **direct action**, as was the case with the movements against the Poll Tax in the 1980s, against the export of live animals in the 1990s and Greenpeace's attempts to destroy experimental tracts of GM crops in 1999–2000. Demonstrations, civil disobedience, major campaigns in the media and even intimidatory tactics are also typical.

Insider and outsider pressure groups – typical methods

Insiders	Outsiders
• Sponsorship of friendly MPs	• Public demonstrations
• Direct links with ministers	• Petitions
• Participation on official committees	• Campaigns of civil disobedience
• Representation on quangos	• Media campaigns
• Influencing parliamentary standing committees to amend legislation	• Illegal activities to achieve publicity
• Testifying before departmental select committees	

Fighting elections

During the 1997 general elections it became apparent that a new phenomenon was emerging. This was the practice of pressure groups putting up candidates for election. They had no hope of having any of their candidates returned to Parliament, but it meant that they received extensive publicity. The anti-abortion Pro-Life Group adopted this tactic, as did the anti-European movement with the Referendum Party. The formation of single-issue parties like this might become a useful tactic for pressure groups in future.

The most dramatic example of a successful election campaign occurred in 2001. On this occasion, however, it was a local pressure group that was involved. A campaign to stop the closure of Kidderminster Hospital put up a candidate in the Wyre Forest constituency. To the surprise of all but local people, he won a decisive victory. This is likely to encourage other groups in future.

Parliamentary action

Since the nineteenth century, various groups have sought to exercise influence through Parliament. Even as parliamentary influence waned during the twentieth century, it remained as a channel for pressure.

The clearest example of the use of this route occurred in 1900, when the trade union movement formed a Parliamentary Representation Committee with the expressed purpose of opening up a new channel of communication to government. Since then many Labour MPs have continued to be 'sponsored' (in terms of expense payments rather than an extra salary) by trade unions, in return for which it is expected that they will defend and fight for the interests of their union.

In a similar way, other MPs often receive retainers in return for representation of a whole variety of interests and causes. These include large businesses, employer groups, professional associations, promotional pressure groups, foreign governments and sports associations.

In recent years there has been a growth in the number and activities of professional political lobbying organisations. These lobbyists organise parliamentary exposure by MPs on behalf of smaller groups and companies that could not make such arrangements themselves. In 1994 the extent of their activities was highlighted by revelations of payments to MPs in return for asking questions in the House in order to draw attention to particular issues on behalf of external groups. Although this practice infringes the rules of the House of Commons, it was clear that similar, more acceptable practices were common.

MPs have a variety of means of raising an issue or promoting an interest group. Asking questions of ministers is common, but speeches during debates, special motions proposed during gaps in parliamentary procedures and direct meetings with officials and ministers are also used. The only truly effective form of parliamentary action is the passage of a Private Member's Bill. Time for such bills is scarce and the Government has a number of ways to thwart them. Nevertheless, successful reform of laws relating to homosexuality (led by Edwina Currie MP) and to abortion (David Alton MP) in the 1990s demonstrates that pressure groups can succeed through the parliamentary route.

Very occasionally, pressure groups have also succeeded in thwarting a government itself by organising a sufficiently large back-bench revolt to defeat proposed legislation. Unions were successful in preventing legislative reform in 1969 by mobilising enough Labour MPs to oppose their leadership before the measures known as 'In Place of Strife' were presented to the House of Commons. More dramatically, a combination of church and union groups organised the defeat of a Bill to allow Sunday trading in 1986, the only defeat of the second reading of a Government Bill since the Second World War.

During the later years of the 1990s, the House of Lords also emerged as fertile ground for pressure group campaigns. Campaigns against the repeal of Clause 28, concerning the inclusion of homosexual issues in education, against a ban on fox hunting, against the reduction in the use of trial by jury and for the strengthening of freedom of information provisions were all carried out in the Lords. In each case, considerable success was achieved. Measures have been dropped, postponed or seriously amended as a result.

When most of the hereditary peers lost their voting rights in 1999, the House enjoyed a rise in its authority and pressure groups recognised this. When the Government has a decisive majority in the Commons, as occurred after 1997, it is inevitable that attention swings to the Lords as the main potential opposition to government. As the hereditary peers disappeared, there was also a corresponding increase in the appointment of life peers. Some of these represent important interests, so even greater influence may be channelled in this direction. Lord Winston, one of the most eminent medical authorities of his day, for example, certainly went some way to encouraging higher health service expenditure when he criticised the Government (the same government that had appointed him!) for its lack of progress in improving medical services. Within a few months the Chancellor announced large increases in NHS spending.

Media campaigns

As part of the mobilisation process, the media provide a useful tool in that both the public and the decision-makers themselves may be influenced. Most significantly, the impact of TV and radio programmes can be decisive. Certainly various environmental pressure groups have been able to attract support in this way.

An essential ingredient in such campaigns is the gathering of information and data to support a group's aims. Such research material is often presented in TV, radio and press features. Issues relating to the environment, smoking, cruelty to animals and transport have all been successfully treated in this way. Celebrities are also an effective addition to these campaigns. Sir Cliff Richard (Viewers' and Listeners' Association, abortion law), Sir Ian McKellen (homosexual law reform and AIDS issues) and the actor Lord Rix (the mentally handicapped) have all fronted high-profile issues.

Direct lobbying

Not only MPs but also leaders of pressure groups and, in some cases, members *en masse* may seek to present their case directly to relevant ministers. Rallies and petitions may be organised, as well as private meetings with the minister concerned or with senior officials. In practice, however, such methods can be significant only if they achieve sufficient exposure to swing public opinion behind the cause.

Why do pressure groups succeed or fail?

As use of the Internet expands, there are new opportunities for pressure and interest groups to mount major campaigns. Furthermore, this is a relatively inexpensive way of mobilising public support for an issue. Governments are now willing to receive e-mails from the public and some politicians have agreed to engage in active dialogue through the medium. Even the Prime Minister, Tony Blair, has subjected himself to electronic questioning. This may be where the future lies.

Size

This may seem obvious at first sight. Clearly, a government is more likely to respond to pressure by large groups simply because there are more potential votes to be won or lost. Thus, such sectional interests as those of motorists or home owners can expect favourable treatment.

Yet the evidence is confusing. During the 1980s, for example, trade unions (total membership about 8 million) and pensioners (about 25 per cent of the population) did not appear to enjoy any political advantage at all. Indeed, in both cases, these large groups suffered considerable discomfort at the hands of ministers.

Government support

The answer to this paradox lies in the question of which party is in government at any particular time. The Government is more likely to be influenced by large numbers of its **own potential supporters** who make up a pressure group's membership. It was, for example, hardly surprising that Conservative administrations of the 1980s and 1990s were unsympathetic to unions as not many of their members were likely to be Conservatives! Home owners, on the other hand, are predominantly Tory supporters and so had to be nurtured.

Some pressure groups will, therefore, expect better treatment from one party than from another. And success or failure will depend largely upon the philosophy of the government in power.

Groups likely to be favoured by a particular party	
Conservative	**Labour**
• National Farmers' Union • CBI • Institute of Directors • Large companies • Financial institutions • Higher income groups • Anti-Europe groups	• Trade unions • Caring professions • Poorer families • Single-parent groups • Education groups • Health Service workers • Pensioner groups • Pro-Europe groups • Groups supporting constitutional reform

Some groups that would be best served by the Liberal Party – those favouring constitutional reform, greater protection for individual rights, open government and environmental protection – are, thus, disadvantaged.

Finance

It is a further truism that finance is a crucial factor. It is also possibly the most controversial issue in this area. The availability of funds does not necessarily indicate numerical strength, nor does it say anything about the justice of a particular argument.

There has been considerable disquiet concerning the financial muscle of large companies such as those producing tobacco, public utilities like gas and electricity, the large brewers and motor manufacturers, retail groups and oil companies. The same can be said of trade unions, which have use of huge quantities of finance raised in subscriptions from their members.

On the one hand, funds can be used to finance political parties and so receive sympathetic treatment. On the other, pressure groups are able to mount expensive campaigns in support of their aims. It is often claimed, for example, that the consistent refusal by governments to ban all advertising on cigarettes is the result of lobbying on a large scale by the big tobacco companies. The same claims are made concerning the lack of action to break the brewers' virtual monopoly over public houses.

Organisation

Inevitably, when pressure groups first come into existence they suffer from a variety of disadvantages. They have no public profile, might lack financial resources and have not established formal links with government bodies.

What they need, therefore, is a strong organisation to achieve all these aims before their cases can be properly presented. Those groups that are able to build up such a strong organisation are at a great advantage over less formal, less organised movements. Some of the important features of the well-organised pressure group are:

- a network for the recruitment of members
- an organised system for raising funds
- research facilities and staff
- decision-making procedures established and widely accepted
- a strong management structure to give policy direction
- established methods for creating publicity
- formal links established with government bodies and/or Parliament.

The fuel lobby, which opposed high petrol duties in autumn 2000, certainly impressed with its level of logistical organisation. The use of the internet on this occasion enabled the campaign to organise a large number of protesters all over the country in a very short time.

Strategic position

Some sectional groups enjoy special status on the grounds that the community is especially reliant upon them. Those who run emergency services are a clear example, but so too are those who supply households and industry with energy and those who produce our food.

In a similar way, there are those on whom government itself relies in order to implement key policies. Trade unions used to hold such a position before their status was seriously undermined by the dramatic reforms of the 1980s. Large businesses and commercial enterprises still do. The banks, financial institutions and the City of London are important factors in the success or failure of financial policy. The co-operation of the farming community, too, is vital to the success of policies related to food production and prices, and the preservation of the countryside.

Key strategic groups that may use their position to exert influence include:

- industries employing large numbers of workers
- firms and unions involved in energy production
- businesses which account for large export volumes
- police, medical and emergency service personnel
- organisations supplying important information to government.

Public opinion

For a variety of reasons, including successful campaigns by pressure groups themselves, public opinion might swing towards a particular issue. As we have seen above, politicians are inevitably sensitive to such movements. Thus, a combination of an effective campaign together with a sympathetic public is a potent combination.

In recent years a number of important policy changes and developments have been the result of such circumstances. For example:

- equal pay for women
- controls over experimentation on animals
- reducing the age of consent for homosexuals to eighteen
- various incentives to reduce harmful vehicle exhaust emissions
- relaxation of the alcohol licensing laws
- small reductions in fuel duties.

Strength of opposition

Pressure groups have been portrayed as simply confronting government with their demands and goals. However, it is often the case that two or more groups are ranged against each other. In these circumstances, the role of the Government may simply be to act as arbiter between competing claims.

Some recent examples of such contests may illustrate this feature:

- animal rights campaigners   v.   the fur trade
- the anti-smoking lobby   v.   the tobacco industry
- the Campaign for Real Ale   v.   the large breweries
- the League Against Cruel Sports v.   the Countryside Alliance
- Transport 2000   v.   the motorcar industry

The result of these struggles, in which the weapons used are a selection of those campaign methods described above, will depend upon both the effectiveness of action and the attitude of the Government of the day. However, it is clear that in some cases like those shown above, the dice are seriously loaded in favour of one of the combatants.

Factors determining the effectiveness of pressure groups
1. Size of membership
2. Which party is in power
3. How much finance is at their disposal
4. How well they are organised
5. How strategic their position is in society or government
6. Whether public opinion is sympathetic
7. Whether there are powerful groups in opposition to their aims

Pluralism, corporatism and democracy

Pluralism The dominance of political parties in Parliament and government in the

importance of pressure groups in our society.

The duopoly of party control had meant that most demands and aspirations within the community were channelled through the parties. Issues came to be seen in adversarial terms – Government versus Opposition, Conservative versus Labour, middle-class demands versus working-class demands. Politicians largely claimed to represent the interests of either one of the great social classes or, alternatively, of the whole nation.

The combination of such dualism and party government left little room for the many competing interests and demands that characterise modern politics. That is not to say that there were no attempts to persuade politicians of either main party to take up a particular cause or interest, but such activities were relatively insignificant in comparison to the great issues that divided the parties.

After the Second World War, the picture began to change. The influence of social class on politics began to wane, the political system became more open and the dominance of party doctrine was reduced. Between 1940 and 1980, in the era of 'consensus politics' when there were relatively few differences between the policies of the main parties, party leaders concentrated on seeking general, or 'consensus', support for their policies. This search for consensus inevitably led to wide consultation with groups representing different interests and views. The dualism of the party system was being replaced by a 'pluralist' environment wherein group, rather than class, interests were generally considered.

Growing prosperity was a further factor in the growth of pluralism. The activities of individuals widened, there was greater access to information, especially with the advent of TV, and an increased awareness that it was possible to exert influence on political leaders.

Even when ideological politics returned under Margaret Thatcher in the 1980s, the greater individualism proliferating in modern society ensured that group membership and activity would continue to grow. Group membership empowered individuals who had previously felt alienated by the party system. Governments have had to respond to these developments and have done so by accepting the pluralistic nature of modern society.

> '*Government, then, has to contend with a society which, in terms of organised interests, is more rather than less pluralist. Furthermore, it has to operate in a political environment in which power is more dispersed than before.*'
> Philip Norton, *New Directions in British Politics*, 1991

Corporatism A number of factors after 1940 led to a period during which the important pressure groups in society were steadily integrated or **incorporated** into the governing process. This process came to be known as 'corporatism'. The factors included:

- the growth of pluralism described above
- the increasing complexity of the governing process, requiring increased information and co-operation from external groups
- the leadership of a group of politicians, including Macmillan, Butler and Gaitskell, who accepted the need for such incorporation
- an understanding that parties alone could not secure widespread acceptance of policy initiatives.

As a result, a number of institutions were set up to accommodate the new corporatist spirit. Most prominent was the **National Economic Development Council** (NEDC), set up in 1961 by Harold Macmillan to discuss economic and industrial policy. Its members included union leaders, business people, civil servants and ministers. In addition, a wide range of **official committees** came into being, with similar membership structures. Group interests were, thus, officially recognised.

The corporatist era largely ended in the 1980s. Successive Conservative governments disbanded hundreds of committees and quangos through which group interests had been represented. The abolition of the NEDC was the most symbolic gesture, but it could not alter an important truth. Although pressure groups had lost many of their seats on official bodies, their influence could not be denied.

Pressure groups and democracy

As long ago as the 1830s, the French writer **Alexis de Tocqueville** (1805–59) expressed the view that intermediate groups in a society were an essential feature of an effective democracy. Should a people fail to organise themselves into an active **civil society** – his collective term for such groups – they become vulnerable to the power of the centralised government. In a modern context, this would imply that the community needs pressure groups to counterbalance the enormously enhanced power of a modern state.

Since Tocqueville, it has become an accepted feature of modern democratic theory that the pluralism represented by pressure group activity must flourish. Indeed, American political scientists in the 1950s and 1960s, such as David Trueman, analysed democracy almost exclusively in terms of the peaceful interplay between such groups.

> *'The total pattern of government over a period of time thus presents a protean complex of crisscrossing relationships that change in strength and direction with alternations in the power and standing of interests, organised and unorganised.'*
> David Trueman, *The Governmental Process*, 1952

However, although pressure group activity appears to serve democracy in a positive way, there are some suggestions that they can operate in opposition to democratic principles. Both sides of the argument are summarised on page 146.

Pressure groups and democracy	
Pressure groups as positive elements in democracy	**Pressure groups as threats to democracy**
• They act as an effective channel of communication between the governed and the Government. They articulate demands and mobilise support for them.	• They can be seen as vehicles for 'vested interests', only concerned with their own welfare and ignoring the broader good of the whole community.
• They provide wide opportunities for people to participate actively in the political process without having to devote excessive amounts of time to such activity.	• Some groups might wield disproportionate amounts of influence as a result of financial resources and links with political parties. This influence might be out of proportion to their true importance in society. Both trade unions and big business have been accused of posing such a threat to the democratic process.
• They ensure that minority groups and interests are represented within the political system.	• Pressure groups themselves might not be internally democratic. The views expressed by their leaders might not reflect those of their members. Unlike the political system itself, which contains democratic guarantees – especially methods of ensuring responsibility – pressure groups may adopt their own internal system. Thus, they might become merely reflections of **elitism** rather than true pluralism. Until the reforms of the 1980s trade unions were again suspected of such undemocratic practices, but the same could be argued of the **Automobile Associations** (private motorists), the **British Medical Association** (doctors) and the **Football Association**, none of which has a well-developed system for consulting its supporters.
• They can act as important checks on the power of the state by mobilising opposition to measures acting against the interests of sections of the community.	
• They help to ensure stability by institutionalising peaceful political conflict, so preventing possible disorder and violence.	

Thus, the case is fairly balanced. Whichever argument holds more truth, there is no doubt that pressure groups have become a central and permanent feature of modern pluralist, liberal democracies.

Future challenges for pressure groups

Europe
Important decision-making processes are steadily being transferred from London to Brussels. This implies two things for pressure groups. One is, clearly, that they must shift some of their operations to the European Commission and the European Parliament. The other is that they must ally themselves with their counterparts in other member countries. This is already occurring.

All large industrial trade unions are affiliated to European federations. The Social Chapter of the Maastricht agreement of 1993 is testament to the influence of these huge organisations. It has improved working conditions, employment protection and other fringe benefits for many millions of workers. A similar development has occurred within the environmental lobby. The European **Green Movement** even boasts representatives in the European Parliament. The movement has made considerable progress in such areas as sea pollution, harmful industrial emissions (including 'greenhouse' gases) and river quality. Some, though fewer, advances have been achieved in the treatment of live farm animals.

Possibly the most powerful of the 'European lobbies' is also the longest established: that is, agriculture. This influential group has succeeded in retaining the **Common Agricultural Policy**, which is designed largely to protect farming groups, despite widespread opposition. It has also succeeded in holding back agreements on a freer world trade system in primary foods. Such an agreement would damage some sections of European agriculture that rely upon tariff protection.

Add to these groups the great industrial complexes, such as steel, motors, oil and gas, shipbuilding and engineering, and we see a picture of increasingly Europeanised pressure group activity. If and when European integration increases, many other lobby groups will have to respond in similar ways.

Ideology
The 1980s saw the return of ideological politics throughout Europe. This style of politics conflicts in some ways with the kind of pluralistic political environment within which group influence may flourish. Governments that take an inflexible, dogmatic approach to policy making are less likely to be influenced by group pressure.

The privatisation of large industries is a case in point. The many vested interests that sought to retain state ownership – particularly trade unions and consumers – were unable to resist the ideological push for such developments. The same has been true of attacks made on aspects of the welfare state. Large interests representing welfare recipients could not compete with the determination of governments to reduce public expenditure and so find scope for tax cutting.

Even some monopoly businesses, traditionally some of the most influential groups, were forced to accept a more competitive trading environment. Public utilities such as electricity, gas, broadcasting and energy production have had to accept compulsory liberalisation measures.

There were signs in the 1990s that ideological rule was weakening and that new consensus, pluralist-style politics would return. In 1994, for example, attempts to privatise the British Post Office were defeated following persistent lobbying. There were also indications that attacks on the welfare system are being stemmed by a combi~~~~~~ ~~ ~~tense lobbying and the in~~~~~~~ ~~ ~~~~ ~~~~~ opinion.

~~ ~~ ~~~~~ that pressure groups must meet the challenges posed by ideologically based governments and there are also signs that they are succeeding after many years of difficulty.

Communications

The explosion in communications technology that is now occurring is less of a threat, more of an opportunity for pressure groups. There is now considerably more access available to the public through new information technology.

Those groups that succeed in harnessing these opportunities to mobilise public support and disseminate information will be the most successful. Not only has there been an expansion in media communications, but also there will be more direct access into people's homes. Pressure groups will learn from the commercial world that the future must lie with these channels of greater communication.

The decline in party identification

Since the 1970s, researchers have noted a marked decline in what is known as 'party alignment': that is, the extent to which people identify with the image and goals of a particular party. There is therefore an opportunity for pressure groups to fill this vacuum of political identification.

To a large extent this has already occurred. As party membership has been steadily declining, membership of pressure groups has increased dramatically. By 1994 membership of the Conservative Party had fallen below one million for the first time since the Second World War, while Labour constituency membership had fallen to an estimated 500,000 from a high point of about one million in the 1960s. Meanwhile, pressure group membership has steadily grown, especially in the environmental field. The 65,000 strength of the Ramblers' Association nearly matches that of the Liberal Democrat Party, while the 540,000 membership of the Royal Society for the Protection of Birds compares well with the two main parties' strength.

It is clear that people's aspirations, goals, concerns and interests are now often served by pressure group activity, rather than by identification with one of the main political parties.

Citizenship

Pressure and interest groups are part of what is often described as **civil society**. Civil society incorporates all the various groups to which people may owe allegiance. They lie between the citizen and the state and are vital in preventing totalitarian rule developing. It may also be true that, in an increasingly individualistic society, they provide a sense of collective identity for people. These phenomena are considered crucial to modern democracy by supporters of Labour's 'Third Way'.

Third Way supporters fear that too much individualism will remove the sense of responsibility that is necessary to hold society together. A free and active civil society can provide a kind of 'cement' to prevent a lack of order. Legitimate pressure groups are, therefore, being encouraged. The **active citizen**, who does have a sense of responsibility to the local and national community, can express and practise that responsibility through such groups.

For exam questions relevant to this unit, see page 555.

Electoral systems

The UK's system for general elections, although having much in common with the US Congressional arrangements, is now relatively rare among democratic states. It is known officially as 'simple majority in single member constituencies', but the more common description is 'first-past-the-post'.

The current British general election system

It is, perhaps, the simplest general election system that can be adopted. Each parliamentary constituency returns a single MP who is elected by a **plurality**: that is, whoever gains the most votes, wins. This can also be described as a 'simple majority'. A few salient points should be noted at this stage:

- Each constituent has only one vote.
- There is no need for a winning candidate to win an absolute majority (i.e. over 50 per cent of the vote).
- Voters have no say in which candidate shall be proposed by any party.

The effects of the British system

We must review the results of recent general elections if we are to draw conclusions from them. These are shown below.

General election results, October 1974–92 (not including Northern Ireland)		
3 May 1979		
Party	**Seats won**	**% of votes won***
Conservative	339	43.9
Labour	269	36.9
Liberal	11	13.8
Scottish Nationalist	2	17.3
Plaid Cymru	2	8.1
Others	0	1.1
9 June 1983		
Conservative	397	42.4
Labour	209	27.6
Liberal/SDP Alliance	23	25.4
Scottish Nationalist	2	11.8
Plaid Cymru	2	7.8
Others	0	0.7

General election results, 1987–2001 (not including Northern Ireland)		
11 June 1987		
Conservative	376	43.4
Labour	229	31.7
Liberal/SDP Alliance	22	23.2
Scottish Nationalist	3	14.0
Plaid Cymru	3	7.3
Others	0	0.5
9 April 1992		
Conservative	336	42.3
Labour	271	35.2
Liberal Democrat	20	18.3
Scottish Nationalist	3	21.5
Plaid Cymru	4	8.8
Others	0	1.0
1 May 1997		
Conservative	165	31.0
Labour	418	44.5
Liberal Democrat	46	17.0
Scottish Nationalist	6	22.5
Plaid Cymru	4	10.0
Others	1**	3.1
7 June 2001		
Conservative	166	31.7
Labour	413	40.7
Liberal Democrat	52	18.3
Scottish Nationalist	5	20.1
Plaid Cymru	4	14.3
Others	19	6.8

* In the cases of the Scottish Nationalists and Plaid Cymru the percentages relate only to Scotland and Wales respectively.
** Martin Bell, an independent anti-corruption candidate.
Source: Based on D. Butler and J. Butler, *British Political Facts 1900–94* (Macmillan, 1995).

Some immediate observations can be made:

• 'Others', which now include mainly Green Party and Referendum Party candidates and the neo-Nazis, have made no significant inroads into gaining voters and are, therefore, scarcely a factor in the results.
• The Liberals, including when they were part of the Alliance with the Social Democrat Party and since they have become Liberal Democrats, are consistently **under-represented** by the system. The starkest result occurred in 1983 when the Alliance (25.4 per cent) was only just beaten by Labour (27.6 per cent) in terms of share of the vote. In

seats, however, Labour (209) won nearly ten times as many as the Alliance (23). In 1992 the Liberal Democrats won over 18 per cent of the total votes, but were awarded only 3 per cent of the seats (20 out of 651). The 1997 general election saw an upturn in their fortunes when tactical voting made the system work in their favour; although their share of the vote actually fell slightly to 17 per cent, they won 46 seats, over twice as many as in 1992.

- Both main parties are **over-represented**. If we study the 1983 result again, we can see that if Labour had been awarded the same percentage of the seats as the percentage of votes that is won, it would have received 179 seats. In fact it received 209. The Conservatives did even better out of the system. They would have won 276 seats on a strict percentage basis, but actually won 397. Interestingly, in 1992 the Conservatives won many fewer seats – down to 336 – although the proportion of the votes they won hardly changed from 1983. Thus, the **disproportionality** of the system is uneven from one election to the next.

- The effect on the nationalist parties is mixed. Taking 1997, it becomes plain that the Scottish Nationalists lost out because of the nature of the system. They gained 22.5 per cent of the Scottish vote, but only 8 per cent of the seats. The Welsh Nationalists (Plaid Cymru), however, did well. Their 10 per cent of the Welsh vote was converted into 10 per cent of the seats available (4 out of 38). The reasons for this apparent anomaly will become apparent below.

- It is even possible for there to be a 'wrong-way-round' result, where a party wins less total votes than its nearest rival, but still wins the election in terms of seats. This occurred in 1929, 1951 and February 1974.

Having established some immediate conclusions, we must look beyond the figures to make some deeper observations.

Charles Kennedy, leader of the Liberal Democrats, after voting in the General Election, June 2001

Safe seats   We may define a 'safe seat' as one where it is extremely unlikely that party control will change hands at a general election. That is, the sitting MP, or a replacement from the same party, is assured of re-election. In the absence of a ~~strict definition of the term 'safe'~~, no exact number of safe seats can be calculated. However, the figure is probably as high as 60 per cent. The reasons for the existence of so many safe seats are twofold. Either one party is always dominant because of the social make-up of the area (i.e. heavily industrial and much poverty = Labour; middle class, wealthy = Conservative), or the opposition to one party is consistently split between the two other main parties.

It should be noted, however, that in by-elections caused by the death, resignation or retirement of an MP between general elections, there is no such thing as a safe seat. Normal voting patterns do not apply and, in theory, any large party may win. Indeed, it is often the governing party that suffers most. After the 1992 election, the Conservatives found themselves incapable of winning **any** by-elections, they were so unpopular. Huge Conservative majorities were overturned on several occasions. This occurred in formerly rock-solid Tory seats such as Eastleigh in 1994 and Christchurch in 1993.

This high proportion of inevitable constituency results in general elections is possibly the most worrying aspect of the electoral system. It means that the majority of voters who live in such constituencies cannot influence the result of the election at all. Their votes are, in short, worthless. Whichever party they choose to support, the overwhelming level of voting for the dominant party in the locality will swamp their own decision. Only in more 'marginal' seats, where there is a realistic chance of a change of party hands, do individual voters feel genuinely empowered. Their vote then does count. But marginal seats are a minority.

Vote counting

The 1997 general election highlighted the tendency of the system to exaggerate a party's victory. Although Labour won only a slightly larger proportion of the vote than the Conservatives had in 1992, it won 82 more seats! This was a Labour landslide in terms of seats, but Labour still won only a minority of the popular vote. However, the Liberal Democrats won over twice as many seats as they had in 1992 (20 up to 46) on a similar share of the vote – an anomaly caused by increased tactical voting.

Differential voting values

We have already seen that a vote in a marginal seat is effectively worth much more than one in a safe seat. We can go further, however, by examining all the votes for the parties. The table below illustrates the point.

2001 general election			
Party	Votes won	Seats won	Votes per seat
Conservative	8,355,267	166	50,333
Labour	10,740,168	413	26,001
Liberal Democrat	4,815,249	52	92,601

The figures demonstrate that it takes, on average, many more Liberal Democrat votes to elect an MP than votes for the other two large parties. This may be interpreted as indicating that each Liberal Democrat vote is worth considerably less than its counterpart for Labour or the Conservatives. Thus, say critics of the system, the principle of 'one-person-one-vote' is distorted in reality by the unequal value of votes.

Falkirk by-election winner, Eric Joyce (Labour) in December 2000

Concentration of party support

The reason why the two main parties profit from the UK's 'first-past-the-post' system is that they enjoy concentrated pockets of support in certain areas. The Liberal Democrats, by contrast, find their ~~tered most~~ ~~across the country.~~

The point may be demonstrated by an absurd, but nevertheless instructive illustration. If every party found that its level of support, as demonstrated in the 2001 general election, was exactly matched in every constituency, Labour would win every seat! The result in each constituency in 2001 would have been as follows:

Candidate A (Labour)	40.7%
Candidate B (Conservative)	31.7%
Candidate C (Lib. Dem.)	18.3%
Others	9.3%

Thus the Labour Party scoop the pool!

Of course, the reality is different. In some places, Labour has concentrated support and so wins most of the seats on offer. Yet the figures can illustrate well what happens to the Liberal Democrats and Scottish Nationalists, who do tend to find the kind of result shown above replicated up and down the country. The areas where they have concentrated support (the West Country for the Liberal Democrats, a variety of localities for the SNP) are few and far between. It is an anomaly that Plaid Cymru, though a small party, benefits because it is a characteristic of Welsh nationalism that it is largely confined to small areas in both the north and south of the principality.

The table below, extracting regional results from the 2001 election, indicates how support for various parties tends to be concentrated in some areas.

2001 general election results by region (seats won)				
Region	**Cons.**	**Labour**	**Lib. Dem.**	**Scots Nats**	**Plaid Cymru**
London	13	55	6		
South-east	73	35	9		
South-west	20	16	15		
West Midlands	13	43	2		
East Midlands	15	28	1		
Yorks. and Humberside	7	47	2		
East Anglia	14	7	1		
North	3	32	1		
North-west	1	60	3		
Scotland	1	56	10	5	
Wales	0	34	2		4

Source: *Observer*, 4 May 1997

Tactical voting   A tactical vote is one that is cast by a voter, not for their preferred party, but for another that they feel has a better chance of winning a seat. Tactical voters normally do this to keep out the candidate of a party that they particularly oppose. Typically, this might be a Liberal Democrat voter supporting a Conservative candidate because she knows her preferred choice has absolutely no chance of winning, but she wants Labour to lose at all costs. So she switches her vote. A number of other combinations can be identified.

As we have seen, the poor showing of smaller parties might lead to large numbers of their supporters defecting because they do not wish to waste their vote. There are no second choices in the British system, so tactical voters are simply trying to make their vote count.

In the 1997 and 2001 general elections, tactical voting was encouraged in critical seats by both Labour and the Liberal Democrats, as well as some newspapers. This resulted in significant gains by the Liberal Democrat Party, which increased its seats at both elections without a significant increase in its popular vote. To balance this, Labour also made gains as Liberal Democrat supporters supported them to oust apparently safe Conservative MPs. In this way Michael Portillo, a right-wing Conservative Cabinet minister, lost the apparently safe seat of Southgate/Enfield.

A further kind of tactical vote is the **negative vote**. This occurs when a voter chooses to support one party simply as a way of indicating opposition to another. He or she may not support the party for which the vote is cast, but is simply determined to keep another candidate out. A lifetime Conservative supporter, for example, may be dissatisfied with the Government's performance and so wish to punish them by supporting Labour or the Liberal Democrats. This phenomenon is most commonly seen in by-elections.

> 'Tactical voting matters because its existence carries a message about the voting system ... it is a symptom of the flaws in the electoral system rather than the root of the problem.'
>
> Helena Catt, 'Tactical Voting in Britain' in
> *Parliamentary Affairs* (October 1989)

Government formation   The most important feature of the British system is its ability to produce decisive outcomes in general elections. This is, of course, at the expense of any sense of fairness towards smaller parties and of giving voters a reasonable degree of choice. Nevertheless, for many this is an acceptable trade-off – clear results in exchange for equity. A review of all the results since 1945 illustrates how the system works.

It can be seen from the table on page 156 that in every election one of the main parties won an overall majority, with the exception of the election of February 1974. That election resulted in a government which was largely powerless, so a fresh election had to be called within a few months. There have, too, been some close calls, notably in 1950, 1951, 1964 and October 1974, but at least a single-party government could be formed.

Election	Winning party	Size of majority
1945	Labour	+146
1950	Labour	+5
1951	Conservative	+17
1955	Conservative	+58
1959	Conservative	+100
1964	Labour	+4
1966	Labour	+96
1970	Conservative	+30
1974 (Feb.)	Labour	−33
1974 (Oct.)	Labour	+3
1979	Conservative	+43
1983	Conservative	+144
1987	Conservative	+102
1992	Conservative	+21
1997	Labour	+179
2001	Labour	+167

Source: Based on D. Butler and J. Butler, *British Political Facts 1900–94* (Macmillan, 1995).

Advantages of first-past-the-post

Before examining the advantages of the British system, a word of warning is required. This is an electoral system operating in the UK and it cannot be separated from the broader political structure. Any conclusions, therefore, can only be applied in the UK. It is important to bear in mind that there is a dominant two-party system, that we expect governments to be drawn from a single party and that we expect to be represented by an MP who clearly represents the community in which we live. The advantages are, therefore, identified in relation to such political principles:

- It is an extremely easy system to understand. Voters have one choice and, on the whole, understand that they are voting for an MP of a particular party and, by implication, a party that they may wish to see in government.
- It produces clear, usually decisive results, as we have seen above. There is rarely uncertainty after an election; one party is normally able to form a government without any hiatus. This is often contrasted with such countries as Italy or Israel, where government formation is frequently difficult as a result of indecisive results and no party being large enough to govern alone.
- The fact that a single party usually wins outright means that the doctrine of mandate and manifesto can operate. This means that parties campaign in elections with a clear manifesto and, if they win, there is no doubt that they have the authority to implement the manifesto. This cannot be said of multiparty government (i.e. coalitions). Voters

can never be certain of which policies, proclaimed by their favourite party, will be retained and which will be dropped during coalition-forming negotiations. It has been strongly argued that in the UK at least 40–45 per cent of the electorate support a specific set of policies adopted by the winning party. With the uncertainties of coalition government and a set of hybrid policies being adopted, **nobody** has voted for the final package.

- There is a strong traditional link between British communities and their MPs. Constituents expect that their MP will represent their interests, irrespective of party allegiance, both in Parliament and directly to the Government. The single-member constituency system safeguards this link.

Disadvantages of the British system

Many of the problems have been described above, or are implied by the figures. Nevertheless, some key points may be emphasised:

- The system is clearly unfair. It discriminates against small parties and does not give equal value to all votes.
- It encourages tactical voting, where voters feel forced into voting for a party they do not support, simply to have a say in the outcome.
- Electors do not have the opportunity to discriminate between candidates from the same party. They must put up with the choice made by a relatively small group of party activists.
- Though the system does produce a single MP to represent constituents, it could be argued that people would prefer to have a representative from the party they support.

In addition to these issues, there is a good deal of controversy concerning the relative merits of single-party government, which is almost guaranteed by the current system, and coalitions, which would almost certainly result if some form of proportional representation were to be introduced in the UK. Such arguments will be analysed after some alternative systems have been considered below.

Alternative systems

The British general election arrangement is known as a **plurality** system. We can divide alternative electoral systems into two other types – these are **majority** systems and **proportional** systems. We can study these in turn.

Majority voting systems

It should be emphasised that these systems are **not** strictly proportional representation, even though the results they produce tend to be slightly more proportional than first-past-the-post. There are three, which are very similar to each other both in the way they work and in the results they tend to produce.

The alternative vote (AV)   Used to elect the Australian House of Representatives, this is like the British general election system in that voters have to return one candidate to represent each constituency. Instead of having one vote, however, as in first-past-the-post, they may place all the candidates in order of preference. If any candidate receives over 50 per cent of **first choice** votes, he or she is automatically elected. If, however, no candidate achieves 50 per cent, the **second preferences** of

the bottom candidate are added to see if anyone can achieve an overall majority. If not, the next lowest candidate's second choices are added and so on until one person has over 50 per cent of the votes. In other words, the successful candidate will b~~~ ~~~~~~~~

even if this is not a majority of first choices.

The system is simple and ensures majority candidates. It helps small party candidates to some, but not a great extent. Therefore it can still produce decisive results as the British system does. But it does give voters more choice and fewer votes are wasted under the system.

The supplementary vote (SV)   Very similar to AV, this system is normally used to elect one single official. It was the method used to elect London's first democratic mayor. Voters have just two choices – first and second. Again, if a candidate wins over 50 per cent of first choices, he or she is elected. However, if not, the top two candidates 'run off'. The second preferences are added to the firsts and one of the two must win. Like AV it ensures majority support for the winner.

The Second Ballot   Used in France, this system is very like the supplementary vote. However, voters only choose one candidate in the first ballot. If anyone gains 50 per cent, they win. If not, a second ballot is held, normally a week later. Usually the top two candidates run off against each other, but now voters are completely free to change either their first or their second choice allegiance. As there are only two candidates left, one of them must win an overall majority. The system favours a three- or four-party contest, but very small parties do not tend to benefit. In France, it has tended to give extreme parties such as the Communists and the National Front some representation in Parliament.

Proportional representation systems (PR)

These are a group of methods, all of which are designed to produce a result that reflects reasonably accurately the proportion of support enjoyed by each political party. PR systems abound. These are the main ones.

Single transferable vote (STV)   This system is used to elect the Republic of Ireland parliament and the Northern Ireland Assembly and local councils. It is a complex system, but one that maximises voter choice. Constituencies are multi-member: normally there are between three and five seats available in each (clearly constituencies tend to be larger than single-member systems). Parties may therefore submit any number of candidates up to the number of seats available. The voters may place all the candidates in their order of preference. They may choose candidates from different parties, show a preference between candidates of the **same** party, or simply follow the advice of the parties and stick to one party's list in the order they recommend. Thereafter the election proceeds in a number of stages:

- The total number of votes cast is counted.
- A 'droop quota' is calculated: the quota is the number of votes plus one divided by the number of seats available plus one.
- Any candidate who achieves the quota on **first preference** votes is elected.
- Thereafter second and subsequent votes are added until all the necessary candidates have achieved the quota.

An example from an Republic of Ireland constituency in 1997 will illustrate the system.

Constituency: Carlow-Kilkenny Quota: 9,409 Seats: 5 First preference votes cast (party in brackets)	
Aylward (Fianna Fail)	11,849
Hogan (Fine Gael)	9,642
Browne (Fine Gael)	6,834
McGuinness (Fianna Fail)	5,990
Nolan (Fianna Fail)	5,975
Pattison (Labour)	5,578
Gibbons (Progressive Democrat)	3,184
White (Green)	3,116
Townsend (Labour)	2,995
Quinn (National)	870
Nolan (Independent)	416
Candidates elected after second and subsequent preferences added	
Aylward (Fianna Fail)	
Hogan (Fine Gael)	
Browne (Fine Gael)	
Pattison (Labour)	
McGuinness (Fianna Fail)	

We can draw a number of conclusions from these interesting figures:

- Had this been five separate constituencies, it seems likely that Fianna Fail would have won three seats, Labour and Fine Gael one each. In other words, the system enabled Labour to win a seat and avoided the over-representation of Fianna Fail.
- Pattison was beaten by Nolan on first preferences, but was still elected owing to a better performance of second and subsequent preferences.
- There was good support for independents (though none was actually elected in this case).

The general conclusions we can draw about the effects of STV are as follows:

- It awards seats more proportionally than first-past-the-post.
- Voters have a great deal more choice. Second and subsequent preferences count and they can show a preference between candidates of the same party.
- Independents and small parties do well. Though none were elected in Carlow-Kilkenny, it is common for independents to win seats all over Ireland.

- Because parties usually put up several candidates, they are more likely to include women and members of minority groups.
- The system removes much of the advantage for larger parties and it is ~~unlikely that~~ ... ~~an overall majority.~~

Coalitions are therefore the norm in Ireland. With small parties and independents winning seats, the coalitions tend to be unstable.

The results of the Republic of Ireland 1997 general election shown in the table below, illustrate these effects.

Party representation in the Parliament of the Republic of Ireland, 1997	
Party	**Seats**
Fianna Fail	77
Fine Gael	54
Labour	17
Independents	6
Progressive Democrat	4
Socialist	4
Green	2
Socialist (Trotskyite)	1
Sinn Fein	1
Total	**166**

No party has overall control and Fianna Fail, which formed the Government, has to rely on the support of small parties and independents. We can also see that five small parties gained some representation, as did six independents.

<u>Party list systems</u>   These are very common. They operate in Israel, Holland and Spain and were used for the 1999 British elections to the European Parliament. There are no real constituencies and voters select from a number of party lists rather than voting for individual candidates. The votes for each list are counted and calculated as a **proportion** of the total vote. The parties are awarded seats in the legislature in exact proportion to the votes cast for their list. There are a number of variations and the main ones are shown in the following chart.

Variations of party list systems

Type	Description
• Regional	• The country is divided into a number of regions. The parties draw up separate lists for each of the regions and seats are awarded according to the proportions of votes in each region. • Used in Spain.
• National	• There are no regions and the lists are national, so **all** representatives come from one single party list. • Used in Israel.
• Closed lists (national or regional)	• The order in which candidates are placed on the list is decided by the party leadership. Those appearing near the top of the list have more chance of being elected than those further down.
• Open lists (regional)	• Here the voters can show a preference between candidates from the **same** party. In other words, they choose the order, not the party leaders.
• Thresholds (all list systems)	• It is normal to operate a threshold, which is a **minimum** proportion of the votes that a party must win to be awarded **any** seats. Thresholds vary in size.

The system used by the UK for its 1999 European Parliament elections was a **closed regional list system**. It is interesting to view the results. The table below shows the number of seats won in the European Parliament by British parties under the regional list. It also shows an **estimate** of how the seats **would have** been distributed had the election been based on first-past-the-post (FPTP).

Seats won in the British European Parliament election, 1999

Party	Seats actually won	Seats won if FPTP used
Conservative	36	49
Labour	29	30
Liberal Democrat	10	0
Scottish Nationalist	2	3
Plaid Cymru	2	2
Green	2	0
UK Independence	3	0

Source: C. Rallings and M. Thrasher, *New Britain: New Elections* (Vacher Dod, 1999).

The difference between the actual list results and the FPTP estimates is remarkable. The Conservatives would have won a comfortable overall majority under FPTP and minor parties would have done badly. Under the proportional list system, however, the results are fragmented and there was no decisive winner (note how the results show a great similarity to the pattern in Ireland under STV). It can also be seen that the SNP and Plaid Cymru, which have concentrated support, do not benefit particularly, if at all. PR does not always favour small parties!

Several general conclusions about list systems can now be drawn:

- They are clearly highly proportional and therefore fairest to all parties.
- No votes are wasted.
- They are unlikely to produce a decisive result.
- Very small parties can gain more representation (except those with concentrated regional support) and might hold the balance of power.
- Closed list systems place a great deal of power in the hands of the party leaderships, as they effectively decide which individuals are elected.
- Open list systems widen voter choice.
- The systems eliminate the idea of constituency representation.

Hybrid systems

The term 'hybrid' refers to any system that is a combination of more than one electoral system. A number exist, but two are considered here.

Additional member systems (AMS) These are combinations of the first-past-the-post system and party lists. There are a number of ways in which they can be combined, but the principles are always the same. Some of the seats in the legislature are filled through single member constituencies, elected in the method used in British general elections. The rest of the seats are elected through a party list system (there are various types, as shown above). Thus electors have two votes – one for the constituency MP, the other for a party list. Candidates from the party lists are returned in proportion to the votes cast in the second vote.

Variations of this system operate in Germany, New Zealand, the Scottish Parliament, the Welsh Assembly and the Greater London Assembly. They are designed to enjoy the best of both worlds. The first-past-the-post element ensures constituency representation and favours the larger parties. The proportional list element awards seats fairly and gives some representation to smaller parties. Results tend to be predictable. The large parties dominate, but they are usually unable to win enough seats to form a majority government. Thus coalitions and minority administrations are common, but they are usually stable because a single large party dominates. Certainly this has been the case in recent times in Germany, Scotland and Wales. The figures below compare the Scottish Parliament elections of 1999 (under AMS) with the results in Scotland of the 1997 general election (under FPTP).

In one sense, the difference is dramatic. The Conservatives moved from no seats at all in 1997 to reasonable representation in 1999, even though the proportion of votes that they won at the two elections was similar. The SNP did considerably better (partly due to a higher total vote). We can also see that some small groups got a look-in under AMS. Despite the radical differences, Labour remained by far the dominant party, so a complete political deadlock was avoided. This is precisely the kind of circumstance which AMS tends to produce.

AV+ In 1998 the **Jenkins Commission** reported to the Labour Government following a long consideration of which electoral system would work best in British general elections. It recommended a hybrid system that it described as AV+. Constituency MPs would be elected by the alternative vote system (as described above). These seats would be topped up by some seats awarded through a party list system. In other words, this is AMS, but it ensures that all constituency MPs achieve a majority of votes.

First-past-the-post and AMS compared in Scotland		
Party	Proportion of seats won under FPTP in 1997	Proportion of seats won under AMS in 1999
Labour	77.8	43.4
Liberal Democrat	13.9	13.2
Conservative	0	14.0
Scottish Nationalist	8.3	27.1
Green	0	0.8
Socialist	0	0.8
Other	0	0.8

The Jenkins Commission itself carried out an exercise to estimate how the 1997 general election results would have been affected had AV+ been used. The results are shown below.

Results of the 1997 general election, actual and under AV+, compared		
Party	Seats actually won in 1997	Estimate of seats likely to have been won under AV+
Labour	419	378
Conservative	165	160
Liberal Democrat	46	88
SNP and Plaid Cymru	10	14
Others (inc. Northern Ireland)	19	19

Two facts are striking here. First, the Labour Party would still have won a majority (59 per cent of the seats). Second, the gainers would clearly have been the Liberal Democrats, whose seats would have nearly doubled. Thus it would have been a more proportional result, but the basic reality of the political outcome – a win for Labour – would not have altered. Clearly the Jenkins Commission hoped these statistics would offer reform without threatening the major parties with serious consequences.

Assessing electoral systems

One of the most common questions asked of students of politics is whether the UK should adopt an alternative electoral system and, if so, which. It is a difficult issue, but can certainly be simplified by taking an organised approach to the subject. If we consider what electoral systems ~~are doing at this time and then determine~~ what we would prefer for the UK, we might be able to make a rational decision.

A typology of electoral systems						
Electoral system	Where used	Does it tend to return decisive governments?	Voter choice? Wasted votes?	Does it preserve constituency representation?	Does it fairly represent parties?	How well are women and minorities represented?
• First-past-the-post	• British general elections	• Yes	• Little choice • Many votes are wasted	• Yes – very strong	• No – small parties suffer severely	• Poorly – parties tend not to nominate women and members of minorities
• AV	• Australia	• Fairly well	• Greater choice	• Yes	• Quite well, but not proportionately	• Not especially well
• Second ballot	• France	• Fairly well	• Greater choice	• Yes	• Quite well, but not totally proportionately	• Not especially well
• STV	• Ireland	• No	• Very wide choice	• Fairly well	• Yes, but not completely	• Considerably
• Party list	• Israel	• No	• Little choice if a closed list • More if open • No votes are wasted	• No	• Excellent	• Good if the list is open; less so if closed
• AMS	• Germany • Scotland • Wales	• Fairly well	• Good choice –two choices for each voter	• Yes	• Fair, but not total	• Fair
• AV+	• Not used yet	• Fair	• Good – two votes on each system	• Yes	• Good but not total	• Potentially good

Electoral systems are methods by which votes are converted into seats in a representative body. If we assess how each system does this and what effect this will have on the voters and on the political system, we can find an answer. First, a list of possible objectives needs to be drawn up. Here is a suggestion:

- Does the electoral system tend to deliver decisive, secure, **majority government**?
- Does it give voters a **reasonable choice** and avoid **wasted votes**?
- Does it preserve **constituency** representation?
- Are the various political parties given **fair representation**?
- Is it likely that **women and minorities** will be given fair representation?

We can now develop a typology of electoral systems that achieve these objectives to a greater or lesser extent.

So it is not practical to review electoral systems without establishing objectives. The table above provides a guide to how well each system meets a variety of these objectives. The choice is, therefore, less a question of 'which is best?' and more a question of whether a system achieves what we are seeking.

Electoral reform in the UK

The parties' attitude

The most enthusiastic supporters of electoral reform have for some time been the **Liberal Democrats**. They have done so out of both principle and practicality. Liberals have always been strong supporters of popular democracy. The first-past-the-post system, they argue, is a denial of democracy in that it makes the value of votes unequal, promotes wasted votes and produces a Parliament and a government neither of which can be said truly to reflect political opinion in the country. It is, in short, not representative. In addition, the two-party system that FPTP sustains produces adversarial politics which is unhealthy. On a practical level, of course, they have recognised that the current system discriminates against smaller parties like themselves. They are inadequately represented and their supporters are often forced to vote for one of the main parties because they understand that a vote for a Liberal Democrat is a wasted vote and gives them no effective say in the result of the election.

The **Labour Party** has often toyed with the idea of proportional representation. Indeed, its 1918 Constitution contained such reform as a party objective. However, once Labour became a viable party of government, having overtaken the Liberals in the 1920s and 1930s, electoral reform seemed a less attractive prospect. Since then, therefore, the party has been split on the issue. The party did not have the political will to consider electoral reform until the 1980s when it seemed to have lost any prospect of winning power under first-past-the-post.

The 1997 election manifesto contained a commitment to consider reform carefully and to hold a referendum on the issue. The first part of the policy – an inquiry – was commissioned and reported in 1998 (see the Jenkins Commission recommendation above). However, having won such a decisive victory in 1997, and with the prospect of a repeat performance in 2001 or 2002, enthusiasm is waning. Furthermore, where proportional representation has been used – in the S~~~~ ~~~~ W~~~~ ~~~~~~~~~~~~~~~~~, ~~~~ ~~~ European Parliament elections of 1999 – Labour performed disappointingly. Small wonder, then, that the party worries about the consequences of reform.

As one might predict, the **Conservatives** are united in their opposition to reform. Only a handful of leading members and MPs support it. Above all, Conservatives oppose change unless they are convinced that it will improve a situation. They do not believe that electoral reform will produce a better political system, so they think it should be rejected. They have also done well out of first-past-the-post, having dominated British politics for the past 80 years. Whoever might be in power, Conservatives prefer strong, decisive government and the current general election system delivers it. Having said that, the Conservatives have not opposed proportional representation for Scotland and Wales. Cynics, of course, might suggest that this was a result of their dismal performance there in the 1992 and 1997 elections. They do, however, remain consistently opposed to a spread of reform.

It is somewhat ironic that the **Welsh Nationalists** (Plaid Cymru) and the **Scottish Nationalists** (SNP) have supported proportional representation, as they do not gain particularly from reform. They have concentrated support and so have done quite well under FPTP. However, they felt it was essential to use PR in the elections to the devolved Welsh Assembly and Scottish Parliament in order to avoid the Labour Party winning unrestrained power there. The results – failure of Labour to secure overall majorities – appeared to justify their position. To be fair, the nationalists have supported reform as a matter of principle, like the Liberal Democrats, and this support has been consistent.

Pressure groups and electoral reform

The key pressure group that has long campaigned for reform is the **Electoral Reform Society**. It argues that some form of proportional representation has to be introduced in the UK believing it to be the fairest, most democratic and most desirable form of electoral system. The Society is concerned, less by which system of PR should be introduced than by its determination to see some kind of reform. **Charter 88** is an organisation that seeks general reforms of the constitution so as to make the UK more democratic and to extend human rights. Electoral reform is only one of a list of demands that the organisation has made since its formation in 1988. As with the Electoral Reform Society, Charter 88 argues that a reformed system would enhance democracy and create a more representative political system.

The pro-reform parties and pressure groups began to win the argument during the 1990s. The introduction of PR in Wales, Scotland and Northern Ireland demonstrates that. However, changing the system for general elections is a more fundamental reform with far-reaching consequences. It may well be that, for the foreseeable future, further change will be difficult to bring about.

The consequences for the UK

In a sense, the UK has become something of a laboratory for experimentation with electoral reform. Five different systems were in use in the year 2000.

Electoral systems in the UK	
System	**Where used**
• First-past-the-post	• General elections, local elections in England and Wales
• Supplementary vote	• London Mayor
• Additional member	• Scottish Parliament, Welsh Assembly, London Assembly
• Single transferable vote	• Northern Ireland
• Closed party lists	• European Parliament elections

We can, therefore, pick up some clues as to what might occur if we were to introduce reform in general elections. The likely consequences of **any** serious reform of the electoral system – probably, but not necessarily – proportional representation, are as follows:

- No party would win an overall majority in the House of Commons. It is possible, under AMS for example, that Labour might have won outright in 1997 and the Conservatives in 1983 or 1987, but this is unlikely.
- As a result, the UK would usually have a minority government, unable to implement controversial measures, or a coalition government with more than one party sharing power.
- Coalitions would probably always contain members of the Liberal Democrat Party in the Cabinet.
- The features of two-party politics, such as adversarial confrontation in Parliament, collective Cabinet responsibility and single-party control over the parliamentary agenda, would largely disappear.
- The doctrine of mandate and manifesto would be eroded. Parties could no longer guarantee the implementation of their election promises because they could only hope, at best, to be in a minority or in a coalition with another party. An illustration of this occurred in Scotland in 1999. The Liberal Democrats had to compromise on their electoral commitment to abolish tuition fees at Scottish universities when they had to share power with the dominant Labour Executive.
- The Liberal Democrats would become a more significant force in British politics.

We can also identify some **possibilities**: that is, some changes which could result from reform, but which are less certain. In some cases, these would depend upon which form of system ~~was adopted~~.

- There might be a growth in the number of small parties contesting elections effectively. These might be extreme parties of the left or the right, they might be single-issue groups.
- It is feasible that the large parties will fragment and actually divide. For example, the Conservatives could split into pro-European and anti-European parties. As things stand, this is unlikely as neither new party would be able to win seats. Under a reformed system, however, smaller versions of the Conservative Party would be able to win seats and enjoy some prospect of sharing power.
- More women and minority candidates might be elected. This is especially likely under STV.
- If a party list system, or a hybrid that included a list system, such as AMS, were adopted, the party leaderships would gain more power. In Scotland and Wales, for example, the London Labour establishment maintained some of its influence through its control of party lists. This was also true in the European Parliament elections.
- The whole basis upon which Parliament operates might change fundamentally. With a large number of smaller parties, there would be marked changes in procedures.

How desirable such developments may be is for the individual observer to decide.

Efforts to make local elections truly local have consistently failed. The introduction of the Poll Tax in 1988 was a partially successful attempt to make councils accountable for their financial behaviour, and by the time of the 1991 polls there were some signs that voters were discriminating between high-spending, high-taxing councils and those that were more frugal. But the Poll Tax was replaced soon afterwards and matters returned to their former state.

More worryingly, turnouts in local elections fell during the 1990s. The 1999 elections saw turnout down to an average of about 30 per cent, a fall of 10 per cent since the 1970s. As usual, voters used local polls to deliver a warning to the Government – in 1999 this was probably because of frustration of Labour's failure to boost public services, education and health in particular. There were Conservative gains and government losses. But it remained clear that, although the results were based on national issues, they did not indicate voter intentions at a future general election. The opinion polls at the beginning of the twenty first century still put Labour firmly ahead.

Parliamentary by-elections

Characteristics

A by-election occurs when a sitting Member of Parliament is, for some reason, unable to retain his or her seat. Most commonly this is due to the death of the member, but it may also result from serious long-term illness, or resignation. Resignation can occur through some form of scandal, but is more commonly for business or family reasons. Bankruptcy and the imprisonment of a member will also result in loss of the seat, but such occurrences are extremely rare. The vacancy must be filled within about three months.

The normal characteristics of a general election simply do not apply in by-elections. There are several reasons for this:

- Constituents are aware that they are not electing a government, which is the case at a general election. They might, therefore, relax their normal party allegiance, safe in the knowledge that their vote will not create any dramatic political change. It follows from this that there is no such thing as a 'safe seat' in a by-election. Certainly not, at least, for the party in government.
- Since they are in 'mid-term' of a government, voters may take the opportunity to pass their verdict on the performance of that government. Often this is critical. Thus, there is a tendency for the governing party to fare badly in by-elections. Some dramatic examples are given below.
- For the reasons described above, smaller parties, especially the Liberal Democrats, tend to do well. Normally a great deal of media attention is paid to by-elections, so candidates from smaller parties often receive more coverage than at a general election.
- Turnouts can be much lower than at a general election – often as low as 50 per cent, compared to 70–75 per cent at a general election. This often distorts the picture of party support. Typically, supporters of the incumbent party (the party of the former MP) stay at home in large numbers, feeling no special urge to vote for a change. In close contests, however, where a major surprise is expected, there might sometimes be a good showing (as much as 80 per cent), as in the Liberal triumph in a formerly Conservative safe seat at Brecon and Radnor in 1985.
- There has been an increasing tendency for 'tactical voting' to take place. This occurs when voters switch their normal allegiance in order to support a party whose candidate has a better chance of winning than their own. The reason is to defeat a candidate whom they particularly oppose, often from the governing party. Certainly three Liberal Democrat victories over the Conservatives after the 1992 general election, at Newbury, Christchurch and Eastleigh, were partly the result of Labour supporters voting tactically for the Liberal Democrat candidate.

Do by-elections matter?

Under most circumstances, the answer is 'not very much'. Of course, they act as a valuable 'barometer' of support for the parties, especially the Government, but for the reasons described above, their results might not be reliable in the long run. Indeed, it is usually the case that, when an incumbent party candidate loses the seat at a by-election, it is regained by the party at the next general election when voting patterns return to 'normal'.

When the Government is faced with a small majority in the House of Commons, however, by-election losses can become crucial. This was never more so than when Labour was elected in October 1974 with a majority of only three. By-election defeats, with seats changing from Labour to Conservative at Woolwich and Walsall North, wiped out the Government's majority, thus reducing it to a weak and largely ineffective administration.

Similar, though less dramatic events overtook the Conservative Government that was elected in 1992 with a 21 majority. By 1995 the Government was so unpopular that it was incapable of holding any of its own seats at a by-election, no matter how large the majority. By-election defeats reduced the Government's majority to eleven and, when a further nine MPs temporarily left the party over its European policies, there was again a minority administration for a short time. Important legislation, including the proposed privatisation of the Post Office, was lost in this difficult period. So the answer to the question concerning the significance of by-elections is that it largely depends upon political circumstances. A government with a comfortable Commons majority need worry little if it suffers mid-term reverses. Most of them can be reclaimed later.

Local elections in the UK

As with by-elections, the normal 'rules' of electoral behaviour do not apply in local council contests. Again, the most convenient way to understand them is to examine the characteristics that differentiate them from general election patterns:

* Turnouts are always much lower, rarely reaching 40 per cent and sometimes being as low as 20 per cent. This means that results can often turn on the switching of a few hundred votes or even less.
* The results owe more to the popularity of the **national** parties than to the performance of local councillors or to their manifestos. As with by-elections, local elections are often used by voters as a rod with which to beat the Government that has lost their confidence. This was particularly true in the 1995 elections in Scotland and the English and Welsh counties. The enormously unpopular Conservative Party under John Major lost most of its remaining council seats in these elections, even driving some Conservative candidates to describe themselves as independent on the ballot papers to try to disguise their true affiliation and so save their seats.
* Voters are largely ignorant of local issues, not even understanding which services are the responsibility of the local authority and which are centrally administered. Thus, unless there are well-publicised local controversies, the patterns of voting are replicated up and down the country; local variations are relatively minor.

Elections to the European Parliament

In 1999 the European elections were held on the basis of a closed regional party list system. In the event, interest tended to centre more on the effect of using such a system than on the campaign or the results. Above all, however, turnout in the 1999 election was very low indeed. Only 23 per cent of the electorate voted, the lowest throughout Europe. The very low turnout was probably caused by a number of factors:

- Many traditional Labour voters had become disenchanted with the Government's performance and therefore decided to stay at home rather than vote for another party.
- There was a general feeling that the European Parliament was an irrelevant body, with no real power.
- Many people were disenchanted with the whole idea of European integration.
- There might have been some voter fatigue. There had been a general election in 1997 and there were local and regional elections in 1999.

Apart from a low turnout the election was also remarkable for turning into almost a single-issue poll. The Conservatives campaigned on a Euro-sceptic ticket and this seemed to strike a chord with those voters who did bother to turn up at the polls.

The results gave hope to a beleaguered Conservative Party and also gave encouragement to some small parties who gained ground. As the election was conducted under a proportional system the small parties gained some seats from a small vote. The results are given in the following table.

Results of the 1999 UK election to the European Parliament		
Party	% of votes won	Seats won
Conservative	35.8	36
Labour	28.0	29
Liberal Democrat	12.7	10
UK Independence	7.0	3
Green	6.3	2
Nationalists	4.6	4
Others	5.6	0

Voting behaviour

The reasons why people choose to vote the way they do has occupied

known – since the 1960s. Clearly, political parties are interested in voting behaviour, but it is also important to the student of politics. This is because it can tell us a great deal about the nature of the political culture and the type and scale of the changes taking place within that culture. Needless to say, the nature of voting patterns is complex and is constantly changing. We can, nevertheless, identify some of the principal trends of recent years.

Social class   When voting behaviour first came under scrutiny in the 1960s, it was clear that the main determinant of party allegiance was social class. Most members of the working class, defined as manual workers, whether skilled, semi-skilled or unskilled, closely identified with the Labour Party and voted for it without fail. About one-third of this class did have a tendency to vote Conservative out of **deference** – a belief that Conservatives were members of a superior ruling class who could be trusted to govern in the interests of all – but the rest were staunch Labour.

Similarly, most members of the middle class – that is, those broadly in 'white-collar' occupations, from clerks and secretaries to senior business managers – were confirmed Conservative supporters. The Liberals at this time were relatively insignificant, picking up a small percentage of votes from the intellectual middle classes and some independent-minded workers.

The incidence of so-called **deviant** voting – voters supporting a party not normally associated with their class – was relatively rare. There were certainly observable instances of people placing themselves in a different social class to the one in which they objectively belonged (typically, members of the working class considering themselves as middle class for reasons of status). This **self-assigned** class placement, as it is known, can certainly lead to 'deviant' voting, as can individuals moving from one class to another and from one generation to the next. An educated son or daughter of working-class parents might become middle class, but retain working-class attitudes including Labour Party allegiance. Yet it could still be said in the 1960s that social class was the deciding factor in party identification.

> *'Class is the basis of British party politics; all else is embellishment and detail.'*
> Peter Pulzer, *Political Representation and Elections in Britain*, 1967

No sooner had Pulzer written his key work on voting than the relationship between social class and voting patterns began to break down. This was for a number of reasons.

Class de-alignment

Class de-alignment began to occur: that is, the connection between social classes and parties began to weaken. A number of explanations have been offered, mainly concerning the increasing **affluence** of some sections of the working class, prompting them to disassociate themselves from Labour. Hand in hand with greater affluence has gone **embourgoisement**. This term refers to a tendency for better-off workers to consider themselves as middle class. They may identify a middle-class lifestyle with voting Conservative and so abandon allegiance to Labour.

> 'It might even be argued that the whole process of dealignment represents an attempt by a more pluralist, heterogeneous and less deferential society to break out of the two-party straitjacket.'
> Robert Pinkney, 'Dealignment, Realignment or just Alignment?', *Parliamentary Affairs*, January 1986

Class fragmentation

As traditional industries such as coal, steel, engineering and shipbuilding have declined and increased automation has reduced the number of manual jobs available, the traditional working class has become scattered. Increasing employment in service industries has led to a growth in the lower and central middle classes. As a result, there are simply fewer members of traditional classes who might have been closely allied to one political party.

Partisan de-alignment

Partisan de-alignment describes a process whereby the traditionally strong connections between certain sections of the population and a particular party have become weaker. This has been described as a lower level of identification with a party, a phenomenon that might also be described as an emotional attachment. The reasons, identified by researchers such as David Denver and Ivor Crewe, vary from dissatisfaction with the performance of the two main parties to increased awareness of political issues, resulting in voters making an informed choice rather than merely voting out of habit for the same party. William Wale's research indicates a marked decline since the 1960s in voters who 'strongly identify' with any party at all. This implies that they have become volatile, non-class-based voters.

Having said that, it remains true that one's social class remains something of a clue as to which party one might support. Labour retains its entrenched position among the traditional working class, while the Conservatives achieve most of their support among the rural and suburban middle classes.

Sectoral cleavage

Ivor Crewe's influential contribution to the debate on modern voting tendencies revolves principally around the concept of sectoral cleavage. Instead of the old class analysis of party allegiance, Crewe suggests, we must look in more detail at individuals' place in the economic structure and in their lifestyle. Thus, he identifies strong Labour support among those who live in council-provided accommodation, work in the public, rather than private sector, and are members of a trade union. On the other hand, people who own their own homes, work for private companies and are not union members are more likely to vote Conservative or even Liberal Democrat. Thus, the cleavage, or division, of support between the parties is based less on class than on the 'section' of the population that people belong to.

Of course, if Crewe's analysis is valid, the traditional Labour Party was certainly doomed to permanent electoral decline, since the kind of voters he identifies as typical Labour supporters are in sharp decline. It is not surprising, therefore, that the modernisation of the Labour Party became inevitable if it was to survive.

Instrumental voting

As society experiences social fragmentation and voters become better informed about political issues, there is a tendency for more voters to choose the party that is likely to bring them most personal benefits. This is known as **instrumental** voting. Property owners, therefore, are likely to support a party that is committed to helping them financially and to maintaining a strong position on law and order. Similarly, high-income groups look for tax-cutting parties. The poor, on the other hand, are more interested in welfare and employment policies. The elderly are concerned about health and pensions, young families about education, and so on.

The concept of voters developing a 'shopping list' of demands that will suit them and comparing this list with party manifestos poses a new challenge for politicians, who must then attempt to find policies that will maximise their appeal. It is also likely to contribute to more volatile voting behaviour.

Other factors

As we have seen, little about voting behaviour is simple any more. There are now many factors that seem to have some effect on voting trends. To begin with, we can identify those factors that seem to have a negligible effect. These include age, sex and religion. There are some trends – a slight tendency for the young to support Labour, for members of ethnic minority groups also to vote Labour, for women and members of the Church of England to be Conservative, while Catholics tend to support Labour more often. However, it is likely that other factors discussed above are the real causes of these slight biases.

The question of region is becoming more important. Irrespective of social class, there are important differences in the strength of party support in different parts of the country. The statistics bear this out, as the following table shows.

Seats won in the 2001 general election				
Region	Labour	Conservative	Lib Dem	Other
London and south-east	86	90	15	0
South-west	16	20	15	0
East Anglia	7	14	1	0
Midlands	71	28	3	1
North	139	17	6	1
Scotland	56	1	10	6
Wales	34	0	2	4

We can see that two regions – the south-east and the south-west of England – are closely contested by the two main parties, while in the latter, the West Country, the Liberal Democrats make a traditionally strong showing. East Anglia remains strongly Conservative, but the bigger regions of the Midlands and the north of England are staunchly Labour.

In Scotland and Wales, the striking feature was the total eclipse of the Conservatives. Even the nationalists were unable to dislodge the Labour domination in Scotland and Wales. Clearly, regional variations in voting can be quite stark. As the political climate stood after the 1997 and 2001 elections, it was the Conservatives who faced the biggest problem in overcoming the crucial bias towards Labour in the north of England, the Midlands, Scotland and Wales.

The Scots, Welsh and northerners commonly believe that Conservative governments have consistently ignored their demands. The Conservatives are very much seen as the party of 'the south'. The reverse is true in the south of England, where Labour is not seen as the appropriate vehicle for voters' demands.

Summary

If we draw these threads together, we can now make some generalisations about the nature of voting behaviour:

- Social class is still an important factor, but a declining one.
- A decreasing number of voters have a strong permanent allegiance to one party or another.
- Voters tend, in increasing numbers, to 'shop around' for the best party to meet their particular needs.
- There is a greater tendency today for voters to understand the issues and to allow them to determine voting rather than relying on traditional allegiances.
- A person's lifestyle and economic status remain key factors in voting behaviour.
- Such factors as religion, age and sex have a relatively minor influence.
- There are marked regional variations in voting patterns.

What determines election results?

Although, as we have seen above, voting is more volatile and unpre-

know which way they will vote even before an election campaign begins and will, therefore, be unaffected by any short-term factors. This proportion may still be as high as 50 per cent. What of the rest? What makes their minds up? A number of factors may be at work together.

The media   The British media have traditionally been biased towards the Conservative Party. Certainly the campaigns waged by the *Sun, Daily Mail, Daily Express* and *Daily Telegraph* helped to underpin support for the Tories throughout the 1980s and in 1992. With the decline in traditional party support, as described above, voters are more open-minded and susceptible to persuasion. The newspapers have filled some of the vacuum left by the reduction in the importance of social class in voting behaviour. The *Sun*'s unexpected support for Labour in 1997 may certainly have contributed towards the size of the Conservative defeat.

Party image   Commentators such as Dennis Kavanagh have noted that the general image of a party can be as important as the detailed issues which it raises. For example, a disunited party presents a negative impression; if it cannot act concertedly in a campaign, how will it handle government?

Certainly Labour in the 1980s suffered from the image of a working-class party, committed to trade unionism, high taxes and wasteful expenditure. The 'antics' of the so-called 'loony left' of extreme socialists, much publicised in the popular press, had a disproportionately powerful effect on voters, well beyond its true significance in the party.

Tony Blair and family outside 10 Downing Street after the 2001 general election

By contrast, the Conservatives presented themselves as responsible and united, solid attributes with which voters could easily identify. In the closely fought 1992 election, it was the spectre of high taxes that went a long way to ensuring a Labour defeat.

In 1997 the air of corruption and 'sleaze' surrounding the Tories, together with the open split on the European issue, presented a poor image to the electors, who punished them with a heavy defeat.

Party leaders

During the 1983 election campaign, the contrast between the dynamic, determined and practical Margaret Thatcher, and the intellectual, but slightly eccentric Michael Foot could not have been more marked. By 1987 Neil Kinnock was in charge of Labour, but he still could not compete with the charismatic image presented by Thatcher.

Neil Kinnock put up a better fight in 1992 against John Major, but still failed to pull off a victory. Kinnock presented a slick, self-assured image by this time, but could still not quite match the trustworthy image that Major conjured up. In 1997 the contest between the party leaders was closer than the landslide result would suggest, with Major representing honesty and reliability against the younger, more dynamic Blair. In 2001 William Hague fell well behind both Charles Kennedy and Tony Blair in the personal popularity stakes. His poor showing was seen as a key factor in Labour's huge victory.

Party performance

It is often said that the incumbent Government cannot win an election, but it can certainly lose one. This implies a negative side to electioneering that has come to the fore in recent times. Increasingly, elections are fought on the basis of the record of the Government rather than the plans of opposition parties. If there are sufficient negative images, the opposition wins. Thus, despite economic success, the Conservative Government of 1992–7 suffered from a record of broken tax promises and the declining state of education and health services.

The Labour Government that lost in 1979 had enjoyed a moderately successful period of economic management in the second half of the 1970s, notably bringing inflation down from peak levels of 22 per cent to single figures. In the autumn of 1978 it was expected to win the forthcoming election comfortably. The notorious 'Winter of Discontent' in 1978–9, when a series of public sector strikes over pay led to severe disruption in British life, put an end to this. The voters were left with a strongly negative image of Labour. By 2001, however, it was Labour's perceived competence in stabilising the economy and promoting prosperity and security which was seen as a decisive factor.

The campaign

With voters more willing to switch allegiance, the election campaign itself has taken on a new significance. All the parties now hire consultants (the 'spin doctors') and advertising agencies to manage the public campaign. In the 1980s, Margaret Thatcher's association with the advertising agency of Saatchi and Saatchi was seen as a key factor in three successful campaigns. News conferences, speeches by front-bench spokespersons, walkabouts, rallies and conferences are carefully orchestrated to achieve maximum impact. Despite all these carefully laid plans, however, events can be unpredictable.

In the 1992 campaign, for example, Labour believed it had stolen a march on the Tories by finding a child who was suffering because of the failure of the National Health Service to treat her (the state of the Health Service was an important issue that year). This backfired when the whole incident appeared to be an elaborate set-up, with little basis in reality. Labour suffered badly from the publicity. Similarly, an ineptly managed rally for Labour a few days before polling day received much negative publicity. Finally, John Major's idea to give speeches in the street from a soapbox was warmly received. Thus, unpredictable incidents can have an important influence on party fortunes. In the end, the 1992 election was probably won because of the success that the Conservative campaign organisers achieved in persuading the voters that they could expect sharp tax increases if Labour won. In contrast, the lacklustre campaign of 2001 appeared to have little effect on the result. Longer term factors had been at work.

Turnout

As election turnouts fell steadily during the 1990s, it became apparent that the level of voting was affecting the actual results. Before examining the link, the causes of declining turnouts should be reviewed. They are as follows:

- There is some disillusionment with the performance of the parties, particularly Labour and the Conservatives. Of course, this phenomenon ebbs and flows, but there is evidence of a long-term drift.
- There are now more elections than in the past, so some voter fatigue is setting in.
- Membership of parties has declined and been largely replaced by increased membership of pressure groups. This reduces general interest in parties, but also means that there are fewer activists who can work to persuade people to come out and vote.
- As the two main parties have come closer together in their policies, voters find it difficult to distinguish between them and so are disinclined to vote.

There is a perception that 'lower order' elections for local councils, devolved assemblies and the European Parliament do not really 'matter', as the bodies being elected have little power. The recent statistics given below illustrate the nature of the problem of falling turnouts.

Election	Turnout (%)
1987 general election	75.4
1992 general election	77.9
1997 general election	71.6
1999 Scottish Parliament election	58.5
1999 Welsh Assembly election	46.2
1999 England & Wales local elections	32.0
1999 European Parliament election	24.1
2001 general election	59.4

We can now ask how turnouts affect results. The general wisdom is that whoever is in government does badly when the turnout is low. This is the result of complacency and a general lack of enthusiasm. Certainly Labour's poor showing in all the 1999 elections was largely put down to a general sense of contentment among the Government's supporters about the way the economy in particular was being run. It is also natural that the opposition parties will show more determination in order to wrest power from the ruling administration.

There is a further theory that Labour supporters are less likely to vote than their Conservative counterparts. It is suggested that, being more likely to be from a 'lower' socioeconomic group with lower educational attainment, they are less politically aware. This is a declining factor, but possibly still influential.

However, the shockingly low turnout in the 2001 general election appeared to affect none of the parties favourably or adversely. All three main parties suffered from voter apathy, complacency or general disillusionment with politics.

The lessons of the 1997 and 2001 elections

Put together, Labour's two decisive election victories in 1997 and 2001 mark a major shift in party identification. The old assumption that the Conservatives are the 'natural party of government' has been finally dismissed. The fact that the Conservatives gained barely more than 30 per cent of the popular vote in two consecutive national polls demonstrates that they cannot rely upon more support than their traditional solid bedrock.

To place these results in perspective, we must divide our conclusions into short-term and long-term factors.

Short-term factors and the campaigns

- It is clear that economic competence is a key factor. In 1997 it was Conservative *perceived* mismanagement of the economy which damaged their electoral support. In 2001, however, Labour was seen as a 'safe pair of hands' and so benefited from its reputation.
- Tactical voting is now an important feature of elections. The Liberal Democrat 'breakthrough' was made possible by widespread tactical voting by Labour supporters who changed their support in order to keep Conservative candidates out. This was repeated in 2001 to maintain the position.
- The electorate showed no appetite for tax cuts if this meant a reduction in the standard of public services.
- Leadership is an issue. Blair was seen as a very positive factor in 1997 while the unfashionable Conservative leader, William Hague, was a negative influence in 2001.
- The support of newspapers appeared to have little impact. There was a swing in media support towards Labour in 2001, but this is thought to have reinforced Labour support rather than adding to it.
- 'Sleaze' was an important factor in 1997, but in 2001 a number of less serious allegations of financial misconduct among Labour ministers were largely ignored by the voters.
- In both elections, unity of the party played a part. Labour was totally focused on all major issues in both 1997 and 2001. In contrast the Conservatives were split on European issues on both occasions.

Long-term factors

<u>Volatility</u>   It is generally agreed that the British electorate are becoming more flexible or volatile in the way they choose the political party that they wish to support. It used to be the case that most voters would stick to one party throughout their lives. This figure was as high as 80 per cent. The o̶t̶h̶e̶r̶s̶ were either 'floating voters' – those who were likely to change their allegiance – or in transition from supp̶o̶r̶t̶i̶n̶g̶ one party to supporting another. It was this group who determined the outcome of elections. By 1997, however, it had become clear that many more of the electorate were willing to change allegiance.

As an illustration, an NOP/BBC exit poll on the night of the 1997 election revealed that the Conservatives had lost 29 per cent of their 1992 support. The Liberal Democrats, whose overall support had remained steady since 1992, still lost 34 per cent of their voters from the previous election (they gained a similar number from the other parties). Even the Labour Party, which enjoyed a huge victory, lost 11 per cent of its 1992 voters.

<u>Tactical voting</u>   The year 1997 saw the first general election where tactical voting played a major part in the result. Labour and Liberal Democrat supporters showed a willingness to drop their primary allegiance and vote for another party just to ensure a Conservative defeat.

The Liberal Democrats were the particular beneficiaries of the tactical vote. They won almost the same proportion of the vote in 1997 as they had done in 1992, but almost doubled their seats tally. The main reason was that many Labour voters in marginal seats decided to support the Liberal Democrats. This was especially true in the south-west.

Tactical voting is here to stay as long as the first-past-the-post system is used. A by-election in Romsey in May 2000 illustrated this. A 'safe' Conservative seat was lost to the Liberal Democrats when most of the Labour voters in the constituency voted tactically to defeat the Conservatives. With weaker party allegiances and the experience of 1997, there is every reason to believe that tactical voting will persist and might influence election outcomes.

<u>The attitude of the press</u>   More attention is paid in modern elections to the role of the press. Throughout the 1980s and even in 1992, the majority of the big circulation newspapers supported the Conservatives, who duly won. In 1997 the balance shifted to Labour. The table on page 181 shows how the daily newspapers gave their support in 1997.

The influence of the British press should not be exaggerated, but there is no doubt that the political parties see newspapers as highly influential and increasingly court their support. They will feature greatly in elections for the foreseeable future.

Daily newspapers' support for the parties in 2001		
Newspaper	Circulation (millions)	Party supported
Daily Mirror	2.19	Labour
Sun	3.45	Labour
Daily Express	0.96	Labour
Daily Mail	2.42	Conservative
Daily Star	0.59	Labour
Daily Telegraph	1.02	Conservative
Guardian	0.40	Labour
The Times	0.71	Labour
Independent	0.23	None

Source: Adapted from D. Butler and D. Kavanagh, *The British General Election of 1997* (Macmillan, 1997).

Summary of key factors in general election results

Factor	Detail
• Party performance	• How well does the electorate believe the ruling party has governed? • How convincing has the other party been in opposition?
• Party image	• Is a party united? • Can it be trusted to deliver its commitments? • Are its leaders trustworthy?
• Party leaders	• Are they charismatic? • Do they inspire confidence? • Have they performed well in government or opposition? • Do they control their own party?
• Turnout	• A low turnout is thought to favour the opposition party in particular and the Conservatives in general. • High turnouts favour Labour.
• The Government's record	• Mainly the state of the economy. • The state of public services. • Its record on law and order. • Specific policy successes or failures.
• The media	• Whom will the key newspapers support? • Tabloids are seen as particularly influential.
• The election campaign	• How successfully have the parties delivered their messages? • How effective have their media campaigns been?

Public opinion polls

Two questions may be asked of ~~opinion polls. First,~~ are they accurate ~~enough to be~~ of any use? Second, do they affect the way in which people view politics and, in particular, the way in which they vote?

The accuracy of opinion polls

The unexpected result of the 1992 general election, when a narrow Conservative victory shocked the experts who were expecting a comfortable Labour win a few days before polling day, brought into question the accuracy of such polls. Some statistics might be helpful here.

Error levels of two leading opinion polls		Gallup	NOP
1987	Conservative	−2.3%	−1.3%
	Labour	+2.5%	+3.5%
1992	Conservative	−4.3%	−3.8%
	Labour	+2.8%	+6.8%
1997	Conservative	+1.0%	−3.0%
	Labour	+1.0%	+5.0%
2001	Conservative	−1.7%	−1.7%
	Labour	+6.3%	+6.3%

Source: D. Butler and J. Butler, *British Political Facts 1900–94*, (Macmillan, 1995); *Independent*, 3 May 1997.

Where the figure shows a plus, it indicates that the polling organisation over-estimated the strength of voting support for a party. A minus indicates an under-estimate. The sample used normally varies between 1000 and 2500 respondents and a possible 4 per cent error in sampling is usually accepted. If we take this 4 per cent margin, we can see that the polls were **always** within their accepted error band, with the exception of NOP's 1992 prediction for Labour.

This suggests a remarkable degree of accuracy, bearing in mind the relatively small size of the samples used and the fact that the actual voting took place a few days after the final poll was taken – time enough for many to change their minds. Indeed, it was understood that the relative inaccuracy of the 1992 polls was not due to poor techniques in opinion research, but rather to a very late swing in voting intention away from Labour towards the Conservatives. Evidently many voters were still making up their minds as they entered the polling stations.

Doubts about the accuracy of the polls were largely dispelled at the 1997 election. Though the polls consistently showed a large Labour lead for months before the election, many felt that the events of 1992 would be repeated. In the event, however, the opinion polls demonstrated a remarkable success rate. Gallup was extremely close to the final result in its overall estimates. NOP, though apparently a little way off in its prediction, successfully identified a larger Labour surge in marginal constituencies. Above all, there was no late change in opinion to embarrass the pollsters. In 2001 the polls tended to over-estimate Labour support, but were very accurate on Conservative and Liberal Democrat showings.

Do opinion polls affect voting?

The French clearly believe so, along with a number of other democracies, as they ban the publication of opinion poll findings a week before an actual election. They fear two effects. One is a 'bandwagon' effect, often observed in the USA, where some undecided voters might throw their support behind the candidate they feel is most likely to win. This is an irrational form of behaviour, but some fear that it happens. Second, there is the possibility of tactical voting, which has been described and discussed above. This is a more realistic threat. Opinion polls give voters the information that is necessary for them to plan their voting tactics. Without it they might simply vote for their genuine preference.

There is, however, little evidence to suggest that opinion polls have any significant effect on British elections. They can help the politicians, of course, by telling them whether their current campaigning is gaining or losing ground. It must also be noted that the parties commission their own private opinion polls. But if they do have an influence, it seems to be too small to be discernible.

For exam questions relevant to this unit, see page 556.

Introduction

The term 'Parliament' actually refers to three institutions grouped into one. These are:

- the Queen-in-Parliament
- the House of Commons
- the House of Lords.

We may dispense quickly with references to the Queen. This is largely an historical hangover from times when Parliament's role was to sustain and legitimise the activities, mostly financial, of the Crown. This role effectively ceased at the end of the seventeenth century. The monarch has not been allowed in the House of Commons since Charles I attempted to arrest a group of rebellious MPs in 1641. Indeed, to this day, the reigning monarch is only permitted to enter the House of Lords once a year to deliver the 'Queen's Speech', a statement of the Government's legislative programme for the year.

Today the monarch's only legislative role is to grant the Royal Assent to (i.e. sign) Bills after they have passed through all the parliamentary stages required. Royal Assent turns a Bill into a statute or law and indicates that the courts should now enforce its measures. Since Royal Assent has not been withheld since 1707, we may assume that it is now merely a formal procedure. The Queen, in reality, has no choice in the matter.

The House of Commons

Structure

The composition and structure of the Commons (also known as the 'Lower House') is as follows.

Members of Parliament

MPs are elected from constituencies throughout England, Scotland, Wales and Northern Ireland. Those who are not ministers, or senior members of the opposition parties, are commonly known as back-benchers.

The Speaker

The Speaker is chosen from the elected members. This is the result of a ballot of all the MPs. Upon election the Speaker ceases to be a constituency MP or a party politician. Instead he or she becomes Chairperson of the House and must remain politically neutral. Much of this function is simply to organise debates, choose speakers and generally keep order, disciplining MPs if necessary. However, there are rare occasions when the role of the Speaker can be crucial.

There are occasions, for example, when MPs demand an emergency debate of a current issue. The Government might wish to speed up the passage of a Bill through the House by introducing a 'Guillotine Motion'. Such a device cuts short opportunities for debate in the interests of speed. There might also be a variety of procedural disputes that could affect the fortunes of legislation. In these, and in a variety of other cases, the Speaker might become involved in controversial political issues, but must still remain neutral.

A typical back-bench MP's week

Monday morning
- Answer correspondence.
- Attend party policy committee meeting.

Monday lunch
- Entertain members of lobby group.

Monday afternoon
- Attend debate on important Bill followed by administrative work.

Monday evening
- Attend further debate.
- Stay for a series of divisions.
- Dinner with party colleagues.
- Return to London flat after 10 p.m.

Tuesday morning
- Answer correspondence.
- Meet delegation from constituency concerning road-building scheme.

Tuesday lunch
- Entertain delegation from a foreign Parliament.

Tuesday afternoon
- Attend Transport Minister's questions. Ask question about road plans in constituency.
- Administrative work.

Tuesday evening
- Attend dinner given by a large business.
- Attend debate in the House.
- Stay for series of divisions until 2 a.m.

Wednesday morning
- Answer correspondence.
- Attend Standing Committee.

Wednesday lunch
- Entertain chairman of constituency party visiting the House.

Wednesday afternoon
- Attend Prime Minister's question time. Unsuccessful attempt to ask question.
- Administrative work.

Wednesday evening
- Free.

Thursday morning
- Answer correspondence.
- Attend back-benchers' meeting.

Thursday lunch
- Outside speaking engagement at school in London.

Thursday afternoon
- Attend Treasury Minister's question time. Do not table a question but hear replies.

Thursday evening
- Attend outside transport committee meeting.
- Dinner alone.
- Return to House for divisions until midnight.

Friday morning
- Answer correspondence.
- Party policy committee meeting.
- Meeting with senior officials at Department of Transport about road plans in constituency.

Friday afternoon
- Return to constituency.
- Attend surgery to hear constituents' problems.

Friday evening
- Attend dinner with local business people.

Saturday morning
- Interview with local newspaper journalist.

Saturday lunch
- Entertained by senior members of constituency party.

Saturday afternoon
- Open fête at school in constituency.

Saturday evening
- Home with family.

Sunday
- Home with family.

Sunday evening
- Return to London.

The front-benches The front-benches comprise senior members of the two major parties. In the case of the governing party, these are ministers, while in the Opposition party they are described as 'shadow ministers' or 'spokespersons'. The name 'front-benches' is self-explanatory.

Leader of the House The Leader of the House is a Cabinet ~~minister~~ ~~whose main role is to~~ organise the business of the House on behalf of the Government. Virtually all of the Commons' programme is controlled by the Cabinet. Time allotted to opposition parties or to individual MPs' concerns is a minority of the total. The Leader of the House, after consultation with the full Cabinet at its weekly meetings, arranges business with the Speaker, including which front-bench members will speak. He or she then informs the government whips, who pass information on to the MPs. The Official Opposition party has a 'shadow leader' who organises the small amount of time allotted to the party.

Whips The whips derive their name from fox-hunting circles where the hounds need to be organised and kept in order. This is an appropriate analogy in the context of the Commons. The Chief Whip (a senior member of his or her party) with several assistants has the responsibility of ensuring that MPs are informed about parliamentary business, turn up at important debates and, most importantly, remain loyal to the party line. In practice, this means ensuring that MPs vote in line with the Government's wishes. MPs who may be prepared to defy the official party line can expect a visit from a whip, who will give them a hard time if they remain obstinate. The role of the whips is central to the operation of government in the UK and will be discussed in some depth below. Whips of the non-governing parties play a similar role, but since the Government's policy is not at stake among the other parties, their function is less critical.

Whips are described as the 'eyes and ears of the Prime Minister'. They also report to the 'Cabinet enforcer,' a new Cabinet position created after 1997, for the purpose of maintaining party unity. It is expected of them to report on the mood of MPs, and to provide answers to such questions as 'Will they support the party leadership?', 'Can a rebellion be headed off?' and 'Can a deal be done to avoid trouble on the backbenches?' The whips shuttle back and forth between ministers and backbenchers to ensure that government control over the House is maintained. In the critical days of the minority Labour Government of 1977–9, during the great debates over the introduction of the Poll Tax in the 1980s and when John Major's Government of 1992–7 lost its Commons majority, the whips were fully employed, with varying degrees of success.

Select committees These have existed in the House since the nineteenth century, but were given a great boost to their authority after 1979 when additional departmental select committees were set up with enhanced powers. The committees have powers to call witnesses, including ministers, civil servants, MPs and representatives of interested groups. Though ministers and civil servants are constrained by rules on collective responsibility and anonymity, questioning is remarkably open. Sometimes the committees can be confrontational and exchanges can be heated. Unlike question time for ministers in the main chamber of the House, the committees are free to question as much as they like and to challenge answers quite freely. A selection of the responsibilities and powers of the committees, as described in the original standing orders which set them up, illustrates their work:

> 'To examine the expenditure, administration and policy of the principal government departments ... and associated public bodies.'

> '[They shall have the power] to send for persons, papers and records, to sit notwithstanding any adjournment of the House, to adjourn from place to place, and to report from time to time.'
>
> House of Commons, Standing Order Number 152

At the end of a committee investigation, a report is issued to the whole House. Some of these reports can prove to be controversial, often embarrassing the Government and sometimes prompting changes in policy. In this sense they have been more successful in making government **accountable** than the House of Commons as a whole. Above all, the committees try to operate away from the pressure of the party whips. Wherever possible they attempt to produce unanimous reports, or at least to achieve cross-party support for their reports. They have varying success in this regard. In some cases, the chair is a member of the Opposition, a way of demonstrating the committees' independence.

Select committees also have inherent weaknesses. These include the following factors:

- Party loyalty still plays a part. However independent MPs might feel, they will still be reluctant to criticise their own party.
- They have a small research staff, but not enough to be able to gather sufficient information to challenge the government machine.
- They have no means of enforcing any of their recommendations.

It is difficult to obtain meaningful information from civil servants and ministers because of the traditional secrecy of government and the constitutional rules that restrain them. It remains to be seen how far the Freedom of Information Act and the Human Rights Act, both of 2000, will help the work of the select committees.

Of the non-departmental select committees, by far the most important is Public Accounts, a powerful, influential body that is, by tradition, always chaired by a member of the Opposition. It often produces controversial reports into the way in which government uses taxpayers' money. Most notably, the Public Accounts Committee issued a report in 1994 suggesting that £300 million had been wasted by government departments in the previous ten years. This led to a major investigation into civil service procedures.

A flavour of the work of select committees in general can be shown by a selection of the investigations carried out by a few of them in the first half of 2000.

Departmental select committees in operation in May 2000	
Departmental committees	**No. of members**
Agriculture	11
Culture, Media and Sport	11
Defence	11
Education and Employment	17
Environment, Transport, Regions	17
Foreign Affairs	12
Health	11
Home Affairs	11
International Development	11
Northern Ireland	11
Science and Technology	11
Scotland	11
Social Security	11
Trade and Industry	11
Treasury	11
Wales	11

Examples of select committee investigations	
Committee	**Topic for investigation**
Foreign Affairs	British involvement in the Sierra Leone Civil War
Foreign Affairs	British role in peacekeeping in Kosovo
Treasury	Investigating the breakdown in the Stock Exchange computer system
Treasury	Reports on the Bank of England, interest rate policy
Public Accounts	Competition in the gas industry
Health	The role of the new Food Standards Agency

Standing committees These are larger than select committees, with up to 40 members. Their role is to consider possible amendments to legislation during its passage through the House. On the face of it, this appears to be a key role, but in practice these committees are very much controlled by the government whips. The Government has a majority of loyal MPs on each committee so that only those amendments of which the Government approves are likely to be adopted. Proposed legislation does have to be tidied up, clarified and modified to take into account various demands for change by interested groups, so it is an important role. However, the standing committees lack independence and, in any case, all their proposals must be approved by the whole House at the 'report stage' of a Bill. A new committee is formed for each separate Bill and, on the whole, MPs treat membership as a chore, however necessary it might be.

Functions

Although Parliament is described as the 'legislature', suggesting that its main role is to make laws, in fact the legislative process is a relatively small part of its functions. The House of Commons in particular plays a much wider role in the British political system than the term 'legislature' suggests. We can identify the range of functions as follows.

An electoral college

Since the UK has no formal constitution to determine how a government should be formed following a general election, we must rely on the House of Commons to ensure stable government. Effectively, a government consists of a Prime Minister and Cabinet which can enjoy the regular support of the majority of the House of Commons. In this sense, the House 'elects' the Government. Since general elections nearly always produce one party that has a majority of the seats in the House of Commons, an actual vote is not required. We simply assume that the leader of the majority party in the House will form a government and that it will be supported by the majority of MPs. Of course, should no party have an overall majority, the House **would** be required to approve a new government by a vote (this would be in the form of a vote of confidence in the proposed government).

Thus, the function of being an electoral college is only **implied**. In those states where clear majorities are rare and coalition governments are common, Parliaments play a key role in deciding who shall form a government. The Commons reserves that function for a time when it might be needed.

It should also not be forgotten that the House of Commons can 'un-elect' a government and occasionally does so. Thus, in 1979, the Callaghan Labour government was ousted by the Commons after its failure to secure a measure of autonomous government for Scotland and Wales. In that year a vote of 'no confidence' was passed and, shortly afterwards, Callaghan resigned.

Sustaining government

This role is not generally understood or appreciated. It was the nineteenth-century journalist Walter Bagehot who discovered a fundamental truth about the British political system. He argued that the system has 'efficient secrets' – aspects which ensure that it runs smoothly and effectively. The power of the Cabinet was the main secret, but the role of the House of Commons was almost as important, he argued. The Commons usually supports the Government (even more so now than in Bagehot's day) and, in so doing, gives it **authority** and **legitimacy**. The House of Commons has been elected by the people. If it grants approval to what the Government is doing, it is granting authority from the people, albeit indirectly. This strengthens and sustains the Government, since it can claim that all its actions have the authority of the people as long as Parliament, in particular the Commons, will support it. It may appear from televised debates in the Commons that there is a constant battle raging between Parliament and Government, but this is largely generated by the Opposition. Most of the time the Commons majority supports its own government.

Legislation This refers to the formal process of passing laws. In order for a law to be enforced in the courts, it must have passed through the formal procedures of both Houses of Parliament. Much of this is a ritual, since the governing majority in the House of Commons nearly always has its way. Indeed, if the Government suspects it may not be able to carry the support of its own party on a Bill, it will normally drop the measure rather than face a defeat on the floor of the House of Commons. Thus, the Labour Government abandoned proposals to reform trade unions in 1969, fearing defeat in the Commons, while the Conservative administration miscalculated in 1986 and was defeated on its Bill proposing to allow all shops to open on Sundays (since passed). The fact that the only serious defeat of a Government Bill since the Second World War was in 1986 is an indication of how much the legislative process is a formality.

Debates on legislation may be interesting, informed and often hotly contested, but the result of a vote in the Commons is rarely in doubt. Nevertheless, the passage of legislation is required to give legitimacy to the laws. Just as Parliament gives authority to government in general, it also grants authority to individual statutes.

The actual legislative procedures are shown in the following box.

Legislative process

First Reading: Purely formal. No vote is taken.

Second Reading: A full debate on the principles of the Bill. A vote (called a Division) follows the debate.

Committee Stage: A standing committee considers possible amendments.

Report Stage: The proposed amendments are presented to the whole House. A Division is taken on each.

Third Reading: A further debate on the Bill including amendments. Another Division follows.

Further Stages: The Bill is passed to the Lords and thence for Royal Assent.

Making government accountable It is a basic principle of the British system of parliamentary government that ministers answer to Parliament, the Commons in particular, for what they do. Accountability effectively means that actions and policies must be explained, justified and open to debate. It also implies that errors may be exposed and, in extreme circumstances, ministers or the Government as a whole may be forced to resign by the Commons. Governments are accountable to the people at general elections, but it is Parliament that makes them answerable on a day-to-day basis.

This function is most apparent during question times in the House, either to the Prime Minister every week, or to individual ministers from time to time. Many questions and answers are written and thus never see the public light of day. Nevertheless, the process is taking place continually. General and legislative debates are further opportunities to force government to justify its actions.

The select committees have begun to take over much of this function from the whole House. Here ministers and their officials are subject to questioning, often of an inquisitorial nature. An appearance before such a committee can be a searching test for members of the Government.

The House of Commons
in session

Law making   This must be distinguished from the process of 'legislation', which occurs when the Government itself introduces a Bill. There are, however, occasions when laws are not developed by government. Two circumstances give raise to this:

- Bills may be introduced by an individual MP. These are known as **Private Members' Bills**. As long as there is sufficient support for the Bill, as long as the government has no objection to it and provided there is parliamentary time available, there is a chance that a Private Member's Bill will become law. However, success is rare and MPs know this. They realise that even introducing a Bill with no chance of success gives publicity to a particular issue. Nevertheless some important legislation has appeared in this way, notably the 1967 Abortion Act and homosexual law reform measures.
- There have been occasions when the Government has allowed a **free vote** on a subject. The whips will be called off and MPs will be allowed to make up their own mind. When the Sunday Trading Bill was introduced (to allow most shops to open on Sundays) in 1994, a free vote was allowed to take account of the fact that some MPs had religious objections to the measure. However, it would be an error to describe the British House of Commons as a law-maker in the true sense of the word.

Representation

In a broad sense, the House of Commons represents the nation and, as such, when it debates an issue, the people as a whole are indirectly involved. Of course, this function is considerably flawed by two features. First, the Commons is far from being a social microcosm of our society. Less than 10 per cent of its members are women, there are only a handful of members of ethnic minorities and the rest are predominantly of middle-class, professional backgrounds. However much MPs might consult with their constituents, they cannot be expected to be truly representative, given such distortions in membership. Second, party loyalties are so strong that MPs are often reluctant to express independent views that might contradict the philosophy of their political superiors. Nevertheless, during the great debates of recent years on the issues surrounding wars in the Falklands, Iraq and Bosnia, the death penalty, Northern Ireland and law and order issues, the House of Commons has been seen at its best. Measured arguments have mingled with impassioned debate and the public have been informed and educated by the experience.

Redress of grievances

This function has been described by Professor Philip Norton as 'tension release'. Norton points out that individuals need to feel that, if they are dissatisfied by the way they have been treated by a governing body, there is some means by which their grievance can be voiced. Whether or not anything is actually done, it is important that there is an outlet for complaints. MPs frequently take up issues raised by constituents with relevant ministers or officials, occasionally achieving some success. Matters concerning planning applications, health care, social security and immigration are common examples. Not only must individuals be given help, but also constituencies as a whole might need representation. MPs have had some success in protecting their constituencies from such problems as intrusive road and rail developments, nuclear-waste dumping and environmental damage.

Influence

Government is subject to a variety of influences in its policy-making procedures. Pressure groups, the media, public opinion in general and committees of experts all have access to ministers. The influence of Parliament is more difficult to assess. However, the fact that many MPs are sponsored by pressure and interest groups, by trade unions, by industrial and commercial concerns and the like suggests that they have some influence. In the 1990s, there was a proliferation of professional lobby groups who employed MPs to help them to gain the ear of the Government. At the same time, the departmental select committees grew in status and began to take a more active role in policy initiation. Despite this, influence is not power, so where key policies are concerned, decision making remains firmly in the hands of the governing party's leadership.

The House of Lords

Structure

The character of the Lords is largely determined by its membership. In many ways it is the most unusual Second Chamber of any political system in the world that claims to be democratic. The membership and structure are as follows.

Hereditary peers

Before 1999 hereditary peers made up the large majority of the House. These are members of the British aristocracy who have inherited a title that gives the holder the right to sit in the House. In that year, however, reform of the membership of the Lords began. The number of hereditary peers with the right to sit and vote in the House was reduced to 92. Most of these 92 are elected to sit by the other hereditary peers. This was intended as a temporary measure pending the abolition of the voting rights of all hereditaries at a later date.

Life peers

Since 1958 the Prime Minister (acting in the name of the monarch) has been able to create life peers, whose titles are not passed on to their children. There are about 350 of these at any one time, the number being topped up as life peers die.

Some life peerages are simply granted to prominent citizens as a reward for a deserving career. These are not political appointments and most such peers remain politically independent, declaring themselves 'cross-benchers'. Notable examples have been Lord Olivier, the celebrated actor, and Lord Jacobovits, the former Chief Rabbi.

Most, however, are political appointments, made within the convention that each party may nominate peers in accordance with its relative strength in the House of Commons. Politicians who wish to move into semi-retirement without completely losing touch with politics are included, such as former Prime Ministers Lord Callaghan and Baroness Thatcher. Lifelong supporters of the party, though not necessarily former MPs, might wish to serve, such as former trade union leader Lord Feather, or Conservative industrialist Lord Weinstock. In some cases life peerage can be a useful device to bring a colleague into the Government who is not an MP. Since ministers must be members of one of the two Houses (under the doctrine of ministerial responsibility), such a device is occasionally necessary. Mrs Thatcher's close supporter Lord David Young was brought into Cabinet in this way in the 1980s.

Lords Spiritual

The Church of England is still the 'established' church of the state and, as such, is entitled to send its two archbishops and 24 other bishops to sit in the Lords. No other religions have an automatic right to have representatives there. This might seem strange in a multicultural society, but it is the result of the historic links between church and state. Normally the bishops sit as cross-benchers.

Law Lords

Twelve senior judges are entitled to sit in the Lords. These judges also make up (in groups of five at a time) the highest Appeal Court in the UK, considering cases of great legal or political significance that have been passed up from lower courts of appeal. It is important to stress that when we refer to the House of Lords as a 'court' it is only the Law

Lords who are concerned, and the House is here performing a completely different function. At this stage we are considering the House only as part of the legislature, where all its members are potentially involved.

Lord Chancellor

The Lord Chancellor is unique in British politics, and possibly in the world, in being a member of all three branches of government. The Lord Chancellor is the most senior judge and is thus a member of the judiciary; he or she is the Speaker, or Chairperson, of the House of Lords and so takes part in the legislature; and finally, he or she is a Cabinet Minister and so is part of the executive.

In the Cabinet, the Lord Chancellor is the Government's senior law officer, advising on legal matters. He or she is also head of their own department, which administers much of the legal system and profession. As a judge, the Lord Chancellor sometimes presides over major appeals. In the Lords he or she mostly acts as a neutral Speaker, organising debates and general business. (Discipline rarely applies, since the House of Lords is nothing if not well behaved, unlike the Commons!) However, from time to time, the Lord Chancellor may descend from his or her seat (known as the 'Woolsack') and represent the Government in debates. Thus the Lord Chancellor is expected to play a multifaceted role and to switch readily from a neutral to a partisan role. Rare qualities are certainly required.

Business managers

As in the Commons, there are whips in the Lords and a Leader of the House who organise its business and attempt to maintain party discipline. With many independent cross-benchers and much less party unity (peers are essentially amateur politicians, so the power of patronage is very weak), the job for the party bosses is much harder in the Lords than in the Commons. Fortunately for the Government, as we shall see, debates and votes in the Upper House are much less critical than in the Commons.

The House of Lords in session

Committees As in the Commons, each Bill requires a stage at which amendments are considered in the Upper House. However, unlike the Commons, the Lords does not form committees as such, but instead the whole House (in practice a relatively small number of interested members) sits as one large committee to consider changes. The fact that all the peers may sit in committee makes it difficult for the government whips to maintain unity so that small defeats for the Government (all later overturned in the Commons) are not uncommon.

There is a much less developed system of **select committees** in the Lords – this is not considered the proper place for close scrutiny of government – so just two committees of the House have political significance. These are the committees on Science and Technology and on the European Union. Here the most committed and experienced peers undertake significant work on scrutiny. They have no exact equivalent in the Commons, which gives them greater authority.

House of Lords composition, April 2000				
Party	**Life peers**	**Hereditary peers**	**Bishops**	**Total**
Conservative	180	52		**232**
Labour	177	4		**181**
Liberal Democrat	49	5		**54**
Cross-benchers*	135	31	26	192
Others	6			**6**
Total	**547**	**92**	**26**	**665**

*No party allegiance. It is assumed all bishops are cross-benchers.
Source: Stationery Office.

We can see from the table above that the political make-up of the House of Lords, after the removal of most of the hereditaries, was well balanced, though it did not reflect Labour's considerable superiority in the elected House of Commons.

Functions Before we study the functions of the Lords it is important to understand its limitations. There are essentially three realities that control the operation of the Upper House:

- **The Parliament Acts of 1911 and 1949.** These two Acts declare that the Lords has no control over Money Bills (those involving the raising or spending of public money), that it can only delay any other Bill for up to a year (in practice this means that any Bill passed in two consecutive sessions of Parliament cannot be blocked by the Lords), and that any proposed Lords' amendments require the aproval of the Commons.
- **The Salisbury Convention.** These were the words of the Marquess of Salisbury in August 1945 when the House of Lords had heard the new Labour Government's proposals for the parliamentary session:

  'Whatever our personal views, we should frankly recognise that these proposals were put before the country at the recent general election and that the people of this country, with full knowledge of these proposals, returned the Labour Party to power. The Government may, therefore, I think, fairly claim that they have a mandate to introduce these proposals.

I believe that it would be constitutionally wrong, when the country has so recently expressed its views, for this House [of Lords] to oppose proposals which have been definitely put before the electorate.'

The Salisbury Convention still holds true today. His grandson, Viscount Cranborne, had to reconfirm the principle in 1999 when accepting that the removal of hereditary peers from the House had to be approved as it was a Labour manifesto pledge in the 1997 election. Thus most of the hereditary peers voted to abolish their own voting rights, tied, as they were, by the historic convention.

- **The threat of reform or swampage.** Here the elected Government might threaten to reform the Lords so as to make it compliant to the wishes of the Commons, or to swamp it with newly created peers sympathetic to the policies of the Government. (In the 1960s Tony Benn referred to them as his 'thousand peers' taken almost literally off the streets to support the Labour Government.) This threat was to be used to great effect in forcing through the Great Reform Act in 1832, the Liberal Budget of 1909, and sanctions against the rebel regime in the then British colony of Rhodesia (now Zimbabwe) in 1967.

Thus the opportunities for significant action by the Lords are strictly limited. What is left?

Delaying
As we have seen above, the Parliament Acts effectively prevent the Lords from blocking legislation coming out of the Commons. Thus, all it can effectively do is delay the passage of laws, in essence making the Government and the House of Commons think again. This occurred in 1990–1 when the Government's **War Crimes Bill** was rejected in the Lords. The following year the Parliament Act was invoked and the Bill passed automatically into law having been passed again in the Commons. The same principle applies to amendments. Although the Lords cannot force the Commons to amend its legislation, it can cause so many problems with proposed changes that the Government might be forced to reconsider its proposals. This was certainly the case when the Welfare Reform Bill of 1999 was held up for several months while proposed House of Lords amendments shuttled backwards and forwards between the two Houses. In this case the Lords was telling the Government to give further thought to the interests of several groups who were affected by the proposals.

Amending
While it is clearly the case that the Lords is rarely in a position to defy the legislative powers of the Commons, peers often feel free to make amendments to legislation. In many cases this arises from the fact that the Upper House contains a large number of experts who can recognise faults in legislation. This is particularly the case where technical matters are concerned. Many former or current lawyers can recognise when the wording of legislation is unclear or difficult to apply.

More fundamentally, the Lords often seek to defend the interests of minority groups. This was the case in the welfare reform measures referred to above. Similar activity was undertaken in debates on the 1999 Transport Bill, mainly to reflect the particular interests of various transport groups. In these cases, the House of Lords hopes that it will win the arguments. Failing that, however, amendments might so frustrate the Government that it is eventually forced to give in to the demands of the amenders.

During the 1990s there was a marked increase in the amending activities of the House of Lords. Between 1992 and 1997 a weakened Conservative Government with a tiny Commons majority was vulnerable to attacks on its legislation in the Lords. The Criminal Justice and Public Order Act of 1994, for example, was heavily amended in the interests of civil liberties. After the 1997 election, members of the Lords became alarmed that the huge government majority left the country without effective opposition. They therefore took it upon themselves to become a kind of second opposition. Amendments to measures on transport, welfare, criminal justice, freedom of information and House of Lords reform itself were forced on a government that was reluctant to face indefinite delays in the implementation of its programme.

Debating

Many of the great issues of the day have been the subject of impressive debates in the Lords. These have included questions such as the abolition of the Greater London Council in the 1980s, regular deliberation over the causes of crime, and the conduct of economic policy, which came to prominence in the early and darker economic days of the Thatcher administration.

We might ask, however, whether such discussions have any real influence on our decision-makers. In the case of all the examples described above, the Government had its way because of its control over the Commons majority.

Safeguarding human rights

There is an assumption that, should a dominant government seek to use its power to threaten individual liberties, the more independent House of Lords stands as a bulwark against what Lord Hailsham called, in 1976, the 'elective dictatorship' of government. Yet once again the Lords' record here is unimpressive. While it is true that an attempt to cancel Greater London Council elections in 1985 was successfully blocked by the Lords, it has failed to hold back steady increases in the powers of the police, despite expressing serious misgivings. Its most notorious defeat concerned the implementation of the Poll Tax legislation in 1988. It was quite clear that the peers considered the tax to be unjust and contrary to the basic principle of taxation that it should be related to the ability to pay. It was clear that they wished to make fundamental changes to the proposals. Faced with the prospect of a disastrous defeat, the Government called up hundreds of normally absent hereditary peers to force the Bill through. Some of the members were so unfamiliar with the Palace of Westminster that they had to be directed to the correct lobby by the whips. Similarly, the Lords tried to refuse to accept the War Crimes Bill in 1990 on the grounds that no suspected person could be sure of a fair trial when evidence was over 50 years old. Yet, the Lords having voted against it, the Bill was simply returned in the same form the following year. Under the Parliament Act rules, the Lords was thwarted once again, being unable to vote against it a second consecutive time.

Thus the evidence suggests that a determined government with a solid Commons majority can defy the Lords whatever it might to do.

An assessment of Parliament

We cannot attempt any discussion of the importance of Parliament
the House of Commons. There are a number of factors involved:

- The Government normally enjoys an overall majority in the
  Commons. For 47 of the 50 years since 1945, the governing party has
  enjoyed such an overall majority of MPs. Thus normal party loyalties
  invariably mean that unity is preserved. Naturally the **size** of the
  Government's majority is significant, but nevertheless, simple arithmetic indicates that even a small advantage is crucial.
- Patronage is a key factor in government control. The Prime Minister
  has about a hundred government posts at his or her personal disposal,
  together with a large number of other appointments and honours,
  notably peerages. Since one of the principal qualifications for political
  advancement is loyalty, this ensures that a majority of MPs would not
  think of jeopardising their promotion prospects by defying the
  instructions of the whips. If we add this group of ambitious members
  to the ministers and junior ministers themselves who are bound to
  support the Government under the doctrine of collective responsibility (the 'payroll vote'), few are left as potential rebels. Only when
  there is a powerful point of principle at stake, such as European
  integration, are members likely to oppose their political superiors.
- In extreme circumstances, a Prime Minister may threaten to resign
  along with the whole government and so provoke a general election.
  MPs with marginal seats are certainly likely to be sobered by threat of
  defeat, but even those in a secure position would prefer not to fight an
  election. Furthermore, members generally prefer their own party to be
  in government. A members' revolt leading to a resignation of the
  Government is more than likely to result in electoral defeat.
- A relatively new phenomenon within the Conservative Party is the
  pressure placed upon members by their own Constituency Associations. In the great uncertainty over the Maastricht Treaty in 1993,
  grass-roots members played their part in bringing a number of dissidents into line. Indeed, in the 1990s new alliances were forged
  between the whips and some constituency parties to persuade
  members that compliance would be a wise course of action. This is
  not a particular feature of the Labour Party, but it should be noted
  however, since constituency parties are often supportive if their
  member takes a radical, anti-government line.
- The doctrine of manifesto and mandate generally denies MPs the
  authority to defy their own government. It is accepted that most of
  the electorate vote for a party and its manifesto, rather than for the
  individual candidates. MPs who then choose to oppose the manifesto
  of their own party will be reminded by the whips that they might be
  betraying the Government's mandate.
- As we have seen above, there are a number of constitutional and
  political reasons for the weakness of the House of Lords. Apart from
  embarrassing defeats on amendments, therefore, the Upper House is
  not a real threat to government power.

For 30 years after the Second World War, relatively little attention was paid to Parliament by political commentators. Apart from occasional disputes between a Conservative-dominated Lords and Labour governments, and short periods during which governments were vulnerable because of their small majority, Parliament was considered largely irrelevant.

The attitude of MPs themselves tended to confirm such a view. Many continued to pursue other careers almost full time – often in business or the law. They rarely used research assistants and often shared secretarial staff. The practice of holding regular 'surgeries' to hear comments and complaints from constituents did not become common until the 1970s. Select committees, apart from Public Accounts, held little status and government defeats were rarely even threatened.

More recently, however, attention has returned to Westminster and there is considerable controversy over its current importance. Attitudes fall generally into two camps, typified by the work of two prominent contemporary experts on parliamentary affairs – Professor Philip Norton and Dr Andrew Adonis.

The Norton view

Professor Norton identifies the approximate date of 1970 as a watershed in the behaviour of the House of Commons. He suggests that there have been attitudinal, behavioural and institutional changes in the activities of MPs since that time. He also suggests that the House of Lords has become more professional and independent in its outlook. The result of these changes is that Parliament has been transformed from a supine, unimportant institution into a policy-influencing body. It cannot yet rival the United States' Congress in importance, but has certainly grown immensely in political significance. Thus he suggests:

- MPs expect government to listen to them. The experience of Edward Heath's premiership, when they were rarely consulted, led MPs to insist that they should play a more active role in policy formulation, both as a whole and through various policy committees.
- MPs accept to a greater extent that they must represent the interests of their constituents actively and thoroughly. They hold regular consultations with constituents and are commonly active in campaigns to protect their constituencies from potentially damaging policies, such as the creation of new motorways or rail routes, or the dumping of nuclear waste. They ask more questions of ministers and are willing to raise local issues in debates on the floor of the House.
- Members consider participation in the work of a departmental select committee to be highly prestigious and useful. In such committees they have a rare glimpse of real influence, normally reserved only for ministers. Seats, and chairmanships in particular, are much coveted. Here they can interrogate ministers and officials without the normal constraints of parliamentary ritual and the reports of such committees have become highly influential on policy.
- The frequency of government defeats, particularly over amendments, has increased. The 1986 defeat of the Sunday Trading Bill on the Second Reading was a major event in Commons history, but there have been many occasions when governments have had a difficult time in passing legislation, often being forced to make important

concessions. Thus the Bill to ratify the Maastricht Treaty was only passed on the understanding that the UK would try to hold back the process of European integration. Similarly, the Poll Tax legisla-
~~tion was only passed when 30 or so MPs were 'bought off' with~~
agreement to give certain vulnerable groups of citizens large rebates. MPs no longer consider themselves 'lobby fodder', as they used to be known.

- The House of Lords, with an increasingly representative mix of life peers, has developed what has become known as a 'new professionalism'. As we have seen, it is extremely active in the scrutiny of proposed European legislation. It is also more willing to challenge government policy, largely through the device of proposed amendments. While such obstructions can be overcome, the Lords has become an important factor in the consideration of future policy making.

Thus, the days when the Government's business managers could disregard Parliament when planning policy implementation have gone. MPs must be consulted fully and concessions are often needed if potential revolts are to be avoided.

The Adonis view

Adonis accepts the Norton analysis in so far as it suggests that Parliament is more important now than it was before 1970. However, he insists that it is still only a very small player in the game of policy formulation and implementation. Thus he argues:

- The House of Lords is indeed more active than it used to be and governments can no longer rely on the smooth passage of legislation through the Upper House. Nevertheless, a Conservative administration can still create a comfortable majority if it so wishes. At the same time, most of its obstruction is little more than a nuisance. Amendments, when successful, are limited in scope and do not alter the fundamental nature of policy.
- The select committees in the Commons are indeed a useful development, but their powers are limited and their influence on policy is yet to be proved.
- There is still no prospect of any major item of public policy being thwarted by the House of Commons. The whips will still have their way. The fact that two key pieces of legislation – the Maastricht Treaty terms and the Poll Tax – were passed despite widespread parliamentary and public opposition, proves that the Commons is still largely politically impotent.
- MPs are still inhibited by the inefficient and archaic procedures of Parliament. There is very limited time for them to raise and pursue issues and the parliamentary agenda is very much controlled by the Cabinet. Private Members' Bills may have wide support, but the Government can block them if it wishes merely by manipulating the procedures. Thus a popular Bill to grant important rights to the disabled was cynically 'killed' by the Conservative Government in 1994, simply by ensuring that it ran out of time.

The 'Adonis view' has many allies in the political arena, notably in the Liberal Democrat Party, but also among politicians of both the left and the right, including Tony Benn and Nicholas Winterton respectively. Before we consider the possibilities for reform, we can summarise the apparent strengths and weaknesses of the modern Parliament.

Strength and weaknesses of Parliament		
Function	**Strengths**	**Weaknesses**
Legitimation	• Parliament is respected by the Government and all policies require the approval of the Commons • Proof of this respect is demonstrated by the need to recall Parliament in times of major crises such as the Iraq War. Even foreign treaties are eventually put before the Commons for its approval. • There is the reserve power to defeat legislation as indicated by the defeat of the Sunday Trading Bill.	• The process of approval is possibly only a ritual meaning little, since the Government is so dominant. Although there is an 'appearance' of conflict, the result of nearly every vote is inevitable.
Ensuring government accountability	• Select committees have become influential and even feared by ministers and officials. • They undertake investigations on such issues as the basis upon which overseas aid is given or the sinking of the troopship *Belgrano* in the Falklands War. • They have wide powers and research facilities and are fairly free of the influence of the whips.	• Ministers' question time is largely ritualised and little information is extracted. • The limitations of collective responsibility and the traditional secrecy of government makes ministers wary of being too forthcoming. • Select committees find it difficult to obtain information from civil servants, who hide behind their constitutional anonymity. • In many cases only official government policy is revealed. • Committees have no way of finding out what information may have been withheld by witnesses.

continued

Strength and weaknesses of Parliament (*continued*)		
Function	**Strengths**	**Weaknesses**
Representation	• The House of Commons is geographically representative. • MPs spend a good deal of time and effort caring for the interests of their constituencies. • Many of the major interests in the country are represented by both MPs and active peers in the Lords.	• The Commons does not accurately represent the strength of support for some parties because of the unproportionality of the electoral system. • Liberal Democrats and other small parties are under-represented. • Socially neither the Lords nor the Commons is representative. • There are relatively few women or members of ethnic minorities. • The Commons is dominated by middle-class professional groups and the Lords is dominated by older and wealthier members. • The hereditary peerage is a denial of democratic principles.
Law making	• The Commons has the power to amend legislation and the reserve power to block Bills. • Some Private Members' Bills have been passed that have proved to be popular. • Prominent examples have been abortion and homosexual law reform.	• The Government dominates the parliamentary agenda and so is able to block any legislation to which it is opposed. • The House of Lords finds it virtually impossible to introduce legislation with any success.
Safeguarding rights	• Although Parliament rarely exercises a veto on legislation that might threaten rights and liberties, the very fact that it does have the power to do so might affect the Government's deliberations.	• The whips have great powers to ensure loyalty among the governing party's MPs. • Where there is a large government majority in the Commons, rebellions are easily thwarted, while in situations where the Government is vulnerable, the strength of party loyalty and executive patronage usually wins the day. • The Lords suffers from the knowledge that it can always be forced into compliance by the Commons majority.

Whichever view we might take on the relative strengths and weaknesses of Parliament, proposals for the reform of either or both chambers are numerous. Some of the principal suggestions are summarised in the next section.

Reform of the House of Commons

We can consider House of Commons reform on two levels. First, relatively minor changes could be introduced that would help to improve its performance, but **without fundamentally changing its role or status**. This might be described as 'tinkering' with the system. Second, there could be far-reaching reforms that would **revolutionise the powers and activities of the Lower House**.

Minor reforms

- The working hours of the House could be modified. MPs suffer from long working hours – estimated at fourteen hours per day during the week, much of that time largely unproductive, often simply waiting for Divisions to be called at all hours of the night or in the early hours of the morning. Morning sittings, together with general streamlining of procedures and the elimination of unnecessary rituals, could lighten the load. It should be noted at this stage that it is partly these burdensome hours which prevent more women who have families from seeking to enter Parliament.

- MPs could be supplied with more research and administrative facilities. Much progress has been made in this regard over the last decade, but members still have poor back-up support to reduce their workload or, more importantly, to enable them to be more effective in their scrutinising and representative functions. Even the physical working environment is considered to be an inhibition to efficiency, so sparse is office space.

- The legislative process could be altered and, to a large extent, reduced. The more radical suggestions have included moving the Committee Stage – when amendments are considered – to the start of the procedure, thus reducing many time-consuming disputes later in the legislative process. This is the basis of the system in the USA and is considered to offer a potentially crucial increase in the influence of the House. However, in the USA members of Congress may 'kill' a Bill in this way and it is unlikely that such a power would be accorded to MPs. A second common suggestion is the removal of a whole stage from the process of the passage of a Bill. This would probably be the Third Reading, which largely duplicates the second stage.

- The problem of the socially unrepresentative nature of the membership centres largely on the lack of women. One solution is suggested above, but a 'quota' system has also been proposed. Thus, devices might be put in place to ensure that a minimum number of women are elected. Similar systems for members of ethnic minorities, or indeed any kind of minority, might also be desirable, but they are likely to be less practical than a women's quota.

Major reforms

- The greatest change in the status and powers of the House of Commons would be achieved by changing the electoral system. Proportional representation, of whatever type, would increase the representation of smaller parties. Above all, however, PR might very well result in permanently 'hung' Parliaments and coalition or minority governments in addition to all the political changes that would accompany such developments. The full implications of the introduction of PR are considered on pages 158–62, but it can clearly be seen that the possible inability of future governments to control the House of Commons majority would result in a fundamental change in the nature of executive–legislature relationships. Similarly, greater numerical strength among smaller parties, notably nationalists, would also have profound political consequences.

- The select committees have been an acknowledged success in terms of the effective scrutiny of government. Further 'beefing up' of the committee system is, therefore, also a popular proposal. More committees with greater powers, extra payments for members or at least chairpeople, and the passage of a 'Freedom of Information Act' to improve their ability to obtain official papers, are some of the suggestions that have been considered.

- The introduction of 'fixed-term' parliaments could have implications that are more far-reaching than might at first appear to be the case. However, the notion of fixed periods between general elections – the Liberal Democrat Party suggests four years – could have great significance. One of the realities that prevents MPs of the governing party from risking defeat for their own government is the fear that the Prime Minister might call an election and so put all their seats in jeopardy. Indeed, John Major made just such a threat in 1993 in order to bring dissident anti-European MPs in his own party into line over ratification of the Maastricht Treaty. The comfortable knowledge that even an important government defeat would not result in an election might encourage MPs to be more independent in their actions.

'If it [Parliament] is not proving truly effective at passing legislation that works and if it is only a second-rate scrutineer of the executive, then it is failing at its central tasks.'
Andrew Marr, *Ruling Britannia*, 1995

Reform of the House of Lords

The issue of House of Lords reform burst to the forefront of British politics after the 1997 general election. A confident Labour Party with an overwhelming majority in the House of Commons was determined to succeed where so many had failed before. It was going to reform the House of Lords. The problem was how to do it.

A Commission was set up under Lord Wakeham to look into the issue during 1998–9. Before it reached its conclusion, however, it was decided to remove the voting rights of the hereditary peers. Whatever Wakeham would suggest later, this was seen as a key interim measure. So, as described above, most of the hereditaries were removed. In order to avoid excessive delay and controversy, the Government agreed to a demand to allow some of hereditary peers to remain, at least for the time being. The compromise number was 92. Thereafter the problems mounted up.

A number of broad possibilities have been supported, the principles of which are as follows.

Abolition This would make the UK a **unicameral** parliamentary system, with just one House. The attraction of this option is that it would streamline legislation, remove many of the uncertainties that now exist and save a good deal of money. Its supporters argue that the House of Commons, and the Government that is drawn from it, have a clear democratic mandate from the voters. As such, they suggest, a second chamber simply interferes with the democratic process. Whether elected or appointed, the second chamber would inevitably have less authority than the Commons.

Unicameral systems are very rare. Only Israel and New Zealand are important examples in the modern democratic world. The reason for the popularity of **bicameralism** (two chambers) is the fear that an elected majority might ride roughshod over the rights and interests of individuals and groups in a society. There is, therefore, a need for some kind of safeguard in case the main legislative chamber exercises too much unbridled power. In other words, if legislative power can be divided, it can also be controlled.

A wholly elected second chamber This is very much the choice of liberal politicians. They insist that any part of the legislature must be elected in order to have political authority. However, this presents two main problems:

- The second chamber might have the same party make-up as the House of Commons. It would therefore be unable and unwilling to challenge the authority of the first House. In other words, it would have no point.
- If it were elected in such a way that its political balance differed markedly from the Commons – say, it was elected by proportional representation or at different times to the first House – it would certainly challenge the authority of the Commons and therefore the Government. This would be confusing as there would be two separate electoral mandates in opposition to each other.

Nevertheless, liberals still suggest that an elected body with specialised, limited functions would be useful without challenging the fundamental principle that the Government has a clear mandate from the House of Commons. If, for example, it enjoyed only delaying and amending powers, as at present, it would have more, but not too much, authority. It might also specialise in constitutional issues that need a consensus, and leave normal government policy largely to the Commons.

A wholly appointed second chamber

This popular solution has the attractions of being relatively simple, avoiding fundamental changes to the current system and being much more flexible than the elective solution. An appointed chamber – effectively made up wholly of life peers – could bring in the variety of experts and interest group representatives that is seen as vital to meaningful debate. It would never challenge the authority of the elected House of Commons, but it would be influential through the quality of its members.

The main objection to this concerns the method by which members would be appointed. What would stop a determined government manipulating the appointments to avoid too much opposition? How could political balance be ensured? This solution has, in fact, been dubbed a kind of 'super-quango' – a government-appointed body with virtually no claims to being democratic and under the effective control of the Government.

A mixed chamber – the Wakeham plan

The Wakeham Commission, which reported in 1999, proposed a compromise solution. It recognised the problems of a wholly elected chamber, but wanted to ensure that it did include a democratic element. On the other hand, the Commission was worried about the method of appointing peers, so further reform was suggested. Otherwise, however, the report was relatively moderate. Its main recommendations were as follows:

- The powers of the House of Lords would remain largely unchanged. There would be some minor enhancements, but these were to be modest.
- A 'substantial minority' would be elected. Elections would be regionally based, so these members were to represent the interests of the English and other national regions. The Commission did not recommend one specific type of election.
- Most of the members would be appointed.
- An Appointments Commission would be formed, independent of government. This Commission would determine who would be acceptable.
- At least 20 per cent of the members would have no party allegiance.
- The others, who were connected with a party, would reflect the strength of the parties in the House of Commons.
- The various religious groupings in the UK were also to be fully represented.

In its opening recommendations, the Wakeham Commission summarised its feelings on a new House of Lords:

> *'The new second chamber should have the capacity to offer counsel from a range of sources. It should be broadly representative of society in the United Kingdom at the beginning of the twenty-first century. It should work with the House of Commons to provide an effective check upon the government. It should give the United Kingdom's constituent nations and regions, for the first time, a formally constituted voice in the Westminster Parliament.*

Royal Commission on the Reform of the House of Lords,
Cm 4534, 1999

Summary of arguments concerning House of Lords reform		
Reform	**Arguments for**	**Arguments against**
• Increasing powers	• Balance the excessive power of the Government. • Control extreme policies. • Safeguard rights of individuals and minorities.	• Will reduce the authority of the Government's democratic mandate. • If not elected, it would not be accountable.
• Wholly elected	• More democratic. • Could balance the power of the Commons. • Might be more representative.	• Would challenge the authority of the Commons and the Government. • Might simply reflect the electoral strength of the government and so be meaningless.
• Wholly appointed	• Could bring in experts and representatives of various groups.	• Could be controlled by government through patronage. • Would lack a democratic mandate.
• Mixed elected and appointed	• A balance between democracy and use of talented experts and representatives.	• Purpose might be unclear. • Difficulty of creating political balance.
• Abolition	• Simpler. • Less expensive. • Would speed up the legislative process. • Would remove challenges to the government's electoral mandate.	• Would remove an important check on the power of the Commons and the Government. • Would exclude worthy people from politics.

Lord Wakeham faces
the press

Conclusion

There is no doubt that Parliament is more important than it was twenty years ago, both the Commons and the Lords. Yet the fundamental truths about its position in the political system remain in place. Both Houses are still dominated by the Government except in exceptional circumstances; there is still no real separation of powers between the executive and legislative branches of government; opportunities for the proper scrutiny of government are still limited.

The televising of both Houses, including departmental select committees, has had a dual effect. On the one hand, public awareness of the work of Parliament has increased, while the political profile of backbenchers such as Dennis Skinner, Edwina Currie and David Alton has been raised. On the other, the poor behaviour of MPs and the apparent weakness of peers has reduced public respect for the institutions. Once the novelty had worn off, the rather ritualised conflict of the Commons became the subject of some ridicule, as did the often sleepy atmosphere in the Lords.

The question of reform is still confined to the problem of what we want in terms of executive–legislature relations. If we wish to continue to experience strong, dominant governments that are able to take decisive action without undue obstruction, we should leave Parliament largely alone. If, however, we believe the Government is too powerful, too secretive and needs to be the subject of greater control, then Parliament does need more authority and power.

For exam questions relevant to this unit, see page 556.

Introduction

Over 100 years ago, the English commentator Walter Bagehot wrote in his great work *The English Constitution* that the Cabinet was the **efficient secret** of the British political system. What he meant was that while much of the British system, such as the monarchy and the House of Lords, was purely ritualised and ceremonial, it had at its centre something that made everything work. This was the Cabinet. He did not mean it was **literally** a secret (although the deliberations of Cabinet remain confidential for at least 30 years by law). What he did mean was that it is not immediately apparent **why** Cabinet should hold such a strategic position.

The UK has no codified constitution, which makes it difficult to identify the precise role of any of its political institutions. In the case of the Cabinet there is an extra difficulty, which is that it is never mentioned in British laws, nor does it appear in any of the country's great constitutional documents. When the British political system was being shaped in the seventeenth and eighteenth centuries, the Cabinet certainly did not exist in its present form. Nevertheless, it has become a central element in the system. Thus, it is no secret, but there is an air of mystery about its development.

Bagehot's use of the adjective 'efficient' was clearer. The whole system of policy formulation, law making and policy implementation depends upon the existence of Cabinet and its particular characteristics. Were it absent, or at least relatively weak, the UK might find itself in a similar situation to that of the USA. There, the political system might be extremely open and pluralist, but Bagehot would certainly not have called it 'efficient'. The Americans have great difficulty creating political coherence in policy making and implementation. This is because political power in the USA is so dispersed. The British Cabinet concentrates huge power in one place and this is its 'efficient secret'.

The office of Prime Minister is almost as old as Cabinet itself, dating back to 1721. The Prime Minister was then simply the most senior member of the Cabinet and this is still true today. We must, therefore, consider the two together. However, the Prime Minister's office has also become a separate institution in modern times, so we must also consider it separately, which we will do in the second part of this unit.

Although the Prime Minister and Cabinet have a long history, the two have only existed in their **present form** since Bagehot's day – 1867 or thereabouts. What took place before then is more the concern of historians than of political scientists. It was the development of the modern party system that created the modern Cabinet. In that regard Disraeli and Gladstone, great Conservative and Liberal Prime Ministers respectively, were key figures. Their Cabinets in the latter part of the nineteenth century resembled more the modern Cabinet than those which had gone before.

The Cabinet

The Labour cabinet,
June 2001

The principles of collective decision making

The theories of individual ministerial and collective responsibility are described in Unit 1. The discussion below refers to the practical application of these doctrines. Cabinet government relies totally on the notion of collective decision making, also known as **collegiality**. Superficially, it is simply a matter of a group of people who come together in order to reach a series of decisions. It might be a case of several heads being better than one, or it might be that the members of the group represent a variety of views so that a balance is struck. A single voice might be too extreme. Cabinet implies both of these things, but it is much more. It also represents the collective leadership of the ruling party. By constantly repeating demonstrations of unity, the Cabinet is able to translate collegiality into parliamentary control. The MPs and peers of the ruling party can rest assured that all the relevant arguments, including their own, have been aired in Downing Street. Thus they can support the resulting decisions. Ministers and whips will constantly remind them of this principle.

> '*For all that passes in Cabinet, every member of it who does not resign is absolutely and irretrievably responsible, and has no right afterwards to say that he agreed in one case to a compromise, while in another he was persuaded by his colleagues.*'
> Lord Salisbury, 1878, quoted in Peter Dorey, 'The Changing Character of Collective Responsibility', *Talking Politics*, Vol. 7, No. 2 (Winter 1994/5).

The practicalities of collegiality in the Cabinet Room are also not simple. It is not sufficient for the Cabinet to obtain a majority and then ask all its members to concur. Nor is it necessary to continue discussions until all members have been persuaded of the rightness of one view, as might occur with a jury. Dissenting ministers who find themselves in a minority are not obliged to **agree** with the opposing view. All they are required to do is to keep their opposition to themselves and, in public, to **defend the decision that has been taken as if they agree with it**. This might seem dishonest, and indeed radical politicians such as Tony Benn have said so. On the other hand, it could be argued that this kind of 'false' unanimity is understood by other members of the political community. The feeling is that, if the Government cannot present a united front to Parliament, it cannot survive. Splits in the Government would be easily exploited by the Opposition and would also ultimately result in the splitting of the governing party itself. Thus, whether we call it a necessary evil or part of the 'efficient secret' of the system, without the Cabinet British political life would be very different.

We can gain some clues as to the nature and importance of collective decision making by reviewing three occasions when the system broke down.

British membership of the European Community, 1975

The UK had joined the Community in 1973 under the leadership of Ted Heath. In the 1974 elections, the Labour Party manifesto committed a future Labour Government to renegotiate the terms of British membership and to put the issue before the people in a referendum. Accordingly, when Labour came to power, negotiations were completed and our membership was confirmed on better terms. However, the Labour Party and the Cabinet itself were hopelessly split on the issue of our membership. The principles of collegiality and collective responsibility could not survive this split. It had been hoped that the Government would be able, **collectively**, to recommend acceptance of the new terms and continued membership. However, there were seven dissidents in the Cabinet who refused to be bound by the rules of collective responsibility. They included several of the party's most powerful and popular leaders: Michael Foot, Barbara Castle, Peter Shore and Tony Benn. A novel response had to be found to this crisis of government. The answer was to suspend the rules of collective responsibility for the duration of the referendum campaign. In this way the 'rebels' could take part in the campaign without inhibitions.

The referendum approved the UK's membership with a two-thirds majority. The split in Labour was not healed by the referendum, although there was only one ministerial casualty – Eric Heffer, who refused to accept the decision and the strictures of collective responsibility, was dismissed. Two main lessons can be learned from the episode. First, collective responsibility is vulnerable to a government split on fundamental issues. Second, its survival suggests that there was an acceptance that government cannot operate effectively without it.

The Westland dispute, 1985–6

In 1985 it was clear that the British-owned Westland helicopter company was in financial difficulties and about to collapse. As it was the main supplier of helicopters to the British armed forces, this was a major crisis. In Cabinet Michael Heseltine, the Defence Secretary, argued for the amalgamation of Westland with a European company. His colleague Leon Brittan, Secretary for Trade and Industry, favoured links with the American Sikorsky company. The issue concerned both British jobs and the question of whether the UK should be promoting closer defence links with Europe or the USA.

Under normal circumstances, Cabinet should have settled the dispute – one of its prime functions. However, the crisis exploded into the public sphere when Heseltine revealed openly that the principles of collective decision making were being undermined by the Prime Minister, who clearly supported Brittan. In the aftermath, Brittan ordered the leaking of critical information about Heseltine which should have been confidential. Meanwhile, Heseltine chose to resign on the grounds that 'proper' collective government had broken down. Brittan followed suit when the dubious nature of his activities was revealed.

Westland unearthed a number of weaknesses in the traditional view of Cabinet government. It indicated how the Prime Minister could subvert the rules in her own interests. It also confirmed the suspicion that ministers can avoid the rules of collective responsibility simply by leaking their views to the press and then denying any knowledge of it. As a postscript, the resignation speeches of two of Heseltine's colleagues, Nigel Lawson in 1989 and Sir Geoffrey Howe in 1990, also contained complaints that collective decision making had been undermined by Margaret Thatcher.

The UK and the single European currency

After the Conservative Party, led by John Major, unexpectedly won the 1992 general election, a split within his Cabinet opened up almost immediately. The issue of whether the UK should enter the proposed single European currency was the cause. Some ministers, such as John Redwood and Michael Portillo, were fundamentally opposed to entry. Others, including Kenneth Clarke and Michael Heseltine, wished to see a more positive approach. The dispute became increasingly public, threatening both the doctrine of collective responsibility and the leadership of John Major itself. A patched-up compromise held together precariously, but the open split was a key factor in the defeat of the Government in the 1997 election.

The membership of the Cabinet

It is the sole responsibility of the Prime Minister to appoint and dismiss members of Cabinet. In constructing the Cabinet, the Prime Minister is engaged in two tasks:

- Selecting the senior ministers, such as Chancellor of the Exchequer and Foreign Secretary, who will automatically sit in the Cabinet simply because they hold high office.
- Constructing a team who will lead the Government. The formation of the team is one of the most crucial roles for any Prime Minister.

He or she has a number of considerations to take into account. These include the following:

- There might be senior members of the ruling party who are so experienced and popular that to exclude them would be unthinkable. This was true of John Prescott in Tony Blair's first Cabinet, and of Douglas Hurd in several of Margaret Thatcher's.

- There are ministers who have enjoyed an excellent record as managers of their departments. It may be, then, that such a 'safe pair of hands' is an automatic choice. Sir Geoffrey Howe had such a record in the 1980s until he came into conflict with Margaret Thatcher.
- A leading politician might have an important following within the party. His or her inclusion in the Cabinet, therefore, recognises the group of supporters and may secure their co-operation. Thus Margaret Thatcher kept Peter Walker in her teams, even though they were often political adversaries, he being one of the 'wets' who opposed her right-wing laissez-faire policies. More dramatically, Michael Heseltine was promoted to Deputy Prime Minister and First Secretary of State in 1995 as a reward for his commitment to support John Major in the Conservative leadership election of July 1995. Not only did Heseltine support Major, but also he delivered the votes of his own followers.
- It is always a temptation for a Prime Minister to promote one or two leading rebels in order to 'buy their silence'. The rules of collective responsibility mean that potential rebels are forced to toe the official line and are prevented from stirring up trouble on the back-benches. This is very much more a Labour Party problem than a Conservative one. Tony Blair's appointment of left-winger Clare Short in 1997 falls into this category. It is probably also true that John Major was more comfortable with right-wingers Michael Portillo and Peter Lilley inside his Cabinet than outside it. On the other hand, John Redwood was excluded from Cabinet as a result of his unsuccessful bid for the leadership in 1995. There are limits to how much opposition a Prime Minister will tolerate!

Mo Mowlam, once a cabinet 'enforcer'

- A confident Prime Minister might feel happier if the Cabinet is packed with his or her own close allies. Margaret Thatcher was able to achieve this objective after her second election victory in 1983. After several years of struggle against the 'wets', she was able to dismiss their leading representatives, such as Francis Pym, Ian Gilmour and James Prior. In their place she promoted her own allies, such as Norman Tebbit and Cecil Parkinson. Tony Blair's first Cabinet was certainly very much a group of his close allies. Though there remained personal rivalries, nearly all its members were closely associated with the transition from 'Old' to 'New' Labour over the previous decade. They were, in short, all Blairites, symbols of the new party and the new approach. This was probably the most closely knit group of politicians who had been assembled since 1983.
- The alternative is a 'balanced' Cabinet, designed to unify the party and ensure moderate policies. After John Major formed his second Cabinet in 1994, it was clear that such a balance was his preference. Moderate 'liberals' such as Kenneth Clarke and Stephen Dorrell were set against the right-wing 'Thatcherites' such as Lilley and Portillo. At the same time as a left–right balance was required, a pro- and anti-European balance had to be struck so that both sides in the schism within the wider party could be satisfied.

John and Norma Major with campaign staff, after the challenge to his leadership in 1995

A number of government posts automatically carry Cabinet membership with them. On the other hand, some ministers are not senior enough to warrant a place in the Cabinet. Effectively, therefore, there are three kinds of ministerial office – those which automatically carry Cabinet status, those which **may** include a place in Cabinet, and those which are too junior for the holder to expect to be included in the Cabinet. Some examples of each are shown below.

Status of ministerial offices		
Posts *always* in Cabinet	**Posts which *may* be in Cabinet**	**Posts *never* in Cabinet**
• Prime Minister • Chancellor of the Exchequer • Foreign Secretary • Defence Secretary • Energy Secretary • Lord Chancellor • Leader of the House • Health Secretary	• Chief Whip • National Heritage Secretary • Transport Secretary • Housing • Party Chairperson	• All junior ministers • Sports Minister • Local Government Minister

The actual number of Cabinet members varies according to circumstances, but it will normally be between twenty and twenty-five. There are some who argue that this is too big to be effective, but others suggest that there is, in reality, an informal 'inner Cabinet' of close associates of the Prime Minister which is able to manipulate the official Cabinet. If we include those MPs who are 'Parliamentary Private Secretaries' – unpaid assistants to ministers – there are about 110 members of the Government in all. Thus, the Cabinet represents about one-fifth of the whole Government.

We should note certain further characteristics of Cabinet membership:

- All must be members of Parliament, either the Commons or the Lords.
- Most come from the Commons, but there must be some members from the Lords who can represent Cabinet there. Since the Lord Chancellor and Leader of the House of Lords are automatic members, there can be no fewer than two representatives from the Lords.
- Although the Cabinet Secretary, the UK's most senior civil servant, attends all Cabinet meetings, prepares the papers and writes the minutes (i.e. the official account) of the meetings, he or she is not a member and should play no direct part in decision making (though informally, as a close adviser of the Prime Minister, the Cabinet Secretary is an influential figure).

From time to time, junior ministers or civil servants might be invited to address a Cabinet meeting; they too are not members and will be asked to leave once their business has been dealt with. Thus, the Cabinet is a very exclusive 'club'.

Functions of the Cabinet

Although minutes of Cabinet meetings are subject to the 'Thirty-Year Rule', which means that they remain a secret for at least 30 years, a number of former Cabinet ministers, notably Richard Crossman and Barbara Castle, both Labour ministers in the 1960s and 1970s, have written extensive diaries that inform us about the operation of the Cabinet. It is also common today for ministers to 'leak' information that updates our knowledge of goings-on there.

We can identify seven main functions of the modern Cabinet.

Controlling Parliament's agenda

The Cabinet meets, normally, once a week. When Parliament is also in session, the weekly agenda must be organised. This will include which ministers are to speak in debates and dealing with any possible problems with back-benchers. In the medium term, decisions must be made as to when Bills or White Papers (pre-legislative consultation papers) are to be introduced. The standing ~~committees~~ of the House of Commons, which discuss amendments, might also need some discussion.

Dealing with crises and emergencies

All governments must deal with events as they arise. It might be a growing economic crisis, such as excessive inflation or a sudden drop in the value of sterling. Possibly the most serious example of such an emergency was the crisis over speculative selling of the pound on the foreign exchanges in September 1992, known as 'Black Wednesday'. Then the UK's membership of the European Exchange Rate Mechanism – a central element in British economic policy – was threatened and a decision had to be made as to whether to abandon membership and risk a total loss of public confidence. It had to be a collective Cabinet decision, for without it the Government could have been hopelessly split. In the event, the UK did leave the system, but the Cabinet stood firm in its support for the action. Of course, foreign affairs is another common example of the need for rapid decision making. Wars in the Falklands and Iraq became the subjects of many crisis meetings.

Settling interdepartmental disputes

From time to time, problems might arise between government departments and, if the ministers concerned cannot settle their differences privately, the dispute must be brought to Cabinet for the judgement of colleagues. By far the most common type of problem concerns finance. The Treasury, which holds the purse strings, is engaged in a constant battle with departments to hold down public expenditure. Thus, decisions as to whether a minister's cherished programme can be properly funded despite Treasury opposition might have to be made by Cabinet. However, since one department's spending plans might deprive another of much needed funds, the Chancellor of the Exchequer can usually find plenty of Cabinet allies.

Allocating government expenditure

Late summer and autumn are the main seasons for financial disputes in Cabinet. It is then that the Treasury must finalise plans for overall government expenditure in the following financial year. The Chief Secretary to the Treasury (i.e. assistant to the Chancellor of the Exchequer) will attempt to finalise the plans after negotiations with ministers outside Cabinet. Normally, however, there will be a few remaining problems to be resolved inside Cabinet. Usually this will concern a minister who is holding out for his or her share of the budget 'cake' despite pressure from colleagues. It is on these occasions that the strong ministers earn their spurs and the weak ones fall by the wayside. Senior ministers are often judged by MPs, the press, civil servants and their colleagues on the basis of their ability to secure funds against the opposition of Cabinet colleagues. Indeed, Barbara Castle described Cabinet as little more than a 'battleground'. The public view of a happy, united body was usually false, she suggested.

Policy formulation

A number of ministers who served in Margaret Thatcher's Cabinet have reported that there was an almost total absence of discussion of general policy. The Prime Minister considered that a matter for her as party leader and Prime Minister. Cabinet's role was to run the Government on a day-to-day basis. So many ex-ministers and journalists have reported this phenomenon that it seems likely to be the case. There is evidence that, under John Major, there was more discussion of policy. However, under Blair the Cabinet meets for such short periods of time that it seems unlikely that policy discussions ever take place in the true meaning of the term.

Ratifying decisions formulated elsewhere

As we shall see below, much of the work of Cabinet is carried out in smaller committees of ministers. Their recommendations must be approved by the full Cabinet before they become official government policy. In most cases this is a formality; only rarely will committee business cause controversy. It would be an error to believe that Cabinet spends much of its time arguing and agonising over decisions. In fact it is largely a 'clearing house' for business that has been transacted elsewhere.

Political cabinets

John Major's struggling administration of 1992–7 was constantly beset by political crises that threatened its existence. He therefore adopted the practice of holding informal Cabinet meetings whose function was merely to discuss the current political situation. Such meetings have come to be known as 'political cabinets'. The **formal** Cabinet is constitutionally forbidden from discussing the fortunes of the governing party, so these meetings had to be announced specifically and they made no formal decisions. Under Major they were mainly concerned with solving disputes among members and determining how to present contentious policies.

Tony Blair has had little need for political cabinets. However, as we shall see below, there did emerge some blurring between the conventional kind of meeting and the political gatherings developed by John Major. The fact that cabinets began to spend more time discussing the **presentation** rather than the **substance** of policy made them appear to be party political in nature.

Cabinet committees

Until 1992 the existence and importance of Cabinet committees had been one of the worst-kept secrets in Whitehall. It had never been acknowledged that most of Cabinet's work was carried out in committee, nor was it announced which committees existed and who sat on them. Nevertheless, every MP and political journalist knew perfectly well how the system worked and could, if they were determined enough, find out what the committees were doing. In view of this, and as part of his commitment to more open government, John Major decided to publish details. He kept his promise in May 1992 and revealed that there are two types of committee – **standing** and **ad hoc**. The former are permanent or at least will exist for the foreseeable future. Ad hoc committees, on the other hand, are temporary. The ad hoc committees carry the name **MISC** or **GEN**, followed by a number that identifies them.

An addition to the committee system was introduced after 1998. This was the idea of a **ministerial group**. These are less formal committees with a wider membership than merely Cabinet ministers. They are part of the concept of 'joined-up' government that is described in Unit 9. The groups deal with issues that do not fall neatly into the responsibilities of one department, but need a more comprehensive app—

Principal Cabinet committees and ministerial groups in December 2000

Committees	Sub-committees	Ministerial groups
• Economic Affairs	• Welfare to Work	• Genetic Modification
• Public Expenditure	• London	• Better Government
• Environment	• Drug Misuse	• Crime Reduction
• Local Government	• Women's Issues	• Rural Issues
• Home and Social Affairs	• European Convention on Human Rights	• Food Safety
• Legislation	• House of Lords Reform	
• Constitutional Reform	• European Issues	
• Devolution	• Freedom of Information	
• Defence and Overseas		
• Northern Ireland		
• Health		
• Education		

Note: There was also a special committee for consultation with the Liberal Democrat Party – an experiment unique in British government.

The use of committees, which first came into existence under Lloyd George's premiership after 1916, has grown considerably since the 1960s. They are now an integral part of the government machinery. The increased importance of the committees has given rise to several conclusions:

- They have dispersed power away from the full Cabinet to a wider group of ministers, since non-Cabinet ministers staff most of the committees alongside Cabinet colleagues. This is illustrated by the fact that regular Cabinet meetings have been reduced from twice to once weekly.
- Smaller groups of ministers are concerned with many specialised decisions. In a sense this is merely an admission of what has always been true – that most ministers do not have either the knowledge or the interest to become involved in decisions which do not affect their own department's work. In other words, they are the inevitable result of the increasing volume and complexity of government business. The Cabinet alone simply cannot cope any more.

- A criticism, certainly before the details of committees were published, was that they formed a kind of 'secret government' from which many ministers were excluded. Although every committee decision must be ratified by the full Cabinet, as we have said there is insufficient time for most ministers to investigate fully what the committees are doing.
- The key committees, standing and ad hoc, are chaired by the Prime Minister. Commentators have suggested that this is one of the modern ways in which the Prime Minister is able to dominate Cabinet government. In addition to holding the chair and therefore controlling the agenda, it is an additional source of patronage for the Prime Minister. Ambitious ministers will seek places on the key committees and rely on the Prime Minister to place them there. In return, the Prime Minister can expect their loyalty.

A note of caution about the committees needs to be struck here. It could be argued that the growth of committees is not an indication of the decline of Cabinet government; rather, it is part of the development of a 'Cabinet system' – still Cabinet government, but with power being more dispersed.

We can now summarise our discussion of Cabinet committees as follows.

Cabinet committees

1. They have existed for over 70 years, but the main growth in their use has been since the 1960s.

2. They mirror all the main current responsibilities of government.

3. They are either permanent standing committees or temporary ad hoc committees.

4. The structure and membership of standing committees has been public knowledge since 1992. The details of ad hoc committees are still not published.

5. The Prime Minister appoints ministers to committees, determines their agendas and forms new committees when required. The Prime Minister also chairs many of the more important committees.

6. They reflect the increased scope and complexity of government business.

7. They have been criticised on the grounds that they have taken power away from the formal Cabinet and/or that they represent extensions in prime ministerial power.

The rules and political status of the Cabinet

Unlike the complex set of political relationships surrounding the Cabinet, the actual rules of conduct are relatively straightforward. They are governed by a document known as 'Questions of Procedure for Ministers' which is updated from time to time. Some key extracts from Sir Robert Armstrong's 1985 version are shown on page 220.

Extracts from 'Questions of Procedure for Ministers', 1985

Cabinet committees	Finance
The ~~Cabinet~~ ~~supported~~ by a system of ministerial committees which has a twofold purpose. First, it relieves the pressure on the Cabinet itself by settling as much business as possible at a lower level. Second, it buttresses the principle of collective responsibility of the government by ensuring that, even though an important question may not reach Cabinet itself the decision will be fully considered and the final judgement will be sufficiently authoritative to ensure that the government as a whole can be properly expected to accept responsibility for it.	Proposals which involve expenditure or affect ~~financial policy~~ should be discussed with the Treasury before they are submitted to the Cabinet or to a ministerial committee; and the results of those discussions, together with the best possible estimate of the cost to the Exchequer, should be indicated in the memorandum.

Oral proposals	Collective responsibility
When a minister wishes to raise a matter orally at Cabinet, the Prime Minister's consent should be sought through the Secretary of the Cabinet.	Decisions reached by the Cabinet or Cabinet committees are binding on all members of the government. They are however, normally announced and defended by the minister concerned as his own decisions.

The following therefore apply:

- What takes place at Cabinet and at Cabinet committee meetings is secret. The decisions reached, but not the details of discussions or disagreements, are circulated to those ministers and civil servants who need to know for their work. This is covered by the Official Secrets Act, so an offence is committed if the rule is broken.
- All members of the Government (not just Cabinet ministers) are bound by the doctrine of collective responsibility. This means that ministers must defend in public any Cabinet decisions, or decisions made by a Cabinet committee, and must not show any dissent from them. The alternative is to resign or face dismissal.
- Cabinet committees may make minor decisions themselves without referral to full Cabinet. Otherwise their recommendations must be approved by Cabinet.
- The Treasury has special control over any proposals that involve large amounts of public expenditure.
- The Prime Minister has complete control over the agenda and over which matters are discussed in Cabinet. However, firm decisions are reached collectively in such a way that all ministers feel they can defend them even if they disagree.

Having established the basic rules, it is more difficult to define the precise political status of the Cabinet. Since all proposals, with the exception of actions involving the security forces, secret negotiations with foreign governments and the conclusion of treaties, must be approved by Parliament, we must ask why Cabinet has so much authority.

The answer lies in the unity of the parties in Parliament. The governing party can rely on the fact that, other than in exceptional circumstances, the party will support the Cabinet in Parliament. Indeed, if there is a danger that this will not occur, it is the job of the Chief Whip to warn Cabinet. If the problem cannot be overcome, Cabinet will simply drop the policy. This was certainly the case, reported by Crossman in 1969, when the Labour Government was forced to abandon its plans for trade union reform.

Given, then, that Cabinet can count on parliamentary support, its decision becomes both official party and government policy. It is granted authority by the unity of the party that supports its own leadership. It might be asked how and whether the Cabinet system could work if the support of a majority in the House of Commons could not be ensured.

The Cabinet Secretary and Cabinet Office

The Cabinet Office and its chief, the Cabinet Secretary, are housed at 10 Downing Street, where the Cabinet itself meets. The office operates on two levels – administrative and political.

Administrative duties

The Cabinet and its many committees and sub-committees require a huge amount of administrative back-up. Meetings must be organised, agendas drawn up, official papers prepared and distributed to committee members, and minutes of the meetings written and sent to those who 'need to know'. Not only does the Office service ministerial meetings, but also every Cabinet committee is shadowed by an **official committee** of civil servants who prepare the way for their political masters to reach final decisions later. These official committees have a good deal of influence, particularly in specialised areas such as complex European legislation, where ministers do not have sufficient time to investigate fully for themselves. The Cabinet Office organises the official committees too. Most of the work is undertaken by **Assistant Secretaries**, who are fairly senior officials temporarily seconded to the Cabinet Office from other departments. They normally stay for two to three years at Downing Street.

These duties might, at first sight, appear to be neutral and unimportant. This is not always the case. Agendas are important in that their organisation can often influence the amount of discussion given to each topic. The minutes, too, might be written in such a way as to influence final decisions to be reached at a higher level. Indeed, the minutes of Cabinet meetings that are drawn up by the Cabinet Secretary in consultation with the Prime Minister might become crucial. The Cabinet minutes form the official policy decisions of the Government. They are circulated to the relevant ministers and civil servants who will have to implement the decisions. The manner in which they are expressed, therefore, can be influential. Richard Crossman reports in his ministerial diaries of the 1960s that Prime

Minister Harold Wilson and his Cabinet Secretary, Sir Burke Trend, spent considerable time on the minutes to ensure they conformed to Wilson's own view of what had been decided in Cabinet. It should be remembered here that there are not normally formal votes in Cabinet. Agreement is reached informally and it is the Prime Minister's role to sum up discussions in such a ~~~~~~ that all members can support a resolution. There are no strictly worded proposals to be ~~~~~~. Not surprisingly, Wilson denied that he influenced Cabinet minutes, but Crossman was ~~~~~~ he had and even claimed that some committee minutes were 'doctored'.

Harold Wilson (right) with Richard Crossman

It should also be noted at this point that the Cabinet Secretary is Head of the Civil Service. He or she is in charge of the general conduct and conditions of work of the Service. As such Sir Robert Armstrong, Sir Robin Butler and Sir Richard Wilson all had to preside over radical reforms of the civil service in the 1980s and 1990s. Armstrong also found himself in the unusual position of enjoying a high degree of public exposure during his term of office. It is normal for such officials to maintain a low profile, but Armstrong became involved in the Government's attempt to stop publication of *Spycatcher*, an exposure of the British security forces. In this regard he appeared in an Australian court. He also intervened to restore Cabinet unity and confidentiality following extensive leaking of information during the Westland dispute, a major Cabinet split over the proposed purchase of foreign helicopters in preference to British-made Westlands. The result was the 1986 publication of the so-called 'Armstrong Memorandum', which set out the principles of secrecy and collective responsibility in Cabinet.

Political role The extent to which the Cabinet Office and the Cabinet Secretary, its head, carry out a political role has varied from period to period. Technically, they should not have any such role at all. Like the rest of the civil service, the Cabinet Office ought, constitutionally, to be neutral. However, this does not always reflect reality.

Margaret Thatcher used the office to help her control both the civil service and the Cabinet. Under Tony Blair, however, it has assumed even greater significance. Blair is reported to have used the Cabinet Office in the following ways:

- to co-ordinate the modernisation of the government machine
- as a direct instrument of his own control over government
- as the centre of a new machinery of committees, commissions and working groups, which are developing policy on current issues that are not the individual responsibility of departments (see the ministerial groups listed on page 218)
- as an extension of the Prime Minister's Office, especially where it is concerned with policy presentation.

Different views on Cabinet government

Cabinet as a central collective decision-making body

The orthodox, traditional and, indeed, optimistic idea about Cabinet government suggests that, although many routine decisions are reached outside Cabinet, the key policies and strategy of the Government are still discussed and determined in a collegial manner. It was the view suggested in one of the standard works on Cabinet by John P. Mackintosh in 1962, but it is still claimed to be true, even after the onslaught on Cabinet government mounted by Margaret Thatcher in the 1980s.

> 'The major task of the Cabinet is not to lead the party, to manage Parliament or to think out policy; it is to take or review the major decisions, to consider any proposals which might affect the future of the Government and to ensure that no departmental interests are overlooked, thus giving the work of Government a measure of unity.'
>
> John P. Mackintosh, *The British Cabinet*, 1962

> 'Cabinet Government undoubtedly still exists despite rumours sometimes heard to the contrary.'
>
> Hugo Young, article, 1986

Cabinet as a system

Professor George Jones has suggested that it is mistaken to think of the Cabinet in its narrow sense alone. If we do, it will indeed seem to be a remarkably limited body. Instead, he believes, we should think of it as a complete system, with the twenty or so senior ministers merely as the centre around which other elements revolve. The 'satellite' bodies include Cabinet committees, the Cabinet Secretary and Cabinet Office, the Prime Minister, the Prime Minister's Policy Unit, senior members of each government department and the Treasury.

It might be true that the **real** decisions are reached among those people and bodies that surround the Cabinet. Nevertheless, they require Cabinet approval to make them legitimate and, where a decision cannot be finalised, there is still one last forum where the matter can be settled.

Cabinet as a battleground This view suggests that politics is essentially a struggle for power in which the politically strong prevail and the weak fall. At the centre lies the Cabinet, where the final struggles are played out. This was very much the opinion of Barbara Castle in her accounts of government in the 1970s and of Sir Douglas Wass, Permanent Secretary at the Treasury, at the same time. Cabinet ceases to be a collective decision-making body and becomes, instead, a struggle for power.

Departmentalism A common criticism of the modern Cabinet is that ministers are only really interested in their own departments, a characteristic known as 'departmentalism'. According to this view, Cabinet simply becomes the place where ministers must fight for their own interests. Thus, it is suggested that collective decision making, where ministers are concerned with the general picture, suffers at the expense of self-interest.

> 'If collective decisions are to be of the right quality then collective decision making has to be the principal, and not the last call on the time and energy of ministers.'
> Douglas Hurd, lecture, 1986

> 'Ministers in cabinet rarely look at the totality of their responsibilities, at the balance of policy, at the progress of government towards its objectives as a whole.'
> Sir Douglas Wass, Reith Lecture, 1983

Cabinet overload Professor Peter Hennessy has written extensively on the subject of the Cabinet. He believes it has become overloaded with important business, in common with the rest of the central government machinery. It is expected to process so many decisions that it cannot engage in its real purpose – strategic, long-term thinking and planning. The former Conservative minister Lord Hailsham has said much the same, arguing especially that the overload has led to the increasing use of Cabinet committees. Of this development he disapproves.

> 'The volume of work that has to be carried through means that the Prime Minister has tended to govern through smaller sub-groups of Ministers.'
> Lord Hailsham, Granada Lecture, 1987

> 'If the Downing Street 22 are locked into an energy-sapping, relentlessly deepening downward spiral of overload (as I believe a lot of them are for much of the time), it does affect the rest of us in a direct and important fashion. Our economy and society are not in any condition to carry the luxury of Whitehall and Westminster knocking along at a low level of performance while the rest of us get along running our increasingly prosperous and fulfilled lives.'
> Peter Hennessy, article, 1986

Prime ministerial domination

The question of how much British government is now effectively 'prime ministerial government' is discussed fully on pages 235–6. However, we can establish here that it is a common view that the Cabinet is merely an instrument of prime ministerial control. Hennessy has argued that Cabinet is simply what the Prime Minister wishes it to be, so that while Thatcher might have chosen to use it to further her own policies, her successor, John Major, preferred to allow Cabinet to make key domestic decisions. On the other hand, many outgoing Cabinet ministers have claimed that collective decision making no longer exists. Tony Benn and John Biffen, a former Cabinet minister in the 1980s, have been prominent examples.

> 'Cabinet Government remains a putty-like concept. A Prime Minister can make of it very largely what he or she will.'
>
> Peter Hennessy, *Cabinet*, 1986

> 'Thatcher Cabinets, however, have already become political folklore, and rightly so. She is in the corporate mould of the political chairman and chief executive. The days are long gone when, as with Baldwin, the Prime Minister was titular head but gave his great departmental chiefs a free hand.'
>
> John Biffen, article, 1990

Marginalisation

Under Blair, Cabinet meetings have become increasingly short. From a norm of two hours under his predecessors, he has often cut their meetings down to 45 minutes of largely formal or political (but non-party) business. This has been suggested as a sure sign that the role of Cabinet has been marginalised, largely replaced by a tendency for the Prime Minister to settle issue with individual ministers, private advisers or inside the Cabinet Office.

Policy presentation

Alongside the suggestion that Cabinet's role has diminished under Blair have come reports that its role is changing. If policy is being developed elsewhere, and if ministerial disputes have become rare, we are led to the question 'What does Cabinet actually do?' The answer, it appears, is that it has become increasingly concerned with the presentation of policy, to Parliament, to the media and to the public. The apparent obsession that the Blair administration has developed with unity, and the **appearance** of unity, has created a need for close co-ordination. The Cabinet provides such a forum.

As we have said, no study of the British Cabinet can be complete without a full exploration of the position of the Prime Minister. The two institutions are closely tied together.

The Prime Minister

As with the Cabinet, it is difficult to establish the constitutional and political basis of the office of Prime Minister. British constitutional statutes make virtually no mention of the position. At the same time, it is clear that the importance of the Prime Minister in today's politics is considerably greater than one could guess from a straightforward description of his or her powers.

Prime ministerial authority

In our search for answers we can start by establishing the sources of authority of the office. Four sources can be identified:

The Crown

The Prime Minister is, technically, appointed by the monarch and thus carries his or her authority. After a general election the Prime Minister-to-be is summoned to Buckingham Palace and asked to form a government that will enjoy the support of Parliament. Under normal circumstances, where there is clearly a majority party in the House of Commons and that party has an undisputed leader, this process is a formality. Nevertheless, it is still a necessity, for in the absence of strict constitutional rules the new (or reappointed) Prime Minister needs the legitimacy that the ceremony provides.

The party

It is assumed that the Prime Minister is the leader of the party which commands a clear majority in the House of Commons, or leads a minority party which is being allowed to govern by the Commons, or is the leader of the senior party in a coalition (a situation that has not existed since 1945). Of course, it is virtually always the first of the three circumstances that prevails – a majority party with a clear leader.

It follows from this that, to become and remain Prime Minister, an individual must seek authority from his or her party. If we are in any doubt about this principle, we need only remind ourselves of the events of November 1990 when John Major was elected Conservative Party leader in place of Margaret Thatcher. The Conservatives had a new leader and, whether the Queen or the electorate liked it or not, the UK had a new Prime Minister. There had been no election except among Conservative MPs.

Parliament

More specifically, we mean here the **majority** in the House of Commons. The House of Lords is not consulted and we would expect the opposition parties not to approve of the Prime Minister. But being a minority, the opposition view is irrelevant. In principle, it is the whole government, or at least the Cabinet, which requires the support of the Commons majority. However, it is clear that, should the governing party's MPs object to an individual, he or she could not survive for long. Of course, when the Conservatives are in power, the Commons majority is the party as far as leadership selection is concerned. For Labour the situation is different. The party leader is elected by **all** party members. Their choice might not have the support of Labour MPs, who only represent one-third of the votes for the Labour leadership. Thus, a future Labour leader could, in theory, be accepted by the party but still rejected by Parliament.

We have to go back to 1940 to witness the potential power of Parliament over the office. Neville Chamberlain was effectively removed by Parliament over his foreign policy conduct. Largely because the country was at war, the new Prime Minister, Winston Churchill, needed widespread, cross-party support in the Commons.

The people Possibly more accurately, we should say 'electorate' here. Research suggests that there has been an increasing tendency in modern times for voters to be influenced by their opinions of the respective party leaders. It follows that the winning party leader can, to some extent, claim to enjoy the authority of the people. This is less clear and less formal than the other three sources of authority described above. Nevertheless, it is widely acknowledged. In the early years of the Labour Government after 1997, it was certainly true that Tony Blair enjoyed considerable personal authority, at least for the first two years of his administration. Similarly, a Prime Minister who can no longer command the respect of the people at large runs the risk of losing office. Certainly, popular opposition played a part in Margaret Thatcher's downfall in 1990, as it did in Ted Heath's election defeat in 1974. And certainly the Conservatives were quick to remove him from their leadership in the following year.

These descriptions show what impressive underpinning there is to prime ministerial power. Those powers can be divided into two types – formal and informal.

James Callaghan waving from 10 Downing Street after becoming Prime Minister in 1976

> **Prime Minister profile**
>
> **Harold Wilson 1964–70, 1974–6**
>
> Wilson was the first Prime Minister of the 'television age' when ownership of TVs became common-place. He understood how to use the new medium, explaining policies to viewers in an intimate way. He came over as straightforward and down-to-earth and was known as an accomplished communicator.
>
> According to some of his senior ministers, including Tony Benn, Richard Crossman and Barbara Castle, he dominated his Cabinets, frequently using inner Cabinets and personal advisers. Crossman suggested he was an expert manipulator of the Cabinet. He was also admired for his control of Parliament, his skill in debate and his cutting wit.
>
> His more radical economic policies failed, especially attempts to introduce centralised planning. Indeed, his greatest failure was probably the poor handling of the devaluation of sterling in 1967. However, he expanded and revitalised higher education, founded the Open University personally and did much to encourage technological advance, including the development of Concorde.
>
> His second term, from 1974 to 1976, was fraught with difficulty as his party only enjoyed a tiny majority in the House of Commons. In that time, however, he reached a vital agreement with the trade unions to limit pay increases (the 'Social Contract') and so began the process of bringing down inflation. He retired in 1976 at the age of 60, as he had promised, making way for Jim Callaghan.

Formal powers

The principal group of powers that the modern Prime Minister possesses are derived from what are known as **prerogative powers**. These relate to functions historically performed by the monarch on a discretionary basis. In a modern democracy, it is clearly not acceptable that such a state of affairs should continue. First, the monarch is not elected. Second, the monarch cannot be made accountable for his or her actions. It is, therefore, part of the Prime Minister's role to perform these functions on behalf of the monarch. They might be carried out in the Queen's name, but she plays no active part in them. There are no statutes or legal rulings to confirm this state of affairs – it is a so-called **convention**, or widely accepted principle, that this is so.

To complicate the matter further, prerogative powers fall into two categories. There are those which are performed on behalf of the monarch as **Head of State**, and those performed as **Head of Government**. The former are duties that would normally be carried out by a **President** in an elective system and are performed on behalf of the whole nation. That is to say, they are outside the party political arena. The duties of the Head of Government are normally carried out by a Prime Minister or the equivalent, but **do** concern party politics. The distinction between the terms 'government' and 'state' in the UK is extremely blurred and this creates confusion over the two roles, especially as the real Head of State – the monarch – is forbidden from becoming involved in the political arena. The USA is the only other leading democracy where such a dual role is accepted. However, while the American President usually makes it clear in which capacity he is acting, the British Prime Minister often does not and need not. A description of the two types of power will help.

Powers as Head of State

Head of the armed forces We could say 'Commander-in Chief'. This does not mean leadership in the heat of battle, of course, but it does mean direction of the overall conduct of the armed forces. This also includes exclusive control of the Intelligence Services, both at home and abroad.

Negotiation of foreign treaties   This means literally what it says, but also includes general relations with foreign powers and international organisations such as the EU, NATO and the UN.

Granting of honours   This means having the final say as to who should receive peerages, knighthoods and lesser honours. In a minority of cases, the Prime Minister nominates individuals him or herself, but generally has a power of veto.

Head of the civil service   Although most of the administrative control of the service is left to the Cabinet Secretary, the Prime Minister is in overall control of the organisation and conduct of the civil service. The Prime Minister will also be a major influence over the appointment of Permanent Secretaries – the senior officials in each government department.

Appointment of senior judges and archbishops or bishops of the Church of England   Although this duty is carried out on the advice of the Lord Chancellor and Archbishop of Canterbury respectively, the Prime Minister has power of final approval.

Powers as Head of Government

The appointment and dismissal of ministers   This is solely the responsibility of the Prime Minister, giving him or her patronage over more than a hundred senior positions.

The appointment of heads of public bodies   This might include having a significant influence over the choice of chairpersons of public corporations such as the BBC and of leading quangos such as the Arts Council and the Equal Opportunities Commission.

Dissolution of Parliament   It is the sole responsibility of the Prime Minister to decide when to dissolve Parliament and call a general election. Only under the most unusual circumstance of a Parliament running a full five years from the previous election would there be no choice.

Chairperson of the Cabinet   The importance of this role has been discussed on page 219.

Edward Heath signing the Treaty of Accession to the European Community, 22 January 1973

Prime Minister profile

Edward Heath 1970–4

Heath was, surprisingly, elected in 1970, despite being less personally popular than his rival Wilson. He did not possess Wilson's skills in communication and was seen as a rather aloof figure. He governed on a very individualistic basis with the advice and support of a small clique of Cabinet colleagues. Most importantly, he ignored the opinions of the Conservative back-bench MPs, rarely explaining policy to them and refusing to listen to objections.

Despite his refusal to adopt a collective style of government, he recognised that policy making in the Conservative Party was too haphazard. He therefore set up a number of policy committees in the party and developed the Central Policy Review Staff to feed policy initiatives into Cabinet.

On coming to power he set about implementing laissez-faire policies, restoring market forces in the control of wages, prices and employment, and disengaging government from industrial policy. In fact, his initial policies were close to those adopted by the Thatcher Governments of the 1980s. In 1971–2, faced by an alarming increase in inflation and a number of industrial crises, he dramatically reversed policies (the so-called Heath 'U-Turn'). Government adopted a strict wage and price control policy and two firms – Rolls-Royce and Upper Clyde Shipbuilders – were even nationalised. His attempts to control trade unions through the Industrial Relations Act were a failure. Possibly his greatest success was to negotiate the UK's entry into the European Community in 1973.

Faced by a damaging miners' strike over pay restraint in 1973–4, he called an early general election in February 1974 as a kind of referendum on his industrial policies. His own unpopularity and public sympathy for the miners combined to defeat him.

Informal powers

Most of the informal powers of the Prime Minister arise from his or her position as leader of the governing party. Of course, this position relies upon the historical reality that there is a **single** governing party, and the acceptance that the monarch will ask **only** the leader of that party to form a government. Should there be a coalition, or a dispute as to which individual could command the support of the governing party in Parliament, these existing certainties would be missing. There is no doubt that a future Prime Minister not enjoying the luxury of leading a single, united parliamentary party could not claim such wide powers. However, we can assume that the status quo will be maintained for the foreseeable future.

Informal powers include the following:

Chief policy-maker

The actual extent to which a Prime Minister controls government policy depends upon which party he or she leads, and upon their own political command of that party. As we saw in Unit 5, a Conservative leader has a great deal more discretionary power over policy than a Labour leader. Of course, any leader has significant constraints on policy development – from the wider party, from MPs and from the Cabinet – but a Labour Prime Minister has less personal discretion.

We should also take into account the position of the individual concerned. Dominant individuals such as Harold Wilson, Margaret Thatcher and Tony Blair chose, and were able, to play a central role in policy formulation. The less secure, or those who have preferred a collective approach, such as John Major, have played a lesser role.

Chief government spokesperson

The weekly sessions of 'Prime Minister's Question Time' in the House of Commons have become the principal occasion on which the public and the media can see the Government's current attitudes to the prevailing issues of the day, and how the Opposition challenges those attitudes. Here the Prime Minister **as an individual** is placed under constant scrutiny. But it is not only the individual who is under challenge. The whole range of government policies is being questioned. The Prime Minister must, therefore, stand alone on these occasions as mouthpiece for the whole Government.

Add to this the constant media attention that is concentrated on the Prime Minister and we are left in no doubt that ministers must rely on their leader to present the Government case on many occasions. Of course, individual ministers do appear in front of the Commons, the cameras and the microphones, but it is the Prime Minister who has become the key figure.

Leader of the parliamentary party

Whatever his or her position in the wider party, the Prime Minister must lead the party's MPs in the House of Commons. They look to the Prime Minister for unity and direction. He or she in turn expects loyalty from them. This sense of loyalty enables the Prime Minister to implement policies even if they are unpopular in the party and the country at large. Many MPs rely on the Prime Minister for their position as members of the governing party and those with marginal seats depend on the Prime Minister for their very places in the Commons. Naturally, this is a double-edged sword. If the Prime Minister loses the support of MPs, the basis of his or her power is removed, as Margaret Thatcher was to discover.

Summary of the Prime Minister's power

Formal basis of power	Informal basis of power
1. Acting on behalf of the Crown as Head of State: • Foreign policy-maker and treaty negotiator • Control over granting of honours • Head of the civil service • Senior appointments in the judiciary and the Church of England **2.** Head of Government: • Power of appointment and dismissal of ministers • Appointment of heads of public bodies • Choose the date of the dissolution of Parliament • Chairman of the Cabinet	**1.** Leading policy-maker **2.** Chief spokesperson of the Government **3.** Leader of the governing party in Parliament

Sources of advice to the Prime Minister

Unlike other ministers, the Prime Minister has no department of his or her own, and is therefore at a potentially great disadvantage against strong-minded colleagues who can call on an army of officials for advice. **Lloyd George** (Prime Minister 1916–22) recognised the problem and therefore created the Cabinet Office. Since then there has been a steady growth in the scope of advice available to a Prime Minister.

The Cabinet Office and Secretary

Despite its name, the Cabinet Office predominantly serves the Prime Minister (see page 221). Other ministers can rely on their own officials for policy advice and initiatives.

The Prime Minister's Policy Unit

This was set up in 1974 as a result of an overhaul of the services at 10 Downing Street ordered by Edward Heath. It comprises a number of special advisers, across a broad range of policy issues, brought into government to advise the Prime Minister. Its members are acknowledged experts in their fields who would not normally have access to the policy-making process. The Policy Unit reached its height under Margaret Thatcher, with twelve members, most of whom were politically committed to her radical policy agenda.

Four successive Heads of the Unit exemplified the shift towards neo-liberal policies in the Conservative Party under Thatcher. Sir John Hoskyns (1979–82) was a successful businessman who believed strongly that government should disengage itself from control over industry and commerce. He was succeeded by a right-wing journalist, Ferdinand Mount (1982–4), and then by John Redwood (1984–5). Redwood was later to become an MP and by 1993 was in John Major's Cabinet. In 1995 his unsuccessful challenge for the party leadership was based on radical neo-liberal, right-wing policies, the same ideas that had characterised his leadership of the Policy Unit. He and his team did much to generate the 'Thatcher revolution' in the mid-1980s. Professor Brian Griffiths (1985–90) followed Redwood. Griffiths was a convinced monetarist and formed a powerful alliance with Mrs Thatcher's private economic adviser, Sir Alan Walters.

After 1997 the Policy Unit, led by David Miliband, a very close associate of the Prime Minister, Tony Blair, assumed a yet more significant role. It formed part of the new machinery, centred in the Cabinet Office, which was to become the personal instrument of prime ministerial dominance.

Individual advisers

All Prime Ministers have been able to choose a number of personal advisers from outside the machinery of government. The most 'notorious' of modern times was Sir Alan Walters, who was the personal economic adviser to Margaret Thatcher in the 1980s. It was the influence of Walters that led to the bitter resignation of Nigel Lawson as Chancellor of the Exchequer in 1989. Lawson claimed that Walters was virtually running economic policy, a role that should have been properly his in consultation with the Prime Minister. Sir Anthony Parsons was a lower-profile adviser on foreign affairs than Walters in the same period.

There has been considerable disquiet over the use of private advisers, but this has not prevented the growth in their number and significance. Under Major and Blair, many of the advisers have become known as 'spin doctors', manipulators of information and political fixers. By early 2000 there were 77 such advisers serving the Prime Minister and Cabinet ministers.

Technically, they are temporary civil servants, though they are not bound by the same rules as permanent officials: that is, they are not required to be neutral. Their role is, in other words, overtly political. They exist to place the Government in a good light and to prevent disputes **within** government. Indeed, three of them, including the Prime Minister's Press Secretary, Alastair Campbell, have been given the power to instruct civil servants. This might seem a small step, but it has enormous potential significance. In the past, all civil servants have reported only to ministers. Now a few political advisers may also control them. For now, however, the principal effects have been to enhance the political status of ministers and to give the Prime Minister independent sources of advice, the like of which he or she has never had before.

Policy agencies ('think tanks')

As with individual, special advisers, there has been an increase in the use of such bodies as an extra input to the policy-making process. Prominent in the 1980s were the **Adam Smith Institute**, the **Institute of Economic Affairs** (IEA) and the **Centre for Policy Studies** (CPS). Much of the privatisation programme at that time was encouraged by the Adam Smith Institute, while the IEA was an important influence on Margaret Thatcher's economic policies. Labour Prime Ministers will not find such a ready-made group of think tanks to help, but it is possible that such groups as the **Fabian Society**, the **Institute for Public Policy Research**, and the **Commission for Social Justice** will come to the fore.

Inner Cabinets

It was Richard Crossman in the 1960s who first identified the existence of what he called 'inner' Cabinets in government. He suggested that the Prime Minister used the practice of forming small groups of senior ministers to advise and support him. Indeed, Crossman himself claimed to be a member of such a group under Wilson. This is no surprise, for all powerful figures need close advisers who are also 'insiders'. All Prime Ministers since Wilson have certainly used such advisers from time to time. Tony Blair's group has changed from time to time, but such figures as Peter Mandelson, David (Lord) Irvine and Gordon Brown have certainly figured largely in his inner groups.

'Kitchen Cabinet'

The term 'Kitchen Cabinet' was coined to describe the small group of individuals who were intimate political advisers to Harold Wilson. The most prominent members were his Political Secretary, Marcia Williams (afterwards ennobled as Lady Falkender), and his Press Officer, Joe Haines. On the face of it, the positions they held were of relatively minor importance, but they undoubtedly wielded considerable influence. It was the rather closed and domestic nature of their role which gave rise to the title 'Kitchen'. Margaret Thatcher also had an important private team. Again the Press Officer, Sir Bernard Ingham, was involved, as was Charles Powell, a civil servant transferred to her private office. Powell was the driving force behind Thatcher's attempts to distance the UK from the European Community.

When Tony Blair took over as Prime Minister in 1997 there were early signs that a new Kitchen Cabinet was being formed, a combination of Cabinet ministers, officers and other ministers. Its members included John Prescott, Gordon Brown, Robin Cook and Ann Taylor (Cabinet ministers), Alastair Campbell (Press Secretary), Nick Brown (Chief Whip), Jonathan Powell (Chief of Staff) and **Peter Mandelson** (Minister without Portfolio). The key figure appeared to be Mandelson, who masterminded the successful general election campaign. His role was to co-ordinate government policy, an apparent euphemism for acting as adviser to the Prime Minister.

Harold Macmillan.
Prime Minister 1957–63

Prime Minister profile

Margaret Thatcher 1979–90

Margaret Thatcher dominated political life in the UK more than probably any other Prime Minister in the twentieth century. During her term of office she suffered periods of intense unpopularity (1981–2), but also enjoyed extreme popularity and admiration (1983–7). Yet she was elected Conservative leader as a compromise candidate, expected to be a 'caretaker' until some other dominant figure emerged. On taking office she was forced to accept a Cabinet that was largely made up of senior politicians who were philosophically opposed to her radical, right-wing policies. These were the so-called 'wets' and they were a majority until after the 1983 election. Her dominance was the result of three main factors – the dramatic shift to the left of the Labour Party which resulted in great public suspicion, the British victory in the Falklands War of 1982 and her second election victory, with a huge 144 majority, in 1983. She could now complete the task, started in 1981, of ridding the Cabinet of her political opponents. She surrounded herself with close allies and, thus armed, was able to dominate completely. From then on she was continually accused of converting the government machine into an instrument for her own personal rule. She was also accused of 'politicising' the civil service by ensuring that officials sympathetic to her philosophy were promoted to senior positions. Despite her dominance, she had learned from Heath's mistakes. In particular, she was careful to inform and consult with her back-benchers. She knew that, if she could carry them with her, Cabinet opposition could be defeated.

Her policies are well documented elsewhere, but it should also be noted that she placed the UK in the forefront of world affairs, forming a close relationship with the USA and distancing the UK from Europe.

The terms 'populist', 'presidential' and 'overbearing' were all applied to her and there is little doubt that there is some truth in all of these descriptions. Whether she changed the nature of the office of Prime Minister in the long term is, however, open to question.

Prime ministerial government?

Two events in 1962 opened up the question of whether the British system of government had actually become prime ministerial government. The first occurred in July when Prime Minister **Harold Macmillan** dismissed one-third of his Cabinet following a period of unpopularity for the Government. The second was Richard Crossman's controversial introduction to a new edition of Bagehot's *English Constitution*. In it Crossman, sure to be a minister in a future Labour Government, suggested that the term 'Cabinet government' was no longer appropriate. Instead, the term 'prime ministerial government' was more suitable. Since then there has been discussion as to whether we now see government as totally dominated by the Prime Minister. The evidence to suggest that Crossman's view was, and still is, true includes a number of aspects.

Patronage

The Macmillan incident, known as the 'Night of the Long Knives' (after an occasion in 1934 when Hitler had his main political opponents assassinated), illustrated how a strong Prime Minister could use his powers of appointment and dismissal to control his colleagues. The practice of manipulating Cabinet membership to improve prime ministerial dominance was also successfully used by Margaret Thatcher in the 1980s. Between 1981 and 1984 she steadily removed opponents, replacing them with close allies such as Norman Tebbit and Cecil Parkinson. Since the growth of Cabinet committees, an additional source of patronage exists. Membership of the key committees is much sought after and lies in the Prime Minister's hands. Thatcher again, for example, was able to secure the compliance of James Prior, a leading 'wet', in return for his place on the key Economic Committee. Callaghan, too, was able to keep the left wing of the party under control by granting posts to its leading members, Tony Benn and Michael Foot.

When we add the thousands of other honours and appointments at the Prime Minister's disposal, we have a picture of the enormous potential influence that exists.

> 'The present centralisation of power into the hands of one person has gone too far and amounts to a system of personal rule in the very heart of our parliamentary democracy.'
>
> Tony Benn, 1979

Cabinet control

Crossman described how it was possible for a Prime Minister to manage Cabinet affairs in the interest of his own position. This included control over the agenda, the minutes and discussions in general. Heath was also accused of making decisions among his own 'inner Cabinet' and then ensuring that the full Cabinet complied by presenting them with policies as though they were already agreed. Thatcher's principal device was simply to ensure that Cabinet never discussed key policy issues. On the rare occasions when they did, she made it clear what her own views were and that opposition to those ideas would result in sanctions against the offender.

> 'Collective responsibility is based on collective decision-making. Margaret Thatcher is not the first Prime Minister to circumvent her colleagues, nor will she be the last, but this habit is not the sign of a healthy or a happy Government.'
>
> Francis Pym, *The Politics of Consent*, 1984

The reduction in the time that Cabinet is allowed to meet has been Tony Blair's contribution to the prime ministerial science of Cabinet control. In addition, his Press Secretary, Alastair Campbell, attends all meetings (the practice of allowing a non-minister or civil servant to attend meetings is unique in British political history). This serves to remind colleagues that the Government needs to present a united front to the media. Campbell tries to see to that.

Prime Minister's advice As we have seen above, considerably more advice is now available to the modern Prime Minister than hitherto. The Policy Unit, Cabinet Office and special advisers have provided the Prime Minister with enough policy ammunition to be able to challenge even the power of the heads of major ministries. Thus, Wilson, Heath, Thatcher and Blair could all **lead** the policy debate rather than merely **preside** over the deliberations of others.

Media Politics play a greater part in the concerns of the media – broadcast and published – than ever before. The televising of Parliament and the increase in TV programmes dealing with current affairs, together with the press's obsession with political affairs, have thrust politicians increasingly into the limelight. It is, therefore, inevitable that the Prime Minister should have become the main focus of attention. In the case of Margaret Thatcher this was, to some extent, the result of a conscious effort on her part. The media wish to concentrate their attention on someone who represents the Government (and indeed the Opposition). The Prime Minister is the obvious target.

> 'The very forcefulness with which Mrs Thatcher has projected her views and style, separate from those of her Cabinet, has also established a model of premiership.'
> Dennis Kavanagh, *Thatcherism and British Politics*, 1990

Foreign affairs The UK's entry into the European Community (now the European Union) and the end of the Cold War have resulted in the increased importance of foreign policy making. A series of complex and dangerous issues have arisen in recent times, including the Falklands War, the Gulf War, Bosnia and the former Yugoslavia, Kosovo, Hong Kong, the Anglo-Irish Agreement, Rwanda and the Maastricht Treaty. The Prime Minister is chief foreign policy-maker, notwithstanding the role of the Foreign Secretary. It is, therefore, inevitable that the Prime Minister should be thrust increasingly into the public consciousness as the UK's national representative. This was especially noticeable under John Major in view of his relative weakness in domestic affairs. To compensate, he appeared regularly on the world stage with other national leaders, 'batting for Britain', as he was prone to remark.

> 'There is more to Thatcherism than a set of beliefs. It encompasses also a particular style of politics. That style is an aggressive one.'
> Philip Norton, 'Margaret Thatcher and the Conservative Party', *Parliamentary Affairs*, January 1990

Cabinet government?

Despite the weight of evidence, as described above, a number of important political commentators do not subscribe to the view that we now have 'prime ministerial government'.

Peter Hennessy

The view of Professor Peter Hennessy is that, under Thatcher, we did indeed experience prime ministerial domination, but this need not be a permanent feature. It was her dominance and style that created the phenomenon, but there is no reason why any other Prime Minister should behave in the same way. The evidence from John Major's premiership certainly bears out the Hennessy view. Indeed, Major came to office promising to restore 'collective government'. Cynics will suggest that Major simply did not have the charisma to dominate as Thatcher did, but in his defence he did set out to adopt a lower profile. Lord (Sir Geoffrey) Howe has also remarked that any Prime Minister enjoying as long a term of office as Margaret Thatcher did (over eleven years) is bound to become dominant, simply by outlasting most of his or her colleagues.

Hugo Young

In his book *One of Us* (1989) the journalist Hugo Young has suggested that Cabinet government was very much alive under Thatcher. It **appeared** that she was personally in control because she promoted to senior positions in government and civil service individuals who were politically close to her (hence the term 'one of us'). The Cabinet did rule collectively, but they spoke with one voice and it was the same as **her** voice. Thus, it was a different political era, but as Hennessy also points out, it depended upon the dominance of Margaret Thatcher herself. There is no reason why it should be permanent.

> 'The Cabinet may have declined, but the Prime Minister is not the sole beneficiary.'
> Martin Burch, 'The British Cabinet: A Residual Executive',
> *Parliamentary Affairs*, January 1988

George Jones

Professor Jones's main contention is twofold. First, there was an **appearance** of presidential or prime ministerial government, but this was largely a question of **style**. Media attention, the prominence of foreign policy issues and the increased tendency for the Prime Minister to act as government spokesperson gave the premier a president-like status. Yet there was no real substance to the change. Second, the traditional constraints on a Prime Minister's power are still very much in place. The Prime Minister can be, and often still is, outvoted by his or her Cabinet colleagues. Similarly, a Prime Minister who does not have the support of back-bench MPs cannot hope to succeed, as Heath was to discover. The removal of Thatcher in 1990 was all the proof we should need to confirm Jones's view.

> 'Cabinet Government and collective responsibility are not defunct notions. Shared responsibility is still meaningful, for a Prime Minister has to gain the support of the bulk of his Cabinet to carry out his policies. He has to persuade it and convince it that he is right. Its meetings do not merely follow his direction. Debate and conflict are frequent. It cannot be by-passed and he cannot be an autocrat. To attempt to become one presages his political suicide.'
> George Jones, *Parliamentary Affairs*, Spring 1965

Though written 25 years before her downfall, Professor Jones's comments above could be an epitaph to Margaret Thatcher's premiership.

> 'Cabinet is a democracy, not an autocracy ... it is the
> Cabinet, not the Prime Minister, who decides.'
>
> Harold Wilson, *The Governance of Britain*, 1976

The effect of John Major

As we have seen above, John Major came to office promising to restore collective government. The use of the word 'restore' is significant, since it suggests that his predecessor had indeed undermined collegiality. Certainly, it would be hard to accuse Major of establishing his own personal rule. However, whether he restored collective government is doubtful. It appears more likely that he restored power to his ministers as individuals, rather than to the Cabinet as a collective body.

> 'The central policy-making machine was much changed by Mrs Thatcher ... the system has been changed radically again under John Major, with his own hand being felt in the revived collegiality in Cabinet and Number 10, in greater openness, wider consultation and more volatility.'
>
> Anthony Seldon, in *The Major Effect*, 1995

Prime Minister profile

Tony Blair 1997–

When John Smith, leader of the Labour Party, died in 1994 he was succeeded by Tony Blair. Blair was the third in a line of Labour leaders, started by Neil Kinnock, who transformed the party from an unelectable, left-wing, trade union-dominated organisation into a potential government. By moderating policies to accommodate the reforms made by Margaret Thatcher and to attract the support of the middle classes, Blair and the others successfully led an internal revolution within Labour.

Tony Blair came to power with an almost unprecedented collection of advantages. He enjoyed enormous personal popularity and authority; most of his party was united in its determination to win and maintain power; the Opposition was in complete disarray; the economy was strong; and he had won a huge majority in the House of Commons. Even after three years, by which time some of the gloss had worn off his leadership and his lead over the Opposition was being eroded, Labour remained dominant.

The Blair formula is clear. Policies should appeal to as broad a section of the electorate as possible. Extreme policies that might alienate important groups should be avoided. Key policies have been put in the hands of his closest allies. When things have gone wrong he has taken personal control, as was the case with Northern Ireland and the Balkans war. Radical, but popular policies such as devolution, the minimum wage and House of Lords reform were implemented early in his administration. Thereafter he has become cautious and moderate. Emphasis is placed on central control, presentation of policy and party unity. All this has worked well and Labour has remained popular. It remains to be seen whether the Blair style will still work if the Government runs into serious political and economic difficulties.

Tony Blair at a press
conference, 2001

Tony Blair and prime ministerial government

We have seen how, under John Major, a weaker leader than his prede-cessor or his successor, the belief that the UK still enjoys Cabinet government grew. However, everything has changed again since 1997 and the argument about prime ministerial government has re-emerged as an important theme. The following features of Blair's administration have played a part in refuelling the debate:

- There has been a huge growth in the importance of the Cabinet Office and the Prime Minister's Office as sources of support and advice to the Prime Minister. This is part of a general process of centralisation of the government machine at 10 Downing Street. **Peter Hennessy**, who has been cautious in his analysis of prime ministerial power, has described this centralisation process as unprecedented.
- The increased emphasis on policy presentation has enhanced the role of the Prime Minister as government spokesperson. This has increased his personal authority.
- He now has a small army of political advisers at his disposal. They are intensely loyal to him personally.
- The increased number of key committees, ministerial groups, central government quangos and life peerages have all increased the scope for prime ministerial patronage.
- The increased need for government unity has enhanced the Prime Minister's control over his ministers.
- The pre-eminence of the Prime Minister in both foreign and domestic affairs has been described by **Michael Foley** as the **British Presidency**. This analysis sees the Prime Minister as a **spatial leader**: that is, one who is separated from the rest of government. Such figures as Mar-garet Thatcher and Ronald Reagan have achieved a similar position, he suggests. Spatial leaders have more authority than the rest of the Government and are judged separately from it. Where necessary, they are even in a position to criticise government itself. Tony Blair has certainly come close to being just such a leader.

For exam questions relevant to this unit, see page 556.

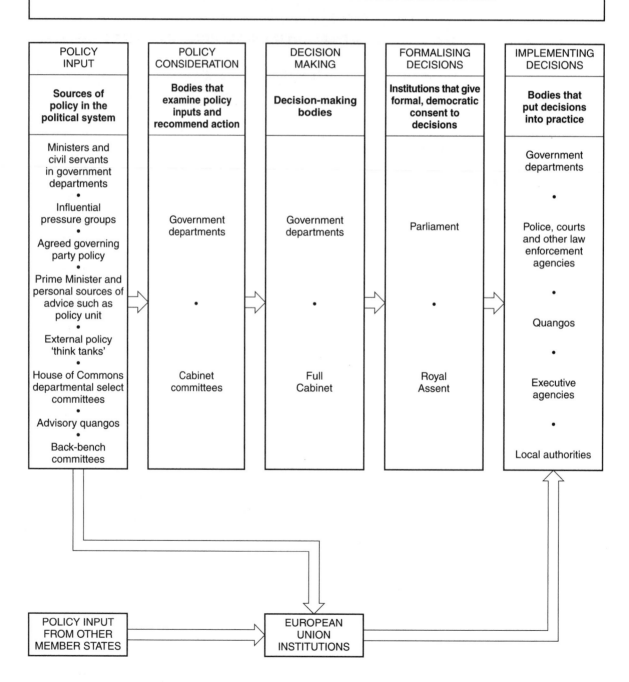

THE MACHINERY OF GOVERNMENT – THE DECISION-MAKING PROCESS

POLICY INPUT	POLICY CONSIDERATION	DECISION MAKING	FORMALISING DECISIONS	IMPLEMENTING DECISIONS
Sources of policy in the political system	**Bodies that examine policy inputs and recommend action**	**Decision-making bodies**	**Institutions that give formal, democratic consent to decisions**	**Bodies that put decisions into practice**
Ministers and civil servants in government departments • Influential pressure groups • Agreed governing party policy • Prime Minister and personal sources of advice such as policy unit • External policy 'think tanks' • House of Commons departmental select committees • Advisory quangos • Back-bench committees	Government departments • Cabinet committees	Government departments • Full Cabinet	Parliament • Royal Assent	Government departments • Police, courts and other law enforcement agencies • Quangos • Executive agencies • Local authorities

POLICY INPUT FROM OTHER MEMBER STATES	EUROPEAN UNION INSTITUTIONS

Who are the civil servants?

Civil servants can be described as all those who are directly employed by central government departments. In the fullest sense, therefore, we might include individuals with no political role whatsoever, such as cleaners, drivers, security guards and maintenance staff. Clearly, we need not concern ourselves with them here, although technically they might fall within our definition. If we include only those who are directly concerned with the development, organisation, drafting and implementation of central government policy and decisions, we have a more realistic definition of the term. The various roles of this narrower definition of civil servant can be described thus:

- **Clerical staff** dealing with the creation and organisation of all the paperwork, computer files and other administrative data that central government generates.
- **Information gatherers** who deal with the routine collection of statistics and facts that are needed for both policy and decision making.
- **Researchers** who are at the forefront of progress. They may be engaged in physical and social sciences, medical research, psychological investigation, criminology, economic theory development and a host of other fields of innovation and progress on behalf of government departments.
- **Executive staff,** who form the largest section of the civil service. They carry out the decisions made by departments on an ongoing basis. Some engage in routine operations while others are managers, sometimes employing hundreds or thousands of other staff. The largest section comprises those who operate the social security system through many local offices. They assess and process claims or manage those who operate the system. The Inland Revenue (direct taxation) and Customs and Excise (VAT and other duties) are two of the other large civil service organisations. Since these offices are located all over the country, most civil servants work outside the capital.
- **Central decision-makers** are civil servants who are close to their minister as they are making decisions **directly** on the minister's behalf. No minister, however conscientious, could hope to give proper considerations to all the matters arising, and must trust senior officials to pass on those matters that need the minister's personal attention, and deal themselves with those that do not. Nevertheless, ministers might sign many documents that contain decisions with which they were not concerned. It becomes clear, therefore, how much they are forced to trust their senior advisers. These same officials are also required to draft parliamentary answers, both written and oral. Typical examples of such work might be sanctioning local authority plans for educational or transport provision, which require ministerial approval; granting export or import licences; and making senior appointments to agencies that come under the jurisdiction of the department.
- **Policy advisers** form the very top levels of the service. It is they who directly advise ministers and the whole Cabinet on government policy. They have weekly contact with their minister, who relies on

them heavily. They operate through a complex system of committees, written memoranda and face-to-face meetings. The information they need is gathered and refined at lower levels so that they are able to distil the decision-making process down to a few manageable options

Top five levels of the civil service

1. Permanent Secretary
2. Deputy Secretary
3. Under Secretary
4. Assistant Secretary
5. Various

Sir Richard Wilson, Cabinet Secretary from 1997

It is with the last two types of civil servant that this unit is concerned. It is they who are of most political significance. While the whole machinery of central government employs over 500,000 people, these senior policy- and decision-making officials number approximately 3000, comprising the top four ranks of the service. If we were to further narrow our definition of policy-makers, this number might be reduced to only about 400 senior officials who deal regularly with the ministers. In general terms, they are the top five ranks of the service, known as the **senior civil service**.

Background to the modern civil service

The structure and operation of the modern civil service has been shaped by three major periods of reform. The first of these took place over a century ago, but the next two occurred during the 1980s and radical reform is still taking place.

Northcote–Trevelyan

In 1854 the Northcote–Trevelyan Report proved to be a damning indictment of the state of the British civil service. It highlighted its corruption and inefficiency and, above all, its recruitment and promotion on the basis of nepotism. That is, posts were granted on the basis of family and social connections rather than ability. It was, therefore, recommended that a complete reform should take place and by 1870 the necessary changes were effected. The basic principles of the service, which were to hold good until the late 1980s, were as follows:

- There were to be three main sections of the service – clerical, executive and administrative. There would be little or no transfer between these levels. The elite group – the administrative class – was to represent the very best brains that could be attracted from the universities (in the event, these came mainly from Oxford and Cambridge).
- Admission was to be by competitive examination and interview. In other words, it was to be based purely on merit.
- Promotion was to be based on a combination of seniority – longer-serving officials were to be given preferment – and merit.
- Posts were permanent. That is, the holder could not be dismissed by a minister on political grounds, but only for misconduct. Thus, it was hoped that political pressure could not be placed on officials who would fear dismissal should they disagree on policy with their political masters. In this way, it was envisaged that neutral advice would be given.
- Neutrality was also safeguarded by the fact that, when a new minister, government or even political party came to office, all officials would retain their position. In other words, civil servants were expected to serve any government with equal care. Officials were also not allowed to participate in party politics.
- Officials were to be anonymous in that they would make no public statements on policy, and not reveal their personal role in any decision- or policy-making process.
- The principle was established that all senior posts should be granted only to those who had already enjoyed a lengthy career in the service. Outsiders would not be allowed into the civil service except at the bottom level. The outlawing of such 'lateral' entry created what was known as the **career civil service**. Put another way, 'civil service' became a closed profession, much as is the case in the law or medicine.

Civil service principles until 1980
1. Recruitment and promotion based on seniority and merit
2. Posts to be held permanently with no political dismissals or appointments
3. Civil servants to be anonymous
4. Civil servants to be neutral and serve any government or minister equally
5. Only career civil servants to be considered for senior posts

For many years the system created by Northcote–Trevelyan appeared to serve British government well. Much admired abroad, the civil service was known for its professionalism, integrity and lack of corruption. By the 1960s, however, concerns began to grow that the service was no longer appropriate in its traditional form to meet the demands of modern government.

The **Fulton Report** of 1968, which was ordered by Prime Minister Harold Wilson as part of his plans to modernise many British institutions, proposed reforms almost as radical as those of Northcote–Trevelyan. However, a stubborn and conservative civil service closed ranks to head off most of Fulton's proposals. There was some tinkering with the system, but overall the existing principles were retained. It was the reforming zeal of Margaret Thatcher that finally brought about dramatic change.

Rayner and FMI

After Fulton, some relatively mild attempts were made to improve the efficiency and management techniques of the civil service, but there was still concern that it was wasteful of public money, inefficient in its operation and certainly larger than it need be.

On taking power in 1979 Margaret Thatcher set up an **Efficiency Unit**, headed by Sir Derek Rayner, Chairman of Marks and Spencer, her favourite successful British company. By 1982 Rayner had produced a major document known as the **Financial Management Initiative** (FMI).

FMI was designed to ensure that civil servants would adopt an approach more similar to that followed by typical business managers. Policies were to be considered on the basis of good value for money, efficiency and the achievement of specific goals. The effect was to remove much of the 'political' consideration that went into making decisions and giving advice, and to concentrate more on making government more efficient and effective.

The role of the Treasury had, of course, always been to reduce wastage and keep public expenditure to a minimum. Now, however, all senior officials were forced to adopt the new management style.

At the same time, the reductions in the sheer size of the civil service that resulted from FMI meant that senior officials suffered reductions in their power and status.

Ibbs and 'The Next Steps'

Sir Robin Ibbs, another former businessman, succeeded Rayner at the Efficiency Unit. His proposals, published in 1988 under the title 'The Next Steps', were more radical than Rayner's. The principal measures affected the provision of services rather than policy making and are discussed in more detail below. Nevertheless, senior officials were affected.

Ibbs suggested that many of the routine administrative tasks undertaken by the service did not need to be under the control of senior civil servants. He therefore proposed that a large number of civil service functions be 'hived off' to semi-independent agencies. These would be funded by their sponsoring department and would come under the general direction of a minister, but would, thereafter, be largely autonomous.

The structure of management was to be similar to that found in business and commerce. Specific performance and financial targets would be set and effectiveness would be judged against these targets. The effect on the civil service was to remove operational responsibility from senior officials and to reduce their authority over a large number of key government functions.

Yet although the power and status of senior civil servants was reduced by the Rayner and Ibbs reforms, they did serve to make a clearer distinction between policy-making and operational roles. The latter were largely removed. The 3000 or so senior officials were clearly now advisers rather than managers.

Reforms in the 1990s

John Major advanced the Rayner and Ibbs reforms still further after 1990. First, he introduced the **Citizens' Charter**, a so-called new deal for those who had contact with public services. The Charter was designed to set standards of service for many public services, including sections of the civil service. Targets of performance were set and published. Failure to meet these service targets could result in damage to the career prospects of public servants and, in some cases, members of the public could be compensated. It would be wrong to see the Citizens' Charter as a dramatic reform by itself, but it has helped to change the way in which many civil servants operate. It is increasingly recognised that they serve the public and should therefore try to serve them well, rather than acting in their own interests.

Major was also interested in the concept of **market testing**. The problem with assessing civil service performance has always been that it is not a commercial operation. There are no profits involved, no sales figures or market shares to worry about. How then can efficiency and effectiveness be measured? One answer has been to review the way in which private enterprise performs in a similar field of operation. By taking similar performance measurements it becomes possible to estimate how well a public service would perform if it were in the private sector. In other words, if it had to operate in a competitive, commercial market, how well would it do? This helps to assess whether public services are giving **value for money** – a popular catchphrase in modern government.

Much of this has applied to local government and to public corporations, but it also applies to the civil service. Under Blair's Labour Government, the term **best value** has tended to be used. The principles of best value are similar to those of market testing. It should also be noted that the Ibbs process of creating new executive agencies has been continuing. In the year 2000, for example, a further thirteen agencies were in the process of being set up.

Criticisms of the senior civil service

Since concern over the role of senior officials began to grow in the 1960s, a number of specific criticisms have been levelled at the civil service.

Excessive power

The traditional version of the role of civil servants states that ministers are the masters and officials are the servants. Ministers are expected to make policy and officials to carry it out without demur. Of course, advice must be given, but this should be confined only to advice and not influence.

A number of former ministers, however, have argued that civil servants seek to wield real power. They are able to do so, it is claimed, because they are permanent and can therefore become experts in their field, while ministers are temporary (on average a minister remains for less than three years in one post) and, essentially, amateurs. It is also true that ministers simply do not have the time to check the nature of all the advice they receive. It has long been accepted that ministers are overloaded with work. Officials are, therefore, able to manipulate information and advice. The view of Richard Crossman, a Labour minister in the 1960s and 1970s, was typical:

> 'This is where one's [a minister's] relationships with the Prime Minister are so all-important. If one doesn't have his backing, or at least the Chancellor's or First Secretary's to the Treasury, the chance of winning against the official view is absolutely nil.'
>
> The Crossman Diaries (under April 1965), 1979

> 'If civil servants are doing their job properly, there is bound, at the very least, to be a creative and probably co-operative tension between the ministers and their official advisers.'
>
> Lord Crowther-Hunt, 'Mandarins and Ministers', Parliamentary Affairs (Autumn 1980)

Nevertheless, it should also be emphasised that no such charge has been levelled against the senior civil service by former Prime Ministers Harold Wilson and Edward Heath. They have argued that only weak ministers can be manipulated by officials.

It must also be remarked that, during the 1980s, a large number of radical reforms were carried through despite considerable civil service opposition. Not least of these are the deep reforms of the machinery of government itself, which are described below and which have considerably weakened the influence of civil servants.

Excessive conservatism

Radical ministers such as Richard Crossman, Tony Benn and Barbara Castle have also suggested that the British civil service is excessively cautious and anti-reformist. As a prime example, they point to attempts to introduce economic planning in the 1960s and 1970s which were thwarted by the stubborn refusal of officials to co-operate. In case we suspect that this is solely a left-wing accusation, it should be emphasised that Margaret Thatcher, on taking prime ministerial office in 1979, brought with her much the same prejudice. Indeed, Thatcher was determined to challenge the deeply rooted 'conservatism' and opposition to reform that she believed to flourish in Whitehall.

It should be noted that, while socialists such as Crossman and Benn viewed the civil service as the natural friend of traditional Toryism, Thatcher believed them to be more left wing and sympathetic to the retention of state power. Hugo Young's observation below illustrates this:

> 'No Government has been elected whose leader [Thatcher] was as deeply seized as this one of the need to overturn the power and presumption of the continuing government of the civil service; to challenge its orthodoxies, cut down its size, reject its assumptions, which were seen as corrosively infected by social democracy, and teach it a lesson in political control.'
>
> Hugo Young, *One of Us*, 1989

In the event, Thatcher succeeded in forcing through most of her radical programme. However, this was achieved by either by-passing civil service advice, turning instead to independent advisers and policy agencies, or appointing senior officials who were openly sympathetic to her views.

Exclusivity

The Northcote–Trevelyan reforms established a system by which only career civil servants could reach senior positions of responsibility. Furthermore, the recruitment practices of the service have ensured that officials are drawn from a relatively narrow range of social and educational backgrounds. It is, therefore, frequently argued that this exclusive and sheltered group is ill-suited to policy making in a complex and technological modern world.

Professor Peter Hennessy's extensive review of the civil service emphasises this particular criticism as one of its most serious shortcomings:

> 'Whitehall failed to attract the rich mixture of human skills it needed, relying overmuch on a single, if refined, stream of generalist graduates, and ... it failed to make full use – and still does – of the human capital already in its possession.'
>
> Peter Hennessy, *Whitehall*, 1989

The solution suggested by Hennessy (and earlier, in 1968, in the Fulton Report) is to make senior positions open to outside entry, with posts advertised generally: in other words, to eliminate the 'career service' principle. In this way, some of the country's more able individuals might become available to give advice to government later in their careers. As occurred in the two world wars, when many experts and academics were drafted into government for the sake of the war effort, ministers might be better served by talented people with wider and deeper experience than career bureaucrats. By 1993 the Conservative Government seemed to have accepted this view and had begun to implement Hennessy's proposals.

Excessive secrecy

The civil service is not immune from the tendency of British government generally to keep its activities out of the public eye. Of course, civil servants are, according to the rules governing their conduct, expected to remain anonymous in terms of their own individual role. They must also sign the **Official Secrets Act**, which places a universal requirement for secrecy on all government work unless a minister expressly sanctions publication. Nevertheless, there is, it is often argued, a 'cult of secrecy' within Whitehall. Again, Hennessy is one of the severest critics:

> *'Secrecy is built into the calcium of the British policy-maker's bones.'*
>
> Peter Hennessy, *Whitehall*, 1989

In practice, this tendency leads officials to attempt to keep policy-making processes from the eyes of both Parliament and the media. Where necessary, reports may be suppressed, information used selectively, and meetings held in private. Letting light into the corridors and committee rooms of Whitehall is certainly discouraged.

Genuine attempts were made by John Major in the 1990s to alter this ethos. Civil servants increasingly appear before select committees of Parliament, although they are rarely able to be completely frank; a minister for open government now exists to find ways of ensuring publication of information that need not be kept secret; some of the workings of the machinery that supports the Cabinet have also been revealed.

Progress, however, is slow. Many, especially Liberal Democrats, believe that only the passage of the **Freedom of Information Act** will solve the problem. In 2001 such an Act is in force, although its advocates are disappointed by the relative weakness of the legislation.

The conduct and loyalty of civil servants

Whom do civil servants serve?

This may seem a simple question at first sight. It is not. Technically, civil servants are servants of the 'Crown'. Does this mean that they serve the monarch and not the Government of the day? Clearly, if the 'Crown' were a truly independent authority, with an active political role, as was the case before the middle of the nineteenth century, the difference between 'Government' and 'Crown' would be crucial. Civil servants would be subject to a higher authority than that of ministers. But 'Government' and 'Crown' are not really separate in a political sense today. Thus, it might seem, civil servants represent the Crown and the Government simultaneously.

What is already a difficult concept becomes more confusing when we consider further alternatives. Officials (and we must remind ourselves here that this concerns the relatively small community of policy advisers and implementers) might act in a manner that serves the interests of any one of the following:

- the whole Government
- the Prime Minister
- their own minister
- their own department, whoever the minister may be
- the ruling party
- some conception of the 'national' or 'public' good.

These possibilities may be examined briefly in turn.

The Government of the day

In 1985, Clive Ponting, a senior official at the Department of Defence, leaked information to an MP that his boss, Secretary of State for Defence Michael Heseltine, had misled Parliament over the UK's conduct of the Falklands War in 1982. Ponting claimed that he was justified in making the revelation by his higher duty to serve the 'public interest'.

Ponting was prosecuted under the Official Secrets Act. The judge, in his remarks to the jury, clearly rejected Ponting's defence. Officials **do** serve the 'national interest', but this can only be interpreted by the Government. It is not for civil servants to decide what is in the national interest.

In the event, Ponting was acquitted. It seems the jury decided that he was **morally** justified even if he might have been technically guilty. Nevertheless, the case established the principle that there is no abstract or independent conception of the national interest. In other words, civil servants serve the Government alone.

The Prime Minister

Part of Margaret Thatcher's domination of the political system in the 1980s was said to be her control of the civil service. Indeed, it has been argued that she eventually controlled all senior appointments in the service personally. Her aim, it was argued, was to ensure that senior officials shared her own political philosophy. In other words, their highest duty was to serve her purposes.

Hugo Young sums this up in the opening lines of his work on the Thatcher years in government:

> *'Is he one of us?' The question became one of the emblematic themes of the Thatcher years. Used by Mrs Thatcher herself, it defined the test which all politicians and other public officials aspiring to her favour were required to pass.'*
>
> Hugo Young, *One of Us*, 1989

There have, certainly, been many fears expressed that the senior civil service was 'politicised' by Thatcher. That is, instead of being appointed on the basis of merit, civil servants were chosen on the basis of their political outlook. The doctrine of a neutral service was, thus, challenged.

Certainly, Sir Robert Armstrong (Cabinet Secretary), Sir Bernard Ingham (Press Secretary) and Sir Charles Powell (Prime Minister's Private Secretary and Foreign Policy Adviser) were seen as her personal political servants; their first loyalty was to the Prime Minister.

We need to be cautious in this area, however, since Margaret Thatcher's premiership was unusual. It seems unlikely that a less dominant Prime Minister could use the civil service in the same way. Even so, it has been of concern that, if the civil service does become politicised in this way, it becomes unable to serve any future government with a different political philosophy. The continuation of 'Thatcherite' policies after her fall in 1990 suggests that there might be some truth in this assumption.

Their own minister

The orthodox view on this question is that civil servants' first duty is to their minister – their political boss. In case there was any doubt, the rules governing conduct were codified by Sir Robert Armstrong, the then Cabinet Secretary and most senior civil servant, in 1985. The 'Armstrong Memorandum' stated clearly that civil servants' first duty was to their minister. Should they have any concerns about their role, about integrity or about policy, they were to consult with their minister for guidance.

This appears straightforward but can cause problems. During the open Cabinet warfare surrounding the dispute over the purchase of Westland helicopters, it was discovered that some civil servants had been serving their ministers somewhat over-zealously. In particular, officials in Sir Leon Brittan's department (Trade) had illegally leaked information to support their minister's case. So it became unclear whether officials were expected to become involved in internal government disputes on behalf of their political masters. However, before Westland, it had appeared that the position was clear:

> *'The constitutional position is both crystal clear and entirely sufficient. Officials propose, Ministers dispose. Officials execute.'*
>
> *The Times*, 15 February 1977

Sir Robert Armstrong,
Cabinet Secretary
1974–87

Their department

One of Richard Crossman's principal criticisms of the civil service was that officials developed a 'departmental view' of various policies. Thus, whoever the minister may be, and whichever party he or she represents, civil servants will attempt to impose this view on the minister. In other words, their first loyalty is to their department.

For example, the Treasury is always concerned with maintaining low public expenditure and a balanced budget; the Foreign Office is more interested in relations with the USA than those with Europe.

These criticisms, however, have been somewhat overtaken by history. The Thatcher reforms have transformed the civil service and all its former certainties have been challenged. There is now little evidence that the Crossman view is still valid.

The ruling party

It is certainly true that official rules forbid civil servants from becoming involved in party, as opposed to governmental, politics. The advice they give and the decisions they make are to be in the national interest as interpreted by ministers, not in the interests of the ruling party alone. The distinction might sometimes be blurred, but it should be made.

The main examples of the problem occur when decisions have to be made that might benefit the community, but might also damage the popularity of the Government. What is a civil servant to do? Let us say a general rise in taxation is indicated by the current state of the economy. This might clearly lose votes in the future for the Government. The question therefore arises: how is the official to advise his or her minister? In theory the official ought to pursue the best interests of the country, but the constitutional rules of conduct say that the public interest is to be judged by elected ministers, not civil servants. This is likely to remain a dilemma as long as civil servants are expected to be neutral.

It does help, of course, that ministers now increasingly use private advisers who are permitted to give political advice. Civil servants can now tell their minister to consult the advisers on the political consequences of an action, while the civil servants themselves can give impartial advice.

The national interest

Finally we return to the Ponting claim – that officials serve the national interest as defined by their own judgement. This has been firmly rejected by constitutional experts and politicians, but it remains an issue, especially for radical politicians such as **Tony Benn**. He and others suggest that an official with the problem of such a conflict of interests should be able to appeal to a parliamentary committee, possibly in confidence.

It seems unlikely that any government will be willing to accept such a proposal. It is in the interests of ministers of any party to be able to rely upon loyal officials. Any weakening of that position is also seen to undermine government itself and so is unlikely to occur.

Higher public profile

The traditional anonymity of the civil service was frequently called into question during the 1980s. The arrival of departmental select committees in the House of Commons in 1979 gave the opportunity for MPs to question civil servants directly. Though officials were under strict instructions to stick firmly to the standard departmental line on policy and avoid voicing their personal opinion, some chinks of light did appear in the dark corners of civil service work.

More importantly, senior officials working for Margaret Thatcher's administrations became increasingly involved in public issues. Her Press Secretary, Sir Bernard Ingham, became a public mouth-piece not just for official government policy but also for the Prime Minister's personal position. Meanwhile, Sir Robert Armstrong, the Cabinet Secretary, appeared both before parliamentary committees and in a court in Australia attempting to block publication there of *Spycatcher*, a highly sensitive book by Peter Wright on the British intelligence community.

A political civil service?

The many problems that have been identified surrounding the relationship between ministers and civil servants have given rise to calls for important changes to the status of officials. Among these is the proposal that ministers should be able to appoint personally a body of advisers in addition to the officials permanently based in their department. These 'political' civil servants would be chosen partly on the basis of their political philosophy. They might be drawn both from within and from outside the existing service.

The inspiration for this idea comes from France, where each minister has his or her own 'Cabinet', numbering about a dozen advisers. These both complement and counterbalance the advice offered by the neutral officials. They also answer those criticisms which suggest that the civil service has its own agenda which it seeks to impose on new ministers.

Largely supported by politicians of the left, such as Tony Benn, the implementation of this plan would break down the traditional barriers in the civil service. Opponents suggest that it is the very neutrality of the existing service which is its great strength. Since the 1970s, however, considerable strains have been placed on that tradition of neutrality.

Political advisers

To some extent the issue of politicisation of the civil service has been overtaken by the growth in the use of private advisers in the 1990s. By 2000, the Government was employing 77 of these 'temporary' civil servants, who are not bound by the rules of neutrality. Three of them – Alastair Campbell (the Prime Minister's Press Secretary), Jonathan Powell (Chief of Staff in the Prime Minister's Office) and David Miliband (Head of the Prime Minister's Policy Unit) are thought to have an unprecedented amount of influence over Tony Blair's Government. They give openly **political** advice and are expected to do so. Their concern is the health of the Government and the ruling party. Their use poses two main problems:

- What is the relationship between political advisers and neutral civil servants? Is there too much tension between them? To whom should ministers pay more attention?
- They are not politically accountable for what they do, or the advice they give. They may, indeed, form a kind of hidden government. Civil servants are made accountable through the doctrine of ministerial responsibility – the minister answers for what they do in Parliament. This is not the case with private advisers.

Four models of the civil service

Dr Kevin Theakston has drawn together a number of views and descriptions of the nature of the civil service and its relationship with ministers. From them he has deduced four 'models' that serve well as a summary.

Theakston's models might conflict with one another, but they do throw light upon many of the different characteristics of the British civil service. In practice, it embodies all of these characteristics in some measure.

The four Theakston models	
1. Formal-constitutional	This is the orthodox view. The service is neutral, loyal, anonymous and professional. It does not serve itself or any other authority, but only the Government and its ministers.
2. Adversarial	The civil service has its own goals and agenda which often involves it in attempting to thwart the plans of new ministers. Included in this model are the radical 'conspiracy theory' and the less extreme notion that officials simply dislike any radical changes in policy. Ministers therefore face a struggle to overcome civil service entrenched power.
3. Village life	Whitehall is like a community. Everyone in the community – ministers and officials – attempts to find a consensus and to work together to retain their power and maintain the status quo. In other words, they all have a vested interest in helping each other. Clearly this is in direct contrast to the adversarial model.
4. Public choice	This is another critical view, suggesting that the civil service acts in its own interests, which are, typically, to retain its own influence, safeguard the career and financial position of its members and attempt to expand its size. It represents the idea of the great bureaucratic machine, of which Margaret Thatcher and her allies were so critical.

The new civil service

The years between 1980 and 2000 have seen radical changes in the nature of the British civil service.

The emergence of rivals

Governments and individual ministers have always used advisers from outside the civil service. The practice was exposed in the years of the Wilson premierships, 1964–70 and 1974–6, when he was known to operate through a 'Kitchen Cabinet' of personal political assistants. In the 1970s and 1980s, however, the process of transferring policy making to private advisers accelerated.

Edward Heath had set up the **Central Policy Review Staff** (CPRS, also known as the 'Think Tank') in 1970 to advise the Cabinet as a whole on key policies. The CPRS drew membership from inside and outside politics and was fully independent of the civil service. Although it was abolished in 1983, the 'Think Tank' established the principle of accepting external advice in an organised way.

The Prime Minister's **Policy Unit** is a similar body comprising a dozen specially selected experts who serve the Head of Government and supplement a number of other individual advisers who are increasingly used by different ministers. Margaret Thatcher's dependence on Professor **Alan Walters** for economic and financial policy became notorious when it appeared to challenge the authority of the Treasury.

At the same time, the Conservative administrations of the 1980s and 1990s made much use of external policy agencies such as the **Adam Smith Institute**, the **Institute of Economic Affairs** and the **Centre for Policy Studies**. The introduction of the Poll Tax, much of the privatisation programme and the basis of Conservative economic policy were all the result of proposals from these bodies.

Reduced responsibilities

The three developments described below – that is, the growth of executive agencies, quangos, and increased privatisation and contracting out of services – have all reduced the jurisdiction of the established civil service. This has tended to reduce the status of many officials simply because they have smaller bureaucracies to manage.

The policy-making functions of senior civil servants have been retained in large measure, but the reduction in executive functions has certainly reduced their power base.

Management style

The civil service has had to accept that its traditional administrative methods are no longer acceptable, especially since the Rayner reforms. Decisions on policy and its implementation must now consider the precise goals to be pursued, the methods by which these will be achieved and reviews of performance once action has been taken.

Officials are subject to the discipline of proving that measures provide value for money and will give rise to specific benefits. Should officials fall short of expectations, they can expect that their shortcomings will be exposed. Promotion will, therefore, be based very much on the quality of management shown rather than on more traditional administrative skills.

Accountability The management style described above is expected to make officials more accountable to their superiors for their performance. At the same time, government departments are now expected to be more responsive to public expectations. The **Citizens' Charter**, created by John Major, has given rise to a new ethos for government officials. It has made it clear that they serve the public as well as their political masters. Performance targets are not, therefore, restricted to purely financial considerations, but also relate to quality of service.

Career structure The old rigid career structure of the civil service has begun to be broken down despite much resistance. There are proposals to bring in outsiders for senior positions; the new agencies, with their own pay and career structures, have disturbed the traditional expectations of officials; and promotion is based more upon performance than on length of service.

With lateral entry and new flexible contracts, it is likely that the old career service will decline. If officials can no longer enjoy the job security that comes with permanence, their practices and attitudes might also change. Whether these reforms will be for the good must remain to be seen.

New Labour and the civil service

In its drive to modernise the machinery of government, the Labour Government that took office in 1997 has made a number of changes to the civil service. None of them has been as radical as the Ibbs reforms, but they have certainly begun to change the general 'culture' and practices of the service.

Joined-up government The most practical change has been the concept of **joined-up government** – a new approach to policy making. Some policy areas do not fit neatly into the responsibility of a single government department. Therefore many new bodies have been set up to co-ordinate the work of various sections of the civil service. In other words, many policy-makers and advisers are being asked to think about whole solutions rather than merely departmental policies. Some examples of these 'policy communities' have been:

- social exclusion (the most deprived sections of society)
- drug misuse
- women's problems
- development of information technology.

In such areas, civil servants cease to be a part of a department and become wholly concerned with the formulation of policy.

Freedom of Information and the Human Rights Act

These two developments, which took place during 2000, will have a major impact on the civil service. **Freedom of Information** will mean two things for civil servants. First, they will have to abandon some aspects of the 'culture of secrecy' that surrounds much of their work. Second, they must be aware that some of the reports that they write and the advice that they give might be open to public scrutiny in the future. They will, therefore, become more directly accountable for what they do and will need to be sure that they are acting in a responsible way.

The **Human Rights Act** will affect policy advice. Civil servants in a wide variety of fields will have to examine all proposals and all actions to decide whether they might contravene the Human Rights Act. If there is a possibility that they will, ministers must be warned and the consequences assessed. It will mean more work, more care and, probably, more caution.

Devolution

When power was devolved to Scotland, Wales and Northern Ireland during 1999–2000, some responsibilities of the British civil service were transferred to the new devolved governments. On the whole, this involved direct transfers and little change in the way in which civil servants were to operate. For those who remained in the service of central UK government, it has had one major effect. Legislation and policy affecting all of the UK has to dovetail with the policies and actions of the devolved governments. There is, therefore, a good deal of co-ordination and co-operation to be managed. What used to be an internal problem has become more complex.

New Labour public services

Professor **George Jones** of the LSE has described the civil service since 1997 as **New Labour public services**. In his description he summarises how the civil service, and indeed the whole of the machinery of central government now operates:

- Citizens should be treated more like consumers than subjects.
- Private businesses must be involved in policy goals, contributing both money and expertise to the process.
- The idea of joined-up government suggested that it was important to strive for successful outcomes to policy and to worry less about how, and by whom, policy was to be implemented.
- Public service would become increasingly involved with the overseeing, inspection and regulation of services, rather than with providing them directly. Thus were spawned a wide variety of new agencies, regulators, inspectorates and commissions for this purpose.
- Government should be more open and transparent. Information technology was to be the cornerstone of economic prosperity in the future and so must be promoted by government, both in education and in business.
- Civil servants should form a small but highly trained elite that could co-ordinate these processes. Members of the public services should accept more individual responsibility for their actions and no longer hide behind anonymity and collective government responsibility.

Executive agencies

The Ibbs Report of 1988 known as 'The Next Steps' resulted an increasing number of governmental functions, formerly carried out by the civil service, being transferred to executive agencies. The agencies were not quite as independent as quangos but were separated from the civil service itself. The civil service has a rigid structure in terms of both pay and careers. The increased flexibility of the agencies, it is assumed, enables them to adjust management performance more effectively. They can also recruit personnel from outside the old civil service.

Examples of executive agencies in the UK	
Agency	**Main functions**
• Benefits Agency	• To assess claimants to a variety of welfare benefits
• Child Support Agency	• To assess the financial liability of absent fathers for their children and to ensure payment
• Drivers and Vehicles Licensing Agency	• To issue and renew vehicle and drivers' licences
• Central Office of Information	• To collect and publish statistical information for educational and research purposes

They have their own targets for both finance and general performance. The outcome of their activities can be measured against these targets so that pay and promotion will depend upon success or failure. This provides incentives that are largely absent from the traditional civil service. In particular, the chief executive, who heads each agency, will have his or her salary determined by the performance of that agency.

Since 1988, there has been a steady transfer of responsibility to these agencies. By the end of 1996, 129 such agencies had been created, employing about one-quarter of all civil servants.

At the beginning of the twenty-first century, Ibbs envisages that the vast majority of government functions will be in the hands of these agencies. This would leave perhaps as few as 20,000 civil servants directly employed by a government department. Only about 10 per cent of this number would be directly involved in policy making.

The effects of the growth of executive agencies are as follows:

- To provide opportunities to assess the efficiency of government.
- To reduce the overall costs of bureaucracy in government.
- To bring a wider variety of skills into the government service.
- To weaken the line of accountability to Parliament, since ministers are not directly in charge of their operation.
- To make a clear separation between the policy-making and the purely executive functions of government.
- To have considerably more financial flexibility, with options to borrow funds from the private sector and to make profits where possible.
- Should a future decision to privatise their operation be made, they are already prepared for full independence from government.

Quangos

What is a quango?

The term 'quango' was coined by journalists in the 1970s. It stands for quasi-autonomous non-government organisation. Their official name has become non-departmental public bodies (NDPBs), but we shall continue to refer to them as quangos.

A quango is a committee or agency that has the following characteristics:

- It is set up by central government.
- It comes under the general oversight of a government department.
- Its members are appointed by a minister or a senior official in the minister's department.
- Members may be full or part time, paid a salary or expenses only.
- Members may be a mixture of local or central government politicians, local or central government officials, experts and academics, community leaders, pressure group representatives, representatives of unions, business, industry or commerce, or even just interested members of the public, i.e. laypersons.
- It is funded by its sponsoring department.
- It is expected to be independent from departmental or other political influence, i.e. it is expected to act in a politically neutral way.

Types of quango

Quangos have a number of different kinds of function. These include the following:

- **Spending agencies.** These are given government funds that they must allocate among competing demands.
- **Advisory committees.** Bodies that give informed and non-political advice to ministers concerning policy, legislation and administration.
- **Regulatory bodies.** For a variety of reasons it might be seen as preferable that legal regulation is carried out by a body which is independent of government. In some cases, these quangos may even be a prosecuting authority with powers to bring possible offenders to court. These bodies might also have powers to grant licences for various types of activity.
- **Administrative bodies.** These are given funds to organise and administer activities set up originally by government departments.

Some quangos perform more than one of the functions described above. Examples of quangos and their functions are shown opposite.

The growth in importance of quangos

There have always been bodies similar to the modern conception of the quango involved in the governing process. Between 1970 and 1980, however, there was a vast increase in their number and scope. A peak of 2167 quangos was reached in 1979 when the new Thatcher administration promised to limit their numbers. This was done and by 1993 there were only 1389. Despite the fall in numbers, however, quangos now control more governmental functions than they have ever done.

Introduction

Definitions Those levels of government which apply to areas of territory that are only a **part** of the whole state may be described as **sub-central government**. This implies that there are decision-making institutions which have some degree of independence from central government.

We must be careful not to confuse sub-central **self-government** with **devolved administration**. Administration only concerns the executing of decisions made elsewhere. There are many examples in the UK of bodies that **appear** to be local or regional government, but these are actually only carrying out policies determined at the centre. The Scottish, Welsh and Northern Ireland Offices are the most prominent examples.

Policy for the national regions is made ultimately by Cabinet, with powers sanctioned by Parliament in Westminster. The three Offices shown above exercise these powers. Of course, they do so with some degree of sensitivity to local opinion, but there is no organised democratic means of consultation and none of the ministers or civil servants involved is locally elected. Similar comments can be made of such devolved administrative bodies as **Area Health Authorities** (which distribute funds for health care) and **Regional Development Agencies** (distributing funds aimed at industrial development).

Sub-central **self-government**, on the other hand, describes the level at which **policy decisions are made**; it is not merely a description of where services are **administered**.

There is no strict distinction between the terms **local** and **regional** government. How do we differentiate between a locality and a region? Clearly the latter is larger than the former, but by how much? A useful pair of definitions might be as follows:

- Local government concerns an area which is small enough that the inhabitants consider themselves a **community**. This might be a group of villages, a town, a city or part of a city, or a county.
- Regional government involves an area that is too big to be considered a community, but does have some distinctive characteristics with which people can identify. These differences might consist of the economic structure (e.g. industrial, commercial, touristic or agricultural), geographical features (an area dominated by a river or mountain range), culture (often concerned with nationality differences) or the pattern of settlement (e.g. rural or urban).

Summary of definitions		
Term	**Definition**	**Example**
• Sub-central government	• Decision-making levels below central government	• All local authorities
• Devolved administration	• The execution, but not the making, of policy decisions at sub-central level	• Scottish Office
• Regional government	• Decision-making bodies below the centre but above local community level	• Isle of Man
• Local government	• Decision making at local community level	• London boroughs

The constitutional position of local government

The UK is a **unitary state**. This means that legislative sovereignty lies only at the centre. Although Parliament is sovereign, it is clearly true that, under normal circumstances, political decision making lies with central government. We can, therefore, make two assertions. One is that **policy** is ultimately made by the **Cabinet**. The other is that all powers can only be granted under **legislation** passed by **Parliament**.

Local government, therefore, has **no sovereign powers**. Local authorities can make by-laws: that is, laws which relate only to the area under their jurisdiction, such as regulations relating to car parking, dogs and parks. However, these by-laws are subject to parliamentary approval and can be overruled at Westminster. They can also make **local policy**, but this is only within powers granted by Parliament and these powers can be altered or removed at any time.

Local government structure in England and Wales

The way in which local government is organised varies only slightly between England and Wales (which can be taken together as their systems are the same), Scotland and Northern Ireland. Since the vast majority of the population live in England and Wales, the description here is confined to them. The general **principles**, however, apply to Scotland too. Northern Ireland remains a special case and cannot be included here.

The structure of English and Welsh local government is no longer the result of any rational organisation. It is, instead, the consequence of a number of piecemeal changes that have taken place since the 1960s. These changes have largely been the result of short-term political considerations and not long-term strategy. The second half of the 1990s have, however, seen more permanent restructuring.

It is necessary to distinguish between three types of area: London, metropolitan conurbations outside London, and non-metropolitan or rural areas.

London

The local government arrangements for London changed dramatically in May 2000 when a mayor, with an assembly of 25 members to support him, was elected. The details of this new development in local government are described in more detail below. However, most local services in London are still in the hands of the **London boroughs**. It is, therefore a two-tier system, but with the second tier considerably more important than the first.

Metropolitan areas

There are six of these areas which, like London, used to have a central authority until abolition in 1986. Since then they have also become essentially single tier. Again, most services are handled by **metropolitan districts** (sometimes called boroughs), with some joint services still controlled by an upper tier of **joint boards**. The six areas in question are: Merseyside, Greater Manchester, West Midlands, West Yorkshire, Tyne and Wear and South Yorkshire.

Non-metropolitan areas

Often known as **shire counties**, these are areas dominated by small towns and rural areas. These are essentially **two-tier**, with a minor **third tier** in the most rural areas. The three tiers are as follows:

1. **County councils** handling larger-scale services.
2. **County districts** dealing with more personal and household services.
3. **Parish councils** in villages. These control a very few minor village and countryside matters.

Services

It is a general principle that the more strategic, broad-scale services are handled by larger authorities. The more personal services, which do not necessarily need large-scale organisation and require a great deal of local sensitivity, are handled at the lower level. Some of the main services and the levels at which they are controlled are shown on page 266.

Structure of local government in England and Wales with examples of main services provided (August 2000)

Area	First tier	Second tier	Third tier
Wales	**Unitary authorities** • Education • Planning • Social services • Housing • Police • Refuse management	**None**	**None**
England (excluding London)	**Unitary authorities** • Education • Planning • Social services • Housing • Police • Refuse management	**None**	**None**
	Counties • Education • Social services • Emergency services	**Districts** • Planning • Refuse collection • Housing	**Parishes** • Footpaths • Planning • Traffic management
	Metropolitan areas • Emergency services • Environmental control • Large planning	**Districts or boroughs** • Education • Planning • Housing • Social services	**None**
London	**Mayor and Greater London Authority** • Public transport • Traffic control • Arts • Police (limited) • Emergency services	**London boroughs** • Education • Housing • Planning • Social Services	**None**

Dilemmas for local government

Before examining the detailed issues concerning British local government, some more general difficulties should be reviewed. The broad, conceptual problems include the following four dilemmas for policy-makers:

Uniformity versus local choice

Individuals might expect that, wherever they live, the same type and quality of local services, such as education, environmental control, child care, traffic management and road maintenance should be available. In other words, some might argue that there should be **uniformity** of local provision in all parts of the country. If this is to be guaranteed, however, there must be strict **central control** of services.

On the other hand, many would also argue that, for democracy to be properly served, there must be genuine local choice in these services. Members of the community might wish to choose how funds are allocated between services and how the services should be run. Thus, one community, for example, might prefer a selective form of education provision, while others might insist on a strict comprehensive system. There could also be significant differences in views on development planning. Should rural areas be preserved or should development be allowed to stimulate employment? Clearly, if **local choice** is to be satisfied, there must be much looser central control and genuinely **independent local government**.

Efficiency versus democracy

This is also a question of scale. It is generally – though not always – true that larger-scale operations are more efficient than smaller ones. Funds can be used more effectively and a wider variety of services can be offered. Economists know this phenomenon as **economies of scale**.

Thus, large scale would seem desirable in the field of local government. However, it is also believed by many that larger organisations are less democratic than smaller ones. It is assumed that there is better public access to small organisations – they are more easily understood and generally closer to the community than large bureaucracies.

So there is a dilemma between the attractions of large scale and the fear that this would reduce the democratic nature of local government.

Politics versus administration

We may define **politics** as the making of choices by different groups between conflicting courses of action. **Administration**, by contrast, is the imposition of decisions based on set rules and guidelines determined elsewhere.

We may then pose the question: should such highly sensitive responsibilities as education, care of the elderly, family support services and mental health provision be left to the uncertainties of party politics, or should they be left to bureaucrats who have no political 'axe to grind'? The Widdicombe Committee on the operation of local which reported in 1986, alluded to this dilemma and recommended that many of these services should be removed from the control of party politicians and instead be administered on a neutral basis.

The national versus the local mandate

Both MPs and local councillors fight elections on the basis of a party manifesto, possibly with a few personal variations. Once elected, these politicians claim they have a mandate to carry out the policies in those manifestos. Unfortunately, it often occurs that local mandates conflict with the national government's mandate. Which has precedence?

In the 1970s, for example, the Labour Government claimed a mandate to introduce comprehensive, non-selective secondary education throughout the country. Many Conservative councils claimed a conflicting mandate to retain selective grammar schools. Similarly, in the 1980s the Conservative Government passed legislation enabling council tenants to buy their own homes from local councils. This time it was Labour councils which argued that their electors wished them to retain the housing stock in public ownership.

Despite the difficulty in judging between the competing claims of local and national mandates, in practice the national claim is likely to prevail. The outcome of the two issues described above illustrates this. In both cases the central government was able to rely on parliamentary legislation to force its measures through. It should also be observed that local election turnouts are roughly half those at general elections, so the national mandate can claim greater popular authority. Nevertheless, problems are presented when local communities choose to make a clear assertion of their wish to defy central policy.

The Thatcher reforms

The problems

When a new Conservative Government came to power in 1979 there were a number of problems with local government which it felt an urgent need to address. The principal perceived difficulties included the following:

- The Greater London Council (GLC) and six other metropolitan counties had become so large and powerful that they had the potential ability to defy central government policy. Furthermore, they were all controlled by the Labour Party and especially by left-wing local cliques within the party (the 'urban left', or 'loony left', as the tabloid press dubbed them).
- The Government was determined to reduce public expenditure, but local government accounted for a large proportion of such expenditure and had shown no sign during the 1970s of being willing or able to curb its own spending.
- It was felt that local councils were insufficiently accountable to their electorates. This was particularly true in the area of finance, where there was widespread ignorance of such matters and apparent indifference to high levels of local expenditure and taxation. (This is described in more detail below in the section on local taxation.)
- There was a commonly held belief that local government was inefficient.
- It was suspected that there was widespread 'political corruption' in local politics. That is, decisions were being taken on purely political grounds, to further the interests of a local party group rather than in the interests of the community itself.

In the light of these problems, reform of local government was undertaken on a broad front.

Structural change

In 1986 the GLC and the six metropolitan counties were abolished. Most of their functions were devolved downwards to second-tier authorities, with some strategic services remaining in the hands of special joint boards.

This was followed in 1990 by the disbanding of the **Inner London Education Authority**, a joint organisation run by the twelve inner London boroughs to administer schooling and some higher education. Education was returned to the jurisdiction of the boroughs.

Thus, a powerful tier of local government was removed, administrative costs were reduced and, above all, a powerful challenge to the authority of central government was eliminated.

Functional changes

In the 1980s and 1990s a large variety of services were transferred **out** of local authority control, while a smaller number of additional functions were transferred **into** their control. The shift in functions represents the greatest change in the nature of government provision of services since the reforms of the second half of the 1940s, when there was widespread nationalisation and many new responsibilities were given to local government. While the changes described below do not form an exhaustive list, they do represent the principal changes.

Functions lost

Education

- The introduction of the National Curriculum f̶o̶r̶ ̶c̶h̶i̶l̶d̶r̶e̶n̶ aged five to sixteen took away l̶o̶c̶a̶l̶ responsibility for the majority of schools' curriculum. Instead the school curriculum was to be established by a central Curriculum Council.
- **Local management of schools** removed control over school budgets from councils. Instead, each school was to manage its own financial arrangements through the headteacher and governors.
- Schools were allowed to 'opt out' of local authority control and instead to take up **grant maintained status**. These schools receive finance and are subject to general oversight by the Department for Education.
- The number of places on school governing bodies available for local authority nominees was reduced, giving **greater parental control**.

Housing

- Local authorities were forced to offer **council houses** for sale to their tenants at preferential terms. Thus, there was a large increase in private ownership and a reduction in local authority housing provision.
- An increasing proportion of central funding for housing was diverted away from local authorities, being channelled instead through the **Housing Corporation** and **Housing Action Trusts**, which finance voluntary housing associations providing low-cost homes for renting.
- Ministers were given discretionary powers to control the level of **rents** charged to council tenants.

Compulsory competitive tendering

- A variety of services such as refuse collection, road repairs, council home maintenance and parks and gardens were no longer automatically undertaken by local authorities. Instead the work would be offered, by tender, to private firms. Councils were forced to accept the best tender. Thus, many functions were **privatised**.

Public transport

- Outside London bus and other transport services under local authority control were **deregulated**: that is, private companies were free to provide the services. In most cases, local authorities became a minority provider of public transport.

Functions gained

Children

- Although councils already had broad responsibility for the welfare and care of children in deprived circumstances, these responsibilities were considerably widened under the **Children Act**. Local authorities were now to accept wide responsibility for identifying and caring for children considered to be at some kind of risk.

The mentally ill

- The scheme known as **Care in the Community** resulted in large-scale closure of centrally funded mental care institutions catering for individuals with low levels of mental illness. Instead, local authorities were to place such people into homes in the community and to supervise their future care.

The elderly

- Funding was also withdrawn from institutions caring for the elderly, and local authorities were given increased responsibility for dealing with this through **private provision** or **sheltered housing**.

Financial controls

During the 1980s there occurred a dramatic increase in the level of control exercised over local authority finance by central government ministers. Limitation powers by ministers over both borrowing and large-scale capital spending projects already existed in 1980 and were fully applied as part of the campaign to create more local financial responsibility. However, four further devices were introduced in an attempt to tighten financial discipline.

Grant Related Expenditure Assessments

Grant Related Expenditure Assessments (GREA) were introduced by the 1979 **Local Government Planning and Land Act**. Before this an agreed level of annual expenditure for each authority was negotiated and central government grants were supplied in order to finance this agreed level. The GREA system (now known as the **Standard Spending Assessment**) changed the situation drastically. Now central government officials alone would assess the spending needs of each authority. This was a fundamental reform. It centralised evaluation of local needs and removed a significant amount of local autonomy.

Local authorities were given greater flexibility than before as to how the central government grant (known as the **Rate Support Grant**) was to be allocated between different services. However, in the event, the assessments were so financially tight that there was relatively little freedom of action in practice.

It was immediately apparent that some local authorities were prepared to escape from these strictures by simply raising local taxation (then known as the 'rates') or by borrowing from the banks. Additional controls were, thus, needed.

Grant penalties

Grant penalties were introduced for those councils that succeeded in spending above the centrally assessed limit. The central government grant was simply reduced by the amount of the overspend. However, even this measure sometimes failed. The most militant of councils would simply raise local taxes even more to make up the penalty. Eventually, the Greater London Council found itself with no central grant at all. Needless to say, it had to demand extremely high taxes. A third measure was, therefore, introduced.

Ratecapping

Ministers were given the power to place a limit on proposed rises in local tax. At the time it was known as 'ratecapping'. Applying a set formula, an authority that was deemed to be raising local rates unnecessarily would be forced to reduce its tax demands. One final attempt to escape from the straitjacket was made by some hard-left councillors. They were prepared to continue to overspend and simply allow the council to become bankrupt.

Surcharges

Councillors who set a budget that would result in bankruptcy were considered to be committing a criminal offence. The penalties included fining or 'surcharging' them, and/or disqualifying them from holding office. A number of councillors in Liverpool and Lambeth fell foul of these rules.

'For many it seemed that local government had, during the 1980s, been subjected to a death of a thousand cuts.'
John Kingdom, *Local Government and Politics in Britain*,
1991

Professor George Jones of the LSE has described this process as the 'Tom and Jerry syndrome'. Each time central government found a new way of financially trapping local authorities, they, in turn, found a new way of escaping. Margaret Thatcher and one of her favourite policy agencies, the Adam Smith Institute, adopted one final measure to try to end the 'cat and mouse' game. This was to force local authorities to control their spending and taxation levels by making them more accountable to the public. Where ministers had failed, the electorate might succeed.

Earlier in the 1980s Michael Heseltine, as Secretary of State for the Environment, had attempted to introduce a system whereby large rises in local taxation would be made subject to approval by a local referendum. A trial vote was held in Coventry, but a very low turnout persuaded him that the system would not work. Margaret Thatcher's plan involved the introduction of the **Community Charge** or **Poll Tax**, as it became known. The principles behind this are described below.

Local taxation

Problems with the rates

Problems over local taxation emerged in the 1960s as it became increasingly apparent that it was neither easy to administer nor levied on a fair basis. Up to 1990 local taxation was known as **rates**. The rates were based roughly upon the size and value of properties. However, only one person in each household was liable to pay the rates and they were largely levied upon home owners. Furthermore, it was pointed out that the size of one's property does not necessarily reflect one's ability to pay. The ultimate problem could be illustrated by the fact that a single poor person living in a large property would pay the same tax as a large, wealthy family living in a modest property.

A rapid increase in the number of families owning their own homes, together with increased pressures on local finance in the 1970s and 1980s, led to the development of the political will to reform local taxation.

Possible solutions

For many years a number of alternative were suggested and rejected:

- Complete replacement by central **government grants** was rejected on the grounds that it would remove local autonomy. Central government would use its financial power to exercise complete control.
- **Local income tax** was attractive as it would be based on ability to pay. However, it was thought too difficult to administer and collect.
- **Local sales tax** is commonly used in the USA, but again it is difficult and expensive to collect. There would also be no room for local variation as people could simply travel to purchase goods where taxes were lower.
- A reformed **property tax** would reduce some of the anomalies presented by the rates, but it was rejected on the old grounds that one's home was not necessarily a reflection of one's ability to pay – one of the fundamental principles of fair taxation.

The Poll Tax

The **Community Charge** or **Poll Tax** was the new form of taxation chosen by the Conservative Government for its 1987 election manifesto. It was an attempt to solve two problems at the same time. First, it was thought to be a fairer form of taxation and second, it might go some way to creating greater public accountability in local government expenditure.

The Poll Tax was to be levied as a single, fixed charge on all adults living within a community. A few groups, such as the very poor, would receive substantial rebates, but, essentially, all were to pay the same amount. Thus, it was thought to be fairer and would spread the tax burden more evenly.

Under the rates system only a minority of individual householders actually paid tax. In some poorer districts, where there were very few home owners, as few as 25 per cent of the adult population were paying local rates at all. Yet, it was pointed out, all adults were consuming local authority services. Why should everyone not contribute?

It was also felt that this simple form of tax, paid by nearly everyone, would make electors realise what was being spent by their local council. High-spending councils would therefore have to face an electorate most of whom were meeting the burden of the expenditure through their tax. This had not been the case with the rates. It was hoped that these 'extravagant' councils would, therefore, be pitched out of office by an angry electorate. There would, in short, be greater local financial accountability.

In the event, the Poll Tax met with widespread, militant opposition. Being totally unrelated to one's ability to pay, it was considered unacceptable, even by many whose tax burden was actually reduced as a result. A campaign of non-payment and serious unrest on the Conservative Party back-benches meant the new tax was doomed. Most dramatically, Margaret Thatcher was removed from office by her own party largely as a result of her refusal to accept abolition of the tax.

John Major became Prime Minister and promptly replaced the Community Charge with a modified property tax known as the **Council Tax**.

Council Tax

By 1992, the Council Tax had replaced the Poll Tax. It was based on property value, but with a large number of payment 'bands' and exemptions to make it more sensitive to people's ability to pay. This has received widespread support and promises to survive for some time into the future.

Conclusions

These problems are not merely arguments about the best form of local taxation. They also represent a number of other issues concerning the relationship between central and local government. It is generally true that the power to raise taxes gives any level of government a degree of independence. It is also a key element in the nature of political responsibility. Tax is, furthermore, one of the oldest features of the process of government. It becomes yet more significant when considering national and regional devolution. Some of these broader issues are discussed below.

The changing nature of local government

Central–local relations

that, since 1979, the control exercised by both central government and a variety of other bodies set up by the Government, has increased markedly. Local authorities have considerably less freedom of action and are subject to greater parliamentary and ministerial control than ever before. The nature of these controls falls into three main categories: legislative control, ministerial control, and financial and administrative control.

Legislative control

The responsibilities that local government must undertake, the services it must provide and the minimum quality of those services are set out in a large number of Acts of Parliament. Local councils must, therefore, operate within the parameters set by Parliament. Some examples of key legislation are as follows:

- **Local Government Acts** set out financial provisions and controls as well as general directives as to the way local administration and decision making should operate. Such Acts are passed at regular intervals in order to update procedures and central–local relations.
- **Town and Country Planning Acts** guide local authorities in their role as controllers of building and transport development. Both requirements and limitations are described in these Acts.
- **Education Acts** are, again, passed at regular intervals. The 1988 Education Reform Act was probably the most significant since 1944, when free secondary education for all was first established. The National Curriculum, together with a host of administrative changes in education provision, was established by such legislation.
- **Local Government Finance Acts** set out the arrangements for central financing, local taxation and ministerial control of central government funding.
- **The Children Act** of 1990 laid a number of extra responsibilities for the welfare of children upon local authorities.

These are only a few examples of a regular stream of new legislation coming out of Westminster with the purpose of controlling local government.

Ministerial control

Various central government ministers have been granted discretionary powers by Parliament to exercise oversight and control. This particularly applies to ministers responsible for the environment, transport, education and housing.

As we have seen above, the level of local taxation may be 'capped' by the Department of the Environment, Transport and the Regions. Additional examples are the ability to overrule planning decisions, to refuse large-scale borrowing or capital spending projects, and to change educational provision.

Financial and administrative control

The principal changes made in the financial arrangements for local government are described on pages 271–2. In addition, however, the **Audit Commission**, set up in 1982, has powers to investigate the manner in which local authorities conduct their administrative affairs. The Commission is charged with the task of inspecting the efficiency and integrity of local authorities' finances.

The principal office concerned with local authority conduct is that of the **District Auditor**, who is particularly concerned with local financial policy and expenditure. During 1994–5 the office became involved in one of the most serious investigations of local authority conduct when it accused Conservative-controlled Westminster Council of manipulating council housing provision in order to ensure that more potential Tory voters were attracted into the borough and so ensure the survival of existing political control.

In 1992 the **Local Government Commission** was established in order to recommend and establish changes to both the internal workings and the general structure of local government, as well as its financial arrangements. Though still in its infancy, the Commission promises to become a further important instrument of central government control.

Local authority services

Just as observers are agreed that there is now much greater central control over local government, they also point to a fundamental change in the way in which local authorities operate.

It is now clear that in the 1990s local authorities changed from being **providers** of services to **enabling bodies**. This means that, instead of actually organising and producing themselves, authorities are acting more as agents of a variety of other bodies that are now involved in the provision of community services. Instead of being providers, they license, employ and supervise others who actually fulfil the necessary functions. This is expressed in the Government's own Citizen's Charter:

> 'Local authorities have historically seen the direct provision of services to the community as one of their major tasks. However, we believe that now is the time for a new approach. The real task for local authorities lies in setting priorities, determining the standards of services which citizens should enjoy, and finding the best way to meet them.'
>
> Citizen's Charter 1991, quoted in David Wilson, 'The Changing Context of Central–Local Government Relationships', *Talking Politics*, Vol. 5, No. 3 (Spring 1995)

This change can best be illustrated by reference to specific services.

Housing

Local authorities used to build council homes, maintain them with their own labour force, regulate and collect rents and be directly responsible for the homeless. In these senses, they were **providers** of housing.

After 1980 the picture changed. Tenants were increasingly encouraged to buy their own homes, thus removing them from the public sector. Building and maintenance of housing was offered out to private contractors under **compulsory competitive tendering**. Increasing amounts of funds, central and local, were channelled through voluntary (i.e. private sector) **housing associations**. The homeless and one-parent families were often housed in private bed-and-breakfast accommodation or hostels. Local authorities retained some planning powers, but with housing becoming an increasing problem, they had little choice but to accept private sector provision.

Public amenities

Various public amenities such as refuse collection, parks maintenance, road repairs and other environmental services, were increasingly put out to **private tender**. The role of the local authorities changed from carrying out these functions to granting tenders, ensuring quality, dismissing contractors and appointing new ones where necessary, and listening to public comments or complaints.

Economic development

Economic development had traditionally been only a marginal local government function, with relatively sparse funds available. However, with a marked increase in the number of agencies set up to distribute both public and private funds, local authorities found themselves at the centre of what has been called a **network** of providers. These have included Development Corporations (such as London Docklands), Enterprise Partnerships (between local government and private enterprise) and Regional Development Agencies (central government-funded). In addition, increasing quantities of development funds for regions and localities are available through the agencies of the **European Union**. Here again, others are responsible for funding, but local authorities must organise the distribution of finance.

> '*Various writers have suggested that in the future local authorities can have a key role in building a network among local organisations and interests to achieve a purpose beyond the ambit of their immediate statutory responsibilities.*'
> Gerry Stoker, *The Politics of Local Government*, 1991

Structure

The structure of local government is constantly changing. It is controlled by the Local Government Commission, whose task it is to ensure that there is a logical and effective system. The Commission created a new structure in England and Wales in 1998, shown on page 266. Changes in the government of London appeared in 2000 and are described below.

In the new devolved governments of Wales, Scotland and Northern Ireland, the structure of local government is now in the hands of those regions' assemblies and executives. Thus English local government structure alone remains under parliamentary control. The principle of reform has been to create **rational** divisions of responsibility. Where a logical region or locality is large enough, it can be a **unitary authority**: that is, it can control all or virtually all services. On the other hand, where communities are smaller, notably in rural areas, a **three-tier** system has been devised so that services can be provided at their appropriate scale. London, of course, does not conform to these general principles, so it is treated differently from the rest of the country. It is a **two-tier** system, reflecting both the unity of London and the relative independence of its 32 boroughs.

Internal organisation

As with the external structure of local government, the internal organisation has also become a subject for reform. Before considering these reforms, however, the traditional model of local democracy and administration must be described.

Councillors

The elected representatives form the **full council**, whose role is twofold:

- discussing and agreeing broad issues – in particular, the setting of financial priorities between services and the establishment of general policy
- ratifying decisions made in the various committees through which all councils operate.

All the detailed work of a council is carried out through committees and sub-committees. On these committees, councillors may specialise and receive expert advice from the permanent officials who are employed by the council. An indication of council work can be gained by reference to some of the main committees that all councils possess:

- Planning
- Housing
- Education
- Environmental Services
- Police
- Transport
- Social Services.

This is by no means an exhaustive list, but the most important are certainly included. In addition, two central bodies play key roles. These are the **Policy and Resources Committee** and its main sub-committee, **Finance**. As their names suggest, they deal with the main priorities of the council, in particular the uses of finance.

A Citizen's Charter leaflet from Wandsworth Council, 1994

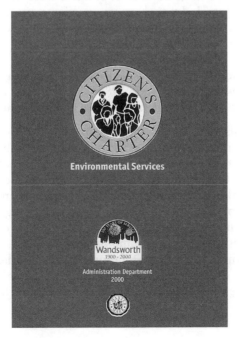

Officials   These are the equivalent of civil servants at local level. Their role is to undertake research, identify problems, suggest alternative courses of action and finally to implement the decisions made by elected councillors. They are expected to be neutral and to avoid becoming involved in party politics.

The structure of local administration largely mirrors the organisation of the councillors. A **Chief Executive** serves the full council and the central Policy and Resources Committee. Below Chief Executive, each committee is served by a **Chief Officer** and his or her staff. Thus, the essentially 'amateur' councillors are guided and serviced by 'professional' officers.

Local parties   In all but the most rural of county districts, most councillors are members of one of the principal political parties. Within the council each party organises itself into groups or 'caucuses', which seek to establish a united party front on every important issue. Thus, before every full council or committee meeting, the party groups discuss the agenda and attempt to enforce collective agreement. Of course, since councillors are not professional politicians, and since there are no highly paid ministerial posts on offer to them, party discipline is more difficult to enforce than is the case at Westminster. Parties on larger councils do have a whip system, but there are few sanctions that can be used to give it real teeth.

Party representation on each committee reflects the relative party strength in the whole council. Thus, if there is a majority party, that same party will enjoy majority membership on every committee and sub-committee. It follows from this that many decisions are actually made within the ruling party caucus and, within this, senior members play a key role.

However, a large number of councils have 'no overall control': that is, they are 'hung'. In such cases, parties must reach agreement among themselves whenever important decisions are to be made. Sometimes a permanent 'coalition' is formed between two parties; sometimes each issue must be resolved on an ad hoc basis.

This picture of local authority organisation remained largely unaltered between 1950 and 1980. Since then, however, a number of significant changes have taken place and still remain in force:

- Councils and their officials have simply less to do, since the responsibilities of local government have, on balance, been reduced.
- Many local services and responsibilities are now shared with other bodies, both in the public and the private sector; this applies at both national and regional level. It has removed much of the independent power of elected councillors. To an increasing extent it must be left to the permanent officials to co-ordinate the work of a wide variety of agencies in the local community context.
- Following the recommendations of the **Widdicombe Report**, political control over officials has been reduced. The general effect has been to increase their authority and to reduce that of local party leaders.

- The **Audit Commission**, as a result of its 1995 report, is now empowered to take steps to force local authorities to introduce greater efficiency and management disciplines within their administration. It is expected that the size of local bureaucracies will be significantly reduced as a result.

Mayors and Cabinets

Since 1998, when a process of reform commenced, local authorities have been given the option of changing their internal structure. Three main proposals have been considered by councils:

- The range of committees would be reduced and many of their responsibilities transferred to a local 'Cabinet'. This would be made up of leading members of the ruling party or coalition. All key decisions would be made by them as well as a strategic plan developed for the authority.
- Council managers – full-time professional executives – could be employed to serve and advise these Cabinets.
- The most radical proposal is that mayors should be elected along the lines of the London mayor. Following a positive referendum result to approve the introduction of such a system, the mayor would effectively become the 'prime minister' of the authority. He or she would chair the Cabinet, represent the authority externally, make key appointments and recommend policy.

By 2000, a handful of councils had adopted the Cabinet system, but there were no elected mayors outside London. Nevertheless, it was clear that important changes were under way.

Best Value and public consultation

The Labour Government elected in 1997 supported the idea that private firms should be used to provide local services where this was appropriate. However, the system of compulsory competitive tendering (CCT), introduced by the Thatcher Government, was replaced by the principle of **Best Value**. CCT **forced** councils to offer some services to private firms. Best Value does not require this, but simply insists that all services should be provided in the most efficient and effective manner, whoever provides them. Furthermore, local people should be consulted on how they want services provided, what standards they expect and how they wish to see funds allocated. The **Audit Commission**, a national government-appointed body, is charged with the task of ensuring that local councils are indeed providing Best Value.

Thus, two objectives are being pursued. One is that public consultation on services should be undertaken. The other is that councils should ensure that services are maintained as effectively as possible within the constraints of limited budgets.

The London mayor and GLA

Ken Livingstone, elected
London mayor in 2000

The mayor

In May 2000, Ken Livingstone was controversially but decisively elected as London's first mayor. Indeed, he is the first mayor ever to be elected in Britain. Existing mayors of towns and cities are appointed by the council and their role is purely ceremonial. This is also true of the Lord Mayor of London. By contrast, London's new mayor was elected by the people and will have some real powers.

On the face of it, the London mayor's powers are very limited. Even where he or she does have responsibilities, they are subject to controls. The main powers of the mayor are to:

- recommend the appointment of the Chief Commissioner of the Metropolitan Police
- influence the way in which the Metropolitan Police uses its resources
- influence the way in which other emergency services operate
- control the way in which London Transport operates
- introduce financial and legislative arrangements to control London traffic
- spend money raised through parking and traffic charges to improve public transport
- negotiate with central government on behalf of London
- negotiate with the European Union on behalf of London
- influence the provision of London arts
- control the public relations and international image of London
- make permanent paid appointments for London government.

The mayor is not able to:

- raise money through taxation
- control the work of the London boroughs
- make any by-laws for London apart from traffic management
- borrow large sums of money to spend in London
- make the final decision on major appointments outside London government
- take powers that have not been granted by Parliament.

It is therefore clear that the mayor will have to make the most of a very narrow set of powers and responsibilities. To some extent, the mayor's power and influence will depend upon his or her relations with central government ministers. The ministers will supply most of the mayor's funds and are in a position to veto most of the proposals the mayor might make.

It remains to be seen how much Mr Livingstone and his successors are able to make the office influential. They will have a good deal of power over transport matters and will do much to create a positive image for London. However, central government ministers are unlikely to want to grant more powers that might reduce their own authority.

The Greater London Authority (GLA)

This is a council of 25 elected members. Its role is to provide advice and policy proposals to the mayor and to the officers whom the mayor has appointed. The GLA is therefore, largely a consultative body. It will have two specific powers:

- to veto the mayor's overall budget and to force him or her to make amendments
- on a two-thirds majority, to overrule decisions by the mayor.

The first GLA is likely to be a difficult body to control. Unlike the central government Parliament and Cabinet, there is no party majority. Far from it, indeed. Mayor Livingstone is an independent, while no party controls the GLA. Its composition in 2000 was as follows:

Labour	9
Conservative	9
Liberal Democrat	4
Green	3

It will, therefore, find it difficult to find a consensus on many issues. This might, in fact, be good news for the mayor. Since the GLA needs an enhanced majority to overturn his decisions, the fragmented nature of its membership makes this unlikely.

So London has a government for the first time since 1986. How important it will be is open to conjecture. However, it is likely to become a model for large authorities in other parts of the country.

Summary of changes in local government since 1979

1. Central government exercises tighter financial control.
2. Ministers have more discretionary powers to control councils.
3. Some local services have been transferred to the private sector.
4. Many services have been transferred to unelected quangos.
5. Tight control over efficiency is exercised by the Audit Commission.
6. Local authorities are increasingly **enablers** and **controllers**, rather than **providers** of services.
7. A new simpler structure of local authorities is in place.
8. Councils are now required to be more sensitive to local needs and demands.
9. New internal organisations are being introduced, including city managers, elected Cabinets and mayors.
10. There is a widely accepted form of local taxation in place – the Council Tax.

For exam questions relevant to this unit, see page 557.

Introduction

Devolution defined

The term 'devolution' is a peculiarly British one. It refers to a way of redistributing political power which is unusual in the modern world. The main reason why it is so different is the fact that the UK has no codified constitution and there are therefore no fixed guidelines as to how the political system should operate. It is also a solution to the problem of how to disperse power to the regions without destroying the sacred **sovereignty of Parliament**. In other words, it was designed in such a way that no power was given away which could not be retrieved.

Devolution is the transfer of substantial **powers** to regional bodies, but it does not transfer any **sovereignty**. What this means is that the powers which have been devolved can be taken back at any time according to the will of Parliament in London. This was illustrated vividly in early 2000 when the newly formed Northern Ireland devolved assembly was suspended and its powers returned to government in London. The temporary failure of the assembly, caused by the refusal of some Unionists to co-operate, meant that it could not continue independently. Under extreme circumstances, the same thing could happen in Scotland and Wales.

Three categories of power can be devolved:

- **Administrative devolution** transfers the power and responsibility to manage and organise public services, such as health, education and social services. The manner in which the services are run, what priorities are set and how funds are allocated are included in such devolution. However, fundamental changes could not be made as this would require legislation, and administrative devolution does not include the power to make and change national laws. Thus, for example, the Welsh devolved executive could not abolish the National Health Service in Wales and replace it with a private system. This would need new laws. Administrative devolution was granted to Scotland, Wales and Northern Ireland in 1999.

- **Financial or fiscal devolution** allows a devolved government to raise its own revenue through taxation. Normally, finance comes from central government through a system of annual grants. Where a regional government has taxation powers, however, it can vary its expenditure up or down according to political circumstances. Only Scotland has such power and this is very limited. The Scottish Executive may vary the standard rate of income tax from that set by central government by 3 per cent upwards or downwards. This enables it to adjust its expenditure plans up or down, but only slightly.

- **Legislative devolution** is the power to make laws. This is not unlimited. Some law making will always be reserved to Parliament in London. For example, laws on the constitution, on drug enforcement and on the death penalty cannot be altered by devolved assemblies. Legislative devolution has been granted to Scotland and Northern Ireland only.

The nature of devolution in the UK is explained further below. On a basic level, however, its meaning can be summarised in the following chart.

Summary of devolved powers		
Type of devolution	**Explanation**	**Where applied**
• Administrative	• The power to run services • Allocate funds • Organise administration	• Wales • Scotland • Northern Ireland
• Financial	• The ability to raise or vary taxation independently	• Scotland
• Legislative	• The power to make, repeal or amend laws	• Scotland • Northern Ireland

Devolution and federalism

It is crucial to make a clear distinction between the concept and operation of devolution and federalism. Devolution involves the transfer of power to regional bodies, but it is understood that those powers may be removed or amended. Under a federal arrangement, powers are granted under a strict constitution and cannot be removed or altered unless there is a constitutional amendment. This distinction might not seem decisive. Closer examination, however, reveals some important differences.

In a **federal** system, it is **sovereignty**, not just power, that is distributed to regional governments. Unlike mere political power, sovereignty cannot be removed or adjusted by simple acts of the legislature. As sovereign powers are guaranteed by a constitution, they can only be changed by changing the constitution. It is always the case that constitutional changes of this kind require a political consensus. In the USA, for example, it needs a two-thirds majority of Congress plus the agreement of three-quarters of the 50 states to change the constitution. This makes it highly unlikely that the sovereign powers of the states could be removed or extended. This is not the case in the UK. Parliament can remove or change devolved powers by a simple Act, which could be passed in just two days. Indeed, in the case of Northern Ireland, the responsible minister – the Secretary of State for Northern Ireland – can take back devolved power with a simple order. Parliament need not be involved.

This leaves us with two distinctions between devolution and federalism:

- Under devolution, only power is devolved; in a federation, sovereignty is distributed.
- Federalism requires special constitutional arrangements, whereas devolution is in the hands of Parliament and is very flexible.

A note on devolution and local government

The distinction between **devolved powers** and those granted to **local government** is less clear. Local government is also granted powers, just as devolved government is, and in both cases they are not sovereign powers. So what is the difference? The answer is twofold:

- Devolution concerns large regions. Local government is what the name implies: it is **local**.
- Regional devolution involves greater powers. In a region, such concerns as health and industrial development must be organised on a large scale. With local government, smaller-scale services can be organised.

When we consider London, the difference is even less clear. Is London a region? If so, the powers granted to the mayor and the assembly are indeed devolved powers. If we consider London to be a locality, then the powers granted to it are still **local government** powers. Whichever, this book treats London government as local rather than devolved government.

How devolution came about

The story of devolution has its origins in the nationalist movements that have existed in Scotland, Wales and Northern Ireland over many decades and even, in the case of Scotland, back to the nineteenth century. However, the suitable place to begin, in a modern context, is the 1970s.

Disillusionment with the poor economic performance of central government in London, together with the decline of traditional industries, has been identified as the main cause of nationalist feeling growing in Scotland and Wales in the 1970s. In the 1974 general elections, the Welsh and Scottish nationalist parties did surprisingly well. Their success was reinforced by gains made in local and parliamentary by-elections. The Labour Government that came to power in 1974 was faced with two political problems that led it to give consideration to devolution.

The first was the possibility that Labour would continue to lose voting support in Scotland and Wales. These two national regions are traditionally strongholds for the Labour Party. To lose their support would mean electoral disaster for the party in the future. By granting devolution, Labour hoped that it could save that vital traditional support. The second reason concerned the position of the Liberal Party. The Liberals had also done well in 1974. This coincided with the fact that the Labour Government was weak. After October 1974, Labour held a tiny House of Commons majority. As part of the price for their support in Parliament, the Liberals pressed the Government to consider devolution. This was a policy that the Liberals had supported for some time and they too felt that they had much to gain. The Conservatives, meanwhile, remained staunchly opposed to the policy.

Plans were laid and the next step was to hold referenda in both countries. At first, it was believed that a simple majority in favour of devolution would be enough to trigger legislation. At this point the weakness of the Labour Government undermined the plans. The Conservatives forced through an amendment to the referendum plan. This insisted that there should be a 'yes to devolution' vote from 40 per cent of the **total electorate**: that is, not 40 per cent of those who voted, but 40 per cent of all those entitled to vote. Since it was expected that there would be a turnout of little more than two-thirds, the 40 per cent would be very difficult to achieve.

The referendum in Wales was unfavourable by any standards. The majority of Scots voted yes, but the 40 per cent figure was not reached. So devolution failed, the Liberals withdrew their support for the Government and the defeat led to the fall of the Government in 1979. The issue then retreated into the background of politics for the next fifteen years. There remained some bitterness among the Scots, but this was insufficient to cause a major revival of nationalism.

In the mid-1990s the Labour Opposition decided to revive the idea of devolution. Nationalism was again on the rise in both countries and Labour saw the issue as a vote winner. The 1997 election proved it correct. The Conservatives, still opposed to devolution, failed to win a single seat in Wales or Scotland in the general election. The Scottish and Welsh nationalists fared well, as did Labour. Once again legislation was prepared, and referenda were held in 1998.

This time there was no wrecking amendment from the weak Conservative Opposition. This time 74 per cent of Scottish voters said yes to devolution. In addition, 64 per cent voted to allow a new Scottish Parliament to vary the rate of income tax by 3 per cent up or down. The Welsh vote was much closer. The majority in favour was only 50.3 per cent. But this was enough and the legislation went ahead. In 1999 the Scottish and Welsh devolved governments took power.

Nationalism and devolution

It is not sufficient merely to detail the **events** leading to Scottish and Welsh devolution. It is also necessary to look at the underlying causes of the rise of nationalist sentiment that occurred in the 1990s. We can clearly understand the political advantages that were seen by the Labour Party in proposing devolution, but the question still arises: why was it a popular policy?

The causes are, not surprisingly, complex and varied. It is also impossible to identify one decisive element. All we can do, therefore, is to understand all the possible factors and accept that each played a greater or lesser role. They are as follows:

- There was a general global rise in nationalism at the end of the Cold War when political ideology declined in importance.
- There was disillusionment in Scotland and Wales with London government. There was a perception that the economic fortunes of the two countries were lagging behind those of England, especially the more prosperous south-east.
- The recession of the early 1990s bit especially hard in the two countries.
- Traditional industries such as agriculture, mining and metals, which were concentrated in Wales and Scotland, began to decline alarmingly. London government was partly blamed for this.
- The increasing centralisation of British government in the 1980s meant that Scotland and Wales felt themselves increasingly isolated.
- There was a feeling that British government was becoming more authoritarian. Nationalism in Wales and Scotland was, to some extent, a liberal movement in opposition to this trend.
- With various kinds of economic help available from the European Union coming on stream, the Scots and the Welsh began to believe that they needed a stronger independent voice in Europe to obtain their fair share.

Of course, devolution stops well short of full independence. At the same time, nationalists do not always want independence. It was therefore understandable that devolution was seen as a way of dealing with nationalist demands without breaking up the UK. More extreme nationalists still want full, sovereign independence for their countries, but there is still no majority for such a move. The question of whether full independence will follow devolution is explored later in this unit.

Northern Ireland

This is a more complex story than those of Wales and Scotland. Much of it is recounted in Unit 15. However, the background can be usefully described here.

When Ireland was granted independence from British rule in 1921, six northern counties were not included. They remained part of the

UK. The reason for the partition of Ireland was that the six counties contained a majority of Ulster Protestants who were both fiercely loyal to the British Crown and afraid of how they would be treated as part of a Catholic Republic of Ireland.

Northern Ireland, as it came to be known, was granted devolved power in 1921 (thus demonstrating that devolution is not a new idea). A parliament (known as **Stormont**) was elected and from it was drawn a government, headed by a Prime Minister. Stormont had limited legislative power, but was given a great deal of control over the running of public services and, most controversially, the police (the **Royal Ulster Constabulary** or RUC). Since the Protestant **loyalists** – also known as **unionists** – were in a majority, they completely dominated government in Northern Ireland up to 1972.

However, representatives of the Catholic minority in Northern Ireland continued to campaign to have Ireland united. This group, known as nationalists or republicans, was represented partly by politicians who wished to see a peaceful political process ending in the uniting of Ireland, and partly by terrorists – the **Irish Republican Army** (IRA). Between 1921 and 1968 the republicans and the IRA periodically burst out into political and violent activity, but was never sustained. All this changed in 1968.

In that year, unrest broke out again. Catholics, who felt that they had been discriminated against by the Protestant majority for nearly 50 years, began a civil rights movement. They wanted fairer treatment by government and especially by the RUC, who were seen as a force dedicated to preserving the position of the Protestant community. The IRA and its political wing, **Sinn Fein**, seized the opportunity to recommence its campaign to reunite Ireland. Unrest turned into violence and then into organised terrorism.

By 1972 it was clear that the situation was out of control and the government of Northern Ireland was dissolved. The province was then run from London – a process known as **direct rule**. The devolution experience was over for the time being.

Several attempts to make a new political settlement failed until the late 1990s. Led by Secretary of State for Northern Ireland, Mo Mowlem, the main parties in the province were finally brought together to negotiate seriously. The result was the **Good Friday Agreement** of April 1998. The agreement was put to a referendum in both Northern Ireland and the Irish Republic. There was an overwhelming positive vote in both countries.

This was really a dual agreement. First, it promised peace for Northern Ireland. The IRA declared peace, the Irish Republic dropped its claim to annexe the territory and the unionists – at least the moderate members – agreed to sit down in government with Sinn Fein, the extreme wing of the nationalist movement. Second, it set up a devolved system of government for the province. This was similar to the Scottish arrangement, but with one key difference. The electoral system – single transferable vote – made it certain that each party received a number of seats close to its appropriate number of votes in the new assembly at Stormont. At the same time, the agreement guaranteed that **all** the main parties would have representatives in the Government. It was, therefore, a **power-sharing system**.

How devolution works

Scotland These are the key features of the political system that was adopted in Scotland in 1999.

- A Parliament is elected by the additional member system of voting. It has 129 seats, of which 73 are from constituencies and the other 56 are allocated on a proportional basis.
- The Scottish Parliament's main roles are to pass legislation, to hold the Scottish Executive (the devolved government) to account, to approve the appointment of members of the Scottish Executive, to debate key issues and to approve the Scottish budget.
- From the Parliament a **First Minister** (effectively the Prime Minister of Scotland) emerges. He or she will normally be leader of the largest party in the Parliament.
- The First Minister will appoint ministers to the Executive. Whether or not this Executive will be acceptable to the Parliament may be put to a vote of confidence.
- The Parliament is chaired by a **Presiding Officer** (effectively the 'Speaker'). He or she will advise the Queen on the appointment of the First Minister.
- The Parliament has a **fixed term**: that is, elections take place every four years.
- Scottish legislation must conform to the British Human Rights Act and must not conflict with any laws made by the UK Parliament.
- The Parliament's powers of legislation and the Executive's administrative powers are limited by UK legislation.

This is effectively the Westminster system on a smaller scale. Of course, the range of issues with which Scottish government can deal is limited, but the operation of the system is very similar.

Division of responsibilities between devolved Scottish Government and the UK Parliament	
Powers reserved to the UK Parliament	**Powers devolved to Scotland**
• Constitutional changes	• Health
• Foreign policy	• Education
• Defence and national security	• Industrial training
• Border controls	• Science research funding
• Economic and financial policy	• Social services
• Trade and commerce	• Local government
• Employment law	• Housing
• Social security policy	• Regeneration of urban areas
• Regulation of professions	• Planning control
• Transport safety	• Varying income tax rates
• Relations with Europe	• Tourism
• Drug laws	• Public transport and waterways
	• Criminal and civil law
	• Law enforcement systems
	• Emergency services
	• Environmental protection
	• Agriculture, forestry and fishing
	• Sports and arts
	• National heritage
	• Animal protection

Wales

The Welsh system has many similarities with that of Scotland. Here the key features are as follows:

- An **Assembly** (it is not called a Parliament, as this would imply that it had legislative powers) is elected by the additional member system, with 60 members.
- Of these, 40 members are elected through constituencies while 20 more are returned on a proportional basis.
- An Executive is drawn from the Assembly, headed by a **First Secretary**. This will have to command the support of the majority of the Assembly.
- The role of the Assembly will be to debate key issues, to advise the Executive on policy, to hold the Executive to account and to act as the source of members of the Executive.
- The Assembly cannot make laws and cannot raise taxation. Therefore it has no control over the Welsh Executive's revenue. However, it does have to approve expenditure plans.

So the Welsh Assembly and Executive have a considerably more limited role than their Scottish counterparts. Rather than list the way in which powers are divided in Wales (they are similar to those in Scotland), it is simpler to consider which powers Welsh government **does not** have, but which Scottish government **does** have. These are as follows:

- legislation
- criminal and civil law
- tax variation
- broadcasting control.

Although it appears that there are few differences, the law-making and tax-varying powers of the Scottish Parliament are extremely significant.

Northern Ireland

The political situation in the province is very different to that of Scotland and Wales. In terms of the responsibilities that have been devolved, there is little difference with the exception of policing and security – clearly critical issues in the province. But the **processes** of devolved government in Northern Ireland vary considerably.

A 108-member Assembly was elected in 1999, with a large number of parties represented. From this Assembly, an Executive has been drawn. It contains representatives from all the major parties. It is headed by a First Minister and a Deputy, who are elected by the assembly. Thereafter the political system contains some important differences from anything seen elsewhere in the UK. The main ones are as follows:

- The First Minister does not choose members of the Executive. They are nominated by the main parties. Thus David Trimble (Unionist) was the first First Minister and his Deputy was Seamus Mallon (Social Democratic and Labour Party – the SDLP – a moderate nationalist party). In addition, the Executive contained a mixture of members of the moderate Alliance Party, Unionists, SDLP and two Sinn Fein representatives.
- Many key resolutions and pieces of legislation require more than simple majority support. There are arrangements to ensure that there is a reasonable level of approval from all main parties for any decisions to be taken.
- The committees of the Northern Ireland Assembly must contain representatives from different sections of the community.
- There are special arrangements to ensure that all decisions of the Assembly or the Executive protect individual rights and safeguard equal treatment for all members of the community.

The areas of responsibility that are devolved to Northern Ireland are similar to those in Scotland and Wales. There are also special arrangements for security matters that concern both Northern Ireland and the Republic of Ireland. Representatives from both sides of the border deal with such issues.

Northern Ireland devolution, therefore, represents a unique experiment in government. This is the concept of governing in such a way that no significant sections of the community are excluded. In most democratic systems, a majority group governs and the minority – all those excluded from government – must accept this. Not so in Northern Ireland. This makes governing difficult, but it is felt essential if peace and co-operation are to be preserved in the troubled province.

Some early features of devolution

elections

in the 1999 elections. This provides us with an immediate and clear distinction from the UK Parliament. The results of the elections are shown in the following table.

Results of elections to devolved assemblies, 1999		
	Party	**Seats won**
Wales	Labour	28
	Plaid Cymru*	17
	Conservative	9
	Liberal Democrat	6
Scotland	Labour	56
	Scottish Nationalist*	35
	Conservative	18
	Liberal Democrat	17
	Others	3
Northern Ireland	Ulster Unionist	28
	Social Democratic and Labour Party*	24
	Democratic Unionist	20
	Sinn Fein*	18
	Alliance Party	6
	Northern Ireland Unionist	3
	United Unionist	3
	Women's Coalition	2
	Progressive Unionist	2
	UK Unionist	1
	Independent Unionist	1

*Nationalist parties

Clearly the proportional representation systems adopted helped the smaller parties, especially the nationalists and the Conservatives in Wales and Scotland. The STV system in Northern Ireland resulted in representation for a number of very small groups.

Government formation

In the three devolved systems, three different arrangements were made. These were as follows:

- In **Scotland,** there was an understanding between the Labour and Liberal Democrat Parties that they would form a **coalition** if there were no overall majority. So it happened. Labour just failed to win 50 per cent of the seats in the Parliament and so had to allow the Liberal Democrats into the Government.

- In **Wales**, Labour also failed to win a majority. On this occasion, however, they decided to form a **minority** government. They understood that this meant that they might lose some votes in the Assembly, but were prepared to risk it. As long as they could gain the support of either Plaid Cymru or the Liberal Democrats, they could make policy. It also has to be noted that the Welsh Assembly cannot make new law, so the absence of a majority is not critical.
- The Northern Ireland system guarantees a **power-sharing coalition**. The Good Friday Agreement, which set up government there, stated that all major parties have to be represented in the Executive. This makes decision making extremely difficult. If all the unionist parties agree, there is a majority, but, as we have seen, important decisions require the approval of nationalists too.

Devolution politics

Devolution is in its infancy. Its true effects and implications will not be known until several years into the twenty-first century. However, there are some early clues as to how events are likely to unfold. We will now consider some of the significant developments.

Government formation

In Northern Ireland, the creation of a power-sharing executive was planned and duly occurred. Less predictable, however, were events in the other devolved systems. In both cases, no party won an overall majority following the first elections. In Scotland, the Labour and Liberal Democrat Parties formed a coalition, with Labour very much the dominant partner. In Wales, however, Labour formed a minority government. It was felt that there would be few controversial issues so that a majority in the Assembly was less essential. It was also felt that most Welsh issues would be the subject of consensus politics.

These were relatively easy arrangements to make. The policies of Labour and the Liberal Democrats were similar enough for coalitions and minority administrations to enjoy relative stability. In future, should no party enjoy Labour's dominant position, and should more controversial issues arise, such developments will prove to be less straightforward.

The Scottish tuition fees dispute

Students at English and Welsh universities had been required to pay a contribution to tuition fees from 1999 onwards. In Scotland, however, the Liberal Democrats opposed such arrangements and had committed themselves in their Scottish election manifesto to vote against them. In coalition with Labour, however, a problem arose. If they were to carry out their election commitment, the coalition itself would be threatened. It was a test for the party's resolve and for the prospects for coalition politics. If the Liberal Democrats gave in to Labour demands for tuition fees, it would make a mockery of the principle of the electoral mandate. In the event, a compromise was reached and honour was preserved. Scottish students were spared the fees, while their English colleagues would be required to pay. This kind of compromise is common to coalition governments. More examples are likely to arise in the future.

The Alun Michael affair The Labour leader in Wales' new assembly, and therefore the likely first First Secretary of the Executive, was Alun Michael. Yet Michael was not the first choice of Labour's Welsh Assembly members. He was, however, the Labour leadership's (especially Tony Blair's) preference and had been elected as a result of an internal voting system which had been constructed to ensure that he won the party contest for its leadership. The preferred choice of the Assembly members was Rhodri Morgan. Morgan had lost narrowly to Michael in the Welsh Labour Party's own leadership contest. The confrontation was, in the end, won by Labour's Assembly members. At almost the first opportunity, a vote of no confidence was proposed against Alun Michael. He was forced to resign and Morgan replaced him as First Secretary of Wales.

The story indicates that a party's central leadership in London might find it difficult to dominate devolved government. The Labour Assembly members had asserted their independence by insisting on their own choice of leader. Party leaderships have learned from this incident that their Welsh and Scottish members will not be easily overruled.

Clause 28 Clause 28 was a section of the 1988 Education Act. It essentially forbade state schools from including positive images of homosexuality in their schools' teaching. The Labour Party was committed to repealing the clause, as it was seen as a homophobic measure. The Labour Government ran into trouble at Westminster, especially with a reluctant House of Lords. In Scotland's single chamber system, however, no such obstruction was forthcoming. Clause 28 was repealed at the first attempt by a large vote in the Scottish Parliament. Thus, for the first time, Scotland had moved ahead of England in its reforming mood. It was a small, but significant step on the road to making Scotland distinct from the rest of the UK.

The Mike Tyson affair When former world boxing champion, Mike Tyson, was contracted to appear in Scotland in the summer of 2000, members of the Scottish Parliament opposed the fight. Tyson, as a convicted rapist, was seen as an undesirable visitor to Scotland. Spurred on by the opposition of women's groups, attempts were made to persuade UK Home Secretary, Jack Straw, to ban Tyson. Straw decided to let him into the UK and thus effectively overruled the Scots. The devolution legislation does not allow the Scots to control who may enter their own country.

The Tyson story illustrates how key areas of sovereignty have not been transferred. The border between England and Scotland is only a symbolic one. Neither goods nor people can be held up there, however much the Scots might wish to do so.

Will devolution lead to independence?

There are two ways of viewing the prospects for full independence in any of the three national regions that have devolved government.

The first is the preferred perspective of the Labour Party, which granted devolution itself. Labour believes that there is no real appetite for full independence, but that there was a desire for some degree of self-government. By granting devolution it is assumed that the Scots and

Welsh will be satisfied. Thus independence has faded into the distance and a suitable compromise has been reached. The Labour Party remains, therefore, committed to keeping the UK together, even though it has agreed to some sacrifice of power to the regions.

The second view is held by the Conservative Party. The Conservatives see devolution as the thin end of the wedge. Once a taste of self-government has been given to the national regions, they believe the demands for full independence will grow. As they are firm in their support for the concept of a united kingdom, Conservatives have opposed devolution and are wary of any further moves towards self-government. The Liberal Democrats accept that a fully federal settlement is likely to follow and this is their preferred solution.

Ultimately, it is highly unlikely in the foreseeable future that Wales and Northern Ireland will enjoy more independence than they currently have. For Scotland, however, the future is less certain. The prospects for full independence might prove to lie in the hands of the Scottish National Party (SNP). The SNP hopes to win a majority in the Scottish Parliament and then to force a referendum on the issue. A 'yes to independence' vote might put irresistible pressure on the Westminster Parliament to give Scotland separate, sovereign status. While Scotland enjoys reasonable economic growth, the SNP is unlikely to gain much ground. However, economic decline and unpopular British governments might fuel the fires of Scottish independence in the future. An independent Scottish voice in Europe – the official SNP policy – is certainly not out of the question in the near future.

English regional devolution

Labour's policy to the English regions is less clear. In principle, the party supports the idea of breaking England up into a number of regions and granting to each some degree of administrative devolution. Any future settlement would most likely be similar to that made in Wales.

To some extent there is already some regional devolution in England. Some large quangos, such as the Arts Council, have a regional structure, while the Regional Development Agencies dispense huge grants to support industry in different parts of England. There are also twelve separate civil service offices to serve the interests of these regions.

In those fields of policy where a separate regional identity is desirable and feasible, English devolution remains a possibility. Transport, industrial and agricultural development, and environmental protection are examples of possibilities for such devolution.

Opponents, on the other hand, especially the Conservative Party, point out that this will add another layer of bureaucracy to an already over-sized government. It is also the case that the European Union already deals with many of England's regional problems, so it can be argued that a further set of institutions is not necessary.

The Labour Party has lost some of its enthusiasm for more devolution since the 1997 election, especially as it won such a huge parliamentary majority at that time. Nevertheless it remains a goal for many party members and for the Liberal Democrats. As with Scottish independence, further progress is likely to depend on the economic prosperity, or otherwise, of the English regions.

For exam questions relevant to this unit, see page 557.

What is a constitution?

Until the late eighteenth century there was no conception of the modern form of 'constitution'. There had been regulated forms of political system in classical Greece and the Roman Republic, but these were elementary and lacked both the sophistication and democratic elements of modern forms.

Through the Dark and Middle Ages, the predominance of monarchy, based on power, order and duty, replaced any need for a constitutional system of government. The development of natural and equal rights, government by consent, limited rule and representative institutions in the eighteenth century introduced the need for a completely new basis for government. Inspired by the ideas of the English philosopher **John Locke**, the notion of a 'social contract' gained support as the political principle upon which future government should be founded.

The contract of which Locke wrote was to be made between the people and their government. For their part, the people agreed upon the manner in which they were to be ruled. The government, in its turn, was to accept limitations to its role and to submit itself to constant examination by the people. Thus, a modern constitution, whatever its form, can be seen as such a contract. This constitution might be considerably more detailed and refined than Locke's original conception, but it is based on the principle that it is an agreement between the government and the governed.

Under what circumstances do such agreements come about? Almost without exception (the UK is an important one) constitutions come about after a major political upheaval such as a revolution, civil war or the achievement of independence from a foreign power. When a people has been forced to dismantle its former government, reform the political system, and rethink and reorganise the way it is governed, a new constitution invariably comes into existence.

We can find a flavour of this idea in the preamble to the American Constitution of 1787, written and established after British colonial rule had been thrown off. This is shown below:

> *'We the people of the United States, in order to form a more perfect Union, establish Justice, insure* domestic Tranquillity, provide for the common Defence, promote the general Welfare, and secure the blessings of Liberty to ourselves and our posterity, do ordain and establish this Constitution for the United States of America.'*   *original spelling

Although we have some clues as to the contractual nature of the American Constitution, it does not explain the several purposes of **any** political constitution. In general, the functions of a constitution can be identified as follows:

- Establishing the distribution of power among the various institutions of government. This also implies a statement of the limits to those powers and the relationships between political institutions.
- Defining the limits to the powers of the state as a whole.
- Guaranteeing the rights of citizens, both against the state and in their relationships with each other.
- Establishing the territory to be governed by the constitution.
- Defining the nature and rules of citizenship of the state.
- Setting out the method by which the constitution can be amended.

Constitution maintenance

Codification At its simplest, codification means 'in written form'. However, it implies more. In particular, we can add that it may be written in a single, organised form. This is more than an administrative distinction. Codification also suggests that constitutional rules are **different** from other rules or laws of conduct.

Entrenchment More crucial than codification, the principle of entrenchment refers to the need to safeguard constitutional laws against the whims of temporary governments and the vagaries of short-term political developments. Parties and governments might come and go, public opinion might change direction with great regularity, but constitutional principles need more stability. They are fundamental and are expected to protect future as well as current generations of citizens.

The practical meaning of entrenchment is that constitutional laws are more difficult to change than other laws. The purposes of such obstacles to change are twofold. First, entrenchment is usually designed to ensure that there is a full and lengthy debate about the desirability of such change. Second, it is important that there is widespread, general agreement about constitutional change. We may describe this as **consensus** – having more than just any majority, but a substantial majority.

Consider, for example, the following issues. Some might be the proper concern of a **temporary** government in its task of maintaining the common good (i.e. **political** matters); others are more fundamental and should, therefore, be subject to entrenchment (i.e. **constitutional** matters).

Suitability of issues for constitutional entrenchment	
Political matters	**Constitutional matters**
• Funding health care	• Establishing equal rights for women
• Student grant levels	• Establishing regional government in Scotland
• Reorganising the armed forces	• Increasing police powers
• Subsidising agriculture	• Altering trade union rights
	• Reforming the House of Lords

A variety of methods exist by which entrenchment may be achieved. In the USA, for example, constitutional amendments require two-thirds majority approval of both Houses of the Senate, plus ratification by three-quarters of the 50 states. The French use referenda to ensure popular support, while other states use various forms of enhanced majority voting.

Superiority

Part of the distinctive nature of constitutional law is that it must be superior to other law. In other words, if some aspect of 'ordinary' law conflicts with constitutional law, the latter is treated as superior and must prevail in that conflict. If this is not the case, constitutional law could not be properly safeguarded from attacks by temporary political opinion. Thus, superiority and entrenchment go hand in hand.

To illustrate, we might envisage a circumstance where Parliament passes a law granting discretionary powers to a government minister to alter prison sentences handed down by the courts. This might conflict with a **constitutional** principle that the law courts must be completely independent of government. If constitutional superiority is respected, the new law would be set aside. The Parliament in question would have to force through a constitutional change, perhaps against entrenched provisions, in order to introduce its new law.

Once again, we may turn to the USA for illustration of this principle. **Chief Justice John Marshall** declared the following in 1805:

> 'That the people have an original right to establish, for their future government, such principles as, in their opinion, shall most conduce to their own happiness, is the basis on which the whole American fabric has been erected ... The principles, therefore, so established, are deemed fundamental. And as the authority from which they proceed is supreme, and can seldom act, they are designed to be permanent.'
>
> John Marshall, *Marbury* v. *Madison*, 1805

The British Constitution

Does the British Constitution exist?

Although reference is commonly made to the term 'British Constitution', examination syllabuses have been so named and a key textbook, written in 1867 by Walter Bagehot, was entitled *English Constitution*, it is open to question whether there is indeed such a thing. In reality, there are persuasive arguments suggesting both that the British Constitution exists **and** that it does not exist. This may appear to be a confusing paradox, but it is understandable if we examine the evidence for both views.

Evidence against

1. There is no single **codified document** entitled the 'British Constitution'. Not only that, but where constitutional statutes do exist, they appear to be no different from any other statute.

2. It is not possible to **entrench** constitutional laws and principles in the UK. This is simply on account of the doctrine of **parliamentary sovereignty**. In this context, the doctrine means that Parliament cannot be limited in its actions by any past statute or agreement. Thus, even where constitutional statutes exist, Parliament is free to repeal or amend them by a simple majority vote.

   A clear example of this occurred in 1994 with the passage of the Criminal Justice Act. Before this Act, it was an accepted principle that accused persons had the right to remain silent under questioning and in court, without any assumptions being made that this might indicate guilt. Such a 'right to silence' is certainly a common element in written constitutions elsewhere. Since the passage of the Act, however, such silence can be used as prosecuting evidence. However much lawyers and campaigners argued that this abused basic individual rights, Parliament had its way.

   By the same principle, of course, lack of entrenchment allows Parliament to **add** to individual rights without excessive difficulty. Thus, race relations and sexual equality have been established through simple, speedy procedures.

3. As we have indicated, there are constitutional statutes in the UK, but these are **not superior** to any other laws. Where there is a conflict between two statutes, Parliament is completely free to determine which shall prevail.

Evidence for

1. There is a general sense in which we understand that there are principles by which the political system operates. When such principles are being threatened, there might be stronger opposition from inside and outside Parliament than would normally be the case.

2. Tradition is a powerful influence in the UK. Those constitutional rules that are traditional, such as the maintenance of freedom of expression, the primacy of the Cabinet, the weakness of the House of Lords and the independence of the judiciary, are challenged rarely and with great reluctance by governments.

3. Governments must face the judgement of the electorate at regular intervals. Those who have challenged such traditional principles must consider whether they can maintain popular approval. Thus, the people themselves act as the guardians of some sort of conception of the 'constitution'.

4. Finally, and perhaps most importantly, many constitutional scholars argue that there is such a thing as the British Constitution even though there is no codified document as such. Instead, it exists in a variety of forms that may be flexible and constantly developing, but which, nevertheless, have enough substance to replace the more formal constitutions that other states possess. These forms are described in the next section.

Does the British Constitution exist?	
No	**Yes**
1. There is no single, codified document.	1. There is a general sense of a Constitution.
2. There is no method of entrenchment.	2. Traditional constitutional principles are strong.
3. Constitutional laws are not superior to others.	3. The people may protect it at election time.
	4. There are accepted forms of constitutional rules.

Form of the British Constitution

As we have seen, constitutional statutes do not look different from any others. They are also passed in the same way, by simple majority of both Houses of Parliament. They are, therefore, only recognisable by the function they are performing.

Some examples will illustrate their range:

Statutes
- The **Parliament Acts** of 1911 and 1949 establish the limitations to the powers of the House of Lords.
- **Criminal Justice Acts** concern the functions of the legal system, rights of accused persons and police powers.
- **Local Government Acts** establish and control the powers of local authorities.
- The **Habeas Corpus Act** protects our rights to a trial when accused of a crime.
- The **Race Relations Acts** establish equal rights for members of all races.
- The **Scotland, Wales and Northern Ireland Acts** of 1998–9 grant devolved powers to those countries.
- The **Human Rights Act** of 1999 incorporates the European Convention on Human Rights into British Law.

Common law
The term 'common law' refers to those laws that have not been passed by Parliament, but which are, nevertheless, recognised as binding. They exist because judges have decided, in past cases, that certain rules of conduct are so firmly rooted in the 'commonly held' traditions of the political system that they have the force of law. But statutes are superior to common law so that, if there is a conflict between statute law and common law, the former must always prevail. However, when statutes are not clear, or when it is not apparent whether a minister or public body is acting lawfully, judges may refer to such common law principles, based on similar disputes in the past.

Common law cases concerning constitutional rules are rare today. They tend to concern the operation of the law courts and the actions of government departments when applying administrative rules.

Essentially, common law insists that courts and public bodies deal with citizens even-handedly, with a natural sense of justice and without prejudice.

Conventions These are unwritten rules which are, nevertheless, considered binding by those who operate them. They have been described as the lubricating oil that makes the machinery of government work, or as a gentleman's agreement to operate the political system in traditional ways. They can only be understood in relation to the **royal prerogative**. The nature of the prerogative and prerogative powers are shown below.

The royal prerogative

Before the powers of Parliament were firmly established in the seventeenth century, the discretionary, personal powers of the monarchy were scarcely controlled. Only in the field of taxation were the powers of the Crown limited. The uncontrolled functions of the monarch were known as the **royal prerogative**. Over the past 300 years these powers have been eroded, being largely replaced by parliamentary sovereignty.

However, some roles still remain. These mainly concern two activities: first, the preservation of the security and integrity of the land, involving control of the armed forces, intelligence operations and maintenance of public order, including the judicial system; and second, the operation of government, such as the appointment of ministers and the calling of elections.

It would, of course, be wrong to assume from this that the reigning monarch actually performs these functions. We do not accept that the monarch has sufficient authority to carry out such vital roles. Instead, therefore, it is up to Parliament or the Prime Minister to exercise prerogative powers on behalf of the Crown. There might still be emergency or unforeseen circumstances when the monarch has to step in and take action, but, on the whole, the royal prerogative has passed into other hands.

Most conventions of the constitution derive from this operation of prerogative powers (see above). They are so rooted in the development of the political system that they appear almost to have the force of law. It is difficult to appreciate how conventions can be enforced if they are not laws. In short, we really do not know. This difficulty is compounded by the fact that there are no modern examples of serious breaches of a convention. Writing in 1885, however, the constitutional theorist A. V. Dicey suggested that such a transgression would **eventually** lead to a conflict with either Parliament or the law courts.

Thus, for example, it is a **convention** that a government must resign if it loses a vote of confidence in the House of Commons. What if a government refused to resign after such a defeat? Dicey suggests that Parliament would refuse to approve any of its future proposals and the courts would not uphold the actions of its ministers.

'But the sanction which constrains the boldest political adventurer to obey the fundamental principles of the constitution and the conventions in which these principles are expressed, is the fact that the breach of these principles and of these conventions will almost immediately bring the offender into conflict with the courts and the law of the land.'
A. V. Dicey, *An Introduction to the Study of the Law of the Constitution*, 1885

The main **conventions** that operate within the British Constitution are as follows:

- The Prime Minister shall be the leader of the majority party in the House of Commons.
- The Prime Minister has the power to appoint all government ministers.
- The Prime Minister shall have sole power to choose the dates of general elections (although there is a limit of five years between elections established by statute).
- A government must resign if it loses a confidence vote in the House of Commons.
- The Prime Minister acts as commander-in-chief of the armed forces and all other security services.
- The Prime Minister negotiates and signs foreign treaties.
- The Prime Minister creates peers, Church of England archbishops and bishops, senior judges and knighthoods, and grants other honours.
- The monarch always gives the Royal Assent to legislation properly passed in Parliament.
- Cabinet ministers must defend government policy or resign from the Government.

These examples illustrate the extent to which the British political system is governed by conventions. It also possibly exaggerates the powers of the Prime Minister. It should be remembered that, although he or she exercises many prerogative powers, the Prime Minister is still subject to the influence of Cabinet colleagues, back-bench MPs and his or her party.

Books and documents of authority

Despite the many statutes and conventions that map out the operation of the British Constitution, some areas have remained the subject of some doubt and confusion. There might be an **awareness** of the existence of such principles as the sovereignty of Parliament and the collective responsibility of the Cabinet, but the **authority** behind such features might be less clear. Here, important documents and theoretical works can help.

- The **Bill of Rights** of 1689 (not to be confused with more recent Bills of Rights, which concern the rights of citizens against the state) was an agreement between Parliament and the new king, William III. Its effect was to confirm parliamentary sovereignty, which has been strengthened considerably since then.
- **Walter Bagehot's** *English Constitution*, published in 1867, went some way to clarifying the status of the Cabinet and the role of party government.
- **Dicey's** *Introduction to the Study of the Law of the Constitution*, published in 1885, established the importance of the **rule of law** and the legal status of **conventions**.

Parliamentary procedures

Many of the rules and regulations of Parliament, largely contained in the reference work *Erskine May's Parliamentary Practice*, are purely administrative, but the book does contain a number of important constitutional principles. Among them are the rights and privileges of MPs, rules concerning their conduct, and the manner in which the Government may control the operations of both Houses. At the same time, parliamentary rules guarantee the independence of the legislature from government.

Rules concerning emergency debates, legislative procedures and the operation of committees affect the political process and must not, therefore, be ignored.

External constitutional agreements

In 1965 the UK agreed to allow its citizens to appeal to the European Court of Human Rights, which administers the European Convention on Human Rights. In 1973 the UK joined the European Community (now the European Union). These two events subjected the UK to constraints that might be described as constitutional, as they affect both the rights of citizens and the jurisdiction of government. They are 'external' in that they affect the UK's constitutional arrangements with other states, individually and collectively.

The **European Convention on Human Rights** is not legally binding on the UK, but the judgments of the European Court of Human Rights carry so much **moral** authority that the British Government normally abides by such rulings. It is, therefore, **quasi-constitutional** in the sense that it has virtually the same force as entrenched principles.

The various treaties governing the jurisdiction of the European Union affect the sovereignty of Parliament and the powers of national governments. Thus, they are an integral part of the British Constitution. The agreements include the **Treaty of Rome**, which the UK signed in 1972, and the **Treaty of Maastricht** of 1993. In addition, the **European Communities Act**, passed by Parliament in 1972, affirmed that all European law automatically became British law and the **Single European Act** of 1986 established the UK's participation in a unified market.

Should European integration deepen in the future, it might be that further constitutional inroads will be made into the British political system.

Sources of the British Constitution

1. Parliamentary statutes
2. Common law
3. Unwritten conventions
4. Books and documents of authority
5. Parliamentary procedures
6. External constitutional constraints

British constitutional features

The fact that the British Constitution is uncodified and unentrenched renders it extremely flexible. The institutions and practices that characterise the political system have, thus, been able to adjust to changing circumstances without any major upheavals.

Flexibility

Over the past 200 years, Britain has seen a number of important changes. These include the following:

- the development of the party system
- the decline in the authority of the monarchy
- the increasing power of the Cabinet
- a reduction in the power of Parliament, especially the House of Lords
- a considerable increase in the functions of the state
- the development of the European Union.

The response to these changes has been the addition of new conventions and the elimination of old ones. Contrast this history with the experience of France, where five constitutions have been created since the 1789 revolution, often accompanied by violence and disruption. The Americans, meanwhile, suffered a cruel civil war and many bitter battles over constitutional amendments. During the same period, Britain remained relatively stable.

Unitary government

The term 'unitary' refers to the fact that legal sovereignty lies in one place – Parliament. It is not divided as is the case in **federal** systems such as those of the USA or Germany. Although Britain has enjoyed a powerful and vigorous local government system in the past, this has not constituted divided sovereignty. The powers of local government have always been merely delegated by Parliament.

The parliamentary system

Parliament is the central feature of the political system. Above all, it is the sovereign body, which means that there can be no higher laws than those made by Parliament, and no higher political authority. In addition, government must be drawn from Parliament and is responsible to it.

Constitutional monarchy

Although, in theory, the Crown has unlimited **prerogative** powers in certain fields, including the maintenance of the security of the realm and the operation of the political system, there are important limitations.

Although there is no written constitution, it is understood that it can only operate within strict legal constraints. Most importantly, the sovereignty of Parliament means that the legislature may pass any statute it wishes, including laws that limit prerogative powers. Thus, for example, the monarch (or government acting on her behalf) may not imprison one of her subjects without trial without infringing the Habeas Corpus Act. At the same time, the powers of the Crown are limited by common law rights. In particular, the monarch may not take over private property without statutory authority.

The weakness of the separation of powers

The eighteenth-century French philosopher **Montesquieu** argued that good government must be self-limiting. The most effective way of achieving this, he added, was to ensure that the three branches of government – **legislature** (the bodies that develop and pass laws), **executive** (the bodies that propose and execute the laws) and **judiciary** (the courts that administer and interpret the laws) – should be strictly separated. Not only that, but they should enjoy powers that limit each other.

Although Montesquieu was describing his perception of the British system of the day, it was the Americans who enshrined his principles in their new Constitution. To them it became known as the system of 'checks and balances', and it has shaped American politics ever since.

Montesquieu's description of Britain was partially correct at the end of the eighteenth century, but since then the separation has been steadily eroded. It can now be said that the principle of the separation of powers no longer holds true in the UK, with the possible exception of the existence of a semi-independent judiciary. The following features can be identified as the causes of this development:

- Members of the Government are all also members of one of the Houses of Parliament.
- The Cabinet invariably dominates the majority in the House of Commons through the party whip system.
- Parliament has surrendered nearly all its genuine law-making functions to the Cabinet.
- Senior judges are appointed by the Prime Minister on the advice of the Lord Chancellor, the Cabinet and party colleagues.
- The Lord Chancellor, the most senior law officer and judge, is a member of the Cabinet and of the House of Lords, thus being unique as a member of all three branches of government.
- The House of Lords, or at least its senior judicial members, acts as the highest appeal court, often considering cases with political significance. Thus, it is part of both the legislature and the judiciary.

The political independence of judges is protected because they cannot be dismissed by the Government, nor can their salaries be reduced. So, it is not possible for any financial or occupational pressure to be placed on them.

The rule of law The principles of the rule of law, confirmed by **A. V. Dicey** in 1885, say much about legal equality and the rights of citizens to a fair trial according to the principles of justice. Their constitutional significance lies in the fact that the Government itself must operate within the laws. It is true, of course, that the laws may be designed by the Government to suit its purposes, so great is executive control over Parliament, but the rule of law ensures that existing statutory limitations will be respected.

EU membership The legal sovereignty of the UK is limited by membership of the European Union. The treaties, laws and regulations of the Union are binding in the UK. Where there is a conflict between European and British law, European law is superior. Where a decision of the European Council of Ministers requires only majority approval, the British Government must accept that decision even if it has voted against it. However, all key issues require unanimous approval. In these cases, the British government may veto a decision, so no sovereignty is lost.

The Human Rights Act This Act is the European Convention on Human Rights brought into British law. It is partly binding and partly advisory only. It has become a key constitutional feature since its introduction in October 2000. The details of the operation of the Act are shown on page 309.

Summary of British constitutional features

1. It is **unwritten**, **unentrenched** and therefore **flexible**.
2. It is **unitary** – sovereignty lies in one place.
3. It is **parliamentary** – Parliament lies at the centre of the system.
4. There is a **constitutional**, or limited, **monarchy**.
5. The **separation of powers** is largely absent.
6. The **rule of law** operates in the main.
7. Sovereignty is limited by **EU membership**.

Does the UK need a codified constitution?

The arguments in favour The principal pressure group currently campaigning for a codified and

and journalists, mostly of a liberal frame of mind, but including a sprinkling of socialists and even Conservatives. To them can be added the campaign group **Liberty** (formerly the National Council for Civil Liberties), eminent constitutional theorist Professor Fred Ridley and the prominent left-wing MP, Tony Benn. These campaigners wish to see major reform of the constitution, but also wish to safeguard those reforms.

The arguments in favour of a written constitution are as follows.

Executive power   There is too much power vested in the executive. A new constitutional settlement is, therefore, needed to disperse power more widely. Most of this redistribution would restore to Parliament much of its former independence.

As we have seen above, the separation of powers between the executive and the legislature has been gradually eroded. No less a Conservative than **Lord Hailsham**, not normally an enthusiast for dramatic reforms, accepted that this was a problem in 1976. His words have become something of a rallying cry for those who have lamented the excessive concentration of power in the Government:

> '*I have reached the conclusion that our Constitution is wearing out. Its central defects are gradually coming to outweigh its merits. I envisage nothing less than a written Constitution for the United Kingdom.*'
> Lord Hailsham, Dimbleby Lecture 1976, in *The Spectator*

In the same lecture, Hailsham described the UK as an 'elective dictatorship', referring to the fact that, once elected, a government can operate without any real controls, so great is its ability to dictate to its own House of Commons majority.

The solution for reformers lies in the adoption of methods to reduce the powers of the executive, including weakening prime ministerial patronage and removing his or her power to dissolve Parliament and call an election if the Government cannot get its way. John Major used this threat twice, in 1993 and 1994, to force through controversial European legislation against the opposition of a group of his own back-benchers.

Centralisation   There is too much power at the centre, in London. During the 1980s, Margaret Thatcher's administrations eroded the powers and independence of local government. More dramatically, a whole tier of local government was removed with the abolition of the Greater London Council, the Inner London Education Authority and six large metropolitan counties.

The rise of Scottish and Welsh nationalism has also heightened interest in regional government. There is a perceived failure by central government to understand or to sympathise with problems in the British regions. The principal of **subsidiarity**, which is gaining adherents, proposes that, in a modern democracy, decisions should be taken as close to the people as is feasible.

A new **entrenched** dispersal of powers to the regions and smaller localities would reverse this process and ensure that such centralisation could not occur again.

Prerogative powers

The prerogative powers exercised by government on behalf of the Crown are ill-defined and uncontrolled. Unlike statutory powers, which fall under parliamentary control, prerogative-based actions can be limited only if the courts judge them to be excessive. Such judicial action is rare. The case of **GCHQ** (Government Communications Headquarters) in 1984 is considered informative in this respect. The Government's decision to ban trade union membership among civil servants at GCHQ was taken under prerogative powers and thus did not require parliamentary approval. Despite widespread public disquiet, the courts upheld the Government's right to take this action.

Such dramatic decisions as declarations of war, the committal of British troops to battle, the signing of foreign treaties and general foreign policy initiatives are all taken under discretionary prerogative powers.

It is time, say campaigners, that these powers are defined and limited in a constitution. Their extent should not be left in the hands of judges, who too often tend to favour state power against individuals. Nor should Parliament be denied the right to exercise some control over such key government functions.

> *'Britain's constitution presents a paradox. We live in a modern world but inhabit a pre-modern, indeed ancient, constitution.'*
> Stephen Haseler, 'Britain's Ancien Régime', *Parliamentary Affairs* (October 1990)

Civil liberties

The rights of citizens are under threat and require greater protection. Although Britain is considered to be one of the longest-standing guardians of individual liberty, with its Anglo-Saxon rights enshrined in the Magna Carta of 1215 and subsequently exported all over the world through the auspices of the Empire, such traditions are unable to withstand the modern challenges of the powerful expanding state and the current challenges to order represented by burgeoning crime levels.

The Human Rights Act (HRA) will help to safeguard rights even more effectively than the European Convention, from which it is derived. However, the HRA is not superior to ordinary law made by the UK Parliament. Parliament remains sovereign. This means that rights **can** still be threatened if a measure has been properly passed by Parliament at Westminster. The following concerns remain important:

- The police have been given increased powers as a result of rising crime rates. Citizens may now be held for lengthy periods without trial. The right to remain silent, under questioning or in court, may now be cited as an indication of guilt under the much-opposed Criminal Justice Act of 1994. Under the same Act, the police also have greater powers to prevent public demonstrations, while the courts may issue severe penalities for trespass. There has also been a steady increase in police powers to stop and search pedestrians, and to detain and question motorists.

- Citizens increasingly come into contact with state institutions and face arbitrary decisions by bureaucracies that are insufficiently controlled. In this way, citizens are exposed to the possibilities of unjust treatment. Social security offices, tax offices, health authorities, local planning authorities, education authorities and housing bodies are all examples of such bureaucratic activity. The individual, it is argued, needs a code of well-protected rights to ensure fair treatment by these bodies.

- An increasing amount of information is held by state institutions about individuals. It is argued that there are dangers that such information might be misused, threatening particularly the privacy of the individual.

- In an increasingly multiracial, multifaith, pluralist society, the rights of the many minorities who now flourish are vulnerable to abuse and discrimination. Legal protection is, therefore, vital to allow our pluralist society to flourish.

- The media have become extremely powerful institutions. On the one hand, it can be argued that newspapers and broadcasters must be guaranteed access to official information where it is in the public interest to know; similarly, they need protection from the censorship that government might attempt to impose upon them in order to protect such information. On the other hand, citizens might need protection from the intrusiveness of the tabloid press in particular.

- The weakening influence of trade unions during the 1980s, coupled with the growing power of multinational corporations, has resulted in workers becoming vulnerable to unfair treatment. Rights in the workplace may, therefore, need firmer guarantees.

- Although the courts offer some protection for individuals from unfair treatment by the state, enforcing, as they do, common law rights, it is often argued that our senior judges are conservative (small 'c') in outlook and generally tend to favour the state against challenges by individuals. Furthermore, even if judges do take the side of the individual, they cannot prevent ministers simply passing laws through the sovereign Parliament to give them powers that might have been denied them by the courts.

- The loss of confidence in the institution of the monarchy experienced during the 1990s has led to demands that its 'political' functions be reduced or even abolished. At its extreme, this belief extends to outright abolition of the monarchy and its replacement by a republic. Full abolition seems unlikely, but even **Jack Straw**, a relatively moderate member of the Labour Party front-bench, proposed a 'slimmed down' monarchy in 1994. Should this be implemented, new constitutional rules would need to be codified to replace the old discretionary powers of the Crown.

The HRA will help to protect rights and the **Freedom of Information Act** of 2000 will address some of the problems listed. Nevertheless supporters of an entrenched constitution point out that the HRA and the Freedom of Information Act cannot disguise the fact that our rights are vulnerable to governments with large parliamentary majorities. Neither of these Acts is **entrenched**. Some say they should be.

> *'It is wrong that any government can change laws affecting civil liberties by ordinary and misrepresentative parliamentary majorities – we do need a Bill of Rights.'*
> Professor Bernard Crick, *Independent*, 19 May 1990

The arguments against

Opponents of a written constitution, and indeed an entrenched Bill of Rights, include virtually all Conservatives and many members of the more radical left. In both cases their main fear is excessive weakening of government as a result of increased constitutional obstacles. In the academic world, Professor Philip Norton leads the 'anti' lobby. Their arguments include the following.

Strong government

The vital quality of British government, much admired in the USA and on the European continent, is its ability to control the legislature, to carry out its electoral mandate without undue delay or opposition and to deal with unforeseen circumstances without encountering the hindrance of too many constitutional restraints.

Control over financial matters is the particular characteristic to which opponents of constitutionally limited government point when illustrating the strength of the current system. With the exception of the budgetary opposition encountered by Chancellor Kenneth Clarke in the 1990s, British governments normally enjoy a relatively free hand in financial and economic policy implementation. This is how it should be, runs the argument.

Flexibility

The very flexibility that is often criticised can be seen as a strength of the status quo. For traditional Conservatives the political system and the features that characterise it must be allowed to evolve naturally with society. Written constitutions and Bills of Rights are based on fixed principles, which such Conservatives oppose.

Certainly, it is true that the British Constitution has been able to adapt to major changes in the setting of British politics. Contrast this with the American experience where responses to the Depression of the 1930s, to economic decline in the 1980s and 1990s, and to a dramatically rising crime rate over the same period have all been hindered by constitutional rigidity. When Presidents and their administrations have attempted to extend their powers to deal with pressing problems, the Supreme Court has been forced to thwart them by enforcing the many constitutional controls over such developments that were put in place in 1787.

Judicial power The experience of the many democracies which have written constitutions is that the courts must frequently become involved in resolving constitutional disputes. Since many of these conflicts concern the powers of government, they are political in nature. We could certainly envisage cases involving the exercise of powers by ministers, or local authorities, becoming the subject of hotly contested political dispute. The question then arises as to whether judges are fit to pronounce on issues with clear political implications. They are unelected and not responsible. Opponents of written constitutions therefore argue that such conflicts must be left to elected politicians at Westminster.

> 'A Bill of Rights would be a cuckoo in the judicial nest.'
> John Biffen (Leader of the House of Commons 1982–7),
> *Independent*, 19 May 1990

Parliamentary sovereignty An entrenched constitution or Bill of Rights would remove the most basic feature of the British political system – the sovereignty of Parliament. Laws and principles that have a higher authority than other legislation would take away part of what Walter Bagehot, in 1867, called the 'efficient secret' of the system. Remove that sovereignty and there is a danger that British government would lose its most powerful tool.

There are some who argue that the creation of entrenched legislation would be futile, since Parliament could simply overturn it when it felt necessary and there exists no authority able to stop Parliament doing so. However, the introduction of a 'real' British Constitution might challenge the most basic and historic of our institutions, including Parliament and the monarchy.

Summary of arguments concerning a written constitution for the UK	
For	**Against**
1. Government is too powerful. Greater controls are needed.	1. Government would lose its power to be able to act decisively.
2. Government is too centralised. Power should be devolved downwards.	2. There would be a loss of flexibility in the political system.
3. The prerogative powers of government are uncontrolled and often abused.	3. The unelected judiciary would be thrust into the political arena.
4. The rights of citizens and groups have been eroded and continue to be threatened by government.	4. The sovereignty of Parliament would be lost.

Rights in the UK

The Human Rights Act

In October 2000 the Human Rights Act (HRA) came into force in the UK. Before considering how the Act works, it is necessary to look at its main provisions. These are summarised below.

Provisions of the Human Rights Act	
Provision	**Explanation**
• The right to life	• Life may only be taken following conviction in a country where the death penalty is legal. Self-defence and the like are allowed.
• Prohibition of torture	• Described as inhuman or degrading treatment.
• Prohibition of slavery	• Essentially forced labour except for legal prisoners.
• Right to liberty	• No unreasonable arrest or imprisonment without a speedy trial.
• Right to a fair trial	• The normal rules of legal justice must apply.
• No illegal punishment	• Any punishments must be in accordance with existing laws.
• Respect for private and family life	• A general, vague provision, open to interpretation.
• Freedom of thought and religion	• Provided the religion does not use illegal practices.
• Freedom of expression	• Including the press and media.
• Freedom of association	• The right to join legal organisations for legal purposes.
• Right to marry	• This also includes the right to create a family.
• Prohibition of discrimination	• On grounds of religion, race, colour, gender, etc.
• Protection of property	• Essentially property may not be seized illegally.
• Right to education	• Effectively no one shall be deprived of education.
• Right to free elections	• They must be regular, with secret ballots, and all adults must be free to vote or stand for office.

How the HRA is applied

It will take many years before the full details of implementation are settled. However, the principles of application are contained in the Act and are as follows:

• If the Government proposes legislation in Parliament, it must declare that, in its opinion, the legislation conforms to the HRA: in other words, that it does not conflict with the rights as laid down. This is known as a **Declaration of Compatibility**. The Government can, on the other hand, admit that the legislation **will** contravene the HRA. In such cases, it must justify its actions as being in the public interest. Here the Government will have to make a **Declaration of Incompatibility**. Governments, it is assumed, will be reluctant to risk such a course of action. Nevertheless, Acts of Parliament do not **have** to conform to the HRA. In this way, the sovereignty of Parliament is preserved. Where a citizen, or group of citizens, believes that an Act of Parliament does contravene the HRA, they can ask for a **judicial**

review by a court (in the first instance, the High Court). If the court decides that the legislation does contravene the HRA, it can declare it incompatible. However, the courts **do not** have the power to set aside or amend the legislation. All the court can do is to urge the Government to change the law to make it conform.

- Legislation made by the Scottish Parliament or Northern Ireland Assembly can be challenged in the courts. Here, however, if the legislation is found to be incompatible, the court **can** order it to be cancelled or amended to make it conform. This is because these legislative bodies are not sovereign.
- Any decision or action by a public body, the Welsh Assembly, local authorities or other organisations can be challenged by a citizen or group. If the action is found to be incompatible with the HRA by the courts, it can be cancelled and, in some cases, compensation may be awarded.
- There is an appeals procedure to the European Court of Human Rights, but this can only be used when all attempts within the British courts (i.e. right up to the House of Lords) have been used up.

The impact of the HRA

The immediate effect of the Act will be to speed up and make easier a process that has existed for many years. Citizens have long been able to appeal to the European Court of Human Rights. However, this is an expensive process, costing tens of thousand of pounds at least. It is also slow, taking up to seven years for the full process to operate. With the right to go to a British court under the HRA, however, everything will be cheaper and quicker.

Perhaps more importantly, the Human Rights Act is the first time the UK has had its own code of rights, clearly stated, as part of its law. Parliament, the media, government and individual citizens can be more directly aware of what rights people have. In other words, it should help to create a **rights culture**, where everyone is aware of rights issues. There will be more direct safeguards in place, more publicity and more sanctions against those who threaten people's rights.

Other ways of protecting rights

The HRA replaced much of the rights protection system that existed up to the end of the twentieth century. However, there are a number of other ways in which individuals and groups may seek remedies for the infringement of their rights.

Judicial review

There are two main examples of when such reviews can be used (other than cases under the HRA, as described above). One concerns cases of **ultra vires** (literally, 'beyond powers'), where a citizen feels a minister or a public body might have acted beyond the powers granted to them by law. During the 1990s, for example, the Home Secretary, Michael Howard, lost a succession of cases when he attempted to extend his powers with relation to the treatment of prisoners. The other type of case arises when a citizen feels that he or she has been unfairly treated by a public body such as the police or the National Health Service. Here the questions asked might be 'Were different cases treated in the same way?' or 'Were the correct procedures followed and all factors taken into consideration when making a decision?' or perhaps 'Were the rules of **natural justice** applied – was the decision a fair one?'

Before the 1980s judicial reviews were very rare, but since then the courts have admitted many more cases. Thousands of judicial reviews were undertaken in the 1980s and 1990s. Although most of them failed, enough succeeded to make ministers and public officials think carefully when dealing with citizens. Indeed, so effective has judicial review been that the Cabinet Office issued a document in the 1980s to all its civil servants, warning them to be careful when making decisions in case an expensive and embarrassing judicial review might follow. The document was known as 'The Judge Over Your Shoulder'. Its name spoke for itself.

> 'Judicial Review is not a perfect jurisdiction, but in the absence of effective, political checks ... it forms a useful part of the system of mixed checks and balances.'
> Dawn Oliver, 'The Judge Over Your Shoulder',
> *Parliamentary Affairs*, July 1989

The European Court of Justice

The European Court of Justice (ECJ) should not be confused with the European Court of Human Rights (ECHR). The ECJ is the main court of the European Union, whereas the ECHR is part of the Council of Europe. The ECJ interprets European Union law and deals with disputes between member states. However, it can also be used as an appeal court when groups of citizens from any EU state feel that their rights, which are guaranteed by European law, have been ignored or abused. Unlike the ECHR, it deals with different, more specialised categories of rights.

Most EU rights concern the treatment of workers, consumers and the recipients of welfare benefits. In recent years, the ECJ has confirmed the right to equal pay and treatment for women workers, the right to equal pension rights for men and a variety of entitlements for groups of workers, especially part-timers. The judgments of the court are binding (unlike those of the ECHR) and have done a great deal to extend and safeguard economic and social rights.

Tribunals

All citizens of the UK have certain rights in relation to public bodies. These may be described as part of **administrative law**. These rights can be categorised as follows:

- The right to be treated equally by public bodies. A claim may be made if, in two very similar cases, decisions have been different so as to discriminate between citizens of equal status: for example, if one home owner is denied planning permission while another has it granted for almost the same alterations.
- The right to be granted the correct procedures when a citizen's case is being considered: for example, over taxation, legal proceedings or a welfare benefit.
- The right to service by a public body, if one qualifies: for example, by the health service, the police or a local authority.
- The right to be treated with natural justice.

In these and similar instances, there is a system of appeals tribunals, which will hear a citizen's case and correct any decisions that do not conform to the principles of administrative rights. Here are some specific examples:

- **Social Security**. Tribunals to deal with appeals concerning social security benefits.
- **Inland Revenue**. Tribunals concerning disputes over income and other direct taxes.
- Mental Health. Tribunals dealing with appeals over the treatment of the mentally ill.
- **Industrial**. Tribunals hearing suspected cases of unfair dismissal from employment.

Tribunals are more accessible to the average citizen than a normal court of law. They are also quicker and cheaper to use.

Ombudsmen

Similar to tribunals, there is a system of commissioners or ombudsmen in the public and private sectors who investigate cases where individuals believe they have been treated unfairly. Typically these are cases that would not fall under the responsibilities of the courts or a tribunal. The most prominent of these work in central government (the **Parliamentary Commissioner for Administration**), local government and the National Health Service. Though they hear relatively few cases, they are an important part of the system that deals with citizens' grievances.

Members of Parliament

It is one of the most ancient functions of MPs to deal with the grievances of their constituents. While tribunals, the courts and ombudsmen may deal with common types of case, MPs will often take up the cause of one or a group of their constituents against what might be seen as unfair treatment by central government (sometimes even local authorities, though MPs have no direct access to them). MPs expect to be given fast access to ministers and senior civil servants. They might also ask awkward questions in Parliament and raise individual cases in the course of debates.

The House of Commons

The House is effectively the sovereign body where law making is concerned. It therefore follows that, in theory at least, it is the guardian of people's rights. It may do this in one of three ways:

- By vetoing a proposed Act of Parliament that might infringe people's rights. This is a very rare event, since any legislation that might not pass the House is normally withdrawn by the Government at an early stage. However, in 1986 the Commons rejected the **Sunday Trading Bill**, introduced to allow more shops to open on Sunday. They did so partly on the grounds that it would abuse the rights of workers to have a day of rest and, for Christians at least, to be able to enjoy the Sabbath Day (the Bill was subsequently passed in the 1990s). However, the power of the government whips and the strength of party discipline normally mean that legislation passes, even when it endangers rights. The **Criminal Justice and Public Order Act** of 1994 is a good example of such an occurrence (see page 315).
- By amending legislation in order to safeguard some rights. This is often done through a process of negotiation with the Government. A

suspicious House of Commons might let a Bill pass in return for concessions. The same Criminal Justice Act referred to above was 'watered down' before it could be passed. Similarly in 2000, Labour MPs forced the Government to strengthen the **Freedom of Information Act** so as to extend citizens' rights further than the Government wished.

- Ultimately, the House of Commons has the power to remove a government by passing a no confidence vote. Though this is extremely rare, it is certainly a check on government's power. If ministers were to attempt to introduce measures that would seriously threaten human rights, they know that the Commons holds the ultimate sanction. The fact that human rights violations in the UK are relatively rare, suggest that this implied threat works.

The House of Lords   When the House of Commons appears to be failing in its duty to uphold people's rights, usually when government has an overwhelming majority there, the Lords can step in as a second line of defence. It is not dominated by the whips, and the Government cannot rely upon a loyal majority. Of course, the House of Lords is limited in its powers compared to the Commons. It can only delay legislation for a year and any amendments it proposes must be returned to the Commons for approval.

Nevertheless the Lords can make such a nuisance of itself that governments often give in to its demands. This was certainly the case when a number of rights to welfare payments were threatened by the **Welfare Reform Bill** in 1999. The House of Lords proposed amendment after amendment, so slowing down the process that the Government was forced to give in to save the Bill.

The reform of the membership of the Lords in 1999 has potentially strengthened its independence, especially when a Conservative Government is in power (the removal of most hereditary peers in that year took away the in-built Conservative majority). On the other hand, a strong, determined government can get its way through the supremacy of the House of Commons.

Civil society   This term refers to the many groups that flourish in society and that might have influence over government. Citizens are either members of these groups, or owe some allegiance to them. The most powerful are the **media** – particularly newspapers – big **pressure or interest groups**, such as Friends of the Earth, Age Concern and trade unions, and **religious establishments**. As long as they are active and independent, they may take up the cause of citizens' rights. Governments have to listen to them because they have influence. Some pressure groups, indeed, have campaigned directly for the protection and extension of rights. **Charter 88** and **Liberty**, for example, have succeeded in bringing the issue of rights to the forefront of public opinion.

If one were to doubt the importance of a free civil society, one would only need to look at the way totalitarian political systems operate. They invariably suppress civil society, banning pressure group activity, censoring the media and often controlling religious activity. They do this because they are potentially influential.

The political sovereignty of the people

In democratic societies, all governments must ultimately account for themselves to the people. At elections, governments are judged on their performance in office. The treatment of human rights will be one of the issues upon which judgement can be made. It has to be said that human rights is a relatively soft issue at elections: that is, it is not a big vote winner or loser compared to economic performance or law and order. Nevertheless, it does provide a discipline upon government. Ministers and MPs are always aware of public opinion and hate to alienate it. As long as substantial numbers of people care about our rights, governments will listen to them.

Summary of how rights in the UK are protected

Method	Weaknesses
• Human Rights Act	• Is not binding on Parliament.
• Judicial Review	• Judges can only recommend, not enforce decisions.
• European Court of Justice	• Limited range of jurisdiction.
• Tribunals	• Limited range of jurisdiction.
• Ombudsmen	• Can only recommened action.
• MPs	• Government need not act on their requests.
• House of Commons	• Government majority is decisive.
• House of Lords	• Can be overruled by the Commons. Can only delay legislation.
• Civil society	• Government need not be influenced.
• Public opinion	• Economic and other issues affect more votes.

The UK's recent record on rights

This is mixed, as is probably the case with most democratic systems. We can review the current position by examining briefly the ways in which British rights have been extended in modern times, and setting them beside examples of ways in which rights have been eroded or where progress has been slow in extending rights.

Extensions of rights
- Legislation has established **equal rights for women**, both in employment and in their general treatment. This has been underpinned by European regulations.
- **Race relations** laws have outlawed discrimination on the grounds of race, colour and creed.
- Discriminatory laws against **homosexuals** have largely been removed.
- **Workers** have extensive protection against unfair treatment by employers. Again, European law has strengthened this.
- **Consumers** now have a wide range of rights against the sellers of goods and services.
- The **Human Rights Act** promises to bring greater safeguards against attacks on people's rights.
- The **Freedom of Information Act**, though weaker than many had hoped, gives citizens rights to view information kept about themselves and gives everyone greater rights to see official documents and reports.
- An increasing number of citizens have been granted the right to **judicial review** of political and administrative decisions that might have infringed their rights.

Negative record
- The UK still lags behind many other democracies in establishing full rights for **homosexuals, disabled people** and **older people**.
- **Trade union** rights were eroded in the 1980s and many of these have not been restored since.
- Government has not really tackled the issue of its tendency to excessive secrecy. The **Official Secrets Act**, which prevents public officials and politicians from discussing the internal workings of central government, remains in full force. The Freedom of Information Act is generally considered to be too weak.
- The **Human Rights Act** was not entrenched or made superior. Though it is a valuable contribution to rights, it can still be ignored by government and Parliament.
- In modern times, the powers of the police have been steadily extended. The **Police and Criminal Evidence Act** of 1984, the **Public Order Act** of 1986 and the **Criminal Justice and Public Order Act** of 1994 are all examples of increasing police powers. They have given the police greater powers to stop and search, to enter premises, to prevent public demonstrations and to hold suspected criminals without trial. In addition, the Criminal Justice Act of 1994 removed the right for prisoners to remain silent without incriminating themselves by so doing. In 2000, in addition, the Government considered reducing the right of accused people to a trial by jury. In other words, some of the most ancient of our rights have now come into question.

These lists are not exhaustive and the student of politics must make up his or her own mind whether they add up to a positive or a negative overall record. There is, however, one certainty. The issue of human rights now plays a far more important role in political life than it did before the 1960s. It seems set to continue to do so.

The judiciary, rights and the Constitution

The senior judiciary

It is not the concern of this book to look at the many magistrates, recorders and county or crown court judges who dispense criminal and civil justice day in and day out. Instead we are interested in those senior judges whose decisions might have far-reaching effects on the Constitution and on the rights of citizens. On the whole, they preside at three levels of court – the High Court, the Courts of Appeal and the House of Lords. A case that has national significance will normally begin life in the High Court. If there is to be an appeal, it will be heard in the Court of Appeal and from there it might reach the House of Lords. Cases sent to the Lords for a final hearing are normally those of greatest significance. This is the final stage unless a case comes under EU jurisdiction, in which case it can go to the European Court of Justice, or when a rights issue is at stake then the European Court of Human Rights can be involved.

The House of Lords, sitting as an appeal court (not to be confused with the House of Lords that is part of the parliamentary process), consists of a group of five of the country's most senior judges, selected from a total panel of twelve. These twelve – officially known as **Lords of Appeal in Ordinary** – are often referred to as the **Law Lords**.

The senior judges are appointed by the Lord Chancellor, who is a member of the Cabinet and therefore a politician. He or she may discuss appointments with the Prime Minister. On the face of it, therefore, judges are **political appointments**. In reality, however, there is little evidence today that there is significant political bias in whom is chosen. If there were, the rest of the judiciary would become well aware of the fact and there would be considerable opposition to such appointments. The basis of choice seems to be legal ability, experience and integrity rather than political views. It is also true that judges cannot be dismissed or punished, or have their salaries reduced, on the basis of the judgments they make. It follows, therefore, that they are able to resist political pressure to make a particular decision.

The principle that separates the judiciary from the political arena is known as the **independence of the judiciary**. The safeguards described above cannot guarantee independence, but, in theory at least, independence is a well-established principle. Whether or not the judges are truly **neutral**, however, is an open question.

Judicial neutrality implies that cases are heard without any political bias. The judges are expected to apply the law in an even-handed way, without favouring any kind of philosophy or beliefs of their own. When a case has political significance, it is vital to neutrality that the judges do not show any special favour towards either the state or individuals, to the Government or the forces of opposition. The traditional view has been that judges are not normally neutral. They have been seen as a conservative (small 'c') body of people who will always tend to favour the status quo and the authority of the state against progressive ideas and the interests of individual citizens. Whether this was ever true or not, it is now clear that an increasing proportion of the judiciary are of a liberal frame of mind. Indeed, the Lord Chief Justice (effectively the UK's most senior judge) appointed in May 2000 – Lord Woolf – had a reputation for defending the rights of individuals and for being suspicious of state power. His predecessor, Lord Bingham, was also on the liberal side of political philosophy.

With the Human Rights Act in force, judicial neutrality will come under even greater scrutiny. Although Parliament does not have the power to criticise individual judgments, public opinion will decide whether judicial neutrality is being preserved.

Judge-made law

There are three main ways in which judges contribute to the making and development of the laws:

- By interpreting the meaning of statutes, orders and regulations, they are effectively clarifying what the law says. This is known as **judicial interpretation**. Typically, this will make clear what powers different political institutions actually have. They might also be indicating the legal relationship between different bodies: for example, between ministers and local government, and between devolved governments and central government.
- By showing how the law should be applied to particular circumstances, they are also making clarifications. This is known as **case law**. Typical examples would be the laws concerning racial and gender discrimination. After many cases have been heard, in many different kinds of situation, we can begin to understand better how laws work in practice. When case law is made, it has to be followed in similar instances in the future, so law is actually being made.
- **Common law** refers to those binding rules of society that have not been established by Parliament, but which have simply grown up through tradition. Common law not being properly codified (i.e. not fully established by statute), it is for judges to interpret what it actually is. Many of our rights are only established by common law, so this is a key element in the unwritten constitution. Once a higher court has declared the meaning of common law, other courts must follow – a process known as **judicial precedent**.

Since many such cases involve relationships between political bodies or deal with the rights of citizens, we can see how judges are involved in political and constitutional controversy.

Should judges establish rights and interpret the Constitution?

This has become a key question for all democratic societies. There are those who oppose the involvement of judges in constitutional affairs. Professors John Griffiths and Philip Norton argue that judges, as they are currently selected, are unsatisfactory figures to be involved in important constitutional affairs. Norton worries because they are not elected and are therefore not accountable; Griffiths is concerned that they are an unrepresentative elite.

Supporters of the judiciary argue that they are politically independent, unlike government and Parliament, so they are the best safeguard of people's rights and of the Constitution. The arguments on either side can be summarised as follows:

Arguments for and against judicial control of the Constitution	
For judicial control	**Against judicial control**
• The judiciary is independent of politics.	• Judges are effectively political appointments.
• Judges are legally qualified to make sound decisions.	• Constitutional and rights issues should be determined by elected politicians.
• Judges are not subject to public pressure.	• Judges are not elected, not accountable and unrepresentative.
• Parliament is controlled by the Government and so is not independent enough to be in control of people's rights and the Constitution.	• Rights and the Constitution must be in the hands of elected representatives.

Whatever the arguments, the passage of the Human Rights Act will undoubtedly throw senior judges into the political arena. High-profile rights cases will be fought out in the courts. The arrival of devolution and the continued importance of the European Union in British affairs also place a burden upon the judiciary. As the distribution of power in the UK steadily changes, judges will continue to be called upon to decide where the divisions of power actually lie.

Conclusion

The period 1997–2001 has been for the UK one of perhaps unprecedented constitutional change. In the past, the British Constitution evolved gradually and slowly. After 1689, when England became a constitutional monarchy, evolution went almost unnoticed. When developments were made, they were small and took place over long periods of time. The Labour Government that took office in 1997, however, was determined to effect a more dramatic change in the distribution of power in the UK. The changes are summarised below.

Summary of constitutional change since 1997	
Change	**Detail**
• Devolution	• The transfer of significant powers to assemblies and executives in Scotland, Wales and Northern Ireland.
• Human Rights Act	• The incorporation of the European Convention on Human Rights in British law. It is binding on all except the British Parliament.
• Freedom of Information Act	• Citizens were given a right to view most information held about them. • Much of the internal work of government is now open to view.
• House of Lords reform	• The right of most hereditary peers to vote in the Lords was taken away. • Further reform is proposed.
• Electoral reform	• Proportional electoral systems were introduced in Scotland, Wales and Northern Ireland.
• Elected city mayors	• A mayor and assembly were elected for London. • Other cities are to be given the same opportunity.
• Referenda	• The principle of using more referenda to determine constitutional change was established. • Referenda on devolution in Wales, Scotland, Northern Ireland and London. • Referenda promised on electoral reform and the single European currency.

For exam questions relevant to this unit, see page 557.

Background to European integration

Ever since Napoleon dreamed of a single European political and legal 'system' at the beginning of the nineteenth century, there have been grand ideas of solving continental problems by permanent, institutional integration. Until the end of the Second World War, however, no such plans ever approached the degree of success that Napoleon nearly achieved.

Two disastrous European wars in the same century finally persuaded politicians that a serious attempt had to be made to eliminate all possibility of a repetition of such events. The key figures were two Frenchmen, **Jean Monnet** and **Robert Schuman**.

Initially, thoughts rested upon an alliance between France and Germany, to avoid future aggression, but Monnet in particular hoped for a broader union to include the UK, Italy and the 'Benelux' countries – Belgium, the Netherlands and Luxembourg. The objectives of European integration were:

- to destroy finally the conditions for future wars between European powers

- to provide stable conditions for increased trade within Europe

- ultimately to create a single, powerful European economy

- to create a single power able to resist military pressure from the Soviet Union.

Such aspirations were clearly long-term aims, requiring radical changes in the political outlook of the peoples and leaders of Europe. Progress has, therefore, been gradual and piecemeal.

The road to union

European Coal and Steel Community

In 1952 six countries signed the **Treaty of Paris**, establishing the European Coal and Steel Community (ECSC). These were France, Germany, Italy, Belgium, the Netherlands and Luxembourg. Presaging later events, the UK decided not to participate, but to wait and see how matters developed. Ever since 1952, British governments have proved to be reluctant partners in Europe.

The ECSC established a system for the control and integration of the coal, iron and steel industries in the member states. It was an important economic step forward, but its greater significance concerns the political institutions that were set up to administer the Community. These became a blueprint for the future closer union. The constituent bodies of the ECSC were as follows:

- A **High Authority** to administer the industries. This was a 'supranational' body whose jurisdiction stood above that of the member states – a unique innovation in international politics. For the first time, domestic governments showed themselves willing to accept transfer of sovereignty to such an institution. There were safeguards, as shown below, but an important principle had been established.
- The **Ministerial Council** comprising representatives from member governments. Its role was to ensure that the High Authority did not act beyond its powers, reserving a veto if necessary.
- A **Parliamentary Assembly**, drawn from the Council of Europe – a consultative body that had existed since 1950 to discuss general progress towards European integration. The Assembly was given no specific powers and was thus a weak body, set up to discuss and propose policy, but little more.
- A **Court**, employing judges from member states, to adjudicate on legal disputes concerning the operation of the rules of the Community.

With the exception of the Ministerial Council, which was later to be given full sovereign status in the Community, these political arrangements were to survive at least until 1996.

The Treaty of Rome

Buoyed up by the success of the ECSC, but determined to widen the scope of economic integration, European leaders now moved towards a broader agreement. In 1957 the **Treaty of Rome** was signed by the six member countries. At the same time, an agreement on co-operation in atomic energy production, known as **Euratom**, was completed.

The Treaty of Rome set up the **European Economic Community** (EEC), often referred to as the **Common Market**. The broad nature of what was agreed in Rome is shown on page 322.

Further functions were added to the EEC after the Treaty of Rome, most notably the **Common Agricultural Policy** in 1967. This was designed to protect European agriculture, stabilise food prices and generally regulate production. The fishing industry was added to the general scheme. Measures to provide help for particular industries which, it is felt, are vital to European prosperity, to give aid to poorer regions and to improve transport facilities are all designed to facilitate trade and greater economic equality between member countries.

Provisions of the Treaty of Rome	
Economic objectives	**Political institutions**
~~1. Eliminate all import tariffs and other barriers~~ between member states. 2. Establish common product descriptions and standards in the Community. 3. Introduce a common external tariff on goods entering from outside the Community.	~~1. The~~ servants, to develop and implement policy. 2. The **Council of Ministers** drawn from each member state. This comprises Heads of Government (i.e. Prime Ministers) for key decisions, and functional ministers for such issues as agriculture, trade and finance. The Council is the **sovereign** body and must agree all laws and regulations. 3. The **European Parliament** (originally this was known as the Assembly). Its role was limited to general debate and consultation. 4. The **European Court of Justice** to settle legal disputes over European law arising in member states.

The treaty did not deal with the thorny problem of finance. International currency exchanges and movements, together with interest rate policy, are vital in the creation of stable trading conditions. These issues were to come to a head in the 1990s.

British membership

As we have seen above, the UK was reluctant to participate in European integration in its early days. Three principal reasons can be identified:

- The UK's tradition of isolation from continental affairs. Historically, the UK has seen itself as a world imperial power rather than a continental European one.
- The close association (the so-called 'special relationship') with the USA, which implied that the UK need not rely on a European alliance.
- The Commonwealth, which provided the UK with a network of special trade agreements, giving it sources of cheap raw materials and imports, together with ready markets for its exports. This, together with extensive trade links with the USA, rendered economic integration with Europe less attractive than maintenance of the status quo.

From a European perspective, British membership was also not wholly supported. The French, in particular, feared that the UK would attempt to dominate the Community, using it for its own purposes. More worrying was a suspicion that a German–British axis might be formed to the detriment of the less wealthy members.

The UK had formed its own European trade community, the **European Free Trade Association** (EFTA) in 1959, which eventually comprised seven members, but as this was made up of much smaller countries (such as Portugal, Austria and Switzerland), it was limited in scope and was of relatively little economic importance. Essentially, by 1960, the UK was isolated in Europe.

It was Harold Macmillan (Prime Minister 1957–63) who made the first attempt to bring the UK into the Community. He was thwarted by the French President, Charles de Gaulle, who vetoed British admission in 1962 following major disagreements over entry conditions. At the time, France was moving closer to Germany in economic and political terms. British membership might have threatened this new accord.

Further tentative overtures were also rejected, but two events renewed British interest. De Gaulle was overthrown in 1969, and this removed the major obstacle to British membership. The following year Edward Heath was elected Prime Minister. Heath was a convinced European, determined to negotiate British entry. Talks reached a successful conclusion in 1972 and on 1 January 1973 the UK joined the EEC.

The Labour Government that took office in 1974 renegotiated the terms of British membership, a largely cosmetic exercise, and then held a referendum on the question of whether membership should be retained. This was politically necessary for the party, as it was hopelessly split on the issue. Only an expression of the popular will could heal the wound. The result was emphatic support for membership, by two to one.

The single market

During 1986 negotiations took place in Luxembourg to complete the task of creating the single market, a process that had started in Rome in 1957. The legislation that was passed – the Single European Act – made a number of political changes within the Community, but its most important provision was to come into effect at the beginning of 1993.

Political changes

- The rules concerning voting in the Council of Ministers were changed. Before the Act, many decisions required **unanimous** approval of the Council to become law. This safeguarded the sovereignty of each state, since there was an effective veto. After the Act most decisions only required a **qualified majority** that is, more than 50 per cent, but less than unanimity. Thus, member states gave up a considerable amount of control. This marked a significant shift in power from member states to this supranational body.
- The European Parliament's influence was enhanced, but only marginally. It was required to approve proposals from the Commission (civil service) and the Council (ministers). It could now force the decision makers to renegotiate proposals, but not stop them altogether. It was also granted the power to decide on the admission of new members and the appointment of senior officials in the Commission.
- The jurisdiction of the Community was widened to include environmental issues, research and development and more extensive regional policy.

Economic changes

One economic principle dominated the Single European Act. This was the establishment of a single market. In practice, this meant that there would be no remaining taxes, regulations or restrictions on the movement of goods, services, people or capital (finance) between member countries. In effect, such movements were to be as free as if they were taking place **within** a single country. This came into effect on 1 January 1993.

The ramifications of this development include the advent of a single currency to apply throughout the Community and a single unified economy. Once these two economic changes have taken place the opportunities for closer political integration will increase.

Expansion 1973–95

There were six original members of the Community. In 1973 Ireland and Denmark joined along with the UK to make nine (Norway was due to join at the same time but a referendum there rejected entry). The nine became twelve when Greece joined in 1981, and Spain and Portugal in 1986. On 1 January 1995 Sweden, Finland and Austria made the total fifteen. Most of western Europe was now included.

Apart from the question of a few other western powers entering, such as Switzerland and Turkey, the main questions over membership at the beginning of the twenty-first century concern the 'new' liberal democracies of eastern and central Europe, such as Hungary, the former Yugoslav states, Poland and Russia. However, it seems unlikely that there can be early entry for these former socialist states. Their economies remain in a transitional state while, at the same time, the question of military alliances has not been resolved. The roles of NATO, a possible future European Defence Establishment and the remaining American forces must be decided before there can be further expansion.

Finance

Hand in hand with economic integration must go closer financial co-operation. As long as national currencies are allowed to fluctuate in value against each other, there will be trade uncertainty and instability. But this is not merely an economic question. Control over currency values and interest rates, which are closely related issues, requires supra-national regulatory bodies which further threaten the sovereignty of member states. Thus, it has vital political significance.

Following earlier modest attempts at monetary regulation, the European **Exchange Rate Mechanism** (ERM) was established in 1980. By 1987 the ERM had developed into a system where each member currency was virtually fixed in value against the value of all the others. The political importance of the ERM was that it required all member states to co-operate in maintaining their currency's exchange rate. This implied that they might have to accept financial constraints for the benefit of maintaining the system, even when this might be damaging to their own economic health. In other words, they might have to accept **short-term national disadvantages** for the sake of **long-term European currency stability**.

This was a price that the UK's Conservative Government was initially not prepared to pay. Sterling was proving particularly unstable, so radical measures would be required to maintain its exchange rate. Thus, the UK stayed out of the ERM. In 1990, however, Margaret Thatcher reluctantly agreed to take the UK in, following intense pressure from other members.

Ironically, it was this event which precipitated the demise of the ERM. Sterling was too weak a currency to maintain its exchange rate without unacceptable measures being taken to protect it. When panic selling of sterling occurred, followed by similar problems for Ireland and Italy, the UK was forced to leave the system in 1992. A discredited Chancellor of the Exchequer, Norman Lamont, resigned, while in Europe the ERM eventually collapsed.

The Treaty of Maastricht

Formally called the **Treaty on European Union,** this agreement was signed in Maastricht, Holland, in 1992. The treaty was a mixture of specific changes and broader, less precise aims. The varied nature of the agreements is summarised below.

The Treaty of Maastricht	
• Institutional changes	• Parliament was to have greater influence over legislation, appointment of Commissioners and other future agreements. • Advisory Committees on the Regions and on Economic and Social Affairs, plus the European Investment Bank, were given increased status. • The name 'the European Community' was changed to 'the European Union'.
• Broadening the scope of the Union	• Greater powers on environmental issues. • More control over social and industrial relations policy (the 'Social Chapter' from which the UK initially opted out). • Increased powers on consumer protection. • More control over transport and regional policy.
• Long-term aims	• Possible future common foreign and defence policy. • Increased democratisation especially increased parliamentary powers. • A single European currency by 1999. • Common legal, political and economic rights for all European citizens.

On balance, Maastricht was more a promise for the future than an immediate radical reform of the Community. It did little to increase democracy in the Union, did not significantly change the role and powers of the Commission or the Council of Ministers, fudged the issue of citizens' rights and left a number of key decisions to the intergovernmental conference scheduled for 1996.

Possibly the most significant measure was the 'Social Chapter'. This section of the treaty gave the Union powers to regulate the rights and conditions of workers, the powers of trade unions, minimum pay and other benefits, with related implications for welfare, pensions, provision for the disabled and a number of other social policies. This represented a major extension of the Union's jurisdiction. So radical was this development that the UK refused to agree and the other members were forced to allow it to be exempt in order to conclude the treaty. As we shall see below, the UK was also permitted to reserve the right to refuse to accept a common currency in the future.

The Treaty of Amsterdam

The Treaty of Amsterdam, signed in 1997, was essentially a follow-up to Maastricht. Most of the treaty concerned arrangements for the single European currency and a number of 'intentions', rather than specific actions. Amsterdam was therefore designed mainly to move the Union forward towards its next stage of integration.

The members decided to move towards a **common defence force** and the integration of members' **foreign policy**. The idea of **European citizenship** was also raised. This suggests a system where all people who are citizens of an EU state have the same civil, economic and social rights. This would have important implications for individual members' policies, since all legislation, in every country, would have to conform. Other measures discussed and agreed in outline at Amsterdam were plans for more police co-ordination and further increases in political integration. In the meantime, a number of categories of decision making were removed from the need for unanimous vote. This had the effect of chipping away further at the sovereignty of individual states.

In essence, therefore, Amsterdam, was a commitment to the future rather than a significant shift in policy. It was signed by the Conservative British Government even though most of its members were extremely sceptical of further integration. The Labour Party, which took office later that year, was more enthusiastic, especially in the field of defence, but little progress has since been made.

The Treaty of Nice

Negotiated in 2000, Nice was intended to be the fourth in a series of stages of development of the EU. However, despite its lofty ideals, it has run into a number of difficulties. The main provision was for a significant enlargement of the Union, admitting new members from central and south-east Europe. Though this was agreed by all the EU ministers, it required ratification by all member states. The Irish Republic, however, rejected the Treaty in a referendum in June 2001. So the issue of enlargement remains 'on hold'. Eurosceptics took heart from the decision of the Irish as it demonstrated that national sovereignty has not been lost by EU membership, at least on major decisions like this.

The treaty also contained a general commitment to a future Bill of Rights for Europe and a stated intention to move towards a common defence and foreign policy. However, insufficient agreement could be reached on these issues for a firm treaty to be signed. In the UK the Conservatives rejected the terms of the Treaty and promised to renegotiate it. However, their failure to win power in the 2001 general election meant that the UK remains committed to the Treaty's terms.

The institutions of the European Union

The Commission

The Commission is, effectively, the civil service of the Union. It is made up of nearly 20,000 permanent officials drawn from member states, the number from each state being in proportion to its size. Whichever country an official represents, he or she is expected to serve the interests of Europe as a whole.

The Commission is divided into seventeen sections, each headed by a **Commissioner**, who is an influential policy developer. The Commissioners are selected by the Council of Ministers, but their appointment must be ratified by the European Parliament. They come from a variety of backgrounds, but are typically civil servants from member states or former politicians. Among the seventeen sections are finance, transport, relations with other states, agriculture and industry.

The role of the Commission divides into two. First, it proposes measures designed to further the long-term general goals of the Union, which have already been set by meetings of ministers. It cannot make law and there is no guarantee that its proposals will be accepted. Second, it is charged with the task of implementing Union policy. In practice, it could not hope to do this itself because it is a relatively small body. In most cases, the Commission relies upon the institutions of the member states themselves to execute decisions. In this sense, its function is largely supervisory.

A European Commission meeting

The Council of Ministers

Though normally referred to in the singular, the Council is not one single body. Instead, it is the collective name for a series of meetings that take place in the EU between representatives from the governments of member states. The key meetings, where the most significant decisions have to be made, are attended by the Heads of Government. In such cases, the title **European Council** is adopted. States take turns to chair

the meetings of this Council for a six-month period each. The most significant effect of chairmanship is that the list of items for discussion – the agenda – is determined by the chairing country. Mostly, however, only functional ministers are required where more, specialised discus-
industry and environment ministers.

The role of the Council, in all its forms, is to ratify decisions that have been proposed by the Commission and discussed by the European Parliament. In short, the Council is the **sovereign** body of the Union. This fact represents the central political feature of Europe. However, it is the system of voting in the Council which is of greatest interest. The basis of the system includes the following arrangements:

- For the most important decisions, such as the admission of new members, currency arrangements, budgetary contributions and changes in the scope of Union jurisdiction, a **unanimous** vote among ministers is essential. In other words, each individual state has a veto on such issues. In this way, there can be no total loss of sovereignty for members.
- Member states are awarded votes in the Council roughly in proportion to their size – obviously larger states have more votes than smaller ones. With the arrival of Sweden, Finland and Austria in 1995, the voting strengths were as follows:

  10 votes – Germany, United Kingdom, France, Italy
  8 votes – Spain
  5 votes – Belgium, Holland, Greece, Portugal
  4 votes – Sweden, Austria
  3 votes – Denmark, Ireland, Finland
  2 votes – Luxembourg

  It can be seen immediately that Germany, by some way the largest state, is under-represented and that tiny Luxembourg receives more votes than its size warrants. This is to prevent excessive domination by larger states.
- Some decisions require a **qualified majority**: that is, more than a simple majority of 50 per cent plus, but less than unanimity. In practice, this is approximately a 70 per cent proportion of the total votes in the Council. Thus, a consensus of support is needed for most agreements.
- For minor matters, a simple majority of 50 per cent plus is acceptable, but only if the vital interests of member states are not involved.

The qualified majority rule results in a great deal of political 'wheeling and dealing' in the Council. Large states can block proposals by gaining the support of just one other big country, or even two of the smaller members. Alliances constantly shift, often with deals being struck between ministers who are in a position to help each other. The key principles are normally, therefore, **consensus** and **compromise**. Confrontational or adversarial politics of the kind practised at Westminster would be a dangerous course of action for any member, as it would run the risk of becoming isolated.

Thus, British support for regional aid to poorer states such as Portugal or Greece could result in their support over issues that affect the UK, such as agricultural quotas and subsidies. Germany might champion protection for the French wine industry against Spanish and Italian competition on the promise of a future French–German alliance in important discussions over budget contributions. Nothing is simple or clear-cut in the Council.

The European Parliament

The intricacies of negotiation within the Council are considerable, but cannot compare with the complexities of the Parliament. It is a large body, divided both by nationality and by party. The structure of the Parliament in 2000 is shown in the table below.

The most significant step after the Maastricht Treaty was to give Parliament the power to force the Council of Ministers into unanimous votes on issues that Parliament disagrees with or wishes to amend. Thus, the Parliament cannot block legislation that the Council of Ministers is determined to approve, but it can place significant obstacles in the way. These new opportunities for parliamentary influence are as follows:

- **Consultation**, which simply ensures that all proposed legislation is discussed by Parliament, and its opinion recorded, before final consideration.
- **Co-operation**, which gives Parliament the chance to interrupt legislation and force reconsideration by the Commission and the Council.
- **Co-decision**, which is required for the most important decisions. Here, Parliament may insist on negotiations between its representatives and those of the Council and Commission before a measure can be approved.

Structure of the European Parliament in 2000										
Political grouping										
	European People's (Cons.)	European Socialists	Liberal/ Democratic/ Reformist	Greens	United left	Europe of Nations Group	Mixed independents	Democratic Alliance	Non-aligned	Total
Austria	7	7		2					5	21
Belgium	6	5	5	7			2			25
Denmark	1	3	6		1	1		4		16
Finland	5	3	5	2	1					16
France	21	22		9	11	12	4	6	1	86
Germany	53	35		5	6					99
Greece	9	9			7					25
Ireland	5	1	1	2		6				15
Italy	34	16	8	2	6	9	11		1	87
Luxembourg	2	2	1	1						6
Netherlands	9	6	8	4	1			3		31
Portugal	9	12			2	2				25
Spain	28	24	3	4	4				1	64
Sweden	7	6	4	2	3					22
UK	37	30	10	6				3	1	87
Total	233	181	51	46	42	30	17	16	9	

European Union members, 1999		
Country	**Population (millions)**	**GNP per capita ($ per annum)**
Austria	8.1	27,920
Belgium	10.2	26,730
Denmark	5.3	34,890
Finland	5.2	24,790
France	59.1	26,300
Germany	82.0	28,280
Greece	10.5	11,640
Ireland	3.7	17,790
Italy	57.7	20,170
Luxembourg	0.4	29,290
Netherlands	15.8	25,830
Portugal	10.0	11,010
Spain	39.4	14,490
Sweden	8.9	26,210
UK	59.4	20,870

The powers of the Parliament after Maastricht remain uncertain, but they are relatively limited. The following chart summarises the basic elements of the Parliament's powers and functions.

European Parliament powers

• New members	• The application for membership of prospective new members must be approved by MEPs.
• The Union Budget	• Parliament may veto the proposed Union Budget, i.e. the level of expenditure and members' contributions. This gives it a lever to exert influence on other issues.
• Appointments	• Before senior Commission members including its President are appointed, Parliament must give its approval.
• Commission proposals	• Each legislative proposal by the Commission is passed first to the Parliament, which gives an 'opinion'. It is hoped that this will influence the Council of Ministers in its deliberations.
• Amendments	• Parliament may propose amendments to legislation. Amendments return to the Commission, which may accept them or return them to the Council of Ministers. The Council can only overturn such a proposed amendment with a unanimous vote.
• Legislative passage*	• If a legislative proposal is accepted by Parliament, it passes to the Council of Ministers for normal approval. However, if Parliament rejects a proposed law, it can only be passed, by a unanimous vote in the Council Occasionally, the Parliament may propose its own legislation.

*These procedures apply to most, but not all legislation.

It should also be noted that, in the 1990s, Parliament increasingly proposed its own legislation, especially on issues concerning social and environmental measures. In order to have any hope of implementation, the Commission must approve such proposals, but this is a possible pointer to a future expanded role for MEPs.

In 1999 the Parliament asserted itself effectively for the first time in its history. Faced by revelations of corruption, nepotism and sleaze within the Commission, Parliament demanded the dismissal of the whole Commission (it did not have the power to censure individual Commissioners). It got its way and all the Commissioners had to resign and apply to be reappointed. Those who appeared to be guilty of the charges were thus removed. The incident points the way to the future development of the Parliament. There are demands for it to be able to hold the Commission, including individual Commissioners, to greater account.

The European Parliament in session

The European Court of Justice

This body should not be confused with the European Court of Human Rights. The latter hears appeals brought under the European Convention on Human Rights, which is not binding on all members of the EU, notably the UK. In fact, the Court of Human Rights is not a European Union institution at all.

The **Court of Justice**, which sits in Luxembourg, is staffed by judges drawn from all member states. Its functions are as follows:

- Adjudicating on claims brought by the Commission that a member state has infringed Union law. Should such a claim be upheld, the Court will order appropriate action.
- Settling disputes between states arising out of the application of Union law. Typically, this might concern taxes, subsidies or quotas being imposed by one state to the detriment of another.
- If a court within a member state requires clarification of European law, the judges in Luxembourg will give an opinion which is binding on that lower court.

It is important to note that it is normally the responsibility of the courts of member states themselves to enforce European law. The Court of Justice only steps in to settle disputes or deal with problems that cannot be handled in those national courts.

Democracy in Europe

The evolving The political system of Europe is still evolving at the beginning of the
~~political system~~ twenty-first century. It is a unique structure in the political world.
fifteen, soon to be more, sovereign nation-states bonded into an economic and political union has never been attempted before. It is, therefore, inevitable that many serious problems will arise.

Every step towards closer union must be painstakingly negotiated in
the European Council and then ratified by each member state. By way of
comparison, the Founding Fathers of the USA established their Constitution in just three months in Philadelphia, while it took only three further
years for agreement by the thirteen member states. This same Constitution is still fundamentally in force in spite of its being created in such a
short time.

The main difficulty in establishing political institutions and processes
in Europe is that all the member states remain sovereign and so retain
the right to veto any developments that they feel might not be in their
national interests. This problem was illustrated graphically by the
process of ratification of the Treaty on European Union (the Maastricht
Treaty). Only unanimous approval by the twelve states that negotiated
the treaty was acceptable. In most states this was not a problem, especially since nine of the states required only parliamentary majorities for
ratification. Only in the UK did this prove a difficulty as a result of the
Government's small majority and a revolt among a sizeable section of its
own back-benchers. However, it was the referenda which three states
were forced to hold that caused the main stumbling block.

In Ireland the people voted decisively in favour of the treaty. In
France there was a nail-biting contest; 51 per cent voted in favour of
France's signing, but the country was clearly split, leading to fears that
future progress towards union might prove difficult. It was the Danes
who nearly destroyed the treaty. By a tiny 40,000-vote majority they
rejected the agreement. Thus, one of the smallest states in the EU threatened to bring progress to a halt. In the event, the treaty was amended to
ease Danish fears, allowing the Danes to opt out of several important
elements. Nearly a year later, a second Danish vote reversed the decision
and the treaty was saved. But the lesson of Maastricht is that future
developments might prove difficult. The UK, France and Denmark are
again likely to prove the main obstacles, as there are serious popular
misgivings in these countries about European integration. Denmark's
rejection of the single currency in a referendum in October 2000 demonstrates that country's resistance to such integration.

A parliamentary The European Union is **not** a parliamentary system. Rather, it is a
system? system with a Parliament. To be truly parliamentary, three features
would need to be present:

- The Parliament would have to be the legislature, i.e. the law-making
  body. The Council of Ministers makes law and the Parliament only
  has an advisory role.

- The government of the Union would be drawn from the Parliament and would thus draw its authority from the assembly. Again, this is not the case. The governing Council is made up instead of representatives from member states.
- The executive branch of the Union – the Council and the Commission – would have to be fully accountable to the Parliament and, in theory at least, removable should they lose the confidence of a majority of MEPs. Even though Maastricht provided increased opportunities for the Parliament to scrutinise the Commission's work, this does not add up to real accountability.

There is little immediate possibility of a truly parliamentary system evolving in Europe. Member states are reluctant to hand over too much sovereignty to a directly elected assembly. In addition, the fact that the Parliament will always be split on both national and party lines suggests that it would be unlikely to be stable enough to sustain a united government.

Subsidiarity and federalism

The Maastricht Treaty declares that the European Union shall operate on the basis of **subsidiarity**. This implies three principles:

- The institutions of the Union shall only be given the powers that they need to carry out the policies of the Union.
- Any powers not granted to Union institutions automatically belong to the member states individually.
- Decisions should be taken as close to the citizen as possible.

It is hoped that this will both limit the powers of central European government and ensure the greatest degree of democracy possible. It is also designed to replace the principle of **federalism**.

Federalism implies a system where the sovereignty of the central government, of the member states and of any further sub-regions that might be established is strictly defined by a constitutional settlement. The difference between subsidiarity and federalism is not readily apparent and might, in practice, turn out to be merely semantic. However, the opponents of such a settlement suggest that federalism would result in a once-and-for-all loss of sovereignty for member states. Subsidiarity, on the other hand, it seen as a more flexible arrangement which ensures that the central Union establishment will never be able to claim powers without the full consent of the members.

There is widespread fear in Europe that there will be a creeping shift in the distribution of power towards Brussels. The principle of subsidiarity, it is hoped, if properly enforced, would prevent such a process. In addition, Liberals especially suggest that subsidiarity would actually result in an **increase** in the powers of regional and local government – powers that are being denied to them by national governments at present.

The 'democratic deficit'

Despite the advances made in the influence of the European Parliament under the Single European Act, which are described above, there continues to be concern that the political system of Europe is not democratic enough. This problem has become known as the 'democratic deficit'.

It can be claimed that democracy is served by the fact that all decisions must be ratified by elected ministers from member governments. Since these ministers are accountable to their own peoples, the argument continues, the requirements of democracy are satisfied.

accountability is too indirect. Member parliaments and electorates simply cannot maintain vigilance over what their ministers are doing in the Council. It is also pointed out that the unelected Commission, which plays a major role in policy formation and implementation, is not accountable at all.

A more pressing concern than the issue of accountability is the problem of **consent**. In domestic general elections, each party produces a manifesto. When a party wins and takes control of government, it has a **mandate** to implement the policies in its manifesto, together with an understanding that it must deal with unforeseen circumstances in accordance with its broad political philosophy. It is the mandate that makes laws **legitimate**. In the European Union, the principles of mandate and manifesto are blurred. The directly elected Parliament has no such mandate and, in any case, does not make law. The ministers in the Council, who do make laws, have a mandate only from their own peoples, not from the electorates of other states. Thus, the status of European laws might be uncertain. The former Conservative Cabinet minister Lord Tebbit expressed these concerns at a Young Conservative Conference in 1995:

> *'But we are now drifting – perhaps being driven – into a situation in which more and more people will regard the decrees emanating from Brussels as unjust laws, laws which do not have the consent of the British people and therefore laws without legitimacy which would not be obeyed.'*
>
> Lord Tebbit, speech, 2 February 1995

Proposals for strengthening European democracy centre largely upon the Parliament, so as to provide the accountability and legitimacy described above. This has two inherent problems, however. First, there is a danger that procedures would become so slow and cumbersome that decision making in the EU would grind to a halt. Second, as we already see, the Parliament itself is an unwieldy body, representing a huge electorate of over 350 million people and still growing. The widely differing economic interests, political philosophies and cultures represented in the Parliament are difficult to reconcile. Agreement on important issues will always be difficult to achieve. The Council and Commission might be less democratic institutions, but they are, at least, more efficient.

Key issues for the EU

What key questions were addressed at the 1997 inter-governmental conference in Amsterdam, which pointed the way towards future developments? Some of them were established at the Maastricht Conference in 1992, but others have longer-running histories.

The single European currency

A number of issues will be thrown up by the development of the single European currency, which comes into full use during 2001–2. Monetary control will pass to the **Central European Bank**. This raises issues about how the bank is to be controlled and how it can be made accountable to all the members of the currency union. There is also likely to be greater harmonisation of some forms of taxation, regulations on savings and control over the budgetary policies of individual states. As new members enter the system – perhaps including the UK – there will be important problems of transition to solve.

Common defence and foreign policy

A common defence and foreign policy, with the institutions necessary to develop such a position, has been considered for some time. Piecemeal attempts have already been made to adopt concerted EU military action in a number of crises, notably the Gulf War of 1991 and the Bosnian civil war. These have been largely futile, with patchy or non-existent co-operation by member states. So the concept of a permanent apparatus that the Maastricht Treaty envisaged appears somewhat utopian at present.

Member states have traditional alliances and views that might be threatened by a common foreign-policy establishment. Austria and Sweden, for example, have retained a position of strict neutrality since the Second World War. The UK has strong links with the USA and its Commonwealth allies, while Spain, France and Italy all have historically close relations with Mediterranean states. Any of these, or others, might cut across attempts to adopt common European attitudes towards the outside world. If troops have to be committed to action, national interests will become all the more sensitive.

Human rights

Maastricht and Amsterdam tentatively moved towards the creation of the concept of **European citizenship**. The free movement of citizens of member states within the Union, EU passports and the existence of many common **economic rights** have gone some way to establishing such a reality. However, it is the prospect of an entrenched, enforceable collection of rights and freedoms, common to all European citizens, which now beckons. Currently, individual rights are safeguarded by domestic constitutions, all of which differ, by the European Convention on Human Rights, which is not legally binding on all, and by a number of Union laws that are limited in scope.

A European **Bill of Rights**, binding on all member states and enforceable in all courts, European or national, would represent a significant shift in sovereignty away from member states. Nevertheless, there are many Liberals, Social Democrats and other radicals in Europe who wish to see it come about.

Widening of membership Since 1957 the European Community has grown from just six to fifteen members, with others waiting in the wings. The question of future widening of membership has been on the agenda since 1996. Turkish membership depends largely upon improvements in the human rights record of that country. The admission of other countries of western Europe, such as Norway, is less contentious. It is the central and eastern European states, formerly communist systems, which present a greater problem.

Part of the difficulty arises from the military and foreign policy issues described above. Many are also concerned, however, that the poor condition of the economies of these countries would represent a severe burden on the more prosperous members. There are some in the UK who would like to see extension in membership, hoping that this will dilute the power of the Union.

Political union It is envisaged that further progress will be made towards greater political union. In the main, this will be effected by increasing the number of decisions that can be made by a majority of ministers in the Council. Unanimous voting prevents the transfer of power from individual member states to the Union. Majority voting, on the other hand, encourages it. Those who wish to see greater political integration will be hoping to extend the scope of qualified majorities. The less enthusiastic countries, such as the UK, might resist such developments.

Common Agricultural Policy The operation of the Common Agricultural Policy (CAP) has come under increasing criticism. Designed to provide protection for farmers, its system of subsidies, quotas and guaranteed prices is seen as a retrogressive device that prevents the operation of a truly free market in food (and indeed fisheries, although there are issues of conservation involved there too). There has been stubborn opposition to reform, especially in France, but countries such as the UK will be determined to persuade enough allies to make significant changes, perhaps even to abolish the CAP.

Immigration Immigration to the Union is a sensitive issue. With the free movement of people allowed in Europe, immigrants from anywhere might end up in members' countries, often when they are not wanted. Most states wish to retain the option of closing their borders to unwelcome immigrants. A common immigration policy will, therefore, be difficult to negotiate.

The UK and Europe

The treaties

The UK's unusual arrangements with regard to foreign treaties create some confusion over its commitment to them. Normally, treaties are signed by a Head of State, which gives **legitimacy** and **permanence** to them. This is not the case in the UK. The prerogative powers of the Crown are exercised by the Government of the day. Thus, treaties are negotiated and ratified only by ministers. Parliament may express a view but is not asked to grant approval.

The problem was illustrated when the UK signed the Maastricht Treaty in 1992. There was a danger that a vote to approve the treaty in the House of Commons would go against the Government. An alliance of the Labour, nationalist and Ulster Unionist parties, together with a group of Conservative anti-Europe MPs, threatened defeat for the Government. Foreign Secretary Douglas Hurd made it clear that the treaty would be ratified even if Parliament did disapprove. It had been agreed under prerogative powers so that parliamentary sovereignty would not apply. In the event, the Government survived the vote, but the incident illustrated the constitutional confusion that exists.

If treaties are negotiated by temporary governments enjoying temporary majorities, and if they do not need the approval of either Parliament or the people, there is a danger that future governments will not accept the legitimacy of the treaty in question. Thus, in 1974 the new Labour Government could demand the right to renegotiate the UK's membership terms. In the future, a Conservative Government might not approve of agreements on social and industrial policy which Labour has signed.

These concerns have led to calls, from all parts of the political spectrum, for a **referendum** to approve any major agreements over Europe that affect the UK's sovereignty and vital interests. Popular approval, it is felt, could provide the permanent legitimacy that current arrangements lack.

Europe and Parliament

The **European Communities Act** of 1972 makes it clear that any European law properly agreed in the Council of Ministers **automatically** becomes UK law that must be enforced in British courts. In other words, Parliament does not have the ability to block EU law after it has been passed.

Parliament's role is, therefore, limited to the following functions:

• In general debates, motions, etc. Parliament has an opportunity to express its view on new proposals in Europe. This may exert some influence on ministers in their negotiations with the Council. However, such influence depends upon voting rules in the Council. Those few key decisions that require unanimous approval could be blocked by Parliament if it can persuade British ministers to dig their heels in and exercise a veto. This was, broadly speaking, the case when the UK refused to sign the Social Chapter (providing a number of protective measures for workers) at Maastricht. When a measure requires only a qualified majority, however, the UK's representative cannot veto the proposal alone, so that Parliament's opposition may prove futile.

- A number of committees, but mainly the House of Lords Select Committee on the European Communities with its functional subcommittees, scrutinise proposed European legislation and pass their opinions to ministers. Much of the work is highly specialised and often technical.

- Parliament may urge British ministers to campaign for changes to European law. For many years, for example, there has been all-party support for reform of both the Common Agricultural Policy and EU policy on fishing quotas. However, success depends upon the determination of those ministers and their ability to persuade their European colleagues to support them.

Europe and the British courts

As we have seen above, European law is British law, which must be enforced in domestic courts. Should a citizen or a body wish to appeal against a decision made under European legislation, they must first exhaust all possible remedies in the UK. Thereafter appeals are passed to the **European Court of Justice** for a final ruling. Its judgments are binding on all courts in the UK.

Should there be a conflict between domestic law and European law, the latter must always prevail. Courts cannot pick and choose which laws to enforce. The most startling example of this principle occurred in 1991 in a case known as **Factortame**. In this judgment, it was ruled that the British Merchant Shipping Act was not valid, as it came into conflict with the European Union's Common Fisheries Policy. This was the first time that a British law was effectively set aside by the ECJ. In some less dramatic cases, British pension laws and some British employment practices have also been declared illegal under EU law.

Europe and the British political parties

The Liberal Democrats, Scottish and Welsh nationalists are the only major parties that unequivocally support greater European union. Both the Labour and Conservative Parties are seriously split on the issue.

Labour

The Labour Party has succeeded in keeping its own internal split over Europe under control since the referendum on membership in 1975. Of course, for most of that time it has been in opposition, so that other matters, related to winning back power, have tended to distract the party from European issues.

The schism cuts largely along left–moderate lines. It is the socialist wing of the party that is mostly suspicious of further European integration. Their beliefs in the necessity of restoring social justice, as they see it, would be hampered by the need to co-operate with our European partners. For them, the rest of Europe is simply not socialist enough, so the UK must go it alone. Moderates, on the other hand, are prepared to accept the march towards European union as inevitable. Many of the measures now being adopted, especially progress towards greater workers' rights, fair wages, better distribution of welfare, consumer protection, industrial competition control and environmental protection, are very much in accord with their own policies. For them Europe is largely social democrat in nature. It is, therefore, an acceptable vehicle for their own aspirations.

When Labour took office in 1997, the potential split over Europe became a matter for more concern. Having delayed any decision on entry into the single European currency, the leadership was able to take a cautious approach. A referendum on entry was promised, but not for several years. Though the Prime Minister and Cabinet were enthusiastic about a common European Defence Force, they remained opposed to the concept of European citizenship. Important questions will confront Labour if they win a further term of office. In the meantime, however, they can afford to adopt a 'wait-and-see' approach.

The Conservatives

The agenda for internal division was established when Margaret Thatcher made a dramatic speech in **Bruges** (Belgium) in 1988. Alarmed by the intentions of the European Commission President, **Jacques Delors**, to speed up progress towards economic and political union, she described the proposals as a prelude to 'a European super-state exercising a new dominance from Brussels'. This Bruges speech (which later spawned an anti-European faction in the party, known as the 'Bruges Group') rallied the Conservative Party's nationalist right wing around the anti-European cause.

As the UK became increasingly isolated in Europe, Margaret Thatcher moved steadily further away from any plans for closer union. In October 1990 she returned from a European Council meeting in Rome and reported her fears to the House of Commons.

> 'The President of the Commission, M. Delors, said at this conference [an EU summit meeting in Rome] the other day that he wanted the European Parliament to be the democratic body of the Community, he wanted the Commission to be the Executive and he wanted the Council of Ministers to be the Senate. No. No. No.'
>
> Margaret Thatcher speaking in the House of Commons, 30 October 1990

This precipitated the resignation of **Sir Geoffrey Howe,** the Leader of the House of Commons, which in turn led to the leadership contest that Mrs Thatcher subsequently lost.

After that the Conservative split on Europe steadily widened. An alliance of authoritarian, nationalist right-wingers, who feared loss of sovereignty for the UK, and neo-liberal 'Thatcherites', who saw Brussels as too bureaucratic and socialist, grew up. There were some, such as **Sir Teddy Taylor**, who would have preferred to see the UK leave the European Union altogether and others, such as **William Cash**, who accepted the benefits of economic union but would not accept political integration.

The pro-Europeans led by **Michael Heseltine** and **Kenneth Clarke**, both Cabinet ministers, were barely able to maintain collective Cabinet responsibility on the issue. They and anti-European Cabinet colleagues, such as **Michael Portillo** and **Jonathan Aitken**, stretched the rules of Cabinet unity to their very limit. So bitter had the issue become that by 1995 it was threatening the integrity of the Cabinet and the Conservative Party.

Defeat for the party in 1997 led to a change in emphasis. The Euro-sceptics became dominant and persuaded the new leader, William Hague, to adopt their approach. Thus the party has teetered on the brink of ruling out monetary union altogether and is opposed to all

plete British withdrawal from the EU also began to gather strength. The party believes it can defeat Labour with a strongly Euro-sceptic approach – a development that has further alienated those such as Kenneth Clarke and Michael Heseltine who remain pro-Europe.

Smaller parties
The **Liberal Democrats** are enthusiasts for closer European integration. Though sovereignty would be lost to Brussels, they believe that more effective regional and local government would also result. They strongly support the principle of **subsidiarity** – that decisions should be taken as close to the citizen as possible – and believe Europe can provide this. They also expect that there will be better protection of citizens' rights and environmental control within Europe.

Scottish and Welsh **nationalists** take a similar line to that of the Liberal Democrats. European union, they hope, will free Scotland and Wales from rule by London. While they too would have to grant a good deal of political and legal sovereignty to Brussels, they believe that the power they would gain from London would more than compensate. **Ulster Unionists**, on the other hand, oppose European integration. This, they fear, would loosen Northern Ireland's ties with the British Crown, the retention of which constitutes their main *raison d'être*.

The **Green Party** sees European integration as its main hope for further progress. Green politics are more prominent in Europe than in the UK and there are a number of Green members of the European Parliament, though none from the UK. Indeed, many environmental issues, such as toxic emissions, sea pollution, farming methods, conservation and energy production can only be treated at the European level.

Europe has never been the major issue at any British general election. In 2001 or 2002 there are some indications that it might well be one of the crucial issues.

Pressure groups
As decision making gradually transfers to the European Union context, so too do the activities of prominent pressure groups. They know that they must lobby the key institutions – the Council of Ministers, Parliament and the Commission – if they are to make an impact. Indeed, the larger groups have set up offices in Europe for that expressed purpose.

In addition, some interest and pressure groups have federated themselves into Europe-wide bodies. This gives them greater strength and is a reflection of the fact that decisions now affect more than narrow national interests, but are directed throughout Europe.

Some examples of groups that operate extensively in Europe are shown on page 341, together with the kind of European policy areas with which they might be concerned.

European pressure groups and policies	
Type of pressure group	**Policy**
• Trade unions	• Employment protection • Workers' rights
• Industrial groups	• Competition policy • Regional grants • Consumer regulations
• Greens	• Environmental protection • Animal rights • Genetic modification
• Farmers	• Common Agricultural Policy • Relations with the World Trade Organisation
• Transport groups	• Public transport • Regional transport grants • Regulations
• Consumer groups	• Consumer protection

A greater problem for pressure groups concerns the mobilisation of European public opinion. Cultural diversity, language differences and sheer expense make it difficult to co-ordinate activities. However, the use of the Internet and better organisation are changing this situation. In recent years, the Green movement has made great progress (as well as winning seats in the European Parliament), as have left-wing organisations campaigning on development and other trade issues.

The process is bound to continue as both Europeanisation and globalisation spread. Pressure groups now face more **levels of government** than ever before – global, European, national, regional and local. Their organisations and operations have, therefore, to become more complex and multilayered.

For exam questions relevant to this unit, see page 558.

The meaning of ideology

Before we embark on an investigation of the various world ideologies that have flourished over the past two hundred years, the term 'ideology' itself needs to be clarified.

The original meaning of the expression, coined by the French philosopher **de Maistre** at the end of the eighteenth century, was the 'science of ideas', in essence the study of the dominant ideas and philosophy of the age. People assumed at that time that there was a single discoverable set of ideas which characterised and moulded the society within which they lived. It was, therefore, a relatively uncontroversial term, though it was a revolutionary notion that such a concept as 'ideology' should exist at all.

At the same time, the German philosopher **Hegel** was also stressing the crucial role of great ideas in the study of history, religion and society. Although he preferred the term 'spirit' or 'zeitgeist' (literally 'spirit of the age'), he was certainly referring to a similar concept.

Karl Marx was a follower of Hegel but took a more critical view of ideology. For him, and for all subsequent Marxist thinkers, the ideology that dominated each age was a product of the ruling class's efforts to ensure that it retained its dominant position and was able to oppress 'inferior' classes. Thus, the ideology of **capitalism** and of **liberalism**, which was associated with it, were views of the world promoted by that ruling class. Unlike de Maistre or Hegel, Marx considered an ideology to be a false picture of society, a version that underpinned class rule.

Nowadays the term is used quite differently. Rather than a single dominant view, whether an objective one as Hegel suggested, or a false one as Marx had claimed, we more often use 'ideology' to refer to **any** established, coherent political philosophy. Thus, there can be more than one ideology in common currency at any time. If a set of political ideas includes the following:

- firm beliefs about the nature of people and society
- a clear set of values that may guide political action
- a coherent vision of how society should be organised,

it may then be described as an 'ideology'. Beliefs held by individuals or political parties that are less precise than this should not be described as ideologies. Rather, they are merely philosophies or perhaps doctrines.

Thus, we may describe socialism, feminism, Marxism itself and even 'Thatcherism' as modern ideologies that compete with each other and attract large numbers of followers. All might claim to be an accurate view of the world, but, as objective observers, we may take a more detached attitude and see them as competing sets of beliefs that contain both clear truths and mere theories.

Communism

Introduction

Though most people associate the term 'communism' with Marxism, **Karl Marx** (1818–83) himself did not 'invent' it. He drew his inspiration for the name from some of the more radical elements during the French Revolution of 50 years or so earlier. Indeed, the basic **principles** of communism can be traced still further back in history. The English 'diggers' of the mid-seventeenth century, for example, organised land sharing and social equality very much along Marxist lines. During the nineteenth century, too, the 'Narodnik' movement stirred up the Russian peasantry, encouraging them to seize and redistribute land among themselves.

It should further be stressed that, in the middle of the nineteenth century when Marx was writing, anarchism was growing in popularity, especially in Germany, France and Russia. The anarchists themselves, as we shall see below, were often described as 'communists'. It was not until the 1870s, when Marx split with the great anarchist revolutionary **Mikhail Bakunin** (1814–76), that Marxism and anarchism could be fully distinguished. At that time, communism referred to the practice of setting up small-scale, self-governing communes, with common ownership of property, internal democracy and economic equality. If we adhere strictly to this definition, as Bakunin himself argued, Marx was not really a communist at all! Nevertheless, when the workers of Paris set up their own government in 1871 just as the city was about to fall to the invading Prussian army, and called it the **Paris Commune**, their main inspiration was Marx. Thus, Marxism and communism have become almost synonymous.

Since regimes calling themselves 'communist', 'socialist' or 'people's republic' have all claimed to be based upon the ideology developed by Marx, any study of communism must begin with an analysis of his philosophy.

The historical analysis

Economic determinism

All societies, argued Marx, have their own distinctive economic structure. By this he meant the manner in which the production and distribution of goods was organised. This might involve such questions as: Who owned land and who did not? How was the land held – was it owned or rented? How were goods sold? Who controlled other forms of production? How was trade organised? This economic structure determined the whole character of society. Its political system, its ideology and dominant beliefs, its social structure and even its religion were all determined by economics. Thus, Marx was an 'economic determinist'. Once one understood the nature of a society's economic 'infrastructure', one could understand the whole of that society.

> 'The history of humanity must therefore always be studied and treated in relation to the history of industry and exchange.'
> Karl Marx, *The German Ideology*, 1845

Dialectic materialism

Marx made a detailed empirical study (that is, with reference to observable events and processes) of the processes of historical change. He argued that history moves in discernible cycles. These cycles or 'epochs' may last for hundreds of years. At the beginning of a cycle there is a state of **harmony**. The organisation of production and distribution, and the economic relationships that arise from production, do not contain conflicts in such a state of harmony. When great civilisations in the past reached their height, such stability could be recognised, as in the classical Greek and Roman periods.

However, as such societies mature, they develop internal conflicts, or **contradictions**. Put simply, this results in the interests of one or more **social classes** coming into conflict with the interests of other classes. In general, Marx suggested that there is always one small dominant **ruling class** and another large **exploited class**. There might be other smaller social classes, but they are of less significance. At first, the exploited class does not appreciate its position and, indeed, believes it is benefiting from the economic system. But it is inevitable that exploitation increases and intensifies. As this occurs, the exploited class becomes aware of its true situation. The result is growing social conflict.

The class conflicts, or 'contradictions', which arise sooner or later in all societies are known as a 'dialectic' process. That is, one sector in a society is confronted by its own opposite, or 'negation'. In this case, the ruling class is confronted by the exploited class, whose interests are totally opposed to its own. Eventually, the conflict becomes so intense and violent that the whole system collapses. A new order is ultimately established, with a new harmony. But the whole process then begins again. Since these changes are taking place within the **material** economic world (as opposed to the world of ideas, philosophy and religion), the process is known as **dialectic materialism**.

The feudal age – a Marxist model			
Productive system	**Class structure**	**Politics and religion**	**Contradictions**
• A hierarchy of land tenure, with land granted in return for a proportion of its output or duties such as military service • Trade carried on for the sale of surplus production in towns including imports and exports	• A ruling class made up of the monarch, aristocracy and feudal nobility • An exploited class of peasants or serfs • A small class of yeomen or independent small farmers • An additional small class of merchants and craftsmen	• Absolute monarchy ruling with the support of the aristocracy • Mostly Catholic or related churches, teaching the importance of obedience and the worthiness of poverty and meekness • Dominant philosophy is 'conservative', stressing the need for order and a natural hierarchy	• Exploitation of serfs becomes intolerable, resulting in increasing revolts and unrest. Food production becomes inadequate under feudal conditions • Traders and merchants become more economically significant, challenging aristocratic power • Emerging primitive capitalism cannot operate in a feudal environment. Result is outbreak of 'bourgeois' revolutions

'The history of all hitherto existing society is the history of class struggles.'

Karl Marx and Friedrich Engels, *The Communist Manifesto*, 1848

All the other phenomena that we can observe in a society – its religious conflicts, political events, wars, civil wars, revolutions and rebellions – are merely **reflections** of the economic, material conflict taking place all the time. Thus, Marx claimed to be a truly **scientific** historian, claiming that he understood the true processes of history. He maintained that others merely observed the superficial changes taking place and analysed them in unscientific ways. Indeed, he went on to charge historians with explaining history in such a way as to justify the position of the ruling class. Marx viewed history very much from the point of view of 'exploited' classes.

The analysis of capitalism

Marx applied the same principles of analysis to the capitalist age (at the height of which he lived and worked), just as he had done for all other historical epochs. Productive forces and economic relations were its basis. The class structure was typical, and progress towards its demise was predictable.

Before describing Marx's analysis, it should be stressed that he was observing capitalism in the middle of the nineteenth century, largely as it operated in Britain, the most advanced industrial country of the day. The nature of capitalism has changed markedly since then. Some would say that the changes have been so radical that Marx's analysis is no longer valid. Nevertheless, it forms the basis of the philosophy of subsequent Marxism and is therefore essential to an understanding of the ideology.

Class under capitalism

There are two great classes. The **bourgeoisie** own and control all the means of production: that is, the factories, mines, workshops, banks, etc. These 'capitalists' are the ruling class, who also control the dominant ideology, religion and political system of capitalism. The **proletariat**, or working class, own none of the means of production. They must sell their labour to the bourgeoisie in return for money wages. For Marx, this is the exploited class.

Marx identified a smaller class – the **petit bourgeois** – consisting of those who earn their living independently, such as individual craftsmen, professionals, tradesmen and merchants. These, he suggested, were relatively insignificant, but, more importantly, would be absorbed into the other great classes. This process was known as **class polarisation**. As more and more people were drawn into the two great economic classes, the antagonism between them would intensify.

The class system on the land, the remnants of the dying feudal age, was of less concern to Marx. The landlords, or **rentier** class, were losing their economic and political power and would continue to do so. The **peasants**, another exploited class but with less revolutionary potential than the industrial working class, would ultimately attempt to free themselves, but their fortunes were of less concern to Marx than those of the proletariat.

It was a key element of Marx's criticism of capitalism that the interests of the two main classes would come increasingly into conflict. This would occur as capitalism developed and became more productive.

Surplus value

Capitalism extracts from its workers a surplus value, argued Marx. The system is organised so that workers are paid only a fraction of the true value of their own production. The rest is surplus value, which is expropriated, or stolen, by the capitalists. Furthermore, as the productive capacity of capitalism increases, and the value of workers' output grows, the degree of surplus also increases. The workers do not, however, benefit.

Wages were determined in free labour markets. These markets ensured, claimed Marx, that wages remained at subsistence (minimum) or certainly very low levels. This was guaranteed by the fact that workers would compete with each other for scarce jobs and so employers could pay low wages. A permanent pool of the unemployed, women and even children was maintained to ensure that workers who claimed higher wages could always be replaced. Thus, even though workers' productivity constantly increased, wages did not. The degree of surplus value extracted steadily grew.

It was largely this fact, however, which sounded the death knell of capitalism. As the exploitation of workers increased, and the gap in living standards between the classes widened, the proletariat would become steadily more aware of the nature of that exploitation. The overthrow of the ruling class by the oppressed class would surely follow.

Alienation

The term 'alienation' is not exclusive to Marxism. It refers to any state of mind where an individual feels that the world around them is strange and alien; they are not at home in it; it confronts them as something hostile and threatening. In Marxist analysis, particularly, it referred to the condition of workers under capitalism.

For Marx, the activity of labour is central to man's existence – it is his 'life force'. Under capitalism he is forced to sell his labour to somebody else. Thus, it is no longer his own, but has been exchanged for money. Furthermore, the workers have no personal interest in the goods they are producing, often being unable to afford to buy them. The **division of labour**, whereby workers become increasingly specialised in the productive process, adds to the alienation, since the worker is further separated from what he is producing. Thus, herded into factories, mines and offices to produce goods and services at the behest of the capitalist, having no control over production or financial rewards, workers are alienated in the workplace. For Marx, this was the principal evil of capitalism. Modern Marxists believe much the same, while suggesting that the precise nature of the alienation has changed under modern conditions.

> *'The worker feels himself at home only during his leisure, whereas at work he feels homeless. His work is not voluntary but imposed, forced labour. It is not the satisfaction of a need, but only a means for satisfying other needs.'*
> Karl Marx, *Economic and Philosophical Manuscripts*, 1844

The capitalist state

Every epoch has its own particular form of state, but all have one feature in common, argued Marx. The state is always the agent of the ruling class. Its main purpose is to maintain class rule. This is an easy concept to understand when considering absolute monarchies, or the oligarchies of wealthy citizens that governed the classical world. Less clear, however, is the charge laid against representative democracy – the typical kind of state operating in capitalist societies. Of course, at the time Marx was writing, universal suffrage was extremely rare. Voting normally carried a property or income qualification. Thus, it was understandable that he should claim that this represented merely bourgeois rule under the guise of democracy. Marx's claims, however, have been transferred to political systems where the working classes were granted the vote.

> 'The State is the form in which the individuals of a ruling class assert their common interest.'
>
> Karl Marx, *The German Ideology*, 1845

For Marx, democracy as a whole was a charade. The real apparatus of the state – its bureaucracy, legal system, armed forces and police – were the truly permanent instruments of class rule. Their role was to maintain the status quo and ensure the continued oppression of the exploited class. Passing governments were of no lasting significance. It followed from this analysis that if capitalism were to be destroyed, so too must the state that supports it be swept away.

The destruction of capitalism

Marx was largely a **determinist**. He asserted that there are social and economic forces which are beyond man's control. He is, therefore, not in control of his own future. But the same uncontrolled forces which sustained capitalism, he insisted, would also destroy it. Capitalism contained the seeds of its own destruction – principally the exploited working class – and these seeds would steadily grow into a lethal force. Thus he identified a clear road to revolution.

Class consciousness

In the early stages of capitalism, the proletariat were not aware of the position in which they found themselves. They saw themselves as individuals, in competition with each other for scarce employment and wages. They did not understand that they might have common interests. As their exploitation intensified, however, **social solidarity** began to grow. The common experience of exploitation would breed class consciousness. This involved both an understanding of the nature of their oppression and the appreciation that there was more to bind them than divide them.

The symptoms of growing class consciousness were the formation of trade unions, frequency of strikes and demonstrations, and political agitation. At first, the state was able to contain such unrest, but capitalism, he suggested, could not prevent its own development, which brought with it greater exploitation and, therefore, deeper working-class consciousness.

The crises of capitalism

Marx foresaw the passage of capitalism through a number of stages leading to its final end. It suffers from an inherent tendency to overproduce, he observed. This led to periods of falling prices and profits, unemployment and declining wages. The working classes, faced with these slumps, would naturally become increasingly discontented. The true nature of capitalism would be increasingly apparent to them.

Intense competition for scarce markets among capitalists would lead to two further developments. First, countries would seek to create or expand empires abroad. Second, a series of wars would ensue, both for control of these empires and directly as a result of market rivalry. As an ultimate irony, the working classes would be asked to fight and risk their lives defending a system that exploits them. The Franco-Prussian War of 1870–1 was just such an example. The First World War represents the most dramatic example to illustrate Marx's predictions.

Increasingly intense booms and slumps, wars and imperial rivalry, and growing unrest among the working classes would all be signs of the impending final crisis of capitalism.

Revolution

As class consciousness grew among the proletariat, the development of revolutionary parties, and some bourgeois intellectuals joining the working-class cause, represented the prelude to revolution. Marx was certain that the ultimate revolution would be a violent one, since the capitalist state, he believed, would defend itself with all the coercive forces at its command. He suggested that Britain, possessing the most mature democracy in the world, might achieve a transition to socialism by peaceful, democratic means, but in other cases only bloody revolt would destroy capitalism.

> 'The communist revolution ... abolishes all class rule, along with the classes themselves.
>
> Karl Marx, *The German Ideology*, 1845

There has been controversy surrounding Marx's revolutionary theory. Some argue that he believed it to be inevitable. Others, however, suggest that this was not so. Rather, the **conditions** for revolution would certainly arise, but it would require the organised efforts of leading members of the proletariat to overthrow the state. Should the latter be true, it can go some way to explaining why so few capitalist states were destroyed. If the working class failed to organise, the state could perhaps survive.

The dictatorship of the proletariat

Possibly the most controversial aspect of Marx's theories concerns his vision of the post-revolutionary world. He insisted that society could not move directly to communism. There would, instead, be a transitional phase. This he describes as the **dictatorship of the proletariat** or the **socialist** phase.

The old capitalist state would be replaced by a new state, charged with the task of first building socialism and then creating the conditions for the transition to a communist society. All states are instruments of class rule, Marx asserted. This would be no exception. The formerly oppressed class would become the rulers. They would now oppress the old ruling class – the bourgeoisie. The powers of the new workers' state would be used for this purpose. This form of socialist state, apparently lacking in democratic institutions, individual liberties or any pluralist institutions, was to characterise the practical application of communism for over 70 years after the Russian Revolution.

Marx intended that the dictatorship of the proletariat would persist until the last remnants of capitalism had been abolished and, even more importantly, all forms of 'bourgeois consciousness' had disappeared. In other words, society would have become totally classless, without private property and with no possibility of capitalist tendencies re-emerging. Then, and only then, would the state be able to 'wither away'. Complete economic equality would exist and all the means of production would be in common ownership. Without the need for any government or coercion, each would receive rewards according to need and all would contribute freely to society without the need of compulsion. Communism would then ensue.

The nature of communism

Marx is less clear about the nature of communism. His description of it is full of generalities and lacking in practicalities. A number of clear features do, however, emerge from his work:

- All property (though not personal possessions) would be in common ownership.
- There would be no classes, as every individual would have the same relationship to the means of production.
- There would be no political state. Thus, there would be no coercive power in the form of law enforcement or sovereign government.
- Rewards would be distributed strictly on the basis of equality.
- The division of labour would cease to exist. Workers would be free to choose their occupation, avoid specialisation and possibly even undertake a number of different occupations at the same time.
- Problems of alienation would have disappeared.
- Communism would contain no internal contradictions. Thus, the dialectic process of history would be at an end. The communist epoch would last for the foreseeable future.

It should be noted that those states which espoused the Marxist creed often referred to themselves as 'communist'. Their systems, however, clearly did not conform to Marx's description of communism. In fact, the term 'communist' was used to express long-term goals. In reality, all these states were in the 'socialist' phase of development.

The Soviet experiment

V. I. Lenin (1870–1924)

In 1917 Lenin led the first successful revolution that was openly inspired by Marxist theory. Yet this revolution took place in a largely peasant-based, neo-feudal society. There was a small industrial working class in a population dominated mostly by poor peasants. Capitalism was still in its early stages. It was true that there was a powerful, autocratic state under tsarist rule and the small proletariat who existed were certainly treated badly by their employers. Russia was also heavily involved in a war which, in terms of Marxist analysis, was a symptom of competition between capitalist powers. Yet these were far from the conditions that Marx had described as the prelude to revolution. Much of Lenin's contribution to Marxist thought was, therefore, to explain how socialism, and ultimately communism, could be established in such an undeveloped economy. Broadly, his justifications for such a revolution were as follows:

- Marx had underestimated the ability of a well-organised, professional revolutionary party to overthrow the state even when the 'classic' conditions for the destruction of capitalism were absent. In other words, Lenin was more of a 'voluntarist' than Marx, insisting that

- His theory of **imperialism**, a truly original contribution to Marxism, saw the world increasingly divided into exploiting and exploited nations. Russia was one of the latter countries and so might never develop a fully capitalist system. Only by striking quickly could the Russian workers prevent this development. Simply waiting for economic progress to take its course would prove futile.

- Third World Marxists were particularly influenced by his concept of **uneven development**. This suggested that countries could move towards socialism at any stage of their economic development. As long as there were large exploited classes – mainly peasants and workers – they should take control of events and overthrow their oppressors. Thereafter socialism could be built alongside industrialisation and the new workers' state. The industrial proletariat was always, for Lenin, the principal vehicle for socialist development, but this did not disqualify other classes from revolutionary activity.

The more controversial elements of Lenin's career concern his political beliefs and actions. He created a state in Russia on the principles of **democratic centralism**. Originally, this was designed to be a two-way flow of power and influence. A party hierarchy was formed, with free access for anyone who wished to be politically active. Each level would nominate members to represent them at the higher level. This continued up to the top level – later to be known as the **Politburo** – at which all key national decisions were to be made. The demands and interests of the people, as long as they conformed to broad socialist principles, were to be passed up through the system. However, once decisions at the higher levels were made, they were imposed on society strictly. Thus, he envisaged a combination of a **workers' democracy** and the **dictatorship of the proletariat**.

As events in Russia unfolded and Lenin was beset by economic and political problems, the system evolved into a mere dictatorship. Influence from below was steadily cut off and, instead, the leading members of the party simply imposed their policies on Russian society. The government – a hierarchy of committees or 'soviets', which were theoretically democratic – was steadily brought under the ruthless control of the Communist Party. The notorious Soviet form of dictatorship was virtually in place by the time Lenin died in 1924.

It remains an open question whether Lenin intended to create the autocratic, oppressive regime that the Soviet Union became, or whether he was a sincere democrat who was forced to adopt temporary authoritarian methods to overcome his country's immediate problems. Whichever is true, his successor, Joseph Stalin, completed the development of a totalitarian regime that had begun to emerge under Lenin.

Joseph Stalin (1879–1953) After Lenin's death, Stalin engaged in a long-drawn-out struggle for power with his rivals in the Communist Party, notably Leon Trotsky. By 1927 he was in control. The very method by which he achieved power established a political feature of the Soviet Union which was to attract a good deal of criticism. There was no open, democratic competition for power in which large sections of the population could take part. Instead, there was a closed, secretive struggle among a few leaders about whom little was known. The Soviet Union was to retain its undemocratic methods of transferring power until the late 1980s.

The system that was ultimately to become known as 'Stalinism' included the following features, all of which were the personal creation of Stalin:

- **Socialism in one country** was Stalin's description of his belief that the Soviet Union must protect itself at all costs from the antagonism of the capitalist world. Its principal role was to build socialism and to ensure that it outdid capitalism in terms of production and developed sufficient military strength to protect itself. Rather than actively supporting revolutions in other parts of the world, the Soviet Union was to provide a perfect 'model' for other working-class movements to emulate. So he cut the country off from the outside world, adopting an inward-looking, isolationist approach to world affairs.
- Stalin preferred **bureaucratic rule** to democratic institutions. Unelected officials, or bureaucrats, could be easily controlled by ensuring that they operated to set procedures imposed from above. Politicians, on the other hand, could be influenced from below and so become unreliable. Thus, he created a hugely bureaucratic state, unresponsive to the demands of the people, but strictly under party control.
- He was determined that his own position as party leader and, therefore, his country's **absolute** ruler, should not be challenged. He saw himself as the pure embodiment of orthodox Marxist thought. Thus, the fortunes of the working class and the future road to communism were in his hands. Those who opposed him were branded as **revisionists** – enemies of socialism and the working class. The party was regularly purged to ensure absolute obedience to its leader.
- The population was kept under control through the use of **terror** – the public use of force, propaganda achieved by total control of the media and the use of an extensive secret police to root out any signs of dissidence.
- The position of the **peasantry** was a major problem for Stalin. Like Lenin before him, Stalin mistrusted them, often describing them as basically petit bourgeois in outlook. He suspected that most of them were only interested in acquiring their own land and working it for their own benefit. He did not accept that they might become true socialists in the way that industrial workers could. His answer was to introduce enforced **collectivisation** of the land. Land was organised into huge collective farms, which employed peasants as though they were factory workers. The total product of the collective farms belonged to the state and the workers were paid a wage. No peasant was allowed to own his own land. The disruption and ruthlessness of this process led to millions of deaths in the 1930s, but it solved the problem of how to control the Soviet Union's masses.

The notorious Stalinist regime brooked no internal opposition and no alternative interpretation of the works of Marx and Lenin, but it did have one implacable enemy – Leon Trotsky.

Leon Trotsky (1879–1940)

Trotsky was one of Lenin's closest associates and, many say, his chosen political heir. But Stalin defeated him in the struggle for power that followed Lenin's death. He was exiled and ultimately assassinated by a Stalinist agent in Mexico in 1940. While in exile, he maintained a campaign of criticism of the Stalinist system. For those who professed to be Marxists, but could not stomach the excesses of Stalinism, Trotsky became a hero. He was to inspire communists from the 1930s to the 1980s.

Much of his thought was in diametric opposition to Stalinism. His principal ideas included the following:

- The communist revolution should not be a single event, but a longer process wherein various aspects of capitalism and bourgeois thought would be attacked. He termed this proposal **permanent revolution**. Stalin, by contrast, had created a static political system which had ceased to develop. Indeed, many of the evils of capitalism had re-emerged, such as the oppressive state, alienation of workers, an unfair wage system and the creation of a new ruling class – the party elite.
- Instead of 'socialism in one country', with an inward-looking, isolated Soviet Union, Trotsky urged **world revolution**. Unless the capitalist world were to be converted to socialism, its intense opposition to the Soviet Union would ultimately prevail. The task of the Soviet Communist Party must, therefore, be to sponsor revolution wherever possible. Thus, revolution was to be permanent and universal.
- Trotsky described Stalin's proposed road to socialism as 'socialism from above': that is, it was imposed by the ruling party elite. He preferred 'revolution from below'. Here the spontaneous actions and demands of the masses should be involved in building socialism. He accepted popular democracy as a positive force. Stalin had feared and therefore suppressed it. The bureaucratic 'monster' that Stalin created in the Soviet Union was a denial of real proletarian democracy, Trotsky insisted. He added that the workers must govern themselves. The faceless machine of the Soviet state created a form of alienation as damaging as anything capitalism had produced.

Trotsky's popular version of socialist revolution and his rejection of any limits to action were attractive to New Left communists of the 1960s and beyond. The notion that all alienated groups – including workers, the young, ethnic minorities, the poor, oppressed women and Third World peasants – could have a role to play in overthrowing capitalism was preferable to the undynamic Stalinist world of orthodoxy and strict adherence to the political line set by a ruling party elite.

Other modern Marxists

Outside the Soviet Union, Marxist-inspired communists were developing alternative applications of the basic philosophy. The persistence of capitalism after the Russian Revolution, and a number of other failed socialist revolts that followed it, required new explanations and there was no shortage of them. Some are described below.

Antonio Gramsci (1891–1937)

The founder of the Italian Communist Party, Gramsci sought to explain why capitalism had not collapsed when Marxist theory suggested it should. He identified two particular reasons for its survival.

First, capitalism had learned to **control its own development**; it had not, as Marx suggested, simply intensified its exploitation of the proletariat to the point where it was bound to be overthrown. Instead, capitalists were able to head off revolution by avoiding the worst excesses of industrialisation. Popular democracy, tolerance of trade unions, improved wages and some social reforms were introduced. When democracy failed to prevent the advance of socialism and communism, capitalism developed a distortion of itself in the form of fascism.

Second, his theory of cultural **hegemony** analysed the very deep hold bourgeois ideas were able to exert upon working-class consciousness. Through the institutions that transmit cultural values – schools, the arts, the media and the political system itself – capitalist ideas were rooted deeply into society. They exerted a domination, or hegemony, over the industrial workers. To combat this hegemony, Gramsci, along with the contemporary **Council Communist** movement, urged the setting up of workers' councils, educational institutions and other cultural organisations to counter bourgeois culture. After its hold had been loosened, progress could be made towards revolution.

Gramsci's ideas were somewhat discredited after the defeat of fascism and the restoration of liberal democracy through most of the capitalist world. Interest in them revived, however, within the New Left movement of the 1960s and 1970s. Gramsci provided a cogent explanation for capitalism's durability as well as pathways towards its future destruction. The creation of 'counter-cultures' within capitalist societies was inspired in part by his writings.

Mao Tse-tung (1893–1976)

Mao led an extensive peasant communist movement in China between 1928 and 1949, at which time his forces overthrew the weak and corrupt Nationalist Government. He was partly a land reformer working among discontented peasants, and partly a Marxist. But his modifications of Marx's ideas proved so radical that 'Marxist' was scarcely an accurate description. He was, however, broadly a 'communist', as he supported the self-sufficient commune, with common ownership of land as the ideal form of economic organisation.

His main contributions to communist thought are as follows:

- In any society the most exploited class is the most revolutionary. Thus, in societies such as that of China, the peasants were the true vehicles of the revolution. By the same token, the principal enemies of the people were the landlords who exploited the peasants.

- Although the Communist Party must play a leading role in society, it should maintain close links with the people, be guided by them as well as guiding them, and avoid becoming separated from them and over-bureaucratic.

Communist Party could interpret and impose Marxist theory, Mao believed that the masses, if broadly guided, could develop true social solidarity spontaneously. Instead of the sullen, obedient population that Stalin commanded, Mao encouraged a highly volatile, enthusiastic and sometimes violent reaction to social problems among the masses. Unfortunately, his mass campaigns frequently ran totally out of control!

- Third World societies are all subject to direct political or indirect economic imperialism, Mao observed. There must, therefore, be a constant struggle by communists against domination by foreign, capitalist powers. In China itself, he saw the external threat of western powers such as the UK and the USA as more dangerous than internal revisionism.

- Although he had a warm relationship with China's masses, Mao was a ruthless dictator. Despite his anti-bureaucratic, anti-elitist and anti-intellectual ideas, he would brook no opposition to his personal rule. Like Stalin, he claimed to be the ultimate embodiment of true communism.

Mao's faith in the revolutionary potential of the peasantry and his awareness of the dangers of western imperialism ensured that he became an inspirational figure for Third World communist movements. In addition, his experience and writings on guerrilla warfare tactics became guides for those carrying out communist actions in Asia, Africa and South America.

Franz Fanon (1925–61) In addition to Mao, Fanon, a French West Indian, proved to be a champion for Third World Marxists. He, too, recognised the international power of capitalist imperialism and believed that freedom fighters should, therefore, concentrate on undermining its hold as well as seeking to overthrow colonial and post-colonial governments that encouraged imperial penetration of their countries.

Fanon also analysed the nature of the developed world's exploitation of poorer countries. He revealed the complex trade and financial systems through which Third World countries were exploited. Indeed, he pointed out, the proletarians of the developed world, far from feeling themselves exploited, threw in their lot with their capitalist masters. They now believed that their best interests lay in co-operating with capitalism's international conspiracy against the exploited masses in Africa and Asia. Thus, the revolutionaries of the future would be not the industrial workers of developed capitalist countries – the classical Marxist model – but what he called the 'wretched of the earth' – the Third World peasantry.

The synthesis of intense nationalism – the struggle against imperialism – and socialism, which Mao and Fanon advocated, was to be the main inspiration for movements led by revolutionaries such as **Fidel Castro** in

Cuba and **Ho Chi Minh** in Vietnam. It was also popular among western Marxists since, like Gramsci, Fanon provided an alternative way forward to replace the traditional models of revolution provided by Marx.

Herbert Marcuse (1906–79)

The left-wing-inspired youth protest movements of the late 1960s and early 1970s acknowledged a number of 'gurus', among whom Marcuse was a leading example. He moved further away from traditional Marxist analysis of capitalist society. He de-emphasised the role of class – a central feature of Marxist ideology – developing instead a theory of **mass society**.

According to Marcuse, all parts of society have become exploited, as consumers as well as workers. He described capitalism's control of society as a new type of totalitarianism. The political form of totalitarianism – fascism – had failed, but been replaced by a more subtle, economic and psychological type of control. He argued that we adopt lifestyles and consumption patterns that have been created for us by capitalism's need to produce more and more. Our lifestyles are not, therefore, of our own choosing; we are manipulated and exploited. Thus, there is still alienation under capitalism, but of a different, more sinister form than had existed before.

Marcuse was pessimistic about the prospects of overthrowing capitalism and the society of the masses. He therefore suggested that individuals must seek to liberate themselves by choosing their own, distinctive lifestyles. In the age of sexual liberation and hallucinatory drugs, these ideas were, understandably, popular among young radicals.

The decline of communism

The destruction of the Soviet political system which **Mikhail Gorbachev** set in motion in the mid-1980s led to a 'domino effect', causing one communist regime after another to collapse, to be replaced by more liberal democratic forms of government. At the same time, the centralised, planned socialist economies in such states have been largely dismantled and transformed, fully or partially, into capitalist states. In short, Marxism appears to be in full retreat.

Some modern socialist writers, such as **Ralph Miliband** and **Nicos Poulantzas**, have always argued that capitalism continues to be an exploitative system, disguised by the façade of liberal institutions. It follows that, although communist regimes are in decline throughout the world, Marxist-inspired socialism is still relevant. However, there can be little doubt that, at the beginning of the twenty-first century, communism is largely a historical phenomenon. It is an open question as to whether it may re-emerge in the future.

Anarchism

Introduction

The term 'anarchy' literally means 'an absence of government'. It does not mean, as many might suppose, 'a state of chaos'. We often use the word to mean disorder, but this is a distortion of the real philosophy known as anarchism. Nor does anarchism automatically imply violence. The image of the bomb-throwing or gun-wielding assassin actually represents very few anarchists.

Rather, as we have observed above, anarchists are, on the whole, essentially communists who have a well-developed sense of order and peace. It is true that many anarchists have been revolutionaries, but for them violence is merely a means to a peaceful end. It is also true that there have been violent anarcho-individualists who have wreaked havoc in civilised society and attracted much hostile attention. But these are a minority, most of whom can be described as 'nihilists'. The analysis shown below will concentrate on mainstream, social forms of anarchism – a **positive** rather than a negative philosophy.

Basic principles

No understanding of anarchism can be achieved without prior comprehension of how anarchists see the basic nature of human beings.

Human nature

'From his birth not a single human being is either good or bad.'
Mikhail Bakunin

There are four different conceptions of natural human beings to be found among the prominent exponents of anarchism:

- The most common view is that people are basically good, sociable and display natural empathy towards their fellow human beings. The fact that they do not always do so is because imperfect societies have corrupted them.
- Similar to this is the notion that people are born neither good nor bad. A person is, rather, a **tabula rasa**, a blank sheet upon which any characteristics may be inscribed by the social environment. Thus, if they live in a corrupted society, they will be corrupt, while in a good society they will be good.
- Less optimistic anarchists have suggested that people have two sides to their natural character. On the one hand, they are egotistical and individualistic; on the other they are sociable and sympathetic to others. Such characteristics give rise to co-operation and mutual aid.
- The most radical anarchist philosophers suggest that people are pure egotists. For these 'nihilists' any form of social organisation is unnatural and cannot, therefore, be justified.

The first three conceptions all have in common the hope that human beings are perfectible. Either they are naturally good and simply need to be returned to such a natural state, or they possess the **capacity** to be good and sociable if a perfect social order can be established. Only the nihilists and extreme anarcho-individualists take a pessimistic view of the possibility of the creation of a truly 'communist' society.

Freedom   As with liberalism, anarchists see individual liberty as a key value, so much so that some have claimed that anarchism is simply an extreme form of liberalism. This is to misunderstand the anarchist conception of freedom, which is fundamentally different from that of liberalism.

Liberals distinguish carefully between **licence** and **freedom**. 'Licence' refers to a state where there are absolutely no restrictions on human action. In these circumstances, they argue, there is no true freedom, since the exercise of licence by one person will inevitably lead to interference with the actions of others. A simple example concerns private property. As soon as one person claims some land for themselves, they deprive another person of enjoyment of that same land. The problem becomes particularly acute when land is scarce. To deal with it, liberals argue that there must be legal regulation of property distribution and ownership.

Thus, 'freedom' can exist only where people operate within laws that protect them from each other. People can only be **free** to enjoy their property if it is protected from encroachment by others. This gives rise to an apparent paradox. In order to be truly free, people must accept restrictions. Of course, liberals argue that this is an acceptable trade-off. In addition, the laws must be openly agreed by the people, so that there is full **consent** to the restrictions. Anarchists reject this proposition. They argue instead that there need be no distinction between licence and freedom.

Anarchists start from the basic premise that, in a natural, uncorrupted state, people will **not** interfere with the liberty of others. Furthermore, they would deal with such problems as scarcity through natural co-operation and equality, rather than through legally controlled competition. Returning to the problem of private property, for example, anarchists believe that **common** and not **private** ownership is natural. Thus, laws regulating the ownership of property should not be needed at all. Freedom for the anarchist consists of **private judgement** – individuals making their own decisions concerning their conduct. If the social conditions can be created within which such private judgement conforms to **natural law**, there is no need for artificial human laws.

> 'Social solidarity is the first human law; freedom is the second.'
> Mikhail Bakunin

Liberals have a similar conception of natural law – the way in which individuals would behave in a natural state – to that of anarchists. Both philosophies suggest that mutual respect and tolerance, justice, the protection of life and the importance of co-operation to overcome social and economic problems are natural. The difference lies in how such natural laws can be applied. Liberals argue that they must be enshrined in human laws, underpinned by coercion. Anarchists maintain that if human beings are morally perfected, everyone will follow natural laws without compulsion. It is possibly this particular aspect of the anarchist philosophy that has been most often criticised as **utopian** and, therefore, unattainable.

The anarchist critique of modern society

Since anarchists insist on the creation of a free society in which all may exercise private judgement, there can be no place for the state in their philosophy. The fundamental purpose of the state is to concentrate coercive power in its institutions in order to enforce laws (even though they

The state

right to exercise power in any form over anyone else. Some anarchists shared the Marxist analysis of the state as the means by which a ruling class is able to maintain its dominant position. Nevertheless, it was the anarchist insistence on the complete removal of any form of state which was the main cause of their split with the Marxists around 1870.

'Anarchy means the government of each by himself.'
Pierre-Joseph Proudhon

Laws

Since laws restrict the anarchist conception of freedom, as we have seen above, they clearly could not be justified. Liberals counter this argument by suggesting that, if laws are the result of a freely made agreement, nobody can claim to have been coerced. Yet **social contract theory**, as this is usually described, is also not accepted by anarchists. Individuals, cannot be coerced by the group to which they belong, even when there is unanimous agreement. There is no guarantee that the individual will always agree and he or she may, at the outset, have been unduly influenced by others.

This is not to say that anarchists reject law as a concept. For them, it is a natural phenomenon, not an artificial creation. Either people are born with the sense of natural law that limits their activities, or they will be forced to obey social laws that are necessary to their survival and well-being. In both cases, they should know or learn how to act spontaneously. They should not be coerced.

Private property

For many anarchists the existence of private property is both the most corrupting influence upon human society and the root of a number of other evils that have emerged since the first time a man placed a barrier around some land and claimed it as his own. Again, there is a sharp contrast with liberalism here, as the latter sees ownership and enjoyment of private property as a basic right.

The anarchist view is that the idea of private property is **not** natural and runs contrary to natural law. Furthermore, its existence gives rise to laws that are needed to protect that property. The need for laws also necessitates the existence of the state to enforce them. Private property also provides opportunities for those who possess it to exploit those who are propertyless.

There is a sense that all the fruits of nature belong to all human beings collectively. Thus, common ownership of all resources is natural, as is equal distribution of the rewards gained from it.

Artificial communities

Modern societies, argue the anarchists, have created a number of artificial groupings into which people are forced to gather. The industrial factory system clearly herded workers together into artificial working communities, but it also gave rise to the proliferation of cities, another unnatural phenomenon. On a larger scale, even the concept of 'nation' was criticised by most anarchists. It is understandable that the political manifestation of nations – the state – should be condemned as coercive, but the nation appears at first sight to be natural. Not so, they suggest. Even common culture, language, religion and history are false values; communities, therefore, should not be based upon them. Furthermore, nationalism has given rise to rivalries, aggression and warfare.

It is essential that any community is voluntary if the anarchist ideal of a society without coercion is to be achieved. Only then can it be guaranteed that all will conform to the norms of the community. Should they not wish to do so, they should be free to leave and join a different group with which they can identify more clearly. Only complete social outcasts would, therefore, be excluded.

Capitalism and industrialisation

The anarchists' objection to capitalism is clear. It is based on private property, exploits workers and underpins the coercive modern state, they complain. There is another criticism of capitalism, however, which not all anarchists share. This concerns the nature of industrialisation that has accompanied the growth of capitalism.

The division of labour, the nature of the modern workplace and the loss of much of the creative element in work are all aspects of modern economic progress that must be reversed. Workers have become brutalised and automated by modern work methods. Long hours, poor conditions and low wages are also to be abhorred, of course, but the alienation experienced by the unskilled, production-line worker can be removed only if the whole system is dismantled. This is a romantic aspect of the anarchist creed, since it suggests a return to a simpler form of existence in which the creative instincts of workers are released and production is organised on a smaller scale.

Summary of anarchist beliefs

1. Mostly there is a belief that people are naturally good and sociable or at least are perfectible.
2. Liberty consists not of freedom within artificial laws but of the exercise of private judgement, which leads, in the uncorrupted individual, to good acts.
3. No one has a right to exercise power over another person.
4. The state and government should not be tolerated, even if they are established by consent.
5. Since the existence of a state cannot be justified there can be no artificial laws. People should, however, conform to natural laws.
6. Private property is unnatural and should, therefore, be replaced by common ownership.
7. All communities should be natural and voluntary.
8. Capitalism and possibly many of the features of industrialisation, should be abolished.

Conceptions of an anarchist order

It is at this point in our analysis of anarchism that a clear distinction must be made between **anarcho-individualism** and **anarcho-communism**, together with its related forms. Both share many common basic beliefs, but their prescriptions for the creation of a new order differ markedly.

Anarcho-individualism The anarcho-individualists stress the egotistical aspects of people's character. For them, all forms of social organisation are unjustified limitations upon people's liberty, even if they are voluntary associations. Instead, they wish to see a world where individuals are sovereign beings, free to exercise their own judgement as to how they behave. Within this tradition there are two further sub-divisions of belief, each of which is dependent upon the anarchist's conception of human nature.

Social Darwinists, sometimes described as **anarcho-capitalists**, draw their inspiration from the biological theories of Charles Darwin, applying them to life in human society. In this analysis each individual is engaged in a personal struggle against their natural and social environment. They must compete in order to survive, or at least succeed at the expense of others. In some ways, this is a logical extension of the intensely individualistic liberalism that flourished in the nineteenth century at the height of the development of capitalism. In the USA it has a longer tradition, arising out of the 'frontier' spirit of the early days of the Union. There, on the edges of civilised society, the influence of government and laws was especially weak. Every individual was, therefore, responsible for themselves.

In its modern form, anarcho-individualism is considered to be a right-wing phenomenon, sometimes described as libertarianism. Here there is an intense suspicion of the activities of the state. It is seen as an instrument of repression, seeking to impose artificial values and to inhibit people's natural instincts for survival.

A gentler individualist tradition also flourished in nineteenth-century America. There, genuine anarchists believed it was possible for absolute individual liberty to exist alongside peaceful community life. Each could, therefore, choose to be self-sufficient or to co-operate with their fellow human beings. This was seen as a world of mutual respect and peace, but without social organisation. People's natural egotism would not bring them into fierce competition with others, but would simply allow them to withdraw from social life.

Anarcho-communism The more influential and widespread form of anarchism that proliferated in the nineteenth century was a communist form, which, as we have seen above, was closely associated with more radical forms of revolutionary socialism. This tradition stressed the sociable nature of people's natural character. Instead of individualism, the anarcho-communists stressed social solidarity and mutual aid. In contrast to the Darwinian approach, they stressed people's desire to live in voluntary communities. The emphasis lay, therefore, in communal living and economic co-operation. Although this has formed a philosophy rich in its diversity, certain common characteristics can be discerned:

- People can live in communities without need of state organisation or laws.
- Wherever possible, these communities should be self-sufficient.
- If communities were forced to co-operate, systems of mutual benefit and fair exchange would be developed.
- Although individual sovereignty would be maintained, each member of the community would naturally conform to its norms of behaviour.

- Decisions would be made by direct democracy with all members participating.
- All property would be in common ownership.
- Goods would be distributed on the basis of absolute equality.

Two principal variants of this theme also flourished. The most popular was known as **anarcho-syndicalism**. This movement based its prospective social and economic organisation upon the existing trade union structure. The nature of people's occupation was seen as the most powerful force that binds them together. It was therefore logical that social organisation should be based upon that criterion. The union structure was also ideal, having in place its own internal democratic structure. The syndicalists enjoyed an additional advantage since, in order to destroy the existing political and social order, trade unions were ideally placed to organise the working classes.

The proposed post-revolutionary social structure was, in essence, to be a highly decentralised form of socialism. Workers were to enjoy common ownership of their own industries. These were to be managed in a highly democratic manner, with economic and social equality respected. The industries would find it necessary to co-operate with each other on a voluntary basis, using a series of trade agreements created for mutual benefit. The more idealistic of the syndicalists – the anarchists themselves – believed that this could be achieved without the need for any form of coercive state.

The most developed form of such a decentralised system was known as **federalism**. In this conception a multilayered hierarchy of communities, ranging from the very small locality to a world system, would be formed on the basis of occupational groupings. At each level, co-operation would take place freely. At the highest level, a federation of workers would be formed on a worldwide basis. Thus, the nation-state would also be abolished as an entity.

So it can be seen that communist forms of anarchism range from conceptions of very small, autonomous, voluntary communities with relatively little to do with each other, through to a great international workers' co-operative with a complex system of trading and mutual aid in place to support it.

Some prominent anarchists

Since there are almost as many anarchist proposals as there are anarchists, and since it is a philosophy with so much diversity, a review of the beliefs of some of the principal anarchists is the most effective way to illustrate the many ideas that have flourished.

William Godwin (1756–1836) (English)

Godwin developed the notion of private judgement, allying it to the principles of utilitarianism. Thus, he argued, individual people should make a decision each time they act. Will the result of the action do more good to others than harm? If so, it should be undertaken. He differed from the mainstream utilitarians such as Bentham, however, in that he believed that it was for individuals to determine for themselves whether the results of their actions would be beneficial.

Godwin shared with Rousseau the belief that, in an ideal world, people should be able to govern themselves, so that there should be no need of government, even of the most democratic kind. The difference between these two close contemporaries, however, was that, while Rousseau was pessimistic about people becoming moral and wise enough to govern themselves, Godwin was more idealistic and looked forward to a world without government. For him, people are completely perfectible, given the appropriate social environment. Thus, while his critics described him as intensely utopian, he saw himself as realistic. His most influential work was entitled *An Enquiry Concerning Political Justice* (1793).

Michael Bakunin (1814–76) (Russian)

Bakunin's principal contribution to the anarchist tradition was the notion of federalism, as described above. He was a close associate of Marx until they split over the issue of the dictatorship of the proletariat. He broadly shared Marx's analysis of capitalism and his vision of a communist world. He could not, however, accept the need for an interim state – the dictatorship of the proletariat.

Like Marx, he saw labour as people's fundamental activity. Thus, the nature of people's work – their occupation – should also form the basis of social communities. In common with many other anarchists of his time, Bakunin was a revolutionary who saw the destruction of the existing repressive state as the first priority for his movement.

Peter Kropotkin (1842–1921) (Russian)

Kropotkin was Bakunin's fellow revolutionary and possibly the purest example of an anarcho-communist. In his book *Fields, Factories and Workshops* (1901) Kropotkin extolled the virtues of the small, voluntary community based on the village. It was, he argued, the breakdown of such small communities that had led to the development of the modern repressive state.

The post-revolutionary world would, for him, be concerned with the restoration of such voluntary communities. If possible, they were to be self-sufficient, but he accepted the need for some large-scale industrial organisations. Like Bakunin, he was an internationalist, viewing the nation as an artificial community. These two Russian anarchists were also scathing in their condemnation of religion as a means by which people have been repressed by a ruling class.

Georges Sorel (1847–1922) (French)

One of the most violent of the anarchists, Sorel developed the political creed of anarcho-syndicalism. For him, people are constrained not only by laws and governments, but also by moral scruples. In order to see society for what it is and to be able to act effectively to destroy it, these moral restraints must be removed. The exercise of one's individual will through extreme violence is the means of achieving this.

The state was the instrument of the will of a ruling elite, he argued, so that only the superior will of the mass of the working class could secure its downfall. Thereafter, a stateless society based on self-governing trade unions could be achieved. His stress on the importance of individual will and decisive action endeared him also to later fascist philosophers as well as modern existentialists.

Pierre Proudhon (1809–65) (French)

As well as being one of the more scientific of the anarchist philosophers, Proudhon was responsible for its best-known maxim – 'All property is theft.' Yet, despite his apparent opposition to the concept of private property, he did not, unlike virtually all other anarchists, recommend its abolition. He understood that property ownership was the principal cause of the existence of the oppressive state and its attendant laws. Property, once established, had to be protected by force. But he also accepted that its ownership was so deeply rooted in society that it could not, realistically, be abolished, however desirable this might be.

His practical theories became known as mutualism and were a compromise between capitalism and socialism. Each person would produce goods either as an individual or in voluntary association with other workers. These goods would be sold, not in free markets, but at prices determined by the amount of labour that had been put into their production. Instead of money, therefore, goods would be priced in 'labour value'. In this way, a free semi-capitalist system would be retained, but neither workers nor consumers would be exploited. The fact that there was no exploitation meant there would be no need for a state, since a state only exists in order to maintain conventional forms of capitalist exploitation.

Proudhon rejected other forms of socialism or communism on the grounds that they were collectivist doctrines, forcing people into mutual co-operation. His scheme, he claimed, gave rise to voluntary mutual arrangements with individuals retaining their own personal liberty.

Henry Thoreau (1817–62) (American)

During the late 1960s and early 1970s interest in certain forms of anarcho-individualism was rekindled within the youth protest movement. Thoreau, and in particular his most celebrated book, *Walden*, became one of the inspirations among radicals of the left. In his early years as a philosopher he did not propose any detailed form of alternative order to that of the modern state, but rather recommended that each individual should free themselves from its restrictions by withdrawing from it and becoming self-sufficient. He practised this philosophy himself in rural America, where he was considered an amiable eccentric. Later, he was to become more militant, recommending that protesters should engage in civil disobedience against the oppressive nature of the modern state.

His combination of individualism and self-sufficiency appealed to those radical thinkers who wished to escape from the restrictions of the all-powerful state, and who were concerned by the destruction of the environment caused by modern production methods.

Max Stirner (1806–56) (German)

Stirner's rejection of all forms of social organisation as a denial of the human ego earned him the title 'nihilist', one of those extreme anarchists who became notorious for their radicalism. His view of human nature was that people have two sides to their character, egoism and sociability. In an ideal society, the opportunities for people's social nature to manifest itself would be maximised, but he recognised this aspiration to be utopian. The alternative was to accept people's egoism and to give it full rein.

In *The Ego and His Own* (1845) Stirner rejected all social theories on the grounds that they would result in alienation for the individual. Thus, governments, laws, morality, religion and society itself must be rejected by people, who will then take control of their own life. The extreme negativity of Stirner's philosophy was too much even for most other anarchists to stomach, but he remained an important philosophical inspiration for the anarcho-individualists.

Robert Nozick (1938–)
(American)

Nozick represents contemporary interest in **libertarianism**, which is both a form of anarcho-individualism and an extreme type of conservatism. For him, every individual should be responsible for their own actions and, most importantly, should also be responsible for their own self-protection. The notion that the state and its laws exist to protect free individuals from each other is rejected in favour of self-help of a kind that had been advocated by the nineteenth-century English essayist **Samuel Smiles**.

In Nozick's world there would be only a minimal state, preferably no state at all. Capitalism would be virtually uncontrolled and a number of voluntary agencies, to which individuals could subscribe for their own protection and welfare, would replace state institutions. Rewards in such a society would be distributed purely on the basis of power in the market place. Popular among many modern libertarians, Nozick's ideas flourish at the confluence of individualist anarchist, New Right conservative and extreme liberal traditions.

The relevance of anarchism

In nineteenth-century Russia, largely among the peasantry, anarchist ideas did enjoy a certain degree of support. There was, during the Spanish Civil War in the 1930s, a substantial anarchist presence, members of which actually controlled Barcelona for a short period. Yet no large-scale community has ever been established for any length of time along anarchist lines. Furthermore, the movement has never attracted mass support. It may, therefore, be asked whether it has any great significance as a world philosophy.

There can be two responses to these observations. First, anarchism must be recognised as having inspired many of the alternative lifestyles that have sprung up since the 1960s. The 'hippy' commune movement and its modern successors, the New Age Travellers, certainly espouse many anarchist principles. So, too, do some environmental groups who have been attempting to establish self-sufficient, sustainable and simple forms of lifestyle in small voluntary groups. Though still on a small scale, interest in such new lifestyles continues to grow steadily as a reaction to modern living.

Second, anarchism serves as a challenging and diverse philosophical criticism of modern society. Though most of its proposals might seem impractical today, many of its observations upon such institutions as the state, property and capitalism are still relevant and stimulating. If it is true that the sovereignty of individuals continues to be challenged by these institutions, then reference to anarchist ideals could serve to remind us of what might be lost.

Totalitarianism

Introduction

The term 'totalitarianism' refers to a political and social system rather than to any specific ideology. We could argue in some instances that the mere exercise of absolute power by a regime can become an end in itself and, therefore, an ideology, but few rulers would admit to this. George Orwell's novel *Nineteen Eighty-Four* suggests that the dictatorship portrayed there was only interested in the pursuit of power and had no other reason for its existence, but the book is a political allegory so we must be wary of generalising on the basis of what it says.

Certainly, as we shall see below, all totalitarian regimes claim to be motivated by ideology, and it is this that drives them to exert total control, rather than the enjoyment of power alone. It is therefore useful to include an analysis of totalitarianism in this section rather than elsewhere. Having done so, we may examine three ideologies that have been most closely associated with absolute regimes. These are fascism, Nazism and Soviet socialism.

Totalitarianism and autocracy

Between the two world wars, it became apparent that a new form of political regime had come about. The term 'autocracy' could be used to describe those systems that did not conform to the new ideas of liberal democracy, but it was inadequate in describing the dictatorial governments of the likes of the Soviet Union, fascist Italy and Nazi Germany.

Hannah Arendt, the historian, and herself a refugee from the Third Reich, provided a clear distinction between the two forms of rule, thus:

- Autocracy is merely a form of government that denies democratic and individual rights. Totalitarianism, on the other hand, is a complete social system, not just a style of government.
- With autocracy a clear distinction is made between what is in the public sphere, i.e. the concern of government, and what is private and therefore not to be interfered with by the state. For totalitarian rulers, no such distinction is recognised. Everything is relevant and may be subject to control or transformation.
- Ideology might not be paramount in an autocratic system. Totalitarians always espouse an ideology, using it as the guide by which they wish to transform society and bend it to their will.
- The autocratic ruler seeks fear and obedience among the governed, but is not necessarily concerned with any deeper control or even enthusiastic support. Those who have led totalitarian states, by contrast, have attempted to exert psychological control over their subject peoples, sometimes resulting in adulation and absolute faith in the ruling ideology and its embodiment – the leader.

Thus, Arendt stresses the 'totalness' of such regimes. She emphasises total relevance of the ideology, total control and total obedience to a single leader. **Bernard Crick** summed up this idea some time later:

'The totalitarian believes that everything is relevant to govern- ment and that the task of government is to reconstruct society utterly according to the goals of an ideology.'
Bernard Crick, *In Defence of Politics*, 1962

The nature of totalitarianism

A distinctive phenomenon?

Scholars have entered into much dispute as to whether there is a distinct form of state that can be described as 'totalitarian'. Some have suggested that it is merely a distorted form of democracy which arose out of the peculiar historical conditions that existed during the inter-war period in Europe. The conditions necessary for its emergence have been variously identified as:

- an unstable political system
- a series of economic crises
- the imminent threat of socialist revolution feared by the middle classes
- in larger countries, difficulty being experienced in maintaining national unity
- perceived threats to the dominant culture of the society.

Certainly, many of these phenomena could be discerned in Germany, Italy, Russia and Spain in the first part of the twentieth century. In the UK, France and the USA, the main victors in the First World War, most of the conditions were, by contrast, absent. Only the Great Depression was experienced by all the European powers.

Thus, there is a strong argument for suggesting that this was merely a passing historical phenomenon arising from the failure of democracy to deal with pressing national problems. However, the counter-theory – that it was a distinctive form of regime arising largely out of adherence to a dominant ideology – remains the more popular.

Theories of totalitarianism

The belief that totalitarianism is indeed a distinct form of society is asserted by a variety of schools of thought.

Talmon, a historian, sees much in the work of Rousseau to provide clues as to the origins of the system. The concept of a **general will**, which Rousseau developed, gave the people a collective voice that could cut through the confusions and majoritarianism of democracy. Thus, minorities would not feel persecuted, majorities could not persecute them and each individual could feel part of an organic whole rather than drifting in a competitive sea. The problem of how to determine such a collective will, if indeed one can exist at all, cannot be solved by demo- cratic methods, Rousseau feared, so a single ruler with perfect know- ledge and understanding of his people must be found to declare the 'general will'. Thus, when democracy appeared to fail in certain coun- tries, this notion was put forward as an explanation. In each case a dynamic individual emerged as the embodiment of the popular will. This, suggests Talmon, is what characterises totalitarian rule.

Friedrich proposed a more detailed version, but at the same time a less sophisticated one. For him, totalitarianism arose out of a combination of the **desire** for a more concentrated form of rule, arising from various economic and political problems, and technological advances that enabled such a concentration of power to be successfully attained. Thus, it is the result of a coincidence of phenomena. He expressed the results in a six-point scheme:

1. There is a single state ideology. No alternative is tolerated.

2. The state has a monopoly of the communications media.

3. There is a similar monopoly of economic power.

4. The state employs terror – the public use of force – to maintain obedience.

5. All significant weapons are in the hands of the state.

6. There is single-party rule, which uses an obedient bureaucracy in order to govern.

It has been suggested that these phenomena are not distinctive enough, that they represent merely exaggerated forms of autocracy, but they certainly conform closely to the characteristics of Nazi Germany and the Soviet Union.

Arendt, as we have seen above, stresses the psychological nature of totalitarianism, as well as its totalness. She observed how 'civil society' – the intermediate social groups such as families, religions, political parties, interest groups and trade unions – are broken down by the state. They are either absent or replaced by 'puppets' which are not independent at all but compliant to the will of the Government. There is, therefore, no social organisation between the central state and individuals. The minds of the people are, thus, laid open to both psychological and coercive control.

This view also lays great stress upon the role of the governing ideology, since its goals must be attained at all costs and no private interests can be allowed to stand in its path.

We can now move on to review the two principal forms of totalitarian regime that flourished in the twentieth century. Since Marxist ideology, which underpinned the Stalinist system in the Soviet Union, is described elsewhere, it is appropriate to begin with fascism.

Fascism

The most important philosopher to have inspired twentieth-century fascists has undoubtedly been **Friedrich Nietzsche** (1844–1900). This strange, complex and, ultimately, insane thinker was largely concerned with the struggle between rational thought and action. For him, the world was being ill-served by rational thinkers who developed such ideologies as democracy and liberalism. He maintained that individuals should not be fettered by the disciplines of rationality, but be free-spirited and ready to engage in a struggle against their fellow human being, a battle of wills in which only the strong can succeed. In this way, society is guided by strength and purpose rather than by weak ideology.

Democracy was the subject of Nietzsche's most scathing criticism. Slavish adherence to the wishes of the majority would render society directionless and without noble purposes. Furthermore, each individual, by subjecting themselves to the will of the majority, denies their own individual will. This Darwinian world which he envisaged, and in which only the fittest can succeed, must yield up a superior being in each society, an individual whose personal will is superior to all others. This being he describes as the *übermensch* or 'superman', an individual who can inspire whole nations into dynamic action. When we add Nietzsche's love of war and conquest to this philosophy, it is easy to understand why such characters as Hitler and Mussolini were so influenced by Nietzschean ideas.

The anarchist **Georges Sorel** (1847–1922) adopted a similar Darwinian approach to that of Nietzsche. He saw politics in terms of the struggle between competing elites. The elite that holds power is able to retain it through the strength of its will. Aspiring elites who wish to take over power must, therefore, demonstrate superior dynamism to succeed. In this way, modern states can guarantee to be ruled by powerful leaders, for it becomes inevitable that the weak must fail. Both Sorel and Nietzsche echo the much earlier works of the Italian Renaissance writer **Niccolo Machiavelli** (1469–1527), whose most celebrated work, *The Prince*, exhorted rulers to exhibit more ruthlessness, cruelty, cunning and, if necessary, deceitfulness than their rivals. All these 'evils' cannot be justified, he admitted, unless they are used for the purpose of defending the state. But if the state is threatened – and it frequently is, both internally and externally – there are no limits to what the ruler can do.

Like Sorel, **Friedrich Hegel** (1770–1831) did not belong strictly to any totalitarian movement, being more in the continental conservative tradition, but he nevertheless provided much inspiration in his philosophical works for later fascists. Hegel's historical theories (which also heavily influenced Marx) suggested that the alienation and disharmony that had characterised all past societies could be eliminated, heralding a new age of peace and freedom. This could only occur, however, if the will of every individual could become identical to the will of the whole society. There would then be no contradiction between individual freedom and the collective purposes of the state. Nobody would feel constricted and individual liberty would not interfere with the harmony of the whole community. Though Hegel almost certainly would have opposed modern fascism, his ideas were used by the fascists to justify the practice of submitting individuals to a subservient role in relation to the state. In other words, what Hegel intended to be a perfect form of collective freedom was interpreted by fascists to be the complete abolition of individual liberty.

Features of fascism

As we have already seen, the nature of fascist regimes has been totalitarian, demonstrating the characteristics described by Arendt, Friedrich, Talmon and the like. However, these phenomena do not present us with a complete picture. Thus, although all fascist regimes have been totalitarian, they have also displayed a number of other distinguishing features.

Will and action

The ruler of a fascist regime does not claim to be its legitimate leader on the grounds that he has been elected or that he represents a political party that has been installed in power by the people. Rather, he claims the right to govern on the grounds of his superior will, his ability to act decisively and to move the nation in a direction that is the result of his own inspiration and not of a democratic process. Mussolini was, thus, prone to remind his people that he might not have observed the rules of democratic politics, but he had succeeded in making Italian trains run on time.

The leader principle

This term, coined by Hitler, refers to the claim that the leader of a fascist regime is the single embodiment of the will of its people. The granting of all power to one personality ensured that there would be a singularity of purpose that is lacking in more pluralist political systems. If a nation is to move decisively towards its future goals, it must have this single-mindedness, claimed the fascist dictator. Hitler argued that his will was merely a reflection of the clear destiny of the German people – to create a superior civilisation and to conquer inferior races. Mussolini, on the other hand, was prepared to admit that he was creating his own myths concerning the Italian people, heralding a new imperialist age for them. In both cases, however, the principle was the same – clarity of purpose and direction.

The implications of this principle were twofold. First, those who chose to defy the will of the leader were, automatically, traitors against their own people. Second, it denied any possibility of organised opposition or democratic processes. Mass participation in politics was allowed and, indeed, encouraged, but this could only manifest itself in demonstrations of enthusiastic support, not in meaningful dialogue.

> 'Fascism insists that government be entrusted to men capable of rising above their own private interests and of realising the aspirations of the whole collectivity.'
> Alfredo Rocco (adviser to Mussolini), 1937

The state

In democratically based political systems, the state – the permanent apparatus of government – is subject to the will of the majority of the people as expressed through their representatives. This is not so in a fascist system. There, everything is subservient to the purposes of the state; everything, that is, except the leader himself, who is the embodiment of the state.

It was Mussolini's closest associate, **Giovanni Gentile** (1875–1944), who brought this concept of the state to its highest form. For him, the state can take on a life of its own and become an individual on its own account, provided that the people collectively bury their own individual-

democratic tradition, this is a difficult concept to understand, since individual liberty, pluralism and tolerance are stressed by democrats. The fascists attempted to break out of this mode of thinking. 'Statism' became a kind of religion within which there could be only one form of allegiance. Naturally, since fascist regimes were totalitarian, everything was the concern of the state. There was no private sphere, no independent civil society and no higher authority.

Nationalism The most powerful synthesis of fascism and nationalism occurred in Hitler's Third Reich and is described in more detail below. However, all the prominent fascist regimes used nationalism as a means by which the solidarity of the state could be maintained.

An important distinction needs to be drawn at this point between German and Italian fascism. For Hitler, there was a higher purpose than the consolidation of state control, which was the greater glory of the German people and their culture. Thus, the state was to **serve** German nationalism. In Italy, on the other hand, Mussolini and Gentile used nationalism as a means to maintain allegiance to the state. So the positions of state and nation were reversed.

Nevertheless, in both cases nationalism was a powerful instrument for maintaining state unity. The belief that a people are bound together by common ancestry, culture, language and history sits well with the struggle to create an organic state. Indeed, the term 'fasces' derives from the Latin noun describing a roped bundle of sticks, symbol of the need to bind disparate peoples under one authority in the Roman Empire. The concept of 'nation' and 'national destiny' proved an easier idea with which to inspire people than the more abstract notion of an organised political state.

> 'It is not nationality which creates the state, but the state which creates nationality, by setting the seal of actual existence on it. It is through the conquest of unity and independence that the nation gives proof of its political will, and establishes its existence as a state.'
> Giovanni Gentile, *The Genesis and Structure of Society*, 1937

Economics Though fascism is generally thought of as a right-wing philosophy, it is not sympathetic to the free operation of capitalism. The economic forces exerted by free markets are seen as a denial of the individual will. Each person should be able to engage in an unfettered struggle against the social and economic environment. Capitalism threatens this process. It is also the case that market capitalism conflicts with the fascist obsession with state power. It becomes a contradiction in terms to have absolute state power but a free, individualistic economic system.

Similarly, though fascism is a collectivist doctrine, its adherents oppose socialism and its extreme form, Marxism. This is not to say that fascists reject all the principles of socialism. Many fascists admire the social solidarity and collective principles of socialism. Indeed, the three most 'successful' fascist leaders – Hitler, Mussolini and Franco – displayed socialist tendencies in their earlier years. The principal objections to socialism are twofold. First, its reliance upon a rational ideology threatens the operation of free individual will. Second, it is a class-based movement, which divides society into at least two social groupings. Fascists pursue a complete, undivided organic state, so class conflict is not acceptable. Of course, the goals of fascism and Marxism might appear to be similar in that they are seeking a classless society, but this is as far as the similarity goes. The persistence of the all-powerful, coercive state is not acceptable to Marxists.

To replace both free market capitalism and state socialism, the fascists developed a theory of economic management of their own, known as the 'corporate state' or 'corporativism'. Its most developed form was introduced in Italy by Mussolini. Here, economic enterprises remained under private control, but their relations with the workforce were to be overseen by 'syndicates' or 'corporations' that would ensure that all interests were served by each industry, i.e. those of employers, workers, consumers and, above all, the state. Thus, there was neither complete state control nor absolute laissez-faire capitalism. In the event, only in Italy was the corporate state created in the full sense of the term. Even there it was corrupted by the domination of the fascist party in every corporation, and war soon overtook their operations. In wartime, although private enterprise was maintained, the purposes of the state became ever more pressing, so the semi-independence of the corporations was largely lost.

Irrationality and myth
As we saw in the philosophy of Nietzsche, fascists are opposed to the application of rational theories in politics. They have, therefore, been described as 'irrational' thinkers, not in the sense of being socially maladjusted, but in that all appeals to reason are rejected.

Instead of appealing to the people on rational grounds, fascists prefer to play on emotions, fears and prejudices. Thus, for example, xenophobia (fear of foreigners or strangers) was seen as a more powerful force in moving the masses than economic self-interest. Similarly, the fostering of a sense of racial superiority could inspire people more effectively than drives for greater efficiency in production. Neither of these emotions, any more than religious bigotry, historical destiny or conspiracy theories, had any basis in reason, but, for the fascist, this is less important than the effect they have on the people.

It was Hitler who was to use the device of national and racial mythology as the most potent form of irrational appeal. The theories of the superior 'Aryan' race, whose culture and will were superior to those of all other peoples, were to become the basis of his own version of the fascist creed – National Socialism.

These theories are described more fully below. Both Franco in Spain and Mussolini in Italy persuaded their people that they were leading them to a new 'Golden Age' whose origins lay in dubious historical interpretations. Neither, however, was to develop the extensive mythology that Hitler's advisers were able to achieve.

War and conquest   Nietzsche had proclaimed that 'the Nation which gives up war and conquest is ready for the rule of shopkeepers and democracy', a condemnation born out of his belief that a people are at their most dynamic and purposeful when they are at war. He saw the conquest of weaker

free because they subordinate their ego and their interests completely to those of the state. Their will and that of the state become one; there are no contradictions to hold people back.

This was very much the fascist view, especially that of Hitler. War and conquest were noble aspirations. There was a natural duty for members of a superior culture to impose themselves on the world. Not to do so would be a denial of their destiny. To the last days of the Second World War, Hitler believed that failure was the result of a lack of will. Death was, therefore, preferable to defeat.

Summary of fascist beliefs

1. The state must be totalitarian in form. Everything becomes the concern of the state.

2. The state should be driven forward by the force of people's will and their ability to act decisively.

3. Democracy is an unjustified denial of the human spirit, based on reason, and it is therefore too weak to serve the state.

4. If a state is founded on the basis of the competitive struggle of wills a superior leader is bound to emerge.

5. The state is superior to all other organisations and individuals except the leader. All activity must be directed to the purposes of the state.

6. The most effective means of creating the collective, organic state is to emphasise nationalism as a popular binding force.

7. Both state socialism and free market capitalism are detrimental. Corporativism – state-led co-operation among all sectors of industry – is preferred.

8. Leaders use irrational emotional appeals and the creation of myths to inspire the people to action.

9. Warfare is exalted as the supreme act of service to the state.

National socialism

National Socialism, or **Nazism**, as it became known, was that particular form of fascism which was developed by Adolf Hitler and his associates, notably **Alfred Rosenberg**. It should be stressed at the outset that the Nazis were fascists in every respect, but added a number of features to that philosophy to give it its distinctive German form.

A description of its principal beliefs need not, therefore, repeat the characteristics described above. The main additional features were as follows.

Racism
The German race was superior to all other races. That was, claimed Hitler, its historical legacy. Following the theories of the nineteenth-century French philosopher **Count Gobineau**, he accepted that the dynamism of the German people had been weakened over the centuries by the mixing of blood with inferior races. If Germany were to re-establish the superior culture that had existed in the Middle Ages, blood purity would have to be restored. In other words, the classic Aryan 'type' was to be recreated.

In addition to these quasi-scientific theories, Hitler was influenced by the ideas of an English adviser, **Houston Chamberlain** (no close relation to the British politician of the same name). Chamberlain suggested that the Aryan (also known as Teutonic) people had long been engaged in a struggle for supremacy against the Jews. These myths were attractive to the Nazi Party, since the theory of a Jewish conspiracy was an ideal explanation for Germany's misfortunes in the First World War and the subsequent economic slump.

These two beliefs concerning race and racial superiority led to the horrific persecution of the Jewish and other 'inferior' peoples, as well as the strict race laws that were designed to ensure racial purity. Indeed, those modern fascists who are described as 'neo-Nazis' still proclaim similar beliefs about race.

Volkism
As we have seen, fascists have always emphasised the key role of national-ism. The Nazis were to take this a stage further. For them, the basis of nationhood was predominantly race. It was blood, not merely common experiences, which truly binds a people together. Thus, mere traditional nationalism is seen as a largely rational idea. Racial purity, on the other hand, is intensely romantic and therefore irrational. It becomes – naturally for a fascist – a superior aspiration to the liberal-democratic forms of nationalism that were common in the nineteenth and twentieth centuries.

In addition to race, the term *Volk* suggested several other qualities that defined a people's superiority. Such attributes as intellect, artistic talent, honour and dynamic will were stressed. Since this *Kultur* – a specifically German term for such a collection of qualities – was indeed superior, those who displayed it were entitled to conquer other peoples and so obtain territory (*Lebensraum*) where their culture would have more room to flourish. Indeed, a people who have spilled their blood in a noble struggle to conquer land are entitled to possess it. Thus, a com-bination of race, culture and territorial claims characterises Volkism as a special form of nationalism.

Socialism To some extent, as many historians will confirm, Hitler added the term 'socialist' to his party's name purely in the hope that this would attract support from Germany's working class. However, it was not merely an exercise in opportunism. Hitler did admire the social solidarity of the working class movement and his speeches often referred to the 'heroism' of the workers. Unlike the peasantry and the middle classes, who were largely driven by self-interest, the workers could claim to be a genuinely collective social group.

The Nazis did develop notions of social equality, abhorred the vested interests of capitalism and the bourgeois state, and preferred the enthusiasm of the masses to the intellectualism of the educated middle classes. So, in very general terms, the Nazis were rudimentary socialists. Certainly, Nazism is a philosophy of collectivism and not individualism, so the term is not wholly inappropriate. It should be stressed, however, that Hitler completely rejected the scientific socialism of Marx and his followers. As we have seen above, the romantic and utopian anarchist Sorel was to prove a more attractive inspiration.

Soviet socialism

The basic principles of Stalinist thought and practice are described above in the section on communism. However, the Soviet system needs to be examined specifically in terms of the nature of totalitarian rule.

While there is no doubt that the Soviet Union under Stalin and his successors conformed largely to Friedrich's six-point scheme (see above), some additional features need to be emphasised:

- Great stress was laid upon **ideology** – in this case, Marxist-Leninism. The relentless adherence to the orthodox interpretation of the doctrines led to extreme repression of even the slightest variance from the 'official line'. Such revision was ruthlessly put down.
- The power of the party **bureaucracy** was raised to new levels under Stalin. Party membership became an essential prerequisite to opportunities and a good standard of living. Furthermore, since all official action had to be sanctioned by party officials, initiative was stifled in favour of procedural correctness.
- As Orwell observed in his allegorical work *Nineteen Eighty-Four*, the Soviet regime made a practice of manipulating history, current news and statistics to justify its own exaggerated claims. **Propaganda** was used extensively, not merely on an emotional level, as fascists practised it, but also by the publication of false production figures and inflated achievements of the party machine.
- Possibly the most important distinction that can be identified was the total control of the **economy** exercised by the state. The totalitarian economy forbade all forms of private enterprise and would not allow any free markets to operate. Even at its height the Third Reich did not attempt to wield such power.

Nationalism

Before examining the several strands of nationalism that have flourished, and that still do flourish, around the world, two terms must be defined. These are 'nation' and 'state'.

The nation

The concept of the nation is a relatively modern one, dating from the latter part of the eighteenth century. Before then peoples were differentiated by territorial boundaries and the jurisdiction of monarchs. Thus, the 'French' were deemed so because they were subjects of the French King and inhabited those territories over which he ruled. Of course, they displayed some elements of national pride and common experience and, of course, mostly spoke the same language, but there was no real sense of 'nation' that could stand above political rule.

The modern idea of what constitutes a nation, however, does suggest that people have forces which bind them other than the fact of a common ruler. Among these forces are the following:

- **Race or ethnicity** is possibly the most popular criterion for identifying a particular nation. The Chinese and the Arabs certainly place this factor above all others in expressing their national heritage.
- Common **ancestry**. In some extreme cases, even a single common ancestor can be a criterion, as is the case with the Jewish nation. This is also true among peoples who describe themselves in terms of 'clan' or 'tribe'.
- Common **historical experience** refers to an understanding that a people have been bound together over a long period of time. The English display this sentiment particularly strongly.
- **Language** might be an important factor. The Welsh stress this feature, as do the Basques.
- **Geography** can play a significant part with island nations often being created by their isolation.
- More difficult to define, but no less powerful for that, is **culture**. The Irish nationalist movement was especially affected by the cultural traditions of the Irish people, which were very distinct from those of their English masters. This had always been a significant force in Germany even before the Third Reich.
- Finally, we can identify **religion** as an important factor in some cases. Jews and Muslims are clear examples of where religion can be a key factor in national sentiment.

Of course, various combinations of these features can be identified in different forms of nationalism. What is important in all cases, however, is that the idea of 'nation' is a state of mind. It might not derive from objective historical truths and might be based on mythology, but this is not crucial. All that matters is that when a people think of themselves as a nation, they then become a potent political force.

The state

While, as we have seen, the idea of **nation** is largely a collective state of mind, the **state** is a political reality. It embodies the existence of a specific territory that is governed by political institutions. Nothing need be said about the legitimacy of this political phenomenon, since all that concerns us here is whether the state has the necessary coercive power to maintain control over its defined territory. If it does, then it is a reality. We can, therefore, say with certainty that France is a state, and so are Italy, Germany and Israel. This could not be said of Bosnia in 1995, however, since no single political entity was able to maintain control.

On the other hand, arguments might rage as to whether some nations are indeed nations as they claim. Does the term apply to the Arabs, for example, or to Catalans in Spain or Tamils in Sri Lanka? Nobody can doubt the **claim** of these peoples to be genuine national groupings, but the reality is more difficult to establish. This is not true with states. The acid test is whether some institutions do indeed exert a monopoly of coercive power within a territory.

The nation-state

It was Napoleon who first attempted to put together the relatively new ideas of nation and state into practical form. His vision of a Europe with common legal and political systems, but within which each nation should possess its own government, was futuristic but undoubtedly realistic.

It was at the end of the First World War that the notion of the nation-state came to fruition. The two great multinational empires of the nineteenth century – the Ottoman and the Austro-Hungarian – had collapsed. America's President **Woodrow Wilson** declared the principle that every nation should also become a state with its own sovereign institutions. Most of the European powers concurred and the concept of the nation-state was realised. However, the principle was to have little credence outside Europe. Colonial possessions still persisted, national groupings were denied statehood in the Middle East, and the great Russian (later Soviet) Empire still held sway over subjugated peoples.

After the Second World War, new life was given to the movement towards nation-states. The United Nations Organisation declared the principle of national self-determination, colonial empires were beginning to break up – a process almost complete by 1990 – and eventually, in the 1990s, the Soviet Empire collapsed, freeing many nationalities to struggle for full statehood.

Despite the great progress towards the achievement of independent nation-states on a universal basis, it is still true that there are nations which are not yet states. The Palestinians have nearly achieved territorial sovereignty, but groups as disparate as the Scots, Kurds and Basques are still searching for nation-statehood. It is also true that there are some states which are not nations. The clearest example is the USA. Despite the intense patriotism displayed by most Americans, they are not one nation and are unlikely to be so for many years. The ethnic and cultural backgrounds of the American peoples are so diverse that true nationhood is far off. Yet they are a state in every sense of the word. This was also true of the former states of Yugoslavia and Czechoslovakia, as their subsequent disintegration indicates.

Having established our terms, we may now investigate the different branches of nationalism that have flourished.

Liberal nationalism

In its early life, nationalism was an exclusively liberal movement. It was concerned with the problems of government by consent and the self-determination of peoples. Having removed the traditional authority of hereditary monarchies in the late eighteenth and nineteenth centuries, liberals faced the difficulty of how to define the political community. Under monarchy the question was answered by establishing the extent of the territory that was rightfully controlled by the ruler. All those living within that territory thus formed the state. The issues of consent or sense of collective identity did not normally arise except as devices used in warfare in order to inspire troops.

In the liberal age, the state could only be founded upon consent, but how were boundaries to be set? The concept of nation provided the solution. Here was a force that was able to bind a people together and justify the establishment of such a political community – the nation-state. For those nations who already enjoyed independence and unity, nationalism was not particularly important in establishing popular governments. In Britain and France, for example, the nation was well established so it was only necessary to transform the system of government for the new kind of state to come into existence. Elsewhere, however, there were greater problems to surmount before a nation-state could be formed. These difficulties were of three main types:

- Independence from a foreign power had to be established. This was particularly the case in the crumbling Austro-Hungarian Empire of the nineteenth century. Hungarians, Serbs, Slovaks, Slavs, Czechs and a host of other national groups sought to establish freedom, self-government and, in most cases, popular democracy. It was their nationalist sentiments which bound and inspired them to seek their freedom. A parallel scenario occurred after 1990 when, the Soviet Empire collapsed. Then it was the likes of Georgians, Uzbeks, Latvians, Lithuanians and Estonians who were, simultaneously, seeking to express their nationhood as well as their release from domination by a foreign power. Indeed, this liberal form of nationalism was to become one of the dominant ideologies of the 1990s.
- In the nineteenth century, there were several peoples who had become divided into a number of separate states, largely through the splitting of inheritances among unstable monarchies. The two prime examples were Germans and Italians. The unification movements in those two regions were not exclusively liberal, but a desire for full self-determination was the driving force behind movements led by Bismarck and Mazzini, the two great unifying nationalists of their age. The desire for a union of Slavic peoples was not successful in the nineteenth century, nor was the desire for the establishment of an Arab nation in the second half of the twentieth century fulfilled.
- Finally, some liberal nationalist movements have been described as 'republican' in nature. Here, the state already exists as a discrete entity, but is governed by rulers – normally hereditary – who are considered to be alien and an obstacle to the exercise of fully popular democracy. In the British Isles this is an apt description of both Irish and Scottish nationalism. Similar movements flourish in Spain (the Catalans) and in Belgium (the Flemish). One of the characteristics of this kind of nationalism is that it may not be permanent. After its main goals have been achieved, there is no particular reason for its existence. It might persist in other forms – national pride and patriotism – but not as a specifically liberal movement.

Anti-colonial nationalism

This kind of movement is very specific in its goals and therefore easier to define. Clearly, peoples who have been subjected to colonial rule might develop nationalist sentiments in order to throw off the yoke of foreign rule. The dissolution of most of the great empires after the Second World War gave rise to a large number of such movements.

However, the desire to remove colonial rule has been the one common feature of such nationalists. Thereafter, they have taken a variety of forms. These have included:

- socialist, as in Zimbabwe and Vietnam
- liberal democratic, as in Kenya and India
- religious, as in Pakistan.

It is also true that the claims to genuine nationhood have varied in strength from one case to another. Since colonial boundaries were often drawn up on an arbitrary basis, with little regard to history or ethnic and tribal divisions, newly independent territories were not natural nations. The problem of fostering national sentiment was, therefore, one that had to be continued long after the anti-colonial struggle had succeeded. Very often this post-colonial form of nationalism has led to the formation of authoritarian, one-party states. The need to create national unity among disparate peoples has eliminated the possibility of tolerating pluralist systems. That would be too much of a threat to the building of the successful nation.

Socialist nationalism

As a response to the economic imperialism experienced by many poorer developing countries, as well as by some long-established societies such as China, there have been revolutionary movements that have created a synthesis between the goals of nationalism and socialism. The ultimate objective has been the establishment of a new order to replace the economic domination of the foreign powers.

In order to move such oppressed peoples to rise up against their governments, which have been unable or unwilling to free themselves from dependence upon richer countries and multinational corporations, a sense of national identity has had to be fostered as a rallying force. It might have **appeared** in such states as Cuba, El Salvador, Nicaragua and Algeria that foreign companies were providing employment and export markets while international banks were providing credit, but socialist nationalists argued that only dependence had been created. Independent economic life, sponsored largely by state socialism, was seen as the solution to inferior status and relative poverty. Thus, there was a symbiotic, interdependent relationship between nationalism and socialism. Its most successful exponents – Fidel Castro (Cuba) and Franz Fanon (Algeria) – were able to overcome the natural suspicion of nationalist sentiment that most socialists harbour.

Conservative, right-wing nationalism

It is tempting to presume that all forms of right-wing nationalism are to be deplored on the grounds that they are associated with totalitarian regimes which have displayed aggressive, expansionist tendencies. Nazism was certainly the example *par excellence* of such a distasteful system, with Italian fascism and, more recently, Serbian nationalism in the Balkans following closely behind. This would, however, be a false picture, as there have been conservative nationalist movements that have not demonstrated such extreme forms of behaviour.

Any political system that has an overwhelming desire to unite a people who show an inclination to disintegrate is likely to attempt to foster an organic society by using nationalistic symbols and forces. By stressing the factors that give people a common identity, there is a hope that such unity will prevail. The concept of an organic society led by a powerful state has been a conservative goal throughout the developed world since the early nineteenth century. Disraeli stressed such sentiments at a time when class conflict threatened the fabric of English society in the 1870s. So, too, did Bismarck in Germany. There was certainly little that could be described as sinister about such philosophies. It might be true that right-wing conservatives suggested that nationalist sentiments sponsored by a dominant ruling class could replace popular democracy, but this did not amount to totalitarianism. At worst, it could lead to benevolent despotism.

Nevertheless, conservative nationalism of this kind has had a tendency to drift towards totalitarianism. If the demands for national identity and pride are overwhelming, they might become as powerful as any other ideology. As we have seen above, the determined imposition of ideological rule of this kind does tend to lead towards a totalitarian society. China under **Chiang Kai-shek** before the 1949 revolution, Spain under **Franco** after 1939 and Chile under **Pinochet** in the 1970s and 1980s may serve as examples. Such nationalist, semi-totalitarian, almost fascist systems have also become endemic in Africa and South America.

In the latter cases, fear of socialism has been a further motivation in the creation of an authoritarian system. Nationalism has been seen as a valuable replacement for emerging class consciousness.

Apart from the development of authoritarianism, right-wing nationalism has also manifested itself in expansionist tendencies. Yet the apparent desire of such regimes for warfare is not merely born out of dreams of conquest. Paranoia – the fear that the country is suffering a constant external threat – can also be the seedbed of nationalism. **Nasser** in Egypt in the 1950s and Iraq under **Saddam Hussein** more recently have been typical in this regard.

We can, therefore, summarise the bases of right-wing nationalism as follows:

- a pressing need to unite a disparate people
- a conservative desire to create an ordered, organic society
- the need to replace socialist sentiments with an alternative form of social consciousness
- in extreme cases, a need to underpin the development of a totalitarian system
- a desire to reinforce expansionist tendencies
- a need to inspire a people to defend the state against a perceived external threat.

Ideas related to nationalism

Patriotism

Patriotism should not be confused with nationalism. The term 'patriotism' can be defined as a strong sense of pride and attachment to a **state**: that is, a political **reality**, not a mere dream or future goal. Where a people aspire to statehood, such as Palestinians or Kurds, we should refer to their sentiments as 'nationalism', not 'patriotism'. Conversely, it is possible to feel patriotic towards one's state even if no nation exists.

This is best illustrated by reference to the USA, which is a multinational society characterised, nevertheless, by a well-developed sense of patriotism. Indeed, to a large extent these sentiments have been deliberately fostered by government in order to unite its disparate peoples. Thus, schoolchildren regularly salute the flag *en masse*, are taught sections of the Constitution and revere the office of the Presidency, even when the incumbent is personally unpopular. Similarly, we might find many Scottish nationalists who are, nevertheless, British **patriots**. In other words, they accept the existence of the British **state** and are loyal to it, but their **national** allegiance is to Scotland. The same analysis could be applied to such states as the former Soviet Union, Yugoslavia and Czechoslovakia, perhaps even South Africa.

Chauvinism

Where patriotism becomes extremely exaggerated, the term 'chauvinism' can be applied. There are overtones of superiority attached to chauvinism, especially where patriotism becomes associated with nationalism, or even racism. The manifestations of chauvinism include sporting fanaticism, racial prejudice and exaggerated attachment to symbols such as patriotic songs and flags. Where the symbolism becomes overwhelming, the term 'jingoism' applies. Very often personality cult and heavy satirical criticism of foreigners may occur. Mao Tse-tung, China's great communist leader, was able to inspire many millions of his people to violent action by use of jingoism, largely directed at the USA and the UK.

Racialism and racism

These two terms are often treated as interchangeable and clearly they are closely related, both being concerned with racial issues. However, we can distinguish between the two.

<u>Racialism</u>   This refers to a number of scientific or quasi-scientific theories about racial or ethnic differences between peoples. The theories presume that racial differences are significant in terms of human behaviour and/or characteristics. If racial origin does indeed influence behaviour in any meaningful way, it follows that it becomes relevant to political theory. Racialism can, therefore, be defined as any political philosophy that bases some or all of its principles upon racial differences.

Racialism existed in possibly its purest form in the white-dominated regime that governed South Africa for over 30 years until it was deposed in 1994. Its policy of **apartheid** (literally 'separateness') actually proposed that different racial groups could not exist together in the same society. The culture, religion and abilities of different races were seen as eternally different, so that peaceful co-existence would prove impossible. It became a by-product of this belief that, if separate states could not be established, the 'superior' white race should deny the other ethnic groups full citizenship and force them to live in separate areas.

While the white South Africans were unable to establish fully separate, racially segregated states, Hitler in Germany certainly did see such an aspiration as a realistic goal. It was, indeed, a central feature of Nazi philosophy and played a large part in most other fascist regimes. There are many historical examples of states or civilisations that have considered themselves to be of a superior race. The ancient Greek and traditional Chinese Empires, for example, certainly took the view that all other peoples were 'barbarians'.

There are also some examples of racialist thinking that have been of a more benign character. Moderate Zionism, for example, bases the existence of the state of Israel upon ethnic/religious origin. Similarly, some Arab regimes have attempted to achieve a degree of racial exclusivity. Saudi Arabia and other Arabian Gulf states demonstrate such a tendency. Of course, all these examples also have their militant wings.

<u>Racism</u>   This represents more an emotional response to race than a political one. Certainly, racists have a highly developed sense of racial superiority and a disdain for what they perceive to be inferior races. Racism's most important manifestation is, as we have seen above, a desire for racial exclusivity, and it is normally the case that racists wish to rid their native country of foreigners. More commonly, however, racism shows itself in the form of prejudice, sometimes expressed violently, and systematic intimidation. It is also important to stress that, while racism is an utterly irrational mode of thinking (racists, for example, tend to place great store by skin colour alone), racialism does at least claim some scientific basis, however tenuous it may be.

Feminism

Origins   Despite the legendary existence of matriarchal (female-dominated) societies such as the warrior race of women known as 'Amazons', ideas concerning female equality did not emerge until the seventeenth century. The English 'diggers', for example, a quasi-communist movement that reached its height in the 1640s, did include some supporters of improved property and political rights for women. After that, only minor evidence of early feminist ideas can be found until the period of the French Revolution. Some, at that time, did argue that equal rights should be extended to women. In the same period in England, Mary Wollstonecraft (the wife of William Godwin, one of the first anarchist philosophers, and mother of Mary Shelley, the novelist who created the character Frankenstein) was campaigning for women's rights, notably for equal opportunities to obtain a good education and to pursue meaningful careers. The great liberal thinker John Stuart Mill, together with his wife, led a campaign to achieve property rights for married women. His work *The Subjugation of Women* (1869) was an immediate precursor of the **Married Women's Property Act**, passed in the following year. This Act gave married women the right, for the first time, to own their own property. It was a significant step in freeing women (at least wealthier middle-class women) from financial reliance upon men.

However, it was the campaigns for women's suffrage – voting rights – that brought the question of the status of women to the fore in political circles. The suffrage movement gained momentum during the 1890s and the early twentieth century, but it was not until 1918 in Britain, 1920 in the USA, that votes for women were guaranteed. Elsewhere, in the fields of education, career opportunities, family law and finance, progress was slow. Indeed, it has been suggested that the achievement of women's suffrage actually set back the cause of women's rights. It had been assumed that with votes would come representation. More women in Parliament would, the campaigners believed, result in political progress towards further rights and opportunities. As a result of this confidence, the movement was largely disbanded, but the expected advances in the women's cause did not arrive. Few women entered parliamentary politics, and women did not use their votes to further their own interests, but tended to persist with the same class-based allegiances to parties as men.

During and between the two world wars, although relatively little legislative progress was made, changes were taking place that were to transform attitudes towards women irrevocably. Among them were the following:

• Many women worked during the wars, often in responsible jobs formerly monopolised by men.
• The spread of knowledge and increased practice of family planning among women enabled them to take more control over their own lives and to limit the burden of childbearing.
• A great deal of literature was increasing public awareness of the inferior status of women. The liberally inspired 'Bloomsbury Group' of writers and artists and the novelist D.H. Lawrence were prominent examples.
• Some information about the improved status of women in the Soviet Union was filtering into the West. News of high numbers of female undergraduates, managers, workers, party officials and even officers in the armed forces inspired many middle-class intellectuals.

Nevertheless, the women's movement remained both small and almost exclusively middle class until the 1960s. It was at that time that modern, more radical forms of feminism were to emerge.

> 'The primary goal [of feminism] is women gaining power in order to eliminate patriarchy and create a more humane society.'
>
> Charlotte Bunch, *Class and Feminism*, 1974

Feminism and the New Left

During the 1960s a new political movement emerged in Europe and the USA which was to become known as the 'New Left'. It was partly Marxist-inspired, but was also a reaction not only to post-industrial capitalism, but also to the totalitarian, state-controlled socialism that had been established in eastern Europe. This was a more individualistic, anti-state group of philosophies, closer to anarchism than Marxism and with a more pluralist outlook upon modern society. Instead of viewing society from the point of view of economic class distinctions, New Left thinkers were concerned with the position of the many minority groups who appeared to be alienated from the dominant culture.

The ruling culture, argued the New Left, was dominated by white, middle-class, male, heterosexual society. Thus, the poor members of ethnic minorities, gays and women were alienated from such a culture. It was as part of this new political movement that modern radical forms of feminism came into existence. At the same time, interest was aroused in more liberal branches of the women's movement. Thus, as the 1960s came to a close, it was clear that two developments were taking place. First, there was a dramatic increase in interest in issues concerned with women. Second, the movement itself was fragmented into a number of different philosophies. We may now examine these various strands of feminism.

Liberal feminism

In common with all other philosophies that are based upon liberal principles, this branch of feminism is limited in its scope. Such feminists recognise that there are aspects of life which are not their concern. In other words, there is a clear distinction between public and private spheres. Thus, for example, individual sexual orientation, the structure of the family, and sexual and romantic relationships between individuals are the private concern of those involved and no one else. However, where there is systematic discrimination against women in the workplace or in education, or if women are portrayed as inferior, liberal feminists in any medium claim the right to campaign for reform.

Similarly, we can say that liberal feminism is a reforming but not a revolutionary movement. There is no desire to transform the structure of society in order to realise women's goals. Rather, there are specific aspects of society that are seen to require reform. The kind of reforms that are proposed are suggested by the following liberal goals:

- Women should enjoy absolutely equal legal and political rights. This objective had been virtually completely achieved in the UK by 1990.
- There should be equal opportunity for girls in education. This implies that girls should have equal access with boys to the whole school curriculum. In addition, there is a need to change attitudes among teachers and parents who might have lower expectations of girls.
- There should also be equal opportunities for women in virtually all forms of occupation. In recruitment and promotion practices, women should be given equal treatment.
- The principle of equal pay for equal work should be established. The European Union had developed laws to provide for this by 1992.
- The state should provide pre-school education for children to enable women with young children to take up paid employment should they so desire.
- Financial help should be offered to single parents so that they may choose either to take up employment or to concentrate on child rearing.
- Abortion should be available on demand.
- References in the media and the arts which overtly encourage attitudes suggesting male superiority should be outlawed.
- More women should be encouraged and enabled to enter active politics.

The above list is not exhaustive, but it summarises the broad objectives of liberal feminism. However, one further aspiration must be emphasised. Betty Friedan, whose 1963 book *The Feminine Mystique* was a key early work of authority for feminists, suggested that women themselves must liberate their own minds. Her original contribution to feminist thought was to maintain that the inferior status of women was not solely due to men's desire to dominate society. Rather, she suggested, the attitude of women towards themselves has caused them to be regarded as inferior. The proposed remedy – that women should demand the right to pursue occupations outside the home – has been a central feature of liberal feminism ever since.

Radical feminism

Although Friedan's work was a crucial element in the early years of the modern women's movement, it was to be overtaken by considerably more radical writings after 1970. In that year, two books were published that together were to transform feminism completely. These were *The Dialectic of Sex* by Shulamith Firestone and *Sexual Politics* by Kate Millett.

Firestone, as the title of her book suggests, adapted Marx's dialectic approach to historical development, but substituted sexual conflict for class conflict as the crucial driving force behind social change. Similarly, while Marx had seen economics as the basis of all societies, Firestone identified the nature of male–female relations as the most significant characteristic of any community.

Millett focused upon sexual relations between men and women as the key factor in patriarchal, or male-dominated, society. She defined such relations as 'political' in nature and claimed that, for this reason, they were the root cause of the conflict between the sexes. For her, domination began not in school, the workplace or the kitchen, but in the conjugal bed.

These two extraordinarily radical feminist tracts demonstrate the two features of this kind of feminism which distinguish it from the liberal variety:

- Patriarchy is seen as a complete **system** of domination of women by men. It pervades all aspects of life. It is not, as liberals suggested, one undesirable aspect of society, but its whole basis.
- There is nothing in society that is not the concern of feminist politics. Even the most private aspects of sexual relations are relevant and, indeed, may form the very basis of female oppression.

It follows from this that radical feminism is a revolutionary philosophy. This does not necessarily mean that there is likely to be a violent uprising by women against their male masters. Instead, it suggests that such feminists are seeking a complete transformation of existing, patriarchal society.

Just as radical feminism's critiques of patriarchal society are fundamental, so too are the solutions that have been proposed. The principal examples are described below.

Radical reform These measures include all the liberal proposals shown above, but go considerably further. For example, all 'sexist' (meaning the display of attitudes demeaning to women or which express male domination) pornography, or sexist portrayals of women in theatre, films, literature and on television are to be outlawed. The militant antipornography campaigner, **Andrea Dworkin**, sees sexist portrayals of women as not merely distasteful, but actually violent, opposed to equal rights and exploitative. Similarly, Millett attacks the way in which women have been encouraged by men to appear feminine and 'sexy', thus accepting inferior status. It was this view that led to notorious 'bra burning' episodes and a tendency for feminists to dress in an asexual manner.

These attacks on attitudes that express male superiority have largely given rise to what is now known as 'political correctness'. Here, the use of language is seen as crucial, since it is language that conveys so many of our cultural attitudes and transmits them from one generation to the next. Germaine Greer, in *The Female Eunuch*, referred to the importance of cultural transmitters as long ago as 1972. For the radical feminist reformer then, all sexist allusions in the written and spoken word should be eliminated.

Separation Those who are less optimistic about the chances of destroying patriarchal society have suggested that women must set up their own social groupings, from which men are excluded. In this way, female consciousness can be heightened and solutions to women's problems found without having to use institutions that are patriarchal.

Women's communes have been set up, the most celebrated of which in the UK joined the permanent resident protest against the siting of American Cruise missiles at Greenham Common. So too have consciousness-raising groups, refuges for women suffering physical abuse by male partners and a variety of other community initiatives.

Lesbianism For those feminists who stress the exploitative nature of heterosexual relations, believing them to be intrinsically characterised by male domination, the only resort has been to encourage lesbianism as a means of freeing women from the most basic aspects of patriarchy. This has also been associated with the notion of separateness described above.

There is an assumption that lesbian relations are not exploitative and are, therefore, the most natural form of human bonding. It might be difficult to accept that this is a call for heterosexual women to **become** lesbians even when their sexual orientation points elsewhere, but the most radical of feminists are suggesting just that.

Matriarchy In a parallel of Marx's hopes that the oppressed working class would one day rise up and become the masters of the class that formerly oppressed them, some feminists wish to see women replace men in dominant social roles. Underlying this aim is an assumption that women are different from men and are, indeed, superior.

Feminists claim that the nature of this superiority lies to some extent in biological differences and that women's genetic attributes that are designed to aid child-rearing also give rise to natural humanity, goodness and a lack of aggression. Feminists criticise men's aggressiveness and militarism, blaming them for many of the world's social ills. Women do not normally possess such characteristics, they argue. A matriarchal world, therefore, is likely to be peaceful and contain true social justice.

Marxist or socialist feminism

This branch of feminism is inspired to some extent by Marxism, but it is not necessarily as militant, so it can take the milder title 'socialist'. In either case, it is a philosophy which suggests that the inferior position of women is based largely upon economic factors. Marx's close collaborator, Friedrich Engels, had suggested such an idea in the 1880s and continues to provide inspiration for women on the left of politics.

This economic branch of the feminist movement propounds the following ideas:

- The traditional nuclear family is, in itself, a repressive institution. Women are forced to provide a cheap source of labour in child-rearing and care of the home. Men are the beneficiaries in the home as they are freed from this burden at relatively little financial cost. Juliet Mitchell in *Women's Estate* (1971) drew attention to these domestic aspects of women's exploitation at a time when radical feminists were concentrating on what were considered 'big' issues, such as employment opportunities and education. She maintained that exploitation begins in the home.
- A more Marxist-led account of economic exploitation considers that women have been used in capitalist systems to provide a cheap source of labour. Marx had pointed out that a labour surplus was essential under capitalism to ensure that there would never be labour shortages which might cause wages to rise and profits to fall. Thus, an army of unskilled women waiting to step into vacancies would keep wages down.
- It is noted that much of the large accumulation of private property has been monopolised by men. This in turn deprives women of that property and, therefore, reinforces economic inequality for women. The answer is seen as the redistribution of that property without any question of preferences between the genders.

Broadly, therefore, the Marxist and socialist feminists believe that a complete transformation of society along socialist lines is required to liberate women. Like radical feminism, it is a 'revolutionary' movement.

Summary of feminist beliefs		
Liberal feminism	**Radical feminism**	**Socialist/Marxist feminism**
• Women must enjoy equal legal and political rights. • There should be equal opportunities for women. • Overtly sexist attitudes should be discouraged. • Women should have wide choice as to how they lead their lives. • There should be equal economic rights for women. • There should be a more female-led focus on such issues as rape, abortion, pornography and violence in the home.	• Patriarchy is a complete system affecting all aspects of society. • Even private sexual relations are political in nature. • There must be a complete transformation of society to achieve feminist aims. • Radical measures are required to rid institutions, the language, the arts and culture generally of sexist attitudes. • Women should choose to set up a separate culture and/or develop purely lesbian sexual relationships to free themselves from male domination. • Society should be matriarchal, which would result in it being more humane, peaceful and just.	• The oppression of women is fundamentally economic in nature. • The traditional family is itself an oppressive and exploitative economic institution. • Women are used by capitalism as a cheap source of labour to be exploited for greater profit. • Private property is largely owned and controlled by men, thus depriving women of economic opportunities. • Only the creation of a socialist society will liberate women.

Environmentalism

Introduction   Just as socialism or feminism can be conveniently divided into broadly liberal and radical wings, so too can two distinct forms of environmentalism be identified. The liberal form is reformist, but not revolutionary. It proposes important changes in the way we treat the natural environment and the living things within it, but stops short of suggesting that we need radical changes to the nature of our society. Radical environmentalists, also known as **ecologists**, on the other hand, insist that a far-reaching transformation in our thinking and way of life is essential if we are to survive as a species.

Both movements, however, have their origins in the New Left movement of the 1960s, to which we alluded in the section on feminism above. As we have seen, the dominant theme of the New Left was **alienation**. In the case of the environmental or 'Green' movement, it was alienation from our natural environment which was of concern. All Greens, radical and liberal, believe that we are in danger of losing sight of the fact that man as a species is intricately connected with the living and physical world. If we lose this perspective – become alienated from the natural earth – serious or irreparable damage will be done to human society.

Liberal environmentalism

It is within this philosophy that most of the groups which form the broad Green movement operate. They are, for example, European Green Parties, Friends of the Earth, Greenpeace and The Council for the Protection of Rural England. Each tends to concentrate upon a relatively limited range of environmental issues, but all are essentially liberal in nature. The kind of issues concerned are as follows:

- Protection for the atmosphere through controls on air pollution: in particular, those gases and chemicals that damage the ozone layer, cause the 'greenhouse effect' of global warming, and are responsible for a variety of human, animal and plant health damage.
- Control over industrial, transport and residential development in order to protect the rural environment.
- The elimination of all forms of water pollution, affecting the sea, lakes and rivers.
- Protection for endangered species of plant and animal life.
- Controls on the depletion of the world's natural resources, including fossil fuels, forests, fish and wild animals, and rare minerals. This is known as the theory of 'sustainable growth': that is, that economic progress should be pursued only if it is not at the expense of our natural resources.
- Decent treatment for wild, farm and domestic animals.
- A halt to the spread of economic development that endangers the traditional culture of primitive communities such as South American, Arctic and African tribal peoples.

All of these objectives, the less radical environmentalists argue, could be achieved within existing economic, social and political structures. Changes in policy and practice are needed, but this does not necessarily involve fundamental changes. The groups involved in seeking to bring about such reform have adopted a variety of tactics to achieve their goals, including lobbying politicians, publicity campaigns, civil disobedience, putting up candidates for election to representative institutions and placing representatives on administrative bodies that are concerned with environmental protection. However, none of these methods can be described as especially radical. It is **ecologism** that engages in such fundamental thought and practice.

Radical environmentalism or ecologism

At the heart of this movement lies the concept of **Gaia**, developed largely by the radical thinker James Lovelock in 1972. This 'hypothesis', as he titled it, suggests that the earth is one single organic whole. In short, it is a complete living thing. Everything, both living and inanimate, is interdependent. This 'biosphere', as it is also called, is in desperate need of protection and it is man's duty to provide that.

Arising out of the Gaia hypothesis is the startling suggestion that human beings are not the centre of this biosphere called earth, but merely one part of it. We therefore have no special rights to treat the earth as if it exists solely for our own benefit. Jonathon Porritt describes the belief that human beings are pre-eminent as 'anthropocentrism' and he rejects it outright.

Underpinning the hypothesis stands a new kind of physical science, a prominent adherent of which was **Fritjof Capra**. Instead of treating physical phenomena as separate entities, Capra and his followers saw everything in nature as connected and interdependent. If anything happens to one part, there will be some effect on all the other parts, however disconnected they might appear to be. It follows from this that we cannot predict the effects of any change to any single part of the earth (sometimes this is described as 'chaos theory', according to which phenomena can occur without any possibility of adequate explanation or prediction). Traditional physical science had suggested that all changing phenomena could be explained. The environmental application of Capra's ideas lies in the fear that human activity which affects the natural environment is unpredictable in its results. We are, in short, interfering with nature without any idea of the ultimate effects of our actions.

Whether or not we accept the Gaia hypothesis, the implications are clear. There must be a fundamental change in our thinking about the way in which we interact with the earth. This, in turn, will involve us in a deep rethinking about the way we organise society. The principal aims and beliefs of radical environmentalism are as follows:

- Much of the cause of environmental damage lies with capitalism. Its constant need for economic growth gives rise to a reckless exploitation of the natural environment. Only if capitalism is abolished, probably to be replaced by socialism, can this relentless desire for economic growth be checked. Thus, sustainable growth does not go far enough. The concept of growth itself must be attacked.
- With regard to the critique of the capitalist obsession with growth, the radicals wish to put an end to the assumption that there will always be a steady increase in prosperity. Indeed, it is noted that much prosperity is achieved at the expense not only of the natural environment, but also of the poorer sectors of the world's population.
- The earth's resources may only be exploited in a sustainable manner: that is, people should not use any natural resources unless they can replace them.
- Industrialisation should be reduced or even abolished. This presupposes a return to an simpler way of life and, in this regard, ecologism can be equated with some forms of anarcho-communism.
- Since humans are not considered to have higher status than any other living organism, we must show respect for all other living things.
- The exploitation of poor Third World countries is not only an economic evil, but also an example of the abuse of the planet's natural ecology. Susan George, the celebrated modern campaigner for Third World protection, notes how the compulsion of developing countries to grow cash crops for export instead of natural local products disturbs the natural relationship between people and their environment.

Of course, the radical environmentalists share virtually all the goals of the liberals, but their views are considerably more philosophical and even spiritual. In many ways, ecologism is the most fundamental of all political ideologies.

For exam questions relevant to this unit, see page 558.

Introduction

Those political issues that concern the operation of government and the Constitution themselves are to be found in other units of this book, as follows:

This unit, however, is concerned with political issues of an economic and social nature: in other words, those issues that affect the ways in which society itself operates. Not all recent political concerns can be covered in a book of this scale. Those which are described, therefore, are the principal issues that have shaped British society and politics in general. They also reflect the main topics that are to be found in current examination syllabuses.

Economic policy

Constraints Before reviewing the way in which economic policy has been conducted in the modern era, it is important to understand the nature of the constraints that have been experienced by decision-makers. These are as follows:

- The British economy is increasingly integrated with that of the European Union as a whole and, in the longer term, with the global economy. This means that decisions have to be taken with regard to decisions made elsewhere. It is also the case that the British economy is affected, for good or ill, by international cycles of activity. The world recession of the late 1980s is an example. The decline in world trade which resulted from this meant that a slump in the UK's economy was inevitable.
- Many markets are now truly global. The markets for currencies, for business finance, for commodities and for shares operate on a world-wide basis. Movements in interest rates, raw material prices and exchange rates are largely out of the control of the Government.
- Much of the economy lies in the hands of multinational corporations such as Ford, Nissan, Vodafone, Sony and Siemens. Some of these companies are British, of course, but most are foreign-based. The Government must, therefore, take into account the fact that the commercial decisions which such companies make will be based on world, not just British, conditions.

- Many decisions have literally been taken out of the hands of the national Government and transferred to the European Union. Issues concerning trade, agriculture, consumer protection, employment law and the environment are dealt with by the Commission and the Council of Ministers. British ministers and officials have an input, but they must take into account the actions and policies of our European partners. To a lesser extent, the UK's external economic policy is also determined in consultation with such bodies as the International Monetary Fund, the World Bank and the World Trade Organisation.

These constraints mean that politicians can never truthfully claim that they are able to control the economy fully. Conversely, their critics are also mistaken if they argue that economic ills are the full responsibility of the government of the day.

Having set the scene, we may now review economic policy since 1945. It is useful to divide the period into four sections. They are 1945–65, 1965–79, 1979–97 and 1997 to the present.

1945–65   The twenty years after the Second World War were characterised by the following features:

- It was known as the era of **consensus**. The two main parties agreed on four principal objectives of economic policy: the maintenance of full employment, low inflation, balance of payments stability and steady economic growth (expected to be about 2–4 per cent per annum).
- There was also general agreement on how these aims were to be realised. The basis of policy was known as **Keynesian demand management**. When the economy was in danger of growing too quickly, bringing the danger of inflation, taxes were raised and government expenditure was reduced. This took spending power out of the economy and was known as deflationary policy. Conversely, when the economy slowed down and unemployment grew, the opposite measures were adopted. Otherwise, few controls were needed.
- It was indeed a period of steady growth and stability in prices and unemployment. However, the British economy performed poorly compared to most of western Europe, the USA and Japan. British policy has been described, therefore, as the **management of economic decline**.
- The UK relinquished most of its **colonial possessions** in this period. The result was more difficult trading conditions and the decline of traditional markets and sources of cheap raw materials.
- After the Labour Government of 1945–51 had brought many large industries, such as coal, steel, railways and energy, into public ownership, it was accepted that the UK should operate a **mixed economy**. Roughly half the economy came under public ownership, so the state became a major economic force in its own right.
- There was a loose political agreement that **class divisions** – the gap in prosperity between rich and poor – should be narrowed. This was to be achieved through the tax and welfare systems. Of course, the Labour Party laid more stress on this objective, but the Conservatives also understood that they had to be seen as a party which supported the interests of all classes.

1965–79 It was during this time that the post-war economic consensus broke down. The slow, steady and stable progress in the economy ceased. In its place, worryingly large fluctuations in economic activity began to appear. Short bursts of rapid growth – for example, in the mid-1960s and mid-1970s – were interspersed with regular crises. The problems were invariably bouts of inflation or problems with the balance of payments. As described above, the UK's trade position weakened in this period. The pound sterling itself became unstable and was the subject of much speculative buying and selling. Both main parties found themselves in power at this time, but neither seemed able to cure the instability.

The period began with a small economic boom, but this only resulted in rising inflation and a worsening balance of payments crisis. The UK was consistently importing more than it was exporting. The value of sterling was clearly too high and British exports were therefore over-priced. The Labour Government of the day, led by Harold Wilson, was forced to adopt drastic measures. The value of sterling was devalued by 14 per cent in 1967 and a system known as **prices and incomes policy** was introduced.

Prices and incomes policies were **direct** measures designed to control the rise in wages and product prices, which seemed to be out of control. Keynesian management was not abandoned, but it was not direct enough to deal with serious inflation. Both parties, when in government, pursued the new direct methods right up until 1978. A variety of systems were adopted, such as wage freezes, price controls, and legislation to limit wages and other forms of income. Edward Heath, Prime Minister between 1970 and 1974, did attempt a short experiment to escape from this mixture of Keynesian demand management and direct controls over wages and prices during 1970–1. He effectively abandoned most controls over the economy in the hope that free market forces would solve the problems. However, this resulted in failure.

By the middle of 1971, the British economy seemed to be out of control. Inflation was rising alarmingly and many British businesses were struggling to survive. Heath lost his nerve and reversed policy. After the 'U-Turn' of 1971, a complete freeze on wage rises, together with stringent regulation of prices, was introduced. Heath also stepped in to support failing industries with government aid. Two large companies – Rolls-Royce and Upper Clyde Shipbuilders – were even nationalised, something that no Conservative Government had ever before contemplated!

The Labour Government that followed in 1974 fared little better. Having inherited record inflation levels – reaching 22 per cent in 1975 – it struggled with rebellious trade unions and inefficient industries to try to restore stability. By 1978–9, however, it became clear that a new economic phenomenon was emerging. This was the spectre of inflation **combined with** rising unemployment, sometimes known as **stagflation**. Economists had believed that this was an impossible combination, but no longer. Defeat for the failing Labour Government in 1979 was therefore inevitable. But defeat not only brought in a new government under Margaret Thatcher; it also heralded in a new era of economic policy.

Before describing the Thatcher era, the preceding period of 1965–79 can be summarised:

- It was known as the period of **stop–go**. The economy lurched from booms to slumps in a regular cycle. Government could not allow rapid growth because the economy was highly prone to inflation in such circumstances. But whenever the Government put the brakes on to avoid inflation, the economy ground to a halt and unemployment mounted. There seemed no answer to the problem of maintaining steady growth.
- The policies of the main parties rarely differed greatly. However, political divisions over economic policy became increasingly bitter. **Adversarial politics** intensified and the economy became the battleground.
- Some economists have argued that the UK's declining economic fortunes were the result of failure to join the **European Community** during its early development. By the time the UK joined in 1973, the damage had been done, it has been argued.
- The desire of successive governments to intervene in the economy to an increasing degree had led, during the period, to steady rises in levels of **taxation and public expenditure**.
- The UK **failed to modernise** its industry at this time. Investment levels remained low and the nationalised industries proved to be undynamic and slow to adapt.
- It was a period of growing **industrial unrest**. The constant attempts by government to bring wages under control helped to make trade unions ever more militant. Strikes and other forms of industrial unrest became commonplace. Managements proved unable to deal with the deteriorating state of industrial relations. They too were finding it difficult to adapt to new conditions. This, together with the lack of development in industry described above, led to the UK becoming less and less competitive in world markets.

By 1979, therefore, when Labour lost power following the 'Winter of Discontent' – several months of major strikes by public sector workers – the economic prospects looked bleak. At this point, Margaret Thatcher appeared on the scene. Thus began over a decade of radical reforms in the nature of the British economy and its management by government.

1979–97

Neo-liberalism

It took Margaret Thatcher three years to establish herself sufficiently in power to begin the task of turning the economy round. Until 1982 she faced alarming rises in both unemployment and inflation, political unpopularity and opposition to her ideas from a substantial portion of her party. Thatcher had radical ideas and remembered the lesson of Edward Heath during 1970–1, in whose government she had served in a minor capacity. Heath had attempted radical change, but had lost his nerve before the changes had had time to work. She would not make the same mistake. At this time, the radical reformers such as Keith Joseph, her close adviser, were known as 'drys'. Their opponents in the Conservative Party, who were afraid of the new ideas and opposed them, were known as 'wets'. By 1982 most of the 'wets' had been dismissed from government. The rest formed a small, weak minority. Thatcher was ready to effect her reforms.

The new policies were a combination of three main strands of economic thought. Together, they may be described as **neo-liberalism**. This was a modern version of the dominant liberal economic ideas of the nineteenth century. Its main components are summarised in the following chart.

Neo-liberal economic ideas	
• Monetarism	• A belief that inflation had one basic cause – too much money in circulation. Money supply represents spending power. If there is too much spending power in the economy, prices will be forced up. All other apparent causes of inflation were fuelled by too much money supply. It therefore followed that the main government policy should be to control money supply. Once inflation was controlled, it was argued, general economic stability would follow.
• Supply-side	• Keynesian policies involved attempts to manipulate the total level of **demand** in the economy: that is, the spending of government, firms and households. Supply-side economics, on the other hand, suggests that it is vital to ensure that the **production** or **supply** side of the economy is efficient and flexible enough to deal with market conditions. In order to achieve the objectives of supply-side economics, the measures shown below are normally adopted.
• Laissez-faire	• Too much government interference was thought to stifle economic activity and inhibit innovation. In particular, high taxation, especially on personal incomes and business profits, was seen as a disincentive to wealth creation. Excessive regulation was also a barrier to growth. The state should interfere as little as possible in industry and commerce. Nationalisation was, therefore, the greatest evil, but aid or subsidies to ailing private firms were also opposed.
• Free markets	• The operation of free markets was believed to be the most effective way of restoring efficiency and of distributing income and wealth to the more deserving sections of society. In particular, neo-liberals hoped to restore freedom, with little or no state interference, in labour, product and financial markets.

These strands were interconnected to form a cohesive, single economic philosophy. From 1982, for the next ten years, they gradually captured the centre ground of politics and came to form a new consensus in economic thought. The chart below shows how Conservative governments under Thatcher and Major (who took over in 1990) put the new ideas into practice. It also indicates the degree to which success was achieved.

Neo-liberal policies in the 1980s and 1990s		
Policy	**Implementation**	**Effectiveness**
• Monetarism	• Keynesian policies were largely abandoned. • Public borrowing was to be brought under control to reduce money supply. • British industry was subjected to a high value of sterling to force it to be more efficient.	• Money supply was never brought under control. Public expenditure also rose in both the early 1980s and the early 1990s. • British industry did gradually become more efficient.
• Laissez-faire	• Most of the nationalised industries were privatised. • Declining industries were allowed to decline, releasing resources to growing industries. • Income and business taxes were reduced. • Regulation of the financial markets was drastically reduced.	• Privatisation proved largely successful and popular. • The British economy began to adapt to decline in manufacturing but growth in the service sector. • Financial markets in the City of London grew enormously and became more dynamic.
• Free markets	• The influence and legal freedom of trade unions was reduced to open up labour markets to competition. . • Financial markets were deregulated. This was known as the 'Big Bang'. • Small businesses were encouraged to increase competition. • Subsidies to industry were reduced, so businesses were forced to become efficient or go under.	• Labour markets were opened up. Wage costs in Britain were brought under control. Unions ceased to inhibit technological progress. Industrial relations settled down and strikes became increasingly rare. • The City of London grew and began to dominate world financial markets. • Industry did slowly begin to compete more successfully in world markets.

The Labour reaction The story of how the Labour Party reacted to these changes represents the change from 'Old' to 'New' Labour. Until the late 1980s, the Labour Party opposed virtually all the economic reforms. Dominated by left-wingers such as Michael Foot (Labour's leader from 1979 to 1984), Tony Benn and miners' leader Arthur Scargill, the party raised fundamental, ideological objections to neo-liberalism. Their main criticisms were as follows:

• Privatisation of large industries had changed their operation. They were now run for profit rather than in the wider interests of the public.
• The deregulation of markets meant that the divide between rich and poor was growing. The business classes, in other words, profited from free markets, but workers suffered from lower wages.

- The reduction in trade union power led to worsening working conditions, relatively lower wages and the loss of basic rights for workers.
- The decline in traditional industries when state support was withdrawn led to unemployment and hardship in poorer areas where such industries were concentrated. This was particularly noticeable in those areas specialising in coal, steel, shipbuilding and textiles.
- Growing inequality also manifested itself in a disparity between the wealthy south and the rest of the country. This was known as the 'North–South Divide'.
- Reductions in public expenditure to finance tax cuts led to declining standards in public services such as health and education.

But the reality of two heavy election defeats in 1983 and 1987, and the UK's economic recovery, demoralised the Labour left-wingers and brought to the fore new leaders who wished to accept the reforms and to enter a new consensus. Neil Kinnock, who took over the Labour leadership in 1984, his successors John Smith and Tony Blair, together with Roy Hattersley, Gordon Brown and Peter Mandelson, began to change the culture of the Labour Party.

The symbolic struggle within Labour concerned **Clause IV** of the party's constitution. Clause IV was an aim that the party had pursued since its foundation, to bring all main industries under public ownership. It was not until the mid-1990s that Tony Blair succeeded in removing the clause, by which time New Labour had already been born.

Meanwhile the Conservatives, under John Major after 1990, began to lose ground. As we have seen above, the British economy is somewhat at the mercy of global circumstances. The world recession of the late 1980s and early 1990s led to a slump at home. But it was an incident in September 1992, known as '**Black Wednesday**', which spelled the effective end of Conservative ascendancy.

In 1990 a reluctant Margaret Thatcher had taken the UK into the European **Exchange Rate Mechanism** (ERM). The ERM was a system of fixed exchange rates among all leading European currencies. Membership promised the UK currency stability after decades of suffering from a weak currency. Unfortunately, the exchange rate at which sterling entered the system was relatively high. For monetarists this did not present a problem. A high-valued currency makes exports expensive and thus forces domestic industry to become more efficient in order to compete internationally. But speculators believed that sterling was drastically overvalued and they began to sell the currency on the currency markets. In September 1992 selling of sterling throughout the world escalated. The system could not stand the strain, but the Government, particularly Chancellor Norman Lamont, refused to give in and leave the ERM. After weeks of indecision during which sterling was severely damaged, the UK at last pulled out.

This represented a humiliation for the Government and destroyed public confidence in its ability to run the economy effectively. Ironically, sterling fell dramatically in value after the UK left the ERM. Exports were suddenly cheaper and the British economy picked up. Indeed, the UK emerged from the world recession in better economic health than most of its competitors. The reforms of the 1980s seemed to have worked. But the Conservatives were not benefiting from the success and their own popularity slumped. Neo-liberal policies remained popular, but there were doubts about whether the Conservatives could run the economy. At the same time, there were growing concerns that inequality in incomes was growing and that public services were suffering. The situation was fertile ground for the reformers in New Labour and they swept to victory in 1997.

New Labour after 1997

New Labour's philosophical position is described in some depth in Unit 3. However, it is useful here to review the areas of neo-liberal economic policy that Labour accepted and was willing to develop further, together with the modifications and reversals that they have been committed to make. These are summarised in the following chart.

New Labour and neo-liberalism	
Consensus policies	**Reversals and modifications**
1. Privatisation is accepted. No industries have been renationalised and more privatisation is planned, including air traffic control.	1. Where full privatisation is not acceptable, public–private sector partnerships are proposed with joint funding and operation. London Underground is an example.
2. The power and privileges of trade unions have not been restored and labour markets remain flexible.	2. The minimum wage was introduced to ensure that no workers suffer from extremely low pay as a result of free labour markets and weak unions.
3. Personal and business taxes remain low and are being further reduced. Special arrangements have been made to help small and newly established businesses.	3. Indirect taxes on expenditure, e.g. on petrol, insurance and energy, have been increased in order to fund increased expenditure on public services.
4. Labour follows the monetarist policy of maintaining a government balanced budget or a surplus. Government borrowing is either unnecessary or minimised, and is justified only if it is used for investment. This is the 'Golden Rule'. By being cautious on public spending, excessive money supply is avoided.	4. Labour follows the Conservative policy of using the level of interest rates to control spending and therefore inflation. However, control over interest rates was transferred to an independent committee of the Bank of England. This avoids the possibility of ministers manipulating interest rates for the purposes of their own popularity.
5. Labour accepts that low taxes are an incentive for economic growth, but believes that this increases the danger of greater inequality in incomes.	5. New welfare policies have been introduced to prevent working families from falling into poverty.
6. Failing industries are rarely to be bailed out with government subsidies.	6. Training arrangements are encouraged to enable workers to gain skills and move from declining to growing industries.
7. Labour accepts that if the value of sterling is high, it will encourage industry to be more efficient, so no attempts are made to reduce exchange rates.	

By the end of the twentieth century, the Labour Government faced a dilemma that no government had experienced since the 1950s. This was the prospect of several years in which there was a large government surplus, allowing the Government to raise public spending without running the risk of getting into debt. Margaret Thatcher had experienced this to a lesser degree in the mid-1980s, when the proceeds of privatisations began to fill up the Government's coffers. However, this was relatively short-lived and not on the same scale as Labour's good fortune. Margaret Thatcher chose to spend most of the money on tax cuts. Labour has a greater problem. Its own members prefer to see increased expenditure on public services, notably health care, public transport and education. The general public, on the other hand, might have a continued appetite for more tax cuts.

One reality colours all current Labour policy, however. This concerns the single European currency. In order to join, the UK must remain within the **convergence criteria** for entry. The criteria include low inflation and interest rates and tight control over public expenditure. All current policy must avoid jeopardising the UK's achievement of these objectives. When we add the convergence criteria to Labour's other policy issues, we can summarise the main concerns about the economy that are faced at the start of the twenty-first century:

- How should the UK's new-found prosperity be distributed? Should taxes be cut further or should public expenditure on public services be increased significantly?
- To what extent should tax and welfare policies be used to reduce inequalities in incomes?
- Should the state intervene to arrest any further decline in the UK's manufacturing industries?
- How should demands for improved workers' rights and conditions be balanced with the need to maintain the flexibility of labour markets?

But, whatever decisions are made, it is the UK's relationship with Europe that will continue to dominate.

The welfare state

Much of the welfare state, which was established in the UK during the 1940s, is administered by local government. This unit, however, confines itself to those aspects of welfare that come under the jurisdiction of central government or are shared between local and central government. These are education, health and social security. The policy issues described below have, in the past, applied throughout the UK. Since the devolution of power to Scotland, Wales and Northern Ireland, however, developments in these areas might begin to diverge as the national regions begin to implement their own distinct policies.

Education

Selection

The 1944 Education Act, which was supported by all three parties in government at the time, established a tripartite system of education. This entitled all children to a free education up to the age of fifteen. At the age of eleven, all primary school pupils sat an examination (known as the **11-plus**) in English, Mathematics and Intelligence. Depending on how well children fared in the 11-plus, they were assigned to one of three types of school. These were:

- **grammar schools** for about 25 per cent of the more able pupils
- **secondary modern schools** for the majority of the rest of the pupils
- **technical schools** for a small number who might benefit from an education that concentrated on manual skills.

In the event, very few technical schools were created, so the vast majority of children went to a grammar or secondary modern school. The process of dividing pupils on the basis of ability is known as selection. The issue of whether this is desirable has remained at the forefront of education controversy ever since. Nevertheless, the system survived without major challenge for twenty years. University education was also available free, with tuition fees paid by the state and needy families given fairly generous grants to enable their children to study for three additional years.

During the 1960s, concern began to be expressed by sociologists and educationalists that the system was socially divisive. The problem was that, although the 11-plus exam was based on pure academic ability, it was almost exclusively children from middle-class homes who were securing places at the prestigious grammar schools. It became clear that many children with high potential were being excluded from grammar schools because of a number of disadvantages resulting from their background. In addition, it was felt that the age of eleven was too young to judge academic potential. What of those who developed late? These concerns were shared by the Labour Party, which developed an alternative policy to replace selection at eleven. This was known as comprehensive education.

Comprehensive education

To replace the existing split between grammar and secondary modern schools Labour proposed a system of schools, known as comprehensives, which **all** children would attend after eleven (with the exception of those in private schools). The comprehensive system was designed to abolish selection at any age and to cater for children of all abilities. In other words, every child would enjoy equal opportunities in education. As an added incentive, many believed that benefits would result from the increased mixing of children from a variety of social backgrounds.

The new proposals encountered considerable opposition. Understandably, many middle-class families whose children were attending grammar schools, or were likely to do so in the future, were concerned at the loss of grammar schools. There was a view that comprehensives would result in a levelling **down** of academic standards, rather than more equality. But public opinion moved decisively in favour of the comprehensive system (bear in mind that most children were attending secondary moderns). When Labour came to power in 1964, therefore, it set about introducing comprehensive schools.

It is an interesting commentary on relations between central and local government at the time that the Labour Government decided not to **impose** comprehensive education on local authorities. Instead a number of experiments were run, after which local councils were **requested** to move over to the new system. During the 1960s and 1970s, therefore, comprehensive education gradually replaced selection at eleven. Naturally, many Conservative-controlled councils either dragged their feet or refused to co-operate altogether. They were subjected to pressure from Labour education ministers, especially Shirley Williams after 1974, notably with threats of reduced funding if they refused to play ball. By 1978, therefore, most councils – there were only six exceptions – had either gone over completely to comprehensive schooling or were in the process of doing so.

In that year the Labour Government did introduce legislation to **force** councils to abolish the remaining grammar schools. But before the law could be implemented, Labour lost power and the whole process slowed down.

The Conservatives and education in the 1980s

Under Labour in the 1970s there had been a great expansion in higher education. Many new universities were coming into existence and the 'tertiary', post-16 sector of education was also growing. It was a clear policy that as large a number of sixteen-year-olds should stay in education as possible. The Conservatives continued this process of expansion. However, under pressure to reduce public expenditure, successive Conservative education ministers reduced the real value of student grants and eventually introduced student loans, repayable after graduation, to replace outright grants for all but the poorest families.

The Conservative Party's attitude to comprehensive education has been mixed in the modern era. The party has recognised the popularity of comprehensives, but also remains committed to providing choice in educational provision. During the 1980s, therefore, relatively little action was taken to disturb the new balance in education. The abolition of grammar schools all but ceased, but very few new grammars were created. The problem for Conservatives was deciding how to retain comprehensive schools while also introducing more choice for parents.

The Education Act 1988

By 1988 Conservative ideas had become clarified enough for the introduction of a major piece of legislation – the 1988 Education Act. This Act had a number of provisions, as follows:

- The National Curriculum was introduced. This was a requirement on all state-run schools to provide minimum standards of education in a number of basic subjects, including Maths, English and Science. Children were to be tested at various ages to ensure that standards were being maintained. Failing teachers and schools could thus be identified and various remedial measures adopted.
- Grant-maintained schools were introduced. If a sufficient number of parents were agreed, schools could apply to opt out of local authority control and be funded instead directly by central government. The plan was that these schools would have greater freedom over how they admitted pupils and how they organised themselves. In this way, more choice was to be introduced.
- In order further to weaken local authority control over schools, the system of **local management of schools** (LMS) was introduced. Head-teachers and boards of governors were able to manage their own budgets. It was assumed that more variety, and therefore choice, would then be introduced into schooling.

The Act did not discuss grammar schools directly, but it was clear that the Government was happy to see the reintroduction of selection at eleven if local authorities or grant-maintained schools were keen to do so.

After 1988 the vast majority of schools remained comprehensive and under local authority control. However, the effects of Conservative policies in the 1980s and 1990s were to loosen local council control, to increase the participation of parent governors and to create a good deal of variety in non-comprehensive schools. The main problem that remained was a wide variation in the nature and quality of education from one district to another.

New Labour and education
The Labour Government that came to power in 1997 made education a key element in its vision. Tony Blair's assertion that he had three priorities, 'education, education and education', exemplified this view. Indeed, educational priority was seen as part of a broader economic policy. If the UK was to compete in the new global market place, it was argued, it would need a well-educated population.

But New Labour also agreed to much of what the Conservatives had done. Indeed, they supported the National Curriculum with greater enthusiasm than the Conservatives themselves. No new grant-maintained schools were to come into existence, but the increased number of selective grammar schools under the Conservatives was accepted, albeit with some reluctance. In some areas, however, change under New Labour is under way. The new initiatives are as follows:

- The National Curriculum has been strengthened and standards have been tightened. Measures against failing schools and teachers have become more severe, with some schools being closed and others having their management completely replaced.
- In 2000 a degree of performance related pay was introduced for teachers. Those with longer experience and a proven record of achievement were given large cash incentives and an improved pay structure. This was also designed to drive up standards.

- Successful schools have been given additional funding as a general incentive for all.
- Large-scale funding has been made available for information technology education.

offered to graduates who are willing to train to be teachers.

- In the university sector, student tuition fees, originally £1000 per annum, have been introduced. This proved the most controversial of New Labour's policies. Arguments that the additional income was vital to maintain standards went largely unheard compared with opposition on the grounds that such fees are a disincentive for poorer students to continue in education.
- All children are entitled to 'pre-school' (nursery) education: that is, one year in schools preparing for their more formal learning process. John Major's Conservative administration began the extension of nursery provision, but the Labour Government has made pre-school education universal.

The issue of selective education still rumbles on. New Labour has remained undecided what to do about the continued existence of selective grammar schools, although most of the party members are philosophically opposed to selection. In 1998 a scheme was introduced that allowed ballots of prospective parents to determine whether they wished to see grammar schools abolished in their locality. However, these polls require a large majority and have proved difficult to organise. By 2000, no grammar schools had been abolished in this way, despite determined attempts to do so in Kent and north London.

Public expenditure on education under Blair's Government has risen, but, like health, it appears a bottomless pit. Many school buildings are in gross disrepair, teachers' pay remains poor and there is a growing bill to deal with the increasing numbers of children with special needs who are entering schools. There is also increasing pressure on higher education spending, despite the introduction of student fees. With competing calls on government expenditure, Blair's commitment to education is likely to be sorely tested.

Health

The National Health Service

In 1948, when the National Health Service (NHS) was set up, the principle of free health care on demand, according to need, was established. Since then this basic principle has never been seriously challenged in British politics. There have been a number of reforms in its management, priorities have been frequently reviewed and some medical services have been charged for. But the fundamental system has not been challenged. Briefly, in the Thatcher era of the 1980s, some radical thinkers in the Conservative Party floated the notion that the UK should introduce a private health scheme, but it was immediately clear that such a policy would not be accepted by the British people. The NHS remains a source of national pride and politicians beware of challenging it. A World Health Organisation survey in 2000 placed the UK only fourteenth in a league table of health care provision, but commented that the principle of free health care on demand was the envy of the world.

As a political issue, therefore, debate on health provision has tended to centre on areas that do not question the central system itself. Since the 1950s, the main areas of controversy have been as follows:

- **Which services can be legitimately charged for?** Prescriptions for most adults were the first example of charging, introduced soon after the NHS's formation, and followed more recently by charging for some forms of dental care and eye tests. However, in all cases the very young and old, together with the poorest sections of society, remained exempt.
- **What services should be provided by the NHS?** There is a certain amount of controversy over what is, and what is not, a real health issue. So, for example, how much public money should be spent on helping childless couples conceive, what forms of cosmetic surgery should be supplied free, and whether abortion on demand should be provided are all important issues.
- **What should be the priorities in health care?** It is impossible to meet all the calls made on the service, although life-saving procedures are bound to come first. But when we consider appropriate fields for medical research, expenditure on procedures to cure non-life threatening illness and preventive medicine, it is more difficult to decide.
- **Who should set these priorities?** Should it be central government politicians, who are accountable for their decisions and are able to take a national perspective? Should it be local organisations, which might be more sensitive to local public opinion and understand regional variations in need? Or should it be 'the market' – the public themselves, who should set priorities and decide which services are purchased for them by the state? The medical professions themselves have also argued that they are best placed to decide.
- **How is the huge system of the NHS to be managed?** A number of schemes have been tried, but a consensus has yet to be reached. The underlying problem in determining a management system lies in the dilemma as to whether the service should aim mainly for efficiency, or whether it should only consider the general health of the nation, whatever the cost.
- **What proportion of the national budget should be devoted to the NHS?** This has held steady in recent years at about 24 per cent of total government spending. This is clearly a very large figure, but the UK does not compare well with most western European countries or with the USA in terms of the proportion of national income devoted to health care. The main reason is, of course, as the World Health Organisation has pointed out, that it is mostly taxpayers who pay the bill. Increases in health expenditure, therefore, impact directly on them. It is difficult for politicians to persuade the public to pay more tax, however worthy the cause might be.

So, the absence of a debate about the fundamental nature of the NHS has not prevented many other issues from taking the political stage.

The Conservatives and health

Until the 1980s, the Conservatives had formed part of a consensus on health care in the UK. Political arguments did break out from time to time over such issues as prescription and dental charges, and over relatively small changes in health expenditure, but the Conservatives did not hold distinctive policies until the later years of Margaret Thatcher's administration.

The neo-liberal attitude towards the economy suggested that the most ~~efficient way to allocate resources in any field was through the mechan~~ ism of the market. But the provision of health care seemed to be resistant to this principle. First, as we have seen, the NHS is precious to the British people, so any attempt to privatise it and put it in the market place was unacceptable. Second, health care was seen as so vital to the nation that it was felt it should remain under political, and therefore democratic, control. Until the late 1980s, therefore the NHS remained largely untouched by the new philosophy.

By 1988, however, a plan had been devised to introduce market forces, but to retain the NHS in public control. This plan was known as the **internal market**. A market needs buyers and sellers, but neither existed in the NHS. It was therefore decided to create them artificially. The buyers were to be regional health authorities, staffed by a mixture of local politicians, nominated members of the community and health experts. The sellers were to be NHS Trusts. The trusts, again run by a mixture of medical practitioners, managers, community representatives and business people, were effectively non-profit-making businesses. In addition, family doctors, or groups of doctors, could become 'fund holders', meaning that they were given their own budget with which to buy services from the trusts on behalf of their patients. The system came into practice in 1990.

The single market was a complex system with a simple principle. By creating the buyers, who could choose from whom they bought medical services (i.e. a number of one type of operation or clinical procedure over the course of a year), competition was introduced. Competition, it was believed, created both efficiency and quality. Thus, public money, channelled through the health authorities, would be used more effectively, it was hoped. At the same time, the system was decentralised so that regional and local needs could be directly assessed. There remained national services for research, training of medical staff and major life-saving procedures, but the routine side of health care remained regionally organised.

The dividend for the Conservatives in such a system was the hope of lower health expenditure at a time when the party saw further tax cuts as essential. This proved an elusive goal. Waiting lists for serious, but routine procedures steadily grew. A number of trusts effectively went bankrupt as they failed to compete successfully. Regional variations appeared in the quality of service and there were even charges of corruption in some trusts. Under John Major the Conservatives hung on to the internal market, but its problems were mounting by the time Labour took power in 1997.

New Labour and health Labour came to power in 1997 with two main policies on health. One was to abolish the internal market and simplify the system of funding and management. The other was to increase expenditure on health in general.

The first commitment was carried out immediately. Many of the NHS Trusts were retained, but not as competitive sellers of health services.

Instead they became one level of management that would determine local priorities. However, Labour's hopes that it could reduce levels of management in the service and divert the resources to direct health care proved more difficult to fulfil. The issue of health spending remained a problem. The new government had committed itself to following the three-year spending plans of its Conservative predecessor. This made it difficult to increase expenditure on health. In 1999 the brakes were released and a five-year programme of growing expenditure – 6 per cent per annum – was at last announced. But this did not spell the end of Labour's problems.

The difficulties that all modern governments face in health policy have steadily grown. Some of the main problems are as follows:

- The UK has an ageing population. A steadily higher proportion of the population is over 60 years old. This inevitably means that calls on the health service are bound to increase. As long as prosperity is improving, the rise in demands for health care can be met without raising taxes. However, should economic growth slow down, hard decisions on priorities will have to be made.
- Ironically, progress in medical treatments creates greater pressure on the NHS. Diseases that could not formerly be cured are now treatable. This applies to such conditions as cancer, heart disease, HIV infection, kidney conditions and hip replacement. This leads to more demands for more treatments, both in hospitals and also with drugs.
- The medical professions have become demoralised after years of underfunding and heavy workloads. There are also staff shortages in some medical disciplines. There are, therefore, problems of recruitment, working conditions, career development and pay in the health service.
- Waiting lists for a variety of operations, both serious and routine, have grown in recent years. This places an increased burden on spending, as there is a double requirement – to keep up with current demands and to make inroads into the huge backlog.
- There will always be disputes over priorities. Today, nearly every major disease and many minor ones have pressure groups that run campaigns for increased funding for research and care facilities. The media are now increasingly interested in health issues and so have become willing to highlight any shortcomings in the system. Not least among such dilemmas is how to divide expenditure between preventive measures and cures or treatments.
- Public opinion has consistently supported more spending on health. But public opinion also opposes tax increases. The Liberal Democrats claim that the public will put up with higher taxes if they are sure that the proceeds will be spent on such services as education and health, but this proposition has yet to be tested.

Health has pushed its way gradually towards the top of the political agenda. Yet an examination of the policies of the main parties reveals only small differences of emphasis. However, it does seem likely that there will be considerable political rewards for any government that can begin to tackle effectively the problems described above.

Social security

From cradle to grave

A comprehensive system of social security was established in 1946. Its principal architect was the Liberal civil servant and peer, William Beveridge, but it required a radical pioneering Labour Party to make it a reality. Its principles were that all those in work should contribute to a national insurance scheme and that a variety of benefits would be available from the insurance fund. Employers were also bound to contribute some payments on behalf of their employees. Some benefits were available to all, no matter what their circumstances; others depended on circumstances. When the circumstances included poverty, a so-called **means test** was established. This meant that a claimant had to prove that he or she was in need. The main benefits that have been available are summarised below.

Principal social security benefits	
Benefit	**Description**
• Pensions	• Available to all above retirement age. This was 60 for women, 65 for men. However, the European Union has declared that this discriminates against men, so the pensionable age remains under review. Pensions are not means tested.
• Unemployment benefit	• For those unable to find work, but willing and able to work. The test is whether a person is genuinely seeking work.
• Income support	• A variety of benefits, in the form of cash, preferential loans, grants and specific help, such as with school lunches or uniforms. These are means tested as they are only for those in poverty.
• Sickness benefit	• Help available for those deprived of wages because of long-term illness. This is not means tested.
• Disability benefits	• Clearly for the disabled. It is means tested.
• Housing benefit	• A means-tested benefit designed to help poorer families with housing costs, whether rents or mortgages.
• Child benefit	• This is, controversially, not means tested. Originally, families with children were given tax allowances. Since the 1970s, the benefit has been paid directly.

As we can see, this is an extremely comprehensive system of benefits. It was said that the welfare state cared for people 'from the cradle to the grave'. This was particularly poignant, as even a death grant is available to help pay for funerals. As with the NHS, no political party has dared to suggest that social security should be abandoned. There have, however, been reforms and modifications over the 50 or so years of its life.

The post-war consensus

The main parties soon came to form a consensus on this aspect of the welfare state. Indeed, during the 1950s the ruling Conservatives actually extended some of its provisions. Despite this agreement, however, there was a distinct difference in attitudes towards social security in particular and the welfare state in general.

For Labour, welfare was a device to reduce the inequalities in living standards which were the natural result of capitalism. The wealthy were expected to contribute more and receive less. The less well off, on the other hand, paid a minimum, but enjoyed a wide range of benefits. For the Conservatives, welfare was seen as a safety net to catch those who became deprived through no fault of their own. The parties disagreed on where the net should be placed. Labour naturally wanted it higher, but the Conservatives never questioned its existence – not until the 1980s, that is. It was not long before Margaret Thatcher's Government turned its attention to the largest item of public expenditure.

Welfare and neo-liberalism

The neo-liberalism of New Right conservatism under Thatcher and Major was naturally suspicious of the role of the state in the field of welfare. This was not just because of its effects on public expenditure and therefore taxation. Their concerns were more fundamental than that.

Neo-liberals believe, like their nineteenth-century predecessors, that welfare creates a **dependency culture** – a whole section of the community who are so used to depending on state support that they become incapable of ever fending for themselves. Worse still, this attitude might be passed down from one generation to the next. Furthermore, the welfare system involves the state in the manipulation of society – a feature to which liberals are basically opposed. When we add to this the fact that a comprehensive welfare system entails high taxation, we see the first serious opposition to social security since 1946.

The attack on the social security system under Thatcher and Major took a number of forms:

- The level of a number of benefits was eroded. This was done by ensuring that any increases did not keep up with inflation, so that their **real** value fell over time. This happened with child benefit and unemployment support.
- Some grants to poor families were replaced by loans.
- Housing benefits were reduced in scope.
- The real value of the state pension was eroded and increased tax breaks were introduced for private pension schemes.
- The criteria by which the disabled were entitled to benefit were tightened.
- The job seeker's allowance replaced unemployment benefit, ensuring that payments were only made to those who were actively seeking and available for work.

In practice, however, spending on social security remained stubbornly high. For many of the Conservative years from 1979 to 1997, there was a high level of unemployment. The restoration of free markets also began to create a large 'underclass' who were dependent on state aid. The attempts to destroy the dependency culture therefore largely failed. As economic inequality increased, the burden placed on the welfare state continued to grow.

The social security system that Labour inherited in 1997 was, therefore, considerably reduced in scope and was failing to achieve William Beveridge's original goals – to remove poverty, unemployment and deprivation. New Labour therefore decided to make welfare reform one of its principal objectives.

New Labour reforms

Labour perceived the problems in the social security system to be as follows:

- There was a serious **poverty trap** in operation, which prevented progress in attacking unemployment and poverty. The poverty trap was a circumstance where unemployed people had no incentive to find work. If they were to find a job, they would indeed earn an income; but if this were very low (which is usually the case for the unemployed), much of it would be eroded by taxation and by the loss of many benefits which would result from having an income. For many families, indeed, starting work could mean an effective **fall** in their living standards. They were therefore in a trap from which there was no escape.
- The growing 'underclass' of poor and unemployed was creating a whole series of related burdens on other state services. The children of such families typically failed at school, often entered lives of crime and/or became involved in substance abuse. The problems of the poor are multifaceted. They concern dependency on welfare, poor educational performance, poor housing and recurring health problems, sometimes physical, sometimes mental. This phenomenon is known by New Labour as **social exclusion**.
- The system was, as Conservatives had also suggested, encouraging groups to remain dependent rather than becoming independent. This applied to single parents, the young unemployed, the disabled and the poor who were in the poverty trap. Reform was therefore needed to give people incentives to find work and support themselves, rather than relying on the state.

A programme of radical reforms was, therefore, developed. At first, the Government was unable to reach agreement on change. Two ministers – Harriet Harman and Frank Field – were removed from Cabinet as a result of their failure to agree. It was left to their successors, led by Alistair Darling, to produce a new reform package in the Welfare Reform and Pensions Act of 1999 and other related orders. The detailed pro-

New Labour and welfare reform	
Welfare category	**Main reform**
• Pensions	• Stakeholder pensions introduced: a system whereby every worker is entitled to a secondary pension to which he or she can contribute. These pensions are run by private companies, but the state will guarantee them for all. • In addition, pensioners were guaranteed a minimum income, starting at £75 per week.
• Unemployment	• The rules on benefits to the unemployed were further tightened. Job seekers were forced to attend interviews on jobs to secure benefit. All were forced to prove their availability for work. • Employers were offered a weekly subsidy (beginning at £60 per week) to take on young unemployed people.
• Poverty	• The working family tax credit scheme was introduced. This was designed to eliminate the poverty trap. All families with at least one working member were guaranteed a minimum income, depending on circumstances. This was pitched at a high enough level to create an incentive to work. • In addition, the minimum wage encourages work. • New lower-level tax band at 10 per cent.
• Children	• The real value of child benefit was increased substantially.
• Single parents and the disabled	• Single parents opting for work were guaranteed a minimum income and child care was to be subsidised. • The disabled were also encouraged to seek work with a minimum income.

posals are extremely complex, but a summary of Labour's main reforms is given on page 409.

These reforms, combined with a number of other minor modifications to the social security system, were all designed to make a fundamental change in the role of welfare. It was now directed at providing incentives and opportunities rather than disincentives. However, the price was that welfare benefits for most groups have become more difficult to obtain and the means and needs tests involved have become much more stringent.

The Conservatives have opposed much of the reform, but their objections are not fundamental. Many of the measures accord with neo-liberal ideas of self-reliance and a reduced role for the state. The pensions provisions, transferring much of the responsibility to the private sector, have also found sympathetic ears among Conservatives. With pensions becoming a major burden on taxpayers in the future (because of the ageing population), the growth of private pensions was bound to be welcomed.

Law and order

Ideological
attitudes

Before studying in detail the modern politics of law and order, it will be useful to review the main philosophical positions on the issues which underlie the attitudes of the main parties. These are summarised below.

Ideological attitudes to law and order

• Conservatism
  • Conservatives consider the rights of the community to be superior to those of individuals. This results in a view that strong measures need to be taken to protect the community and its property against attacks by individual criminals or by the mass actions of protest groups and any others engaged in anti-social behaviour. They also believe that criminal behaviour is the responsibility of the individual, not of his or her social environment. In other words, we are responsible for our own actions and so must accept the consequences.

• Socialism
  • Here much more emphasis is placed upon the economic and social circumstances that cause crime. While criminals must be dealt with, so must the conditions that cause their crimes. Thus unemployment, racial disharmony and general social alienation need to be reduced if crime is to be effectively reduced.

• Liberalism
  • Liberals share the socialist view of the causes of crime. In addition, they are concerned that measures to combat crime and disorder should not damage basic civil liberties such as freedom of movement, association and expression. A balance has to be struck in crime measures between the rights of individuals and those of the community. This is also true when judging the kind of mass actions of which Conservatives are so suspicious.

These beliefs, and various shades of opinion between them, have informed the debate on law and order that has grown steadily since the 1960s.

The experience of the 1980s

A number of developments during the 1980s brought the issue of law and order to the forefront of British politics in a way unheard of before. These were as follows:

- There was a steady rise in the crime rate, notably among the young and in crimes of violence or against cars and property.
- There were a number of periods of breakdowns in public order: in particular, the riots in inner cities, especially London, Birmingham and Liverpool. These were the results largely of high unemployment and dissatisfaction with policing methods. There were also two miners' strikes which resulted in a degree of violence, especially during 1984. Finally, in 1989 a number of demonstrations against the Poll Tax became dangerously threatening and a great deal of property was damaged.

- Police forces, faced with decreasing public expenditure on the service, found it increasingly difficult to deal with rising crime and so placed pressure on government for increased powers.
- Football hooliganism, which had grown up during the 1970s, was proving difficult to combat and became a persistent problem for police forces everywhere.

The Conservative Government was not only concerned by these occurrences, it was also philosophically sympathetic to calls for a firmer stance on law and issue. It was therefore natural that a series of legislative initiatives were taken. These stretched into the 1990s under John Major. Three main pieces of legislation demonstrate the Conservative attitude to the issue:

- **Police and Criminal Evidence Act** 1984 gave the police increased powers to stop and search people, including the setting up of road blocks. The police were also given the right to hold suspects for questioning for up to four days, doubling the existing period.
- **The Public Order Act** 1986 gave the police powers to prevent demonstrations and public meetings if they believed they would cause major disruption or damage to the local community.
- **The Criminal Justice and Public Order Act** 1994 was possibly the most radical of all the measures taken since 1979. It took away the right of accused people to remain silent without that silence incriminating them. It also reduced the right of groups to hold open air ('rave' parties) or meetings and of travellers to pitch camp on private land.

These and other detailed measures concerning the prison service, treatment of suspected terrorists and the introduction of more severe sentences for a range of crimes exemplified a considerably tougher attitude to crime and public order than even Conservatives had proposed before. The Liberal Democrats raged against the measures, civil rights pressure groups campaigned against the legislation and Labour MPs trooped into the 'No' lobbies in Parliament, but nothing stopped the new policy.

In 1992–3, however, the Labour Party, led by John Smith and with Tony Blair as shadow Home Secretary, began to see law and order issues in a new light. Realising that tougher measures struck a chord with the voters, and believing that they would soon be in government and so be forced to deal with the problems, the party leadership began to change its attitude.

Jack Straw and New Labour's hard line

Once in power, with Jack Straw at the Home Office, Labour was true to its word that it would follow the Conservative lead. Although some categories of crime were declining, notably burglaries (believed to be the result of falling unemployment) and car crime, violence was still on the increase. In addition, hooliganism associated with football began to re-emerge during 1999–2000.

Labour was not prepared to introduce legislation as radical as that of the Conservatives, but a variety of proposals were introduced to combat crime. The most important and comprehensive were the **Youth Justice** 1998. Among other provisions, these Acts introduced the following:

- Restraints could be placed on individuals who were proved to engage in consistent anti-social behaviour.
- Local authorities could evict from council homes those who committed frequent offences.
- Parents could be held criminally responsible for the behaviour of their young children.
- Curfews could be introduced for young offenders.
- Those convicted of child sex offences were to be kept under special surveillance by police.
- DNA samples of all offenders and suspects could be held on record.

The hard new measures did not, however, satisfy public opinion's desire for yet more anti-crime policies. In 2000 the Government introduced proposals to reduce the right of accused people to opt for trial by jury rather than a magistrate. Tough new measures were also being considered against suspected and convicted football hooligans, including the removal of passports. So-called zero-tolerance policing against drunken or rowdy behaviour was also being discussed.

The one issue that Labour found difficulty in addressing was the question of police numbers. Policing had been a massive drain on public finances since the 1970s when crime began to rise alarmingly. Successive governments tried to keep police expenditure down by seeking ways of making policing more efficient. New Labour was no exception. By the beginning of the new century, however, it became clear that the police were seriously overstretched in many areas. In 2000, therefore, an increase in police numbers approaching 5000 was finally announced.

It is clear from the record of both recent Labour and Conservative governments that there is a consensus on most law and order issues. Naturally there remain policy differences, but these are largely ones of detail only. Both main parties are united in agreeing that draconian measures are now needed to arrest the growth in criminal behaviour. Only the Liberal Democrats stand out in proposing more social remedies to crime and in opposing the extension of police powers.

Race and racism

Background

The problem of racism in the UK emerged as a major issue in the late 1950s. Earlier in the decade there had been a large influx of immigrants, mostly from the Caribbean. They had been encouraged to come to the UK in order to fill many thousands of job vacancies that then existed in the public services. At that time, the UK enjoyed full employment, so there were insufficient workers to staff such state enterprises as the National Health Service, public transport and other nationalised industries. This was followed in the 1960s and 1970s by further waves of immigrants from the Indian subcontinent and the newly independent former British colonies in Africa. Asians and Africans were able to come because they held British passports under agreements made with the new independent governments.

As the larger cities gained new populations from various ethnic groupings, race relations became increasingly strained. As early as the late 1950s, riots in London and Liverpool had broken out, with white youths protesting at the influx of new immigrants. During the 1960s tension mounted again, especially when unemployment began to grow. Ethnic minorities were blamed for 'stealing' jobs formerly taken by white workers. Conversely, the new immigrants found that they were experiencing widespread discrimination in housing, jobs, education and relations with the police.

Standing on the right wing of the Conservative Party, **Enoch Powell** fanned the flames of racial tension in 1967 when he delivered a speech in Birmingham which sent shock waves through all the big cities with large immigrant populations. Powell warned that further immigration would lead to racial violence. He added words to the effect that 'rivers of blood' would flow through city streets if action were not taken. No new immigration should be allowed and existing ethnic minorities should be encouraged to return to their original homelands, he urged. The growing unrest and Powell's stirrings forced the Labour Government of the day into more drastic action to combat racism than it had already taken. So began a long process of ridding the UK of racial disharmony.

The Race Relations Acts

Three main pieces of legislation have set the scene for race relations in the UK. They are the **Race Relations Acts** of 1965, 1968 and 1976. Together with a Conservative measure – the **Public Order Act** of 1986 – they had the following effects:

- Discrimination on the grounds of race or skin colour in such fields as employment, housing and the selling of goods and services was outlawed.
- A race relations body – originally a Race Relations Board, later the **Commission for Racial Equality** (CRE) – was set up to research into racial problems, to advise the Government and to prosecute important cases of discrimination.

- The use of words or activities in public designed to cause racial hatred or violence became a criminal offence. This was strengthened to include words or actions that had the **effect**, whether intended or not,

In 1998 a further racial measure was introduced when the **Crime and Disorder Act** included a section that made some classes of offence more serious, therefore carrying heavier punishments, if they contained a racial element. This is the principle known as 'racial aggravation'.

While this legislation was being enacted, governments of both main parties steadily reduced the flow of legal immigrants into the UK. A series of Immigration and Nationality Acts has reduced the flow to a fraction of 1960s levels. Powell's warning, though heavily criticised at the time, has struck home and it is recognised that high levels of immigration are likely to cause further problems.

The battle against racism

It would be a mistake to believe that legislation is the only way in which governments have sought to combat racism. The phenomenon is far too complex and deep rooted to be dealt with by laws alone. Some of the other measures taken to combat racism are as follows:

- Black and Asian pupils have suffered discrimination in schools. It is therefore a requirement on all schools to ensure equal opportunities for members of all ethnic groups.
- Employers cannot be compelled to take on members of ethnic minorities, even though they can be prosecuted for active discrimination. The Government and other public bodies, therefore, have taken a lead in ensuring that a fair proportion of such minorities are employed. The Labour Party has flirted with the idea of creating quotas (known as black sections) of ethnic minorities in its institutions, but has never implemented them officially.
- Deeply rooted attitudes cause racist sentiments. Schools are therefore required to adopt anti-racist elements in their curricula. Racial incidents in schools must, by law, be reported to a local authority and action taken against them.
- Racism is recognised as a major problem within the police service. The report into the Stephen Lawrence case in 1999 threw this problem into sharp focus. Stephen Lawrence was a black teenager murdered by white youths. The police were found to be negligent in failing to prosecute the killers even though there was probably enough evidence to convict them. Part of the report insisted that there was 'institutional racism' in the police force. When added to the common incidence of black suspects dying in custody, and other racially motivated crimes not prosecuted thoroughly, the Lawrence inquiry signalled the need for drastic action. Retraining of the police, the removal of racist officers and recruitment targets for members of ethnic minorities are seen as the main solutions.
- All government departments are required to promote a positive image of ethnic minority groups.
- Local authorities are required to employ racial community officers to promote racial harmony and co-operation in their districts.

Party attitudes

The Liberal Democrat and Labour Parties have virtually identical policies on racial matters. They perceive the UK to be a multicultural society and view this as a positive feature rather than a problem. The Labour Government, post 1997, believes that further large-scale immigration is undesirable, but remains willing to accept genuine refugees fleeing from persecution at home. Both parties are committed to changing public attitudes to race and to taking a hard line on racially motivated crime. Neither, however, is in favour of any system of **positive discrimination** (known as 'affirmative action' in the USA). Positive discrimination would effectively force all large employers to accept a minimum number of workers from ethnic minorities. The measure is seen as divisive and unworkable.

The Conservative Party has long been troubled by right-wing, excessively nationalist elements within its own ranks. The leadership has disowned such sentiments and rejected the idea of repatriating (i.e. deporting) immigrant groups. It has also come to accept the fact that the UK's multiracial culture is here to stay. While the Conservatives have no strong record of taking positive measures to combat racism, it is also true that they have not seriously opposed Labour Party measures in that direction.

Racism remains a serious problem in the UK. Any attempts to reduce it are bound to be long term. However, a political consensus has gradually emerged and very few mainstream politicians will publicly express racially motivated views. Despite the unity, progress remains slow.

Northern Ireland

The historical background to the Northern Ireland problem is described in Unit 11. This should be referred to as an introduction. The various attempts to solve the 'troubles' since 1968 are also described there. Here we shall review the more recent developments, together with some of the difficulties that are likely to be faced in the future.

The parties and other groups in Northern Ireland

An understanding of the politics of Northern Ireland cannot be attempted until the various political and other groupings have been described. The main protagonists are summarised on page 416.

Bringing peace

Between 1968 and 1994 all attempts to bring peace to Northern Ireland failed. Both the Catholic, nationalist community and the Protestant unionists felt threatened by each other's political aspirations. When direct rule from London was introduced after 1972, British forces, together with the Royal Ulster Constabulary (RUC), dominated as it was by Protestants, were seen by Catholic nationalists as agents of unionism. The nationalists therefore gave considerable support to the IRA, whom they saw as their defenders. In 1972 the killing of thirteen demonstrators, mostly Catholic, by British soldiers when a demonstration became unruly (known as the **Bloody Sunday** incident) did much to create further antagonism.

Political parties and groups in Northern Ireland	
• **Unionists**	• Usually, though not necessarily, Protestant members of the community, who wish to see Northern Ireland remain a part of the UK under the British Crown. They do not necessarily insist on being governed from London, but are loyal to the Crown. Originally there was one Unionist Party, but there are now several splinter groups, such as the Democratic Unionists (led by Ian Paisley) and the Progressive Unionists. They differ from the main Ulster Unionist Party in their attitudes towards the peace process and the future government of the province. Some are more moderate; others are militant and favour resistance to change. Paisley's Democratic Unionist Party is the main group opposing any government that includes Sinn Fein.
• **Loyalists**	• A very general term for all those members of the community who wish to see Northern Ireland remain under the rule of the British Crown.
• **Loyalist paramilitaries**	• Groups such as the Ulster Volunteer Force (UVF) and the Ulster Freedom Fighters (UFF) who take terrorist action to defend the loyalist position.
• **Nationalists**	• A general term for all those who have, as a political objective, the reuniting of Ireland into one country.
• **Republicans**	• The same as nationalists, but the term 'republican' implies a more militant attitude to the objective.
• **Irish Republican Army (IRA)**	• An organised terrorist army, dedicated to throw off British rule and to protect the nationalist community from any attacks from loyalists. Since the 1994 ceasefire a number of splinter groups from the IRA, such as the 'Real IRA', have continued with terrorist acts.
• **Sinn Fein**	• A political party that is either the political wing of the IRA (as is claimed by its opponents) or that merely shares the objectives of the IRA and tends to speak on its behalf.
• **The Irish National Liberation Army (INLA)**	• A republican terrorist group even more militant that the IRA.
• **Social Democratic and Labour Party (SDLP)**	• A nationalist party, dedicated to peaceful means to uniting Ireland. It has been led for many years by John Hume.
• **Orange Order**	• A traditional society, dedicated to keeping alive the memory of British and Protestant supremacy in Northern Ireland. It holds regular marches in the province, an action that often creates tension among Catholics, who see the marches as threatening to them. The Order is closely associated with unionist parties.

Until John Major came to power, the role of the British Government presented a problem. Protestants saw it as their protector. It was assumed that London government – especially if it was Conservative – was unionist and would therefore always oppose attempts at Irish unity. Conversely, the more militant members of the Catholic community viewed British troops as an occupying force. The IRA was, therefore, seen as fighting a war. Major, and his Secretary of State for the province, Patrick Mayhew, understood this problem. They set about persuading the Catholic minority that the British Government was actually neutral. The troops were there to keep the peace, not to perpetuate British rule. Major assured the Protestants, meanwhile, that no change in the constitutional status of Northern Ireland would occur without the approval of a referendum.

In 1994 the IRA declared a ceasefire. They agreed to pursue their objectives peacefully as long as the British Government retained its neutral position. A few weeks later, the loyalist paramilitaries followed suit. An uneasy peace descended on Northern Ireland. A few militant splinter groups continued to commit terrorist acts, but they were minor compared to what had gone before. Despite the peace, however, progress on a political settlement remained elusive.

The IRA ceasefire was briefly suspended in the mid-1990s, but was restored after Labour came to power. Tony Blair made a political settlement in Northern Ireland an immediate priority.

A political settlement

Blair worked during 1997–8 with a group of politicians who were all committed to finding an agreement. A key to their apparent success was that they were largely trusted by the leaders of both communities. It was trust that had always been lacking in the past. American President Bill Clinton, special US envoy Senator George Mitchell, Irish Prime Minister Bertie Aherne and Secretary of State Mo Mowlem formed a team working for the settlement. A further factor in their success was a major shift in public opinion in Northern Ireland. The deaths and devastation caused by a bomb in the small town of Omagh in 1997 (planted by an offshoot of the IRA who did not recognise the ceasefire) resulted in a new determination to bring permanent peace.

The **Good Friday (or Belfast) Agreement** of 1998 was the result of a number of factors at work. The principal ones were as follows:

- The Ulster unionist leader, David Trimble, was a moderate who believed that the only viable future for Northern Ireland lay in a permanent political agreement.
- A referendum held in 1998 showed overwhelming support for the settlement. Approximately 75 per cent of the electorate voted in favour. This isolated the militant loyalists and republicans, and gave momentum to the peace process.
- The use of a neutral third party – George Mitchell – had been a success. He was trusted by both sides even when unionist faith in Mo Mowlem had declined.
- The Labour Government was untainted by the belief that the Conservative Party was fundamentally unionist and anti-devolution.
- The upturn in the British economy led people in Northern Ireland to believe that they could share in the prosperity. But this was possible only if order was restored.
- The Sinn Fein leaders – Gerry Adams and Martin McGinnis – were relative moderates in the republican movement. They clearly had sufficient influence on the IRA to persuade them to accept the new arrangements even though they fell short of reuniting Ireland, their ultimate goal.
- The agreement was fully supported by the Government of the Republic of Ireland and its people. The Republic, as part of the Good Friday Agreement, agreed to drop its historic claim to the territory of

Northern Ireland. This vital step undermined the republican position in the province, especially that of the IRA, which had always counted on Irish support abroad.

The details of the Agreement are described in Unit 11 above. Its continuing problems, however, are noteworthy here. The main difficulty in maintaining peace and political stability is the issue of the decommissioning of arms held by terrorist groups.

Decommissioning

The delays that occurred in the process of the IRA giving up its weapons caused the Northern Ireland Assembly to be suspended by Peter Mandelson (the then Secretary of State) in early 2000. The Ulster Unionist Party withdrew over the delays and government could not continue with the largest political party missing. However, the IRA rescued the situation that spring by finding a new definition for decommissioning.

It was agreed that the terrorists would not hand in their weapons, but would allow a neutral commission to inspect arms dumps, reveal what was there, and ensure that the weapons could not actually be used. This was not decommissioning as originally defined, but it satisfied the Ulster Unionists for the time being. Mandelson restored the Assembly and the work of trying to govern the province recommenced.

The future for Northern Ireland

This has to remain uncertain. A number of problems are unresolved. Among them are the following:

- The province is still full of hidden terrorist weapons. Neither community will feel completely safe until they disappear.
- The devolved government is still divided. The most serious issue is the policing of the province. The RUC is subject to reform proposals, but the unionists wish to see it retained in its current form, while the nationalists wish to see it completely re-formed.
- There are a number of militant splinter groups – loyalist and republican – who remain committed to violence and threaten the situation.
- The Orange Order is determined to maintain its ancient rights and customs. This is provocative to Catholics and creates tension.

Despite the many problems which remained at the time of the Good Friday Agreement, the general picture appeared optimistic until the general election of 2001. At that election serious developments emerged which have threatened the whole future of the peace process. A number of moderate members of the SDLP and the Ulster Unionists were ousted in favour of Sinn Fein and Democratic Unionist candidates. Similar results occurred in the local elections of the same year. These more extreme politicians were much more sceptical of the prospects for a lasting settlement. The balance of power in the province was shifting away from the moderates and back towards extremists again. The future looks less certain than it had done in the high point of optimism in 1999–2000.

For exam questions relevant to this unit, see page 558.

The social and political context of American government

Introduction

The United States of America came effectively into existence with the creation of the Constitution in 1787. At that time, there were 13 member states. Since then a further 37 states have joined the Union, making a total of 50. The last two to be added were Alaska and Hawaii in 1959. The states vary greatly in size and population. California, the largest, has a population close to 25 million, while Alaska has about 300,000 inhabitants.

Each state has its own constitution, legislature and government. These must all operate within the boundaries laid down in the federal Constitution. Each state elects two Senators to attend the federal Senate and a number of Representatives, depending on the size of its population, who pursue the interests of their constituencies in the House of Representatives.

The states are divided into **counties** and **cities**, which form the most local form of government. These smaller units enjoy a considerable degree of independence from the state government. The term 'city' must be treated with caution. Geographically, of course, the expression refers to a large urban conurbation and this is true in the USA, but **politically** a city is a small unit of local government; American 'cities' can be just small towns as well as great metropolises such as New York.

The **District of Columbia** (the 'DC' in Washington DC) is not a state, but the territory immediately surrounding the capital city. It is administered directly by Congress and, thus, does not have its own government.

The USA has never possessed overseas colonies in the way that European powers have. However, a number of territories fall under American protection and are, broadly speaking, administered by Washington. The Pacific island of Guam, the American Virgin Islands and Puerto Rico in the Caribbean come into this category.

A multinational country

The USA is not a 'nation' in the true sense of the word. Its people come from too many cultural and ethnic backgrounds for nationhood to be claimed. Americans often refer to themselves as a nation, but this relates more to their aspirations to unity than to any historical reality.

Although the largest 'ethnic' group consists of the white descendants of the original British colonists, there are also substantial communities of other origins. These include:

Black Americans	Mostly descended from slaves
Hispanics	Immigrants from Mexico, Central America, the Philippines, Cuba, etc.
Asians	Mostly from Japan, China, Korea and Pacific islands
Jews	Largely refugees from oppression in Europe
Irish	The result of several migrations in hard times
Various Europeans	Escaping oppression and poverty at home

These groups are all 'Americans' and remain, on the whole, loyal and patriotic. This is not to say, however, that ethnic differences have no political significance. Their origins and sensitivities must be taken account of. Apart from the clear educational needs of more recent immigrants, politicians must also take heed of national sentiments. Modern examples have included the following:

- Policy in the Middle East is tempered by the need to maintain support from the large, influential Jewish population. The USA's relations with Israel are extremely delicate for this reason.
- In order to placate the largely Irish Catholic population, American politicians have been tempted to involve themselves in the Northern Ireland troubles. Indeed, it has been a common practice among Presidents, notably J.F. Kennedy and Ronald Reagan, to stress their Irish origins.
- The strong anti-communist position that the USA has taken in Central America and Asia has partly been driven by the demands of immigrants from those regions, notably Cubans, who came to the USA to escape such regimes.
- All immigrant groups have a tendency to suffer discrimination from the white majority. There is, therefore, a constant need to develop political measures to combat the abuse of civil rights.

The importance of section

The British term 'region' is described by Americans as 'section'. The USA is extremely large geographically, but more importantly, its sections have experienced different patterns of development, both economically and ethnically. Account must, therefore, be taken of the very different conditions that prevail in different parts of the country. A brief description of the main sections will give an indication of the political significance of 'sectionalism'.

The South

This really refers to the south-east corner. Texas dominates the South economically, but not culturally. It is, untypically, a mixture of conservatism and liberalism. Most of the South comprises old-established states such as Mississippi, Arkansas and Alabama. This is the heart of the former slave-owning part of the country. It has, therefore, a large black population. The white inhabitants are largely descended from English and French origins. It is also the least prosperous part of the USA – the result of the decline of agriculture and decades of economic neglect there following the Civil War and the freeing of the slaves in the 1860s.

The white, often poor, population tends to be deeply conservative in outlook, often racist and anti-federal government. These poor whites (also known as 'rednecks' or 'good ole boys') resisted civil rights legislation in the 1950s and 1960s and consistently discriminated against the equally poor blacks. There was some economic recovery towards the end of the century and some degree of liberalisation of politics there. However, it remains an isolated, untypical part of the political map.

The East Coast

Dominated by New York, Washington and nearby Philadelphia, this is one of the oldest-established parts of the country, and includes some parts of the original British and Dutch colonies. It is more cosmopolitan than elsewhere, an extremely rich mixture of ethnic groups, especially in the cities. Its prosperity is based upon industry, finance and business, which are, in turn, dependent upon international trade. This is middle-class America, but **liberal** middle class, not conservative.

The people here, therefore, tend to be more progressive and international in their outlook. Until the growth of California in the middle of the twentieth century, the East Coast was the centre of American commercial and political life. To some extent it still is, though the West Coast is now an important rival.

New England

This is the most 'English' part of the USA – hence its name – and also one of the wealthiest regions. It comprises the north-eastern states, such as Massachusetts, Maine, New Hampshire, Vermont and Maryland. Boston is the principal city. The old-established families there, including the Kennedys, are the nearest thing the Americans have to an aristocracy and they have certainly played a dominant role in American life in modern times.

The people are, broadly speaking, liberal in their political outlook, but above all they tend to be parochial. There is a very old, established tradition of independent local government within the hundreds of small communities. Many decisions are still made at 'town meetings' where the whole population gathers to exercise the most direct form of democracy known. This is a throwback to the way in which the original settlers carried on their politics, demonstrating how much tradition still

A New England town meeting

The Mid-west

The term 'Mid-west' describes the great states in the centre of the country, with scattered populations and great empty spaces – the landscapes so often seen in 'western' films. Illinois dominates the area, which also includes Ohio and Indiana. It is largely agricultural, although much of its former prosperity has moved further west to California as a result of 'over-farming' in the early part of the twentieth century. In the 1930s a large proportion of the rural inhabitants moved west (the subject of John Steinbeck's epic novel, *The Grapes of Wrath*), as a result of which parts of the region have become seriously depopulated.

Outside its larger cities, such as Indianapolis, Cleveland and Chicago, most Mid-westerners live in small isolated communities. Not surprisingly, they tend to be inward-looking, conservative people. They generally oppose American involvement in the outside world and have supported firm policies of protection for agriculture against international competition.

The West Coast

This is 'new' America – the later additions to the Union, now becoming the most prosperous. It is dominated by California and its three largest cities: Los Angeles, San Diego and San Francisco. It is here that the USA's newer and most modern industries – the 'sunrise' economy – are centred, including electronics (the original 'Silicon Valley' is in California), wine and exotic agriculture, and, of course, entertainment. In some ways, California and its neighbouring states are cut off from the rest of the USA. They are becoming increasingly more prosperous than the rest of the country and now look more to the Far East, towards Japan and China, than to Europe for their trading links.

Politically, the West Coast is very much a microcosm of the rest of the country. The liberal, urban middle classes in the north of the region are contrasted by the conservatives of Los Angeles and the agricultural communities.

Religion

Religious observance is more established in the USA than in most of Europe. Furthermore, there is developing an increasing diversity of faiths. The Christian religion is widely followed, but is gradually becoming more fragmented as there develops a steady increase in the number of sects and splinter groups. We have already seen how the Jewish and Irish Catholic communities can affect politics, but the revival of religious interest goes still further.

Many of the new fundamentalist Christian groups are deeply conservative in their moral outlook, taking a reactionary line on such issues as divorce, abortion, crime and even welfare. The New Right movement that grew during the 1980s, under the protection of Ronald Reagan's presidency, was partly religious in its inspiration. It regretted the loosening of morals, blaming rising crime, homosexuality and divorce rates on liberal social and moral attitudes. Many of the new members of Congress who swept into power as part of the Republican triumph in the 1994 elections were motivated by a deep religious sense of morality, which was opposed to President Clinton's progressive social outlook.

At the same time, an increasing number of the black population are turning to Islam as the answer to the problem of their persistently low status in American society. Leading members of the black community, such as world boxing champions Mohammed Ali and Mike Tyson, have followed in the footsteps of more radical black leaders of the 1960s and 1970s, so rendering Islamic belief more respectable. The move to Islam threatens to usher in a new radical era in black politics. Adherence to the Muslim faith poses a challenge to traditional American social and political values.

The economy

Although the USA remains the most prosperous large country on earth, it still suffers a number of chronic economic problems. It has not experienced the same extremes of unemployment and inflation, the twin evils that have dogged Europe since the 1960s, but this does not signify a healthy economy. There are pockets of serious unemployment in the big cities, resulting in crime and other social problems, but these are not considered as pressing as the longer-term imbalances in the American economy.

The main problem in the American economy is debt, both domestic and international. For many years the federal government has run a huge deficit: that is, its spending has far exceeded its revenue from taxation. The accumulated debt – largely raised by borrowing from the public (in the form of bonds) and from the banks – places an enormous burden on the American taxpayer. There is a vast amount of interest to pay on the debt every year, as well as a proportion of the original sum which must regularly be repaid. Repeated attempts by Presidents and Congress have failed to make inroads into the debt. There is heavy pressure not to raise taxes on the one hand, but also resistance to reductions in public spending on the other. So the problem persists from one year to the next.

The USA has also suffered a long-term deficit in its balance of payments account. Put simply, there is a constant tendency to import more goods than it is exporting. This also results in debt, much of it overseas

imports of cheap food from the Third World and manufactured goods, especially cars, from Japan and the Far East. But American governments recognise the importance of trade and are reluctant to jeopardise links with their allies. Attempts to make American industry and agriculture more competitive have also failed. The once almighty dollar has become a weak currency, prone to bouts of selling which cause disruption to the financial life of the country.

It would be mistaken to suggest that the American economy is in crisis, though it suffers from periodic recessions as the other major world economies do. Rather, it is the case that the political system finds it increasingly difficult to maintain smooth economic growth in the way that the country is used to.

The media

As is the case with the political system in general, the American media is largely decentralised. Newspapers are all localised to cities and states, as are most of the TV and radio stations. There are a few network organisations, such as ABC and CNN, as well as some public service (non-commercial) broadcasting, but most coverage is regional. The effect is to ensure that local political issues are given a prominent place in the media, often rivalling all but the most dramatic national and international issues.

The press is extremely independent and the great newspapers all have a strong tradition of investigative journalism. The openness of the political system gives extensive access to journalists and they put it to full use. This was never more evident than when two reporters – Woodward and Bernstein – were able to reveal the full extent of the dishonest practices adopted by President Nixon's staff in the Watergate scandal of the 1970s. The USA now has a Freedom of Information Act, which ensures that the press is able to see official documents, ensuring that the work of journalists, such as the Watergate investigators, can continue to be an effective check on government.

The broadcasting media are similarly independent, though there is less political involvement than that undertaken by the press. TV and radio are seen predominantly as providers of entertainment rather than information. Documentary or investigative programmes are, therefore, relatively rare. Politicians are able to buy time on TV and radio, and this has become one of the most important forms of political campaigning. Although there are statutory limits to spending by individual candidates, there is, essentially, open access to the broadcasting media for candidates for election of all kinds.

Social problems

Crime

Of all the economically developed democracies in the western world, the USA suffers most from high levels of endemic crime. It is widely assumed that liberal gun laws are partly to blame – the right to carry weapons for self-defence is safeguarded by the Constitution – but this is not the only cause.

A popular explanation proposes that the main culprit is the wide gulf between the ostentatious wealth of many sections of the population and the extreme poverty of other groups, often from ethnic minorities and frequently concentrated in the cities. There is an assumption that large numbers of the urban poor, especially the young, have become alienated from the rest of the USA's prosperous society. Some look more critically at the American culture, suggesting that the extreme individualism that it has always promoted (as exemplified by the western 'cowboy' tradition) can lead to self-seeking criminal behaviour.

Whatever the true explanations, there is a considerable split within the political community concerning remedies. The conservative right suggests draconian punishments to act as a deterrent to crime. Extensive use of the death penalty, long custodial sentences and tougher prison regimes have all been suggested. The liberal response is that there should be a greater focus on the economic and social causes of crime, including measures to relieve inner-city poverty and unemployment, to provide better social education and to curb the sale of guns. Though the problem continues to grow, political deadlock prevents dramatic action in either direction.

Inner-city decay

It would be a mistake to assume that the USA is completely riddled with criminal behaviour. In fact, most crime is concentrated in the centres of the great cities, notably New York, Los Angeles, Miami, Washington, Chicago and New Orleans. It is no mere coincidence that the rise in crime has coincided with the continued decline in both the social fabric and the physical environment of these cities.

Housing is run-down, schools are deprived and disordered, there are few employment opportunities and there is little hope for the young to improve their living conditions. In addition, there are ghettos where members of ethnic minorities are heavily concentrated, so that there is constant tension and violence between neighbouring communities. Finally, and perhaps most seriously, drug abuse has become a serious and growing problem, leading to both criminal behaviour and broken lives.

Homelessness and poverty are major problems in many inner cities in the USA

As life in the cities has become less tolerable, there has been a growing exodus to the suburbs, especially by the middle classes, leaving poverty yet more concentrated in the city centres. Presidents Kennedy and Johnson began to tackle the problem of the inner cities in the 1960s, but since then the economic problems referred to on pages 423–4 have prevented serious attempts to make inroads into the crisis. Bill Clinton declared, on his election in 1992, that he intended to tackle the problem of the cities, but a reluctant Congress is unwilling to release the huge funds needed to relieve the deprivation and decay. The high levels of crime and periodic rioting that have been seen of late seem set to continue.

Drugs

Wars on the drug problem are periodically declared by American politicians, but progress has been slow. As with crime, its most severe incidence occurs in the cities and among the poor, but it has become an issue that now affects all levels of American society.

The USA has a huge coastline and land border, making it extremely difficult to prevent the import of drugs. Being so prosperous, it is also seen as an ideal target for the commercial interests associated with drugs. So, the problem appears to be intractable and no political party or leader has been able to propose viable solutions. There has been some entanglement with the USA's chief suppliers of drugs, such as Colombia and Panama, but these have resulted only in embarrassment and failure.

The political culture

Politically, the USA is extremely complex. This is mainly the result of a political culture that is full of paradoxes and subtle variations. As we have seen above, too, generalisations must be treated with caution, as there are wide sectional variations in the political life of the country. Nevertheless, some general observations might be useful to gaining an understanding of American politics.

Suspicion of governments

On the whole, Americans are extremely suspicious of governments. This sentiment can be traced right back to the origins of the Union, when British rule became very discredited, and even further back to the origins of the first settlers. Many of them arrived to escape from governments that had been oppressing them. Ever since then, new waves of immigrant groups have followed, many of whom have also suffered from tyranny. It was, indeed, small wonder that the Founding Fathers ensured that the Constitution placed large obstacles in the way of any future administration with ambitions to extend federal power.

There are variations in anti-government feeling, from the very conservative 'states'-rights' campaigners, who wish to see more power transferred from Washington to the state capitals, to more moderate politicians who simply wish to protect the constitutional safeguards against centralised power from being further eroded. All have in common, however, a determination to prevent government becoming overbearing.

The relatively low turnouts at presidential and congressional elections may be seen as symptoms of the traditional dislike of big government. It is common for only 40–50 per cent of the electorate to vote in such elections, compared to about 75 per cent in the UK. A close parallel may be drawn between the British electorate's relative indifference to campaigns in European parliamentary polls (turnouts close to those of the USA) and that of the electorate in the USA. The reasons are similar. Governments in both Washington and Brussels are viewed as remote, ineffective and wasteful. By contrast, however, Americans are enthusiastic participants in local politics, especially where interest and pressure groups come into conflict with governmental institutions such as school boards, water authorities and police departments. They might be reluctant to vote for party politicians, but not to exercise their right to take direct political action.

Individualism

Few, if any, western democratic countries give greater rein to the freedom of the individual than the USA. Individual liberties are firmly protected by the Constitution. Economic enterprise is not only protected, but also actively encouraged. Americans tend to like people who take responsibility for their own lives and are unsympathetic to those who rely on others when they could help themselves.

For this reason, collectivism has never been popular as a way of achieving goals among Americans. There is no organised public health service, little publicly provided housing, only a basic welfare system and trade union membership is not widespread. Not surprisingly, socialism, even social democracy, has never gained a significant toehold in the political scene.

Parochialism

Despite the existence of many huge cities, the USA is basically a country of small towns. In these towns the sense of community tends to be very strong. The level of political activity on a national scale is relatively low when compared to European democracies. National election turnouts only reach about 50 per cent and there are few national party activists. At local level, however, the story is very different.

Local politics is extremely vigorous and well supported. Community interest and pressure groups abound. Local issues are often hotly disputed through the media and in the form of direct action. As we shall see below, many local officials are elected, whereas in Europe they would be appointed. This makes for a lively and interesting local political environment.

The story is similar at state level. As we have seen, many Americans see federal government as remote and largely irrelevant. What goes on in their state and their country, on the other hand, affects them more directly. For these reasons, American politics is mostly parochial in nature.

Conservatism

One of the paradoxes of American political life is the fact that, in a country that has proved to be one of the most dynamic and innovative societies in the modern world, the people are, on the whole, conservative in outlook. Radical politicians are treated with great suspicion, as are the radical measures that they might propose.

The recent revival in religious observance has underpinned this deep-seated conservatism, since most of the new Christian groups are fundamentalist in character. The media, too, tend to avoid too many radical positions, though this may be the result, rather than a cause of, American moderation.

Some caution needs to be expressed at this point, since there are regional variations on this issue. As we have seen above, the states of New England, the Deep South and the Mid-west are largely conservative, but there have been pockets of political radicalism in the eastern cities and on the West Coast which have emerged from time to time – never more so than in the 1960s, when the USA appeared to be taking a political turn to the left. By the mid-1970s, however, the apparently stronger conservative tradition had reasserted itself.

Patriotism

Few nations can rival the USA in the love its people show for their country. Patriotic symbolism is heavily stressed in American schools. The flag, the anthem and the Declaration of Independence are well-known images to all American children. Yet patriotism is also a reflection of a natural sentiment that was noted as long ago as 1830 by the visiting French political philosopher Alexis de Tocqueville. For him, it was one of the country's most endearing qualities and he saw it as essential to the stability of the political system.

Even when government is unpopular, the President receives a loyal welcome wherever he travels. Most Americans understand that there is a difference between the **office** of the President, which they respect, and the policies of the **individual** who holds that office, which they might oppose. Similarly, they might fight to defend the **Constitution** even when they find government repugnant.

In a country that is the home of citizens with such diverse ethnic origins, cultures and religions, patriotism becomes the key to the unity of the country. As we have said above, the USA is not really a nation, but it is able to compensate for that through the degree of loyalty to the country shown by most of its people. Apart from its powerful patriotic symbols, the USA has also come to embody the 'American dream'. The dream is that anybody, no matter how humble their origins, has the opportunity to realise their full potential. In a free society, with no social or ethnic barriers to success, Americans believe that every individual has the same life-chances. Though aspects of American life might fall some way short of the dream, it sustains many of the people in their love of the country.

For exam questions relevant to this unit, see page 558.

Background

Historical development

In 1765 British America was comprised of thirteen colonies that came under the jurisdiction of Parliament in London, and whose people were subjects of the King (George III at that time). Each of the colonies had its own political institutions, but these were relatively powerless, with no legislative and few executive powers.

In that year Parliament in London passed the notorious **Stamp Act**, effectively a tax on all official documents and contracts. What might seem a relatively unimportant event was to light a spark that became a conflagration. The tax was bitterly resented and gave rise to calls for greater American control over such matters. The maxim 'No taxation without representation' was born at this time. The colonists pointed to the long English history of allowing Parliament, with its representatives from the towns and counties, to oversee the King's use of taxation and public expenditure. Why were they denied such representative rights?

Unrest led to the **Boston Massacre** in 1770, when British troops fired on a crowd protesting over British monopolies in trading rights. Three years later the famous **Boston Tea Party** saw the destruction of tea imports taking place for similar reasons. The stories – largely exaggerated – of the exploits of the Bostonians and the British repression that followed it, gave rise to the calling of the first **Continental Congress** in 1774. Representatives from twelve of the colonies met in what became the first seedbed of independent American government. They called on George III and his government to grant a number of rights to the colonists. These calls went unheeded, however, and unrest grew in the colonies.

By the time the second Continental Congress met in 1775, the War of Independence had begun. On 19 April the battles of **Concord** and **Lexington** took place. The Congress lasted for five years and was, effectively, the provisional government of the American revolutionaries. Its most important achievement, other than the raising of an army to fight the British, was the publication of the **Declaration of Independence** on 4 July 1776. The Declaration was largely written by **Thomas Jefferson** of Virginia, who was to become the effective leader of the new country. Though **George Washington** was later to become its first President, Jefferson was the dominant political figure.

After the Declaration, all the states claimed to be sovereign political units and most of them adopted written constitutions. These events of 1776–81, therefore, were to prove to be key historical moments in the development of the concept of constitutional government. The **Massachusetts State Constitution** of 1780 still exists today (albeit with many amendments) and is the oldest codified constitution still in force anywhere in the world.

By 1781 a constitution for all the thirteen states had been established, known as the **Articles of Confederacy**. This created a loose union between the states, each of which retained its own sovereignty. The

Confederacy was to control the armed forces, foreign affairs and treaties on behalf of all the states, exercise broad economic and currency control, and deal with disputes between states. However, it did not deny the claim of the thirteen former colonies to be independent sovereign states. The Confederate Congress was drawn from delegates from the states and no true executive government was set up. It was, in short, a compromise between a **unitary**, centralised state, as Britain was, and a **federal** system, which was to evolve in America after 1787.

The **Treaty of Paris** in 1783 formally brought to an end the War of Independence, which had effectively been won two years earlier. Britain accepted the independent status of the thirteen states. It was soon clear, however, that the Confederate system could not work. The states were too weak, militarily and economically, to survive alone. A closer union was needed, with some sort of centralised leadership. If America were to join the international community of states, it needed a new political structure. After an abortive attempt to create a union at **Annapolis** in 1786, representatives from the thirteen states met at Philadelphia in the summer of 1787, charged with the task of creating the United States of America.

The 'Founding Fathers', as the Philadelphia gathering became known, worked quickly (and in secret, which explains much of their efficiency), producing the **United States' Constitution** in the autumn. There then began a long process by which each of the thirteen states' assemblies had to ratify the document. By the time the state of Rhode Island narrowly approved the new Constitution in May 1790, all the other thirteen states had ratified it. Before that, however, the first President, George Washington, had been sworn in on 30 April 1789. And it is this date that marks the creation of the United States.

The road to the Constitution – a chronology of events	
1765	Passage of the Stamp Act
1770	Boston Massacre
1773	Boston Tea Party
1774	First Continental Congress
1775	War of Independence begins Second Continental Congress
1776	Declaration of Independence
1781	Articles of Confederacy signed War of Independence ends
1783	Treaty of Paris formally ends war
1786	Annapolis Convention
1787	Constitution written at Philadelphia
1789	Washington sworn in as President
1790	All thirteen states ratify the Constitution

Philosophical principles

Democracy

It might seem obvious today that the Founding Fathers should choose democracy as the basic form of government to be adopted. However, in 1787 the matter was less clear. The French Revolution had not yet occurred, so no large scale democratic political system had been established. Many feared the power of the mass of the people and the disorder that might result from the abandonment of absolute government.

But it was the democrats who won the day decisively. Of course, it was to be a democracy of property owners and not the mass of the people. Slaves were certainly excluded, as were women. For free men the issue was less clear. In fact, it was not until later in the nineteenth century that universal male adult suffrage was established. Yet this does not alter the fact that the American Constitution was firmly rooted in the concept that citizens of the state should be able to influence and participate in government.

Government by consent

The principal objection that the American colonists had laid against the Government of George III was that it gave no opportunities for those who were governed – the subjects of the Crown – to give their agreement to the power being exercised over them. A hundred years before, the English philosopher **John Locke** had insisted that any government could be legitimate only if it enjoyed the consent of the people. Thus, the Constitution was designed to ensure that there would be mechanisms for establishing such consent. The system chosen was for an elected legislative body (Congress) to agree to laws or taxation **on behalf** of the people.

> 'Nor can any edict of anybody else, in whatever form soever conceived, or by what power soever backed, have the force and obligation of the law which has not its sanction from the legislative which the public has chosen and appointed.'
> John Locke, *Second Treatise of Civil Government*, 1691

Individual rights

It was something of an oversight that the original Constitution of 1787 did not contain a clear statement of the rights of individuals. Nor did it include provision for the protection of such rights. During the ratification process, however, there was an insistence that such a provision be included. The revolutionaries had clearly been motivated largely by a desire to grant such rights to the people of America – rights that had been denied by British government. In the event, the first ten Amendments to the Constitution expressed the need for the entrenchment of individual rights. These amendments have become known as the **Bill of Rights.**

They arose from two traditions. One was the historical development of 'common law' rights that were part of Anglo-Saxon culture. In the early days of the USA, most of the citizens were of Anglo-Saxon stock, so they understood the principles. Such rights as trial by jury, private enjoyment of property and freedom from imprisonment without trial were ancient privileges that had been enjoyed by free Englishmen for centuries. They had been enshrined in the Magna Carta of 1215, but the

Americans added the device of entrenchment as an added safeguard. Thus, rights were not only stated clearly, but also protected from encroachment by government.

The second origin of the protection of rights in the Constitution arose out of the conception of natural rights that had been developed by such philosophers as Thomas Hobbes, John Locke, Jean-Jacques Rousseau and, above all, **Tom Paine**, an Englishman who had, despite his nationality, joined the American cause.

The inspiration for the Declaration of Independence had come largely from Paine's revolutionary pamphlet *Common Sense*, published in 1775. The Bill of Rights arose largely out of his later work, *The Rights of Man*.

> 'The end of all political associations is the preservation of the natural and imprescriptible rights of man ... liberty, property, security and resistance of oppression.'
>
> Tom Paine, *The Rights of Man*, 1790

Political principles

Limited government

The American colonists had suffered from the experience of the arbitrary government of the British monarchy and the uncontrolled sovereignty of Parliament in London. It was, therefore, hardly surprising that the Founding Fathers wished to establish the principle of limited government. They developed a concept that was, at the time, completely unique. This was the use of a written constitution to establish the limitations upon government.

Philosophers such as Locke had suggested that the way in which government could be controlled was through the ability of the people to remove it. However, this ignored the possibility that a tyrannical government might simply refuse to be so removed. By making government subject to the limitations of a constitution, underpinned by the principle that its laws would be unenforceable if they did not conform to constitutional rules, the problem was largely solved.

The principle, also known as 'constitutionalism', establishes that part of the Constitution will clearly set out the boundaries within which each branch of government may operate. Its authority will not run beyond these boundaries.

Judicial review

Associated with the concept of constitutionalism stands the principle of judicial review. This establishes that any dispute concerning the meaning or application of the Constitution must be resolved by a review carried out in the courts, ultimately the Supreme Court. Such review, however, does not take place **before** a law is passed or a government order made. Rather, it must first be challenged by an individual, an organisation or a state through the courts and later, if necessary, through an appeals procedure.

If a law or government action is deemed to have contravened the Constitution, it is declared **unconstitutional**. The courts will not enforce it and so it must be set aside.

The separation of powers The French philosopher **Montesquieu**, one of the inspirations behind the French Revolution, had argued that, if tyrannical government was to be avoided, it was necessary for it to be **internally** limited. The principle of

Montesquieu was more concerned with the nature of government itself.

Montesquieu first identified the three branches of government as **legislative** (law making – the Congress), **executive** (policy making and implementing laws – the President and the agencies he or she controls), and **judicial** (law interpretation – the courts, especially the Supreme Court). He then suggested that each branch should possess powers that would limit the other two. As long as they were separate and mutually powerful, there would be an automatic mechanism whereby no single branch of government could become too powerful. The concentration of power in too few hands was to be avoided for the sake of balanced and controlled administration of the laws.

The American version of Montesquieu's principles has become known as 'checks and balances'. The powers granted by the Constitution to each branch of government were carefully matched against those granted to a rival branch. To illustrate, the President has the power to veto laws passed by Congress. This is balanced by the fact that the President can issue no laws without congressional approval. Thus, they control and rely on each other.

Similarly, the President may appoint judges to the Supreme Court, but this is balanced and controlled by the fact that the President's nominations may be set aside by Congress. In addition, since judges are appointed for life, the President cannot remove them if he or she is dissatisfied with their decisions.

> 'US government is in reality based not on separated but on shared powers which give each branch of government considerable powers in the legislative, executive and judicial functions of government.'
> Howard Elcock, 'American Government in the 1990s'
> *Talking Politics*, Vol. 6, No. 2 (Winter 1994)

Federalism The biggest problem that the Founding Fathers faced in 1787 was how to reconcile the demands of the thirteen states to retain some autonomy while, at the same time, creating a strong union that would not disintegrate at the first sign of political controversy. Allied to this difficulty stood the danger that the new union could be dominated by the larger, richer states. The result, forged out of a number of compromises, was known as the 'federal settlement'. It should be immediately apparent that the kind of controversies that raged in Philadelphia over 200 years ago are still being played out in the struggle to find a structure for the European Union in the 1990s.

The nature of the federal compromise was something of a masterpiece of both legal theory and political reality. The legal device used was to split sovereignty between the central institutions of government and the several states. The division of sovereignty was protected by the extremely entrenched nature of the Constitution itself. It was made so difficult, as we shall see below, to alter the terms of the Constitution that the states were satisfied that their sovereignty would be safeguarded except in highly unusual and unlikely circumstances.

Two particular principles were designed to protect what are called 'states' rights'. One was a limitation upon the powers of the federal Congress and the Presidency so that there could be no significant erosion of state power. The other was to assert that any powers not covered by the Constitution would automatically be granted to individual states. Thus, even if the scope and functions of future government were to increase, it would not automatically lead to greater centralised power.

The Founding Fathers were, however, also realists and understood that the Constitution should not be too rigid in its division of sovereignty. Thus, some of the wording remains vague and capable of future interpretation. Terms such as 'trade' and 'commerce' are prominent examples of the compromise.

Despite some problems during over two hundred years of its life, the federal settlement has proved such a successful constitutional device in reconciling political unity with regional autonomy that many other states have adopted similar devices since. Germany, India and Russia have been important examples of federalism.

The structure of the Constitution

The Articles The Articles of the Constitution (effectively sections) reflect the thoughts of the founders on the appropriate nature of constitutional government, together with the philosophical principles established by the likes of John Locke, Tom Paine and Montesquieu. There are seven Articles in all, as listed below.

Article 1 The powers and limitations of the Federal Congress
Article 2 The powers and limitations of the President and his Administration
Article 3 The role of the judiciary, especially the Supreme Court
Article 4 The nature of membership of the Union and citizenship defined
Article 5 Procedures for amendment of the Constitution
Article 6 An affirmation of the supreme authority of the Constitution
Article 7 Arrangements for the original ratification of the Constitution

One area was omitted – a clear statement of the rights of citizens. This was put right before the ratification procedure was completed. The ten amendments forming the Bill of Rights are described below.

The Bill of Rights These amendments (confusingly, also known as 'Articles') are a description, varying in clarity, of the rights that American citizens can expect to enjoy. Article 6 of the main Constitution makes it clear that all laws and

rights. The rights that are established are as follows:

- freedom of religion
- freedom of speech and expression
- freedom of association and assembly
- freedom to petition government for redress of grievances
- the right to carry arms for self-protection
- freedom from enforced billeting of troops in private houses in peacetime
- protection from searches of private homes, except following legal procedure
- the right of accused persons in serious cases to have a preliminary hearing before a 'grand jury' – effectively a randomly selected group of members of the public
- the right of accused persons to remain silent during interrogation and trial in case they should incriminate themselves (the famous 'fifth amendment', hence the term 'pleading the fifth' when a defendant refuses to answer questions)
- protection from being tried for the same crime twice ('double jeopardy')
- accused persons must be quickly brought to trial and not held in custody without such a trial
- the right to trial by jury in serious cases
- the right to be represented by a lawyer in criminal cases
- protection from excessive bail and 'cruel and unusual punishments'
- any other rights enjoyed by individuals or the states are automatically protected unless expressly removed by consent of the people.

Though this forms an impressive list, the Bill of Rights still leaves a number of important questions unanswered. Examples of these issues include:

- Do these terms grant the right to privacy?
- Should there be limits to the right to carry weapons?
- Does 'cruel and unusual punishment' include all judicial executions, some types or none at all?

Apart from these open issues, which have continued to exercise the minds of lawyers, judges and politicians ever since, a number of further rights issues have come to light, with some being resolved and others not. Voting rights were left out and the issue of slavery was fudged. Discrimination against racial minorities and women was to become a key issue in the 1950s and 1960s and the latter remains to be resolved. Freedom of information has become an issue with the growth of government functions in recent times. So, too, has the question of censorship and pornography. Yet, apart from questions arising specifically out of modern developments, unforeseeable by the Constitution writers, the Bill of Rights remains a guide against which all legislation must be judged.

Amendments Any amendment to the Constitution requires the approval of two-thirds of both Houses of Congress, together with ratification by the legislative assemblies of three-quarters of the states (38 out of 50). It is a long and difficult procedure, as was fully intended when the Constitution was drawn up. This is an entrenched constitution. Changes were only to be considered if there was a broad consensus of support for such changes. The principle of 'government by consent' lives on in these amendment procedures.

During its life of just over two hundred years the Constitution has only been amended 27 times. This is testimony both to the complexity of the amendment procedures and the skill of the Founding Fathers in creating such an enduring system. Some of the most important amendments are shown in the table below.

Constitutional amendments		
Number	**Year**	**Detail**
13	1865	The abolition of slavery
14	1868	Establishment of equal rights, including their right to vote, for all males over 21
15	1870	Voting rights not to be denied to anyone on the grounds of race, colour or religion
18	1919	Prohibition of manufacture and sale of alcohol
19	1920	Voting rights for women established
21	1933	Repeal of the 18th Amendment (Prohibition)
22	1951	Presidents to have a maximum of two terms of office (8 years)
26	1971	Voting age reduced to 18

The difficulty in amending the Constitution can be illustrated by the problems encountered by two important proposals in recent times. The Equal Rights Amendment (ERA) was designed to force all states to outlaw discrimination against women. Having passed both Houses of Congress successfully, its ratification journey was halted in 1982 after 35 states had given their approval. Thus, it fell just three states short of enactment. In 1995 a proposal by Republican Senate leader Robert Dole to force future administrations to achieve a balanced budget (where government expenditure would be matched by revenue from taxation) fell two votes short of success in the Senate, having passed through the House of Representatives with a large majority.

438 ■ Success in Politics

The status of the Constitution

1803

Chief Justice John Marshall was possibly the USA's greatest constitutional lawyer and judge. He was Chief Justice of the Supreme Court from 1801 to 1835 at a time when a number of important cases were heard – cases that shaped the meaning and status of the Constitution. The most significant of these cases was *Marbury* v. *Madison* in 1803.

The case was a dispute over the appointment of judges. In making his judgment, Marshall made a declaration concerning the status of the Court and the Constitution which has been considered binding ever since. Three main principles were established:

- The Supreme Court has the right to undertake **judicial review** of cases brought before it in which constitutional principles are at stake.
- If the Supreme Court declares a law to be unconstitutional, it has no force and must be set aside.
- If there is a conflict between any ordinary law and a constitutional law, the latter must prevail.

The key section of Marshall's judgment is shown below:

> '*It is emphatically the province and duty of the judicial department to say what the law is. Those who apply the rule to particular cases, must of necessity expound and interpret that rule. If two laws conflict with each other, the courts must decide on the operation of each.*'
> Chief Justice John Marshall, *Marbury* v. *Madison*, 1803

McCulloch v. Maryland,
1819

It was Marshall again who enhanced the status of the federal Constitution in 1819 in a case where the state of Maryland was attempting to defy federal law. The state was brought before the Supreme Court where a far-reaching judgment was made.

Marshall ruled that, in any dispute between the laws of the federal Constitution and the laws of a particular state, the federal Constitution must prevail. Thus, although legal sovereignty is divided in the USA, there can be no doubt that the central authority of the Constitution is supreme. Marshall's words are clear in their implication:

> '*This great principle is, that the Constitution and the laws made in pursuance thereof are supreme; that they control the Constitution and laws of the respective states, and cannot be controlled by them.*'
> Chief Justice John Marshall, *McCulloch* v. *Maryland*, 1819

The living Constitution

The Supreme Court and the Constitution

John Marshall's term of office confirmed the status of the Supreme Court in the maintenance and development of the Constitution. Although, as we have seen, there have only been 27 **formal** amendments to the Constitution, this should not be interpreted to mean that it is a fixed, rigid document. On the contrary, it is constantly evolving and changing its practical applications.

The reasons for the evolving nature of the Constitution are threefold:

- Circumstances are constantly changing; fresh situations arise that have not been addressed by the terms of the Constitution. For example, the development of the communications media has thrown up new problems concerning censorship, privacy and federal control of broadcasting.
- The make-up of the Supreme Court itself is permanently changing. As judges retire or die and new members are appointed by the President, the political balance of the Court alters. Thus, for example, while a 'conservative' Court might allow capital punishment to be imposed, a more liberal bench might outlaw it. Similarly, some of the judges have been sympathetic to federal power and have, therefore, allowed a degree of centralisation; others have been staunch defenders of the rights of the individual states.
- The nature of American public opinion is in a permanent state of flux. Political sentiments and moral views do change over time. Thus, during the 1980s and 1990s a new moral movement took hold. This is reflected in a series of cases over such issues as abortion in which individual rights were reconsidered from a constitutional point of view. When the USA is in a liberal mood it is also civil liberties that often take the attention of the Supreme Court. Although some 'conservative' legal commentators have argued that the Supreme Court should not be influenced by movements in political and moral opinion among the general public, it has always been true that the judges have reflected changing public feeling.

Thus, the nature of the Supreme Court and its use of judicial review ensures that the Constitution is always evolving. To illustrate, some of the most celebrated constitutional cases are described briefly below.

Gibbons v. Ogden, 1824

The Constitution gives power to the federal government to **regulate commerce** but does not explain the precise meaning of the term 'commerce'. The pioneering Chief Justice John Marshall ruled in this case that commerce should be interpreted widely to include trade between the states and therefore, by implication, the general regulation of industrial and commercial activity. His words were clear: 'Commerce undoubtedly is traffic, but it is something more – it is intercourse. It describes the commercial intercourse between nations and parts of nations, in all its branches, and is regulated by prescribing rules for carrying on that intercourse.' The limited interpretation of federal power was, therefore, rejected by the ruling, and central government power has tended to increase ever since.

Dred Scott v. Sandford, 1857

A conservative Court was asked to judge whether black slaves could become citizens if they resided in a state where slavery was outlawed. It was ruled that, as slaves were 'property', they could not claim the same ~~r~~ ~~The decision~~ ~~f the factors that led to the~~ Civil War when the southern states sought to protect their right to maintain slavery. Though seen as a retrograde decision, the Court had opened the issue to public debate and, ultimately, the Constitution was amended to end slavery.

Pollock v. Farmers' Loan and Trust Company, 1895

This test case affirmed that the federal government did **not** have the constitutional right to levy taxes on income. The resultant debate over the issue led to the ultimate passage of the sixteenth amendment in 1913, allowing government to raise such tax.

Schechter Poultry Corporation v. United States, 1935

President F. D. Roosevelt's attempts to extend the power of the federal government into the field of industrial relations during the Great Depression (as part of his **New Deal** policies designed to regenerate American industry) was stopped in its tracks by this judgment. The **National Industrial Recovery Act** (NIRA) included measures to restrict working hours and so provide increased employment opportunities. Schechter challenged the Act on the grounds that the Constitution did not allow federal government to take such powers. The Court, which was unsympathetic to the New Deal policies, found in favour of Schechter. The NIRA was now virtually useless and it took Roosevelt a further two years, when a more friendly Court was in place, to restore his programme.

Brown v. Topeka Board of Education, 1954

In a number of the ultraconservative southern states, schools were usually segregated until the 1950s, to avoid the mixing of black and white pupils. In this case the practice was challenged and the Court held that blacks had the right to attend any school. The civil rights movement was, thus, given a boost which was to culminate in President Lyndon Johnson's Civil Rights Act of 1964, securing equal rights for all races.

Baker v. Carr, 1962

This case illustrated the ability of the Court to interpret constitutional principles broadly. The fifteenth amendment states that there must be equal voting rights for all. *Baker v. Carr*, however, concerned a claim that electoral boundaries were being manipulated to favour one political party – a practice known as **gerrymandering**. It was considered that such gerrymandering denied certain voters equal rights, since they were disadvantaged by the artificial creation of the electoral boundaries. This was indeed a liberal interpretation of the wording in the Constitution, but was still effective in establishing a new political principle – that the creation of such electoral boundaries must be seen to be neutral and fair to all parties.

Furman v. Georgia, 1972

The Court specifically abolished the use of the death penalty in this case on the grounds that its use varied so much from state to state and from court to court that it had become a matter of pure good or bad fortune whether a convicted murderer was put to death or not. Thus, it constituted an 'unusual' punishment, forbidden by the Constitution.

Gregg v. Georgia, 1976

A protracted debate followed the Furman case, as a result of which the Court reconsidered its earlier decision. Public opinion was also slowly returning to supporting the use of capital punishment. The Court finally declared that, under most circumstances, execution for capital crimes could be constitutional after all.

Roe v. Wade, 1973

This case, concerning abortion, reflected the rising power of feminism in the USA. By forbidding anti-abortion laws it affirmed the right of women to seek an abortion during the first three months of pregnancy.

Casey v. Planned Parenthood of Pennsylvania, 1992

As opinions on abortion began to change in the 1980s away from the liberal stance of the previous two decades, the Supreme Court was asked to reconsider the earlier *Roe* v. *Wade* judgment. The Casey case was a compromise whereby states were given powers to limit the circumstances under which abortions could be performed, without allowing them to introduce outright prohibition.

Adarand Constructors v. Pena, 1995

This case concerned a challenge to the principle of 'affirmative action', or positive discrimination, which is commonly implemented in American states. Normally, there is a legal requirement that larger employees take on a certain 'quota' of members of ethnic minorities in order to counteract the apparent negative discrimination that such groups suffer. Despite President Clinton's appointment of two liberal justices who might have supported this kind of device, a 5–4 majority outlawed many forms of affirmative action as an unconstitutional interference in commercial practice. Indeed, even the Court's one black judge voted with the conservative majority. The decision further confirmed the 1990s conservative reaction to civil rights progress.

This brief selection of Supreme Court cases illustrates the breadth of judicial action on developing the meaning and applications of the Constitution. Among them we can find examples of interpretation, responses to shifting public opinion and adaptation to changing circumstances. Thus, the Constitution is, indeed, alive and growing.

Legislation

The twin processes of constitutional amendment and judicial review ensure that the Constitution is constantly evolving, but these procedures are not enough to ensure that the business of government and politics can develop quickly enough to meet shorter-term contingencies. More flexible devices are necessary to deal with rapidly changing circumstances. Here, ordinary legislation can be used to flesh out the skeleton of the Constitution. Though Acts of Congress do not carry special labels if they are of constitutional significance, we can recognise them as such from the nature of their content. They form a part of the 'living' Constitution in the same way as the other devices that have been described above. Some of the most important constitutional Acts are shown below.

Federal Regulation of Lobbying Act, 1946

Responding to the growth in the activities of pressure and interest groups in Congress, this Act requires all such groups to register with Congress in order to have access to legislators. It also forces them to declare the nature of their activities, the sources of their funds and the use to which they have been put.

This was a clear case of legislation being needed to meet a fresh cir-

detailed regulation, it was not practical to use the method of constitutional amendment. In addition, the Act can be easily adjusted by Congress in the future without recourse to the long and complex constitutional amendment procedures.

Civil Rights Act, 1964

President John F. Kennedy was the architect of this legislation, but was assassinated before he was able to enact it. His successor, Lyndon Johnson, guided it through a sympathetic Congress a year after Kennedy's death.

In essence, the Act prevented federal funds being given to any enterprise where racial discrimination was practised. Although its main effect was on educational provision, which relies heavily on such funds, by outlawing racial discrimination it had the broader effect of bringing southern states into line with the rest of the country. The constitutional provisions had not proved clear or detailed enough to prevent discriminatory practices, so additional legislation had been required.

War powers resolution, 1973

The Constitution asserts that war may only be **officially** declared by Congress – a requirement that delayed the USA's entry into both world wars. However, the Constitution also clearly states that the President is Commander-in-Chief of the armed forces. The question therefore arises: who has constitutional authority when war is **undeclared**?

This question was brought into focus when President Nixon engaged in increasingly secret armed operations in Vietnam and Cambodia against communist insurgents during the 1970s. Congress demanded the right to be informed and consulted, while Nixon quoted his own constitutional powers to justify his actions. Congress passed the War Powers Resolution in 1973, despite the President's attempts to veto it. This Act requires the President to inform congressional leaders immediately after he has committed American troops to combat. Thereafter Congress may order withdrawal after 60 days, giving the President a further 60 days to comply. Effectively, this means that the President may commit troops to combat for a period of four to five months without declaring war and without being forced by Congress to withdraw.

The constitutionality of the Resolution is still in doubt, but there has not been an opportunity for the Supreme Court to test its validity. Operations by American forces since the end of the Vietnam War have been short and limited. Invasions of Grenada (1983), Lebanon (1983–4) and Haiti (1994) in attempts to restore ordered government, the bombing of specific targets in Libya (1986) in retaliation for acts of terrorism, and the Gulf War (1991) were all too restricted to present a threat to the Resolution. Nevertheless, it is a clear example of how legislation can redefine constitutional statements.

Gramm–Rudman–Hollings (GRH) Act, 1985

Named after its congressional sponsors, the GRH Act was a response to the growing fiscal deficit being experienced by the federal government. The deficit – an excess of public spending over receipts from taxation – had grown to alarming proportions when President **Reagan** came to office in 1983. He was, therefore, happy to support such legislation.

It required that the President and Congress should adopt a medium-term strategy for bringing down the deficit and, eventually, eliminating it altogether. It was a 'constitutional' measure in that it sought to place important restrictions on the activities of central government in the interests of taxpayers and inflation control.

In the event, the Act proved to be virtually unworkable and the deficit has since continued to grow. Senator Bob Dole's attempts to convert the basis of the GRH Act into a constitutional amendment narrowly failed in 1995, but the issue remains a priority for the Republican Party.

Foreign policy declarations

The Constitution makes no mention of specific foreign policy issues, other than to describe the powers of President and Congress in the conduct of war and the negotiation of treaties. The actual **objectives** of American foreign policy have never been declared in constitutional form. There have, however, been two key doctrines established which shape such policy.

The Monroe Doctrine, 1823

Alarmed by political disorders in Central and South American countries, resulting in interference by European powers, President **Monroe** resolved to establish the USA's place in its own hemisphere, or 'back-yard' as it has come to be known.

In the interests of the security and self-defence of the USA, Monroe declared that western hemisphere affairs were the rightful concern of the USA and that it would, henceforth, claim the right to intervene to maintain order in that part of the world. The blockade of Cuba in 1963 by John Kennedy in order to force the removal of Soviet missiles, and the invasions of Grenada and Haiti described above, are clear recent examples of the operation of the doctrine.

> 'The United States looks on any attempt on their [foreign powers'] part to extend their system to any portion of this hemisphere as dangerous to our peace and safety.'
> President James Monroe, 1823

The Truman Doctrine, 1947

After the end of the Second World War, it became apparent that the Soviet Union was engaged in a programme of expansionism. President Truman met this threat by committing the USA to the defence of the 'free world'.

Since then there have been several examples of American forces being used in response to the need to defend vulnerable peoples from external invasion. Clear examples are the defence of West Berlin in 1949, Korea 1950–3, Vietnam in the 1960s and 1970s, and Kuwait in 1991. (Technically Kuwait and Korea were United Nations operations, but there was no doubting that the USA was the driving force.)

> 'It is the policy of the United States to support free peoples who are resisting subjugation by armed minorities or outside pressures.'
> President Harry Truman, Address to Congress, 1947

These doctrines are neither constitutional requirements nor Acts of Congress. Nevertheless, they have been considered so powerful that Presidents since have considered them binding in foreign policy

Informal amendments

As in the UK, written principles do not give the full picture of how the United States' Constitution works. There are also 'conventions' or informal practices that determine the real operation of government.

Executive agreements are a typical example. These are pacts or contracts made by the President with foreign powers. Not being classed as 'treaties', they do not require the formal approval of Congress. It is understood that, in the conduct of foreign policy, the President must have some flexibility and this device provides him or her with such freedom. Yet we will not find regulations governing such agreements written down formally in the archives of Congress.

There are similar 'conventions' affecting the operation of Congress. Though both Houses have similar powers with regard to the development of the federal budget, it is understood that the House of Representatives plays a leading role and the Senate will be led by the House. In foreign affairs the position is reversed. The House may debate such foreign issues, but is not expected to attempt to usurp the Senate's pre-eminence in the field.

The doctrine of the separation of powers, enshrined in the Constitution, also disguises the existence of an important political practice. Although, unlike in the UK, the executive branch is not strictly **responsible** to Congress and its members, including the President, and cannot be removed by Congress for purely political reasons, it is clear that there is a constant requirement for officers of the administration to report to Congress and respond to its criticisms. Powerful congressional committees regularly submit Department Heads to close scrutiny and it is understood that, should criticism become severe enough, the President must remove the individual in question although neither constitutionally nor legally obliged to do so. This particular development in the practical operation of government has simply arisen over the years and is, therefore, an informal, gradual amendment to constitutional doctrine.

Summary of constitutional development and change

1. Formal amendment, such as women's voting rights, 1920

2. Interpretations by the Supreme Court such as *Roe* v. *Wade*, 1973

3. Legislation, such as Gramm–Rudman–Hollings, 1985

4. Presidential doctrines, such as the Truman Doctrine, 1947

5. Informal amendment, such as the growth of executive agreements

The British and American Constitutions compared

Philosophical principles

The American Constitution is predominantly a **liberal** document, while the UK's counterpart is essentially **conservative** in nature. The implications of this difference are deep and far-reaching.

Such liberal ideas as limited government, government by consent, the separation of powers, the desire to safeguard individual rights and the need to establish legal and political equality are all fixed for the foreseeable future in the American Constitution. It was never expected that these principles would be threatened, and so it has proved.

In the UK, by contrast, the conservative traditions of the political establishment have demanded that the system should not be subject to such unchanging, abstract principles. For a conservative, the Constitution is a part of the living, changing society and culture. It is rooted within them. It should, therefore, be allowed to grow and develop in sympathy with social change. Thus, it cannot be a fixed set of principles, but should, instead, be allowed to reflect constantly shifting public sentiment. So when it is felt that some individual rights should be sacrificed in the interests of public order – when there is a marked rise in crime, for example – the British Constitution is flexible enough to allow this to occur. Similarly, when it is widely accepted that government should be granted more powers – such as at the time of the creation of the welfare state – this can be achieved without major constitutional upheaval. American leaders and legislators are hampered by the rigid liberal principles of their Constitution, and while this reassures the people, it makes fundamental political change difficult. Though liberals and socialists in the UK might disagree with this philosophy, the pre-eminence of conservatism over the past two centuries has ensured the retention of the traditional character of the Constitution.

Status

The different philosophical foundations of the two constitutions, as described above, give rise to important contrasts in their status. In the USA it is clear that the Constitution is absolutely supreme. All laws and Acts of government are subordinate to it. Where there is a conflict, the Constitution must always prevail. So declared Chief Justice John Marshall nearly two hundred years ago.

In the UK it is accepted that, while constitutional principles are important, they can be subordinated to the needs of government and the wishes of Parliament. Provided the correct procedures are adopted, ordinary law and decisions taken under properly delegated powers cannot be constrained by the Constitution. This principle will always be upheld by the courts.

Codification

The clearest difference that can be discerned lies in the very clear way in which the American document is laid out, with all the major aspects of the political system included. The British Constitution is not codified at all, there being no single document entitled 'The Constitution'.

This is not the same as not being 'written', however. Parts of the British Constitution are written in the form of statutes and important documents. It is also not the case that the whole of the American Constitution is written. As we have seen above, there are elements that are purely 'convention', in particular the relationships between the executive and legislative branches of government.

It may be, however, that the closer links with the European Union which [...]

tutional constraints. The original Treaty of Rome and the Maastricht Treaty of 1992 are both examples of quasi-constitutional codification.

Entrenchment

Here again a wide difference can be seen. The American Constitution is exceptionally deeply entrenched, possibly the most stubbornly safeguarded of all the major constitutions in the democratic world. This is far from the case in the UK.

The sovereignty of the British Parliament, its inability to bind its successors to constitutional principles, renders the Constitution extremely flexible. It can mean changes being made merely through the passage of a statute – an event that can take less than two days and requires only a simple majority of both Houses of Parliament. Some entrenchment does exist in the unwritten conventions that make up so much of the British Constitution. Since conventions only develop over long periods of time, and certainly need a consensus of support in order to become established, they are, in practice, entrenched through tradition. However, it still remains true that, in most cases, a statute could overturn a convention if there were enough support.

The extensive increase in the scope of government in the 1940s, and the dramatic changes that took place in the balance of power between central and local government in the 1980s, bear testimony to the flexibility of the British Constitution. In the USA, such reforms would have required a considerably longer period of time to effect and, indeed, could probably not have been contemplated. The rigidity of rules governing the distribution of political power in the USA is difficult to overcome. President Clinton's vain attempts to increase federal responsibility for health care in the 1990s demonstrate the difficulties involved.

Though the British Constitution remains flexible, those European regulations that now apply in the UK are deeply entrenched, often requiring the unanimous approval of all the member states of the EU. The advent of a European Constitution, similar in its status to that of the USA, might not be far off.

Judicial review

Despite the key differences in the nature of the entrenchment of the two constitutions, there are a number of similarities in the processes of change. Of course, formal amendment is far more difficult in the USA than in the UK, but the less formal processes are similar.

Judicial review is carried out in the British courts – usually the Court of Appeal or the House of Lords – in much the same way as the Supreme Court operates. Challenges may be made to the constitutional validity of executive actions and the judges are required to test those actions against established constitutional principles. In both countries the courts have the power to set aside governmental decisions. Even in the UK, the Government is always loath to risk incurring unfavourable judgments by the courts.

What is more important about judicial review, however, is that it provides opportunities in both systems for the Constitution to be interpreted and reinterpreted according to circumstances. Parliament plays a bigger role in the process than does Congress, but it remains true that both constitutions rely heavily on judges to ensure their systems remain up to date.

For exam questions relevant to this unit, see page 559.

18 The United States' Congress

Key selections from the United States' Constitution, Article 1

Section 1	All legislative powers granted shall be vested in a Congress of the United States which shall consist of a Senate and a House of Representatives.
Section 2(1)	The House of Representatives shall be composed of Members chosen every second year by the people of the several States.
Section 2(5)	The House of Representatives shall choose their Speaker and other Officers, and shall have the sole power of impeachment.
Section 3(1)	The Senate of the United States shall be composed of two Senators from each State . . . thereof, for six years and each Senator shall have one vote.
Section 3(4)	The Vice President of the United States shall be President of the Senate, but shall have no vote, unless they be equally divided.
Section 3(6)	The Senate shall have the sole power to try impeachments.
Section 6(2)	No Senator or Representative shall, during the time for which he was elected, be appointed to any civil office under the authority of the United States, which shall have been created, or the emoluments whereof shall have been increased during such time; and no person holding any office under the United States, shall be a member of either House during his continuance in office.
Section 7(1)	All Bills for raising revenue shall originate in the House of Representatives; but the Senate may propose or concur with amendments as on other Bills.
Section 7(2)	Every Bill which shall have passed the House of Representatives and the Senate shall, before it becomes law, be presented to the President of the United States; if he approves he shall sign it, but if not he shall return it with his objections to the House in which it shall have originated, who shall enter the objections at large on their journal, and proceed to reconsider it. If, after such reconsideration, two-thirds of the House shall agree to pass the Bill it shall be sent, together with the objections, to the other House, by which it shall likewise be reconsidered, and if approved by two-thirds of that House, it shall become law.
Section 8(1)	The Congress shall have power to lay and collect taxes, duties, imposts and excises to pay the debts and provide for the common defence and general welfare of the United States; but all duties, imposts and excises shall be uniform throughout the United States.
Section 8(3)	The Congress shall have power to regulate commerce with foreign Nations, and among the several States, and with the Indian Tribes.
Section 8(11)	The Congress shall have power to declare War.
Section 8(12)	The Congress shall have power to raise and support armies, but no appropriation of money to that use shall be for a longer term than two years.
Section 9(8)	No title of nobility shall be granted by the United States.

Introduction

The US Congress is unlike any other legislature. In particular, it possibly deserves the term 'law-making body' more than any of its rivals. While Congress initiates, debates, amends and creates laws; other assemblies are either mere charades, as is the case in many one-party systems, or so dominated by the executive branch that they cannot claim to be truly independent, as is the case in the UK. Such assemblies might have adopted formal procedures for the passage and legitimisation of legislation, but none of them can claim to be a genuine law-maker. Not so Congress. In respect of its other functions – scrutiny and control of government and representation of interests and political philosophies – it might not appear to be extraordinary. It is its ability to develop law that singles it out from the rest.

We can find few clues to this special quality in the Constitution. While it is true that all Congress's current functions are to be found, explicitly or implicitly, in the provisions of the Constitution, it is not immediately clear why Congress has not developed in the way that legislatures in other liberal democracies have done. It may help us to consider first why other legislative assemblies have failed to become true law-makers. Having developed some theories, we might discover what it is about Congress that makes it so different. Three features are apparent:

- **The committee system**. Most elected assemblies are too large to be able to develop coherent legislative programmes. Of course, Congress is also very large, but it has developed a committee system which ensures that legislation with widespread support **can** be created and passed without the organisation and discipline, normally provided by government. Each committee becomes a relatively small policy community in itself.
- **Checks and balances**. It is normally the case that the executive branch dominates the legislature. Not unexpectedly, governments will use their control to demand a virtual monopoly over law making. Indeed, most democratic governments claim an electoral mandate for their legislative programmes. They argue that their authority is derived from the electorate. Representative assemblies are also elected, of course, but they cannot assert the same authority as the governing party or coalition, which owes its position to public support for specific policies. Such domination of the legislature by the executive is not possible in the USA. The system of 'checks and balances' that was included so carefully in the Constitution gives Congress its independence. While the President can claim a separate electoral mandate, he or she is aware that members of the Congress have a continuous direct line of communication to the electorate through the open access that it allows to the many interest and pressure groups which form the lobby. The balance of power is, thus, both a constitutional and a political reality.
- **The party system**. American parties are considerably less coherent and unified than most other democratic parties. They might be efficient in such functions as candidate selection, electioneering and finance raising, but as policy-making machines they make little impact. Where

parties are concentrated, disciplined centres of policy development, legislative power can be retained by them when they achieve governmental office. In the USA there are few effective party institutions in the field of law making. The vacuum is filled not only by the President and his or her administration, but equally by Congress.

The Constitution clearly intended that Congress should exercise a great deal of control over public finance, both the raising of taxes and government expenditure. So it has proved. Taxation had been a particularly sensitive issue in the Americans' dissatisfaction with British rule, so it was hardly surprising that special provisions regarding this were included when the Union Constitution was written. What was perhaps not envisaged was the effect that financial control would have over general policy. Most government programmes require large amounts of money to make them work. Congress's control over such funds has the effect of giving it power over the policies themselves. Such programmes as health care, welfare, defence and transport initiatives may be proposed by the President, who might obtain congressional approval for them **in principle**. Yet if the necessary funds are not approved, the exercise might prove futile.

Newt Gingrich's 'Contract with America'

Shortly before the congressional elections in November 1994, over 300 Republican Party candidates for the House signed a document known as the 'Contract with America'. Newt Gingrich, the inspiration behind the Contract, insisted that it be read before every session of the House to remind members of their promise.

  The Contract detailed ten key measures that were to be enacted within four months of the new Congress and, with the Republicans having won a majority, there was a good possibility that a number of the proposed Acts would reach the statute book. The ten terms of the Contract were as follows:

1. The Fiscal Responsibility Act to ensure a balanced government budget by 2002.
2. Congressmen's terms of office to be restricted to six years in total, Senators' to twelve.
3. Tougher anti-crime measures, including more use of the death penalty.
4. Tightening up of the rules entitling various groups to welfare benefits.
5. Reduced taxes for middle-income groups.
6. Increased defence expenditure but reduced contributions to the United Nations.
7. Reductions in the amounts of damages paid in civil disputes.
8. Reduced taxes on capital gains to encourage investment.
9. Reduced taxes on pensioners.
10. Banning of homosexuals in the armed forces.

The significance of the Contract is that it was the first attempt by an American party to create a detailed election manifesto along the lines of those produced by British parties. Presidential vetoes and something of a Democratic recovery in the 1996 congressional elections ultimately undermined the Contract. Nevertheless, the swing to the right in American politics in 1994 is illustrated by the radical nature of the Contract.

As we have suggested above, all legislatures assert the right to exercise some degree of control over government. The Congress is no exception. There can be little doubt that most of the Founding Fathers would have been delighted by the way in which Congress has developed its scrutiny role. The traditional American fear of central government power is expressed in modern times through the way in which members of Congress insist on regular questioning, even interrogation, of representatives of the federal government.

Newt Gingrich, holding a copy of the 'Contract with America', 11 January 1995

It is normal for the representation of interests to operate largely within government agencies. In democratic systems, it is recognised that policy is largely in the hands of senior officials and ministers, so that pressure must be concentrated there. Legislatures are subject to lobbying everywhere, of course, but this is invariably a secondary activity. The greater influence that the American Congress enjoys forces lobbyists to split their efforts between the administration at the White House and Congress on Capitol Hill. The American system is remarkable for the open access it allows to all those who legitimately seek to influence. Indeed, the institutions of Congress, principally its committees, operate as the forum within which the three main elements of policy development can meet. Here, representatives of interest groups, members of Congress and senior office-holders in the administration can communicate and negotiate. The term 'pluralism' is possibly most aptly used in this context. Congress is not simply a legislative assembly, it is very much a market place in which demands, influence and political decisions are traded.

We can now summarise the principal features of Congress. These are shown below.

Main features of Congress

1. It is very much involved with the process of making law.
2. It is a forum of negotiation between the administration, interest groups and elected members over legislation and finance.
3. There is open access to interest and pressure groups.
4. It exercises close scrutiny and control over the executive branch.
5. Its power is balanced delicately against that of the President.
6. The party system is relatively weak and diffused.

The composition of the Senate

Senators

There are 100 Senators, two from each state. Since each state has the same representation, some small states, such as Alaska and Wyoming, are 'over-represented', while larger states, such as Texas and California, are relatively 'under-represented'. Senators are elected on a six-year term of office, but Senate seats are not all contested in the same year. Every two years one-third of the seats are contested. Thus, the composition of the Senate changes gradually. For each state, the Senator who has served for the longer period is called 'Senior Senator', while his or her colleague is called 'Junior Senator'.

The reason for the uneven representation of states is largely historical. The smaller members of the original Union in 1787, such as Rhode Island, feared the power of their larger neighbours, notably Virginia. Had there been representation on the basis of population, two or three states of the original thirteen would have been able to dominate proceedings by holding a permanent majority in the legislature. As we shall see, the House of Representatives is based on equal geographical representation, but the Senate, with virtually equal powers, acts as a balance against the power of the big states. Although this is less critical today, with 50 states in the Union, the system offers some protection against the powerful majority. It is interesting to note at this stage that the same kind of problem faces the European Union as it seeks to develop democratic institutions. For Virginia read Germany, and for Rhode Island read Portugal, and the difficulty becomes clear.

President of the Senate

The President of the Senate is the Vice President of the USA. Effectively, this makes him or her the equivalent of the 'Speaker' in the House of Representatives or in the British House of Commons. In this role the President of the Senate is expected to be neutral, maintaining good order, organising debates and dealing with procedural disputes. He or she is, of course, in an ideal position to act as the President's representative in the Senate. However, since neutrality is required, this must be handled with some degree of subtlety and sensitivity. The President of the Senate cannot vote, not being an elected Senator, but will resolve a tied vote. Normally an irrelevant function, this power suddenly became vital when the Senate was tied 50–50 between Democrats and Republicans from January 2001. Since the Vice President must inevitably be absent for much of the time on duties of State, he or she is often replaced by the **President Pro Tempore**. This is a senior Senator of the majority party who, although neutral in maintaining discipline and organisation, is allowed to vote.

Senate majority leader

The Senate majority leader is the key party leader in the Senate. As the name suggests, he or she is chosen by the Senators of whichever party holds the majority of the seats in the Senate. In modern times this has usually been the Democrats, although there was a significant period from 1981 to 1988 when the Republicans were in the ascendancy during the Reagan years (at that time the House was still Democrat dominated). The majority leader has a number of roles, as described below:

- Attempting to ensure that legislation to which his or her party is sympathetic receives sufficient debating time to stand a chance of success.
- Mobilising support, particularly within his or her own party, for such legislation. It should be noted here that achieving ~~~~~~~~~~~ unity behind a measure is deemed to be a success in congressional politics. Republican **Howard Baker** (majority leader 1981–5) achieved an average of 80 per cent unity for President Reagan's proposals in the Senate and was thus a key figure in the reforms of that period.
- Mobilising support for the President's proposals, provided, of course, that the President is of the same party. There might be a few occasions when the majority leader and a President of the same party might disagree, but this is unusual.
- Playing a leading role in the appointment of his or her own party's members on committees.

Senate Republican leader Robert Dole in 1994

Thus, while the President might have a higher profile on the international scene, the Senate majority leader, and his or her equivalent in the House, is a key personality in American domestic politics, carrying great authority and influence. Republican **Bob Dole** took over in 1995, forming a powerful alliance with the Speaker of the House of Representatives, **Newt Gingrich**. This extremely conservative alliance acted as a strong barrier to presidential influence.

The events of 1996–8, however, turned matters in Clinton's favour. The key factors were as follows:

- Newt Gingrich was replaced by the more moderate Dennis Hastert.
- Clinton won a second term in office quite comfortably against Republican Bob Dole.
- Despite the growing Monica Lewinski scandal, Clinton remained a popular leader.
- The economy was booming. This meant that the Republicans' determination to force the President to 'balance the budget' (i.e. spend no more than he was collecting in taxation) became irrelevant. The budget soon balanced itself and Clinton was seen as a responsible President.
- Congress's attempts to bring American government to a standstill by refusing to agree the presidential budget in 1997 backfired. Public opinion saw it as a negative response and Clinton profited as the perceived victim.
- Clinton was extremely cautious in his legislative programme and so did not suffer major defeats.

These events demonstrate that, whatever the political make-up of the Congress, a President can assert his or her authority given favourable political circumstances.

Possibly the most successful majority leader of modern times was Lyndon Johnson (1953–61), who was to become Vice President and later President. He was a Democrat confronted by a Republican President (Eisenhower). Nevertheless, he was able to lay the groundwork for the civil rights and welfare programmes that he and President Kennedy were to complete in the following decade. Indeed, Johnson himself formed a vital alliance with majority leader Mike Mansfield (1961–77) to steer through many liberal reforms.

Senate minority leader

The Senate minority leader, as the name suggests, does not enjoy the luxury of a party majority. Even so, several of his or her functions are similar to those of the Senate majority leader. Of particular importance are those occasions when the minority leader is of the same party as the President – a situation that occurred during the Republican presidencies of Richard Nixon and Gerald Ford (1968–76). With a Democrat majority in both Houses of Congress, the role became particularly difficult, especially during the complex foreign policy issues caused by the Vietnam conflict and the continuing Cold War.

The minority leader has relatively little influence over the legislative programme, but is still expected to attempt to mobilise his or her party, either in opposition to, or support of, particular measures. The minority leader's party will also enjoy fewer committee seats than the opposing party. It is largely up to him or her to allocate such places.

The importance of the Senate majority position was thrown into dramatic focus in May 2001 when a unique set of circumstances came together. Senator Jeffords of Vermont, a moderate Republican, decided he had no stomach for the policies of the new President, George W. Bush. He therefore became an independent, the only one of his kind in the Senate.

Before this event the evenly split Senate (50–50 between Democrats and Republicans) was effectively Republican controlled because of the casting vote of the Vice President (like his boss, Bush, a Republican). Now, however, the Democrats enjoyed majority status by 50–49 (Vice President Chainey's casting vote no longer being operational). As a result, control of all the key committees, in particular the Senate Policy Committee, fell into Democrat hands. From now on Bush would have infinitely more difficulty in forcing his legislation through the Senate. In other words, the actions of one individual had completely shifted the balance of power away from the ruling Republicans towards the opposition Democrats. Perhaps never before had the US system of checks and balances worked so effectively.

Whips

Both parties have whips who have the unenviable task of attempting to maintain party discipline in a system where members are notoriously independent. The whips of both parties have little hope of persuading Senators to change their mind over an issue when they are being placed under great pressure from constituents, lobbyists or Policy Action Committees, upon whom they depend for re-election sooner or later. In practice, the whips become the principal assistants to both the majority and minority leaders. They might help to persuade, cajole or forge deals with wavering Senators, but they cannot bully them into compliance.

Party committees

Party committees should not be confused with the standing and select committees of the Senate. As we have seen, party organisation in Congress is notoriously weak and this is reflected in the relative lack of importance of party committees. Nevertheless, both parties attempt to influence the course and fortunes of legislation through such committees. The **Democrats** have a **Policy Committee** that seeks to determine which legislation has a chance of success, and a **Steering Committee** to ease the passage of such Bills. The **Republicans** limit themselves to a **Policy Committee** with both functions. Unlike the Democrats, Republicans have a **Committee on Committees**, which largely determines which Senators sit on which congressional committees. Its chairperson wields considerable influence in the party, since patronage over committee seats is an important element in political authority.

Party caucuses

From time to time, all Senators from the respective parties will meet to discuss matters of common concern. Such sessions are known as party **caucuses**, or **conferences**. Once again, we must take into account the relative lack of party unity and discipline in the USA. The caucuses might be the scene of heated debates from time to time, but the real horse trading and persuasion goes on in private committee rooms and offices.

Before we move on to describe the congressional committee system, the most important feature of the politics of the legislature, we must examine the House of Representatives.

The composition of the House of Representatives

Congressional Districts

Unlike Senators, members of the House represent roughly equal constituencies, known as Congressional Districts. The size of each district is between 550,000 and 600,000 people. Although districts are inevitably smaller in very small states, there must be at least two members from each state. In 1994 there were 435 members. They must seek re-election every two years when the whole House goes to the polls. This is perhaps the shortest term of office of any representative assembly in the West. We shall see its effects later, but it is immediately apparent that membership may change more rapidly than that of the Senate.

Speaker

The affairs of the House are presided over by a Speaker who is, by tradition though not by law, a leading member of the majority party. He or she has a dual role. When chairing the House, the Speaker is expected to be even-handed and will not take part in debate, although he or she is allowed to vote. As a senior member of his or her party, however, the Speaker has considerable patronage over committee posts and is influential in determining what legislation is likely to survive to reach the statute book. The Speaker is also expected to play a leading part in keeping the party together and is, thus, an auxiliary whip.

The best-known modern Speaker was **Tip O'Neill**, a Democrat who did much to thwart the plans of his own party's President (Carter), and then did little to stop President Reagan, in theory an opponent, gaining control over the federal budget. However, in 1995, following the success of his party in the 1994 congressional elections, Republican **Newt Gingrich** took over the post. Gingrich, a right-winger with a strong antipathy to federal government power, held something of a stranglehold over presidential proposals in the House.

US House of Representatives

But Gingrich did not last long. Discredited in his personal life and, having failed to gain significant support for his own personal manifesto, he gave way to the more moderate Dennis Hastert. Hastert understood that the Republicans would have to make compromises with any of their plans. There was not the two-thirds conservative majority necessary to overturn the presidential veto, so Hastert was forced to deal with Clinton rather than confront him, as Gingrich had done.

Floor leader and whip

As in the Senate, the majority party elects a 'floor leader' and a whip. Their role, jointly, is to try to maintain, some degree of party unity and to engineer support for Bills that the party as a whole can support. Assisted by a small army of assistant whips, they engage in much the same negotiating and persuasion that characterises the Senate. Representatives are perhaps even more independent-minded than Senators. Their short term of office means that they are virtually fighting a permanent election campaign. They are under pressure from constituents and financial sponsors alike. Their voting records are well publicised and may determine their ability to raise funds and win votes for the next election campaign. Thus, the floor leader and whips have their work cut out in creating party cohesion. The minority party has a similar team with the same role, although, being in a minority, they are often fighting a rearguard action.

Both floor leaders have a special relationship with the President, whether he or she is of the same party or not. If the President can gain the support of either or both floor leaders, his or her chances of implementing policies successfully are considerably increased.

Party caucuses

The two parties have similar structures to those of the Senate, with a caucus of all members, together with **Policy** and **Steering Committees**. Both parties, but especially the Democrats who invariably hold a majority in the House, have attempted to make these institutions into a more formalised and centralised structure for the sake of greater party unity. Little success has been achieved, however, so the formal structure is of much less importance than their equivalents in many European legislatures.

We can now summarise the structure of the two Houses, excluding the standing and select committee systems.

Structure of the Senate and House of Representatives	
Senate	**House of Representatives**
• Senate President (US Vice President)	• Speaker
• Majority leader	• Majority floor leader
• Minority leader	• Minority floor leader
• Majority whip	• Majority whip
• Minority whip	• Minority whip
• Party conferences (caucuses)	• Party conferences
• Party Policy Committees	• Party Policy Committees
• Democratic Steering Committee	• Democratic Steering Committee
• Republican Committee on Committees	• Republican Committee on Committees
• 100 Senators (six-year term)	• 435 Representatives (two-year term)

The committee system in Congress

The committees in their setting

The Constitution of the USA makes no mention of congressional committees. This is hardly surprising since, with only thirteen states in the Union and a relatively limited population, Congress was very small to begin with. Add to this the fact that the volume of business was relatively limited at that time, and we can see that committees were scarcely necessary. Today, by contrast, several thousand measures are proposed in each session of Congress. Many of these are extremely complex and often contentious. They must all be studied, sifted and filtered. The small number that do receive a hearing require careful consideration and often radical amendment. Congress as a whole cannot hope to perform such an enormous task without resorting to a form of streamlining. Hence there are committees – in particular, the standing committees.

The standing committees in both Houses are listed below.

Standing Committees in the Senate and House of Representatives	
Senate	**House of Representatives**
• Appropriations	• Appropriations
• Finance	• Ways and Means
• Foreign Relations	• Foreign Affairs
• Armed Services	• Armed Services
• Budget	• Rules
• Agriculture etc.	• Agriculture
• Banking, Housing and Urban Affairs	• Banking, Finance and Urban Affairs
• Commerce, Science and Transport	• Education and Labor
• Energy and Natural Resources	• Government Operations
• Environment and Public Works	• House Administration
• Government Affairs	• Judiciary
• Judiciary	• Merchant, Marine and Fisheries
• Labor and Human Resources	• Natural Resources
• Rules and Administration	• Post Office and Civil Service
• Science and Space	• Public Works and Transport
• Small Business	
• Standards of Official Conduct	
• Veterans' Affairs	
• Ways and Means	

This impressive list of committees goes some way to illustrating the complexity of Congress. Indeed, the legislative process is often described as a labyrinth, with many avenues and dead ends. As we shall see, few proposals are able to make a successful passage through it.

If we are to enter the maze, we will need a map. The following procedure refers to a Bill originating in the House. Bills beginning in the Senate have the same procedure, with the Senate stages taken first.

The US legislative
process

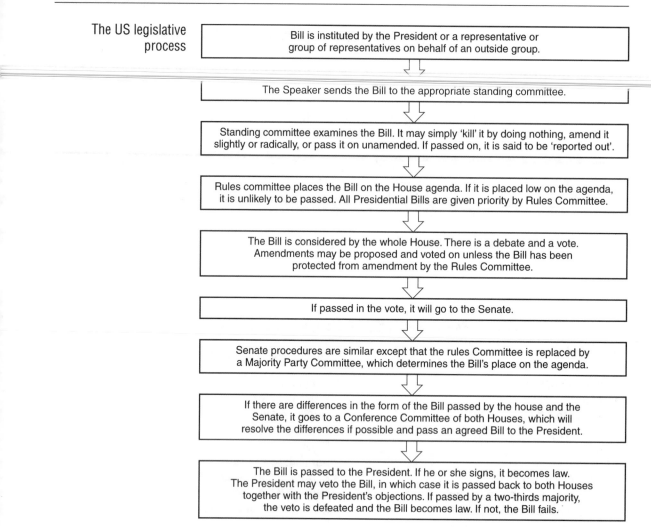

Bill is instituted by the President or a representative or
group of representatives on behalf of an outside group.

The Speaker sends the Bill to the appropriate standing committee.

Standing committee examines the Bill. It may simply 'kill' it by doing nothing, amend it
slightly or radically, or pass it on unamended. If passed on, it is said to be 'reported out'.

Rules committee places the Bill on the House agenda. If it is placed low on the agenda,
it is unlikely to be passed. All Presidential Bills are given priority by Rules Committee.

The Bill is considered by the whole House. There is a debate and a vote.
Amendments may be proposed and voted on unless the Bill has been
protected from amendment by the Rules Committee.

If passed in the vote, it will go to the Senate.

Senate procedures are similar except that the rules Committee is replaced by
a Majority Party Committee, which determines the Bill's place on the agenda.

If there are differences in the form of the Bill passed by the house and the
Senate, it goes to a Conference Committee of both Houses, which will
resolve the differences if possible and pass an agreed Bill to the President.

The Bill is passed to the President. If he or she signs, it becomes law.
The President may veto the Bill, in which case it is passed back to both Houses
together with the President's objections. If passed by a two-thirds majority,
the veto is defeated and the Bill becomes law. If not, the Bill fails.

Subject standing committees

Every aspect of governmental and legislative activity is covered by a congressional committee. Since these committees are permanent, with some members spending most or all of their careers on the same committees, they become considerable experts in their field. They have access to a large research staff, which may be augmented from time to time for special consideration of legislation, and extensive finance is available. Members may travel around the country, or even abroad when appropriate, in pursuit of information and opinion. They may also commission major private investigations.

Although their principal role is to consider and amend legislation, committees are engaged in a permanent scrutiny of those government agencies that deal with their work. They get to know officials well and have the right to demand to know what is going on in policy formulation. The USA has a tradition and, indeed, laws of freedom of information. The chronic secrecy that characterises British government is largely absent. Questioning of officials might be inquisitorial or friendly, depending on the situation, but whichever obtains, there is a relatively free flow of information between executive and legislature.

When a committee is considering a Bill, it will call witnesses from a variety of sources to assist in its work. Thus, other members of Congress not already on the committee might appear, together with government officials and representatives of interest and pressure groups who have a vested interest in the legislation. Add to this impressive list any number of outside experts or academics who might be required, and we have a picture of a full-scale inquiry every time a new law is proposed. Where a matter of great public concern and interest is at stake, hearings might be broadcast, sometimes on live TV. Where necessary, votes are taken among the members and again these are matters of public record.

The committee chairperson is a key figure. He or she has a major influence over the agenda, determining which Bills will be considered and which will be 'shelved'. Committees are presented with far more business than they can possibly transact within the allotted time. If a Bill is put aside for later consideration, it is being effectively killed. The committee chairperson will also have a significant influence over proposed amendments. Again, those considered first will receive a proper hearing; those which are postponed will never see the light of day. The only rule that must be followed is that Bills presented by the President are given priority. This does not mean they have a better chance of success, although the President does have political advantages over other groups. It does mean, however, that everything the President proposes will be given a fair hearing. Were a committee to ignore this courtesy to the President, it would risk the heavy hand of retribution in the form of a storm of vetoes against cherished congressional programmes.

Thus, in some senses, committees are part of the governmental as well as the legislative process. They are not passive bodies, waiting for policy proposals to be presented to them. Indeed, in some cases, committees actually draft Bills themselves. Certainly, they are a permanent element in the policy-making community. In the UK and most other western democratic systems, many of the functions of these committees are carried out by government departments. Consultation, research, drafting, refining and support recruitment, with all the other aspects of creating the necessary legislation to implement policy, are as much the concern of congressional committees as they are of government agencies in the USA.

As we can see above, if the committee majority approves, and when all amendments have been considered, the Bill is 'reported out'. It might be almost unrecognisable from the original proposal if it has been extensively amended, or it might emerge largely untouched. Whichever, it has several hurdles still to encounter. In particular, it must find a prominent place on the congressional agenda. For this it must go to another committee.

House Rules and Senate Majority Policy Committee

If a Bill successfully negotiates its standing committee, it must find a place on the agenda of the relevant House. Its chances of success depend upon how early in the session it will be heard. If it is placed too low down on the agenda, it will suffer one of two fates. Either it will never be debated because time has run out or, if it is only debated in the last ten days of the session (Congress tends to save up a large number of Bills until the end and then rushes them through in a short time), it might fall foul of a presidential **pocket veto**. The pocket veto occurs

congressional session. Normally, the President is required to give reasons for a veto and might therefore be reluctant to use it, usually if the measure is a popular one. A pocket veto is somewhat different. It is operated by the President simply sitting on the Bill (i.e. 'pocketing it') without signing it. Once the congressional session is over, within these last ten days, the Bill simply fails. Here, the President does not need to give reasons for using the veto. Thus, it is an attractive course of action for a President who objects to a Bill and an early 'rule' is much sought-after by supporters of a Bill.

In the House of Representatives it is the function of the **Rules Committee** to place a Bill on the agenda. The House has a more crowded agenda than the Senate, so this is a more critical stage than its counterpart in the Upper House. The chairperson and membership of the Rules Committee is largely in the hands of the House Speaker and majority leader and so is very much controlled by the majority party. The chairperson is one of the most influential politicians in the system. The committee enjoyed its 'heyday' in the 1960s when a congressional majority of liberal legislators found themselves confronted by a conservative House Rules Committee (a coalition of Republicans and conservative southern Democrats). It was not until President Johnson gained control over the Democrat majority that reform could be effected. The Committee may also boost a Bill by granting it a 'closed' rule, which effectively forbids any further amendment by the whole House. Excessive amendment can delay a Bill fatally, or change its character fundamentally, often rendering it worthless. The closed rule is, therefore, a valuable asset.

In the Senate it is the **Policy Committee** that performs the function of the House Rules Committee. Unlike Rules, it is exclusively a party committee, staffed only by members of the majority party. However, it is slightly less influential than its House equivalent. The Senate's agenda is less critical and Senators are less inclined to allow their agenda to be controlled by a small group.

If a Bill has a favourable rule granted, it will be debated and voted on by the whole House. It might seem strange to an outsider that this is a relatively insignificant part of the legislative process, at least in terms of time. Debates are usually formal and brief. Most of the real political action has already taken place long before the full floor debate on a Bill. The arguments have been rehearsed and mostly resolved in the committees. It is true that, if amendments are still being proposed, there might be much to do, but generally there is less contentious material to be considered at this stage. Bills that do not have widespread support will have been filtered out by a committee at an earlier stage of the process. This is not to say that there are not close votes after full sessions of Congress, but it is recognised that this is not the place for detailed debate. Speeches are made largely for public consumption, with members of Congress simply wishing to place on record their attitude to a Bill. Before long they will all have to face re-election and their speaking and voting records will be studied by many of the voters.

Having been passed by both Houses, most Bills will have two different forms, since each House might have made its own amendments. These differences must be resolved and yet another committee is needed.

Conference committee

Such committees are formed when a Bill emerges from Congress in two different forms. Members are drawn from both Houses. If such a conference is needed, the agreed form of the Bill must return to each House where it cannot be amended again. Thus, there is still a stage when a Bill might fail, owing to lack of agreement, even if both Houses approve. However, the days when powerful conference committees were able to change the form of a Bill completely are largely gone. It is usually accepted that the will of Congress must be accepted, so genuine efforts are made to achieve an acceptable compromise.

Sub-committees

As the business of Congress has grown, it has been increasingly necessary to resort to the use of sub-committees to deal with specialised legislation. This has had two effects. On the one hand, it has reduced the power of committee chairpersons and diffused it among the heads of the sub-committees. On the other, it has broadened the opportunities for more members of Congress to become closely involved in the business of law making. The diffusion of power in Congress is not only the result of the development of sub-committees, it is also due to the decline of the seniority system in the selection of committee chairpersons. This is examined below.

Committee chairpersons

In many ways, congressional committee chairpersons are as powerful, perhaps even more so, than the Department Directors and Secretaries who are appointed by the President to run the administration. This is especially true of key committees such as House Rules, Appropriations, Foreign Relations and several others that stand as watchtowers over vital legislative programmes. It used to be the case that chairpersons held the key to the success or failure of government action or congressional legislation. Their position was strengthened by the **Seniority Rule** that was in force until the 1970s. This simply meant that, when a chair became vacant, the post would automatically fall to whichever member of the majority party had served on the committee for the longest period, i.e. the senior member. This prevented much political manoeuvring, but gave such security of tenure to chairpersons that they tended to become politically invincible. The situation today has changed considerably. Chairpersons may lose their position and be replaced by younger, ambitious members of Congress. Vacancies are filled by those who enjoy the support of their party or a faction of that party, rather than by those who have been waiting for the longest period. As we have seen, the development of sub-committees has altered the position of chairpersons, but perhaps the most important change is the advent of public hearings. When committees met in private, manipulation by the chairperson was allowed to continue unchecked. Since the media and public have been allowed to observe proceedings, however, such blatant tactics have become unacceptable. Thus, chairpersons are still key political figures, but lack the influence they used to enjoy.

Select committees

From time to time, one of the Houses of Congress might wish to conduct a special investigation, usually into some aspect of the conduct of the administration, or into a feature of American life that is causing concern. Although such committees are normally temporary, the most notorious example lasted for nearly 40 years before its abolition in 1975. This was the House of Representatives Un-American Activities Committee, set up to investigate groups and individuals who might have been operating against the interests of the USA at best, or who were suspected traitors at worst. Led in the early 1950s by Joe McCarthy, the committee conducted a witch-hunt against suspected communists, especially targeting public figures from the world of entertainment and the arts.

More recently, the so-called 'Watergate' Committee of the Senate attracted much attention. This committee was set up to investigate the alleged spying on Democratic Party Headquarters at the Watergate Building by aides of President Nixon, who was seeking re-election in 1972. The subsequent cover-up and discovery that election funds had been improperly used became the subject of a series of dramatic hearings that were carried live on national TV. The committee chairman, Sam Ervin, and other prominent members such as Howard Baker and Daniel Inouye became household names and, in the last two cases, found their political careers were given a great boost by the episode.

Col. Oliver North taking the oath before the House Foreign Affairs Committee, 9 December 1986

In 1988 the **Iran–Contra** affair received similar media coverage when the Senate investigated it. Here, Colonel Oliver North gave a series of dramatic accounts to his inquisitors about the use of funds from arms sales to the 'Contra' rebels in Nicaragua to secure the release of American hostages in Iran. The concern was that the President, through his representative North, was conducting foreign policy without informing Congress. This has been a particularly sensitive issue in Congress, especially the Senate, since a succession of Presidents – Kennedy, Johnson and Nixon – conducted extensive military and intelligence operations in Vietnam and Cambodia without securing the approval of Congress. In the event, North became something of a folk hero and was adopted as a Republican Senate candidate in 1994.

These are three examples of prominent select committees, but there have been many, less-publicised examples, investigating such matters as penal reform, abortion, the operations of the CIA and the intelligence community, and overseas aid.

We can now summarise the features of committees that we have established so far.

Features of congressional committees

1. They are both legislative and investigatory committees.

2. They may develop, draft and pass their own legislation.

3. Legislation developed elsewhere may be rejected, amended or accepted in full.

4. Committees have large permanent staffs and expensive research facilities, often augmented by special investigators.

5. They may call witnesses from Congress, the administration or outside bodies.

6. Most hearings are in public and the voting record of members is known.

7. The procedural committees – Policy in the Senate, Rules in the House – have the ability to kill or severely hinder legislation.

8. Committee chairpersons are powerful political figures, although less so than twenty years ago. Such positions are much sought after.

9. Select or special committees may be formed by either House.

Congress and public finance

mostly in the form of taxation, together with the allocation of funds to spending programmes – remain largely in the hands of the Government. There will always be public scrutiny of finances, but this is normally **post facto**. In other words, it is a check that money has been spent on the purposes for which expenditure was approved, that it has been spent wisely and that there has been no corrupt use of money. Congress, however, reserves the right to play a more creative role in finance, involving itself **before** money is allocated and spent. There is an understanding here that policy cannot be separated from finance, as nearly all legislation will involve the federal government in expenditure. The control of expenditure exercised by Congress is, thus, another aspect of its influence over public policy. Where taxation is concerned, as we have said above, there are strong historical reasons why Congress should be sensitive to tax proposals, as President Bush (1988–92) was to discover when he wished to break election pledges not to raise taxes. Members of Congress are highly susceptible to pressure from their constituents, and Americans dislike being taxed more than do most people in the West.

Under Clinton, the issue of finance centred on Republican attempts to force the President to bring in a balanced budget. A target of 2002 was set for this goal. Clinton resisted, however, vetoing attempts to make legislation on the issue. When Clinton's budget went into surplus in 1999, the question became one of deciding how to use the windfall – reducing taxes or increasing spending – rather than budgetary conduct. Here again, Clinton used his skill to win the argument. He was able to increase spending on such areas as medical services and transport. Congress, recognising public support for the President, had to concede.

An overview The federal system of budgetary control has a number of inherent problems:

- Although Congress reserves the right to have a major say in the level of taxation and expenditure, it does not have the ability to exercise overall control. Both Houses have Budget Committees that propose a general budget and, in particular, the extent to which expenditure shall be allowed to exceed tax revenue. If these budget proposals were to be accepted, they would form guidelines for total levels of expenditure within which departments of government should work. However, the Budget Committees are weak compared to the specialised standing committees and the Appropriations Committees, which control expenditure within particular areas of policy implementation. Thus, expenditure ceilings become a futile objective.
- Most programmes involve ongoing expenditure. Serious cuts can only be made, therefore, if the programme itself is cancelled. Such a course of action is unlikely to be acceptable to a Congress that originally approved them. Thus, much expenditure control is 'incremental' – each year relatively small adjustments can be made.
- As we have seen, members of Congress are under immense pressure from their constituencies to keep taxes as low as possible, but to protect federal spending programmes that will be of benefit to the

area. So there is always a tendency for taxes to be held down, but for expenditure to creep up.

- While the President has the ability to take an overview of the budget and to develop long-term targets, he or she can only exercise limited control over Congress and its key financial committees. At the same time, during his or her first term, knowing that it will be necessary to seek re-election, the President is limited by the need to nurture public opinion. The American public care more about low taxes than about budget deficits.
- In practice, expenditure and taxation are generally considered separately by Congress. This makes overall control exceedingly difficult.

Appropriations

All legislation or proposed federal programmes require approval for the necessary expenditure from the Appropriations Committees of both Houses. Indeed, if a law has been passed that requires such approval, a further Bill must be presented to approve the necessary funds and the whole process is effectively repeated, albeit more quickly.

Appropriations Committees have huge amounts of business to transact over a wide variety of subjects, from defence to agricultural subsidies, from transport to welfare programmes and inner city reconstruction. Thus, they must divide into a large number of sub-committees, each with a fair degree of independence.

These committees cannot reject legislation and spending programmes, but they may cut, sometimes severely, the funds available for them. The effect might amount to something close to rejection. Certainly, over the past two decades, such programmes as space research, health care, welfare and anti-crime programmes have suffered at the hands of these sub-committees. Indeed, it is normally the case that original requests for funds from the Government are cut, and the vital question is really the extent of these cuts. At the same time, Congress's own measures are more likely to enjoy much fuller funding. There is, thus, a constant tension between the spending plans of the President and those of Congress.

No real target for **overall** expenditure is accepted by Congress, even though the President may propose one. At the same time, the committees and sub-committees are autonomous. The result is that total expenditure for the year is randomly determined, despite all attempts to stay within set limits.

Taxation

Congress does not itself propose tax measures, but those which are presented by the President require congressional approval and may be amended. The **House Ways and Means** and **Senate Finance Committees** deal with taxation, and membership of these committees is much sought after, so crucial is their role. As with appropriations, these committees do not operate with overall budgetary targets. Thus, while appropriations might be allowing expenditure to rise, they might also be determined to keep taxes down. The fact that this could result in a burdensome borrowing problem for the Government is of little concern to them. It is partly traditional and partly practical that the House Ways and Means Committee is the more influential of the two. The shorter term of office of Representatives and the closer scrutiny exercised over them by constituents renders them more sensitive to taxation issues.

The Gramm–Rudman ~~Hollings Act~~

The election of **President Reagan** in 1980 heralded new concerns about the level of borrowing by the Government, in particular the effect it was having on inflation and interest rates. With the help of the three Con-gressmen (Gramm, Rudman and Hollings),

Reagan supported legislation to ensure that the budget deficit would be eliminated by the 1990s. The Republican Party's opposition to higher taxation meant that the objectives of the Act could be met only if spending programmes were cut back.

At first, some progress was made with Appropriations sub-committees co-operating by reducing expenditure. Much of the reduction fell on welfare and housing programmes and thus became the subject of considerable controversy. President Bush (1988–92) was committed to pursuing the Act's goals, although it was becoming increasingly apparent that the problem was not going to be solved by cutbacks in spending alone. Bush's problems were exacerbated by the influx of many new Democratic Senators and Representatives who were opposed to cuts, which were having a devastating effect on the USA's poor, especially in the inner cities where poverty, rising crime and drug abuse, poor housing and education, and declining health care facilities had become endemic.

In the event, Bush was forced to abandon the intentions of the Act, and the goal of a balanced budget – with expenditure equalling tax revenue – was postponed further. At the same time, he was forced to raise taxes in order to protect vital spending programmes. The tax increases proved to be a major factor in Bush's defeat by **Bill Clinton** in the 1992 election.

The election of Clinton brought a fresh view of the budget problem. He asked the American people to accept the prospect of higher taxes both to reduce the budget deficit and to finance vital housing, welfare, law and order and, especially, health care programmes. Having achieved a decisive victory at the polls, and with comfortable Democrat majorities in both Houses, he could set about persuading the key financial committees to back his plans. As we have seen above, Clinton was able both to head off demands for congressional control of the budget and to win support for increased spending right up to the end of his term of office in 2000.

President George W. Bush, Clinton's successor, has re-affirmed his office's determination to maintain a budget surplus, though he will find this a difficult commitment to keep as he also intends to make extensive tax cuts.

Summary of Congress and public finance

1. Congress considers both expenditure and taxation plans before they are finalised.
2. Although an overall federal budget is proposed there is no compulsion for Congress to operate within its limitations.
3. Appropriations Committees in both Houses play a key role in the implementation of legislation as well as federal spending programmes.
4. Taxation must be approved by Senate Finance and House Ways and Means Committees.
5. Congress has found it difficult to engage in budget planning but in the 1990s there was a new resolve to tackle budget problems.
6. There is a constant tension between President and Congress over budgetary control.

Congress and foreign policy

Background

Although the President is understood to be pre-eminent in the field of foreign policy – after all, the President is Head of State as well as Head of Government – Congress now demands a major say in the key foreign policy decisions that arise from time to time. Naturally, Congress cannot hope to be involved in the day-to-day business of foreign policy, but it expects to be concerned at important times. The role of Congress is shaped by three main factors:

- Section 8(11) of the Constitution, which grants to Congress the sole right to declare war.
- Article II, Section 2(2), which deals with presidential powers, states that foreign treaties made by the President require the approval of two-thirds of the Senate.
- The War Powers Act of 1973, which requires the President to inform Congress within 60 days if American troops are committed to action abroad. It also requires that those troops be removed if Congress insists on this.

Until the 1950s, relatively little attention was paid to foreign affairs in Congress. Apart from its reluctance to involve the USA in what were seen as European wars – reluctance that was to be overcome by events in 1917 and 1941 – the USA normally stayed aloof from world affairs. Historically, with the exception of involvement in problems with close neighbours such as Mexico or Cuba, the USA was isolationist in outlook. The wars in Korea (1950–3) and Vietnam (1962–75), together with the onset of the Cold War with the Soviet Union and its allies, signalled a major change in American foreign policy. The House of Representatives has remained reluctant to become involved, but the Senate is closely concerned with presidential action.

It is the power that the Senate has over treaty ratification which has resulted in the Upper House being more concerned with foreign policy than the House of Representatives. The House is usually too embroiled in domestic affairs to look outwards. The President has a traditionally close relationship with the chairperson of the key Senate Foreign Relations Committee. Normally, the President will find an ally here. Congress, and the Senate in particular, recognises that it may be seen as unpatriotic if it places obstacles in the way of presidential policy.

Presidential pre-eminence

Despite the apparently impressive powers that Congress has over the conduct of foreign policy, in practice the balance of power lies firmly with the executive branch. Several developments have been important in this respect:

- The extensive use of **executive agreements** has avoided the need for the President to seek treaty ratification in the Senate. These agreements are not full treaties, even though they commit the USA to a variety of agreements with foreign powers. Most of them concern trade and aid, but such devices are the currency of modern foreign relations. Executive agreements tend to outnumber treaties by over ten to one.

- All three Presidents who were involved in Vietnam discovered that, while the 'war' was undeclared, Congress lost much of its influence. It was Nixon's totally secret invasion of Cambodia in the 1970s that led

examples of 'minor' military actions which have never been considered 'wars', so Congress was unable to prevent them. The invasion of Grenada in 1983 to restore democratic government was such a case.
- Although the War Powers Act theoretically gives Congress the power to order troops home, many actions are so short-lived that the 60-day rule does not apply.
- In recent conflicts, where American troops have been heavily committed – in the Gulf, Bosnia and Kosovo – President Clinton has been able to use American troops and negotiate with NATO, Russia and the European powers with relatively little congressional interference.
- By the summer of 2000, Clinton had so much control over foreign policy that he was able to win perhaps his greatest victory over Congress. After many years of struggle, he gained acceptance for his policy of resuming trade links with China after a gap of over 50 years.

Thus we can see that congressional powers in this area are relatively weak, existing more in theory than in practice.

Additional functions

Advice and consent

The Senate has the power to reject presidential nominations for posts in the Cabinet or for a position on the Supreme Court. This has only proved a major problem for the President in recent years, with Bush having **John Tower**, and Clinton **Zoe Baird** rejected on the grounds of personal conduct. Even President Reagan found difficulty in gaining acceptance for appointments, in his case largely on political grounds. However, it is not the actual rejections that demonstrate Congress's true power. Long before actual committee hearings take place at which nominees are questioned by Senators, the President must discuss his or her plans with important members of the relevant committee. Those who are unlikely to gain approval will never be nominated. Thus, the Senate does have some input into the political and personal make-up of the administration and the Supreme Court.

Impeachment

Before 1974 the removal of a President from office on the grounds of misconduct was simply not envisaged. However, there have been two occasions since Nixon's Presidency when impeachment has taken centre stage in American politics. The Watergate affair and its aftermath led to inevitable talk of Nixon's removal from office. The threat alone was enough to ensure his resignation in 1974. Clinton's Presidency in the 1990s was beset by rumours of scandal and threats of congressional proceedings. The Lewinski affair led to an unsuccessful attempt at impeachment, but the experience severely damaged Clinton's authority. With excessively intensive media interest and question marks over the past of every prominent politician, impeachment has become an important political issue.

Constitutional amendment

The Constitution requires that proposed amendments to the Constitution receive the approval of two-thirds of both Houses of Congress before they are taken to the states for their ratification. This device recognises that constitutional change warrants a consensus rather than a majority of support.

There have only been 27 amendments over the 200-year history of the Constitution, so this is a rarely used function. The last amendment – in 1992 – limited Congress's ability to raise their own salaries. Recent attention has centred on the 'Equal Rights Amendment', which would forbid all laws that are discriminatory on the grounds of gender. Congress passed the proposal in 1972, but it failed to achieve sufficient support in the states. In 1982 a further attempt failed in the House, where it enjoyed a majority, but not a large enough one. The battle continued in the 1990s, but without any final conclusion.

Additional features

The parties in Congress

As we have seen, the parties in Congress are relatively unstructured and disunited. There have, however, been signs in the past 25 years that party unity is increasing. Two main developments are responsible for this. First, there has been a degree of concentration on philosophy in the Republican Party following the rise of the 'New Right' ideas, a movement fronted by President Reagan. Second, the Democratic Party has become more 'nationalised'. Traditionally, Democrats from the southern states have been extremely conservative in outlook. This has partly been a legacy of Civil War days, but, more practically, it was a result of the need to attract the support of the majority of the poor whites in the area. This group's opposition to liberal reforms, especially in the area of racial equality, outweighs the need for social policies to alleviate poverty. The southern Democrats, or 'Dixiecrats', have been in decline. The Republicans in the south have captured their old constituencies, while the increased voting among the black and immigrant population in the South has led them to fall into line with their more liberal colleagues in the north.

The effects can be seen in the voting records of the parties since 1975. Taking the percentage of party members who supported the majority line on voting, we find the following:

Democrats	1975–84	69%
	1985–92	80%
	1993–2000	72%
Republicans	1975–84	71%
	1985–92	75%
	1993–2000	81%

We can see that, in both parties, there has been an increase in party unity. Nevertheless, it is still true that divisions which cut across party lines are often more important than party strength in the Congress. On some issues, especially appropriations, sectional (regional) groups become important. When social legislation is at stake it is the conservative–liberal ~~split~~ ... Committees that **appear** to have a Democrat majority might, in fact, still have a **conservative** majority, which is more crucial.

Congress and the lobby

Provided a group has been registered as an official lobby group, its members have virtually open access to both Houses of Congress. Indeed, they maintain permanent offices on Capitol Hill. Attention centres on the standing committees, with lobbyists seeking to testify in open hearings. They may be promoting legislation, opposing it, or merely seeking to secure important amendments.

Lobbyists are also active in gaining the support of individual members. They have a variety of incentives available, including election funds and the guarantee of electoral support. At the same time, there are sanctions against those who try to resist their overtures. The successful lobbyist is likely to be the one who can persuade a member of Congress that his or her support for, or opposition to, a measure will win the member many votes when seeking re-election. In this regard, extensive campaigns take place to ensure that there is widespread support for the issue in question.

The President and Congress

We will examine the President's role in Congress in Unit 19. However, a few key points might be useful at this stage. The President has six main objectives in dealing with Congress:

1. securing the passage of legislation that he or she has proposed
2. opposing congressional legislation of which he or she disapproves
3. securing funding for spending programmes
4. gaining approval for taxation plans
5. obtaining support for foreign policy initiatives
6. gaining approval for his or her nominations to Government and the Supreme Court.

In order to achieve his or her objectives, the President now has a large congressional office whose job is to lobby the House and the Senate in the interests of the President. The President also relies on the support of key congressional figures, usually from his or her own party, who may be permanent allies.

The President has a number of favourable factors, including the natural loyalty and patriotism accorded to the Head of State and the fact that the President is leader of his or her party. If that party enjoys a majority in the Congress, this is especially useful. The President also carries the threat of the use of the veto to thwart the Congress in its own legislative goals. The veto is the President's greatest weapon, but Congress, especially a Congress whose majority party is not the same as the President's (most Republican Presidents in modern times have had to deal with a Democrat-dominated Congress), can override the veto and defeat the President's own legislation if they wish.

Thus, there is a fine balance in President–Congress relations, as the Founding Fathers intended in 1787.

Pressure on members

Members of Congress, Senators and Representatives alike, face contrasting pressures when deciding which causes to support and how to vote. These include the following:

- **Party loyalty.** Apart from the normal feeling that they ought to support their party, members are aware that they owe their election to the army of party workers at home. They usually **expect** members to toe the party line on most occasions. Members might also wish to continue to enjoy the political companionship of fellow members in Congress. As we have seen, such loyalty in voting is on the increase.

- **From lobbyists.** It requires considerable funds today to fight elections, so the financial contributions offered to sitting members are a great (and perfectly legal) temptation. This is also true of the many Political Action Committees, local pressure groups and corporate backers who seek their support. Today most sitting members can almost guarantee re-election and this is because of the huge financial rewards that are available to them if they are compliant.

- **From constituents.** The voting and speaking record of members is sure to be publicised at election time. Members who defy public opinion in their constituency, therefore, are playing a dangerous game. This factor is more significant for Representatives, who must seek re-election after only two years and whose constituencies are much smaller than those of most Senators. The Senate's longer term of office – six years – releases them from this pressure. Indeed, it used to be the case that Senators were notorious for their defiance of public opinion. Safe in their 'citadel', as the journalist William White called the Senate in the 1950s, Senators formed an exclusive 'club', and were largely immune from external pressure. This is less so today and Senators are more sensitive to public opinion than ever before.

- **Personal philosophies.** Many members have strong personal philosophies, whatever their party allegiance. Thus, Senator **Edward Kennedy**, for example, is a convinced liberal and supporter of social reform and a greater degree of economic equality. At the other end of the spectrum, Republican Representative **Newt Gingrich** is a firm conservative who would oppose most economic and social reform. Personal convictions, in such cases, will often be a more powerful influence than any of the other factors.

Differences between the Senate and House of Representatives

In contrast to most bicameral systems, the two Houses of Congress have remarkably balanced powers. The titles 'upper' and 'lower' House are largely meaningless, unless we accept that Senators enjoy higher political status than Representatives, a development that was spurred by the fact that two great Presidents of modern times – Kennedy and Johnson – were former Senators. However, there are important differences.

Possibly the strangest feature of the Senate that differentiates it from the House is the **filibuster**. Any Bill that runs out of debating time is automatically lost. It follows from this rule that a determined group of ~~Congressmen may seek to defeat a Bill simply by~~ 'filibustering', which means speaking indefinitely (about any subject they choose) until time runs out for further consideration of the Bill. Senators have been known to stay on their feet for over 24 hours to ensure a successful filibuster!

To stop a filibuster, supporters of a Bill must introduce a motion of 'cloture' (a corruption of the word 'closure'). Unfortunately, a cloture motion needs the support of 60 per cent of the Senate. It therefore follows that a Bill effectively needs a 60 per cent majority; 51 per cent will not do if there is serious opposition. In the House of Representatives a simple majority **will** bring a Bill to the vote, so the filibuster would be futile.

The effect of the principle of filibustering is to make the passing of legislation through the Senate slightly more difficult. However, the fact that the Senate is smaller at least means that only 60 Senators need to be persuaded to support a Bill, whereas the simple majority in the House is 218.

All of the distinctions between the Senate and the House can be divided into those of **powers and authority** and those of **characteristics**.

Powers and authority

Senate	House of Representatives
• To impeach the President	• To conduct preliminary impeachment hearings
• To approve or reject presidential nominations to the Cabinet or Supreme Court	• Special power over tax proposals
• Ratification of foreign treaties	• More influence over appropriations
• More say in national issues	• More authority over domestic issues
• Filibuster block available	• No filibuster possible

Characteristics

Senate	House of Representatives
• Senators are less open to pressure from constituents	• Representatives are very sensitive to constituency opinion
• Senators tend to take a 'national' outlook	• Representatives are more concerned with domestic issues
• Party and committee leaders are less powerful	• Power is more in the hands of key party leaders
• There are fewer Senators, so they are better known nationally	• In the bigger House, Representatives have less prestige
• Bills have more chance of success	• Bills are more likely to fall foul of the powerful Rules Committee

---

Conclusion   The US Congress is undoubtedly one of the most pluralist bodies in western democratic politics. Power is extremely diffused and access to the key centres of power is remarkably open. The great question over which American commentators argue is whether these characteristics render the Congress too weak to be effective, or whether this absence of concentrated power is the perfect safeguard against the tyranny of a powerful majority.

The US Congress and British Parliament compared

Contrasts

The relative positions of these two legislatures in their political settings are shaped by four particular features.

The separation of powers

The eighteenth-century French political philosopher **Montesquieu** was a great admirer of the British political system. He believed, with relatively little justification, that the secret of the British system was the separation of the powers of the three branches of government – judiciary, executive and legislature. This separation, he argued, prevented the concentration of power in too few hands. Each branch of government would balance the power of the others. His romantic vision of British government was one of the major influences on the writers of the American Constitution. It is, therefore, ironic that, while the American Constitution insisted on the separation of executive and legislative power, the British system moved steadily away from Montesquieu's vision. What does this imply in practice?

In the USA:

- There are separate elections for the Presidency and the Congress. Thus, each branch has its own source of authority.
- The President is required to attend Congress once a year to make the annual 'State of the Union Address'. Otherwise, the President and other members of the administration may only come to Capitol Hill if invited.
- In addition, members of the administration may not sit as members of Congress.
- The Constitution lays down completely separate powers for the Congress and the President. If one of the two were to attempt to encroach upon the power of the other, the Supreme Court would quickly intervene to prevent it.
- The survival of the administration does not depend upon favourable votes in the Congress. Indeed, Presidents may lose a large proportion of their legislation at the hands of an unfriendly Congress, but must carry on regardless. US Presidents have no record of resigning on the grounds that they are unable to control the legislature.

In the UK:

- Members of the Government are, and indeed **must be**, drawn from either House of Parliament.
- It follows from the above that ministers are invariably present in Parliament and are expected to lead debates if they concern the minister's area of responsibility.
- It is understood that Parliament and Government do not have separate mandates from the electorate. Thus, the party that wins power can claim authority to carry out its manifesto without obstruction from Parliament.

- There being no entrenched and codified Constitution in the UK, there is no clear separation of the responsibilities of Government and Parliament.

~~_____ the continuous support of the major-~~
ity in Parliament.

The party system   The contrast between the parliamentary behaviour of British and American parties could hardly be more striking. Unity scores on legislation among both Democrats and Republicans, as we have seen above, usually lie between 75 per cent and 80 per cent. In the UK, such scores would represent disaster for a government and almost certain resignation. The governing party in the UK invariably marshals over 95 per cent support and often 100 per cent among its MPs. Why is this so? To answer this question, we only have to ask what the respective whips in the two systems have at their disposal to maintain discipline.

In Parliament, MPs may be threatened with loss of career prospects, temporary suspension, the enmity of their colleagues, deselection by their constituency party and even the ultimate sanction of expulsion from the party. Indeed, in the 1993 battles to keep the Conservative Party in line over ratification of the Maastricht Treaty, the whips were said to have used a variety of 'dirty tricks', including revelations of extra-marital affairs, to bring the most stubborn into line. As a last resort, the whips may point out that an issue is a matter of confidence in the Government. If sufficient dissidents insist on defying the party line, resignation of the Government and the threat of an election will usually prove enough to cool down the hotheads. This is indeed an impressive array of weapons!

Pity, then, the poor American whips. They can appeal to the loyalty of the party. If a presidential proposal is at stake, they may appeal to members' patriotism. They may have at their disposal potentially damaging knowledge of members' private or financial affairs to use as a threat. If they are very lucky, they may have something at their disposal with which to strike a bargain – the compliance of a member on one issue may be rewarded with a valuable government contract going to his or her state or district. When whips are representing the President, members' support may be secured in return for the President's sympathy in a different area of policy dear to the members' heart. Yet these are mere bows and arrows compared to the heavy artillery available to British party whips.

There have been a few occasions when the British Labour Party whips have encountered the same kinds of obstacle as their American colleagues. Prominent left-wingers such as **Tony Benn** have felt secure enough in their beliefs to be independent-minded, while others have come under such extreme pressure from militant constituency members or trade union backers that they have been forced to defy the whip. The Conservative Party, less troubled by such pressures, has had a few of its own rebels – **Nicholas Winterton** being a prominent example – but they are relatively rare. Nevertheless, despite such exceptions, the behaviour of British parties in Parliament is markedly different from that of the parties in Congress.

'Damn your principles, stick to your Party,' declared Conservative leader **Benjamin Disraeli** over a hundred years ago. The appeal of this instruction still holds largely true in the UK, and the result is a remarkable degree of predictability about voting in the House of Commons. In Congress, party membership is only one of several forces acting on members, so the outcome of most proposals is uncertain.

Of course, party loyalties are of less importance in the House of Lords than in the Commons. Indeed, for the many cross-benchers, parties are not a consideration. However, as we shall discuss below, the weaknesses of the British Upper House render such comparisons largely irrelevant.

The sovereignty of Parliament or checks and balances

At first sight, it might appear that Parliament has considerably more power than Congress. After all, it enjoys almost unlimited sovereignty, is omnicompetent, having no restraints on its powers over domestic affairs, and is not bound by a supreme Constitution. Congress, by contrast, is strictly limited in its jurisdiction by the terms of the Constitution. But this is only a superficial view.

In effect, the sovereignty of Parliament becomes the sovereignty of Government. Since the Government exercises virtually complete control over its majority in the Commons, the legal strength of Parliament translates into barely limited executive power. On the other hand, Congress's powers are actually **guaranteed** by the Constitution. The executive branch simply **cannot** usurp these powers. The checks and balances built into the system both limit and enhance congressional independence.

Of course, should it become the case that British governments cannot regularly command the support of a majority, which would most probably be the case if 'hung' parliaments became the norm, the circumstances might be very different. For the foreseeable future, however, parliamentary sovereignty results in parliamentary weakness.

The Upper House

In some ways, the House of Lords might appear similar to the two Houses of Congress. Its members enjoy a great degree of independence, debates are less party-dominated and there is considerable concern with legislative amendment. Indeed, the intense controversies over two major pieces of government legislation in 1994 closely resembled the deliberations of American standing committees. The **Police and Magistrates' Courts Bill** and the **Criminal Justice and Public Order Bill** were extensively amended in the Lords, as a result of intensive external lobbying and the concerns of peers with a background in the legal profession.

However, even when the Lords engages in one of its periodic bouts of rebelliousness, it is always in the knowledge that the Government, through its Commons majority, can undo everything it has tried to achieve. By contrast, the powers of the two Houses of Congress are almost equally balanced. A measure that enjoys success in one place may still encounter obstacles in the other.

Having established these points, we may now make some detailed comparisons.

Legislation

Congress	Parliament
• Congress may initiate draft, amend or reject legislation.	• ~~All legislation originates in Parliament.~~ Usually fewer than five Private Members' Bills are successful per session. Most are rejected.
• The executive branch is not guaranteed favourable treatment for its legislation. Carter (1977–80) enjoyed about a 75 per cent success rate. Reagan (1981–8) achieved between 43 per cent and 82 per cent, Clinton achieved 89 per cent success in 1993.	• Virtually all government legislation is guaranteed success. Only one Bill – the Sunday Trading Bill of 1986 – has been defeated on the floor of the Commons since the Second World War.
• There is extensive expert examination of all legislation.	• The amending function in the Commons is largely meaningless, with only government approved changes being accepted.
• External lobby groups have considerable influence.	• Government domination means that the parliamentary lobby is relatively weak.

Finance

Congress	Parliament
• All taxation proposals require congressional approval. There is liable to be significant amendment to tax measures.	• Parliament is remarkably powerless in its consideration of public finance, even though it spends considerable time debating the annual Finance Bill.
• All expenditure for every purpose must be separately approved.	• Even controversial tax proposals can be forced through Parliament. Thus, the Poll Tax (1988) and VAT on domestic fuel bills (1993) were accepted by Parliament despite fierce public opposition.
• Legislation may be favourably or unfavourably affected by appropriations votes.	• Expenditure is not seriously questioned before it is made. The Public Accounts Committee does scrutinise expenditure effectively, but **after** it has taken place.
• Congress does not consider any overall levels of expenditure, taxation or long-term budgetary constraints.	• Parliamentary weakness allows the Government to exercise budgetary control.

Representation of interests

Congress	Parliament
• There is extremely open access for lobbyists.	• Access is allowed to lobbyists, but this is relatively limited.
• Members rely heavily upon interest groups for finance of election campaigns and political support. The weakness of the party system frees members from party commitment, allowing them to support external groups more openly.	• MPs can be sponsored by outside groups, including trade unions, business, and cause groups, but there are many reservations about such influence, as indicated by the disciplining of two Conservative MPs who accepted bribes in return for asking parliamentary questions. Also, individual campaign spending for MPs is very limited by law, so there is little need for financial support from such groups.
• The committee system relies heavily upon information and opinion from interest groups.	• There is limited access to legislative and investigatory committees. Most lobbying activity is centred on government departments.
• Members, especially Representatives, take special care to protect the interests of their constituencies, securing favourable and opposing unfavourable legislation and supporting a fair share of federal spending and government contracts.	• MPs take care to represent the interests of constituencies. Whips accept that this may transcend party loyalty. Thus, members of the governing party have defied government policy over such issues as nuclear waste dumping sites and the siting of motorways and railways.

Scrutiny of government

Congress	Parliament
• Congressional committees have wide powers to call witnesses and see papers. Freedom of Information Act ensures the right to see official documents.	• Select committees have fewer powers to see government witnesses and papers. Official documents might not be forthcoming.
• American government does not have a strong tradition of secrecy.	• The Official Secrets Act and the tradition of secrecy inhibit ministers and officials in their evidence to committees.
• Important hearings are well publicised and broadcast.	• Committees are generally low profile.
• There is no doctrine of collective responsibility, so members of the Government can be more frank.	• The doctrine of collective responsibility prevents ministers from expressing personal views.
• Public officials are freer to express views.	• Civil servants must only repeat official government policy and cannot discuss policy making, their own role in it or their own views.
• Appointment of government members and Supreme Court judges is subject to Senate approval.	• Parliament has no influence on public appointments.
• Congress has the right to investigate the work of the CIA and intelligence services.	• Question Time on the floor of the House has become largely ritualised and government-controlled.

Some similarities

There can be little doubt that there are considerably more contrasts than similarities between Parliament and Congress. They play fundamentally different roles in their political systems. Nevertheless, we can identify a

Social composition

Both bodies are notoriously unrepresentative of the broader population. The table below shows some revealing statistics taken in 1999. (The House of Lords, being an unelected body, is not included in this comparison.)

	Congress	House of Commons
% women	13	18
% ethnic minorities	15	3
% former manual workers	9	10

Figures are rounded to the nearest whole number.

There is also disproportionate representation of professions in both – in 1999, 46 per cent of members of Congress were lawyers, while 48 per cent of British MPs were from a professional background; the average age of members of Congress in that year was 53, remarkably similar to the average of 52 in the House of Commons.

Constituency representation

In both the House of Commons and the Congress it is expected that members should pay special attention to the interests of their constituents, both as individuals and as a whole. While it is true that Congress members have more means at their disposal – notably, influence over the allocation of federal funds and contracts around the country – MPs are also expected to lobby the Government in the interest of their constituents. Certainly, there has been a trend in the UK for such activity to increase in modern times as voting becomes more volatile, but this feature has always been present in the USA, where it is an essential ingredient in re-election campaigns.

Committee work

Although American committees are vastly more influential than their British counterparts, we should still note the similarities that now exist in committee structures. It is true that the House of Commons separates legislative and investigatory committees, but the essential functions exist in both systems. In both countries, the debates on the floor of the House are of considerably less importance than the background work going on in committee rooms (in the case of the UK, often unnoticed).

Legitimation

Both Congress and Parliament have the key role of giving authority to legislation. Neither the people nor the courts will accept laws that have not been legitimised by the elected legislature. It might be largely a meaningless ritual in the UK compared to the hard-fought battle that takes place in the USA, but in both cases it is the central activity.

The future . . . There are some indications that Congress and Parliament might be moving towards a greater similarity in their characteristics. This is not dramatic, but is certainly perceptible:

- Congress is developing greater party unity, as we have seen above. This has always been notable when a new President first takes office. During this period, the President enjoys a 'honeymoon period' and Congress behaves most like the House of Commons. However, there has been a noticeable trend towards greater party discipline at other times.
- The development of departmental select committees in the House of Commons since 1979 has been a significant step in the direction of the congressional system. There are even signs that the committees are beginning to take legislative initiatives, pointing the way to future policy as a result of their investigations.
- The UK's position in Europe being a major policy issue, the main parties have become split across the traditional ideological lines. These have become open wounds in the Conservative Party, but are also significant in the Labour Party, which managed to keep them under the surface while seeking to gain power. The question of devolution – the granting of greater autonomy to Scotland and Wales – represented a further divisive force for Labour. Should issues like these split the parties, the UK will be faced with the same kind of competing schisms that exist in Congress. The traditional north–south split in the Democratic Party, and the centre–right divide among Republicans, have inhibited unity; Europe and devolution may play the same role in the future of British parliamentary parties.
- As Professor Philip Norton has pointed out, since 1970 there has been a new prevailing attitude among British MPs that they are not mere lobby fodder. They are more independent-minded and are willing to defy their party leaderships on such clear issues as taxation, Europe and defence policy. The removal of Margaret Thatcher as Prime Minister by her own MPs was indeed a dramatic development. There has also been a recent increase in the Commons' determination to create some of its own legislation. Important changes to abortion law in 1993 and to laws relating to homosexuality in 1994 are prominent examples.

Over the same period, the House of Lords has become more active in its scrutiny of legislation. While its powers remain limited, it has certainly attempted at times to behave like the American Senate.

Conclusion It is somewhat ironic that, while many British parliamentarians look wistfully across the Atlantic, wishing that they too could enjoy the influence of their American colleagues, American government officials remain envious of the British Government's ability to force even unpopular measures through a weak and compliant Parliament. In many ways these emotions illustrate the principal contrasts between Congress and Parliament.

For exam questions relevant to this unit, see page 559.

19 The United States' Presidency and administration

Introduction

The Founding Fathers faced, in 1787, a number of problems when shaping the future government of the USA. Among them was the precise relationship between Congress and the executive. They were aware of the danger that government might be dominated by one or two large states, notably Virginia and New York, and that there might be no figure who could represent the Union as a whole. The twin objectives of uniting the states and giving government a firm direction seemed to conflict with each other. At the same time, there was a pressing need to establish the USA in the world community (not least, in order to secure some financial credit to pay for the armed forces) and to protect it from external threats. The answer was to create the Presidency.

The office of President of the USA is unique in western democratic politics. It is the only case where the positions of **Head of State** and **Head of Government** are combined in one post. The incumbent is, therefore, expected to perform the two basic functions described below.

Head of State   Here the President must undertake a number of responsibilities:

- to represent the whole country in relationships and negotiations with other states
- to unite the country in times of emergency and crisis
- to understand and further the interests of the whole American community, irrespective of party allegiance; to attempt to take into account the interests of specific groups as well as those of the people collectively
- to undertake the security of the USA from both external and internal threats
- to act as a figurehead, representing the spirit of America, its culture and traditions
- to be able to maintain national unity even in the face of bitter political controversies.

Head of Government   These functions are distinct from those that the President performs as Head of State:

- to promote a specific programme that has been sanctioned during the President's own election, as part of his or her party's political programme
- to support those sections of the Congress that are promoting policies with which the President can concur
- to mediate between competing views on policy arising out of congressional debates
- to ensure the implementation of legislation passed by Congress in such a way that it conforms to the interests of the country
- in some cases, to veto legislation that the President feels is impractical or not in the interests of the people.

There is little doubt that the framers of the Constitution intended that the President's role as Head of State would be the more significant. They saw policy making as largely the preserve of the Congress; the President was to oversee the process of government, appoint its officers and ensure continuity, but little else. Despite James Madison's hopes to the contrary, it was the emergence of political parties that changed the picture. As it became clear during the nineteenth century that the President was becoming head of the majority party, his **political** role as Head of Government began to dominate. By the time **Abraham Lincoln** (1861–5) took on the southern states over the slavery issue, it had become clear that the direction of government was in the hands of the President.

Since the President's role as party leader has become a key factor, our understanding of how the Presidency works must begin with the presidential election.

The election of the President

Party nomination
In theory, any citizen of the USA who meets the necessary constitutional conditions may ~~run for election as President. In practice~~, however, a candidate has no realistic chance of being elected unless he or she is nominated as the official choice of either the Democrat or Republican Party. There are occasions when heroic campaigns have been waged by independent candidates or those representing minor parties, but these have always ended in failure. **John Anderson** won 6.1 per cent of the popular vote in 1980 and **Ross Perot** achieved the remarkable figure of 19.0 per cent in 1992, but neither was a realistic contender once the polls opened. It follows that the first major step on the road to the election of a President is the securing of a major party nomination.

Ross Perot talking to the press during his 1992 election campaign

The process may begin as long as two years before the actual election, which always takes place in November. Indeed, by March 1995 a total of nine prospective Republican candidates were beginning their campaigns for the 1996 election.

The campaign for the 2000 election also began and effectively ended early. By March, with less than half the primaries over (see below), the two parties' candidates were decided – Al Gore, the Democrat Vice President, was to face George Bush junior (son of the former President) for the Republicans.

Both parties choose their candidate at a **National Convention** in the summer before the election. Party delegates from all the states (the number being proportional to the population of the state) assemble and are balloted to determine whom they wish to see as their party's presidential candidate. There is an exhaustive ballot, where losing aspirants drop out until one of the nominees achieves an overall majority of the delegate votes. As we shall see, however, most of the activity takes place before the Convention.

Most of the delegates are committed to support one individual by the time they arrive at the Convention. They are free to switch their support only if their nominee is eliminated in an earlier ballot. The delegates become committed to one nominee by one of two processes, both used by the two parties in much the same way. These are either **primary elections** or **caucuses**.

Primaries These are basically private elections held among the supporters of each party. Voters must register for one or other of the parties to be eligible to take part in a primary. There are a number of variations in the way in which the primaries are organised and in the degree to which they bind delegates to the Convention. In principle, however, they apportion the delegates to various nominees in two main ways. **Either** the nominee who wins a primary receives the support of **all** the party delegates from that state, **or** delegate support is apportioned according to the proportion of votes won by each nominee in the primary. Primaries for the presidential nomination are currently used in 28 states. New Hampshire is traditionally the first primary, usually in February or March, and the rest follow over the next three or four months.

Caucuses These are meetings of party activists rather than open elections. Again, delegates are chosen at the caucuses, some of whom are committed to a nominee, some of whom are not. The delegates chosen attend a state convention that **does** normally bind the delegates to the National Convention to a particular nominee.

The National Convention Both major parties hold their Convention in the summer before a presidential election. This is the most important event in the life of an American political party, serving a number of functions:

- It is a mass rally of key party workers, designed to boost morale before the arduous task in the autumn of campaigning for their candidate – not just the presidential candidate, but all the other office-seekers (at national, state and local level) who are also elected in November.
- It is a public relations exercise with much high-profile publicity. The party and its candidate must appear confident and competent before the election.
- The presidential candidate for the party must be chosen.
- Once a candidate is chosen, a political programme must be approved, and it must be one upon which both the chosen presidential candidate and members of Congress can agree. Most of the process is a formality, but some issues remain to be resolved at the Convention.
- Finally, after the battle for party nomination, the Convention seeks to unite the whole party, including the losing aspirants, behind the nominee.

In some cases, one of the candidates has already secured an absolute majority of the committed delegates **before** the Convention, through successful caucuses and primaries. This was the case with **Walter**

Mondale, the Democratic nominee in 1984 (though this did not prevent his being heavily defeated by Republican **Ronald Reagan** in the real election). In 2000, the candidates for **both** main parties – Gore and Bush – had long since been decided. In such a case, the Convention turns into a triumphal rally and a great show of unity.

If there is to be balloting, each party hopes for a decisive result on the first ballot to avoid damaging in-fighting. A bitterly fought Convention presents a poor image of the party to the public. The Democratic Convention of 1968 in Chicago, for example, in which **Hubert Humphrey** beat off the challenge of **Eugene McCarthy** amid much acrimony, was contrasted with the Republican display of unity behind **Richard Nixon** in Miami. Not surprisingly, therefore, Nixon beat Humphrey, the earlier favourite, in the following November's election.

The election

Every four years, early in November, the whole of the USA is entitled to vote in the presidential election. As we have seen, small party and independent candidates are a distraction, but not a serious factor. This is a contest between the nominated candidates from each of the two main parties. It is not, however, a straightforward popular election. The President is actually elected through the **electoral college** system. This device requires careful explanation.

Ronald and Nancy Reagan at the Republican National Convention, 23 August 1984

Richard Nixon at the
Republican National
Convention, 8 August
1968

The electoral college
Effectively, in a presidential election each state holds its own 'mini-election'. That is, the votes for each candidate are counted **within** the state and a winner is declared. The winner in each state receives **all** the 'electoral college' votes for that state. The number of such electoral college votes gained depends upon the population size of the state. Thus, the very small states have only **three** electoral college votes (the minimum permissible), while the largest – California – has 54 votes. After the election, the electoral college votes of each candidate are added up and the winner is elected. Should no candidate win an overall majority of the college vote, there are procedures for settling the deadlock, but since this did not occur in the twentieth century, we need not describe them here.

The results of three modern presidential elections illustrate the effects of the electoral college system.

Year	Candidate	Total votes gained	Electoral college votes
1980	Carter (Dem.)	35,483,820	49
	Reagan (Rep.)	43,901,812	489
	Anderson (Ind.)	5,719,722	0
1992	Clinton (Dem.)	43,728,275	370
	Bush (Rep.)	38,167,416	168
	Perot (Ind.)	19,237,247	0
1996	Clinton (Dem.)	45,000,000	379
	Dole (Rep.)	37,000,000	159
	Perot (Reform)	8,000,000	0
2000	Gore (Dem.)	50,158,094	267
	Bush (Rep.)	49,820,518	271
	Nader (Green)	2,783,728	0

We can see that the effect of the electoral college is to distort the true popularity of the candidates. Ross Perot's zero score in 1992 disguised a good showing by him in terms of popular support. Similarly, a fairly close contest in 1980 looked like a landslide for Reagan if we only look at the electoral college. However, despite these distortions, in every election since the Second World War, the candidate with the largest popular vote has also won the ~~~~~~~~~~ college system does not produce the 'wrong' winner, it merely exaggerates the size of the victory. Even so, hoping for an unusual result, candidates campaign much harder in those states with most electoral college votes. A narrow victory in California or Illinois is worth much more than a thumping majority in a small state such as Iowa or Rhode Island.

Such an event occurred dramatically in the 2000 election. After the notorious dispute over the counting of votes in Florida, **George W. Bush** was declared the winner by a mere four electoral college votes. His opponent Al Gore, however, achieved a narrow win in the popular vote. A further interesting effect of the system was that Bush won 30 out of 50 states, but his final victory was extremely narrow. Gore won the big states such as California, New York and Illinois, but his opponent won most of the small states.

We can now summarise the stages on the road to the White House:

A successful campaign for the Presidency	
1998	Tentative feelers are put out to test potential strength of support.
March 1999	An announcement of an intention to run for President is made.
Summer 1999	A drive to raise campaign funds is initiated.
Autumn 1999	A firm commitment to run is made. More fundraising activity.
February 2000	Campaigning in the primaries and caucuses begins.
Summer 2000	The National Convention takes place. The candidate becomes the party nominee.
Autumn 2000	Campaigning and fundraising intensity.
November 2000	The presidential election is held.
January 2001	The new President takes the oath of allegiance and takes office.

George W. Bush campaigning in Florida during the 2000 election

The powers of the President

As Head of State These powers concern mostly the conduct of foreign policy, military action and the maintenance of public order within the USA. Although all of the functions performed under the auspices of the President's role as Head of State are subject to constitutional and congressional controls (part of the general principle of 'checks and balances'), it is in this area that the President has most discretionary freedom. Indeed, they are sometimes described as 'prerogative powers', similar to those enjoyed by a British Prime Minister acting on behalf of the Crown. The most important are detailed below.

Treaties The negotiation and signing of treaties is carried out by the President and his or her advisers, notably the Secretary of State. During the Cold War, several issues arose concerning the control of nuclear weapons which required extremely sensitive treatment during discussions with the Soviet Union and its allies. The **Nuclear Test Ban Treaty** (signed by John F. Kennedy in 1963), the **Nuclear Non Proliferation Treaty** (signed by Lyndon Johnson in 1968) and the **Strategic Arms Limitation Treaties** (SALT 1, 1970 and SALT 2, 1977), for example, were negotiated in great secrecy and with relatively little domestic interference.

John F. Kennedy signing the partial Nuclear Test Ban Treaty, 7 October 1963

However, although Presidents may conduct their discussions in relative freedom, the final treaty requires the approval of a two-thirds majority in the Senate. This is by no means automatic. The 1968 Test Ban Treaty was delayed by a year, so Richard Nixon took the credit for Johnson's work; SALT 2 was never ratified owing to the Senate's suspicions that the Soviet Union could not be trusted to comply with the requirement to reduce its weapon stocks.

Executive agreements   Executive agreements replace formal treaties, being arrangements made with other countries concerning trade, military co-operation, mutual friendship and the like. They are binding but, not being ~~subject to~~ ratification by the Senate. These comprise, in the true sense of the phrase, prerogative presidential powers. They must, of course, be reported to Congress, but no formal action can be taken to undo them.

Control of the armed forces   As **Commander-in-chief** of the armed forces, the President also enjoys considerable freedom of action. Congress must approve formal declarations of war but, thereafter, the President is in full control. Indeed, before the **War Powers Resolution** was passed in 1973, Presidents could do as they wished with American forces in undeclared conflicts. The conduct of the Vietnam War between 1962 and 1975 changed this situation. Successive Presidents – Kennedy, Johnson and Nixon – sheltered under their powers as Commander-in-Chief to wage an undeclared war, often under the cloak of secrecy, and even after the support of public opinion for the action had clearly been lost. Congress now demands overall control of such conflicts.

Nevertheless, as we have seen above, several short-term military adventures have been carried out by Presidents, unhindered by the limited terms of the War Powers Resolution. In Grenada, Somalia, the Arabian Gulf, Lebanon and Haiti, Presidents Reagan, Bush and Clinton have felt at liberty to commit and command American forces without hindrance by Congress.

Control of the National Guard   As well as external forces, the President commands the National Guard, a domestic 'army' whose role is to put down major outbreaks of public disorder and to deal with other emergencies, such as natural disasters. During the 'Youth in Protest' movement of the late 1960s and early 1970s, largely directed against the Vietnam War, Presidents Johnson and Nixon were forced to resort to use of the Guard to control student rioting.

More commonly, however, it is the incidence of natural disasters such as major flooding, hurricanes and earthquakes that see the National Guard in action. In the most serious examples, the President may be seen taking personal control.

The intelligence services   The intelligence services are the responsibility of the President. The principal body is the **Central Intelligence Agency** (CIA), whose Director is appointed by and reports directly to the President. This relationship remained relatively uncontroversial until, after the creation of the CIA in 1947, it became clear that its agents were increasingly acting as instruments of clandestine presidential policy abroad. In the 1970s CIA operatives were discovered to be conducting covert operations in Vietnam and Cambodia, in communist-dominated Nicaragua, and in Chile, where the autocratic regime of General Pinochet was said to be supported heavily by the CIA despite its record of human rights violations. As a result, Congress now demands greater information concerning CIA operations and a special committee has powers to demand full information concerning its activities.

Appointment of ambassadors

All American ambassadors are appointed by the President. Of course, a new President does not replace all the ambassadors, but is certainly expected to replace those holding key positions in such capitals as Moscow, Beijing, London and Paris. In this way, Presidents can ensure that ambassadors become their personal envoys and important instruments in their foreign policy plans.

Acting as a figurehead

The President, as we have observed above, is expected to represent all the American people. He or she is, therefore, a figurehead, who will attempt to unite the country at important moments in its history. In times when important domestic and foreign events threaten to have a major impact on American lives, it is the President's role to lead the country. In this regard, the President has total access to the **media** and, in particular, is empowered to take broadcasting time on both TV and radio in order to speak to the people. Presidents are not entitled to use this privilege to promote their own or their party's policies, but they may tell the American people why they feel certain courses of action are necessary. The commitment of American troops to battle is a clear example, as are regular requests for people to show patience in times of economic difficulty.

As Head of Government

We can divide the President's role as head of the executive branch into four areas. These are legislation, appointments, budgetary control and federal expenditure. We examine each in turn.

Legislation

Congress is the principal legislative branch of government. The Constitution states this and it is still, broadly speaking, true. What the Founding Fathers did not anticipate, however, was that Presidents would come to play a key role in law making. Although the Constitution states that Presidents should, from time to time, make recommendations for action to the Congress, the concept of a full legislative programme to be developed by Presidents and their advisers was not expected.

The legislative role of the President falls into two categories. First, they initiate a good deal of legislation, either themselves or through the various executive agencies that they influence. In modern times, for example, we have seen programmes of civil rights protection and poverty relief from Presidents Kennedy and Johnson, of reform in the system of distributing federal funds to the regions (revenue sharing) from Richard Nixon, new energy initiatives by Jimmy Carter, deregulation of the economy by Ronald Reagan and new health and crime initiatives by Bill Clinton.

Second, Presidents have the power to **veto** legislation proposed by Congress. This effectively means that they can block new laws unless they are backed by a two-thirds majority of the legislature. They do this either by refusing to sign the Bill and so denying it legitimacy, or through a **pocket veto**. The pocket veto means that, at the end of a congressional session, they simply delay signing until the session ends; the Bill then runs out of time and is lost simply by default. This device is useful to a President who does not wish to enter into bargaining over a piece of legislation and is possible because there is no opportunity for Congress to overrule the veto with its two-thirds majority. In 1996, the veto power of the President was extended when the **line item veto** was introduced. This allows Presidents to veto **parts** of congressional Bills, not just the whole piece of legislation. Line item vetoes have the effect of ~~increasing the President's negotiating powers, and Bill Clinton used it to~~ good effect several times in his presidency.

At first sight the veto may appear to be a purely negative device, but skilful Presidents can use their power of veto creatively. It may be effective as a bargaining counter with the Congress. In return for withholding a possible veto, Presidents may secure the compliance of the Congress over a piece of their own legislation. Moreover, they can use the new line item veto as a bargaining counter with Congress. Thus, there are subtle ways in which the power of veto can be a useful legislative tool for the President.

How well this can work largely depends upon the political complexion of Congress, whether it is broadly in philosophical sympathy with the President, as was the case with Lyndon Johnson, or whether there is strong opposition, as under Bill Clinton.

The different uses of the veto can be illustrated by the contrast between the presidencies shown below.

President	Office years	Total vetoes	No. overruled	Average per year
F. D. Roosevelt	1933–45	635	9	53
D. Eisenhower	1953–61	181	2	22
R. Nixon	1969–74	43	7	8
G. Bush	1989–93	46	1	12
W. Clinton	1993–6	17	1	4

Roosevelt was faced with a largely sympathetic Congress, supportive of his radical 'New Deal' policies, but there were, nevertheless, frequent stand-offs, illustrated by the high rate of veto. Eisenhower, a traditional Republican, was simply opposed to federal power and interference, so he blocked many congressional initiatives.

Richard Nixon, on the other hand, had good relations with his Congress for much of his presidency and was prepared to let them take the leading role in domestic policy. Thus, he interfered relatively infrequently.

Appointments   When a new President takes office, he or she has the opportunity to make about 4,000 appointments. These comprise ambassadors, as we have seen above, but more importantly, all the senior officials in the President's own office (the White House Staff) together with the Heads and senior officials in the executive agencies that form the new administration. Presidents may select whomsoever they wish and often nominations come from such varied quarters as Congress itself, the universities, business, pressure groups and, of course, from among their own close political supporters. It is generally expected that those who have done most to help in the President's election campaign will obtain a senior post. Even nepotism is acceptable: John Kennedy appointed his brother,

Bobby, as Attorney General, but more controversially, Jimmy Carter chose, amid considerable embarrassment, his hard-drinking brother, Billy, to serve on his personal staff.

Presidents have less discretion over the appointment of judges to the Supreme Court. Here, they must wait until an incumbent judge dies or retires, as there can only be nine judges at any one time. Presidents may not dismiss any judges, so their freedom of action depends largely on circumstance. The nature of the relationship between the President and the Supreme Court is discussed in more detail on pages 497–9.

Budgetary control

In conjunction with the **Bureau of the Budget**, Presidents play a leading role in the formulation of the federal budget each year. They propose tax changes and the new levels of existing taxes, together with appropriate levels of expenditure on the various activities of the federal government. At the same time, Presidents set the agenda for broad economic policy, for which they are also responsible. They might wish to deflate the economy by raising taxes and cutting public expenditure, or to promote expansion by taking the opposite measures.

Presidential freedom of action in this field, however, is heavily limited by congressional action, especially that of the House of Representatives. The annual announcement of the federal budget proposals is the prelude to a prolonged series of negotiations with congressional leaders. Frequently, the Congress will wish to reduce taxes, since constituents invariably judge their representatives on their ability to reduce the financial burden that central government imposes upon them. At the same time, however, many members of Congress and Senators will also be campaigning for increased federal expenditure if it means more jobs and prosperity for the region that they represent. So the President inevitably has difficulty in reaching budgetary agreement with the legislature.

Democrat President **Bill Clinton** faced a more unusual problem with Congress in the 1990s. Confronted by a hostile, Republican-dominated House of Representatives, his plans to raise taxes in order to finance a new health care plan and law and order measures were vehemently opposed. Speaker of the House **Newt Gingrich** and Senate majority leader **Bob Dole** led a campaign to force Clinton to reduce expenditure while also keeping taxes down. Their interest lay in achieving a more balanced budget to combat possible inflation and to reduce the enormous burden of accumulated debt on the federal government. The result was a series of setbacks for Clinton. He was unable to implement his policies, simply for lack of the necessary funds. However, by 1997 Clinton was in the ascendancy and, by skilful use of his veto and his negotiating powers, he was able to bring a reluctant Congress round to accepting a compromise budget.

Federal expenditure (appropriations)

As well as setting an overall sum to be spent by each federal department, the President must determine the allocation of funds to projects within different states and in particular regions. This might include such items as agricultural subsidies, scientific research funds, transport initiatives, environmental projects, industrial grants or the establishment of federal operations in a particular city. In such cases, there are significant implications in terms of job opportunities and the general prosperity of an area.

Appropriations, as such allocations are called, provide the President with a significant weapon in the struggle to win support from members of Congress. The apportionment of large amounts of federal funds to a ~~Congress member's district can work wonders~~ when it comes to seeking their support for a cherished presidential policy.

Bill Clinton in 1993

As with the federal budget, however, the House of Representatives, through its powerful **Appropriations Committee**, can make substantial amendments to the President's plans. Indeed, it can be a bargaining counter for use by Congress itself, as well as by the President. Nowhere within the American political system is the system of checks and balances better illustrated than in the horse trading that takes place over federal appropriations.

Conversely, when Congress itself apportions federal funds to projects that it supports, the President has the power to cancel or **impound** them. Impoundment can be thwarted through the use of legislative vetoes, but only if in both Houses, and the process is difficult and time consuming.

The President and Congress

Party strengths It is in the relationship between a President and the Congress that the system of checks and balances operates most clearly. The careful balance of power that the original writers of the Constitution created is not constant, however; it is significantly affected by the relative party strengths at the White House and on Capitol Hill, where Congress meets.

We can see the variety of combinations of party majorities that can exist by reference to the political make-up of Congress since 1961, shown against the party of the incumbent President.

Term	President	House of Representatives		Senate	
		Democrats	Republicans	Democrats	Republicans
1961–3	Democrat	262	175	64	36
1963–5	Democrat	258	176	67	33
1965–7	Democrat	295	140	68	32
1967–9	Democrat	248	187	64	36
1969–71	Republican	243	192	58	42
1971–3	Republican	255	180	54	44
1973–5	Republican	242	192	56	42
1975–7	Republican	291	144	61	37
1977–9	Democrat	292	143	61	38
1979–81	Democrat	277	158	58	41
1981–3	Republican	243	192	46	53
1983–5	Republican	268	167	46	54
1985–7	Republican	253	182	47	53
1987–9	Republican	258	177	55	45
1989–91	Republican	260	175	55	45
1991–3	Republican	267	167	56	44
1993–5	Democrat	258	175	57	43
1995–7	Democrat	204	230	47	53
1997–9*	Democrat	207	227	45	55
2001–3	Republican	212	221	50	50

*Plus one independent in the House of Representatives

We can also see that it is normal for the Democrats to hold a majority in both Houses of Congress, especially in the House of Representatives, where the first Republican majority since 1955 appeared in 1994. This might suggest that only a Democratic President is able to achieve significant success. It is, indeed, certainly true that one of the most 'productive' Presidencies was that of **Lyndon Johnson**, a Democrat (1963–9), who enjoyed very large Senate and House majorities. At their height (1933–9) the Democrats dominated the Senate by 76 to 16 and the House by 331 to 89; Franklin Roosevelt was able to enact the most extensive legislative programme ever seen in American politics.

Lyndon Johnson
reviewing Vietnam War
troops, 28 December

Nevertheless, the picture is not always so clear. Among the Democrats there is always a sizeable conservative group, especially among Congress members from southern states, who can obstruct a progressive President. **Jimmy Carter** (1977–81) was to experience such opposition. Conversely, **Ronald Reagan** (1985–93), although a right-wing Republican, was able to enact considerable reforms by creating a coalition of support between a united Republican Party and a group of southern Democrats.

The most striking example, however, of how the party balance in Congress can work against a President occurred in the mid-1990s when Democrat Bill Clinton found himself completely blocked by Republican majorities in both Houses from the beginning of 1995. To add to the problem, Clinton was a relatively liberal President, while the new Republican Congress leaders, notably Bob Dole (Senate) and Newt Gingrich (House) were, on the whole, extremely conservative. It remains to be seen how George W. Bush copes with a Senate which is split down the middle and a House where his party has a wafer-thin majority.

Yet the fact that American parties are rarely as united and disciplined as their British counterparts does mean that Presidents can make some headway against an apparently hostile Congress, provided they possess sufficient political skill, the backing of public opinion and a strong team of congressional managers. Of all modern Presidents, Reagan, Johnson and Clinton possessed all three qualities to the greatest degree.

Reciprocal veto power

As we have seen, the President's use the veto over congressional initiatives can be used as both a negative and a positive tool. Thus, a conservative President such as Ronald Reagan was able to keep the progressives in Congress at bay through his use of the veto. At the same time, he could bargain with congressional leaders to ensure that his own policies – mainly in the fields of crime control, welfare and economic management – were given a fair hearing.

On the other hand, Congress has, since 1932, been able to exercise a **legislative veto** over executive actions by the President or one of the President's agencies of government. Apart from lesser executive agreements in foreign policy, it is the appropriation of federal funds for different projects and regions that is most often subjected to such vetoes.

Appropriations and impoundments

Some of the fiercest battles waged between the President and the Congress concern the apportionment of federal funds. The conflict is ensured by the fact that both Congress and the executive branch, led by the President, have power to spend such moneys. Naturally, Congress might wish to spend funds on its favourite projects, such as inner city renovations, anti-crime measures or environmental projects. As representatives, they wish to show their constituents that they have been fighting for the well-being of their area. Members of the House of Representatives are particularly sensitive to federal spending, as they are forced to seek re-election every two years.

At the same time, public expenditure forms a vital part of presidential policy making, especially in the fields of defence and foreign affairs. Apart from the huge expenditure on the armed forces, which the President controls directly, overseas aid must be apportioned to maintain the USA's world-wide network of allies. Space and weapons research are additional favourite items of presidential spending. Both Reagan and Bush, for example, cherished dreams of seeing through the 'Star Wars' project – a fabulously expensive plan to create a laser-based anti-missile defence umbrella for North America.

Presidential–congressional conflict over public expenditure came to a head under President Nixon in the 1970s. The problem had become exacerbated by two features. First, Nixon was spending vast sums on the wars in Vietnam and Cambodia, of which Congress was increasingly disapproving. Second, a liberal and progressive Congress, determined to reduce poverty and urban deprivation, was frequently falling foul of Nixon's conservatism and dislike of excessive domestic spending.

Ultimately, the **Budget and Impoundment Control Act** of 1974 attempted to clarify the issue. Although the financial relationship between the President and Congress remains complex, while the use of impoundments and legislative vetoes is subject to constitutional dispute, some order was restored in 1974. Basically, the President may stop or defer any congressional spending programme through impoundment. However, a legislative veto by **both** Houses of Congress may overturn the impoundment. Similarly, Congress may thwart presidential spending programmes, but the President may simply retaliate by using the veto to make life difficult for the Congress.

It was such a balance of power – some may say 'deadlock' – that faced Bill Clinton in relation to his second Congress, elected in 1994 with a Republican majority in both Houses. His two great spending pro-grammes ~~of welfare and education control~~ were destroyed by an unfriendly Congress.

Advice and consent

As we have seen, the Constitution insists that some presidential actions require the approval of Congress. The Congress describes this stipula-tion as 'advice and consent'. It applies to foreign treaties and the appointment of Supreme Court judges and senior executive officials.

Until the 1970s most Congresses scarcely used their reserve powers to thwart presidential plans. They had been considered very much as 'reserve' powers, for use only if a President appeared to be becoming dictatorial. In more recent times, however, it has become a reflection of the growing authority of Congress in their relations with the Presidency that the advice and consent power has been increasingly used.

George Bush Senior in 1992

In the 1970s, for example, the Senate consistently refused to ratify SALT 2 (the second strategic arms limitation treaty with the Soviet Union), thus usurping some of the President's authority in foreign policy and defence matters. More recently, President **George Bush** found his nominee for Defense Secretary, **John Tower**, rejected in 1989 on the grounds that the Senate did not trust his financial motives for seeking the post. Similarly, Bill Clinton's nomination for Attorney-General (the senior law officer in the administration), **Zoe Baird**, was refused in 1993 as she had employed illegal immigrants in her house, so it was felt she could not be relied upon in a senior post. The highly publicised Tower and Baird rejections represent a tendency for the Senate to question presidential nominations more searchingly now than in the past.

Impeachment

Although Bill Clinton's second term was dominated by Congress's attempts to impeach him over the Lewinski affair, the power of impeachment is not a significant one for Congress. A President, unlike many heads of government in democratic systems, cannot be removed for **political** reasons. A President might lose vote after vote in Congress, lose the support of public opinion and be acknowledged as a weak, ineffective leader, but he or she cannot be voted out of office by Congress. Only the people can do that, and they are only given one opportunity.

Impeachment becomes a possibility when a President is accused of 'high crimes and misdemeanours': in other words, misconduct of a personal nature. It has to be said that the attempt to impeach Clinton was partly politically motivated. A conservative Congress wanted him out of office and was willing to try anything to achieve this. However, it had to prove that he had attempted to subvert the course of justice – in this case, by persuading witnesses not to testify against him in court – to make impeachment successful. (It is a common misunderstanding that Clinton was accused on the grounds of his sexual conduct. This was not the case.)

In the event, Congress – the Senate in particular, for it is they who have the main responsibility for the process – failed to impeach Clinton. Public opinion did not back them and they were unable to muster enough votes. Though damaged and discredited by the hearings, Clinton – often dubbed the 'comeback kid' – survived as popular as ever. All we can learn from the episode is that impeachment is not, strictly speaking, a political act as it is concerned with the personal conduct of the President, rather than his policies. Nevertheless, some opponents of a President might try to use impeachment (or the threat of it) as a political weapon to undermine his authority.

Richard Nixon went through a similar process in the Watergate scandal. Watergate involved a dirty tricks campaign against Nixon's opponents, attempts to cover up the plot and the misuse of campaign funds. Unlike in the Clinton case, this impeachment probably would have succeeded had Nixon not resigned to prevent it in 1974.

The President and the Supreme Court

The Supreme Court judges are, in theory, **neutral** guardians of the spirit of the Constitution. It would be easy to understand that Presidents would prefer to face a Court that is sympathetic to their own political outlook. The political views of prospective candidates for appointment to the Court are often well known, so there are certainly some opportunities to 'pack' a Court with judges of a particular philosophical persuasion. It may be, of course, that only occasionally do cases come before the Court which have great political significance, but any President would want to be ready for such eventualities.

The most important incidence of the key political role of the Court occurred in the 1930s. Franklin D. Roosevelt had swept to power as President in 1932. His 'New Deal' for the USA pledged to bring the country out of the Great Depression, then at its height. This would require, however, great extensions in the powers of the federal government. The question was: would the measures be challenged in the Supreme Court as unconstitutional? Further, would the Court block the President's plans in this way? During Roosevelt's first term these fears were, indeed, realised. A conservative Court, in a series of challenges to extensions in federal authority, thwarted the New Deal policies. Roosevelt threatened to amend the Constitution, possibly even to give himself powers to flood the Court with his own new nominees. In the event, such drastic measures were not needed. By 1937 he had been able to make a number of legitimate appointments, so that he faced a Court generally divided five to four in favour of the new interpretation of federal power.

Though each judge has an equal vote in Court decisions, there is no doubt that the **Chief Justice** is a key figure, leading the discussion and generally setting the tone for the deliberations. We have already referred to the influence of **John Marshall** in the early days of the Constitution's life; more recently, two further Chief Justices have made a significant impact on the American political climate:

- In 1953 **Earl Warren** was appointed Chief Justice by Dwight D. Eisenhower. Warren presided over the Court until 1969. During that time, dramatic changes were effected in the USA's political culture, especially under Presidents Kennedy (1961–3) and Johnson (1963–8). In particular, a string of measures to establish equal rights for racial minorities and increased welfare provision for the poor were implemented. Successive constitutional challenges were rejected by a fundamentally liberal Court.
- Richard Nixon, who succeeded Johnson as President, appointed an apparently conservative Chief Justice, **Warren Burger**, in 1969, in the hope that he would be able to lead the Court towards reversal of many of the liberal decisions made by his predecessor, Earl Warren. Furthermore, a total of six judges had been appointed by Republican Presidents – Nixon, Ford and Reagan – by 1983. The scene was set, apparently, for reaction against the reforms of Kennedy and Johnson. In fact, the very opposite occurred. One after another of the Warren

Court's decisions were confirmed, despite determined challenges. The progress towards civil rights and increased welfare for the poor and underprivileged continued unabated.

The experience of the Burger Court illustrates the uncertainty of the relationship between the President and the judges. Without any means of putting pressure on them, the President cannot guarantee that they will not simply decide to act independently and without regard to their past political record. The conservatism of Burger disappeared once he took office, but this has not been the case with his successor, **William Rehnquist**, who took over in 1986. Rehnquist is a fierce defender of states' rights and illiberal on social and moral issues. Ronald Reagan found a willing political ally in him, in a way that Richard Nixon missed under Burger.

Summary of presidential powers

Power	Limits
• Commander-in-Chief of the armed forces	• Only Congress may declare war • The War Powers Resolution • Congress may withhold appropriations for military purposes
• Negotiation and signing of foreign treaties	• Treaties require support of two-thirds of the Senate
• Making executive agreements with foreign powers	• Legislative vetoes
• Appointment of Supreme Court judges	• May only act when there is a vacancy • Senate must approve all appointments
• Appointment of administration officials	• Senate must approve all appointments
• Setting the federal budget	• Congress may refuse to enact the budget
• Proposing legislation	• Congress may refuse to pass presidential legislation • New law may be declared unconstitutional by the Supreme Court
• Veto of laws passed by Congress	• May be overriden by a two-thirds majority
• Implementation of federal programmes	• May be declared unconstitutional by the Supreme Court • May be limited by a legislative veto in Congress
• Impoundment of congressional spending programmes	• Legislative veto of both Houses of Congress
• Speaking on behalf of the whole country	• None significant
• Using the National Guard in a state of emergency	• None significant

The Presidency – an overview

Two descriptions of the American Presidency reflect the condition of the post in modern times. One refers to ~~two~~ ~~~~ ~~~~ ~~~~ describes the office as the 'separated Presidency'.

Two Presidencies

The American President is often described as the 'most powerful man on earth'. This is how he is seen from the perspective of foreigners, however. The view refers to the fact that the President plays the leading role in American foreign policy and military affairs. It also takes note of the fact that the USA is the world's richest and mightiest country, so its leader is bound to cut an impressive figure on the world stage.

From a domestic standpoint, the picture is very different. Congress makes an equal claim to authority over domestic affairs. As we have seen, the President faces considerably more constraints in policy making at home than when dealing with the rest of the world. At the same time, the President must accept that Congress, too, makes policy and if there is a clash of objectives between Congress and the President, it is often the former that prevails, as Bill Clinton found to his cost.

Thus, there are indeed two Presidencies. One is the powerful world leader who can command great armies, impose American authority on weaker nations, distribute largesse in the form of foreign aid, negotiate treaties with other great nations and is capable of pressing a single button that would initiate a devastating nuclear attack. The other is a domestic policy-maker, often facing an uncooperative Congress, struggling with immense financial constraints, attempting to control volatile public opinion and perhaps facing a struggle to be re-elected four years hence.

The separated Presidency

The separation of powers which was incorporated in the American Constitution works extremely effectively in the field of congressional–presidential relations. This has become increasingly apparent since Richard Nixon alienated his Congress in the early 1970s.

In addition to this widening schism, American public opinion has become less reliable and more independent. The voters treat congressional elections very differently to those occasions when they are choosing the President. There may, therefore, be little in common between the political make-up of the Congress and the philosophy of the President. In other words, the President has become increasingly separated from the world of congressional politics. For a powerful, popular communicator such as Ronald Reagan, this presented fewer problems. But the less popular Jimmy Carter, George Bush and Bill Clinton found that Congress is more of an adversary than a partner.

The Vice President

Powers and functions

It is a cliché, but no less true for that, that the Vice President is a heartbeat away from becoming the most powerful person on earth. Should the President die, resign or become permanently incapacitated, the Vice President automatically steps in until the next scheduled election. Harry Truman in 1945, when Franklin D. Roosevelt died suddenly, Lyndon Johnson in 1963, when John F. Kennedy was assassinated in Dallas, and Gerald Ford, when Richard Nixon resigned in 1974, have experienced these occurrences. Thus the Vice President is a deputy to the President, but only in an emergency situation. Vice Presidents are not expected to make any decisions **on behalf** of their senior, as most deputies do, unless the President is totally unavailable.

The second important function of the Vice President is to preside over, or be Speaker of, the Senate. This is a largely ceremonial position, but it can occasionally carry some responsibility. The Vice President is, for example, a key presidential spokesperson among the Senators and may perform the task of informing and persuading them of the merits of the President's proposals. In the event of a tie in the Senate, the Vice President has the power to give the casting vote. This last occurred in 1993 when Bill Clinton was experiencing difficulty securing the passage of the budget. **Al Gore**, his loyal and respected deputy, was able to break the deadlock in favour of the President.

The presidential 'ticket'

In many ways, the importance of the Vice President is noticed only during the months leading up to a presidential election. In the presidential election, the candidate for President is harnessed to a particular deputy. In other words, voters are presented with a team of two and they cannot vote for one without the other. So the pair must appeal to as wide a spectrum of electoral opinion as possible. It is often the case, therefore, that an attempt is made to 'balance the ticket'.

President Clinton and Vice President Al Gore celebrate election victory in 1992

Should a presidential candidate be, for example, a known progressive liberal, with particular appeal among the poor, ethnic minorities and the educated middle class, he or she may lack appeal in the more conservat-ive southern … It is therefore tempting to choose as a 'running mate' a candidate who is more conservative in outlook. It is also the case that some candidates appeal to a particular part of the country because of their background. Again, a balance is needed. It was for this reason that Jimmy Carter, a southerner and, therefore, mistrusted by the established northern heartland of the Democratic Party, who saw such southerners as conservative, chose Walter Mondale (1977–81) to fight the election with him. Mondale was a more traditional Democrat and may have swung electoral fortunes decisively Carter's way. In 1960 John F. Kennedy selected Lyndon Johnson (1961–3) for the opposite reason. Kennedy was an intellectual northerner (from Massachusetts), while Johnson was a Texan, much respected among the more conservative Democrats in that region. In 2000, George W. Bush chose Dick Cheney, a foreign policy expert, to balance his own lack of interest in, and knowledge of, the subject.

The fact that presidential running mates can have so much influence on voters is largely illogical. Having few functions and, normally, less influence, the choice of Vice President is of little practical consequence. Yet voters might be swayed. More importantly, so too might the key party workers who help to secure the votes for their own candidate. They need to feel that one of the candidates on the presidential ticket is one of their own and not a stranger.

A flexible role Most Vice Presidents have played no significant role in American politics. **Dan Quayle** (1989–93), for example, George Bush's deputy, was allowed only ceremonial duties. Even less was seen of **Spiro Agnew** (1969–73), Richard Nixon's first Vice President, who was to resign over allegations of tax evasion after three years of undistinguished office.

There have, nevertheless, been some deputies who have found a positive role to play. Lyndon Johnson had been Senate Democrat majority leader before Kennedy chose him as running mate. Kennedy's intention was to find an experienced, respected congressional leader who understood the kind of deal making and coalition building that a President needs to control Congress. In the event, Johnson was of little help to Kennedy, but his background was to prove a vital factor during his own Presidency. George Bush (1981–9), Reagan's Vice President, had been a Director of the Central Intelligence Agency. His experience of foreign relations was, therefore, of great use to Reagan, who was a complete beginner in this area. Bush acted as a kind of roving ambassador for the USA during his eight years as Vice President.

Thus, we can see that the post of Vice President can vary in its importance, depending on the incumbent's abilities and background. But, however large a role the Vice President might be given, he or she can never rival the authority of the key figures in congressional party politics, such as the floor leaders and senior committee chairpersons.

**The future
President?**

Either because they have been in office upon the demise of a President, or because they choose later to run for office, a high proportion of Vice Presidents go on to become President. Since the Second World War, the list reads impressively: Harry Truman, Richard Nixon, Lyndon Johnson, Gerald Ford and George Bush.

Lacking in influence they might be, but Vice Presidents do have a privileged position in the White House. They see most of the action from the inside, may be present at high-level discussions and can learn how the office of President works. The position has therefore become one of the several typical 'apprenticeships' that an aspiring President might undertake. In the 2000 presidential election, Vice President Al Gore flew the Democrat flag and so became the latest in a long line of deputies aspiring to the top job.

The executive office of the President

Also known as the White House Office, or Staff, the executive office represents a collection of powerful bodies that serve the President directly, helping to shape policies and advising on the nature of their implementation. The date of its creation by Congress – 1939 – is significant. It followed a period of unprecedented growth in the scope of presidential power during the first half of Franklin D. Roosevelt's incumbency, the New Deal era. With the expanded role of the Presidency, he clearly needed a bureaucracy of his own to be able to sustain all the functions expected of him. At the centre of the White House organisation sits the White House Office itself.

**The White House
Office**

These are the most personal advisers to the President – those who may expect to see him or her on a day-to-day basis when in Washington. The most senior member is the **Chief of Staff**, the President's personal aide, who keeps the President informed of what the rest of the Office staff are doing and, in turn, informs them of the President's current thinking. Behind the Chief of Staff stand a number of **assistants** and **special assistants** who are assigned specific roles in the White House machine. The **Counsel to the President** advises the President on legal matters, while the **Press Secretary** deals with the media on behalf of the White House.

Under normal circumstances, it is expected that these staff are mere reflections of the President's own thinking. During Richard Nixon's Presidency, however, it became clear that several of the White House staff were actually running the policy-making process themselves, often without consulting the President. Three of Nixon's closest advisers, **Bob Haldeman** (Chief of Staff), **John Erlichman** (special assistant) and **John Dean** (legal counsel) formed, with the aid of a number of other officers, notably Attorney-General **John Mitchell**, an inner circle whose legal, semi-legal and even illegal activities formed a kind of 'hidden executive' from which Congress and the public were excluded. The revelations of such a situation, which resulted from the **Watergate** hearings, were to bring about Nixon's downfall. More recently, Ronald Reagan's Chief of Staff, **Donald Regan** (the similarity of names was a mere coincidence), was said to wield considerable influence in White House politics.

The National Security Council

The National Security Council (NSC) chaired by the President and with the Vice President in attendance, deals with White House policy in foreign affairs, national defence and the intelligence services. As such, its members include the Director of the Central Intelligence Agency, the Chairman of the Military Chiefs-of-Staff, the Secretary of State (i.e. Foreign Secretary) and the Secretary for Defense. Backed by a team of experts on defence and foreign affairs, the NSC is the hub of the President's policy-making machinery in all matters related to the security of the USA.

The Office of Management and Budget

The Office of Management and Budget (OMB) is a key office for the President. The preparation, presentation and implementation of the annual federal budget is possibly the most complex operation that the President must undertake. Furthermore, Presidents expect, in a normal year, to face difficulty in negotiations with Congress over the precise terms of the budget. Bill Clinton in the 1990s faced especially heavy opposition to his plans for higher taxes and federal spending, and had to rely heavily on the OMB for support.

The work of the OMB is year-long. It must deal with the various executive secretaries and agency heads who wish to claim a share of the federal expenditure kitty, and also with representations from the 50 states who seek federal help with their spending plans. On the other hand, taxation has to be considered, along with the general economic consequences of budgetary plans. Liaison with the President's economic and financial advisers is, therefore, also needed.

Once a budget proposal has finally been crafted out of this complex set of negotiations and consultations, Congress must be faced, especially the House of Representatives, which has the senior role in budget negotiations. As we have said, in the case of Clinton's progressive budgeting, opposition was so fierce that a virtual reconstruction of his budgets had to take place before Congress would accept them.

The Council of Economic Advisers

Normally, the Council of Economic Advisers (CEA) comprises three economic advisers (whose appointment requires the consent of the Senate) helped by a permanent team of professional economic researchers. Their role is to provide economic information to the President, advise on possible courses of action to deal with economic problems and help prepare the President's annual address to Congress on the state of the national economy.

When it was set up in 1946, the Council had fairly specific tasks, including the maintenance of full employment, monetary stability and a healthy overseas balance of payments. Broadly speaking, these have remained the objectives of the executive branch. During the Presidency of Ronald Reagan, however, it adopted a 'monetarist' stance, concentrating on anti-inflationary policies through control of interest rates and the money supply. It became committed to the reduction of both federal taxation and expenditure. Under President Clinton, attempts were made by the Council to return to expansionary policy, but congressional opposition hindered its work.

A considerable amount of liaison takes place between the CEA and the OMB, as well as with the US Treasury and the Federal Reserve. Although Presidents must mediate between competing policy demands from these bodies, they have come to rely increasingly upon their Chief Economic Adviser for guidance.

Other offices The **Office of Policy Development** is a catch-all organisation, dealing with all the matters of domestic policy not covered in the other sections of the executive office. It is headed by an assistant to the President who must act as guide on a host of miscellaneous concerns. The title of the **Council of Environmental Quality** speaks for itself, as does that of the **Office of the United States Trade Representatives**. The **Office of Science and Technology Policy** has played an important role in advising the President on space and weapons research policy, though the end of the Cold War has reduced these matters to a lower priority. Finally, the **Office of Administration** does what its name suggests – providing administrative back-up for all the other departments.

Conclusion The list of organisations in the executive office of the President makes impressive reading. It comprises a formidable array of expertise and specialist knowledge upon which the President can call. Of all western democratic leaders, American Presidents have, perhaps, the most powerful machine backing them. Yet they certainly need it. In many ways, they stand alone as the chief executive. Presidents are elected separately by the people, who expect them to achieve great progress in a variety of ways. They cannot devolve responsibility elsewhere, to a Cabinet or to their ministers. They must face the electorate alone when the time comes to judge their performance.

At the same time, they face the impressive authority and power of the Congress. They must be able to negotiate and persuade, bully and cajole the legislators into accepting all or part of their plans. These White House advisers must, therefore, be prepared to operate on the floor of Congress, furthering the cause of presidential influence.

The executive departments

The Cabinet Those who have grown up with preconceptions about Cabinet government as it is practised in the UK must not make the error of assuming that its American counterpart is in any way similar. It is different in virtually all respects except its name. When the President's 'Secretaries', who head the departments, meet together from time to time, they might **look** something like the British Cabinet, seated around a large table with the President at its head, but the similarity ends there.

The principal difference is that the Cabinet is **not** a collective decision-making body. Indeed, it makes no decisions at all. Discussion may centre around key elements of the administration's policy, but these consultations do not result in binding decisions. They are discussions and little more. It is clearly understood in American government that all major decisions are made by the President, but that decisions specifically related to the work of one department are made by its Secretary. Some

Presidents, such as Dwight Eisenhower (1953–61) and Ronald Reagan (1981–9), have relied heavily upon the advice of Cabinet colleagues. They both took a limited view of the presidential role, seeing it as more ~~of a public business and a non-policy making one. Others, such as John~~ Kennedy (1961–3) and George Bush (1989–93) have largely ignored the Cabinet, whose meetings became formal and meaningless.

The Cabinet comprises thirteen members, all Secretaries, who are appointed by the President subject to ratification by the Congress. The Constitution specifies that they must not be drawn from the Congress (thus preserving the principle of the separation of powers), so the President must look elsewhere for nominees. Civil servants, retired politicians, academics, pressure group leaders and senior managers from the worlds of finance, business and commerce are favourites, as are successful officials from state governments.

The thirteen positions are the Secretaries of or for:

- State (foreign affairs)
- Commerce
- Treasury
- Labor
- Defense
- Justice (Attorney-General)
- Health and Human Resources
- Housing and Urban Development
- Transportation
- The Interior
- Agriculture
- Energy
- Education.

Each Secretary has a number of assistants and an army of lesser civil servants. The senior officials are also appointed by the President, though in effect the Department Head has the major voice in lesser appointments.

Department Secretaries are considerably limited in their powers by a number of factors. First, they may be overruled by the President as head of the executive branch. Second, their legislative plans may be thwarted by an unsympathetic Congress. Third, and perhaps most importantly, they must rely upon the Congress for the appropriation of funds required for their programmes of action. Thus, it would be a mistake to compare them directly with 'ministers' who lead European-style democracies. They are very much presidential assistants, rather than political leaders in their own right.

There have, nevertheless, been important exceptions to the norm. Some Department Secretaries have played a leading role in American policies. **Henry Kissinger**, for example, was President Nixon's Secretary of State and, as such, played a leading role in the conduct of the Cold War, the Vietnam conflict and American involvement in the Middle East. **Bobby Kennedy**, brother of J.F. Kennedy, was an enormously influential Attorney-General, taking the lead in preparing the ground for important civil rights legislation.

It must also be stressed that these senior officials have the vital task of appearing regularly before Congress to explain administration policy. A good showing before a congressional committee will not only enhance a Secretary's prestige, but also further the cause of presidential power.

Executive agencies

It is a matter of great potential confusion in American government that agencies whose heads are below Cabinet rank have been given a variety of titles, such as 'agency', 'commission' or 'administration'. They have in common, however, the fact that they are operational agencies, charged with the task of implementing policy that has been determined at a higher level. The agencies form the bulk of the federal administration (though not all are based in Washington). They vary in the degree of independence they enjoy, but it must be emphasised that their senior members are appointed and may be removed by the President. They are, therefore, still subject to presidential jurisdiction.

The most significant include:

- Environmental Protection Agency
- Federal Communication Commission
- Federal Reserve System
- Interstate Commerce Commission
- Securities and Exchange Commission
- Tennessee Valley Authority
- Veterans Administration
- National Aeronautics and Space Administration (NASA).

We are now in a position to summarise the structure of the federal administration:

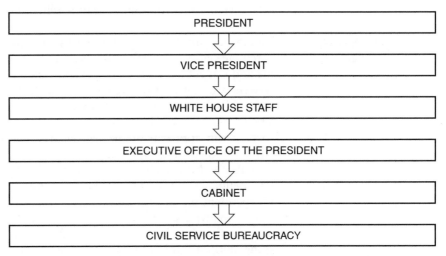

```
┌─────────────────────────────────────────────┐
│                  PRESIDENT                    │
└─────────────────────────────────────────────┘
                      ⇩
┌─────────────────────────────────────────────┐
│               VICE PRESIDENT                  │
└─────────────────────────────────────────────┘
                      ⇩
┌─────────────────────────────────────────────┐
│              WHITE HOUSE STAFF                │
└─────────────────────────────────────────────┘
                      ⇩
┌─────────────────────────────────────────────┐
│        EXECUTIVE OFFICE OF THE PRESIDENT      │
└─────────────────────────────────────────────┘
                      ⇩
┌─────────────────────────────────────────────┐
│                   CABINET                     │
└─────────────────────────────────────────────┘
                      ⇩
┌─────────────────────────────────────────────┐
│            CIVIL SERVICE BUREAUCRACY          │
└─────────────────────────────────────────────┘
```

Comparison of the American President and the British Prime Minister

In some ways such a comparison is spurious, since there is a key difference between the constitutional positions of the two posts. The American President is **both** Head of State and Head of Government. The Prime Minister is **only** Head of Government. Nevertheless, there are a number of respects in which similarities can be found as well as distinctions.

Similarities
- Both have extensive powers of patronage, with hundreds, even thousands, of important political posts at their disposal.
- They are the chief policy-makers within the political community.
- Both are heads of the governing party.
- Foreign policy is very much in their hands.
- Both play the role of Commander-in-Chief of the armed forces.
- In times of crisis and emergency, they may speak on behalf of the country.

Distinctions This is the more complex part of the comparative analysis since, although the similarities are clear, the variations in power are more subtle. The easiest way to deal with this problem is first to identify those ~~powers of the President's role that give him greater power or influence~~ than the Prime Minister, and then to reverse the position and see where a Prime Minister gains in contrast.

Presidential advantages
- Being Head of State, the President has the authority to speak for all American people.
- The President's authority is not shared with the Cabinet. The President dominates it, whereas the Prime Minister is only 'first among equals' in the British Cabinet and can be outvoted by them.
- The whole of the administration serves the President and is subject to direct patronage. He/she does not have to share powers with ministers.
- The President cannot be removed from office for political reasons by the legislature. He/she may suffer political defeats, but remain in office. The Prime Minister constantly relies upon parliamentary support.

Prime ministerial advantages
- The Prime Minister is not limited by an entrenched Constitution. The extensive nature of prerogative powers that he or she exercises is flexible and not subject to legal or parliamentary constraint. The President's powers are constitutionally circumscribed. Since a Prime Minister can control Parliament, his or her powers are enormously enhanced.
- The Prime Minister's powers of patronage are not limited by the need to seek the approval of the legislature. The President must seek the 'advice and consent' of Congress.
- The Prime Minister's party is normally united behind him or her. Presidents, on the other hand, head weak, decentralised and independent party machines.
- The Prime Minister leads a government that is normally able to dominate Parliament. By contrast, the President cannot rely on congressional support and often faces stiff opposition.
- The UK's unitary state means that the Prime Minister does not face strong regional forces, whereas the President has limited jurisdiction among the states.
- The Prime Minister may choose the date of a general election to his or her party's advantage. The President faces a fixed four-year term and so is less in control of his or her political fortunes.

The 'balance sheet' is, therefore, difficult to interpret. However, a reference back to the phenomenon of the 'two Presidencies' described above may help us. In the field of **foreign policy**, we can certainly say that the American President does, indeed, possess unsurpassed powers. If we consider **domestic affairs**, on the other hand, it is evident that the British Prime Minister enjoys considerably enhanced freedom of action and possesses a more impressive array of unconstrained powers. One proviso must, however, still be added. The pre-eminent domestic position of the Prime Minister depends upon his or her ability to control both party and Parliament. A President can still govern despite remarkably severe political opposition; a Prime Minister cannot.

For exam questions relevant to this unit, see page 559.

Parties

Introduction

Unit 4 of this book describes the functions of political parties in general. It was apparent that British parties have as one of their prime functions, perhaps **the** prime function, the articulation of demands. They spend much of their time developing and refining policy programmes that can be placed before the electorate at elections and, if the election is won, that can be turned into government action. Although American parties are concerned with this same process, it is certainly not their principal characteristic. Indeed, all our European preconceptions must be put aside if we are to understand American party politics at all.

The most striking feature which we will notice is that there is considerable variation in the political philosophy of the parties depending upon which part of the country they are operating in. This geographical divergence can be observed to a limited extent in Germany and Italy, but to nothing like the same extent as in the USA. There is also no real concept of the 'election manifesto' in the USA. Individual candidates may produce their own manifestos, but the parties as a whole do not have organised political programmes to put before the electorate.

In some ways, the party system in the USA resembles that which prevailed in Britain in the first half of the nineteenth century. A party label such as 'Tory', 'Whig' or 'Radical' gave a clue to the philosophy of the candidate, but it was only a clue. He was not tied to a fixed set of party policies, nor was he subject to any central discipline. One might be able to predict how he would vote in the House of Commons on such issues as protectionism versus free trade, the Irish question or constitutional reform, but one could guarantee nothing. So it is today in the American Congress at Washington and in the state legislatures.

What we can say with some certainty, however, is that there is a two-party system of sorts. In all but the most local elections, the endorsement of either the Democratic or Republican Party is essential if a candidate for public office is to have a realistic chance of success at the polls. The precise nature of the two-party system might vary from place to place, but there is always the same duopoly.

The origins of the parties

There have been a number of defining periods in American political history which have helped to create the modern Democratic and Republican Parties.

The Civil War

Broadly speaking, it was the Democratic Party that supported the breakaway of the southern states over the issue of slavery in the 1860s. The Republicans, who were determined to maintain the unity of the country, proposed the abolition of slave-holding. Having won the Civil War in 1865, the Republicans dominated the political scene for the next 70 years. Those Democrats who were based in the northern states were virtually completely excluded from power. In the South, however, a strange, more resilient kind of political animal had been born. This was the 'southern Democrat', or 'Dixiecrat', as he was to become known.

In the South, the Democrats completely dominated the political scene

there was little chance of a Democratic candidate being elected President (**Grover Cleveland** in 1884 and 1892 was the only exception). The Dixiecrats were conservative in outlook, unwilling to grant the freed slaves full civil rights and opposed to the power of federal government, which had defeated them militarily. To make matters worse for them, the Republicans were supported by an alliance of business interests, the growing industrial working class and freed slaves. These were all seen as economic threats to the poorer South, which was dominated by estate owners, small tenant farmers and agricultural labourers.

The Industrial Revolution

The old North–South divide that followed the Civil War and determined the two-party system of the day began to break up with the onset of the USA's late but rapid industrial revolution, which became politically significant in the 1890s.

The challenge of **William Jennings Bryant** to the Republicans was based on support from the small, independent farmers, craftsmen and traders who felt threatened by the rise of big business interests. Although Bryant, a Populist by title, was embraced by the Democrats, his real influence was felt among the Republicans. Effectively, they were split over the issue of whether to support the great new industrial and commercial interests, or whether to champion the 'small, independent' man as Bryant had done. Ultimately, the Republicans tried to secure the support of both groups. The northern Democrats, meanwhile, had their eyes firmly on the new, expanding working class who were centred in the growing cities. The Republicans still drew much support from workers, but their hold over them was beginning to slip. The Democrats forged links with the trade unions and the poor sections of the community, both black and white. Meanwhile the southern Democrats, frozen in time, retained their parochial, conservative outlook.

The New Deal era

By the 1930s, the Republicans were still hanging on to their dominant political position, especially in presidential elections. The Great Depression, which struck in 1929–30, changed American politics for the rest of the century. The Republicans appeared to have no answer to the economic slump. **Franklin D. Roosevelt** persuaded the Democrats to nominate him as their candidate in 1932 with a radical programme, proposing massive federal intervention in industry and commerce to bring the USA back to full employment and prosperity.

Roosevelt's dramatic victory, added to the Democratic domination of the Congress that followed it, forged a new coalition of support for the Democrats. This comprised the working classes (particularly in the northern cities), the more educated middle classes and, as before, the poorer elements in urban society. Republican support shrank to comprise only the Mid-west farming interests, owners of small businesses, and the salaried employees of big businesses, banks, etc. The Democrat voters accepted the expanded role of the federal government that Roosevelt had brought about. As long as central government served their economic interests, they were prepared to put aside the traditional American suspicion of governmental power. Republicans, more conservative and traditional in their outlook, were not prepared to see federal interference with economic enterprise and feared the erosion of the independence of the states in the face of growing federal authority.

Once again, while all these changes on the political map were taking place, little changed in the South. The Dixiecrats continued to hold on. Although the South suffered from the Depression along with the rest of the country, their Democratic members of Congress resisted many of Roosevelt's reforms. Like the northern Republicans, they were still fearful of federal power, a legacy of the Civil War. There was, in other words, a conservative anti-Roosevelt coalition, which cut across party lines. This continues to be a common feature of the American political system in Washington.

The civil rights era

The year 1960 saw the election of **John F. Kennedy** as President. He was supported by a new kind of Democratic coalition. This contained, as we would expect, the poor blacks and whites in the cities as he promised to bring civil rights to all and to introduce anti-poverty, welfare and housing programmes to combat the growing problems of the USA's cities. He also attracted the votes of many young Americans, traditionally a politically apathetic group. They saw him as a new kind of politician, a man of vision who promised to break the hold of the old political establishment and so make real changes for the better in American society.

However, as well as attracting new elements of support for the Democrats, Kennedy increasingly broke the hold of conservative Democrats in the South – a process initiated in 1948 by Truman's espousal of civil rights. His civil rights policies, designed to end racial discrimination, angered the poorer whites in the South who opposed such liberal proposals. Indeed, Kennedy's, and his successor Lyndon Johnson's, generally liberal and progressive philosophy was deeply unpopular in the South. The Republicans began, albeit slowly, to pick up support there from defecting Democrats. This change in the political balance of the South was largely responsible for the Republican domination of the White House from 1968 to 1992 (apart from the brief Democratic incumbency of Jimmy Carter from 1977 to 1981).

Modern party alignments

As we have seen, it is an error to think of American parties as single, unified entities. They are highly decentralised organisations whose support varies considerably from one part of the country to another. It used to be the case, therefore, that generalisations about party alignments were dangerous and certainly futile exercises. The regional pattern of party support was at least fairly predictable, but even that has now broken down.

Since the movement to the right of the Republican Party in the 1980s, and the weakening of the conservative Democratic hold over the South, the precise nature of party alignments among the electors has become even less certain. Voters tend to be more volatile, more influenced by the individual candidates than by their party label. As has occurred in the UK, there has been a considerable degree of 'partisan dealignment' in the USA. Traditional attachments to parties are weaker; issues and personalities now rival them in the mind of the typical voter.

Nevertheless, some discernible patterns can still be identified. The principal elements of **national** party support are shown below.

National party allegiances

Republicans	Democrats
• Mid-western farming interests	• Members of ethnic minorities
• Business executives	• Liberal eastern middle classes
• Small business entrepreneurs	• Some poor whites in the South
• Some southern whites	• Industrial workers
• Religious fundamentalists	• Young liberal idealists
• Commercial interests in the East	• Members of caring professions
• Wealthier families in the West	

Party philosophies

The decentralised nature of American parties is not merely an organisational feature. The great sectional variations that exist in the political culture are also reflected in the philosophies of both Democrats and Republicans. Thus, it is dangerous to make any generalised comments about basic beliefs. The clearest example, as we have seen, is the phenomenon of the southern, conservative Democrat. There are also pockets of progressive, more liberal Republicanism in the cities of the East such as New York and Boston.

We must also be aware that every candidate for election is relatively free to create their own political programme, based on their own philosophy and the nature of the constituency that they are seeking to represent. A Republican who is normally opposed to federal government power, for example, would need to modify his views if he were running for the House of Representatives in a district that relied heavily on federal government funds or contracts. Similarly, a normally progressive Democrat, with strong views on civil rights for ethnic minority groups, has to be cautious where there is a high level of racial tension. Her liberal views would need to be tempered by a possibly more conservative view on law and order. In addition, virtually every candidate needs financial help from a variety of sponsors and supporters. The interest groups, business enterprises and individuals who are supporting candidates in this way inevitably expect them to take their views and demands into consideration. Only candidates who are sure of being elected, or who can finance themselves independently, can afford to resist such pressures when developing their personal manifesto.

Thus, any general statement about the philosophies of the two parties must be seen against two important variable factors. These are the region or section in which the party is operating and the nature of individual candidates, who are financing them and what pressures are being placed upon them within the community. Nevertheless, the typical, broad beliefs and goals of the two parties can be summarised as follows.

Typical party philosophies	
Republicans	**Democrats**
• Suspicion of federal power preference for greater independence for the states • Opposition to high levels of taxation and public expenditure • Support for policies favourable to business and commerce • Dislike of government-organised welfare, housing and health schemes • Belief that individuals should be prepared to support themselves • Strong defence of those parts of the Constitution that guarantee individual liberty • Stress on firm policies on law and order • Support for protectionist measures in defence of agriculture and industry against foreign competition • Opposition to American involvement in foreign affairs outside the immediate vicinity of North America • A conservative view on moral issues	• Support for full equal civil rights for all • An acceptance of federal intervention in order to exercise economic control • General sympathy for measures to improve health, welfare and housing provision through positive action by federal government • Concern for the environment and an acceptance that government intervention is needed to curb environmental damage • Opposition to protectionism and an acceptance of the benefits of free trade • Support for stiffer gun control laws but a general belief that the crime problem needs social as well as legal remedies • A stress on education as a key element in social order and prosperity • A generally tolerant liberal attitude on moral issues

Party organisation

American parties do not have single, unified, national organisations as most European parties do. It must also be borne in mind that there is no real concept of party membership in the USA. There are small numbers of regular workers and a larger group of 'activists', who are willing to support party candidates at elections, but who then cease to participate in politics until the next polling day. Without a permanent mass membership, and without a hard core of active workers, there cannot be an extensive established party organisation.

The organisation of the parties can only be understood as a series of layers, which correspond broadly to the various levels at which American government operates. Not only is party organisation multilayered, it is also multifaceted. The character of party activity varies at each of the levels. Descriptions here begin at the most local tier.

Precincts

These are the smallest units within American government. They may be political clubs or caucuses that meet irregularly and might have their own, unique organisations. Their role is largely threefold. First, they might be called on to nominate delegates to the state party convention, whose role is to select the candidates for state positions and to try to create some sort of political programme for the forthcoming elections. Second, they must try to raise funds for the candidates representing their parties at all levels, from local school board members to the presidency itself. Finally, they will campaign locally to try to persuade the voters to turn out in support of their candidates.

Wards, counties and cities The small units of local government, wards (occasionally boroughs), make up the counties and the cities. In each case there is likely to be a ... and a chairperson. Their role only becomes significant when they are required to attend meetings of the state party ... or even the state convention, which plays a crucial role, alongside primary elections, in candidate selection. Otherwise, they are expected to help at election time, raising money and canvassing support, but will largely disappear from view between elections. The big cities used to have more formal and powerful committees in the days of 'machine politics', but these have now declined so that even in such large units of local government as Los Angeles, Chicago and New York, party committees make little impact on the political scene.

The states There is a more formal organisation operating at state level. Each party has a central committee, headed by a chairperson. Their tasks are similar to those at the levels below them – fundraising, candidate nomination and election campaigning. In addition, however, they attempt to co-ordinate the work of the party's various elected representatives within the state. These will include those Senators, Governors, Lieutenant-Generals and members of the House of Representatives who might be members of that party.

Within the state legislature itself, the party representatives organise themselves into as tight a group as they can for the purposes of voting as a block, especially when the State Governor is of their party and so needs their support. Majority or minority leaders are, therefore, chosen by the members, as are party whips whose role it is to try to maintain some sort of disciplined unity. As in Washington, this might not always be possible, but there is more party cohesion at state level than at federal level.

National parties As in the states, there is a national committee, headed by a chairperson. The most important task that these committees carry out is the organisation of the National Convention, at which the party's presidential candidate is chosen. Thus, they are only prominent every four years when those conventions take place. It used to be the case, when leadership of a party carried with it considerable influence, that the national committees were able to interfere with the nomination process at the Convention. This is less true today, since most delegates are now tied to supporting a particular candidate through the results of state primary elections. Thus, their role is now largely ceremonial and symbolic.

Congress and the White House The real party work at national level takes place within Congress. The party whose nominee secures the Presidency is in a special position. The President is automatically head of their party. It becomes their and their staff's role to try to secure the support of colleagues in the House and the Senate. Together with the party floor leaders (both the majority leader and the minority leader) and the whips, attempts are made to create unity. Success in this regard is variable. The Democrats, in particular, find difficulty in forging a coalition between the liberal northerners and the conservatives from the South. To a lesser extent, the Republicans might also find themselves split between their right wing and the moderates within the party.

The Democratic Party
Convention 2000

Where the Presidency is held by its rivals, a party has no real leader. If
they hold a majority in one or both Houses of Congress, however, their
floor leaders become the most powerful members of the party. If they
are able to carry the rest of the party with them, they can put themselves
in a position of parity with the President, who will depend on them to
secure the passage of legislation. In return, congressional party leaders
might gain the President's backing for some of their cherished programmes.

The worst scenario for a party in Washington is to lose the Presidency
and to be in a minority in both Houses of Congress. In these circumstances, it becomes largely impotent, reduced to sniping at the administration, trying to be as obstructive as possible and, in some
circumstances, attempting to link with some disaffected members of the
majority party to form a temporary majority on a specific issue. The
Republicans faced this situation in the 1930s and again in the 1960s. In
both cases the result was a successful programme of radical reforms by
the triumphant Democrats, largely untroubled by their opponents,
except when some conservative southern Democrats were willing to
throw in their lot with the Republicans over a particularly repugnant
measure.

Parties and elections

The parties' task

in the USA a large proportion of these are elected officials who, in other political systems, would be appointed by some sort of superior body. Thus, in any election (November is election season in the USA), the following candidates might be placed before the electorate:

- President
- Senator
- Representative (member of Congress)
- State Governor
- State Lieutenant-General
- State Attorney-General
- county or city mayor
- county judge
- county sheriff
- school board representative.

In addition to this list, there may be other officials whose titles and roles vary from state to state. Thus, the party organisations, loose and informal though they might be, have an enormous task supporting so many candidates.

The workers must organise meetings and rallies, fundraising events, dinners, opportunities for ordinary people to meet the candidate and exposure in the media. On the day of the election itself, it is their job to go out to persuade people to cast their votes. Americans are notoriously reluctant to vote, so a great deal of cajoling needs to be done. The platforms of the candidates must be explained (often in the simplest terms), their personal qualities emphasised and, if they already hold office, the better aspects of their political record highlighted.

Primary elections

As we have seen in Unit 19, the USA enjoys a unique system for determining which individual should represent each party in elections. In European parties, candidates are chosen by the party leadership, by small committees of local party activists or by ballots of registered, permanent members. The American primary election is different in character, which has quite marked effects on the nature of the final ballot. It does not yet operate in all states, but the majority – 38 – now use the procedure.

Primaries can be **open**, where all registered voters may vote, or **closed**, where only those who are registered as a party's supporter can vote. In either case they have the effect of bringing into the candidate selection procedure a broad section of the electorate. For some period before an election, at presidential, congressional and state levels, aspiring party candidates compete with each other, through the primaries, to demonstrate that they can attract sufficient support to be able to win office for their party.

The effects of using primaries are several, and most are considered by Americans to improve the quality of their democracy:

- They widen political participation, allowing ordinary voters to express a preference between candidates of the same party.

- They open up the political system to a wider variety of aspiring office-holders. In British parties, virtually all candidates have to serve a long apprenticeship in a party, otherwise they have little chance of being adopted. In the USA it is possible to enter and win primary contests without such a background. Thus, many more able people may qualify for consideration.
- Since voters are normally more moderate in their political outlook than party activists, their participation in primaries tends to produce more moderate candidates. The 'extremes' are usually filtered out in primary contests.

What determines the result of elections?

The results of elections depend upon a wide variety of factors, many of which cannot always be explained by political tradition.

The individual campaign

The average American voter does not have a strong allegiance to either party. In other words, 'partisan alignment' is relatively weak. It follows then that the character, image and performance of each individual candidate is most important. How well the campaign is conducted, how much exposure there is in the media and how adept the candidate is at avoiding offending important groups of voters, are all of great significance. A charismatic individual can 'buck the trend' against his or her party, just as a poor candidate might help the opposing party, which would have little chance under normal circumstances.

Section

In some areas there is, effectively, a one-party system. There are still parts of the Deep South which are completely controlled by the local Democrats. Arkansas and Alabama are notable in this respect. Some cities, such as Chicago, are also Democrat monopolies. The Republicans, too, have their strongholds, such as Kentucky and Kansas. Here, one party is virtually guaranteed victory in all elections above those at the most local level.

The legacy of city machines

It used to be the case that one or other of the parties maintained a political 'machine' in one of the great cities. The city machines were rare examples of established organisations, more closely related to the European model than to the normal American style of loose-knit party political organisation. In every precinct or ward of the city, the party that dominated the city could boast groups of party supporters on whom they could rely for fundraising and electioneering. In many cases, where Democrats held sway, trade union officials would be recruited in this way. The reward for their work for the party was the promise of a job with one of the city's departments, or some other form of preferential treatment, guaranteed by the party's established control of City Hall. As well as controlling voting patterns in the cities, the machines also determined the way in which delegates to the National Party Convention, where presidential candidates are chosen, voted. Thus, a few powerful party leaders carried considerable influence within the national party.

The machines are all but gone now. It was at the Democratic National Convention of 1968 in Chicago, when the all-powerful mayor,

Dick Daley, openly 'rigged' the result of the nomination process in favour of Senator Hubert Humphrey (standing against the radical candi-

~~date George McGovern), the 'machine politics' was finally discredited~~

Nevertheless, the legacy of that domination of the cities by one party or another still remains. Most cities are still almost dominated by electoral support for one party.

Individual voter circumstances Although social factors are less important in American voting than is the case in the UK, there are still a number of discernible patterns in the USA. Some of the principal factors are shown below.

Personal circumstances affecting voting patterns	
Circumstance	More probable party allegiance
• Protestant	• Republican
• Catholic	• Democrat
• Jewish	• Democrat
• College graduate	• Republican
• Failed to graduate from High School	• Democrat
• Trade union member	• Democrat
• Non-white	• Democrat
• Male	• Republican
• Female	• Democrat
• Young	• Democrat
• Old	• Republican

The social, ethnic and age structure of a particular constituency is, therefore, a significant element in determining how well each party is likely to perform at the polls.

Incumbency More important than all these factors, however, is that of 'incumbency'. There is a considerably greater chance that the incumbent Senator, member of Congress, state assembly member, governor or the like will be elected than a new challenger. Of course, this is largely due to the fact that some constituencies, because of their social make-up, are bound to return a candidate of the same party. Nevertheless, there is still a tendency for voters to prefer the representative they know to one who is an unknown quantity. A word of caution is needed at this point, however. The 1994 congressional elections saw a rout of many apparently 'safe' Democrat seats. There is also a stronger likelihood that the incumbent President will be beaten than used to be the case. Fighting against a President who was seeking a second term was usually seen as a futile exercise. In recent years, however, three Presidents – Ford (1976), Carter (1980) and Bush (1992) – have all been denied such a second term. The incumbency factor, still important within the states, seems to have broken down at federal level.

Ticket voting The sheer mechanics of voting in American elections can be a factor in the behaviour of the electors. At every poll the voter is faced with a ballot paper listing candidates for as many as 50 different posts, for each of which there are at least two, sometimes more, candidates. Faced with a bewildering choice, the voters might prefer simply to cast all their votes for candidates of their preferred party. This is known as 'voting the straight ticket'. To help the voters there is, in many states, a voting machine that allows them to cast a number of votes simultaneously, provided, of course, they are all for the same party. 'Split ticket' voting, where a voter supports different party candidates for different posts, involves more effort and more special knowledge. Clearly, some candidates benefit from this factor, picking up votes simply because they stand for the party that is the voter's choice. Voting machines are not universally used, so this only applies in the more populated districts, often the big cities.

Coat-tailing

In a similar way, a phenomenon known as 'coat-tailing' can occur. Here, a popular party candidate for a senior post – say the Presidency itself, or the post of Senator – might carry along other lesser-known candidates from the same party on their 'coat-tails'. In other words, less popular or less well-known individuals might be elected on the reputation of another candidate. The opposite might happen where there is an unpopular candidate leading a party's challenge.

Hillary Clinton after her election to Senate in 2000

The financial bandwagon

Finance and the 'bandwagon' effect can also go a long way to determining election results. The many pressure groups and businesses that use the financing of candidates' campaigns to help further their cause are extremely sensitive to the chances of success of each of the candidates. They invariably wish to sponsor successful office-seekers, since otherwise they would be of no use to them. Supporting losing candidates is seen as a waste of money. It follows, therefore, that when a candidate seems to be gaining ground during the campaign, he or she will automatically attract more financial support. In the primary elections, which last several months, this effect is especially noticeable. One by one, the less popular candidates drop out through sheer lack of funds. Those who are doing well, on the other hand, gallop ahead with ever-increasing campaign funds swelling their coffers. This is known as a ~~ment~~ ~~effe~~ ~~and more~~ financial supporters climb on the candidate's election train. Of course, the more funds a candidate has, the greater his or her chances of success.

Some comparisons At this point it might be instructive to compare the factors that tend to determine the outcome of American elections with some of those that are influential in the UK. A summary is shown below.

Determining factors in British and American elections		
Factors common to both the USA and the UK	**Factors more influential in the USA**	**Factors more influential in the UK**
1. Regional patterns of party support 2. Influential factors – which policies benefit which voters 3. The political record of existing office-holders 4. Voters' occupations 5. Quality of the campaign itself	1. The incumbency factor 2. Religion 3. Ethnic origin of the voter 4. Success in raising finance 5. Personality of the candidate 6. Coat-tailing and the bandwagon effects 7. Straight ticket voting	1. Social class of the voter 2. Party image 3. Sectoral cleavage – personal circumstances of the voter

Other parties The USA has a two-party system that is more entrenched than possibly any other in the western democratic world. Small parties are remarkably unsuccessful. Independents might win some very localised elections, but at the wider state and federal levels they never win. Indeed, the permanent, 'established' minor parties such as socialists and liberals are totally insignificant. Only temporary 'third' parties, centred round the personality of one individual in presidential elections, gain any substantial numerical support. There are a number of reasons for this lack of success:

- Finance is a vital aspect of party success. Candidates cannot make an impact without huge financial backing to fund media advertising, hiring of support staff and travelling expenses. Those who are willing to back candidates – largely businesses and pressure groups – will only commit money to those whom they think can win, otherwise the exercise would be pointless. They seek political influence and this can only be achieved through those who hold public office. This is unlikely to be a representative of any party other than the Republicans or Democrats.

- Americans are notoriously reluctant to vote. The candidates therefore need a considerable organisation to help cajole and transport supporters to the polls. The established parties have extensive **electoral machines** in place in most parts of the country. This is not the case with other candidates.

- In most states, small parties are not permitted to hold primary elections to determine who will be their candidates. This might not be a problem where there is only one viable candidate, but it does reduce the opportunities for publicity, which are so vital to electoral success.

- All candidates for election must show that they have a reasonable amount of support in order to be placed on the ballot paper at all. This is in the form of a 'petition' signed by electors. In many states this might not present a problem as the numbers required are quite small, but in some states, such as Illinois and California, up to 100,000 signatures may be stipulated in presidential elections.
- Many voters feel a strong emotional sense of attachment to a 'traditional' party. This often causes them to vote for candidates of that party even when they are largely ignorant of the issues at stake. It is difficult for a new party candidate to break these traditional allegiances.
- As we have seen in Unit 16, Americans are notoriously conservative in their political outlook. They do not take easily to new social and philosophical ideas. Radical candidates are, therefore, at an immediate disadvantage.

Despite all these problems, a number of presidential candidates from parties other than the Republicans and Democrats have done tolerably well. Some examples are shown below.

Presidential election year	Candidate	Party	Votes won	Electoral college votes
1912	Theodore Roosevelt	Progressive	4,119,507	88
1948	Strom Thurmond	States' Rights	1,176,125	40
1968	George Wallace	American Ind.	9,906,473	46
1980	John Anderson	Independent	15,719,722	0
1992	Ross Perot	Independent	19,741,065	0
1996	Ross Perot	Reform	8,085,402	0

Comparisons

American parties, as we have clearly seen above, are quite different from their counterparts in the rest of the democratic world. It therefore becomes difficult to make meaningful comparisons. Parties should be judged by reference to their objectives. The very fact that the goals of American parties are somewhat different from those of British parties, for example, hinders analysis.

Nevertheless, if we accept that the organisation and characteristics of American parties are **bound** to be different, given the nature of their objectives, some interesting observations can be made.

Policy formulation

Herein lies the principal distinction between American and British parties. Indeed, it is in this area that respective objectives are so divergent. The typical British party is organised at its centre almost entirely with a view to developing a policy programme that can be placed before the electorate. American parties cannot do this. They possess neither the organisation nor the philosophical cohesion to be able to create a unified programme that most of their candidates could support.

Structure

The second key distinction between British and American parties lies in their structure. The fact that they operate in very different political systems is of vital importance. The American federal system ensures that the parties there have a decentralised structure. They must fight on two or more fronts at the same time. Small wonder then that there are more than a hundred American parties (two per state). The unitary state in the UK, with weak local government, means that the parties must be highly centralised. National politics is much more important than regional and local variations, even after devolution.

Candidate selection

As we have seen, British election candidates come from a narrower range of possible nominees. They must satisfy a relatively small number of party activists to be adopted as the official nomination. It follows from this that British candidates, at both national and local level, are often in the image of the party workers who select them – highly committed, usually loyal and often significantly ideological in their political philosophy. In the USA, access to the ballot is more open. Prospective candidates must appeal to the ordinary voters rather than to party enthusiasts. They are, therefore, likely to be more moderate and more populist in their appeal.

Party systems

The American system boasts only two major parties. This is the result of a series of factors, some historical, some financial and some political. Since about 1970 the UK has had a three-party system with, in Scotland and Wales, the added complication of a fourth significant contender in the form of the nationalists. This results in slightly more complicated electoral arithmetic. In the USA, one party must beat its opponent fair and square. In the UK, one party might gain from two other parties splitting the vote against them. Certainly, the Conservatives in particular have enjoyed the effects of this factor.

Parties and pressure groups

Although there was a marked increase in the importance of pressure groups in British politics in the last quarter of the twentieth century, parties remain the principal means by which demands are articulated. The process of a transfer of activity away from parties towards pressure groups has been in train for much longer in the USA than is the case in the UK and has had more profound effects. The reason lies in both the extreme pluralism of the American political culture and the weakness of parties in being able to promote public policy. Political participation is widespread in the USA, but it is more usually in the form of activity on behalf of pressure and interest groups than in solid work on behalf of a party.

Membership

British parties have been characterised by large mass memberships. The Conservatives have, in the past, been able to boast over one million members, even though many have only been, in truth, social members. The Labour Party, excluding union subscription payers, has reached 600,000 constituency members and even the Liberal Democrats have over 75,000 adherents. Thus, they are in continuous active session and have permanent access to an army of enthusiastic supporters. In the USA, the parties only really mobilise themselves fully at election time. State and National Conventions, where candidates are confirmed, might be impressive occasions, characterised by much publicity and razzmatazz, but they are the only occasions when there appears to be any coherence in party activities.

Pressure groups

Introduction

The USA's political system is generally thought of as perhaps the most pluralist of all democratic systems. This is not to say there is a **broad** spectrum of political opinion that flourishes in the country. That claim can be better made in such countries as France, Italy and Spain. By contrast, the USA's political culture displays a remarkably **narrow** range of political philosophies. Rather, the description 'pluralist' refers to the fact that large numbers of factions, interests and campaigning organisations co-exist in a crowded political forum, jostling for prominence, determined to be heard above the noise made by all the others and sometimes resorting to grand gestures in order to be noticed.

It is customary to point to the relative weakness and lack of ideological coherence of the two great political parties when explaining the extensive nature of pressure group activity. This is undoubtedly true to a degree. Parties and their candidates, from the President downwards, cannot guarantee to fulfil any commitments that they might have made during election campaigns. Power at federal, state and local level is so diffused and so subject to checks and balances that decisive political action becomes extremely hazardous. Individually and in groups, Americans are aware of this. As a response, therefore, they need to take more direct political action in order to further their political goals. Reliance on their elected representatives is simply not enough. So active pressure groups come about.

The causes of pressure group activity

Party weakness is not a sufficient explanation for the abundance of American pressure groups. A number of other reasons – institutional, social and political – must be found.

Institutional

The decentralised nature of American government means that much political action must be conducted at two or more different levels at the same time. Federal government is limited, both by the Constitution and by the relative political independence of the states, so it is not sufficient for pressure to be confined to Washington. The lack of a significant focus of power means that there is a great deal of access available for pressure groups to exercise leverage. Decentralisation, then, is both a challenge and an opportunity for pressure groups. The parties certainly do not have the necessary tight-knit organisation to cope with such an open system. Campaigning and interest groups, on the other hand, are often organised enough at all levels to be able to operate on a broad front.

The first amendment to the Constitution guarantees to American citizens the right of free speech and free association. There have, therefore, never been legal limitations on the establishment of political campaign groups. Alexis de Tocqueville noted this in the 1830s when researching his great work *Democracy in America*. For him, no democratic system could survive if it did not allow and encourage an active 'civil society' – the collective term for the many different groups to which citizens may belong and which act as a 'buffer' between the individual and the state.

Political We have already referred to the loose nature of American parties and the effect this has had on pressure group activity, but other political features are also relevant. It has always been the case that American representative institutions at federal and state level are remarkably open. The traditional suspicion of governmental institutions has resulted in an insistence that they carry out their deliberations in public. Publicity has, however, also come to mean access. American laws do place some restrictions upon the activities of pressure groups, but they also guarantee that political institutions open their doors to the many campaigning groups that seek entry.

Social The USA is a remarkably diverse society. It is divided into many ethnic groups, cultural backgrounds, religions and economic sections. Nevertheless, all of these consider themselves to be American and are proud of American democracy. Most of them, therefore, express their differences and their diverse demands **within** the legitimate arena of democratic politics. There are occasions when some alienated and disaffected groups have sought extra-legal methods to make their demands heard. During the late 1960s, for example, urban black groups, sections of the most poor and many college students resorted to direct, sometimes violent, action to express their opposition to American policy in Vietnam and to what they believed to be a corrupted political system. But it is usually the case that the USA's diversity is contained within the realms of legal activity. The fact that pressure groups enjoy guaranteed liberties and access to political institutions makes this possible.

Types of pressure group We can divide American pressure groups in the same way as we can their counterparts in the UK. Essentially, there are **interest** groups, which represent a particular economic, social or ethnic section of the population, and **cause** groups, which are concerned with a particular issue. Some of the main examples are shown below.

Interest groups have always played a major part in American politics, but it is largely since the 1960s that cause groups have begun to take over the scene. Indeed, there has been a tendency for these campaigns to amalgamate to form conglomerates with others who have similar demands. These are sometimes called 'externality' groups and have large memberships and extensive political influence. **Public Citizen**, run by the veteran consumers' campaigner and presidential candidate in 2000, **Ralph Nader**, is an amalgamation of consumer protection groups, while the **Heritage Foundation** combines a variety of conservative causes in its work.

A further element in lobby group activity is the development of 'think tanks' – organisations that carry out research in a designated area of public policy and that are financed by many of the kinds of interest group described above. The **Urban Institute**, for example, is concerned with welfare, racial and housing issues as they affect life in the poor districts of the cities. The **American Enterprise Institute**, by contrast, prefers to discourage government intervention in order to allow free-market capitalism to flourish.

American pressure groups	
Those representing sectional interests	
Group	**Representing**
• American Federation of Labor – Congress of Industrial Organizations (AFL–CIO) • American Farm Bureau Federation • National Association of Manufacturers • American Bar Association • National Association for the Advancement of Colored People • National Organization for Women	• Trade unions • Agricultural interests • Industry • Legal profession • Black and other non-white minorities • Women's rights
Cause groups	
Group	**Representing**
• National Rifle Association • National Wildlife Federation • National Right to Life Committee • Christian Coalition • Common Cause	• Defending the right to carry guns • Environmental issues • Anti-abortion • Conserving traditional moral values • Rights for consumers and citizens against inefficient or unfair government

A remarkable plurality of organisations therefore operate the American lobby system. This reflects partly the diversity of interest and concerns within the political culture, and partly the fact that there are many different points of access to the political system, which might require different approaches and tactics.

Where pressure groups operate

Local government

At county, school board, and large and small city level, officials are constantly subject to lobbying, both by smaller community groups and by local branches of larger campaigns. Typically, issues will concern education, the environment, transport, agriculture, controversial planning decisions, law and order and public amenities. The very well-developed sense of community spirit that flourishes within American society results inevitably in constant pressure being brought to bear on the lowest level of government. The political parties might not be fully organised at this level, but campaign groups often are, and can raise the finance necessary to make their voices heard.

In addition to high levels of local pressure group participation, the fact that so many local officials are elected gives considerable leverage to campaigners. The record of such officials is very carefully scrutinised and publicised, especially at election time. This renders local representatives extremely sensitive to public opinion within their own communities. Local democracy, therefore, consists very much of pressure group politics.

The states As we have seen, state governments are microcosms of the national political system. State legislatures are extremely open to lobbying, while ~~they also all possess active committee systems,~~ which require a good deal of interaction with lobby groups. ~~Witnesses may be called to~~ provide information to state representatives and evidence of public opinion, and to ensure that issues are seen to be given the fullest deliberation possible. Thus, there is a 'symbiotic' relationship between the state legislatures and the many groups who operate around them. They depend on each other. The groups need influence and this can be provided within the state legislature, but representatives also need the groups, for both financial support in their re-election campaigns and political support to help them with their own programmes.

At the same time, the governments of the states, the department heads and the officials who run the various services supplied at this level are constantly subjected to lobbying. In some cases, a single state might become the target for a national pressure group that is particularly concerned by its activities. Where major environmental damage is threatened, for example, the full weight of a group such as **Friends of the Earth** might be brought to bear on the state government. Similarly, anti-abortion **Right to Life** campaigners might target one state where they feel there is a possibility of restrictive legislation being introduced. It might indeed be difficult for a smaller state political system to resist the pressure of a national campaign group.

Federal Congress It is in this arena that the highest-profile operations of pressure groups, collectively known simply as the 'lobby', operate at their highest level. Approximately 5000 groups are registered with Congress (that is, are given legal access to the members of Congress in general and the committees in particular). A further 10,000 or more may operate without such privileged access, but still consider it useful to be in Washington. The army of lawyers, agents, professional campaigners and public relations executives who operate here were collectively known in the 1980s as 'Gucci Gulch', such was their apparent affluence and fashionability. The lobby can also be described as an industry, so extensive are its activities.

Operations are mainly on two levels. First, individual Senators and members of Congress may be targeted by groups as the most likely to be sympathetic. Members of the House of Representatives are considerably more vulnerable to such pressure. They must face a re-election campaign every two years. Their voting record will be carefully checked during the campaign, as will their congressional speeches. In many congressional districts, certain pressure groups are particularly important. Thus, in industrial areas the support of trade unions must be nurtured; where there are large ethnic minorities, or even majorities, the issues that concern them will come to the fore. The same is true for interest groups concerned with agriculture, business, foreign trade or specific industries. If one of these activities is prominent in a Congress member's district, the groups that represent them gain great influence over the member. Second, congressional committees become a centre of pressure group interest.

Whenever legislation is being considered, the standing committees become involved at one stage or another. This might be to decide whether to devote any time at all to a proposed Bill, whether to give it a favourable place on the agenda or whether to suggest various amendments. Pressure groups will clamour to be heard by the relevant committee if the outcome of the legislation is important to them. At the same time, the committees are happy to call witnesses from the interest groups in order to gather information and to gauge the strength of support or opposition to a measure.

The federal administration

The many departments and agencies that make up the administration, including the executive office of the President and the White House Staff, are almost as open as Congress to pressure group activity. Indeed, in some cases a permanent relationship can be built up between an agency and those groups most affected by its work. Thus, for example, it is vital that the Department of Education is in constant touch with organisations representing teachers, while the same kind of relationship must exist between the Department of Agriculture and the various farm groups who operate in Washington. Sometimes, in fact, the relationship can be too cosy, resulting in a phenomenon known as **agency capture**, where a pressure group seems to have developed so much influence over the agency that it appears to be running it.

Whether or not too much influence can be wielded by the lobby in Washington's bureaucracy, there is no doubt that, as at state level, there is an interdependency between interest groups and government agencies. Information changes hands, deals are done, involving the use of influence and finance, and powerful coalitions may be formed to push through important legislation or, where necessary, to thwart unwanted initiatives from Congress.

Iron triangles

This term refers to the observation that there can develop a strong three-way relationship between interest groups, a government agency and a congressional standing committee. If all three are working towards the same objective, it is argued, the coalition is so strong that it cannot be resisted. The triangles thus become policy-making communities in themselves – 'governments within government'.

Typically, this analysis has been applied to the agriculture lobby, where pressure for protection from world competition has become irresistible. The same was also true of the automobile industry in the 1990s. Energy policy has also been the subject of successful lobby group relationships, with such a triangle being able to thwart even the plans of the President himself.

The iron triangle analysis has been weakened somewhat in recent years, to be replaced by the concept of **issue networks**. This is a more complex concept, suggesting that pressure groups are being forced to operate on a broader front. The standing committees in Congress, it is suggested, are no longer as influential as they were. At the same time, there is considerably more fragmentation within the parties in Congress, so lobby groups must seek the help of smaller groups of Congress members in order to build a wide coalition or 'network' of support. In short, policy making is not as simple as it once was. The groups must be more sophisticated in their campaigns. Power in Congress is more diffuse today and the groups must respond accordingly.

How pressure groups operate

Public campaigns and initiatives

One of the most effective means of putting pressure upon legislators and government officials is to demonstrate that there is widespread public support for a group's proposals, interests or for an issue. Public petitions or write-in campaigns might be organised and demonstrations held – those run by the National Association for the Advancement of Colored People in the 1960s were extremely influential. Write-ins involve large numbers of individuals writing to representatives and officials, all making the same demands, in the hope that the recipient will be persuaded that there is sufficient public support to warrant positive action.

In those states that incorporate an **initiative** system, pressure groups have a more direct form of leverage available to them. They might be able to gather sufficient signatures to trigger an initiative – effectively a referendum – and then have the resources to be able to conduct the resultant campaign for a favourable vote. Anti-tax groups are particularly active in this field.

In some cases, more extreme measures might be adopted. During civil rights campaigns in the Deep South in the 1950s and 1960s, a great deal of civil disobedience was used, especially against segregation in schools, universities and other public places. Later in the 1960s students rioted on their campuses, blacks in the city centres and the poor marched on Washington, squatting in their thousands in front of the White House to publicise their plight. More recently, in the 1990s, anti-abortion groups have attacked abortion clinics and they even assassinated one of the surgeons who had performed terminations. However, public demonstrations remain, on the whole, relatively peaceful and law-abiding.

The media

Access to the media is open to any lobby group that has the funds to pay for the space of the time. Press advertising is a common feature of pressure group activity, as are slots between radio and TV programmes, provided the group in question has the necessary finance. Indeed, on those shows which are unashamedly religious or morally conservative in nature, sympathetic groups might not need to pay for their time. The broadcasting stations might themselves be a prominent feature of the campaign. Such publicity takes three main forms.

First, it might be designed to give information to members of the public. Environmental, moral and legal issues, for example, need to be brought to the attention of viewers and listeners. Statistics, scientific facts and viewpoints may be effectively conveyed through the broadcasting media. Second, attempts might be made to persuade the public to support a cause. Here, an appeal might take on the appearance of any other commercial. Finally, the more subtle campaigns might publicise the personal record of elected officials, especially those who show antipathy to the cause. In this way, pressure is placed on them to conform to the wishes of the lobby group, under the threat that they might lose public support as a result of the campaign.

A civil rights march in
Memphis, Tennessee,
30 March 1968

Through the courts

The USA is an exceptionally **litigious** society. This means that it is relatively easy to have access to the courts and that citizens are not reluctant to use this freedom. At both state and federal level, court orders may be sought to prevent governmental action that may be considered to be contrary to current law or, in extreme circumstances, unconstitutional. If official or legislative actions are thought to offend such principles as individual rights, privacy, freedom of expression or freedom of association and movement, court orders may be used to prevent or merely delay the process.

In these circumstances, where courts, and especially the federal Supreme Court, are judging official actions against fixed legal principles, a lobby group may be considered *amici curiae*, meaning 'friends of the court'. This means that the group may be given the privileged role of adviser to the court, providing facts as well as legal opinion. All large campaign groups employ constitutional lawyers for such purposes. Typically, pro- and anti-abortion groups, law and order campaigners, environmentalists, consumer protectionists and 'Common Cause', the citizen's group described above, use the courts wherever possible. A number of examples of such key cases can be found in Unit 17.

Congressional committees

Of considerably more importance than either House of Congress are the congressional committees, which are the main target for pressure group activity at federal level. Those standing committees that are concerned with agriculture, transport, environment, industry, defence, finance and the economy are constantly pressed by the relevant lobby groups to consider favourable legislation, to resist measures that are considered unfriendly or to amend Bills in ways they consider desirable.

There is a great deal of informal lobbying of committee members, but groups are also frequently required to give evidence at well-publicised formal hearings. Indeed, lobbying might take place well before this stage is reached. When committees are being formed at the beginning of a new

Congress, lobbyists will seek to ensure that representatives and Senators who are known to be sympathetic to their cause will find a place on ~~committees that are relevant to it.~~

The federal administration

Here pressure groups begin by attempting to give themselves a privileged place within the central bureaucracy. First, they might attempt to ensure the appointment of sympathetic officials or to prevent the promotion of less friendly individuals. With favourable officials and congressional committee members, any group places itself at a great advantage. Second, the larger groups will seek a privileged, permanent position within the organisation of the agency. They need to ensure that they are regularly consulted and have ready access to important members of the agency. In the UK this process is known as **incorporation**, but in the USA it is often described as **agency capture**.

The phenomenon of **iron triangles** has been described above, but this depends upon the co-operation of members of Congress. Without them, lobby groups must rely on the ability of administration officials to operate successfully on the Congress floor and in the committee rooms. In these cases, the relationship may be described as a partnership rather than a triangle.

Initiatives

In a number of states, citizens may call for a referendum if they can collect a sufficiently large quantity of names on a petition. If a pressure group can force through such an initiative, causing it to appear on the normal ballot paper in November, there is an excellent chance that public opinion will back its demands. Politicians, faced with such a device, have little choice but to accept the verdict of the people. The best-known example of such an initiative was **Proposition 13**, which was passed in California in 1978. This had been promoted by anti-tax groups and the result was a significant cut in state taxation.

Political Action Committees

Political Action Committees (PACs) are a relatively recent development on the American political scene. They are the result partly of the fragmentation of pressure groups, and partly of legislation limiting the financing of candidates for public office. PACs are umbrella groups that collect finance from a variety of lobby groups that are all concerned with a similar issue. There were as many as 4000 PACs in existence by 1990. Although no individual may give more than $5000 to a particular PAC, there is no limit on how many PACs may receive such funds and no limit on how many PAC contributions any election candidate may receive. This gets round the legal limits on **direct** contributions to candidates, which cannot be made by businesses or any other organisations. PACs can receive such financing, provided no single donation is above $5000.

Typical examples of PAC concerns can be illustrated by their titles:

- Business–Industry PAC
- Committee for Responsible Government
- National Conservative PAC
- AFL–CIO Political Education PAC.

Some PACs are simply representatives of large interest groups, such as employers, farmers, professions, trade unions, women, students, banking, business and commerce. Others are more ideological in nature, pursuing conservative, liberal or progressive causes of one kind or another.

Although PACs operate extensively on the floor of Congress, their principal activity on behalf of their clients is the financing of candidates at all levels of government. They seek out those who are likely to be sympathetic to the cause and try to ensure their election through financial aid to their campaigns. To an increasing extent, PAC work has become one of the prime political methods used by pressure groups.

Are pressure groups in decline?

Since the rise of 'New Right' politics in the 1980s, there has been much speculation that the influence of the lobby is waning. There is an assumption that the return of more ideological politics has closed many points of access to pressure groups. There is little research evidence that the voting patterns of representatives have been particularly affected by PAC contributions to their election campaigns. There has also been something of a reaction by legislators against the activities of pressure groups. Americans may be proud of their pluralist, open democracy, but they have also become concerned by the increasing influence of lobby groups who do not appear to be politically responsible to anyone.

Two incidents in the 1980s illustrate the new conflict between the lobby and Congress in particular, and politicians in general. In 1983 the welfare system was extensively reformed through the **Social Security Reform Act**. This was done in the face of intense pressure from lobby groups to abandon or amend the proposals. More dramatically, in 1986 the **Tax Reform Act** was discussed and passed almost in secrecy in order to avoid pressure group influence. All the lobby could do was to click its heels while decisions were taken behind doors that had been closed to them.

The reaction against pressure group activity is the result of concerns that the enormous financial influence that the lobby wields is unhealthy in a modern democracy. There has also been a feeling that it has had the effect of rendering politicians largely impotent, in that **any** form of political action is likely to meet with so much opposition from lobby groups that it is immensely difficult to achieve any significant change. Issues such as gun control, abortion, anti-crime measures, health reform, public spending cuts, energy policy and agricultural aid have all been subject to the stifling effect of pressure group activity. There are now renewed demands to curb these groups' activities still further.

For exam questions relevant to this unit, see page 559.

21 Federalism and the states

The origins and nature of federalism

The Constitution

During the political manoeuvring that preceded the development of the federal Constitution in 1787, three main groups emerged. The first favoured a continuation of the existing loose **confederation**. Central government would be relatively powerless. A second faction favoured a strong, unified political system – the states would have some independent powers, but sovereignty would reside in the Union capital. Between them lay a party, led by **James Madison**, known as 'federalists', who wished to see either a confederation or a unitary system. Its campaign, centring on a series of political pamphlets known as the 'Federalist Papers', was ultimately successful, and a federal system was introduced. This was the first such political system ever to be fully devised and is the USA's most important contribution to constitutional theory.

Why a federal system was adopted

We can identify three principal reasons why the Founding Fathers opted for a federal solution and, indeed, why their system has only come under serious challenge twice – in the Civil War era of the 1860s and in the modern era of 'New Federalism', which will be discussed below.

- The American people were, and indeed still are, fiercely independent. They view strong government as a threat to their liberty. The experience of British rule left them with a natural antipathy to political authority. Federalism guaranteed a measure of independence while accepting that some form of centralised state was inevitable.
- The thirteen original states varied in character, especially in economic structure from the predominantly agricultural areas such as Virginia, to the trading states of New York and Rhode Island and the 'frontier lands' further west. Federalism reflected this diversity, allowing it to flourish, but within an ordered national framework.
- Madison himself recognised the dangers of concentrating too much power in too few hands. He understood that a method of reducing such a danger was to divide government. Federalism was one way of doing this (separating the powers of the three branches of central government was the other). The guaranteed powers and independence of the states could act as a check on the power of the central state. So an important constitutional principle was born with the creation of the federal union.

'It is a known fact in human nature, that its affections are commonly weak in proportion to the distance of diffusiveness of the object. Upon the same principle that a man is more attached to his family than to his neighbourhood, to his neighbourhood than to his community at large, the people of each state would be apt to feel a stronger bias towards their local governments, than towards the government of the union, unless the force of that principle should be destroyed by a much better administration of the latter.'
Alexander Hamilton, *The Federalist*, 1787

Disputes about the exact **balance** of power between the federal government and the states have continued, but there has never been a serious attempt to end the federal system altogether.

How federalism works

The Constitution and its subsequent amendments establish how **sovereign** powers are to be divided. It is important to stress the term 'sovereignty', since it is clear that, once the Constitution has allocated powers to the federal government, to the states or to a combination of the two, they cannot be taken back or overruled, as is the case in a unitary constitution such as the UK's. The only way in which the division of sovereignty can be altered is by constitutional amendment. Since such an amendment would require not only congressional approval but also the agreement of three-quarters of the states themselves, the federal settlement is safety protected. The states can only be required to give up sovereign powers by their own consent.

The allocation of powers works as follows:

- Some powers are reserved **only** for one or more of the branches of federal government.
- Some are reserved **only** for the states.
- Some are left open for the federal Congress to determine who shall exercise them.
- Any powers not allocated by the Constitution or by Congress are automatically reserved for the states.

In practice, we can see how the system works by enumerating the powers that are now exercised by federal government, by the states or by both.

Powers exercised ONLY by federal government and forbidden to the states	Powers exercised by BOTH federal and state governments	Powers exercised ONLY by the states
• National defence and internal security of the USA • Negotiations and treaty making with foreign powers • Regulating trade with foreign powers • Regulating the American currency • Regulating interstate trade	• Developmental and enforcement of criminal and civil law (mostly controlled by states) • Health care, welfare and housing programmes • Care of the environment • Transport provision • Regulating of broadcasting and the media • Regulating industry and commerce within the state itself • Taxation of individual and corporate incomes • Arrangements and funding of educational provision	• Taxation on property and goods • Control over local government • Control over city government

The list shown above, though not exhaustive, illustrates how few powers are now reserved completely for the states compared to those that only federal government exercises. But the real dynamics of the federal system concern those powers that are shared. It is here that the ebb and flow of the balance of powers between state and federal government takes place. On the whole, there has been a steady shift of power and function towards the centre since the federal system was first estab-

stemmed and a reaction is under way. Calls for transfers of powers back to the states have been growing louder and more insistent.

The changing nature of federalism

Dual federalism

In 1791 the tenth amendment to the Constitution was passed. This was an attempt to clarify the relationship between the states and federal government. The wording of the amendment was as follows:

> *'The powers not delegated to the United States* by the Constitution, nor prohibited by it to the States, are reserved to the States respectively, or to the people.'*
>
> Amendment 10 of the US Constitution, ratified 1791

*Here the term 'United States' refers to federal (central) government.

By granting all 'reserve' powers to the states, it was assumed that the independence of the states would be protected from future encroachments by the federal authorities. This was the establishment of what is known as **dual federalism**. It confirmed the principle that the federal and state governments should run in parallel, each with its own institutions and powers. Relatively little overlapping of powers was envisaged. However, as time has gone by, the principles of dual federalism have been steadily eroded.

The interstate commerce clause

In the case of *Gibbons* v. *Ogden*, which came before the Supreme Court in 1824, the precise meaning of the term 'interstate commerce' came into question. The Constitution states in Article 1, Section 8, that the Congress shall have power to 'regulate commerce **among the several states**'. Does this imply that the federal Congress, and therefore government, should have the power to regulate all forms of trade that affect more than one state (effectively virtually all trade)? Yes, said the Court led by Chief Justice Marshall. Thus was established federal jurisdiction over commerce, later industry, and this ultimately became full economic control.

Five years earlier, in the case of *McCulloch* v. *Maryland*, the pre-eminence of federal government in matters concerning taxation had also been established by the Court. Put together, these two judgments made it clear that, whatever the tenth amendment might say, areas of jurisdiction not covered in the Constitution were, in fact, likely to fall into the hands of the federal Congress or the President.

> *'We admit, as all must admit, that the powers of the government are limited, and that its limits are not to be transcended. But we think the sound construction of the Constitution must allow to the national legislature that discretion, with respect to the means by which the powers it confers are to be carried into execution, which will enable that body to perform the high duties assigned to it, in the manner most beneficial to the people.'*
>
> Chief Justice John Marshall, *McCulloch* v. *Maryland*, 1819

The Civil War

The attempt by a number of southern states to secede from the Union over the slavery issue was not merely about the principles of slavery itself. It was also about the authority of the federal government to dictate to the various states. When proposals were made to instruct all states to end the practice of slavery, the slave states revolted. Here was the most direct confrontation yet between those who claimed the rights of the states to run their own affairs and the power of federal government.

The military victory that Abraham Lincoln, the President, and the supporters of federal power (the 'Union' side in the war) achieved, established the ability, if not the authority, of the federal government to exercise wide powers. Since then, there has been a lingering resentment in the South, so both Democrats and Republicans continue to be suspicious of the power of Washington. When Presidents Nixon and Reagan promised to shift some of the balance of power back to the states in more recent times, they found ready allies in the South.

The sixteenth amendment and taxation

In 1913 the federal government was granted constitutional powers to raise taxation on individual and corporate incomes. This was a significant development, since it enabled the federal government to raise considerably larger amounts of its own funds and thus to initiate more expansive policies. Without these taxation powers, the President, or Congress, was forced to persuade the states to spend their own money if new programmes were to be implemented.

Grants-in-aid and co-operative federalism

This device was first used in the 1860s during Lincoln's Presidency, but it was hampered by lack of funds. With the sixteenth amendment came fresh opportunities and grants-in-aid began to form the main basis for federal–state government relations.

The system had a number of features that all led to increased federal control. In essence, the federal administration can propose a policy to be implemented in a particular state. This might be, typically, road building, agricultural subsidies, welfare programmes, hospital building, an energy production scheme or education initiatives. The funding was to be shared between federal and state sources. Essentially, each dollar used by Washington would be matched by the state government. Although voluntary, any state would be reluctant to refuse a grant-in-aid, as the money, raised from its own citizens, would only then be used for a project in a different state.

This system gave rise to a new term for this kind of federal action. **Co-operative federalism** supplanted the old mutual variety. However, co-operation was not a strictly accurate description. Though it may appear to operate on the basis of voluntary agreements, the projects are invariably controlled by the federal government, which dictates how the money shall be spent and may lay down minimum standards in the provision of services. In addition, the original initiative normally comes from Washington. The states are in a weak position because they cannot themselves propose extensive programmes without the financial co-operation of the federal administration.

As well as grants-in-aid, the new style of federalism also meant that federal government felt freer to use its own funds exclusively, without state involvement, to introduce new schemes. Many of Roosevelt's New

Deal measures, described below, were achieved without matching-fund schemes. So, in one way or another, the period between 1913 and the [marked extension in the responsibilities of] central government and a matching decline in states' independence.

The New Deal

President Roosevelt came to power in the 1930s with a clear popular mandate to extend the scope of federal government into new realms. Social security systems were introduced using federal funds to help poorer families. The creation of the **Tennessee Valley Authority** also opened the way for federal initiatives in state investment, infrastructure development, agricultural subsidies and employment creation schemes. Together with a variety of further measures to ensure fair wages, improved working conditions and recognition of trade union powers, the New Deal policies established the principle that federal government had authority to intervene in the economic and industrial structures of the states, provided, of course, there was an electoral mandate to do so.

A number of challenges were made in the Supreme Court to Roosevelt's policies – challenges that were, at first, successful in holding back progress. By 1937, however, Roosevelt had established greater control in the Court and the New Deal policies were finally granted constitutional approval.

The Great Society

The commitment of **John F. Kennedy** (1961–3) and his successor, **Lyndon Johnson** (1963–9), to further intervention by the federal administration in the fields of welfare, education, medical care for the poor, urban renewal and housing programmes was known as the 'Great Society'. Aided by a friendly, Democrat-dominated Congress, Johnson in particular was determined to ensure that the traditional ear of central government power would not prevent him from reversing what he saw as many years of neglect by state governments in their own social fabric.

Both grants-in-aid and straightforward federal expenditure were used to establish radical increases in the responsibilities of American government. By the time Richard Nixon took over the Presidency in January 1969, the tide of federal power had reached its high point. Nixon was determined to turn this tide back and claimed a clear mandate to do so.

New federalism

Nixon's plan was relatively simple. First, he cancelled a large number of specific grants that could only be spent by the states on programmes specified by federal government. They were replaced by 'block grants', which could be used in whatever ways a state chose. The policy was known as 'general revenue sharing'. This was clearly designed to return a measure of independence to the states. Second, he reduced the number and cost of grants-in-aid. The states were presented with a greater expenditure burden through the loss of federal funds, but at least they were freed from a good deal of federal intervention in their affairs.

After Nixon, **Jimmy Carter** (1977–81), whose term of office proved to be a brief Democratic interlude in a period of Republican domination of the White House, began by promising to restore many of the federal aid programmes, which Nixon had abolished, to the states. However, he was thwarted by determined resistance in both Congress and the state governments. The process of federal disengagement that Nixon had started could not be stopped.

Ronald Reagan (1981–9) introduced the most radical phase of the 'New Federalism' era. He transferred responsibility for a large number of welfare, anti-poverty, housing and health programmes to the states. He also made deep cuts in federal expenditure in order to finance substantial tax cuts. Between 1980 and 1991 federal grants to the states fell by almost 20 per cent, mostly as a result of the 1981 **Omnibus Reconciliation Act**, which set the cuts in motion. Some of the states, notably in the South, were happy to pick up the gauntlet thrown down by Reagan. They took over the programmes relinquished by federal government, even though it involved them in higher financial commitments. This was a fair trade-off in return for greater autonomy. In other cases, however, the expenditure cuts resulted only in hardship. Some of the cities, notably New York, were effectively bankrupt. A number of states had to make severe reductions in police, emergency and social services to make up for the loss of federal funding. Even California, the Union's wealthiest state, struggled to maintain educational and social provisions.

Thus, New Federalism has had its price and the states have had to pay it. Either by raising their own taxes or by reducing services, shortfalls have been made up. But the pressure is still on. Like Carter before him, President **Bill Clinton** hoped, on his election in 1992, to resurrect federal initiatives with his plans for a comprehensive health care scheme and extensive crime control measures. Tax increases and reductions in other items of federal expenditure, such as defence, were to pay for the plans two years later. However, a conservative, Republican-dominated Congress was elected. Its leaders, Bob Dole and Newt Gingrich were determined to resist any further increases in federal expenditure and power. Clearly, the spirit of New Federalism was still alive.

The future for federalism

The rise of New Right conservatism in the 1980s and 1990s has heralded a new era in federal–state relations. Federal government has been under attack for a number of reasons:

- It is thought to be corrupt, inefficient and wasteful.
- It is associated with high taxation that stifles enterprise.
- Rising federal expenditure increases its power and threatens state independence.
- The faulty policies of federal government are blamed for the poor economic performance of the USA in recent years. The failure to 'balance the federal budget' since 1969 is, it is argued, caused by extravagant federal officials.

Apart from these specific criticisms, however, there is a growing feeling that the power of central government is threatening the liberty of individuals. Herein lies a parallel with the British Conservative right wing's fear of the growth of European Union power. Only by restoring autonomy to a lower level of government, argues the right, can individualism be restored. In extreme cases in the USA, calls are beginning to be heard for the complete independence of some states. As yet this is very much an extreme minority view, but centrifugal forces have certainly become more powerful.

Thus, the definite shift in the balance of power between the centre and the states seems set to continue as long as conservatives hold sway in Washington. It may, nevertheless, be that economic recovery will end the criticisms of federal power and equilibrium will be restored.

State government

The state constitutions

most cases, these constitutions were written at around the time when the state became a member of the Union. However, in other cases a completely new document has been written and adopted since. The table below shows when some of the states established their current constitution.

Date of adoption of current state constitutions	
State	Date of current constitution
Massachusetts	1780
New Hampshire	1784
Vermont	1793
Indiana	1851
California	1879
New Mexico	1912
New Jersey	1948
Hawaii	1959
Louisiana	1975

Each of the constitutions contains provisions similar to those in the federal document. They set out the distribution of powers between the counties, cities and other units of local government, and establish the legal limits to the jurisdiction of each level of administration. They also all contain a statement of the rights of citizens in the state. These might not go as far as the federal Bill, but sometimes they might go further. For example, there are states that legally guarantee equal rights for women – a provision not yet established at federal level. Of course, such rights are only mandatory within the borders of the state.

State constitutions are subject to regular amendment and, in many cases, a full rewriting may be required. Louisiana, for example, established its eleventh constitution in 1975! Georgia is close behind with ten and South Carolina has had seven. However, such drastic measures are not normally needed. A number of states, notably Kansas and Oregon, still operate their original constitutions.

Methods for amendment vary. A common method is the **voter initiative** system. Seventeen states operate a system where citizens may collect a petition that calls for constitutional amendment. These petitions are known as 'initiatives'. Provided sufficient names – normally a fixed percentage of the votes cast for Governor at the last election – are forthcoming, the amendment may be included in a ballot. Thereafter, a majority of voters may approve or reject the amendment. Otherwise, proposals for change are often the result of **legislature initiative**. Here the state legislature brings forward the amendment. However, the approval of the voters is still required.

The most dramatic examples of popular democracy at work occur in fourteen states where there is a mechanism for the regular calling of an elected **Constitutional Convention** to review the existing document.

New Hampshire, for example, has held seventeen such conventions since the establishment of the Union. At the most recent convention, 175 amendments were proposed, but only ten were passed.

Although every state constitution must conform to the federal Constitution, their existence and importance illustrate the key role of the principle of **government by consent** in the USA. Whether citizens themselves initiate change, or are simply asked to approve changes proposed by their elected representatives, it is clear that American government remains very much in the hands of its people.

The state administrations

The Governor

Every state elects a Governor, who is the chief executive in the state and head of its administration. The Governors normally operate on four-year terms (three Governors must seek re-election every two years) and voting coincides with congressional elections in November. Broadly speaking, the role of the Governor is similar to that of the federal President, except, of course, that they need not concern themselves with foreign affairs or the defence of the country. These last two roles are forbidden to the Governor by the Constitution.

In most states the Governor's functions include the following:

- Legislative proposals. The Governor is the state's chief policy-maker.
- Exercising a veto over legislation that he or she opposes.
- Oversight of the state's administration.
- Representing the state in negotiations with other states.
- Acting as the state's representative in negotiation with the federal administration and Congress, especially over grants-in-aid. The Governor must attempt to secure funding from Washington for many of the state's key services.
- Appointment of **some** of the state's senior officials, though many, as we shall see below, are directly elected.
- Quasi-judicial functions such as the right to approve paroles or pardon convicted criminals.

The administration

Here, there may be some variation from state to state. However, it is normal for there to be a **Lieutenant-Governor** who is a deputy to the Governor. Like the federal Vice President, he or she must take over if the Governor dies or resigns, but otherwise has few powers or functions. In the main, the Lieutenant-Governor deputises for the Governor on ceremonial occasions.

In addition, there may be a **Treasurer**, in charge of the finances and economy of the state, a **Secretary of State**, another largely ceremonial role, and an **Attorney-General**, controller of the legal and criminal enforcement systems in the state. Otherwise, the precise titles and nature of posts in the administration are subject to considerable differences from one state to the next.

It is difficult to generalise about the manner in which administration officials are chosen. Some may be appointed by the Governor, others are elected. In the latter cases, of course, problems might arise if an official is of a different party to that of the Governor. However, since they are normally elected together, at the same time, voters will normally elect them as a 'team'.

State court systems

Most criminal and civil law in the USA is under the jurisdiction of the states. It is, therefore, inevitable that state courts play a greater role in American life than do their federal counterparts. The basic 'pyramid' of courts is also subject to variation, but in most states courts are organised as follows:

- At the lowest level, where minor criminal cases and civil disputes are heard, there are **Justices of the Peace** or **Magistrates' Courts** in the rural counties and the smaller cities.
- The larger cities have **Municipal Courts** in which more senior judges sit. These courts are further divided into levels depending on the nature of the crime or the financial size of a civil dispute.
- The main state courts are normally called **General Trial Courts**. Here, most criminal and civil cases are heard. The state is divided into a number of **districts** or **circuits**, each presided over by a court. In the criminal district courts, prosecutions are carried out by **district attorneys** who are sometimes elected, sometimes appointed by the state Attorney-General.
- **Appeal Courts** deal with more routine appeals arising from cases in lower courts. Where an appeal concerns important principles of state law, or constitutional matters, it must be carried higher.
- The **State Supreme Court** is the summit of the legal system in the state. It hears the more important appeals which may have wider legal implications. It also considers challenges to state laws and executive actions that may offend the state's own constitution. Despite all this, perhaps its highest-profile role is the consideration of final appeals against the execution of offenders in those states that operate the death penalty.

On rare occasions there might be some conflict between the operation of state laws and those which are federal and therefore apply throughout the USA. This might especially arise in matters concerning government or major commercial civil cases arising out of disputes in more than one state. In these cases, the problem must be resolved in a federal appeal court or, if important enough, in the Supreme Court in Washington itself. It should also be noted that if a crime is committed in more than one state, the case must be heard in a federal court. A fugitive from justice, for example, who crosses a state line, automatically becomes a **federal** criminal and comes under the jurisdiction of the Federal Bureau of Investigation (FBI).

Judges may be appointed in one of three ways, depending on their state. Some are appointed by the Governor or the Governor's Attorney-General. Others are appointed by the state legislature and finally, and most controversially, some states elect their judges. However, it is most common for a combination of these methods to be adopted. Only in thirteen states are all judges elected. Appointment by the Governor is the most common method.

It might seem strange that a supposedly neutral official, such as a judge, should be elected. In fact, most candidates do not stand under a party label, and those who do still claim to be politically impartial. The reason for the persistence of such elections arises simply from the American love affair with direct forms of democracy. It is believed that judges 'represent the people' in the administration of justice. To ensure that this continues, they must be elected. The practice is, however, slowly dying out.

State legislatures

Voting

Until the 1960s, the principle of 'one-person-one-vote' was not finally and irrevocably established in all states. Although the federal Constitution had long since established universal suffrage, some states were able to discriminate against certain classes, mainly blacks, by introducing such barriers to voting as a literacy test. The Supreme Court judgment in *Reynolds* v. *Sims*, a 1964 dispute in Alabama, finally declared that all discriminatory practices were unconstitutional.

Similarly, the drawing of electoral boundaries had often been subject to discrimination by ruling parties. The practice of **gerrymandering** – drawing electoral boundaries to favour one party – was ultimately outlawed in the Supreme Court judgment in *Baker* v. *Carr* in 1962.

Bicameralism

All states have two legislative chambers – a small Upper House and a large Lower House. The practice of bicameralism is a reflection of the American determination to avoid concentrations of power by dividing government into two branches. Systems vary, but on the whole legislation requires the approval of both Houses, which are elected at different times and on different bases. In this way, no party majority can guarantee to govern unopposed for any significant length of time.

The organisation of state legislatures is similar to that of Congress in Washington (though their actual titles vary). There are standing committees dealing with the agenda, rules and amendments. The chairpersons are just as influential as their counterparts in Washington, as are party leaders on the floor of the legislatures. Bills go through a lengthy, often complex procedure and then must be approved by the Governor, who can, and often does, veto them. In a few cases, certain categories of legislation, usually concerning finance and taxation, might have to be put before a referendum of the people for their approval.

State legislatures do not meet as often as the federal Congress, so representatives need not be full time. Indeed, many are paid by the day rather than receiving an annual salary. Most have outside interests, often full-time jobs. However, in some large states such as California, being a legislator is a complete career.

Parties are highly organised at state legislature level. Unlike the national parties, which are extremely fragmented and subject to wide regional variations in philosophy, the state organisations are more cohesive. Indeed, in some states where one party completely dominates, there maybe an extremely tight-knit hierarchy. Party discipline is stronger and, if the Governor is sympathetic, policy programmes can be coherent and predictable. Such party control is based upon patronage and a network of links with local business and interest groups. It is therefore the case that the political system in many states resembles the European picture much more closely than does federal government.

Local government

state. Nevertheless, certain basic institutions and principles can be established which are, more or less, applicable in all cases.

Counties

These are the building blocks of nearly all states. They vary in size a great deal, from a few thousand to over seven million in Los Angeles County, California. Only Connecticut and Rhode Island do not have them. About half the states determine the nature of country government through their constitution, but the other half allow counties to make their own arrangements. It is in the area of county government that state constitutional amendment is often proposed.

Typically, a county board is elected and, in turn, appoints full-time officials to run the county, such as engineers, planning officers, health inspectors and financial controllers. Some officers might be directly elected, including prosecuting attorneys, judges, coroners, treasurers and sheriffs.

The functions of counties normally include law enforcement, prisons, road building and maintenance, planning controls, some welfare for the elderly and the poor, public works, refuse collection and disposal, environmental protection and a variety of other public services. Some schooling is within county jurisdiction.

Counties receive their finance in the form of grants from state government. They collect taxes on behalf of the state authorities.

Towns and townships

These are a throwback to the USA's early origins. They are common in the New England states, in the states of New York and New Jersey, and in the mid-West. Replacing county government, the town or township is a small community, based on one or more small towns or villages. It is characterised by the phenomenon of the 'town meeting'. Here, all voters meet to make decisions directly. This might include the election of town officials, key decisions on transport or public works and even levying of tax. The towns are given a remarkable degree of independence by the states. This can even extend to some financial independence.

Though not a major factor in American local government, the township system is an interesting example of the most direct form of democracy in the modern world, an echo of the market place democracy of ancient Athens and the 'New Leveller' movement in England in the 1640s.

School boards and special districts

Overlaying the local government system sit special authorities (whose officials are normally elected) which run various specialised services. School boards are everywhere, operating with state funds and under the general auspices of the state administration. In addition, some authorities are responsible for providing water, police, environmental protection, emergency services, libraries, sanitation and public transport.

Special districts do not necessarily conform to other local government boundaries and are not normally subject to jurisdiction at county level. The average citizen might be subject to a bewildering variety of county, school board, police, transport and water supply jurisdictions. When they go to vote, they will be presented with a ballot paper listing candidates from several different levels of government.

Cities

As we have observed earlier, caution needs to be exercised when describing American cities. 'City' is more a local government term than a geographical description. Thus, cities vary greatly in size, from huge conurbations such as Chicago to relatively modest towns. Whichever is the case, cities are granted **charters** by state legislatures, allowing them to control their own affairs. It follows that the government of cities varies both between states and within them.

Despite this, a few generalisations can be made. All cities elect a **mayor**. The mayor might be a 'strong' official who is **chief executive**, appoints officials, makes policy and controls the city budget. This applies in New York and Chicago, for example. Such mayors have often become major national figures. Dick Daley of Chicago led a notorious party machine in the 1960s and New York's chief executive is always a high-profile politician. In the states of the South, it is now common for mayors to be black, reflecting the concentration of ethnic minority groups in urban ghettos and their new willingness to vote in larger numbers.

The mayor might also be in a much weaker position, being merely a figurehead. In such cases, the mayor's officials are separately elected and the mayor is not expected to formulate policy. The most celebrated example of such a ceremonial figure was actor Clint Eastwood, who became mayor of Carmel, California, in the 1980s.

Clint Eastwood being sworn in as mayor of Carmel

Councils are elected to run cities alongside the mayor. Where the mayor is weak, the city council is strong, and vice versa. In particular, the strong councils have powers to appoint officials and take the lead in policy making. More than rural areas, the cities rely heavily upon outside financing. In particular, the large conurbations rely upon federal funding for housing renewal, anti-crime measures, relief of the poor and health programmes.

Many of the larger cities experienced severe social problems in the 1980s and 1990s, including drug abuse, general crime, racial tension, poor housing and schools, and general poverty. Since the decline in federal funding that began during Ronald Reagan's Presidency, many cities have found themselves unable to cope. They have been squeezed between increasing problems and declining revenue. Police and medical services have been particularly disadvantaged. The mayor and council might, therefore, appear to be independent and powerful, but in practice they are hampered by financial stringency.

Conclusions on sub-central government
~~in the USA~~

The decentralised nature of American government makes generalisation difficult. However, some useful observations can be made.

The elective principle   Hundreds of thousands of representatives and officials are elected in the American political system. There are approximately 82,000 units of local government alone. Add to this the 50 state governments and legislatures, and the federal system, and we see an impressive array of politicians who owe their position, not to the patronage of party leaderships, but to the approval of the people in their own community. Their record in office is a matter of public concern, they face regular re-election campaigns and may be removed every two, four or six years, depending on their role, if the people are not satisfied. No other political system in the world elects so high a proportion of its politicians and officials.

Decentralisation   We know that the USA is a federal system. This is not unusual. A large number of other states, including Germany, India and Russia, have similar systems. What is remarkable in the USA, however, is the degree of independence enjoyed by levels of government below state level. Counties, towns and cities are broadly self-governing. As we have already observed, the township meeting is the most ancient and direct form of democracy known to mankind. Particularly striking is the extent to which financial independence is allowed. Although taxes are basically only levied at two levels – state and federal – there are three or more tiers of government where expenditure is largely free of controls from superior authorities.

Complexity   The decentralised nature of the political system, and the degree of independence that each level of government enjoys, makes sub-central administration in the USA extremely complicated. Most citizens have a fairly adequate grasp of those local institutions that govern them. Should residents move to another part of the country, however, they must begin a whole new learning process to discover what taxes they must pay and to whom, who supplies their water, public transport, schooling for their children and policing, and which representatives or officials they must elect in November's ballot. If they are especially fortunate, they might even find themselves voting on local taxation or on proposed changes to their state's constitution. The lack of uniformity in government is certainly striking.

Comparison with the UK

The nature of government below the centre in the two countries is radically different. Some of the main distinctions are as follows.

Distribution of sovereignty

The USA is a federal system in which sovereignty is divided between the centre and the regions. The UK is a unitary state, with sovereignty residing in one place – Parliament. Any powers that are passed down to regional or local bodies in the UK are only **delegated**; they may be overruled or withdrawn.

Regionalism

Here the distinction is less clear. Since the devolution of power to Scotland, Wales and Northern Ireland in 1999, the UK has become a regionally governed country. Certainly, too, the powers devolved to Scotland and Northern Ireland, at least, bear a close resemblance to the powers reserved to the American states by the Constitution.

Of course, we must beware. As we saw in Unit 11 no sovereignty has been transferred to the regions in the UK. **Constitutionally**, therefore, there is a great divide between the two systems. **Politically**, however, there are now some similarities.

Local democracy

Although British local government is elected, none of its officials are. Furthermore, turnouts in local elections are notoriously low and the outcome has more to do with national politics than with local issues. People recognise that British local government has little independent power, especially since 1979, so the outcome of electoral contests is of relatively little importance. Local councils are heavily dictated to by ministers in London. They have little control over finance and their actions are heavily circumscribed by legislation and by ministerial controls.

In the USA, if anything, citizens are more interested in the politics of their state and their community than in the goings-on in Washington. Their daily lives are clearly affected more by the nature and performance of local government than those of British citizens. American local democracy is, therefore, more lively, more meaningful and more cherished than it is in the UK.

Federalism in Europe

The problems faced by America's founding fathers, of creating a
country, while at the same time preserving the aspirations of the thirteen
states to maintain their identity, are largely mirrored in the European
Union.

Each member is concerned to preserve its own culture, maintain
control over its economy and determine its own social policies. Two
further complications, not faced by the Americans, are the questions of
language and relations with other countries. Yet, at the same time, there
are powerful forces working towards greater unity.

A federal system is to be established in Europe. Therefore, these questions must be answered:

- What is the acceptable balance between the transfer of sovereignty to
  federal institutions and the maintenance of national self-interest?
- How can a federal settlement be made flexible enough to accommodate change, without being so weak that centralising forces cannot be
  resisted?
- How is it possible to avoid a federation being dominated by one state
  (say Germany), or a few large states (Germany, France, Italy, the
  UK)? In other words, how could the interests of small weaker states
  be protected?
- How can institutions such as the Parliament and the Council of Ministers become genuinely supranational, genuinely **European**, rather
  than mere battlegrounds where the competing national interests of
  individual members are fought out?
- Will it be possible to establish a system for creating a real, single
  Head of State?

The Americans solved some of their similar problems by such devices as:

- the bicameral system, where small states were given equal representation in the Senate, but not in the House;
- the separately elected President as Head of State, whose primary role
  is to unite the country;
- strict constitutional safeguards to protect the sovereignty of the states.

European federalists might learn from this experience, both from those
devices that have been successful, such as the bicameral system, and
from the failures, such as the inability of central government to overcome powerful regional interests.

For exam questions relevant to this unit, see page 559.

Comparative politics

A number of key elements can be used as a means of comparing different political systems. These include:

- the relationship between the legislative and executive branches
- the degree of independent power enjoyed by the Head of Government
- the role of the Head of State
- the operation and functions of the legislature
- the relationship between citizens and the state
- the distribution of power between central government, regions and localities
- the nature of the main political parties within the system.

We can, therefore, place the British system in context by comparing these elements with those that prevail in the USA and in Europe.

Legislative–executive relations

As **Walter Bagehot** commented in 1867 in *The English Constitution*, the fusion between the Government – in the form of the Cabinet – and the legislature – largely the House of Commons – is the 'efficient secret' of the political system. Indeed, since his day, there has been a strengthening of that bond, so much so that by 1976 Lord Hailsham was able to describe British government as an 'elective dictatorship'.

The reason for the ever-increasing strength of government and its growing dominance of Parliament lies predominantly in the development of party discipline and unity. In practice, the House of Commons places a government in power and can remove that same government by a simple majority vote, as occurred in 1979. But this reserve power is rarely exercised to any great effect. A number of factors have contributed to this reality:

- the power of prime ministerial patronage
- the extremely unified nature of the parties
- the constitutional convention that the Government cannot survive an adverse vote on a key issue in the House of Commons
- the frequency with which winning parties achieve comfortable Commons majorities
- the obsessive fear that MPs have of losing their seats at a general election. They are, therefore, reluctant to precipitate an election by defeating their own government.

The manifestations of executive power are clear to see. They include the rarity of defeats on major pieces of legislation (the difficult periods for Labour in the late 1970s and the Conservatives in the mid-1990s were notable exceptions), and the inability of Parliament to force through legislation proposed by back-bench members and of parliamentary committees to pass amendments against the Government's wishes.

committees in 1979, ministers and officials find it relatively easy to evade meaningful investigations in their policy-making procedures. Ministers and civil servants tend to be obsessed with secrecy, and attempts by MPs to open up government to public view have all failed.

In almost all respects, the circumstances in the USA present a marked contrast to the British experience. The powers of the executive and legislative branches control each other; they are both separated and balanced. The causes of this phenomenon can be identified as follows:

- The Constitution guarantees that each branch has powers to limit the other: the system of 'checks and balances'.
- The parties lack unity and discipline. Members of Congress are independent in their thinking and their actions.
- The system of fixed-term Congresses means that the executive (i.e. the President) cannot be removed from office during the four-year term. Legislators, therefore, do not fear to vote against a President even from the same party as themselves.
- Since members of the Government (administration) are often not drawn from Congress, the President's powers of patronage *vis-à-vis* Congress are weak.

Thus, while the British system may be described as **executive dominance**, that of the USA should be seen as **balanced**. This balance is further illustrated by the fact that, although Congress has important powers of scrutiny without the smokescreen of government secrecy that prevails in the UK, the executive, in the form of the President as Head of State, enjoys relatively independent powers in the formulation of foreign policy.

We can find a further contrast in the political system of the European Union. Here, there is very little relationship of any kind between the executive branch – the Commission, the Council of Ministers and the legislature – and the European Parliament. Their sources of authority are completely separate and there is relatively little interplay between them. The Parliament possesses no real powers at all, only nebulous influence.

The EU system can, therefore, be described as **executive dominance** with only **token legislative control**. Nevertheless, it must be remembered that individual members of the Council of Ministers are subject to influence from their own domestic legislature. If their national parliament's power is considerable, as is the case in Spain and Italy, ministers in the Council may find their freedom of action considerably restricted. This is not the case in the UK, however, where parliamentary control over relations with Europe remains notoriously weak, so ministers have a free hand in negotiations.

Heads of Government

The position of a Head of Government (also known as **chief executive**) depends upon a number of factors. These are:

- leadership of a unified, disciplined party that controls government
- ability to control the legislature
- control over the rest of the government machinery, including the bureaucracy
- powers of patronage unencumbered by other bodies
- access to the media.

The British chief executive – the Prime Minister – enjoys most of these privileges. The principal check to this impressive list of powers lies with the Cabinet, which does, from time to time, overrule the Prime Minister. Otherwise, he or she enjoys what may be described as a **dominant** role in all fields. A similar role is played, for example, by the Chancellor of Germany, although the federal nature of German government means that the latter's power may be rivalled by influential provincial leaders.

Presidents of the USA cannot boast the same advantages, even though they combine the roles of chief executive and Head of State. They lead a party (whether it be Democrat or Republican) divided into factions. That party is made up of independent-minded (and independently funded) legislators who all have their own political agendas. Patronage is limited by the Senate's constitutional power to veto the President's nominations for important offices. There is no guarantee that the President's proposed legislation or budgetary proposals will pass successfully through Congress.

French Prime Ministers are in an equally ambiguous position. Their power is rivalled by that of the separately elected President and, indeed, they may be removed from office at any time by that same President. They do not fully control the membership of their own Cabinet and are often not even leader of the principal governing party. French chief executives, frustrated by their lack of independent power, must look enviously across the Channel at their dominant British counterpart.

In the European Union there is no effective chief executive at all! The post which fits this description most closely is that of **President of the Commission,** but this is an unselected official who can only advise, persuade and cajole the Council of Ministers. Presidents of the Commission have no decision-making powers of their own and lack nearly all the advantages enjoyed by the British Prime Minister.

Heads of State

by Heads of State:

- the symbolic figurehead
- the power-sharing Head of State
- the dominant leader.

Clearly, the British monarchy conforms to the first model, with most of the functions of 'Head of State' being performed by the Prime Minister on behalf of the monarch. The fact that the Crown's role is almost entirely ceremonial leads to a number of problems. For example, it might be difficult to separate the **national** interest from the interests of the **Government** itself. Similarly, maintaining national unity on key issues might be difficult for a Government that does not enjoy the support of the majority of the populace. However, as we shall see below, the structured party system enables the processes of government to run smoothly under most circumstances. Were it not for party dominance, the system would often need the intervention of an individual who could stand aloof from short-term political controversy. This would be the role of an active Head of State, which the UK does not possess. Weak monarchical systems also operate in the Netherlands, Belgium, Australia and Canada.

More powerful Heads of State may have to share their power with elected Governments. This is certainly the case in France, where the President has control over foreign policy and defence, but must co-operate in domestic policy making with the Prime Minister and the Government. France, therefore, conforms to the second model.

The dominant leader is exemplified by the new Russian President, Vladimir Putin. He enjoys extensive control over membership of the Government, is clearly the key figure in both domestic and foreign policy and is able, in a number of policy fields, to govern virtually by decree. He does experience some opposition from within the Parliament, but, in the absence of a coherent party system, he is able to avoid significant control by them. With greater reservations, the US President can be classified as a dominant type. However, the President's position depends upon shifting political fortunes. When confronted by a Congress dominated by a party other than their own, as has been the case for Bill Clinton, Presidents become power-sharers. Should they enjoy significant congressional support, on the other hand, they can become the dominant political figure in Washington.

Legislative bodies

How can we compare such institutions? They come – literally – in all shapes and sizes. Indeed, the rectangular form of both Houses of Parliament is often quoted as an illustration of the bipolar, adversarial nature of British politics. By contrast, the typically semi-circular shape of legislatures in Washington and most European capitals is seen as a model of more complex, fragmented party systems. But we should search for less superficial comparative features. The following questions must be answered regarding each legislative body:

- Does it have the power to remove the Government from office?
- Is it able to initiate legislation independently of the executive branch?
- How effective are its powers of scrutiny of government institutions?
- Is it subject to extensive constitutional controls?
- How much power does it have over budgetary measures?
- Can it block legislative proposals emerging from the Government effectively?
- Does it have effective powers to amend legislation?
- Are individual legislators able to represent the interests of their constituents effectively?

On virtually all counts, the British Parliament (principally the House of Commons) scores low marks. Theoretically, it possesses the decisive ability to pitch any government from office by a simple vote of no confidence, but this power is rarely exercised. Instead, over the past century it has surrendered most of its powers of legislation, amendment and budgeting, handing them over to the Cabinet.

On the plus side, the departmental select committees have beefed up Parliament's powers of scrutiny, but they are still hindered by government secrecy and the reluctance of MPs to challenge executive power. Members of the governing party usually avoid drawing attention to their independence of thought, lest they incur the displeasure of the powerful party whips. There are ample opportunities for MPs to raise constituency business and there is increasing evidence of greater activity in this field. Most significantly, however, it is the existence of parliamentary sovereignty that **appears** to invest Parliament with almost complete freedom of action. But the true position is less clear.

In view of executive dominance, which is described above, the unfettered sovereignty of Parliament becomes largely the sovereignty of government. The legislature's very independence is, thus, turned back on itself and contributes to its own weakness.

If Parliament does badly in this scheme of assessment, the US Congress provides a dramatic contrast. It fulfils virtually all the requirements of what might be described as the 'dominant legislature' model. Indeed, Congress suffers from only one important limitation, which is that created by constitutional restraints. It cannot, unlike the UK's sovereign Parliament, claim powers that are denied to it by the Constitution. Nor can it infringe individual liberties without falling foul of those constitutional requirements that guarantee citizens' rights.

Between these two extremes lie most European legislatures. The fragmented Italian Parliament comes closer to the American model, while

Party control in Germany is strong and usually well founded.

Turning to the Parliament of the European Union, however, we find a completely new model. Every political system that describes itself as a democracy must include an elected, representative body. This is also true of the European Union. But the Parliament represents little more than a token claim to real effectiveness. In other words, it is essential to satisfy the democratic requirement, but performs few other functions. The 'charade' parliaments that were set up by the French *ancien régime* in the eighteenth century and by the Russian Tsar in 1905 (the 'Duma') were designed to head off demands for democratic reforms. They were not expected to achieve any real change. Similarly, the European Parliament is little more than a democratic symbol. Its limited role of advice and consultation renders it perhaps the weakest example among modern parliaments. Supporters of further European integration do, nevertheless, understand that any further political progress will have to be accompanied by extensions in parliamentary power. Otherwise, the 'democratic deficit' in Europe will worsen.

The citizen and the state

Throughout Europe, both within individual countries and in the EU as a whole, guarantees of individual rights against the power of the state abound in the form of codified, entrenched constitutions, Bills of Rights, Basic Laws and legal conventions. In the USA the whole Constitution, the Bill of Rights section in particular, plays a similar role. Redress of individual grievances is made possible through powerful constitutional courts and most citizens feel they do have access to such bodies. However, there remains the difficulty that different judges interpret the Bill in different ways.

The UK's lack of constitutionally guaranteed rights stands in dramatic contrast to other democracies. British government, indeed, enjoys prerogative powers that cannot be controlled even by Parliament. Redress through the European Court of Human Rights is possible but, as we have seen, is not binding. Yet it would be wrong to suggest that the British suffer under tyrannical government. The combined forces of tradition and parliamentary representation have succeeded in preventing serious infringements of basic rights. The contrast between the UK and the USA or most of the European democracies is largely confined to the **potential** power of government and the fragile guarantees of civil rights. In **reality**, rights have been preserved in the UK almost as effectively as they have in other constitutional democracies.

The distribution of power

It is useful here to classify political systems in the following way:

- highly centralised systems with no significant regional institutions and with local government enjoying very little independence
- centralised systems, but with strong local and/or regional self-government
- federations where sovereignty is granted to regional government
- loose confederations with strong regional government and limited power at the centre.

The reforms in local government structure and provisions that occurred during the 1980s and 1990s moved the UK from the second category towards the first. The centralisation of power was not complete, with many new regional quangos having been created, but there were marked reductions in the freedom of action of local councils. Much of that local power was transferred to central government ministers and official agencies. While it is true that devolution has brought more autonomy to the UK's national regions, **England's** political system remains essentially centralised, with weak local government persisting.

Italy, though not a federal structure, grants considerable independence to city governments and so has a more decentralised system than the UK. Clearly, the USA, Russia and Germany are federations with constitutional guarantees for regional government. When we consider the European Union, however, we see an example of the fourth category – a loose confederation of states with central government institutions having a remarkably narrow range of jurisdiction.

Parties

The UK and the USA present us with sharp contrasts in the respective roles and structures of their parties. This produces significant effects upon the political system in general. While the American Republicans and Democrats are loose, decentralised organisations, with weak discipline and without the ability or inclination to develop coherent national policy programmes, British parties are notable for their unity and discipline.

Furthermore, these differences can be identified as key determinants of several other political phenomena. The British Parliament and Government are both shaped by the nature of the parties. They could not exist in their present form were it not for the persistence of an ordered two-party system. The lack of a formal, codified constitution means that executive–legislative relations and the process of government formation depend upon the near certainty that a single, unified party is able to win government office decisively and then to maintain itself in power.

No such features exist in the American central government system (though in some states and localities party rule can exist in a similar way to that existing in the UK). Political processes depend, instead, on

constitutional rules, personal patronage and complex sets of relationships between individual legislators, government officials and agencies,
~~and shifting party factions. American parties simply do~~
not have the cohesion to be able to run the system in a meaningful way.

The European Union displays similar characteristics to those found in
the USA. No coherent party system has emerged as yet in Europe. There
are – to add to the complexities of non-party politics – national interests
to take into consideration. The party groupings are, therefore, of minor
political significance. Elsewhere in Europe, party political systems vary
considerably, from the chaotic Italian system where coalitions are
created and destroyed with great regularity, to the stable Swedish
system, dominated as it is by the Social Democrat Party.

Conclusion

What makes the British system so uniquely different from those of the
USA and Europe? All the features described above have played a part,
but which are the more crucial factors? What are, to borrow Bagehot's
words, the 'efficient secrets' today? A few realities stand out:

- the lack of separation of powers between the executive and the legislature
- the strength and unity of the parties
- the ability of a single party to win governmental power on its own
- the concentration of powers in central government
- the accumulation of powers placed in the hands of the Prime Minister
- the sovereignty of Parliament converted into government dominance.

Sample examination questions

These practice questions are written similarly to the form used by the main examination boards for AS and A2-level Government and Politics courses. The marks shown in brackets after each question should be used as a guide to the level of detail required, as should the time available per question.

AS-level questions

All questions: 35 minutes

Unit 2
Political concepts

1 (a) What is meant by the term 'direct democracy'? (5)
  (b) Distinguish between direct and representative democracy. (10)
  (c) Under what circumstances might the use of referenda be justified? (15)
  (d) What are the arguments against the use of referenda to determine political issues? (20)
2 (a) What is meant by the term 'parliamentary democracy'? (5)
  (b) How representative are British MPs? (10)
  (c) Describe any TWO senses in which the UK is NOT a democracy. (15)
  (d) How democratic is the House of Commons? (20)

Unit 3
The ideological context of British politics

1 To what extent is 'New Labour' really 'new'? (50)
2 To what extent has the Conservative Party abandoned the policies of the Thatcher era? (50)
3 (a) What do you understand by the terms 'left wing' and 'right wing' in the context of British politics? (20)
  (b) To what extent have Labour and the Conservatives moved to the 'centre' of British politics in the 1990s? (20)
  (c) Which of the two terms best describes the British party system? (20)
4 (a) What is the role of the Opposition? (6)
  (b) What opportunities does the Opposition have to make its case in Parliament? (12)
  (c) What are the main ways in which the Conservatives have opposed New Labour policies? (22)

Unit 4
Political parties

1 (a) Describe any TWO functions of political parties. (5)
  (b) How do parties support democracy? (10)
  (c) Describe any TWO ways in which parties are a threat to democracy. (15)
  (d) Why is the UK usually described as a two-party system? (20)
2 (a) What is meant by the term 'consensus politics'? (5)
  (b) How does consensus differ from adversarial politics? (10)
  (c) How is adversarial politics played out in Parliament? (15)

Unit 5
Pressure groups

1 (a) What is a pressure group? (5)
  (b) Briefly describe two types of pressure group. (10)
  (c) How do pressure groups differ from parties? (15)
  (d) Why is the distinction between a party and a pressure group often unclear? (20)
2 (a) Distinguish between insider and outsider pressure groups. (6)
  (b) Why do some pressure groups use direct action? (12)

(c) Assess the relative effectiveness of direct and parliamentary action used by pressure groups. (22)

2 (a) Distinguish between cause and sectional pressure groups. (6)

(b) What are the main differences between the ways in which cause and sectional groups normally operate? (12)

(c) Why has the British environmental lobby tended to use direct action? (22)

Unit 6
Elections

1 (a) Briefly describe how the 'first-past-the-post' electoral system works. (5)

(b) Briefly describe one alternative system. (10)

(c) What arguments have been used for maintaining the current British electoral system? (15)

(d) What would be the main political effects of changing the British electoral system to proportional representation? (20)

2 (a) Briefly describe the electoral system used for the developed system in Scotland and Wales. (5)

(b) What were the main effects of using them? (10)

(c) Why were the systems used in Scotland and Wales? (15)

(d) How would the use of this system affect the UK Parliament? (20)

3 (a) Why do some people vote tactically? (6)

(b) What other factors determine the party allegiance of most voters? (12)

(c) What are the main factors that determine the outcome of general elections? (22)

Unit 7
Parliament

1 (a) What is meant by the term 'parliamentary sovereignty'? (5)

(b) In what senses can Parliament be said not to be sovereign? (10)

(c) How does the executive attempt to control the activities of Parliament? (15)

(d) In what ways could government be made more accountable to Parliament? (20)

2 (a) What are the main roles of British MPs? (6)

(b) What factors prevent MPs from playing their role effectively? (12)

(c) How could the effectiveness of MPs be improved? (22)

3 (a) What are the main functions of the House of Lords? (6)

(b) What were the main recommendations of the Wakeham Committee on House of Lords reform? (12)

(c) How could the House of Lords be made a more effective second chamber? (22)

Unit 8
Prime Minister and Cabinet

1 (a) What are the main functions of the Cabinet? (5)

(b) How does the Prime Minister seek to control the Cabinet? (10)

(c) What factors determine the Prime Minister's choice of Cabinet colleagues? (15)

(d) Has prime ministerial government now replaced Cabinet government? (20)

2 (a) Briefly describe two functions of the Prime Minister. (5)

(b) What is meant by the term 'prime ministerial patronage'? (10)

(c) What are the main constraints on prime ministerial power? (15)

(d) Is the Prime Minister now effectively a President? (20)

3 (a) What are the functions of the Cabinet Office? (6)

(b) In what ways has Tony Blair attempted to centralise power? (12)

(c) Does the Prime Minister now have too much power? (22)

Unit 9 **The civil service and the** **machinery of central** **government**	1	(a) What is meant by the term 'individual ministerial responsibility'?	(5)
		(b) How does the principle protect civil servants?	(10)
		(c) In what senses are civil servants neutral?	(15)
		(d) To what extent has the modern civil service been brought under political control?	(20)
	2	(a) In what sense are civil servants permanent?	(5)
		(b) How has permanence been eroded in recent times?	(10)
		(c) How did the 'Next Steps' report change the nature of the civil service?	(15)
		(d) Why was it thought necessary to reform the civil service after 1979?	(20)
	3	(a) Describe the nature of the relationship between ministers and civil servants.	(6)
		(b) How has this relationship come under strain since 1979?	(12)
		(c) How has New Labour changed the way in which the civil service operates?	(22)

Unit 10 **Local government in** **England and Wales**	1	(a) Describe briefly TWO functions of local government.	(5)
		(b) In what ways is local government able to raise its own finances?	(10)
		(c) How does central government attempt to control local government finance?	(15)
		(d) In what ways is English local government truly independent?	(20)
	2	(a) Describe the ways in which the London mayor was elected in 2000.	(6)
		(b) What were the main reasons for the decision to reintroduce local government in London?	(12)
		(c) What are the main powers of the London mayor and assembly?	(22)

Unit 11 **Devolution**	1	(a) What is meant by the term 'devolution'?	(5)
		(b) How does devolution differ from federalism?	(10)
		(c) What were the main powers devolved to the Scottish Parliament?	(15)
		(d) Why were powers devolved to Scotland and Wales in 1999?	(20)
	2	(a) Why did devolution become a major political issue in the 1990s?	(6)
		(b) Why was more power devolved to Scotland than to Wales?	(12)
		(c) Is devolution likely to lead to full independence?	(22)

Unit 12 **Constitutional issues**	1	(a) What is a codified constitution?	(5)
		(b) What are the main sources of the British Constitution?	(10)
		(c) What advantages are there for the UK's uncodified constitution?	(15)
		(d) What are the arguments for introducing a written constitution in the UK?	(20)
	2	(a) In what ways does the judiciary seek to protect rights in the UK?	(6)
		(b) How is the judiciary constrained in its protection of rights?	(12)
		(c) In what other ways are rights protected?	(22)
	3	(a) Why has the European Convention on Human Rights been incorporated into British law?	(6)
		(b) How is this likely to affect the way the British judiciary operates?	(12)
		(c) How might the Human Rights Act affect the way in which government governs?	(22)

Unit 13
The European context

1 (a) How has sovereignty been affected by British membership
     of the EU? (5)

(c) In what ways can British ministers influence the policies of
    the EU? (15)

(d) How do the two main parties differ in their attitude to membership of
    the EU? (20)

2 (a) Why has the EU adopted the principle of the single currency? (6)

(b) What are the main arguments in favour of the UK joining the
    euro system? (12)

(c) How will adoption of the single currency affect British sovereignty? (22)

A2-level questions

These questions are in essay form. Assume 45 minutes per question.

Unit 14
Alternative ideologies

1 How have Liberals and Conservatives differed in their attitude towards the state?
2 How new is 'New Labour'?
3 To what extent is anarchism one single ideology?
4 How have radical feminists sought to erode the distinction between public and private spheres?
5 To what extent was the communism of Lenin and Stalinism a corruption of Marxist ideology?
6 Is Marxism still relevant in modern political thought?
7 Why has nationalism become a major force in the post-Cold War world?
8 Discuss the view that all major parties in the UK are fundamentally liberal in nature.
9 Distinguish between environmentalism and ecologism.
10 Has conservatism become a united philosophy?

Unit 15
Political issues in the modern UK

1 To what extent has economic policy in the UK become a matter of political consensus since 1979?
2 Why did law and order become a major political issue in the UK after 1979?
3 In what senses has the welfare state been eroded since 1979?
4 Why was Northern Ireland a matter for political consensus, while the issue of devolution was hotly contested?
5 In which areas do the main parties agree and disagree over modern educational policy?
6 To what extent has the problem of racism in the UK been attacked through legislation? What other measures have been adopted to improve race relations?
7 To what extent has the National Health Service been 'safe in the hands' of the main parties?

Unit 16
The social and political context of American government

1 Discuss briefly the following features of the American political culture:
  (a) attitudes to central government
  (b) individualism
  (c) rights
  (d) constitutionalism.
2 What factors did the founding fathers take into account when framing the US Constitution?
3 (a) To what extent are the different states in the USA 'different'?
  (b) How is the diversity of the states recognised in the Constitution and the political system?

Unit 17
The United States'
Constitution

1 'The American Constitution appears to be inflexible and set firm in history, but the reality is that it is a living organism.' Explain and discuss.
2 In what ways is the American Constitution at the mercy of the Supreme Court?
3 Discuss the view that the similarities between the American and British Constitutions are greater than the differences.

Unit 18
The United States'
Congress

1 Discuss the view that the USA is effectively governed by Congress rather than the President.
2 Which is more powerful in modern American politics, the Senate or the House?
3 To what extent has the Congress become simply the 'poodle' of powerful pressure groups?
4 'Bicameralism works more effectively in the modern UK than in the USA.' To what extent is this a true statement?
5 What lessons could British parliamentary reformers usefully learn from the experience of the American Congress?

Unit 19
The United States'
Presidency and
administration

1 Why has Bill Clinton been described as a 'successful' President?
2 'Since 1980 the balance of power between Congress and the Presidency has moved decisively in favour of the former.' To what extent is this a true statement?
3 Discuss the view that presidential elections are effectively over by the spring of the election year.
4 'The notion that the British Prime Minister has become effectively like an American President ignores the reality of politics in the USA.' Do you agree?
5 How accountable are American Presidents and British Prime Ministers to public opinion?
6 'For modern heads of government, parties are no longer a serious constraint.' Assess this view with reference to the American President and the British Prime Minister.

Unit 20
Parties and pressure
groups in the USA

1 Discuss the view that modern American pressure groups have made parties largely redundant.
2 Describe and discuss the importance of 'iron triangles' in American politics.
3 'The role of modern American parties is now almost confined to running elections.' To what extent is this true?
4 In what ways is the American President a party leader?
5 Why do small parties consistently fail in American elections?
6 Have British pressure groups become effectively 'Americanised'?
7 To what extent have personality politics taken over from party politics in the British and American political systems?

Unit 21
Federalism and the states

1 To what extent has the power of federal government been eroded since 1968?
2 How and why did Presidents Nixon and Reagan change the relationship between federal and state governments?
3 How similar is British devolution to American federalism?

Some AS- or A2-level examination questions take the form of stimulus–response questions, normally involving either data or one or more passages from leading authorities. Students often have difficulty in approaching such questions. The following guide offers some general practical advice and then looks at two typical questions.

General points

The following practices should be adopted:

- Make sure you read all the information. You are given at least five minutes' allowance for reading, so do not rush and try to cut corners. Examiners take a great deal of time choosing data or commentaries, so it is likely that **all** the information is relevant. Try to respond to **every** aspect of the stimulus material.
- Respond carefully to the division of the marks. Divide your time approximately in the same proportion as the marks. For example, if four sections award 5, 10, 15 and 20 (total 50) marks, and there are 45 minutes available, you should divide your time approximately as follows:

  Reading: 5 minutes
  Part (a): 4 minutes
  Part (b): 8 minutes
  Part (c): 12 minutes
  Part (d): 16 minutes

- It is reasonable to quote directly from the data or passage(s), but do so only briefly and sparingly. Try to adapt the information using your own words.
- Candidates are often not sure how much to restrict themselves to using the information only, and how much to use extra knowledge. A guide to this is shown below. The wording of the question is important.

  '**What does the data (or passage) say about . . .**' In this case, use only the information given.

  '**Using the data . . .**' This implies that you should extract information, but extend it using your own knowledge, perhaps explaining further or giving more information.

  '**Distinguish between the first and second pieces of information concerning . . .**' Only the information given is relevant. If the question does not refer to the information at all, you should be using your own knowledge, but it is important to use any of the information that might be relevant.

We can now apply these principles to two typical questions.

Question 1   45 minutes   See Unit 8.
Study the following two passages and then answer the questions that follow.

> 'It is doubtful that she [Thatcher] has transformed the role of prime minister in British politics. The office is not highly institutionalised and she has not made changes in this respect. Her significance as prime minister is that she has set an example, by pushing to the outer limits of her authority.'
> Dennis Kavanagh, *Thatcherism and British Politics*, 1990

> 'He [Tony Blair] has ruthlessly centralised power, bringing in Mandelson, his trusted lackey, and later Cunningham to co-ordinate policy, as well as Gerry Irvine in a less defined way. While eschewing [rejecting] the lure of a prime minister's department, he has greatly strengthened the Cabinet Office to institutionalize the dominance of Number 10 in the machinery of government. To ensure his writ runs throughout the government, he has appointed in the Fleet Street argot [role], an enforcer – not Mandelson as many had predicted, but the likeable yet tough Geordie, Jack Cunningham.'
> Bill Jones characterising a criticism of Blair, in Bill Jones (ed.), *Political Issues in Britain Today*, 1999

(a) What is the prime minister's 'authority', as the term is used in the first passage? (5)

(b) How do the two passages differ in their views about how Blair and Thatcher have adapted the office of Prime Minister? (10)

(c) Using the two passages, what evidence is there to suggest that the UK now has 'prime ministerial' government? (15)

(d) What evidence is there to suggest that the Cabinet has become an insignificant part of British government? (20)

Guide   (a) About 4 minutes. Clearly little time. This does not require information from the passage. Merely write about the sources of the Prime Minister's authority, such as the party and Parliament.

(b) About 8 minutes. Here information should be taken **only** from the passage, as stated. Identify facts such as that Thatcher pushed authority to its limits but did not make institutional changes. Blair has appointed enforcers and enhanced the Cabinet Office, etc.

(c) About 12 minutes. This allows you to use both information from the passages and your own knowledge. Refer to Blair promoting his own associates, to 'his writ running throughout government', etc. and Thatcher stretching authority to its limits. Also add other factors, such as control over presentation, extended patronage and other evidence.

(d) About 16 minutes. Effectively a 'mini essay'. Use mostly your own knowledge, such as the shortness of modern meetings and the existence of alternative policy communities. However, a little information from the second passage can be used (Cabinet enforcers, etc.).

Question 2 45 minutes   See Unit 7.
Study the following data and answer the questions that follow.

Party	Life peers	Hereditary peers	Bishops	Total
Conservative	180	52		232
Labour	177	4		181
Liberal Democrat	49	5		54
Cross-benchers	135	31	26	192
Others	6			6
Total	547	92	26	665

Composition of the House of Lords, April 2000

Source: Stationery Office.

(a) From the data, comment on the political make-up of the House of Lords in April 2000 (5).
(b) What are 'cross-bench' peers and what is their significance? (10)
(c) What do the data suggest about the need to reform the composition of the House of Lords? (15)
(d) What are the arguments in favour of retaining life and hereditary peers in the House of Lords? (20)

Guide (a) About 4 minutes. Clearly you are expected to quote some of the data. You should say what is significant, e.g. about the balance between main parties' life peers, but the Conservative majority of hereditaries, etc. Don't forget to refer to the bishops and to say that the Church of England is significantly represented.

(b) About 8 minutes. You need to know about cross-bench peers from your own knowledge. However, comment on their numbers from the data and how they hold the balance of power between the main parties.

(c) About 12 minutes. Here you **must** limit yourself to the data, as the question requires. So discuss issues such as the over-representation of Conservatives, the lack of Liberal Democrat representation and the importance of life peers and therefore of government patronage.

(d) This is all your own knowledge. However, you might wish to quote the exact numbers in your answer.

Further reading and research

Journals

Students will find excellent articles to expand and update their knowledge in two journals specifically designed for advanced-level study and beyond:

The Politics Review (Philip Allan Updates)
Talking Politics (The Politics Association)

Subscriptions are available as well as back numbers.

The Internet

Students should beware of unofficial sites on politics. They might be of interest, but should not be used for learning or research purposes. A selection of useful websites is shown below:

www.open.gov.uk/index.htm
The official government website. It covers the whole of the government structure. Very useful indeed.
www.cabinet-office.gov.uk
As above, but specialises in the centres of power.
www.parliament.uk
Speaks for itself. Current developments are included.
www.bbc.co.uk/news
A quick and easy way to keep up with current events.
www.labour.org.uk
The official site of the Labour Party.
www.libdems.org.uk
The official site of the Liberal Democrat Party.
www.tory.org.uk
The official site of the Conservative Party.
www.hansard-society.org.uk
Information on the structure, functions and possible reform of Parliament.
www.civil-service.co.uk
Plenty of statistics and information, including details of reforms.
www.eu.org
A full information service about institutions, treaties and issues in Europe.
www.access.gpo.gov/congress
Up-to-date information about the Congress, including elections, legislation and issues.
www.whitehouse.gov/WH/EOP
Information about the presidential branch and the central executive of the USA.

Books

Studying politics: starting points
British Politics Today, B. Jones and D. Kavanagh (Manchester University Press, 1998)
Half a Century of British Politics, L. Robins and B. Jones (eds) (Manchester University Press, 1997)
British Politics in Focus, D. Roberts (Causeway, 1996)

Unit 2
Political concepts
Politics, A. Heywood (Macmillan, 1997)
In Defence of Politics, B. Crick (Penguin, 1992)
Political Ideas in Modern Britain, R. Barker (Routledge, 1997)

Unit 3
The ideological context of British politics
Ideology and Politics in Britain Today, I. Adams (Manchester University Press, 1998)
Political Ideologies, A. Heywood (Macmillan, 1998)
Contemporary British Ideologies, R. Eccleshall *et al.* (Routledge, 1996)
The Third Way, A. Giddens (Polity, 1998)

Unit 4
Political parties
Political Parties, J. Fisher (Prentice Hall, 1996)
British Political Parties Today, R. Garner and R. Kelly (Manchester University Press, 1998)
UK Political Parties since 1945, A. Seldon (ed.) (Philip Allan Updates, 1991)

Unit 5
Pressure Groups
Pressure Groups, D. Simpson (Hodder and Stoughton, 1999)
Pressure Groups Today, R. Baggott (Manchester University Press, 1995)
Pressure Politics, M. Smith (Baseline, 1995)

Unit 6
Elections
The British General Election of 1997, D. Butler and D. Kavanagh (Macmillan, 1997)
Voting Behaviour and Electoral Systems, C. Robinson (Hodder and Stoughton, 1998)
Elections and Voting Behaviour in Britain, D. Denver (Philip Allan Updates, 1994)
Voting Behaviour, P. Dorey (Sheffield Hallam, 1998)

Unit 7
Parliament
Does Parliament Matter?, P. Norton (Harvester Wheatsheaf, 1993)
Parliament Today, A. Adonis (Manchester University Press, 1993)
Parliament in the 1990s, P. Norton (Blackwell, 1998)

Unit 8
Prime Minister and Cabinet
The Prime Minister and Cabinet, N. McNaughton (Hodder and Stoughton, 1999)
The Rise of the British Presidency, M. Foley (Manchester University Press, 1993)
The British Cabinet System, M. Burch and D. Holliday (Prentice Hall, 1996)
Prime Minister and Cabinet Today, G. Thomas (Manchester University Press, 1998)

Unit 9
The civil service and the machinery of central government
The Civil Service and the Conservatives, D. Richards (Sussex Academic Press, 1997)
The Civil Service, N. McNaughton (Hodder and Stoughton, 2000)
Whitehall, P. Hennessy (Fontana, 1989)
The New Civil Service, J. Tonge (Baseline, 1999)

Unit 10
Local government in England and Wales
Local Government in the United Kingdom, J. Wilson and W. Game (Macmillan, 1995)
Local and Regional Government in Britain, N. McNaughton (Hodder and Stoughton, 1998)
Local Government in Britain, T. Byrne (ed.) (Penguin, 1994)

Unit 11 **Devolution**	*Devolution in the United Kingdom*, V. Bogdanor (Oxford University Press, 1999) *The Battle for Scotland*, A. Marr (Penguin, 1995) *Local and Regional Government in Britain*, N. McNaughton (Hodder and Stoughton, 1996)
Unit 12 **Constitutional issues**	*Protecting Rights in Britain*, D. Watts (Hodder and Stoughton, 1998) *A Bill of Rights*, M. Zander (Sweet and Maxwell, 1997) *The Constitution in Flux*, P. Norton (Blackwell, 1982)
Unit 13 **The European context**	*Britain in the EU Today*, C. Pilkington (Manchester University Press, 1995) *British Politics and Europe*, A. Davies (Hodder and Stoughton, 1999) J. McCormick, *Understanding the EU* (Macmillan, 1999)
Unit 14 **Alternative ideologies**	*Political Ideologies*, A. Heywood (Macmillan, 1998) *Using Political Ideas*, B. Goodwin (Wiley, 1997) *Political Ideologies*, R. Eccleshall *et al.* (Routledge, 1996) *Contemporary Political Ideologies*, R. Eatwell and A. Wright (Pinter, 1993)
Unit 15 **Political issues in the** **modern UK**	*Developments in British Politics*, P. Dunleavey *et al.* (Macmillan, 2000) *Issues in British Politics*, C. Pilkington (Macmillan, 1998) *Political Issues in Britain Today*, W. Jones (ed.) (Manchester University Press, 1999) *New Labour – Politics After Thatcherism*, S. Driver and L. Martell (Polity, 1999) *The Welfare State in Britain since 1945*, R. Lowe (Macmillan, 1999) *Government and the Economy*, S. Lyons (Hodder and Stoughton, 1998) *Northern Ireland since 1945*, S. Wishart (Longman, 1999) *Law, Order and the Judiciary*, P. Joyce (Hodder and Stoughton, 1999)
Unit 16 **The social and political** **context of American** **government**	*US Politics Today*, A. Ashbee and N. Ashford (Manchester University Press, 1999) *Politics USA*, R. McKeever *et al.* (Prentice Hall, 1999) *American Politics and Society*, D. McKay (Blackwell, 1998)
Unit 17 **The United States'** **Constitution**	*The Supreme Court and the United States*, T. Walker and N. Epstein (St Martin's Press, 1993) *American Government*, M. Skidmore (St Martin's Press, 1993)
Unit 18 **The United States'** **Congress**	*Congress Today*, E. Schneier and B. Cross (St Martin's Press, 1993) *The American Political Process*, A. Grant (Ashgate, 1997)
Unit 19 **The United States'** **Presidency and** **administration**	*The President of the United States*, D. Mervin (Harvester Wheatsheaf, 1993) *The Presidential Branch*, I. Hart (Chatham House, 1995) *Congress and the Presidency*, M. Foley and J. Owens (Manchester University Press, 1996)
Unit 20 **Parties and pressure** **groups in the USA**	*Two Parties – Or More?*, J. Bibby and L. Maisel (Westview, 1998) *American Political Parties*, D. McSweeney and I. Zvesper (Routledge, 1991) *Interest Group Politics in America*, R. Hrebener (Sharpe, 1997) *US Elections Today*, P. Davies (Manchester University Press, 1999)
Unit 21 **Federalism and the** **states**	*American Federalism*, T. Dye (Lexington, 1997) *The New Federalism*, M. Reagan and J. Sanzone (Oxford University Press, 1981)
Unit 22 **The British political** **system in a comparative** **context**	*UK Government and Politics in Context*, D. Simpson (Hodder and Stoughton, 1998) *Bring Home the Revolution*, J. Freedland (Fourth Estate, 1999)

Glossary

The following terms may be described in the main text but are included here as a ready reference. Other explanations of terms may be found by reference to the index.

Absolutism A system of rule where a leader or small group holds complete power within a political system. There is no serious, effective opposition.

Adversary politics Periods of political life when the main parties have fundamental disagreements on policy.

Affirmative action See under 'Positive discrimination'.

Autocracy A system of rule where the leader or leaders are not subject to democratic controls or accountability. Internal opposition is not tolerated and decisions are reached without seeking the consent of the people.

Back-bencher Any British MP who is not a senior spokesperson for his or her party.

Best value A principle used in central and local government which requires that services are carried out with both efficiency and high quality.

Bill The formal proposal for legislation before it has been passed by the legislative process.

Bill of Rights A constitutional document that sets out the basic rights of the citizens of a state. Such Bills are normally entrenched by special safeguards and are binding upon law-makers and government. Also the name of an agreement made in 1689 between the English Parliament and King William III, whereby the King gave up the right to make law without the sanction of Parliament.

By-law In the UK, a law passed by a public body subordinate to central government, mostly local authorities or public corporations.

Capitalism An economic system where the distribution of finance, raw materials, incomes and goods is determined by free markets in which there is free movement of goods, labour and money. It has formed the basis of the economic structure of the developed world since the industrial revolution.

Charisma The special ability of an individual to inspire a following through the force of their personality, not merely the plausibility of their message.

Citizenship The right granted to an individual to enjoy the privileges associated with belonging to a particular state. Usually, but not always, it includes the right of abode in a country.

Civil service The body of officials who are directly employed by a central government department.

Classical liberalism That form of liberalism which is concerned with the extension of liberty and tolerance, and which flourished in the middle part of the nineteenth century.

Coalition Specifically a government where ministerial posts are shared among more than one party. Generally it can mean any grouping of politicians with varying beliefs, who come together temporarily to promote some form of action to which they all agree.

Coercion The use of force to achieve a particular end.

Collegiality Where a group is able to make decisions on a genuinely collective basis and not just through a majority vote. Normally related to Cabinet government, it suggests that ministers in the Cabinet can all support the same decision.

Consensus General agreement that is more than a mere majority, but includes the vast majority of a community. In political life, consensus refers to a circumstance where a large proportion of the population and the political community are agreed on certain values. The period 1940–70 is often described in the UK as the 'era of consensus politics'.

Conservative (small 'c') A description of a person who places a high value on traditional institutions, values and ideas, and who is suspicious of excessive amounts of change.

Conservative (capital 'C') A member or supporter of the British Conservative Party.

Constitution A document or set of principles that sets out the distribution of power within a state, establishes the relationship between citizens and the state, and specifies the limits of the Government's jurisdiction.

Corporate state In fascist states, notably Italy, this referred to a system where regional bodies, comprising representatives of unions, industry and the ruling party, planned public policy. In a modern context, it refers to a tendency, noticeable in the UK in the 1960s and 1970s, for government to incorporate important interests into the governing process.

Democratic deficit A situation where, within a political system, there is a gap in the democratic process. Normally, this relates to a circumstance where a governing body is not sufficiently accountable to an elected institution. Most often applied to the relationship between the European Parliament and the rest of the Union's government.

Devolution The transfer of significant powers to regional forms of government, but stopping short of the transfer of sovereignty.

Doctrine A firmly held belief, normally concerned with politics. It is used as the basis, or partial basis, of political action or a wider

Drys The opposite of 'wets' – see below. Those Conservatives who, during the 1980s, were most supportive of Margaret Thatcher's radical policies.

Electoral college A body that is elected with the expressed purpose of itself electing a higher political authority. The best-known example is in the USA, where the electoral college, now only a formal body, is popularly elected to choose a President. In effect, all the votes of this college are fixed in advance by the original election.

Elite A description of a group of people who are considered, for some reason or another to be superior to others. In politics, it refers to those who have achieved some kind of exclusive access to power.

EMU European Monetary Union. The proposal that the European Union should adopt one single currency to be used by all members.

Executive In politics, that part of the state which oversees the implementation of public policy and the laws of that state. Normally, the executive will also be heavily involved in the formulation of policy.

Faction A distinct group within a political party which holds views that differ from the central policies of that party. However, these views are not so incompatible with the norm as to warrant them forming a separate party.

Filibuster A device, commonly used in the American Senate, where a speaker in the legislature continues to talk for so long that a piece of legislation runs out of its apportioned time and so fails.

General will A term associated with the eighteenth-century philosopher Rousseau. It suggests a collective will of the people as opposed merely to the will of the majority.

Gerrymandering The practice – usually illegal – of drawing up electoral boundaries in such a way as to favour one political party.

Government (capital 'G') That group of individuals who control the operation of the state at any particular time. In a democratic system this group will have been elected.

Government (small 'g') The act of governing or a term relating to the broader institutions of government, not just elected ministers. Thus, it includes non-elected civil servants, advisers, public bodies, etc.

Grass roots A description of those supporters of a party who do not hold any office, but do form the basic membership.

Head of State The individual who is able, on appropriate occasions, to represent all the people of a state.

Hereditary peer A member of the House of Lords who has inherited their title from their father.

Hung Parliament In the UK, a situation where no one party is able to command an overall majority in the House of Commons. As with the term 'hung jury', it suggests that it is difficult to reach decisions under such circumstances.

Impeachment A means of removing an individual from public office for reasons that could not be enforced through the conventional law courts. Normally associated with financial or sexual misconduct rather than political errors.

Initiative A referendum that has been called on the initiative of a section of a community, rather than by government itself.

Judiciary The individuals and bodies, normally judges and courts, which administer the laws. This includes the resolution of civil disputes, disputes between citizens and the state, trial of suspected criminals and interpretations of the meaning and applications of the laws.

Laissez-faire A description of a style of government that prefers not to interfere with the life of its people. It refers mainly to the economic and industrial field. It is associated with liberalism, modern neo-liberalism, monetarism, and free trade.

Law A system of rules that are binding on all and enforced by the state.

Legislature The body that formalises the laws of a state. It might also be involved, though not always, in the policy-making and policy-influencing process.

Liberal An individual whose outlook and values include tolerance for the ideas of others, respect for the freedom of others, social justice for all, equal rights and powerful democratic controls over governmental power.

Mandate The authority or consent given by the people of a state to its Government to carry out certain policies. In a democratic system, such a mandate is normally granted at elections. In international politics, it can refer to a situation where one state is given responsibility for governing a territory temporarily while arrangements for permanent sovereignty can be completed.

Manifesto A statement published by a political party, normally before an election, containing its stated philosophy, aims and intentions when it gains public office.

Monetarism An economic philosophy that has as its basis a belief that the only positive interference in the economy that should be undertaken by government is the control of the supply of money and, therefore, of interest rates. Control of taxation and public expenditure for economic reasons should, thus, be avoided. Monetarism is associated with laissez-faire policies and a belief in the operation of free markets.

Neo-liberal A term used to describe one who follows the ideas of so-called right-wing, or 'New Right' thinkers of the late twentieth century. It is an adaptation of classical liberalism, encompassing ideas of laissez-faire economics, monetarism and free trade.

New Left A collection of radical movements that developed in the 1960s and early 1970s. It included feminists, environmentalists, pacifists, black rights activists, anarchists, gay rights campaigners and a broad socialist youth movement.

New Right A conservative movement that arose in the late 1970s, mainly in the USA and the UK. It encompasses neo-liberal ideas (see above), a stress on traditional moral values, a strong position on law and order, and is nationalistic and xenophobic. In the case of the USA, it extols the virtues of Christian religion.

One-nation conservatism A description of a section of the Conservative Party which embraces its traditional values, referring back to Benjamin Disraeli. The term refers to the idea that these values will unite the nation and prevent social conflict.

Paternalism A tendency among some, especially politicians, to claim that they have a deeper understanding of how to improve the condition of individuals and society than the people themselves. They may suggest they know what is best for people who, having inferior knowledge, do not understand what is in their own best interests. The relationship between paternalists and the people can be described as similar to that of father and child. Associated with the idea of a 'superior' ruling class.

Plebiscite A popular vote organised within a community where people vote to decide who shall exercise sovereignty over them: in other words, in which state they shall live.

Political Action Committee An American device to raise funds and to campaign for political action to benefit a section of the community or to further a popular cause. They arose in the 1970s as a way of avoiding tight federal laws on the funding of the campaigns by candidates for public office.

Political culture The dominant political values, attitudes, traditions and emotions that exist within a community.

Poll Tax A tax, used in British local government in the late 1980s, based on a flat rate charge levied on all adults.

Pork Barrel An American term for funds that are available to federal government for distribution among projects in different parts of the country. Regional interests compete strongly for these funds.

Positive discrimination Measures designed to give a section of a community which is considered to suffer unfair disadvantages special privileges to restore the principle of equal opportunities. It may involve special quotas for jobs or political offices for members of ethnic minorities or women. Known in the USA as 'affirmative action'.

Pragmatism A style of decision making that is based not on firm principles, but on an understanding of what appears to be the best course of action in the short term, with the fewest potential problems.

President A name used in politics to describe a Head of State other than a monarch. It is also sometimes used at a lower level to describe a lesser position at the head of an organisation, as in 'President of the Board of Trade'.

Primary An election held within a political party to decide which of a number of competing individuals should be the official candidate of that party in a public election. Most commonly used in the USA.

Proportional representation An electoral system that awards seats in a legislature in close proportion to the votes cast for each party and/or candidate.

Public corporations In the UK, enterprises that are publicly owned and run by the Government. They are separated from the rest of government by having their own management structures, financial arrangements and legal status. There were a large number of such corporations until 1980, but most have now been privatised. The BBC is an example that still remains.

Quango This stands for 'quasi-autonomous non-governmental organisation'. A body established, appointed, overseen and funded by national government to carry out some function or functions of the state on behalf of the Government, yet which is expected to act independently of the Government.

Reactionary One who strongly opposes new ideas and innovations. The reactionary prefers what has gone before to new developments.

Referendum A popular vote organised in a community to decide on an important issue. It may or may not be binding upon the government of that community.

Revolution An event or series of events that brings about a complete transformation of the political system, not merely a change in the personnel of government. It may or may not be violent.

Social contract A philosophical idea associated with such thinkers as John Locke and Jean-Jacques Rousseau. It argues that the appropriate basis of government should be a free agreement between the people, who will submit themselves to the laws, and a Government which agrees to respect natural laws and rights. Thus a political or social contract is formed. It is the basis of all constitutional government. It also relates to a voluntary agreement in the late 1970s between trade unions and the British Government to moderate wage demands.

Spin doctor A government adviser or spokesperson who seeks to put a party's policies or actions in the most favourable light.

State The permanent apparatus of government which enjoys a legal monopoly of the means of coercion. It represents the permanent interests of the whole country in the long term. It expresses where sovereignty lies permanently, whoever may form the temporary Government.

Subsidiarity Where government is carried out at the most local level appropriate to efficient administration. Each level of government has its suitable geographical level. It is believed to enhance democracy.

Suffrage The right to vote in public state elections.

Terror The public demonstration of force used by a state to instil fear and obedience in its people. Typical examples are public executions, open troop movements and public 'show trials'.

Ticket An American expression meaning a list of candidates from the same party appearing on the same ballot paper.

Tory A popular nickname for a member of the Conservative Party. Modern Conservatives often use it to describe one who espouses traditional, rather than modern, Conservative values. A more extreme version is 'High Tory'.

Totalitarianism A system of rule where the leadership maintains complete control over all, or virtually all, aspects of political, social, cultural and economic life, usually on the basis of a ruling ideology.

Trust An American expression for what the British call a 'monopoly'.

Welfare state A national system where all citizens are required to contribute through taxation or other contributions to the provision of social services such as health, education, financial benefits and pensions. These services are available to all according to need on a free or subsidised basis.

Wets A pejorative term used in the 1980s to describe those leading Conservatives who were opposed to the radical policies of Margaret Thatcher. The term 'wet' was used to suggest weakness of resolve.

Index